P9-DHQ-670

Understanding Motivation and Emotion

Third Edition

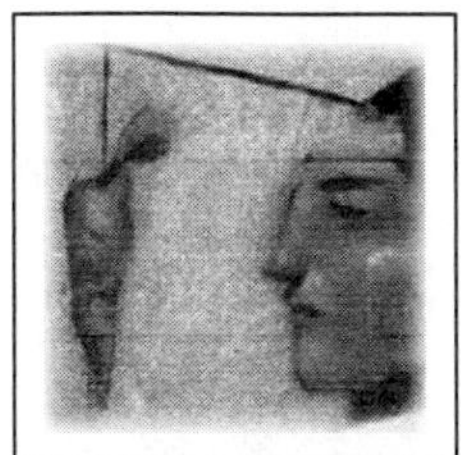

UNDERSTANDING MOTIVATION AND EMOTION

THIRD EDITION

JOHNMARSHALL REEVE | *University of Iowa*

JOHN WILEY & SONS, INC.
New York • Chichester • Weinheim • Brisbane • Singapore • Toronto

Cover: Tim Teekben

This book is printed on acid free paper. ∞

Library of Congress Cataloging-in-Publication Data

Reeve, Johnmarshall

Understanding Motivation and Emotion / Johnmarshall Reeve,—Third Edition

p. cm.

L.C. Card No. 00-102763

ISBN 0-470-00194-1

Printed in the United States of America

10 9 8 7 6 5 4 3 2

Preface

Welcome to the golden age of motivation and emotion. Never in its 100 years of formal study has the field been more exciting than it is today. Every month, new and important findings appear in the scholarly journals, and every year a stream of scholars joins those already studying motivation and emotion. Just 20 years ago, this was not the case, as the field was relatively stagnant and quiet. Something changed in the 1990s. Creative ideas appeared, new theories emerged, life-changing applications became obvious, and the sheer number of people interested in understanding and applying motivation and emotion exploded. All this activity produced an enormous amount of new knowledge, and these advances equipped the field to venture into areas of application that made the academic study of motivation relevant to people's daily lives. Now, as you read this text in the new millennium, you are in a position to benefit from those who have just recently gone before you. Had you taken this same course 10 years ago, the field could not have offered you material that is as exciting and as meaningful as it now can. Now is the best possible time to take a course in motivation and emotion. I hope this book will help identify what we in the field are so terribly enthusiastic about.

You will find in this book some of the most useful information in psychology and in life. Motivation is about human strivings, wants, desires, and aspirations. Its study concerns all conditions that exist within the person and in the environment and culture that explain "why we want what we want" and "why we do what we do." By the end of the book, I hope you will feel comfortable with motivation study at two levels. First, theoretically, an understanding of motivation and emotion provides answers to questions such as, "Why did she do that?" and "From where does the sense of 'want to' come?" Second, practically, an understanding of motivation and emotion provides the means to develop the art of motivating both self and others.

I assumed some background knowledge on the part of the reader, such as an introductory course in psychology. The intended audience is undergraduates enrolled in courses in a department of psychology. I also write for students in other disciplines, such as education and business, as the book concentrates on human, rather than on nonhuman, motivation. The book includes some experiments in which rats, dogs, and monkeys served as research participants, but the information gleaned from these studies is always framed within an analysis of human motivation and emotion.

WHAT'S NEW IN THE THIRD EDITION

Three features represent most of what is new to this edition: (1) clear focus on contemporary motivational constructs, (2) addition of chapter boxes, and (3) expanded recommended readings. The first major change represents a clear focus on contemporary motivational constructs. The second edition included three chapters on emotion, while this edition features only two. This change was necessary not only to accommodate professors' requests for a book with a greater emphasis on motivation, but also to make room for the multitude of new discoveries in motivation that have taken place in just the last few years. In recognition of the growing importance of these new areas, I introduced or expanded the text's discussion on the self-regulation of physiological needs, types of extrinsic motivation, achievement goals, personal strivings, entity and incremental self-theories, and formulation of implementation intentions to supplement goal setting, values, self-efficacy as personal and collective empowerment, perceived control as an individual difference, growth seeking versus validation seeking, the non-Freudian unconscious, object relations theory, the problem of evil, the adaptive functions of emotion, and new insights on motivating both the self and others. I also found it necessary to identify a new set of core themes in the conclusion chapter to reflect the changing emphasis of contemporary researchers.

A second new feature is the addition of chapter boxes. The purpose of each box (one per chapter) is to communicate how motivational principles apply to life. Each box begins with the same question: Why would a person want to learn about the motivational states discussed in this chapter? To provide an answer, I show how the motivational principles introduced in the chapter can be used to enrich the reader's daily life. For instance, the box in chapter 4 helps the reader identify his or her own interpersonal motivating style. Some boxes speak to practical situations, such as how to reduce anxiety in achievement situations (chapter 6) or how to implement an effective goal-setting program (chapter 7). Other boxes provide insights on everyday phenomena, such as understanding romantic love as an attachment process (chapter 12) or understanding the raging obesity epidemic as a manifestation of self-regulation failure. The box in chapter 15 finds meaning in the biology of emotion by identifying cutting-edge computer technology that reads the user's biological states to know (and adapt to) her current emotional state. Each box makes an explicit attempt to demonstrate the practical utility of understanding motivation and emotion.

A third new feature includes subject-specific recommended readings. That is, while the second edition listed ten recommended readings for physiological needs, the third edition lists three or four readings targeted specifically to the individual physiological needs of pain, thirst, hunger, and sex. The recommended readings can play an important role in the course because many of the ideas and theories will be new to the reader. My experience in working with students teaches me that many desire suggestions to guide their own personal study. For those occasions in which you seek a deeper understanding of the subject matter, I selected recommended readings that fit four criteria: (1) topic appeals to a wide audience and is central to the contents of the chapter; (2) length is short so that the reader will have time to read several articles rather than just one or two; (3) methodology and data analysis are reader-friendly; and (4) journals central to motivation study are showcased.

The recommended readings provide two opportunities. First, each reading offers a firsthand exposure to an original article in motivation. In reading the original article the reader gains the perspective and insight of the study's authors and therefore hears an additional voice in the conversation about motivation and emotion. Second, each reading offers a potential to satisfy curiosity in ways that are beyond the scope of this book. While this book overviews the study of motivation and emotion, the depth of the field lies within these recommended readings.

INSTRUCTOR'S MANUAL/TEST BANK

For the third edition, I expanded the test bank to include lecture suggestions, questions for discussion, recommended activities, and other tools to help instructors teach their students. interested instructors should contact their John Wiley & Sons representative for more information on the Instructor's Manual/Test Bank.

ACKNOWLEDGMENTS

Many voices speak within the pages of the book. Much of what I write emerged from conversations with colleagues and through reading their work. I have heard and benefited from so many colleagues that I now find it impossible to acknowledge them all. Still, I want to try. So, my first expression of gratitude goes to all those colleagues who, formally or casually, intentionally or inadvertently, knowingly or unknowingly, shared their ideas in conversation: Roy Baumesiter, Daniel Berlyne, Virginia Blankenship, Jerry Burger, Steven G. Cole, Mihaly Csikszentmihalyi, Richard deCharms, Ed Deci, Andrew Elliot, Paula Gottlieb, Wendy Grolnick, Diane Hamm, Alice Isen, Carroll Izard, Richard Koestner, Randy Larsen, Wayne Ludvigson, David McClelland, Henry Newell, Glen Nix, Angela O'Donnell, Brad Olson, Dawn Robinson, Tom Rocklin, Richard Ryan, Carl Rogers, Lynn Smith-Lovin, Richard Solomon, Silvan Tomkins, Robert Vallerand, and Dan Wegner. I consider each of these contributors to be my colleague, mentor, and kindred spirit in the fun and struggle to understand human strivings. My second expression of gratitude goes to those who explicitly donated their time and energy to reviewing the early drafts of the book, including Sandor B. Brent, Robert Emmons, Wayne Harrison, John Hinson, Wesley J. Kasprow, John Kounios, Michael McCall, James J. Ryan, Peter Senkowski, Michael Sylvester, and A. Bond Woodruff. My third expression of gratitude goes to those colleagues who provided valuable comments and suggestions for this edition: Gustavo Carlo, University of Nebraska; Valeri Farmer-Dougan, Illinois State University; Eddie Harmon-Jones, University of Wisconsin; Carol A. Hayes, Delta State University; Mark S. Hoyert, Indiana University Northwest; Norman E. Kinney, Southeast Missouri State University; Robert Madigan, University of Alaska; Randall Martin, Northern Illinois University; Jim McMartin, California State University; and Ronald R. Ulm, Salisbury State University.

I sincerely thank all the students I have had the pleasure to know over the years. It was back at Ithaca College that I first became convinced that my students wanted and needed such a book. In a very real sense, I wrote the first edition for them. The students who occupy my thoughts today are those with me at the University of Iowa, here in Iowa City. For readers familiar with the earlier editions, this third edition presents a tone that is decidedly more practical and applied. Every chapter now reflects an equal balance between, on the one hand, what motivation researchers know and, on the other hand, what students see as most worth learning.

Ithaca is doubly important to me, because it was in this beautiful town in upstate New York that I met Deborah Van Patten of Harcourt College Publishers. Deborah was every bit as responsible for getting this book off the ground as I was. Though 10 years have now passed, I still want to express my deep gratitude to you, Deborah. The professionals at Harcourt have been wonderful. Everyone at Harcourt has been both a valuable resource and a source of pleasure, especially Elaine Richards, Katie Matthews, Megan McDaniel, Serena Sipho, and Brian Salisbury.

I am especially grateful for the advice, patience, assistance, and direction provided by Christine Abshire. Thanks.

—Johnmarshall Reeve

To Richard Troelstrup, who introduced me to psychology.

To Edwin Guthrie, who interested me in psychology.

To Steven Cole, who mentored me so I could participate in this wonderful profession.

Brief Contents

Detailed Contents

I

INTRODUCTION TO THE STUDY OF MOTIVATION

What is motivation? What is emotion? What is the difference between motivation and emotion? Are there differences between the two? One reason to read this book is, of course, to find answers to such questions. But as a way of beginning the journey, pause for a moment and generate your own answers, however preliminary or tentative. Perhaps scribble a definition for motivation and a definition for emotion in the margins of this book.

To define motivation and emotion, notice that you first need to come up with a noun to begin your definition (as in motivation is a ___). Is motivation a feeling? a way of thinking? a sense of striving? an urge? a desire for something? Is it a need or a collection of needs? In three pages, the text offers a definition of motivation, in the section "Subject Matter," that almost everyone who studies it would agree with. The first part of chapter 14, "What Is an Emotion?" presents a detailed definition for emotion.

For most people, trying to understand motivation and its mysteries is an inherently interesting thing to do. And this seems to be so for two reasons. First, few topics spark and entertain the imagination as well as does motivation. Anything that tells us about who we are, why we want what we want, and how we can improve our lives is going to be interesting. Anything that helps us understand other people, why they want what they want, and how we can improve their lives is also going to be interesting. When stumped in trying to explain why people do what they do, we can turn to theories of motivation to see what they have to say about topics such as human nature, strivings for achievement and power, desires for biological sex and for psychological intimacy, emotions like fear and anger, acts of altruism and acts of aggression, and the psychophysiology of hunger and of eating disorders like obesity and bulimia. Investigating these topics and asking questions like, "Why is desire sometimes strong and resilient but other times wanes and disappears altogether?" is what motivation researchers do.

Second, few topics are more important and relevant to our lives than motivation. Its study can be an extremely practical and worthwhile undertaking. It can be quite useful to know where motivation comes from, why it sometimes changes and why other times it does not, under what conditions motivation increases or decreases, what aspects of motivation can and cannot be changed, and what types of motivation are associated with productive engagement and what types are not? Such understandings apply nicely to situations such as trying to tutor students, motivate employees, coach athletes, counsel clients, raise children, or change our own ways of thinking, feeling, and behaving. To the extent that a study of motivation can tell us how we can improve our lives and also how we can improve the lives of those we love, learning about motivation then promises to be time well spent.

The utility of studying motivation is that it promises to equip us with both the theoretical knowledge and the practical know-how needed to understand and to accomplish whatever it is we think is important. As a case in point, consider exercise. Think about it for a moment—why would anyone *want* to exercise? From where does the motivation to exercise come? Are people more willing to exercise under some conditions than under other conditions? Can anything be done to increase people's motivation to exercise? If someone hates exercising, can another encourage in him or her a truly volitional sense of wanting to exercise? The following paragraph is about exercising, but actually, it could be about the motivation underlying almost any other activity—studying, developing a talent, learning to read, practicing the piano, graduating from school, eating less, improving a tennis serve, and so on. In each case, the same question would linger—why do people want to do things?

Why run laps around a track, jump up and down during aerobics, walk briskly in the park, or swim laps in a pool? Why run when you know your lungs will collapse for want of air; why jump and stretch when you know your muscles will rip and tear; why take an hour out of the day for a brisk walk when your schedule will not allow it; and why exercise when life offers so many other interesting things to do? Of course, plenty of good reasons exist in answering these questions.

Children exercise spontaneously—they run and jump and chase, and they do so simply for the sheer fun of it (i.e., intrinsic motivation). Most of us exercise, however, for more utilitarian reasons, such as to please a coach or to win a scholarship (i.e., extrinsic motivation). Goal setting can motivate exercise, as some people care very much whether they can run a mile in 6 minutes or less. Other people can and sometimes do inspire us to exercise, such as an athlete we want to be like or a model who is slim and trim (i.e., possible selves). And exercise sometimes offers us a challenge—a standard of excellence—to pursue, such as a skier racing to the bottom of the mountain against the clock (achievement strivings; flow). Some of the motivation to exercise grows out of a sense of accomplishment and satisfaction from a job well done (competence; effectance motivation). Some people say that jogging gives them an emotional kick, a runner's high (opponent process theory). Sometimes beautiful weather can pick up our mood and invigorate exercise spontaneously, as we skip along or walk briskly without even knowing why (positive affect). Others exercise to relieve stress, silence depression, and gain a sense of personal control in their lives (personal control beliefs). And exercise is often a social event, a time simply to enjoy hanging out with friends (relatedness), or a chance to test our skills against others (social comparison).

For those who value exercise (or studying, developing a talent, learning to read, etc.), paying attention to why people want to exercise becomes both an interesting and a practical undertaking. What motivation research revolves around is the effort to generate and then test the accuracy and viability of hypotheses and theories in explaining motivational phenomena, such as those listed above for exercise. For instance, motivation researchers could ask any or all of the following questions: Which of the above explanations are valid and which are erroneous? Can we produce any evidence that people will want to exercise more when they adopt a goal? Does exercise really relieve stress, reduce depression, provide a sense of accomplishment, or produce a "runner's high"? If exercise produces any of these effects, then under what conditions does it do so? Once a hypothesis can be validated, it not only allows us to gain a deeper understanding of the phenomenon (i.e., gain theoretical knowledge), but it also helps us construct workable solutions to solve the problems we and others face in our lives (i.e., gain practical know-how).

TWO PERENNIAL QUESTIONS

The study of motivation revolves around providing the best possible answers for two fundamental questions:

1. What causes behavior?
2. Why does behavior vary in its intensity?

Motivation's first fundamental question is, "What causes behavior?" (Or alternatively, "Why did she do that?") We see people behave, but we cannot see the underlying causes of their behavior. We watch people show great effort and persistence (or none at all), but the reasons why they show great effort and persistence remain unobserved. The chief reason why motivation has such an important place in the general field of psychology is that motivation helps explain the behavior we observe.

To really explain the underlying causes of behavior, however, we need to expand this general question into a series of more specific questions: How does behavior start? Once begun, how is behavior sustained over time? From where does the psychological experience of "want" come? Why is behavior directed toward some goals yet away from others? Why does behavior change its direction? or its intensity? Why does behavior stop? In other words, it is not enough to ask why a person practices a sport, why a child reads books, or why an adolescent refuses to sing in the choir. We must also ask why athletes begin to practice in the first place. What energizes their effort hour after hour, day after day, season after season? Why do they practice that sport rather than another? Why are they practicing now rather than, say, hanging out with their friends? When they do practice, why do they quit either during the day or during their lifetimes? These same questions can be asked for children as they read their books: Why begin? Why continue reading past the first page? past the first chapter? Why pick that particular book rather than one of the other books sitting on the shelf? Why stop reading? Will their reading continue in the years to come? For a more personal example, why did you begin to read this book today? Will you continue reading to the end of the chapter? Will you continue reading until the end of the book? If you do stop before the end, at what point will you stop? Why? After reading, what will you do next? Why?

Motivation's first perennial question—What causes behavior?—can, therefore, be elaborated into the study of how motivation affects behavior's initiation, persistence, change, goal directedness, and eventual termination. This question is either one grand question, or it is five interrelated questions. Either way, the first essential problem in a motivational analysis of behavior is to understand how motivation participates in, influences, and helps explain the stream of behavior.

Motivation's second fundamental question is, "Why does behavior vary in its intensity?" Behavior varies both within the individual and between different individuals. The idea that motivation can vary within the individual means that at one time a person can be actively engaged yet at another time can be passive and listless. The idea that motivation can vary between individuals means that, even in the same situation, some people can be actively engaged while others are passive and listless.

Within any one individual, motivation varies over time. Behavior almost always varies in its intensity, such as showing high or low effort, persistence, intensity, promptness, or liveliness. Some days an employee works rapidly and diligently; other days the work is lethargic. One day a student shows strong enthusiasm, strives for excellence, and shows determined goal-directed striving; yet the next day, the same student is listless, does only the minimal amount of work, and avoids being challenged academically. Why the same person shows strong and persistent motivation at one time yet weak and unenthusiastic motivation at another time needs to be explained and understood. Why does the worker perform so well on Monday but not on Tuesday? Why do children say they are not hungry in the morning, yet the same children complain of urgent hunger in the afternoon? Why does the driver get so angry and upset when stuck in traffic at one time yet remain undisturbed at another? Behavior's intensity varies from time to time and from day to day, so the second essential problem in a motivational analysis of behavior is to understand why behavior varies in intensity from one moment to the next, from one day to the next, and from one year to the next.

Between different people, motivation varies even in the same situation. We all share the same basic motivations (hunger, need for affiliation, anger, and so on), but people do clearly differ in what motivates them. Many motives are relatively strong for one person yet relatively weak for another. Why is one person a sensation seeker who continually seeks out strong sources of stimulation, such as riding a motorcycle, whereas another person is a sensation avoider who finds such strong stimulation more of an irritant than a source of excitement? In a contest, why do some people strive diligently to win, whereas others care little about winning and strive more to make friends? Some people seem so easy to anger, whereas others seem rarely upset. For those motives in which wide individual differences exist, motivation study investigates how such differences arise and what implications they hold. So another motivational problem to solve is to recognize that individuals differ in what motivates them and to explain why one person shows intense behavioral engagement while another does not.

SUBJECT MATTER

To explain why people do what they do, we need a theory of motivation. The usefulness of a motivation theory is that it allows us to explain what gives a person's behavior its energy and its direction. It is some motive that energizes the athlete, and it is some motive that directs the student's behavior toward a particular goal. *The study of motivation concerns those processes that give behavior its energy and direction.* Energy implies that behavior has strength—that it is relatively strong, intense, and persistent. Direction implies that behavior has purpose—that it is aimed toward achieving a particular goal.

The processes that energize and direct behavior emanate from forces in the individual and in the environment, as shown in Figure 1.1. Motives are internal experiences—needs, cognitions, and emotions—that energize the individual's approach and avoidance

FIGURE 1.1 **Hierarchy of the Four Sources of Motivation**

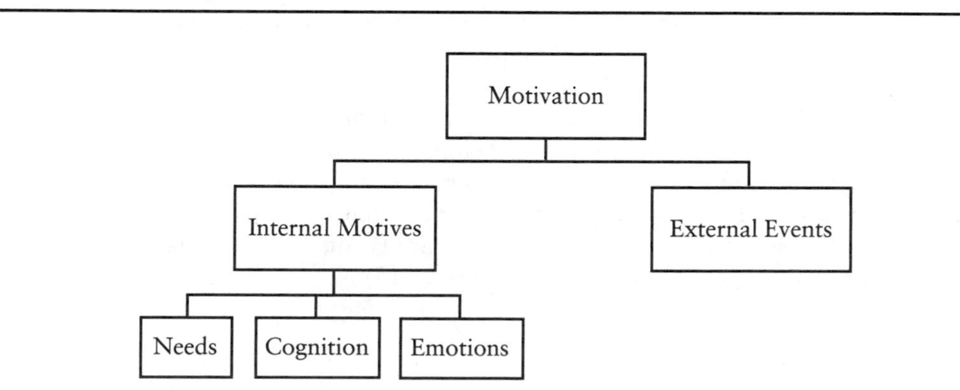

tendencies. External events are environmental incentives that attract or repel the individual in engaging or not engaging in behavior.

MOTIVES

Motive is a general term that identifies the common ground shared by needs, cognitions, and emotions (each is an internal process that energizes and directs behavior). The difference between a motive and a need, cognition, or emotion is simply the level of analysis (general versus specific, as needs, cognitions, and emotions are specific types of motives; see Figure 1.1).

Needs are conditions within the individual that are essential and necessary for the maintenance of life and for the nurturance of growth and well-being. Hunger and thirst exemplify two motivational states that arise from the physiological needs for food and water. Both food and water are essential and necessary for biological maintenance, well-being, and growth. Competence and belongingness exemplify two motivational states that arise from psychological needs for environmental mastery and warm interpersonal relationships. Both competence and belongingness are essential and necessary for psychological maintenance, well-being, and growth. Needs serve the organism by generating wants, desires, and strivings that motivate whatever behaviors are necessary for the maintenance of life and for the promotion of well-being and growth. Part I discusses specific types of needs: physiological needs (chapter 3), organismic psychological needs (chapter 4), and acquired social needs (chapter 6).

Cognitions refer to specific mental events, such as beliefs and expectations, and to organized structures of beliefs, such as the self-concept. Cognitive sources of motivation revolve around the person's relatively enduring ways of thinking. For instance, as students, athletes, or salespersons engage in a task, they have in mind some plan or goal and they hold beliefs about their abilities, expectations for success and failure, ways of explaining their successes and failures, and an understanding of who they are and what their role in the larger society is, and so forth. Part II discusses specific cognitive sources of motivation: plans and goals (chapter 7), expectancies (chapter 8), attributions and values (chapter 9), and the self (chapter 10).

Emotions organize and orchestrate four interrelated aspects of experience: feelings, physiological preparedness (how our body becomes mobilized to meet situational demands), function (what we want to accomplish), and expression (how we communicate our inner experience publicly to others). By orchestrating these four aspects of experience into a coherent pattern, emotions allow us to react adaptively to the important events in our lives. When facing a threat to our well-being, for instance, we feel afraid, our heart rate increases, we strive to escape, and the corners of our lips are drawn backward in such a way that others can recognize and respond to our experience. Other emotions, such as anger and joy, show similar coherent patterns. Part IV discusses the nature of emotion (chapter 14) as well as its different aspects (chapter 15).

EXTERNAL EVENTS

External events are environmental incentives and consequences that provide behavior with energy and direction. For instance, offering money often energizes approach behavior, hostile audiences energize defensive avoidance, and public recognition directs people's behavior toward striving harder at events such as a sporting competition. The incentive (money, audience, and public recognition) signals information that a particular behavior will likely produce rewarding or punishing consequences. In doing so, incentives create motivation for those particular behaviors. Consequences (i.e., actually receiving the money, hostility, or recognition) strengthen whatever behaviors produce the consequences. Consequences, therefore, direct behavior by making some goals and some behaviors more probable (i.e., doing what one gets rewarded for doing) and other goals and behaviors less probable (i.e., ignoring everything else).

From a broader perspective, external events also include environmental contexts, social situations, climates (e.g., those that emerge in the classroom, family, and workplace), and sociological forces such as culture. Chapter 5 discusses how incentives, consequences, and larger social contexts add to a motivational analysis of behavior.

EXPRESSIONS OF MOTIVATION

In addition to identifying motivation's perennial problems and its subject matter, one more introductory task remains—namely, specifying how motivation expresses itself. In other words, how can you tell when someone is or is not motivated? Or as you watch the behavior of two people, how do you know that one person is more motivated than the other?

Two primary means exist to infer motivation in another person. The first way is to observe motivation's behavioral manifestations. To infer hunger, for instance, we watch to see whether Joe eats more quickly than usual, chews vigorously, talks about eating during conversation, and forgoes social manners for the opportunity to eat. Behaving quickly, vigorously, and narrowly implies that some force must be energizing and directing Joe's consummatory behavior. The second way to infer motivation is to pay close attention to the antecedents known to give rise to motivational states. After 72 hours of food deprivation, a person will be hungry; after feeling threatened, a person will feel fear; after winning a competition, a person will feel competent; and so on. Food deprivation leads to hunger, a threat appraisal leads to fear, and objective messages of effectance lead to feeling competent. Because the antecedents to many motivational states are known, we are not always left in the precarious position of having to infer motivation from behavior. That is, we can predict people's motivational states in advance with confidence as we take notice that the person has gone without food, been threatened, or just won the championship. But these antecedents are not always known. Sometimes, motivation must be inferred from its expressions—its behavior, physiology, and self-report.

Behavior

Seven aspects of behavior express both the presence and intensity of motivation (Atkinson & Birch, 1970, 1978; Bolles, 1975; Ekman & Friesen, 1975): effort, latency, persistence, choice, probability of response, facial expressions, and bodily gestures.

Effort

Effort is the extent of exertion put forth while trying to accomplish a task. Often, the phrase "expenditure of effort" is used to mark high motivation, as expenditure of effort varies in proportion to the environmental demands placed on the individual. As demands rise, the person must utilize more of her total capacity to cope effectively (Kahneman, 1973). Thus, when challenged, people utilize more attention, more arousal, and more muscular exertion than when not challenged. Putting forth high effort essentially means putting forth a good deal of one's total capacity. Similar to effort is intensity, which is the amplitude of the individual's response to a stimulus event. In a study of the joy emotion, for instance, researchers watched participants' facial expressions to infer how much joy they felt. The more intensely each person pulled back his zygomatic muscles of the cheek and mouth (the smile muscles), the stronger was his inferred joy (Pope & Smith, 1994). As a rule of thumb, the more one uses her capacity (i.e., the greater the expenditure of effort) and the greater is the intensity of the behavior, the greater is the strength of the underlying motive.

Latency

Latency is the time a person delays a response following an initial exposure to a stimulus event. For example, if a child cries immediately after separation from the mother, such a quick reaction (i.e., a short latency to respond) allows an observer to infer high separation anxiety, relative to another child who cries moments or hours after such a separation. Or if a child walks into a room, sees a toy, and wastes no time in picking up that toy to play with, then such a quick reaction allows the observer to infer high task interest. In these examples, latency is the elapsed time between separation from the mother and the crying or the elapsed time between seeing the toy and picking it up. As a rule of thumb, as response latency decreases, the presence and intensity of the underlying motive increases.

Persistence

Persistence is the time between the initiation of a response until its cessation. In the previous two examples, persistence is the number of seconds or minutes the child continues to cry and the number of seconds or minutes the child continues to play with the toy. Persistence is proportional to the intensity of the underlying motive for that activity (and inversely proportional to the intensity of the motives to engage in alternative activities). The person who continues a goal-directed act for an extended period expresses the more intense motive than does the person who quickly quits. Notice that persistence and effort are not the same thing, though persistence is essentially effort over time. Persistence and effort are not interchangeable, however, because a person can be persistent at a task for a long period of time yet sustain a low daily rate of effort, as with students working on their degrees, savers working to achieve their fortunes, and musicians honing their talents.

Choice

Choice, or preference for one course of action over another, presents the individual with two or more options in which she selects one particular course of action. At any given time, we typically face a large number of options from which to choose. For instance, you can read this book, go to the refrigerator for a drink, pick up the phone to call a friend, take a nap, listen to music, and so on. Preference of one course of action over another expresses the strength of the motives underlying each course of action (i.e., reading, drinking, affiliating, sleeping, and sensation seeking). In designing an experiment on altruism, for instance, a researcher might give the participant the choice between either helping or not helping, and the participants who choose to help express the greater underlying motive for altruism.

Probability of Response

Probability of response refers to the number of occasions a goal-directed response occurs per number of opportunities the response had an opportunity to occur. If two people are put into a situation 10 times, the person who performs the response 8 times expresses the more intense motive than does the person who performs the response only 3 times. Thus, other things being equal, the person who telephones his friends 8 nights out of 10 expresses the stronger need for affiliation than does the person who telephones his friends only 3 nights out of 10 (Lansing & Heyns, 1959).

Facial Expressions

Facial muscle movements communicate the specific content of feelings and emotions (Ekman & Friesen, 1975; Ekman & Rosenberg, 1997). People communicate a feeling of fear when they raise and draw together their eyebrows, wrinkle the center of their forehead, and tensely draw back and stretch their lips. People communicate a feeling of disgust when they wrinkle their nose, raise their upper lip, and lower their brow a bit. People communicate a feeling of anger when they lower and draw together their eyebrows, tense their lips, and show a hard stare with their eyes. People communicate a feeling of joy when they draw up and back the corners of their lips, raise their cheeks, and show wrinkles below their lower eyelids. And people communicate a feeling of sadness when they draw up the inner corners of their eyebrows, raise the inner corners of their upper eyelids, and turn down the corners of their lips. Thus, the nonverbal behavior of the face communicates the existence of, and the intensity of, an underlying emotion.

Bodily Gestures

Bodily gestures like posture, weight shifts, and the movements of the legs, arms, and hands (e.g., a clenched fist) communicate underlying desires and preferences. Consider, for example, the next time you find yourself engaged in a rather boring face-to-face conversation. When you wish to terminate the conversation, consciously or unconsciously, you will signal your desire to depart by (1) shifting your weight from an equal to an unequal distribution, (2) crossing your legs (while standing), and (3) moving away from the other person (Lockard et al., 1978). Shifting your weight, crossing your legs, and increasing the distance between yourself and your conversant all express a desire to escape from the interaction.

Overview

These seven aspects of behavior provide the observer with data to infer the presence and intensity of another person's motivation. When behavior shows intense effort, short latency, long persistence, high probability of occurrence, facial or gestural expressiveness, or when the individual pursues a specific goal-object in lieu of another, such is the evidence to infer the presence of a relatively intense motive. When behavior shows lackadaisical effort, long latency, short persistence, low probability of occurrence, minimal facial and gestural expressiveness, or the individual pursues an alternative goal-object, such is the evidence to infer an absence of a motive or at least a relatively weak motive. The term "engagement" nicely captures an overview sense of how intense a person's motivation is. Engagement refers to the intensity and emotional quality of a person's involvement with an activity (Connell & Wellborn, 1991; Skinner & Belmont, 1993). It features both behavioral and emotional aspects, such that an engaged student expresses not only high effort, persistence, attention, and the like, but also a positive emotional tone (e.g., high interest, low anxiety) during that effort.

PHYSIOLOGY

As people and animals prepare to engage in various activities, the nervous and endocrine systems manufacture and release various chemical substances (e.g., neurotransmitters, hormones) that provide the biological underpinnings of motivational and emotional states (Andreassi, 1986; Coles, Ponchin, & Porges, 1986). Some parallels exists between neurotransmitters and hormones; both are chemical substances that operate within a communication network, as cells release neurotransmitters to affect other cells while glands secrete hormones to affect bodily organs. In the course of a public speech, for example, speakers experience acute emotional stress to various degrees, and that emotionality manifests itself physiologically through a rise in plasma catecholamines (e.g., adrenaline; Bolm-Avdorff et al., 1989). The rise in catecholamines serves as the biological underpinning of the felt stress. To measure various neural and hormonal changes, researchers use blood tests, saliva tests, urine analyses, and a host of psychophysiological measures involving complex electrical equipment (e.g., electromyograph, galvanic skin response). Using these measures, motivation researchers monitor a person's heart rate, blood pressure, respiratory rate, pupil diameter, skin conductance, contents of blood plasma, and other indices of physiological functioning to infer the presence and intensity of underlying motivational and emotional states.

Psychophysiology

Psychophysiology is an amalgamation of psychology and physiology. The goals of psychophysiological experiments are (1) to observe how the body prepares its biological systems to perform psychologically and behaviorally and (2) to use that knowledge to understand the physiology of motivation and emotion. The five bodily arousal systems that express motivation and emotion are cardiovascular, plasma, ocular (eye), electrodermal, and skeletal muscle activity.

Cardiovascular activity (cardia, heart; vascular, blood vessels) increases with the pursuit of difficult/challenging tasks and attractive incentives (Fowles, 1983). For instance, intensity of cardiac activity is proportional to intensity of a monetary incentive (Fowles, Fisher, & Tranel, 1982; Tranel, Fisher, & Fowles, 1982) and therefore expresses extent of want or desire.[1] *Plasma activity* involves the contents of the blood stream, particularly the catecholamines of epinephrine and norepinephrine, which regulate the fight-or-flight reaction. Epinephrine (or adrenaline) coincides with feelings of tension and anxiety, whereas norepinephrine (or noradrenaline) coincides with aggressive strivings and perceptions of control (Dimsdale & Moss, 1980). *Ocular activity* involves eye behavior—pupil size, eye blinks, and eye movements. Pupil size correlates with the extent of mental activity required to complete a task (Beatty, 1982, 1986; Kahneman, 1973; Stern, Walrath, & Goldstein, 1984); eye blinks (the involuntary ones) express changing cognitive states, allocation of attention, and transition points in the information processing flow (Stern et al., 1984); and lateral eye movements increase in frequency during reflective thought (Woods, Beecher, & Ris, 1978), as during an interview (Meskin & Singer, 1974; Woods & Steigman, 1978). *Electrodermal activity* refers to the electrical changes on the surface of the skin, as during sweating. Novel, emotional, threatening, and attention-getting stimuli all evoke electrodermal activity (Raskin, 1973) and therefore express threat, aversion, and stimulus significance. *Skeletal activity* involves the musculature, and as discussed earlier in the section "Facial Expressions," researchers routinely record skeletal muscular activity in the face to collect information about emotional states (Cacioppo et al., 1986; Fridlund & Izard, 1983; Larsen, Kasimatis, & Frey, 1992; Russell & Fernandez-Dols, 1997; Sackeim, Gur, & Saucy, 1978; Schwartz, 1986; Schwartz, Brown, & Ahern, 1980).

SELF-REPORT

A third way to collect data to infer the presence and intensity of motivation is simply to ask. Typically people can introspect and self-report their level of motivation, as in an interview or on a questionnaire. An interviewer might assess anxiety, for instance, by asking how anxious the interviewee feels in particular settings or by asking the interviewee to report anxiety-related symptoms such as an upset stomach or thoughts of failure. These same questions could also be asked on a pencil-and-paper or computerized questionnaire. For instance, a questionnaire might ask, "When interacting with strangers, how anxious do you feel?" and include a one-to-four response scale in which one indicates "not at all," two indicates "a little," three indicates "some," and four indicates "very much."

Questionnaires have several advantages. They are easy to administer, can be given to many people simultaneously, and can target very specific information (Carlsmith, Ellsworth, & Aronson, 1976). At least four reasons exist, however, to suggest self-report ratings might not reflect a person's true underlying motivation (Mitchell & Jolley, 1988). First, people might intentionally distort their self-reports to produce socially desirable,

[1] On the other hand, cardiac activity decreases when the individual pays close attention to some aspect of the environment (Lacey et al., 1963; Reeve, 1993) and therefore may express interest.

rather than actual, ratings. Recognizing this, questionnaire developers go to great lengths to validate their measures. Second, people may not know their own motives (Nisbett & Wilson, 1977). It is a difficult task, even when being fully honest, to report precisely what one's underlying sex drive, achievement striving, or fear is at any moment. Third, self-report ratings frequently ask for a retrospective account (e.g., "How nervous do you feel when talking to strangers?") and therefore depend on a person's memory for their accuracy. Fourth, self-report questionnaires are not applicable to animals, infants, or verbally handicapped individuals (Plutchik, 1980).

While questionnaires have advantages, they also have pitfalls that raise a red flag of caution as to their usefulness. Many researchers lament the lack of correspondence between what people say they do and what they actually do (for reviews see Quattrone, 1985; Wicker, 1969). Further, there is also a lack of correspondence between how people say they feel and what their psychophysiological activity indicates they probably feel (Hodgson & Rachman, 1974; Rachman & Hodgson, 1974). Hence, what people say their motives are sometimes are not what people's behavioral and physiological expressions suggest their motives are. What conclusion, for instance, can one draw when a person verbally reports low anger but shows a quick latency to aggress with eyebrows that are drawn tightly downward and together and a rapid acceleration in heart rate? Because of such discrepancies, motivation researchers typically rely on only a conservative use of self-report measures. In contrast, these same researchers trust and rely heavily on behavioral and physiological measures. Therefore, self-report measures are used mostly to confirm the validity of behavioral and physiological measures.

THEMES IN THE STUDY OF MOTIVATION

Motivation study includes a wide range of assumptions, hypotheses, theories, findings, and domains of application. But motivation study also has a number of unifying themes that integrate these assumptions, hypotheses, theories, findings, and applications into a coherent field of study. The following are nine themes that run throughout this text and throughout the contemporary study of motivation:

- Motivation Benefits Adaptation
- Motives Affect Behavior by Directing Attention
- Motive Strengths Vary Over Time and Influence the Stream of Behavior
- Motivation Includes Both Approach and Avoidance Tendencies
- Motivation Study Reveals the Contents of Human Nature
- Motivation Varies Not Only in Its Intensity but Also in Its Type
- We Are Not Always Consciously Aware of the Motivational Basis of Our Behavior
- Motivational Principles Can Be Applied
- There Is Nothing So Practical As a Good Theory

MOTIVATION BENEFITS ADAPTATION

For anyone who has taken a course in psychology or biology, one lesson you probably learned is that humans and animals are complex adaptive systems. Another lesson in psychology and biology is that environments always change. Job demands rise and fall, educational opportunities change, relationships change, athletic seasons change, personal health status changes, and so on. Motivation benefits adaptation to ever-changing circumstances because motivational states arise whenever discrepancies occur between one's well-being and moment-to-moment demands.

When people go for hours without food and when food supply is scarce, biological and psychological states create hunger motivation. When deadlines become too numerous, biological and psychological states create stress. When a person gains control over a difficult problem, biological and psychological states create a sense of mastery, achievement, and well-being. When the sunshine and warm temperatures are surprising, biological and psychological states create a good mood. Therefore, one theme that runs throughout this book is that motivational states (e.g., hunger, stress, achievement, good mood) provide a key means for the individual to cope successfully with life's inevitable demands. Take away the motivational states, and people would quickly lose a vital resource they rely on constantly to adapt and maintain their well-being.

When motivation sours, personal adaptation suffers. People who feel helpless in exerting control over their fates tend to give up quickly when challenged (Peterson, Maier, & Seligman, 1993). People who face challenges with more doubt than confidence tend to avoid interacting with their surroundings (Bandura, 1997). And people who are bossed around, coerced, and controlled tend to become emotionally flat and numb to the hopes and aspirations embedded within their inner psychological needs (Deci, 1995). In contrast, when the quality of a person's motivational states is strong and purposive, personal adaptation thrives.[2] As a case in point, when kids are excited about school, when workers try hard, and when athletes gain confidence, and teachers, supervisors, and coaches can rest assured each of these persons will be able to adapt successfully to his unique environment. Hence, the quality of motivation benefits the quality of personal adaptation.

Motives Affect Behavior by Directing Attention

Environments constantly demand our attention in a multitude of ways. Just driving down the road, for instance, we have many things to do—avoid hitting the other cars, listen and respond to our passenger's interesting story, find some particular destination, keep our bodies warm from the cold, avoid spilling our coffee, and arrive at a destination in a limited amount of time. Similarly, a college student must simultaneously make good grades, maintain old friendships, eat healthy, balance budgets of money and time, plan for the future, wash clothes, develop artistic talents, keep abreast of world news, and so on. Who is to say whether our attention is allocated in one direction or the other? Much of that "say" comes from motivational states. Motives have a way of gaining, and sometimes

---

[2] One useful indicator of how well or how poorly people are currently adapting to the demands placed on them can be found in their emotional states. When people adapt successfully and when development progresses, people experience and express positive emotions such as joy, hope, interest, and optimism. But when people are overwhelmed by their environment and when development stagnates, people experience and express negative emotions such as sadness, hopelessness, frustration, and stress.

demanding, our attention so that we attend to one aspect of the environment and to one course of behavior rather than to other aspects and behaviors.

Motives affect behavior by directing attention to select some behaviors over others. An illustration of how motives grab our attention and channel our behavior appears in Table 1.1. The table's four columns list, from left to right, (a) a half-dozen aspects of the environment, (b) a motive typically aroused under those conditions, (c) a motive-satisfying course of action, and (d) a hypothetical priority or sense of urgency given to each course of action as determined by the intensity of the underlying motivational state. While six courses of action are possible, attention is not allocated equally to each behavior because the motive strengths associated with each environmental condition vary (as denoted by the number of asterisks in the far right column). Because rest and thirst are not urgent at that particular time (one asterisk), their salience is low and they fail to grab attention. The motive to avoid pain, aroused by a headache, however, is highly salient (five asterisks) and will grab attention and direct behavior toward taking aspirin. Motives, therefore, influence behavior by capturing attention, interrupting what we are doing, distracting us from doing other things, and imposing a priority onto our behaviors that is relevant to a particular motive.

MOTIVE STRENGTHS VARY OVER TIME AND INFLUENCE THE STREAM OF BEHAVIOR

Motivation is a dynamic process—always changing, always rising and falling—rather than a discrete event or static condition. Not only do motive strengths constantly rise and fall, but people always harbor a multitude of different motives at any one point in time. One motive is typically strongest, while others are relatively subordinate (i.e., one motive dominates our attention, while others lie relatively dormant, as in Table 1.1). The strongest motive typically has the greatest influence on our behavior, but each subordinate motive can become dominant and can therefore influence the ongoing stream of behavior.

As an illustration, consider a typical study session in which a student sits at a desk with book in hand. Our scholar's goal is to read the book, a relatively strong motive on this occasion because of an upcoming examination. The student reads for an hour, but during this time, curiosity becomes satisfied, fatigue sets in, and various subordinate

TABLE 1.1 **How Motives Influence Behavior for a Student Sitting at a Desk**

ENVIRONMENTAL EVENT	AROUSED MOTIVE	MOTIVE-RELEVANT COURSE OF ACTION	MOTIVE'S URGENCY ATTENTION-GETTING STATUS
Book	Interest	Read chapter.	*
Cola	Thirst	Drink beverage.	*
Familiar voices	Affiliation	Talk with friends.	* * *
Headache	Pain avoidance	Take aspirin.	* * * * *
Lack of sleep	Rest	Lie down, nap.	*
Upcoming competition	Achievement	Practice skill.	* *

Note: The number of asterisks in column 4 represents the intensity of the aroused motive. One asterisk denotes the lowest intensity level, while five asterisks denote the highest intensity level.

motives—such as hunger and affiliation—begin to increase in strength. Perhaps the smell of popcorn from a neighbor's room makes its way down the hallway, or perhaps the sight of a close friend passing by in the hallway increases the relative strength of an affiliation motive. If the affiliation motive increases in strength to a dominant level, then our scholar's stream of behavior will shift direction from studying to affiliating.

A stream of behavior in which a person performs a set of three behaviors, X, Y, and Z (e.g., studying, eating, and affiliating; Atkinson, Bongort, & Price, 1977) appears in Figure 1.2. The figure plots the changes in the strength of each of these three motives that produce the observed stream of behavior. At time 1, motive X (studying) is the dominant motive, while motives Y and Z are relatively subordinate. At time 2, motive Y (eating) has increased in strength above motive X, while motive Z remains subordinate. At time 3, motive Z (affiliating) gains relative dominance and exerts its influence on the stream of behavior. Overall, Figure 1.2 illustrates that (a) motive strengths change over time, (b) people forever harbor a multitude of motives of various intensities, any one of which might at some time grab attention and participate in the stream of behavior, given the appropriate circumstances, and (c) motives are not something a person either does or does not have, but instead, these motives rise and fall during a cycle of lying dormant, emerging into consciousness, being satisfied or frustrated, and growing or fading in intensity.

Motivation Includes Both Approach and Avoidance Tendencies

Generally speaking, people presuppose that to be motivated is better than to be unmotivated. Indeed, the two most frequent questions in motivation are, "How can I motivate myself to do better (or more)?" and "How can I motivate another person to do better (or

Figure 1.2 **Stream of Behavior and the Changes in the Strength of Its Underlying Motives**

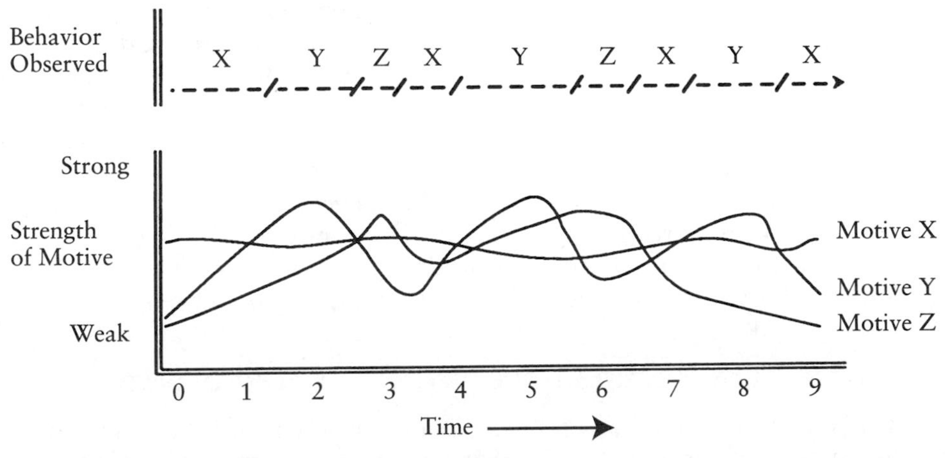

Source: Adapted from "Cognitive Control of Action," by D. Birch, J. W. Atkinson, and K. Bongort, in *Cognitive View of Human Motivation* (pp. 71–84), B. Weiners (ed.), 1974, New York: Academic Press.

more)?" In other words, how might one get more motivation than one presently has, either for oneself or for others? Clearly, motivation is a state that people long to achieve for themselves and for others.

The problem is that sometimes you get what you wish for. In actuality, several motivational systems are aversive in nature—pain, hunger, distress, fear, dissonance, anxiety, pressure, and so on. In fact, the early motivation theorists (who will be presented in chapter 2) conceptualized human beings as continually struggling to ward off noxious states of affairs. In Freudian theory, for example, the individual is perpetually warding off instinctual energies of sex and aggression, and behavior occurs because people need to cope with, escape from, and defend against these anxieties. In Hullian theory, motivation occurs with biological deprivation states (e.g., deprivation of food, deprivation of water), and behavior serves as the means by which survival continues for another day. In cognitive dissonance theory (Harmon-Jones & Mills, 1999), inconsistent beliefs (i.e., "I believe X, but non-X also seems to be true") create an averse emotional state that pokes a psychological needle in one's side until the person adjusts either his way of thinking or way of behaving (e.g., either pick up that litter you just dropped on the ground, or drop your pro-environmentalist attitude—one or the other). In all these theories, the body harbors a multitude of response potentials that lie in wait until ignited to activity by some aversive motivation (i.e., hunger, thirst, dissonance). And "the greater the irritation, the greater the change" (in motivation, emotion, and behavior; Kimble, 1990, p. 36). Therefore, when others ask how they can motivate themselves or how they can motivate others more, they probably do not have in mind an answer like instinctual urges, biological deprivations, or inconsistencies between beliefs and behaviors.

As a point of illustration, monitor your own motivational tendencies during achievement settings, such as taking a test or playing a sport. If you are like the majority, a part of you will likely feel a hope for success and a desire to approach the activity with enthusiasm. Yet, another part of you will likely fear the possibility of failure that creates an anxious desire to avoid the upcoming challenge. The same approach-avoidance motivational conflict accompanies many of our daily motivational experiences (e.g., dating, interviewing for a job, reading this book, riding a motorcycle, going to the doctor).

Human beings are curious, intrinsically motivated, sensation-seeking animals with goals and plans for striving to master challenges, for developing warm interpersonal relationships, and for moving towards attractive incentives, psychological development, and growth. It is also true, however, that people are stressed, frustrated, plagued by insecurities, pressured, afraid, in pain, and depressed and encounter aversive situations from which they wish to flee. Further, people often, and perhaps even typically, feel these positive and negative motivational and emotional states at the same time. To adapt optimally, both positive and negative motivational states need to be part of our repertoire.

Motivation Study Reveals the Contents of Human Nature

The study of motivation reveals why people (and animals) want what they want. But it also reveals the contents of human nature. The subject matter of motivation and emotion concerns what we all hope for, desire, want, need, and fear. It examines questions such as whether people are essentially good or evil, naturally active or passive, brotherly or aggressive, altruistic or egocentric, free to choose or determined by biological demands, and whether or not people harbor within themselves tendencies to grow and to self-actualize.

Theories of motivation reveal what is common within the strivings of all human beings by identifying the commonalities among people from different cultures and from varied experiences. All of us harbor physiological needs such as hunger, thirst, sex, and pain. All of us inherit biological dispositions such as temperament and neural circuits in the brain for pleasure and aversion. We all share a small number of basic emotions, and we all feel these emotions under the same conditions, such as feeling fear when threatened and distress after losing something or someone of high value. As children, we all interact with our surroundings with the same constellation of needs as we explore our surroundings, develop our competencies, refine our skills, and form close attachments to our caregivers. Unconscious processes also exist within us all, and they exert their influence on how we think, feel, and behave.

Theories of motivation also reveal those motivations that are learned. For example, beliefs about our abilities are learned, as is the habitual way we explain life's successes and failures, the long-term goals to which we commit, and the value we place on money and fame. These are needs and wants that we internalized from experience (i.e., people have to learn and internalize the long-term goal of "becoming a teacher"). We also acquire motivations from social and cultural forces, such as the identities we adopt, the possible selves we try to become, and whether we react to environmental objects with attraction or with repulsion. The study of motivation informs us of what part of want and desire stem from human nature and of what part of want and desire stem from personal, social, and cultural learning. In doing both, motivation study reveals the contents of human nature.

Motivation Varies Not Only in Its Intensity but Also in Its Type

In many people's mind, motivation is a unitary concept. In other words, the only feature of motivation that varies is its amount or intensity, and the only concern about motivation is "how much?" In contrast, several motivation theorists suggest that important types of motivations can be distinguished (Ames, 1987; Ames & Archer, 1988; Atkinson, 1964; Condry & Stokker, 1992; Deci, 1992a). For instance, Deci (1992a) distinguished between intrinsic motivation and extrinsic motivation. Ames and Archer (1988) distinguished between motivation to learn and motivation to perform. Atkinson (1964) distinguished between the motivation to approach success and the motivation to avoid failure.

It is important and helpful to pay attention to motivation's intensity, but it can be at least as fruitful to think about types of motivation. Watch as an athlete practices, a student studies, an employee works, and a doctor cares for a patient, and you will see variations in the intensity of motivation. But an equally important observation to make and question to ask is why the athlete practices, why the student studies, why the employee works, and why the doctor provides care. The question of why a person is motivated is an important one to ask and answer because some types of motivation are associated with more productive and psychologically healthier outcomes than are other types of motivation. For instance, students who learn out of an intrinsic motivation (via interest, challenge, curiosity) show more creativity and positive emotionality than do students who learn out of an extrinsic motivation (via grades, stickers, deadlines; Deci & Ryan, 1987). Emotions as well show that the type of motivation matters at least as much as its intensity. For instance, a person who is intensely angry behaves quite differently from a person who is intensely afraid. It helps to know that a person is experiencing an intense emotion, but it helps even more to know which emotion the person is experiencing. So a complete motivational analysis of behavior answers both questions—How much? What type?

We Are Not Always Consciously Aware of the Motivational Basis of Our Behavior

Motives vary in how accessible they are to consciousness and to verbal report. Some motives originate in language structures (e.g., goals) and are thus readily available to conscious awareness (e.g., "I have a goal to sell three insurance policies today"). And if you ask a person why she selected that particular goal (or particular college major, or particular marriage partner, etc.), she more often than not can confidently list the rational and logical reason or reasons. Despite the fact that people can sometimes provide prompt and satisfying motives to explain their behaviors, some acts are impulsive, and the reasons we do what we do are not clear. Some motives have their origins in nonlanguage structures and are thus much less available to consciousness and to verbal report. There is little to be gained by suggesting that some motives reside in "the conscious" while other motives reside in "the unconscious," but the theme here is that motives vary in the degree to which they are available to consciousness and to verbal report.

Consider one study that showed that motives can be obvious or not so obvious. Participants were positioned into either a slumped or an erect posture while they worked on an experimental task (Riskind & Gotay, 1982). The task was unsolvable because the researchers wanted to know what effect posture would have on each performer's persistence. Erect participants persisted significantly longer than did slumped participants, although the two groups did not report any differences in their emotions. In a similar study and after the experimenter manipulated participants' postures as either erect or slumped, participants solved a problem and reported how much pride they felt after solving the problem. Erect achievers reported significantly more pride than did slumped achievers (Stepper & Strack, 1993). Thus, posture affected persistence and pride, but it did so in a way that the performer remained fully unaware.

Many additional experimental findings can be offered in making this point. Consider that people who feel good after receiving an unexpected gift are more likely to help a stranger in need than are people in neutral moods (Isen, 1987). People are more sociable on a sunny day than they are on a cloudy day (Kraut & Johnston, 1979). People commit more acts of violence in summer months than in other times of the year (Anderson, 1989). Major league baseball pitchers are more likely to intentionally hit batters on the opposing team when the temperature is hot rather than cold or moderate (Reifman, Larrick, & Fein, 1991). And after receiving from a therapist a suggestion during hypnosis, people commit acts without knowing why (Hilgard & Hilgard, 1983). In each of these examples, the person is not consciously aware of why he committed the social or antisocial act. Few people, for instance, would say they helped a stranger because they felt good, and few say they commit murder or throw baseballs at the heads of opponents because of the hot temperature. Still, these are conditions that cause motivations. The brief lesson behind these empirical examples is that the motives that regulate human behavior are not always immediately obvious. This theme of hidden motives is one of the primary reasons motivation researchers rely heavily on behavioral and physiological measures and only lightly on self-report measures.

Motivational Principles Can Be Applied

This book provides ideas, information, interpretations, and empirical evidence to help the reader gain a relatively sophisticated understanding of motivation and emotion. Understanding motivation and emotion entails becoming familiar enough with motivational concepts to answer perennial questions (e.g., "What causes behavior?) and to know in advance what effect various conditions will have on people's motivational states (e.g., How does praise affect motivation?). In addition, this book provides illustrations, examples, and food for thought to help the reader feel comfortable in the attempt to apply principles of motivation.

Four areas of application are stressed in this book: (1) education, (2) work, (3) sports, and (4) therapy. And each area of application is based on the assumption that the study of motivation can provide insights in how to attain the objectives sought and, in doing so, help create a better, happier society (McClelland, 1978). In education, an understanding of motivation can be applied to promote students' classroom engagement, to foster the motivation necessary to develop talents like those in music or foreign language, and to inform teachers of how to provide a supportive classroom that will nurture the needs of students at different ages. In work, an understanding of motivation can be applied to improve worker productivity and satisfaction; to structure jobs so that they offer workers optimal levels of challenge, variety, and relatedness with their coworkers; and to identify the role of individual differences in areas such as entrepreneurship and leadership. In sports, an understanding of motivation can be applied to identify the reasons youths participate in sports, to design exercise programs that promote long-term adherence, and to predict the effects on performance of factors such as interpersonal competition, performance feedback, and goal-setting. In therapy, an understanding of motivation can be applied to improve mental and emotional well-being, to appreciate why the quality of interpersonal relationships is so fundamentally important to well-being, and to explain the paradox of why mental control and self-regulation strategies so often backfire.

The tricky part of motivating the self and others is that there are at least two markedly different approaches in doing so (Ryan, Connell, & Grolnick, 1992). One approach assumes that motivation is something people lack, and it therefore needs to be produced from the outside. A teacher, employer, coach, or the like uses incentives and rewards as means for creating enthusiasm about working toward a particular goal. An alternative approach is to support the motivations of students, workers, athletes, and clients from within. This more humanistic approach assumes that motivation is something inherent in us all and that the means of facilitating motivation is to nurture the inner motivational resources people already possess (e.g., competence, curiosity, interest). As you watch one person try to motivate another (e.g., teacher motivating a student, coach motivating an athlete), classify the strategies and techniques you see. As you watch others,

Why We Do What We Do

Question: Why would a person want to learn about the motivational states discussed in this chapter?

Answer: To become aware of motivation theories that *really* explain why people do what they do.

Explaining motivation—why people do what they do—is difficult. People have no shortage of possible motivation theories ("He did that because . . ."), but the problem is that while some of those theories explain behavior well, many of them are erroneous.

By far, the most common theory people hold to motivate others is to increase their self-esteem. The view on self-esteem sounds something like, "Find a way to make them feel good about themselves, and then good things will start to happen." Praise them, reward them, compliment them, give them stickers or trophies; give them some affirmation that they are worthy as a person and that brighter days are ahead." The problem with this strategy is that it is wrong. It is wrong because there is practically no empirical evidence to support it. Educational psychologists, for instance, routinely find that increases in students' self-esteem do not produce increases in their academic achievement (Marsh, 1990; Scheier & Kraut, 1979; Shaalvik & Hagtvet, 1990). One motivation researcher went so far as to conclude that "there are almost no findings that self-esteem causes anything at all" (Seligman, quoted in Azar, 1994, p. 4).

There is a certain value of self-esteem, however. It's ludicrous to wish low self-esteem on someone. The problem is that self-esteem is not a causal variable. Instead, it is an effect—a reflection on how our lives are going. It is a barometer of

or as you participate in these interactions yourself (e.g., at work, in school), monitor how active versus passive the person being motivated seems, how she reacts emotionally, and whether performance improves or only suffers. You will observe that not all attempts to motivate the self and others are successful and that there really is an art to motivating the self and others. This is an important forewarning because while motivational principles can be put into practice, it seems that they can be applied in ways that are ineffective just as easily as they can be applied in ways that are effective. In the chapters to come, some of the text will be devoted to the art of motivating others.

THERE IS NOTHING SO PRACTICAL AS A GOOD THEORY

Consider how you might answer a motivational question such as, "What causes Joe to study so hard and for so long?" To generate an answer, you might begin with a commonsense analysis. Additionally, you might recall a similar instance from your personal experience when you tried very hard, and you might then generalize that experience to this particular situation. A third strategy might be to find an expert on the topic and ask her (e.g., My neighbor is a teacher, I'll ask her why she thinks Joe might be studying so well-being. When life is going well, self-esteem rises; when life is going poorly, self-esteem drops. This is very different from saying that self-esteem causes life to go well, however. The logical flaw in thinking about self-esteem as a source of motivation is the act of putting the proverbial cart before the horse. Self-esteem is an expression, rather than a cause, of motivation. By analogy, consider when you are in a sour mood, and somebody walks up to you and says, "Smile, let's see that happy face!" Smiling does not create happiness any more than self-esteem creates motivation.

If motivation does not flow outward from a reservoir of high self-esteem, then one has to wonder where this motivation comes from. How do people succeed in their attempts to study more, start exercising, reverse bad habits, resist temptation, or overcome impulses and appetites like alcohol abuse, overeating, smoking, gambling, shopping, and aggression? To understand the sources of motivation that can influence behavior in a causal way, consider shifting some of your attention away from self-esteem as a motivation theory toward the theories listed in Table 1.2. These are the theories that empirical evidence shows are the ways to change the way people think, feel, and behave. Some theories revolve around supporting people's needs, other theories revolve around cultivating optimistic and resilient ways of thinking (cognitions), other theories establish conditions that promote positive emotions, and still other theories address the judicious management of incentives and consequences. Thus, in making this argument, the reader should entertain the potential merits of putting self-esteem somewhere on the back shelf of the ways for explaining motivation and should make room for new theories that use needs, cognitions, emotions, and incentives to explain motivated action.

hard). These are all fine and informative resources for helping answer motivational questions, but a good theory is yet another resource.

A theory is a set of variables (e.g., ability beliefs, goals, effort) and the relationships that are assumed to exist among those variables (e.g., strong ability beliefs encourage people to set goals, and once set, goals encourage high effort). Theories provide a conceptual framework for interpreting behavioral observations and function as intellectual bridges that link motivational questions and problems with satisfying answers and solutions. With a motivation theory in mind, the researcher approaches a question or problem along the lines of, "Well, according to goal-setting theory, . . ." or "According to the attributional theory of achievement motivation, . . ." As you read through the pages of each chapter, become familiar with each motivation theory and consider its usefulness in answering the motivational questions you care about most.

Table 1.2 introduces the names of 24 motivation theories that appear in the chapters to come. The theories are listed here for two reasons. First, the list introduces the idea that the heart and soul of a motivational analysis of behavior is its theories. Instead of existing as dry and abstract playthings of scientists, a good theory is the most practical, useable tool for solving the problems faced by students, teachers, workers, employers,

TABLE 1.2 **Twenty-four Theories in the Study of Motivation and Emotion (With a Supportive Reference Citation)**

MOTIVATION THEORY	SUPPORTIVE REFERENCE CITATION
Achievement motivation	Atkinson (1964)
Arousal	Berlyne (1967)
Attribution	Weiner (1986)
Cognitive dissonance	Harmon-Jones and Mills (1999)
Cognitive evaluation	Deci and Ryan (1985a)
Differential emotions	Izard (1991)
Drive	Bolles (1975)
Dynamics of action	Atkinson and Birch (1978)
Effectance motivation	Harter (1981)
Ego development	Loevinger (1976)
Expectancy × value	Vroom (1964)
Facial feedback hypothesis	Laird (1974)
Flow	Csikszentmihalyi (1997)
Goal setting	Locke and Latham (1990)
Learned helplessness	Peterson, Maier, and Seligman (1993)
Opponent process	Solomon (1980)
Positive affect	Isen (1987)
Psychodynamics	Westin (1997)
Reactance	Wortman and Brehm (1975)
Self-actualization	Rogers (1959)
Self-determination	Rigby, Deci, Patrick, and Ryan (1992)
Self-efficacy	Bandura (1997)
Sensation seeking	Zuckerman (1994)
Stress and coping	Lazarus (1991a)

managers, athletes, coaches, parents, therapists, and clients. To paraphrase Kurt Lewin (chapter 7), there is nothing so practical as a good theory.

Second, the theories listed here can serve as a means for monitoring your growing familiarity and comprehensive understanding of contemporary motivation study as you turn the pages from one chapter to the next. At the present time, you probably recognize very few of the theories listed in the table, but your familiarity will grow week by week. Months from now, to the extent that you feel comfortable with the two dozen theories listed in Table 1.2, you can then be confident that you are developing a sophisticated and complete understanding of motivation and emotion. When you know motivation theories, you know motivation.

SUMMARY

The journey to understand motivation and emotion begins by asking the perennial question, "What causes behavior?" This question invites the asking of more specific questions, ones that constitute the core problems to be solved in a motivational analysis of behavior: What starts behavior? From where does a sense of want come? How is behavior sustained over time? Why is behavior directed toward some ends but away from others? Why does behavior stop? What are the forces that determine behavior's intensity? Why does a person behave one way in a particular situation at one time yet behave in a different way at another time? What are the motivational differences among individuals, and how do such differences arise?

The subject matter of motivation concerns those processes that give behavior its energy and direction. The four processes capable of giving behavior strength and purpose—its energy and direction—are needs, cognitions, emotions, and external events. Needs are conditions within the individual that are essential and necessary for the maintenance of life and for growth and well-being. Cognitions are mental events, such as beliefs, expectations, and self-concept, that represent rather enduring ways of thinking. Emotions organize feelings, physiology, purpose, and expression (how we feel, how our body reacts, our sense of purpose, and how we express our experience to others) into a coherent response to an environmental condition, such as a threat. External events are environmental incentives that energize and direct behavior toward those events that signal positive consequences and away from those that signal aversive consequences. When considered broadly, external events include environmental contexts, situations, and climates, as well as sociological forces such as culture.

Both in its presence and in its intensity, motivation can be expressed in three ways: behavior, physiology, and self-report. The seven aspects of motivated behavior include effort, latency, persistence, choice, probability of response, facial expressions, and bodily gestures. Psychophysiological states express the activity of the central nervous and hormonal systems, and they provide further data to infer the biological underpinnings of motivation and emotion. Self-report ratings, as from an interview or a questionnaire, also measure motivational states. All three of these expressions of motivation can be helpful in inferring motivation, but researchers rely heavily on behavioral and physiological measures and only lightly on self-report ratings.

Nine themes run through motivation study. These themes are as follows: (1) motivation benefits adaptation, (2) motives affect behavior by directing attention, (3) motive strengths vary over time and influence the stream of behavior, (4) motivation includes both approach and avoidance tendencies, (5) motivation study reveals the contents of human nature, (6) motivation varies not only in intensity but also in its type, (7) we are not always consciously aware of the motivational basis of our behavior, (8) motivational principles can be applied, and (9) there is nothing so practical as a good theory. These principles are important because they provide an overall perspective for unifying motivation study's diverse assumptions, hypotheses, perspectives, theories, findings, and applications into a coherent, interesting, and practical field of study.

2

Motivation in Historical Perspective

Have you seen the Michael J. Fox movie *Back to the Future?* If so, imagine having the science-fiction technology to go back to the 1950s to see what a college motivation course looked like. Besides all the funny haircuts of the students, one item to notice would be the lack of a textbook. The first textbook in motivation was not written until 1964 (Cofer & Appley, 1964). Another item to notice would be the syllabus. Featured topics would be drive theory, incentives and reinforcement, acquired drives, conflict, and emotion. You could search the entire syllabus all you wanted, but none of the really interesting stuff about how to apply motivation would be included—nothing about motivation in the schools, sports psychology, work motivation, obesity and dieting, personal control beliefs, and so on. The course would, however, likely include psychoanalytic and self-actualization concepts. The third item to notice would be a weekly laboratory assignment. In such a lab, each student would receive a rat and would spend her time testing what effects manipulations such as 24 hours of food deprivation had on the rat's running speed toward a goal box filled with sunflower seeds. Once you returned back to today, you would probably agree that the study of motivation has changed and improved itself even more than have the fashions.

PHILOSOPHICAL ORIGINS OF MOTIVATIONAL CONCEPTS

If our science-fiction technology sent you back more than 100 years, then you would probably have no motivation course to look into. Motivation courses first appeared in psychology departments about 100 years ago. Still, the study of motivation can be traced back to at least the ancient Greeks—Socrates, Plato, and Aristotle. Plato (Socrates' student) proposed that motivation flowed from a tripartite, hierarchically arranged soul (or mind, psyche). At the most primitive level was the soul's appetitive aspect, which contributed bodily appetites and desires such as hunger and sex. At a second level was the competitive aspect, which contributed socially referenced standards such as feeling honored or shamed. At the highest level was the calculating aspect, which contributed the soul's decision-making capacities such as reason and choosing. For Plato, different aspects of the soul motivated different realms of behavior (e.g., hunger motivation was regulated by the soul's appetitive aspect). But each higher aspect could regulate the motives of the lower aspects (e.g., reason could keep bodily appetites in check). Interestingly, Plato's portrayal anticipated Sigmund Freud's psychodynamics (e.g., see Plato's Book IX, pp. 280–281): Roughly speaking, Plato's appetitive aspect corresponds to Freud's id, the competitive aspect to the superego, and the calculating aspect to the ego (Erdelyi, 1985).

Aristotle endorsed Plato's hierarchically organized, tripartite soul (appetitive, competitive, and calculating), though he preferred different terminology (nutritive, sensitive, and rational). The nutritive aspect was the most impulsive, irrational, and animal-like as it contributed bodily urges necessary for the maintenance of life. The sensitive aspect was also bodily related and regulated pleasure and pain. The soul's rational component was unique to human beings, and it was idea-related, intellectual, and featured the will. The will operated as the soul's highest level as it utilized intention, choice, and that which is divine and immortal.

Hundreds of years later, the Greek's tripartite psyche was reduced to a dualism—the passions of the body and the reason of the mind. The two-part soul retained the same hierarchical nature as it made its chief distinction between that which was impulsive, irrational, animate, and biological versus that which was inanimate, intelligent, rational, and spiritual. The impetus for this reinterpretation rested mostly in the era's intellectual commitment to motivational dichotomies, such as passion versus reason, good versus evil, and animal nature versus human soul. Thomas Aquinas, for example, suggested that the body provided irrational, pleasure-based motivational impulses, whereas the mind provided rational, will-based motivations.

In the post-Renaissance era, René Descartes, a French philosopher, added to this mind-body dualism by distinguishing between the passive and active aspects of motivation. The body was a mechanical and motivationally passive agent, whereas the will was an immaterial and motivationally active agent. As a physical entity, the body possessed nutritive needs and responded to the environment in mechanistic ways through its senses, reflexes, and physiology. The mind, however, was a spiritual, immaterial, and thinking entity that possessed a purposive will. This distinction was a tremendously important one because it set the agenda for motivation study over the next 300 years. What was needed to understand the passive and reactive motives was a mechanistic analysis of the body (i.e., the study of physiology). What was needed to understand active and purposive motives was an intellectual analysis of the will (i.e., the study of philosophy).

WILL: THE FIRST GRAND THEORY

For Descartes, the ultimate motivational force was the will. Descartes reasoned that if he could understand the will, then he could understand motivation. The will initiated and directed action; it chose both whether to act and what to do when acting. Bodily needs, passions, pleasures, and pains certainly created impulses to action, but these impulses only excited the will. The will was a faculty (a power) of the mind that controlled the bodily appetites and passions in the interests of virtue and salvation by exercising its powers of choice and of striving. By assigning exclusive powers of motivation to the will, Descartes provided motivation with its first grand theory.

The phrase "grand theory" is used here and throughout the chapter to connote an all-encompassing theory, one that seeks to explain the full range of motivated action—why we eat, drink, work, play, compete, fear certain things, read, fall in love, and so on. The statement that "the will motivates all action" is a grand theory of motivation in the same way that "the love of money is the root of all evil" is a grand theory of evil. Both identify a single, all-encompassing cause that explains why we do what we do.

Descartes' hope was that once the will was understood, then an understanding of motivation would inevitably unfold. Understanding motivation was reduced to, and became synonymous with, understanding the will. For this reason, a great deal of philosophical energy was invested in the study of the will. Some progress was made as the acts of willing were identified to be choosing (i.e., deciding whether to act or not; Rand, 1964), striving (i.e., creating impulses to act; Ruckmick, 1936), and resisting (i.e., self-denial or resisting temptation). In the end, two centuries of philosophical analysis yielded disappointing results. The will turned out to be an ill-understood faculty of the mind that arose, somehow, out of a congeries of innate capacities, environmental sensations, life experience, and reflections upon itself and its ideas. Further, once the will emerged, it somehow became endowed with intentions and purposes. And it turned out that some people showed more willpower than did other people.

To make a long story short, philosophers found the will to be as mysterious and as difficult to explain as was the motivation it supposedly generated. Philosophers discovered neither the will's nature nor the laws by which it operated. Essentially, philosophers painted themselves into the proverbial corner by multiplying the problem they were trying to solve. In using the will, philosophers now had to explain not only motivation but also the motivator—the will. As you can see, the problem only multiplied in its difficulty. For this reason, those involved with the new science of psychology, which emerged in the 1870s, (Schultz, 1987) found themselves in search of a less mysterious motivational principle. They found one, not within philosophy, but within physiology—the instinct.

Before leaving the historical discussion on the will, consider that contemporary psychologists fully recognize that the mind (the will) does think, plan, and form intentions that precede action. If it is not the will that is doing the thinking and planning, then from where is all this thinking and planning coming? In other words, how do people resist temptation (Mischel, 1996), sustain effort (Locke & Kristof, 1996), exercise self-control (Mischel & Mischel, 1983), control their thoughts and emotions (Wegner, 1994), form intentions to act (Gollwitzer, 1993), and concentrate attention (Rand, 1964)? Consider two explanations. In the first, consider how children summon the willpower they need to delay gratification and resist temptation (Mischel, et al., 1989; Patterson & Mischel, 1976). In one experiment that attempted to answer such a dilemma, a preschool child sits alone at a table with a tempting cookie. The experimenter gives the child a choice—one cookie now or two cookies after waiting 20 minutes. Rather than calling on their willpower (i.e., self-denial, grim determination), children successfully resist temptation and delay gratification by converting the frustrating wait into something more tolerable or enjoyable (i.e., playing a game, singing, or even taking a nap). Children who intentionally use such strategies resist temptation, whereas children with no such strategies act on impulse (eat the available cookie immediately). In the second example, college students took an exam as researchers tried to predict how well or poorly they would do (Locke & Kristof, 1996). The researchers recorded each student's goals (the desired grade) and study methods. Only students with clear plans and sophisticated study methods performed as well as they had hoped. Thus, goals and strategies, not personal willpower, produced effective performance. Therefore, in the contemporary study of motivation, researchers study mental processes like plans, goals, and strategies, rather than the self-denial and grim determination of the mysterious will (Gollwitzer & Bargh, 1996).

INSTINCT: THE SECOND GRAND THEORY

Charles Darwin's biological determinism had two major effects on scientific thinking. It provided biology with its most important idea (evolution), and it turned the mood of scientists away from mentalistic motivational concepts (i.e., will) toward mechanistic and genetic ones. It also ended the man-animal dualism that pervaded motivation study by introducing such questions as how animals use their resources (i.e., motivation) to adapt to the prevailing demands of an environment. For Darwin, animal behavior seemed to be largely unlearned, automated, and mechanistic (Darwin, 1859, 1872). With or without experience, animals adapted to their prevailing environments: Birds built nests, hens brooded, dogs chased hares, and rabbits ran from dogs. To explain prewired adaptive behavior, Darwin proposed the instinct.

Darwin's achievement was that his motivational concept could explain what the philosopher's will could not—namely, where the motivational force came from in the first place. Instincts arose from a physical substance, from the genetic endowment. Instincts were in the genes, and therefore they existed as an inherited tendency to act in a specific way. Given the presence of the appropriate stimulus, instincts expressed themselves through inherited bodily reflexes—the bird built a nest, the hen brooded, and the dog hunted, all because each had a genetically endowed, biologically aroused impulse to do so. Essentially, motivation thinkers in the 19th century stripped away the inanimate part of the philosopher's dualism (i.e., the rational soul) and kept that which remained, namely the biological urges, impulses, and appetites.

Borrowing heavily from the intellectual climate of Darwin and his contemporaries, William James (1890) was the first psychologist to popularize an instinct theory of motivation. James endowed human beings with a generous number of physical (e.g., sucking, locomotion) and mental (e.g., imitation, play, sociability) instincts. All that was needed to translate an instinct into a specific course of goal-directed behavior was the presence of an appropriate stimulus. Cats chase mice, run from dogs, avoid fires simply because they biologically must (i.e., because a mouse brings out the cat's instinct to chase, a dog brings out the instinct to flee, and the fire's flames bring out the instinct to protect). That is, the sight of a mouse (or dog or fire) activates in the cat a complex set of inherited reflexes that generated impulses to specific actions (e.g., chasing, running). Through the instinct, animals inherited a nature endowed with impulses to act and the reflexes needed to produce that purposive action.

Psychology's affection for, and commitment to, its second grand theory of motivation grew rapidly. A generation after James, William McDougall (1908, 1930) proposed an instinct theory that featured instincts to explore, to fight, to care for the young (i.e., mothering), and so on. McDougall regarded instincts as irrational and impulsive motivational forces that oriented a person toward one particular goal. It was the instinct that "determines its possessor to perceive, and to pay attention to, objects of a certain class, to experience an emotional excitement of a particular quality upon perceiving such an object, and to act in regard to it in a particular manner, or, at least, to experience an impulse to such action" (McDougall, 1908, p. 30). Thus, instincts (and their associated emotions) explained the goal-directed quality so readily apparent in human behavior. In many respects, McDougall's instinct doctrine paralleled that of James' theories. The greatest difference between the two was McDougall's rather extreme assertion that without instincts human beings would initiate no action. Without these "prime movers," human beings would be inert lumps, bodies without any impulses to action. In other words, all of human motivation owes its origin to a collection of genetically endowed instincts.

Once researchers accepted the instinct as an agent of motivation, the next task became identifying how many instincts human beings possessed. The instinct doctrine soon became hopelessly out of control as different lists of instincts grew to include over 6,000 different instincts (Bernard, 1924; Dunlap, 1919). In the practice of compiling lists of instincts, intellectual promiscuity reigned: "If he goes with his fellows, it is the 'herd instinct' which activates him; if he walks alone, it is the 'antisocial instinct'; if he twiddles his thumbs, it is the 'thumb-twiddling instinct'; if he does not twiddle his thumbs, it is the 'thumb-not-twiddling instinct'" (Holt, 1931, p. 428). The problem here is the tendency to confuse naming with explaining (e.g., the reason people are aggressive is because they have an instinct to be aggressive). As David McClelland (1987, p. 33) put it, "It is like saying that . . . the apple falls because it wants to fall." Confusing naming with explaining adds nothing to the understanding of motivation and emotion.

In addition, the logic underlying instinct theory was exposed as circular (Kuo, 1921; Tolman, 1923). Consider the explanation of how the instinct to fight motivates acts of aggression. The only evidence that people possess an instinct to fight is that they behave in ways that are aggressive. For the theorist, this is the worst kind of circularity: The cause explains the behavior (instinct→ behavior), but the behavior is evidence for its cause (behavior → instinct). What is lacking here is some independent way to determine if the instinct really exists. One way to determine this is to raise two very similar animals (i.e., animals endowed with similar instincts) in a way that gives them different life experiences. Then wait until the animals mature into adulthood, and check if their behaviors are essentially the same. If instincts direct behavior, then two genetically matched animals should behave in essentially the same way, despite the differences in their life circumstances and experiences. When researchers performed such experiments, the animals mostly acted in ways that were different from one another.

Consider the mothering instinct in rats (Birch, 1956) and the handiness (right- or left-handed) instinct in humans (Watson, 1924). During pregnancy, female rats engage in frequent licking of their own genitalia, and during birth, they smear their vaginal tissues on their pups. Thus, two possibilities exist to explain a rat's mothering behavior—a mothering instinct and the presence of a familiar odor. To test his odor hypothesis, Birch placed cuffs on some females' forepaws to prevent self-licking and, hence, the means to transfer their familiar odor to the pups. The rats had normal pregnancies, but after giving birth, these mothers paid little attention to their pups. When they did attend to their odorless pups, they ate them. Surely the mothers did not have an instinct to eat their pups. As for the handiness instinct, John Watson meticulously measured infants' preferences for using one hand over the other on all sorts of tasks (i.e., reaching for a toy, holding onto a bar) and found that infantile preferences to use one hand over the other did not predict childhood and adulthood hand preference. Instead, children learned a handedness preference from their early training and from their parents' socialization.

Originally, the instinct concept arose to fill a gap of what motivation is and from where it came (Beach, 1955). Psychology's affair with instinct theory began with wholehearted acceptance but ended with sweeping denial.[1] Just as psychology previously abandoned the will, it abandoned the instinct and found itself in search of a substitute motivational concept to explain behavior's purposive nature.

DRIVE: THE THIRD GRAND THEORY

The motivational concept that arose to replace instinct was drive (introduced by Woodworth, 1918). Drive as a motivational concept arose from a functional biology, one that understood that the function of behavior was to service bodily needs. As biological

---

[1] Contemporary psychology no longer uses the instinct to explain complex human behavior. Nonetheless, the proposition that nonhuman animals show consistent, unlearned, stereotypical patterns of behavior is an undeniable observation. Bees build hexagonal cells, male stickleback fish attack red coloration, and birds build nests. Contemporary psychologists (but especially ethologists) concede that such stereotypical acts can be attributed to instincts in animals. As James wrote over a century ago, "that instincts . . . exist on an enormous scale in the animal kingdom needs no proof" (1890, p. 383). In using the term "instinct," ethologists (Eibl-Eibesfeldt, 1989; Lorenz, 1965; Moltz, 1965) now speak of inherited neuronal structures that are unmodified by the environment during development. These inherited neuronal structures give rise not to general patterns of behavior but to particular bits of situationally specific behavior, referred to as "fixed action patterns." Changing instinct's focus from the cause of complex behavior to the cause of bits of behavior (fixed action patterns) proved to be a comfortable theoretical compromise. While theoretically expedient, such a compromise clearly shows the decline of a grand theory. Explaining bits of behavior or bits of motivation is just not the same as explaining all of behavior and all of motivation.

imbalances occurred (e.g., lack of food and water), animals experienced these need deficits psychologically as "drive." Drive motivated whatever behavior was instrumental to servicing the body's needs (e.g., eating and drinking). The two most widely embraced drive theories came from Sigmund Freud (1915) and Clark Hull (1943).

FREUD'S DRIVE THEORY

Freud, a physiologist by training, believed that all behavior was motivated and that the purpose of behavior was to serve the satisfaction of needs. Freud's view of the nervous system was that biological urges (e.g., hunger) were constantly and inevitably recurring conditions that produced energy buildups within a nervous system that revolved around an inherited tendency to maintain a constant low level of energy. While the nervous system tried to maintain a constant and low energy level, it was perpetually being displaced from this objective by the emergence of biological urges. Each energy buildup upset nervous system stability and produced psychological discomfort (i.e., anxiety). If the energy buildup rose unchecked, it could threaten physical and psychological health. To protect one's health, drive arose as a sort of emergency warning urge so that the individual would take action. Behavior continued until the drive or urge that motivated it was satisfied. In other words, behavior served the nervous system, and drive acted as a sort of middleman for ensuring that behavior satisfied the bodily needs.

Freud (1915) summarized his drive theory with four components: source, impetus, aim, and object. The *source* of drive was the bodily deficit. Drive had an *impetus* (force) that possessed the *aim* of satisfaction, which was the removal (via satisfaction) of the underlying bodily deficit. To accomplish this aim, it motivated the behavioral search for an *object* capable of removing the bodily deficit. One way to understand Freud's view of nervous system energy (i.e., "libido") is through the analogy of a hydraulic system in which energy (like constantly flowing water) continues to rise and rise. As the bodily drives continue to build up energy, the anxious urge to discharge that energy becomes increasingly urgent and expedient (i.e., or else the water would overflow). The desire to release the energy (i.e., drive) generates an impulse to action. Adaptive behavior quieted the drive, for a time, but the ever-constant buildup of nervous-system energy would return (i.e., the water's inflow never shuts off).

Despite its creativity, Freud's drive theory suffered at least three criticisms: (1) a relative overestimation of the contribution of biological forces to motivation (and hence, a relative underestimation of factors related to learning and experience); (2) an overreliance on data taken from case studies of disturbed individuals (and hence, an underreliance on data taken from experimental research with more representative samples); and (3) ideas that were not scientifically (i.e., experimentally) testable (e.g., How can you test whether or not people possess a drive toward aggression?). None of these three criticisms applied, however, to the second major drive theory, that by Clark Hull.

HULL'S DRIVE THEORY

For Hull (1943, 1952), drive was a pooled energy source composed of all current bodily disturbances. In other words, particular needs for food, water, sex, sleep, and so forth summed to constitute a total bodily need. For Hull, as for Freud, motivation (i.e., drive) had a purely physiological basis and bodily need was the ultimate basis of motivation.

Hull's drive theory had one outstanding feature that no motivation theory before it had ever possessed—namely motivation could be predicted *before it occurred* from antecedent conditions in the environment. With the instinct and with the will, it was impossible to predict in an *a priori* fashion when and whether or not a person would be motivated. But if an animal was deprived of food, water, sex, or sleep, then drive would inevitably increase in accordance with the duration of that deprivation. Drive was an increasing monotonic function of total bodily need, and total bodily need was an increasing monotonic function of hours of deprivation. The fact that drive could be known from antecedent environmental conditions explains much of why drive was able to replace instinct as motivation's third grand theory. After all, a list of Hull's primary drives does not sound overly discrepant from a list of the major instincts: hunger, thirst, sex, air, temperature regulation, defecation, urination, rest (following exertion), sleep, activity, nest building, care of one's young, and pain avoidance (Hull, 1943, pp. 59–60).

Once drive arose, it energized behavior (Bolles, 1975). Although drive energized behavior, it did not direct it. Habit, not drive, directed behavior. As one contemporary phrased it, "Drive is an energizer, not a guide" (Hebb, 1955, p. 249). Behavior-guiding habits came from learning, and learning occurred as a consequence of reinforcement. Hull's research led him to argue that if a response was followed quickly by a reduction in drive, learning occurred and habit was reinforced. Any response that decreased drive (e.g., eating, drinking, mating) produced reinforcement, and the animal learned which response produced drive reduction in that particular situation. To show how habit and drive (i.e., learning and motivation) produced behavior, Hull (1943) developed the following formula:

$$sEr = sHr \times D$$

The variable *sEr* is the strength of behavior (*E* stands for "excitatory potential") in the presence of a particular stimulus; *sHr* is habit strength (i.e., probability of a particular drive-reducing response given a particular stimulus); and *D* is drive.[2] The observable aspects of behavior—running, persisting, etc.—are denoted by *sEr*. The variables *sHr* and *D* refer to behavior's underlying, unobservable causes. The multiplication sign is important in that behavior occurred only when habit and drive were at nonzero levels. In other words, without drive (D = 0) or without habit (H = 0), there is no excitatory potential (E = 0).

Later, Hull (1952) extended his behavior system beyond H × D to include a third cause of behavior: incentive motivation, abbreviated as K.[3] In addition to the motivational properties of D, the incentive value of a goal object (its quality, its quantity, or

[2] The subscripts *s* and *r* stand for "stimulus" and "response" to communicate that *sHr* refers to a particular response in the presence of a particular stimulus. Similarly, the subscripts joined with *sEr* refer to the potential "energy" of that response in the presence of that particular stimulus.

[3] Incidentally, if you happen to wonder why incentive motivation was abbreviated as *K* instead of as *I*, *K* stood for Kenneth Spence (Weiner, 1972). Spence convinced Hull of the necessity of incorporating incentive motivation into his behavior system. Besides, *I* was used for another variable, inhibition, which is not discussed here.

both) also energized the animal. After all, people generally work harder for $50 than they do for $1. Because he recognized that motivation could arise from either internal (D) or external (K) sources, Hull (1952) proposed the following formula:

$$sEr = sHr \times D \times K$$

Both *D* and *K* were motivational terms. The principal difference between the two was that *D* was rooted in internal stimulation via bodily disturbances, whereas *K* was rooted in external stimulation via the quality of the incentive.

Hull's behavior theory gained enormous popularity. In its zenith, his drive theory was as popular as any theory in the history of psychology. That is obviously a strong statement, but consider three historical occurrences. First, approximately half of all the articles published in the leading psychology journals in the early 1950s (e.g., *Psychological Review, Journal of Experimental Psychology)* included a reference to Hull's 1943 book. Second, books on motivation went from being practically nonexistent at mid-century to commonplace 10 years later (Atkinson, 1964; Bindra, 1959; Brown, 1961; Hall, 1961; Lindzey, 1958; Madsen, 1959; McClelland, 1955; Maslow, 1954; Olds, 1956a; Peters, 1958; Stacey & DeMartino, 1958; Toman, 1960; Young, 1961). And third, in the 1950s the American Psychological Association (APA) invited its members to list the most important figures in the history of psychology through mid-century. The survey rankings appear in Table 2.1. Notice that the two names at the top of the list are drive theorists.

DECLINE OF DRIVE THEORY

Drive theory—including both the Freudian and Hullian versions—rested on three fundamental assumptions: (1) Drive emerged from bodily needs; (2) drive reduction was reinforcing and produced learning; and (3) drive energized behavior. Throughout the 1950s, empirical tests of these assumptions revealed much support but also some reason for concern. First, some motives existed with or without any corresponding biological need. For instance, anorexics do not eat (and do not want to eat) despite a strong biological need to

TABLE 2.1 **Mid-Century Rankings of the 10 Most Important Historical Figures in Psychology**

1. Sigmund Freud
2. Clark Hull
3. Wilhelm Wundt
4. Ivan Pavlov
5. John Watson
6. Edward Thorndike
7. William James
8. Max Wertheimer
9. Edward Tolman
10. Kurt Lewin

do so (Klien, 1954). Thus, motivation must also emerge from sources other than one's bodily disturbances. Second, learning often occurred without any corresponding experience of drive reduction. Hungry rats, for instance, learn even when reinforced only by a nonnutritive saccharin reward (Sheffield & Roby, 1950). Because saccharin has no nutritional benefit, it cannot reduce drive (i.e., cannot serve the needs of the body). Other research showed learning from drive induction (i.e., with drive increase; Harlow, 1953). Clearly, learning could occur in ways unrelated to drive reduction. Third, research recognized the importance of external (nonphysiological) sources of motivation. For example, a person who is not necessarily thirsty can feel a rather strong motive to drink upon tasting (or seeing or smelling) a favorite beverage. While Hull included incentive motivation (K), the important point here for drive theory is that motives arose from more than just bodily physiology. To explain motivational phenomena like eating, drinking, and having sex, it became increasingly clear that attention had to be focused not only on internal physiological sources of motivation (i.e., D) but on external environmental sources as well (i.e., K).

Hull's drive theory was not wrong. The research conducted within its framework was sound research that showed each of its three major assumptions was correct, at least to a degree. Some motivation does emerge from bodily needs, drive reduction does reinforce learning, and drive does energize behavior. Rather than being wrong, drive theory simply proved to be unnecessarily limited in its scope of application. It just had too many exceptions and loopholes to permit it to serve as the theoretical explanation for all motivated behavior (i.e., to serve as a grand theory for all of motivation).

Post-Drive Theory Years

The 1950s and 1960s were transitional decades in the study of motivation. In the early 1950s, the prevalent motivation theories were the well-known, historically entrenched grand theories. The prominent mid-century motivational theories centered on drive (Hull, 1952; Bolles, 1975), optimal level of arousal (Hebb, 1955; Berlyne, 1967), pleasure centers in the brain (Olds, 1956b, 1969; Olds & Milner, 1954), approach-avoidance conflicts (Miller, 1959), universal needs (Murray, 1938), conditioned motives (Miller, 1948), self-actualization (Rogers, 1959), and psychoanalysis (Freud, 1915; Rapaport, 1960). As motivation study progressed, it became clear that if progress was to be made, the field was going to have to step outside the boundaries of its grand theories. In the 1960s and 1970s, psychologists began to embrace mini-theories of motivation (Dember, 1965). The next section discusses these mini-theories, but the late 1950s and 1960s proved to be important transitional years. As drive theory declined in support and popularity, three motivational principles were offered as possible replacements: incentive, arousal, and discrepancy.

Consider first the motivational principle of incentive. An incentive is an external event (or stimulus) that energizes and directs approach or avoidance behavior. The incentive theories that emerged in the 1960s fundamentally sought to explain why people approached positive incentives and why they avoided negative ones. These theories rested on the concept of hedonism, which essentially postulates that organisms approach pleasure and avoid pain. Through learning, people formed associations (or expectancies) that some environmental objects were gratifying and thus deserved approach responses, whereas other objects were pain-inflicting and thus deserved avoidance responses.

Incentive theories offered three new features: (1) new motivational concepts, such as environmental incentives, (2) the idea that motivational states could be acquired through experience, and (3) a portrayal of motivation that highlighted moment-to-moment changes because environmental incentives can change from one moment to the next, as with praise and criticism, for example.

Second, consider the motivational principle of arousal. The rising disaffection with drive theory was countered by a rising affection for arousal theory. The discovery that lay the foundation for this transition came from the neurophysiological finding of an arousal system in the brain stem (discovered by Moruzzi & Magoun, 1949; translated into a theory of emotion by Lindsley, 1957). The central ideas were that (1) aspects of the environment (how stimulating, novel, stressful) affected how aroused the brain was, and (2) variations in level of arousal had a curvilinear (the famous inverted-U shape) relationship to behavior. That is, environments that did not stimulate generated low levels of arousal and emotional states like boredom; somewhat surprising, challenging, and stimulating environments generated optimal levels of arousal and emotional states like interest; and overly stimulating, unfamiliar, and conflict-endowed environments generated high levels of arousal and emotional states like fear. Eventually, level of arousal came to be understood as something "synonymous with a general drive state" (Hebb, 1955, p. 249). But notice what happened to drive theory—it had been reinterpreted away from its biological roots and brought into the age of neurophysiology and cognition in the form of arousal. In doing so, arousal theory highlighted the "central stimulation" of motivational states rather than either the physiological stimulation of biological need or the environmental stimulation of incentives. Notice that the motivational psychologist of the day could then focus on physiological sources of motivation (drive), environmental sources of motivation (incentives), or central/brain sources of motivation (arousal).

Finally, consider the motivational principle of discrepancy, or equilibrium. Equilibrium is based on the ideas that (1) an optimal level of each motivational state exists and (2) organisms are motivated to maintain that equilibrium. An optimal level of arousal is one example of equilibrium. Discrepancy is therefore any detectable deviation from equilibrium. Discrepancies are motivational in that when they occur, they energize and direct the organism to engage in whatever behavior is necessary to restore the lost equilibrium (Appley, 1991; Carver & Scheier, 1981; Hunt, 1965; Stagner, 1977). Many contemporary theories of motivation (e.g., goal-setting, cognitive dissonance) are in essence discrepancy theories, as will be discussed in chapters 7 and 10. What is most important in a historical understanding of motivation and emotion is that the focus of attention shifted from maintaining an optimal level of arousal to detecting (and acting on) discrepancies from any desired states, such as level of hunger, level of competence, level of progress toward a goal, and so on.

With the growing disaffection with drive theory and the growing affection for motivational principles like incentive, arousal, and discrepancy, it became increasingly evident that any one grand theory was simply unable to carry the whole burden of explaining motivation. Even concepts like arousal and discrepancy, which both harbored a potential for becoming a fourth grand theory of motivation, were recognized rather quickly as being insufficient principles to stretch far enough to cover the full range of motivational phenomena (Appley, 1991). In its attempt to cover the full range of motivational phenomena, the contemporary landscape of motivation study is now characterized by a wide-ranging diversity of theories ("mini-theories") rather than by any consensus to a single grand theory.

RISE OF THE MINI-THEORIES

Unlike grand theories that try to explain the full range of motivation, mini-theories limit their attention to specific motivational phenomenon. Mini-theories seek to understand or investigate one particular behavioral phenomenon (e.g., doing well versus poorly in school), the motivational significance of a particular set of circumstances (e.g., failure feedback, the presence of an audience), a theoretical question (e.g., What is the relationship between cognition and emotion?), or the motivational problems or tendencies of a particular group of people (e.g., extraverts, children, workers). A mini-theory explains some but not all of motivated behavior. Thus, achievement motivation theory (a mini-theory) arose to explain why some people seek out ability-testing challenges, whereas others go out of their way to avoid them; the cognitive dissonance mini-theory arose to explain why people strive for consistency in their attitudes and behaviors; and research on sensation seekers arose to explain why some people find pleasure in novel, intense, and risky activities, such as riding motorcycles and engaging in promiscuous sex. The following list identifies some of the mini-theories (with its seminal reference) that emerged in the 1960s and 1970s and replaced the fading grand theories:

- Achievement motivation theory (Atkinson, 1964)
- Attributional theory of achievement motivation (Weiner, 1972)
- Cognitive dissonance theory (Festinger, 1957)
- Effectance motivation (White, 1959; Harter, 1978a)
- Expectancy × value theory (Vroom, 1964)
- Intrinsic motivation (Deci, 1975)
- Goal-setting theory (Locke, 1968)
- Learned helplessness theory (Seligman, 1975)
- Reactance theory (Brehm, 1966)
- Self-efficacy theory (Bandura, 1977)
- Self-schemas (Markus, 1977)

Three historical trends explain why motivation study left behind its tradition of the grand theories in favor of mini-theories. First, motivation researchers reevaluated the wisdom of the idea that human beings are inherently passive. The next section discusses this trend. Second, motivation, like all of psychology, turned markedly cognitive in its emphasis. This trend became known as the cognitive revolution. And third, motivation researchers became increasingly interested in applied, socially relevant questions and problems. In addition to these historical trends, the first journal devoted exclusively to the topic of motivation emerged in 1977, *Motivation and Emotion.* This journal has focused almost all of its attention on the empirical exploration of mini-theories of motivation. A second journal, *Cognition and Emotion,* which debuted in 1987, focuses on the empirical study of how mental processes affect emotional experience.

ACTIVE NATURE OF THE PERSON

The purpose of drive theory was to explain how an animal went from inactive to active (Weiner, 1990). The mid-century assumption was that animals (including human beings) were naturally inactive—inert. The role of motivation was to arouse the passive into the active. Indeed, the term "motive" derives from the Latin word meaning "to move"; so drive, like all other early motivational constructs, explained the instigating motor of behavior. For instance, a common mid-century definition of motivation was, "the process of arousing action, sustaining the activity in progress, and regulating the pattern of activity" (Young, 1961, p. 24). Motivation was the study of induced motion.

The psychologists of the second half of the century saw things differently, emphasizing that the person was always getting to and doing something. The human organism was inherently active and always motivated. According to one of the first proponents of inherent activity, "Sound motivational theory should . . . assume that motivation is constant, never ending, fluctuating, and complex, and that it is an almost universal characteristic of practically every organismic state of affairs" (Maslow, 1954, p. 69). Perhaps there is no place where this is more evident than in little children. "They pick things up, shake them, smell them, taste them, throw them across the room, and keep asking, 'What's this?' They are unendingly curious" (Deci & Ryan, 1985a, p. 11).

In their mid-1960s review of motivation theories, Charles Cofer and Mortimer Appley (1964) divided the motivation theories of the day into those that assumed a passive, energy-conserving organism and those that assumed an active, growth-seeking organism. While the passive-oriented portrayals outnumbered the active-oriented portrayals by 10 to 1, theories assuming an active organism were beginning to emerge and gain acceptance. Throughout the 1970s, motivation theories increasingly adopted the notion of the active organism. Today's ideas about motivation and emotion have less and less to do with deficit motivations (e.g., tension reduction, homeostasis, equilibrium) and more and more to do with growth motivations (e.g., creativity, competence, possible selves, self-actualization; Appley, 1991; Benjamin & Jones, 1978; Rapaport, 1960; White, 1960).

COGNITIVE REVOLUTION

The early motivational concepts—drive, need, hunger, arousal, homeostasis—were grounded in biology and physiology. Much of the thinking about motivation was therefore molded by a biological heritage and perspective. Contemporary motivation study maintains a close allegiance with the study of genetics, biology, physiology, and sociobiology. In the early 1970s, however, psychology's Zeitgeist (its intellectual climate) turned decidedly cognitive (Gardner, 1985), and the cognitive revolution spilled into motivation just as it spilled into virtually all areas of psychology (D'Amato, 1974; Dember, 1974). Motivation researchers began to supplement, and sometimes even replace, their biological concepts with those that emphasized internal mental processes (such as arousal replacing drive). Throughout this book (especially chapters 7 through 10), the following fruits of the cognitive revolution in mentalistic motivational constructs will be explained in further detail: plans (Miller, Galanter, & Pribram, 1960), goals (Locke & Latham, 1990), expectations and beliefs (Bandura, 1977), attributions (Weiner, 1972), and the self-concept (Markus, 1977).

The cognitive revolution had two additional, more subtle, effects on thinking about motivation. First, intellectual discussions about motivation emphasized cognitive constructs (e.g., expectancies, goals) and de-emphasized structural constructs (e.g., incentives, rewards). These discussions changed psychology's image of human functioning to become "human rather than mechanical" (McKeachie, 1976, p. 831). This ideological shift from mechanical to dynamic portrayals of motivation (Carver & Scheier, 1981, 1990; Marcus & Wurf, 1987) was captured nicely in the title of one of the popular motivation texts of the day, *Theories of Motivation: From Mechanism to Cognition* (Weiner, 1972). In addition, a review of motivation studies from the 1960s and 1970s shows a marked decline in experiments manipulating the deprivation states of rats and shows a marked increase in experiments manipulating success or failure feedback given to human performance (Weiner, 1990). The experimental design is not much different, but the focus on human, instead of nonhuman, animals is unmistakable.

Second, the cognitive revolution and its corresponding de-emphasis on mechanical, structural portrayals of motivation complemented the emerging movement of humanism. Humanistic psychologists critiqued the prevailing motivation theories of the 1960s as decidedly not related to humans. Humanists resist the machine metaphor that portrays motivation in a deterministic fashion in response to unyielding biological forces, developmental fates (e.g., traumatic childhood experiences), or controls in the environment or in society (Bugental, 1967; Wertheimer, 1978). Ideas about motivation from Abraham Maslow and Carl Rogers (chapter 12) expressed psychology's new understanding of human beings as inherently active, cognitively flexible, and growth motivated (Berlyne, 1975; Maslow, 1987; Rogers, 1961).

Applied, Socially Relevant Research

A third important change occurred to usher in the mini-theories era: Researchers turned their attention to questions that were relevant to solving the motivational problems people faced in their lives (McClelland, 1978)—at work (Locke & Latham, 1984), in school (Weiner, 1979), in coping with stress (Lazarus, 1966), in reversing depression (Seligman, 1975), and so on. As researchers turned from nonhuman animals to humans, they discovered a wealth of naturally occurring instances of motivation outside the laboratory, particularly in domains such as achievement and affiliation and in settings such as work and school. Hence, motivation researchers began focusing increasingly on socially relevant, applied questions and problems. Overall, the field became less interested in studying, for instance, hunger as a motive and more interested in studying the motivations underlying eating, dieting, obesity, and bulimia (Rodin, 1981; Taubes, 1998).

BENEFITS OF A HISTORICAL ANALYSIS OF MOTIVATION

There is much to gain by wading through 24 centuries of thinking about motivation. Consider the ancient questions that define the study of human motivation: Why behave? Why

The Many Voices in Motivation Study

Question: Why would a person want to learn about the motivational states discussed in this chapter?

Answer: Because in reading the history of motivation, one hears from the full range of voices trying to understand motivation.

Most social conversations and most laboratory experiments rely on a single perspective for understanding motivation. For instance, when a teenager loses interest in schooling, a parent might rely on one motivational perspective to understand why. For instance, the parent might think school is an unrewarding place and then might offer the teenager an attractive incentive if she will engage herself more in school. The parent might also help the teenager forge a sense of identity and find a way for school to support that identity. The parent might also pull an inspirational pep talk out of his pocket to bolster the youngster's sense of confidence. The point is that in thinking about motivation, people often choose the first logical idea that comes to mind. Another way to think about motivation, however, is to become aware of a fuller range of possible ideas about motivation and then select those that best fit the particular problem.

A historical analysis of motivation is one way to become aware of all the different possibilities. While many voices participate in contemporary motivation study, six perspectives are particularly prominent throughout motivation's history:

Behavioral	How motives emerge from incentives and rewards (e.g., money)
Biological/physiological	How motives emerge from brain and hormonal systems (e.g., hunger)
Cognitive	How motives emerge from the way we think and process information (e.g., goals)

do anything—why get out of the bed in the morning and do anything? Given these questions, the history of motivation begins with the search for the instigators of behavior—that is, the search to identify that which initiates behavior. For two millennia (from Plato [ca. 428–348 B.C.]) to Descartes [ca. 1596–1650]), the intellectual effort to understand motivation focused on the will, which resided within the immaterial and elusive soul. Studying an immaterial, spiritual substance proved to be too difficult an undertaking for the new science of psychology. Biology (including genetics and physiology) proved to be a more suitable alternative because its subject matter was material and measurable. In answering the "Why behave?" question, the answer came to be that behavior serviced the needs of the organism. Instinct, drive, and arousal all gained appeal because each clearly energized and directed behavior that served the needs of the organism (i.e., people get out of bed because they are hungry and need to eat something). Incentive added to these motivational constructs because hedonism (approach pleasure, avoid pain) explained why

Evolutionary	How motives emerge from our genetic endowment (e.g., extraversion)
Humanistic	How motives emerge from encouraging human potential (e.g., self-actualization)
Psychoanalytical	How motives emerge from unconscious mental life (e.g., anxiety)

As a point of illustration, consider the many ways to think about a motivation that is near and dear to the hearts of many college students: sexual motivation. Behaviorists would point out that part of desire stems from how attractive another person is, as in physical attractiveness, a pleasing smell, or a pleasing sense of humor. Biologists would point out that desire depends on the underlying presence of hormones to stimulate arousal. Cognitivists would add that desire further comes from sexual scripts, fantasies, expectancies, and beliefs with roots in religion, morals, and culture. Evolutionists would add that men and women have different mating strategies and therefore desire different qualities in a mate. Humanists would point out that part of desire stems from the opportunity to participate in an intimate, growth-promoting relationship. And psychoanalysts would add that we desire relationships with those who fit our childhood-rooted mental model of what an ideal romantic partner should be.

In listening to the many voices that participate in the conversation about motivation, one gains the opportunity to put together more pieces of the puzzle, so to speak. And researchers from different perspectives ask different questions about motivation, many of which you might never have thought to consider had they not first been raised by others. All the answers will not be satisfactory, but the idea is to first put all the knowledge on the table and then select that which is most empirically defensible and most personally useable.

environmental events (incentives, rewards, punishers) could energize behavior (i.e., people get out of bed to approach pleasure and to avoid pain). Finally, discrepancy seemed to pull everything nicely together by postulating that motivation arose under any condition in which discrepancy existed between the organism's present state (current need or level of pleasure) and ideal state. People get out of bed to attain ideal states. Century by century, thinkers were improving their answers to the question of what instigates behavior: will, instinct, drive, arousal, incentive, discrepancy.

The whole process was going along rather nicely until a critical mass of motivation researchers realized that they were asking and pursing the wrong question. The question of the instigation of behavior presumes a passive and biologically regulated organism, that is, one who is asleep and upon awaking, needs some motive to get into behaving mode. At some point, motivation thinkers realized that sleeping was behaving and that the proverbial sleeper was actively engaged in his environment. The realization was that to be alive is to be active: Organisms are always active, organisms are always behaving, and there is no time in which a live organism is not behaving. Since there is no time in which a live organism is not showing both energy and direction, the fundamental questions of motivation shifted to the following: Why does behavior vary in its intensity? Why does the person do one thing rather than another?

These two questions expand the charge of motivation study by focusing not only on behavior's energy but also on its direction. This is why the three historical trends, (1) the active organism, (2) cognitive revolution, and (3) concern for applied, socially relevant research, are so important because the field became less entrenched in the instigators of behavior, biology, and animal laboratory experimentation and increasingly interested in the directors of behavior, cognition, and human motivational problems.

CURRENT ERA: MINI-THEORIES

Thomas Kuhn (1962) described the history of most sciences as a cyclical pattern in which progress occurs both continuously and discontinuously. With continuous progress, new data add to and supplant old data, and new ideas add to and supplant outworn ideas. Through ongoing modification, the scientific discipline grows and matures. With discontinuous progress, radical ideas appear and rival old ideas rather than add to old ideas. The new ideas reveal the shortcomings of the old ideas. If the radical ideas gain acceptance, researchers' ways of thinking change, sometimes drastically, as old models are torn down and brand-new models are reconstructed to take their place.

In Kuhn's terminology, the continuous growth of a discipline represents a "normal stage," whereas discontinuous growth represents a "crisis stage." In the normal stage, contributors share a common theoretical and methodological framework. This shared framework (a "paradigm") allows each contributor to understand the science's subject matter and subsequently guides emerging theories and research. As the discipline increases its knowledge base and makes new discoveries, the inadequacies of the prevalent modes of thinking eventually become apparent. Anomalies pop up—findings that simply cannot be explained with the prevailing paradigm. These newly found inadequacies give rise to a general discomfort that soon runs throughout the field. With ever-increasing discomfort, the discipline enters a crisis stage—a tug of war between ideas and paradigms. As a result, fresh insights and new discoveries arise, and these insights and discoveries breed a new way of thinking (a "paradigm shift"). Armed with their new way of thinking, researchers then settle into a new and improved paradigm, and the scientific process returns to normal, a process that typically takes decades and multiple generations of scientists. Two classic examples of paradigm shifts, for instance, occurred when the Copernican revolution replaced astronomers' ideas of earth centrality and when Einstein's general theory of relativity unseated Euclidean geometry.

As a field, motivation study has participated in the rise and fall of (at least) three major focuses of thinking: will, instinct, and drive. Each of these motivational concepts gained wide acceptance, but as new data emerged, each concept proved to be too limiting for further progress. Eventually, each was replaced by the next new-and-improved radical idea. The field's theoretical fallout with drive theory initiated its third historical crisis stage. Despite the general popularity of incentive, arousal, and discrepancy as major motivational principles, contemporary motivation remains theoretically discontent and in want of fresh ideas and new discoveries that can help the field progress to a fourth normal stage.

The "crisis stage" transition from drive theory to the mini-theories produced consequences that were both good and bad. On the bad side, motivation was dethroned as perhaps psychology's most important discipline to a sort of second-class field of study. The dethronement of motivation was so severe that, to some degree, the field disappeared for a decade and a half. If that statement sounds too strong, then try the following demonstration. Ask the psychology professors in almost any department in the world (including your own school) what their special field of study is. You will probably find a good number of cognitive, perceptual, physiological, health, clinical, counseling, personality, social, developmental, educational, and industrial/organizational specialists. You probably will not find many motivation specialists. The downside was rather severe.

Motivation study, however, has not disappeared. The questions that define motivation, discussed in chapter 1, endured. Instead of disappearing, motivation specialists dispersed themselves into virtually all areas of psychology. Learning theorists, personality psychologists, social psychologists, clinicians, and others were unable to explain all the behavior they sought to explain without motivational concepts. In other words, psychology's other fields needed answers to their motivational questions. What emerged were theories of social motivation (Pittman & Heller, 1988), of physiological motivation (Stellar & Stellar, 1985), of cognitive motivation (Sorrentino & Higgins, 1986), of developmental motivation (Kagan, 1972), and so on. Further, motivation theories specific to particular domains of application emerged: theories to explain the motivation underlying dieting and bingeing (Polivy & Herman, 1985), work (Locke & Latham, 1984, 1990; Vroom, 1964), sports (Roberts, 1992; Straub & Williams, 1984), education (Weiner, 1979), and so on. By 1980, motivation psychologists were in literally every area of psychology investigating the motivational underpinnings of cognition, of social interaction, of health, of personality, of education, and so on. While motivation did not exist as its own coherent field, its problems proved to be significant for and relevant to practically every aspect of psychology. The end result of motivation branching out and forming alliances with other fields resulted in motivation's dispersion into a loose network of researchers who shared a common concern and commitment to motivationally relevant questions and problems.

Given the prevailing "crisis stage," there are two ways to conceptualize contemporary motivation study. Figure 1.1 (from chapter 1) represents the first way by arguing that four constructs define the subject matter of motivation: needs, cognitions, emotions, and external events. All motivation researchers emphasize the contribution of one or more of these constructs to explain behavior's energy and direction. In the study of needs, for instance, some theorists argue that "the study of human motivation is the study of human needs and the dynamic processes related to these needs" (Deci, 1980, p. 31). Emotion-minded motivational theorists argue that "emotions are the primary motivation system" (Tomkins, 1970, p. 101). A cognitive study of motivation assumes "people's . . . beliefs determine their level of motivation" (Bandura, 1989, p. 1176). Other theorists focus on the motivational properties of external events and favor a careful analysis of how environmental stimuli and social incentives energize and direct behavior (Baldwin & Baldwin, 1986; Skinner, 1953). The organization of chapters in this book reflects this first conceptualization of motivation study.

A second way to conceptualize contemporary motivation study focuses on the relationships and alliances between motivation and other fields in psychology, as depicted in Figure 2.1. The figure has two purposes. First, it illustrates the loose boundaries that currently exist between motivation and related fields. Second, it illustrates explicitly how motivation links itself with the reader's other courses in psychology. That is, courses in social psychology, personality, and educational psychology will have some content that is decidedly motivational. Because of this overlap, it is sometimes difficult to say where the study of cognition ends and where the study of motivation begins (Sorrentino & Higgins, 1986) or where the study of perception ends and where the study of motivation begins (Bindra, 1979). Weak boundaries between motivation and allied fields generally suggest an identity crisis within motivation study, but in practice, the absence of sharp boundaries facilitated the exchange of ideas and fostered an exposure to different perspectives and methodologies (Feshbach, 1984), including those outside of psychology (e.g., sociology; Turner, 1987). As a consequence, contemporary motivation study has a special richness and interest.

THE RETURN OF MOTIVATION STUDY

Starting in 1952, the University of Nebraska invited the most prominent motivation theorists of the day to gather annually for a symposium on motivational topics. In its inau-

FIGURE 2.1 **Relationship of Motivation and Emotion to Other Fields in Psychology**

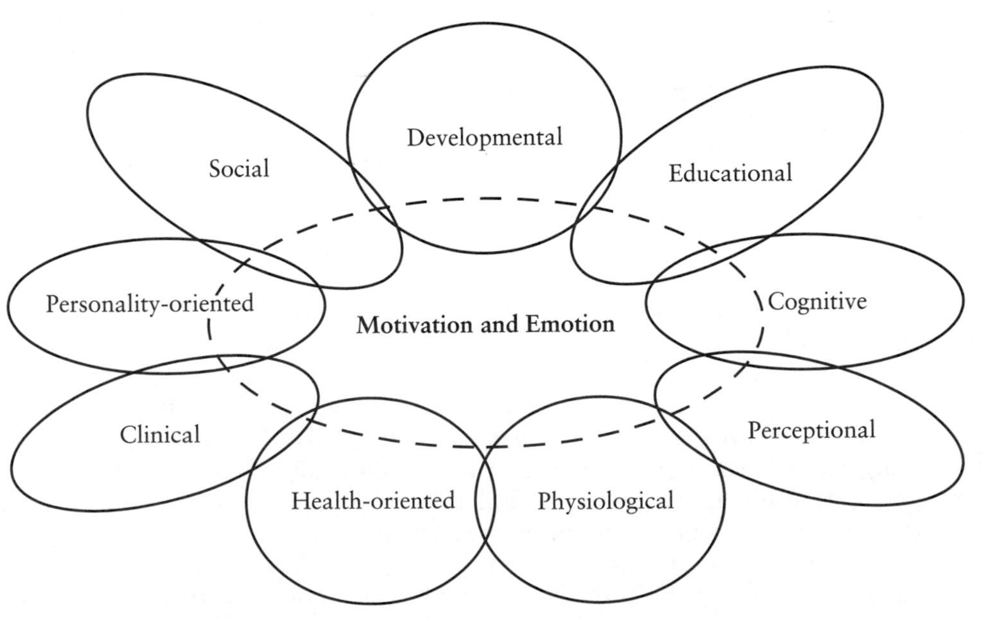

gural year, contributors included Harry Harlow, Judson Brown, and Hobart Mowrer (rather famous names in motivation study). The next year, John Atkinson and Leon Festinger presented papers, and Abraham Maslow, David McClelland, James Olds, and Jullian Rotter presented papers in the third year (again, all famous names in motivation study, as will be evident in the chapters to come). The symposium quickly became a success and served a leadership role in defining and reflecting the field. The symposium continued uninterrupted for 25 years, until a fundamental change occurred in 1978 (Benjamin & Jones, 1978). In 1979, the symposium discontinued its motivational theme and, instead, considered topics that changed from one year to the next, none of which had much if anything to do with motivation. The 1979 symposium focused on attitudes and values, and later symposiums focused on topics such as socioemotional development, psychology and gender, alcohol and addictive behaviors, and psychology and aging. Recall that these years correspond to motivation's dethronement as perhaps psychology's most important field to a sort of second-class field. Basically, the Nebraska Symposium, like psychology in general, lost interest in the study of motivation (for reasons described earlier). With the decline of drive theory, motivation study lost its focus and identity.

The story does not end with motivation in hopeless crisis, however. In recognition of motivation's revival and its contemporary accomplishments (i.e., the mini-theories era), the organizers of the 1990 Nebraska Symposium once again invited prominent motivation researchers to gather for a symposium devoted exclusively to the concept of motivation (Dienstbier, 1991). During that conference, the organizers asked the participants—Mortimer Appley, Albert Bandura, Edward L. Deci, Douglas Derryberry, Carol Dweck, Don Tucker, Richard Ryan, and Bernard Weiner—if they thought motivation was once again strong enough and mature enough as a field to support an exclusive return to motivation topics. Unanimously and enthusiastically, the contributors agreed that motivation was once again a rich enough field of study to justify an annual gathering in Nebraska. The organizers agreed and, in doing so, gave motivation study a vote of confidence and a sense of public identity. Every year since, the symposium has continued its focus on motivation.

In the 1970s, motivation study was on the brink of extinction, "flat on its back," as one pair of researchers put it (Sorrentino & Higgins, 1986, p. 8). It survived by allying itself with other fields of study, and the 1990 Nebraska Symposium symbolically heralds its return as an integrated, coherent field of study. As the new millennium has come, motivation study once again has its critical mass of interested and prominent participants (see Table 1.1 from chapter 1).To document such an optimistic conclusion, the reader can glance through psychology's major journals (e.g., *Psychological Review, Psychological Bulletin*) and expect to find an article related to motivation in almost every issue. And the same can be said for journals in a number of specialty areas as well (e.g., *Journal of Educational Psychology, Journal of Personality and Social Psychology*). As the new millennium has begun, motivation is clearly back at the frontier of psychology. In the 14 chapters to come, the reader can expect to encounter a growing field in its prime.

SUMMARY

A historical view of motivation study allows the reader to consider how the concept of motivation came to prominence, how it changed and developed, how ideas were challenged and replaced, and finally, how the field of motivation reemerged and brought together various disciplines within psychology (Bolles, 1975). Ideas about motivation have philosophical origins. From the ancient Greeks through the European Renaissance, motivation was understood within the two themes of that which is good, rational, immaterial, and active (i.e., the will) and that which is primitive, impulsive, biological, and reactive (i.e., bodily desires). The principal motivational construct within the study of motivation for these two millennia was the will. Unfortunately, the will turned out to be a dead end that explained very little about motivation, and it actually raised more questions than it answered. The hope of explaining motivation passed from philosophy to physiology and psychology in the late 1800s.

To explain motivation, the new field of psychology chose the mechanistic, genetically endowed concept of the instinct. The appeal of the instinct doctrine was its ability to explain unlearned behavior that had energy and purpose (i.e., goal-directed biological impulses). Despite two decades of popularity, the instinct proved to be an intellectual dead end as well, at least in terms of its capacity to serve as a grand theory of motivation. Its logic was hopelessly circular, and its usefulness was more in the naming, not in the explaining, of motivated action. Motivation's third grand theory was drive. In the concept of drive, behavior was motivated to the extent that it served the needs of the organism and restored a biological homeostasis. Like will and instinct, drive appeared to be full of promise, especially because drive theory could do what no motivation theory had ever done before—namely, predict motivation before it occurred from antecedent conditions in the environment (e.g., hours of deprivation). Consequently, the theory enjoyed wide acceptance, especially as manifest in the theories of Freud and Hull. In the end, drive theory too proved itself to be overly limited in scope, and with its rejection came the field's disillusionment with grand theories in general, though several additional motivational principles soon emerged in the spirit of a grand theory, including incentive, arousal, and discrepancy.

Eventually, it became clear that if progress was to be made in understanding motivation, the field had to be willing to step outside the boundaries of its grand theories and embrace the less ambitious, but more promising, mini-theories. While motivation researchers were stepping gently out of their past, they got a strong shove to speed things up from three historical trends. First, motivation study rejected its commitment to a passive view of human nature and adopted a more active portrayal of human beings. Second, motivation turned decidedly cognitive and somewhat humanistic in its subject matter. Third, the field focused on applied, socially relevant problems. The outcome of all this stepping and shoving was part disaster and part good fortune. As to disaster, motivation lost its comfortable status as psychology's flagship discipline and descended into a second-class status. In reaction, motivation researchers dispersed into virtually all areas of psychology (e.g., social, developmental, clinical) and forged alliances with other fields to share ideas, constructs, methodologies, and perspectives. This turned out to be motivation's good fortune because the field successfully developed a host of enlightening mini-theories. Contemporary motivation study is now characterized by mini-theories that are so theoretically and practically enriching that they collectively restored motivation study to a first-class, widely appealing field of study.

The theme throughout this chapter is that motivation study has undergone a constant, albeit turbulent, developmental process. In retrospect, motivation study progressed from relatively simplistic conceptualizations of motivation to an ever-increasing collection of sophisticated and empirically defensible insights about the forces that energize and direct behavior. With the turn of the new millennium, the grand theories have passed. No single theory is going to be general enough to encompass all the sources of human motivation, including those that are genetic, physiological, biological, cognitive, emotional, social, and sociological-cultural. What has arisen to replace a once unified field dominated by a consensus commitment to a series of grand theories is an eclectic group of researchers who embrace three commonalities: (1) core questions (e.g., What causes energetic and directed behavior?); (2) core constructs (i.e., needs, cognitions, emotions, and external events), and (3) a shared history.

RECOMMENDED READINGS

History During the Grand Theories Era

Bolles, R. C. (1975). Historical origins of motivational concepts. In *A theory of motivation* (2nd ed., pp. 21–50). New York: Harper & Row.

Cofer, C. N., & Appley, M. H. (1964). Motivation in historical perspective. In *Motivation: Theory and research* (pp. 19–55). New York: Wiley.

Hull, C. L. (1943). Primary motivation and reaction potential. In *Principles of behavior* (pp. 238–253). New York: Appleton-Century-Crofts.

Koch, S. (1951). The current status of motivational psychology. *Psychological Review, 58,* 147–154.

Kuo, Z. Y. (1921). Giving up instincts in psychology. *Journal of Philosophy, 17,* 645–664.

History During the Mini-Theories Era

Appley, M. H. (1991). Motivation, equilibration, and stress. In R. A. Dienstbier (Ed.), *Nebraska symposium on motivation* (Vol. 38, pp. 1–67). Lincoln: University of Nebraska Press.

Benjamin, L. T., Jr., & Jones, M. R. (1978). From motivational theory to social cognitive development: Twenty-five years of the Nebraska Symposium. *Nebraska symposium on motivation* (Vol. 26, pp. ix–xix). Lincoln: University of Nebraska Press.

Berlyne, D. E. (1975). Behaviorism? Cognitive theory? Humanistic psychology—To Hull with them all! *Canadian Psychological Review, 16,* 69–90.

Dember, W. N. (1965). The new look in motivation. *American Scientist, 53,* 409–427.

Dember, W. N. (1974). Motivation and the cognitive revolution. *American Psychologist, 29,* 161–168.

Weiner, B. (1990). History of motivational research in education. *Journal of Educational Psychology, 82,* 616–622.

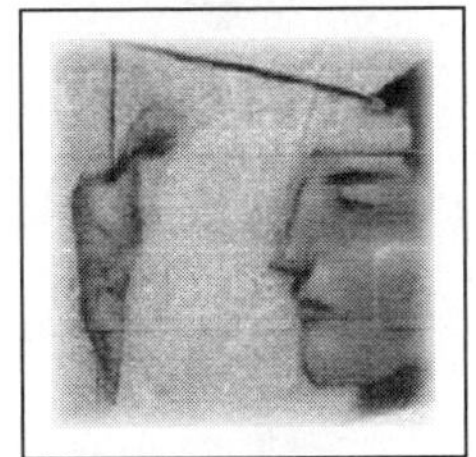

I

Needs

3

Physiological Needs

Consider the following: A researcher invites you to participate in an experiment, and she promises that you will be paid handsomely for your effort. All you have to do is try to gain 10% of your present body weight. It sounds easy and profitable enough, so you accept. At first, all goes well and you gain four pounds in week 1 and two more in week 2. By week 3, however, your appetite wanes and at times disappears altogether. It becomes increasingly difficult to gain another pound, let alone the nine still needed to achieve your 10% increase. Food has lost its appeal, as your body seems to be putting up defenses to counter the weight gain attempt. Plus, your active lifestyle has slowed to a sedentary pace, as you want to exercise less and use elevators more. It takes two months, but you gain the 10%.

With time, your body weight and lifestyle recover. But, alas, the experimenter has another offer. This time, she wants to see if you can lose 10% of your body weight. Confident in your previous success, you accept and begin a strict diet. While too much food took away your appetite, the food deprivation is just plain miserable. Gone are the body's kind and gentle defenses. This time your body is not fooling around. You feel cranky and irritable, and your appetite is forever at the center of your attention. After two months of continual effort with daily exercise and a low-fat diet, you begin to realize that you might be in over your head on this one. The more you restrain yourself and the more you ignore your bodily cues to eat, the grouchier you feel and the more tempting high-calorie food seems. Because you have too many other important things to do and because this constant irritation is getting in your way of daily functioning, you call the experiment off after a month. A return to your normal weight coincides with the departure of your misery and midnight fantasies of pizza.

After the experiments are over, two things have changed. On the one hand, you have a lot more money. But on the other hand, you think about hunger, eating, and weight control a little differently. Your experience shows that the body has a predispositional, somewhat automated guide to how much it should weigh. As you will see, the body does indeed feature many self-regulatory guides, and when these self-regulatory guides are upset, ignored, or outright rejected, motivational states arise. Such motivational states (e.g., hunger, misery) will continue, and even intensify, until the individual acts to correct the upset regulatory guides. Thus, the thesis of the present chapter is that physiological needs, biological systems, and behavior act in concert with one another to achieve stable physiological regulation.

NEED

A need is any condition of a person that is essential and necessary for life, growth, and well-being. If neglected or frustrated, the need's thwarting will produce damage that disrupts biological or psychological well-being. Motivational states therefore provide the impetus to act before damage occurs.

Damage can be to biological systems, so motivational states arise from physiological needs to avoid tissue damage and to maintain bodily water and energy (e.g., pain alleviation, thirst, hunger, and sex). Damage can be to developmental potentials and trajectories, so motivational conditions arise from organismic psychological needs to orient development toward growth and adaptation (e.g., self-determination, competence, and relatedness). Damage can also occur to beliefs, values, and sense of self, so motivational conditions arise from acquired psychological needs to preserve our identities, priorities, and interpersonal relationships (e.g., achievement, affiliation, intimacy, and power). Together, physiological, organismic psychological, and acquired psychological needs provide

FIGURE 3.1 **Relationships Among Categories of Needs**

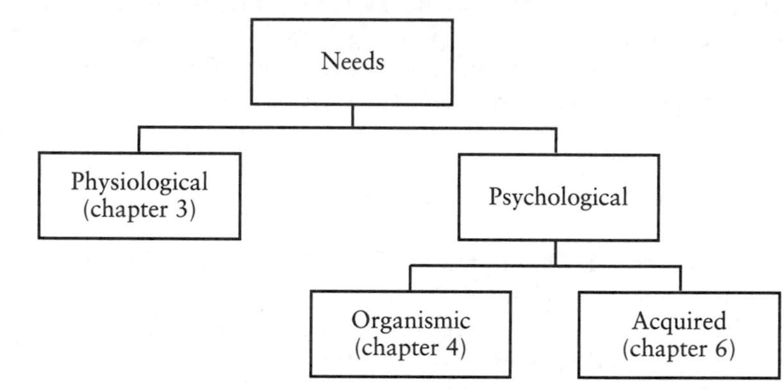

a range of conditions that serve the individual's life, growth, and well-being. The relationships among the three categories of needs appear in Figure 3.1.

Physiological needs involve biological systems such as neural brain circuits, hormones, and bodily organs. When unmet for an extended period, physiological needs constitute life-threatening emergencies and therefore generate motivational states that can dominate consciousness. When gratified, their salience in consciousness fades, and these needs are forgotten about, at least for a while. Psychological needs involve central nervous system processes. Instead of conforming to a cyclical time course (rise, fall, and rise again) like physiological needs do, psychological needs are forever present in consciousness, at least to a degree. They gain salience in consciousness mostly in the presence of the environmental conditions the individual believes are capable of involving and satisfying these needs. For instance, hanging out with friends makes the need for affiliation salient, while being bossed around frustrates a person's need for self-determination. Notice that two kinds of psychological needs exists, and the distinction between organismic and acquired psychological needs is that the former needs are innate and that all people inherit basically the same constellation of organismic psychological needs, whereas the latter needs exist within each individual as a unique constellation of personality characteristics that reflect each individual's unique life experience and socialization history.

All needs generate energy. How one need differs from another is through its directional effects on behavior (Murray, 1937). For instance, a hunger need is different from a thirst need, not in the amount of energy it generates but in its ability to direct attention and action toward seeking out food rather than water. Similarly, a competence need is different from a relatedness need not in the amount of motivation aroused but in the ensuing desire to seek out optimal challenges rather than intimate relationships. Another way that needs differ from one another is that some generate deficiency motivation whereas others generate growth motivation (Maslow, 1987). With deficiency needs, life goes along just fine until some state of deprivation (i.e., it's been 10 hours since your last meal) activates a need to interact with the world in a way that will quiet the deficit (i.e., consume food). With growth needs, motivational states energize and direct behavior to nurture development (seek out challenges, improve interpersonal relationships). The telltale sign to differentiate a deficiency-based need from a growth-based need is by the emotions each generates. Deficiency needs typically generate tension-packed, urgency-laden emotions, such as anxiety, frustration, pain, stress, and relief. Growth needs typically generate positive emotions, such as interest, enjoyment, and vitality.

FUNDAMENTALS OF REGULATION

A half century ago, Clark Hull (1943) described a biologically based theory of motivation referred to as drive theory (see chapter 2). According to drive theory, physiological deprivations and deficits (e.g., lack of water, food, and sleep) create biological needs. If the need continues unsatisfied, the biological deprivation becomes potent enough to occupy attention and generate psychological drive. "Drive" is a theoretical term used to depict the psychological discomfort (felt tension and restlessness) stemming from the underlying and persistent biological deficit. Drive energizes the animal to engage in behaviors that service its physiological needs.

Figure 3.2 illustrates the physiological need–psychological drive–behavioral action process. After drinking a glass of water or having breakfast, an individual experiences a satiated (i.e., full) biological condition in which neither thirst nor hunger is of motiva-

FIGURE 3.2 **Model of Need-Drive-Behavior Sequence**

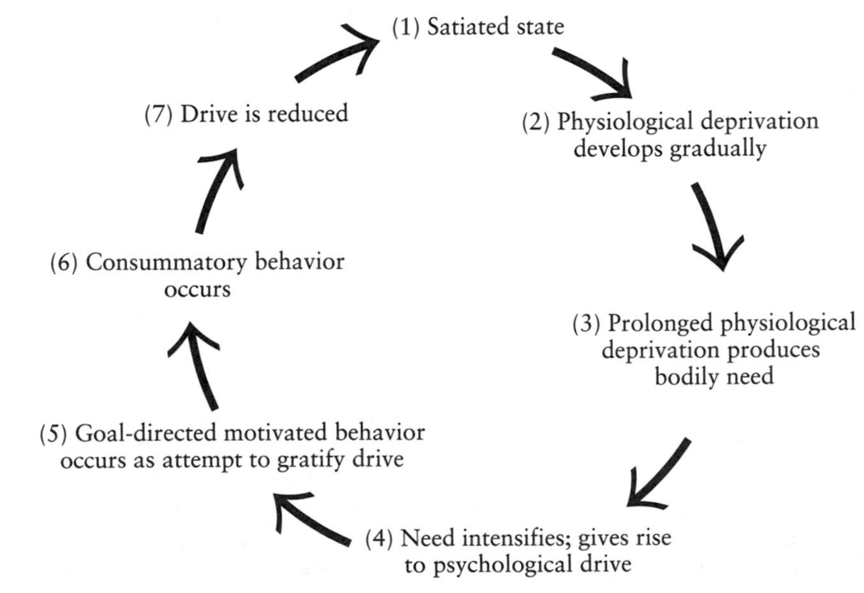

tional consequence, as depicted in (1) in the figure. As time goes by, the individual evaporates water and expends calories. With the loss of water and nutrients, physiological imbalance develops (2). If the physiological imbalance persists and intensifies, then continued deprivation produces a physiological need for water or calories (3). In time, the physiological need intensifies enough to produce felt tension and restlessness, which is the psychological drive (4). Once motivated by drive, the person engages in goal-directed action (5). When the thirsty person finds and drinks water, or when the hungry person locates and consumes food, consummatory behavior occurs (6). The water and food intake satisfies and removes the underlying physiological need, which quiets the psychological drive, through a process called drive reduction (7). Following drive reduction, the individual returns to a satiated (i.e., unmotivated) state (1).

Physiological Need

The cyclical pattern depicting the rise and fall of psychological drive (Figure 3.2) involves seven core processes: need, drive, homeostasis, negative feedback, multiple inputs/multiple outputs, intra-organismic mechanisms, and extra-organismic mechanisms. Physiological need describes a deficient biological condition. Physiological needs occur with tissue and bloodstream deficits, as from water loss, nutrient deprivation, or physical injury. If neglected to the point that the need endures and intensifies, bodily harm or pathology follows. Hence, physiological needs when unmet and intense represent life-threatening emergencies. Restoration of water or food or recovery from physical injury removes the physiological need (and thus the biological emergency).

Drive

Drive is a psychological, not a biological, term. It is the conscious manifestation of an underlying biological need. Drive, not physiological needs per se, has motivational properties in that it produces the energy and direction for behavior. For instance, our urge to eat comes from a felt appetite, not necessarily from low blood sugar or shrunken fat cells. In other words, we are aware of psychological drive, not actual bodily need. When salient enough to grab the attention of an individual, drive readies that individual to perform a particular set of goal-directed behaviors capable of yielding drive reduction.

Homeostasis

Bodily systems show a remarkable capacity for maintaining a steady state of equilibrium, even as these systems perform their functions and are exposed to widely differing and stressful environmental conditions. The term that describes the body's tendency to maintain a steady state is homeostasis. The bloodstream, for instance, shows a remarkable constancy in its level of water, salt, sugar, calcium, oxygen, temperature, acidity, as well as constant levels of proteins and fats (Cannon, 1932, Dempsey, 1951). People constantly face changing external and internal environments, and the mere passage of time brings conditions of deprivation. And people sometimes eat, drink, and sleep to excess. Hence, bodily systems are inevitably and continually displaced from homeostasis. Homeostasis is essentially the body's ability to return a system (i.e., bloodstream) to its basal state. To do so, bodily systems generate motivational states for goal-directed, homeostasis-restoring behavior.

Homeostasis for the body's temperature, for instance, is 98.6°F. If the body temperature drops below 98.6°, the body can shiver its musculature and break down fats to generate a compensatory amount of heat. In addition, a psychological drive of feeling too cold energizes and directs behaviors like exercising vigorously, putting on a coat, and staying inside a warm house. Similarly, if the body temperature rises above 98.6°, the body can perspire. It can also generate a psychological drive of feeling too hot that energizes and directs acts like turning on the air conditioner, drinking fluids, and going swimming. Thus, the body has both a tendency to maintain a steady state as well as the means to generate the motivation necessary to enact homeostasis-restoring behaviors.

Negative Feedback

Negative feedback refers to homeostasis' physiological stop system (Mook, 1988). People eat and sleep but only until they are no longer hungry or sleepy. Drive activates behavior; negative feedback stops behavior.

Without feedback and without a way of inhibiting drive-motivated behavior once the underlying need was satiated, human beings would be like the fabled sorcerer's apprentice (from Dukas' poem popularized by Walt Disney's *Fantasia;* Cofer & Appley, 1964). As the story goes, the apprentice, by imitating the sorcerer, learned how to command a broom to bring a bucket of water. The broom obeyed and brought the apprentice a bucket of water. After a couple of buckets, the apprentice had enough water, but the broom continued to bring bucket after bucket after bucket. Most regrettably, the apprentice forgot to learn how to command the broom to quit bringing water. Were the body unable to inhibit a drive, bodily disaster would result. If people were unable to shut off hunger, they might literally eat themselves to death.

The household furnace provides a mechanically engineered analogy for how feedback operates in concert with homeostasis. The temperature setting on the thermostat determines the optimal (i.e., homeostatic) room temperature, and a mechanical feedback system controls the furnace output. If the room temperature is the same as the thermostat setting, furnace output remains constant. If the room temperature falls below the thermostat setting, furnace output increases and heat pours into the room. The furnace continues to heat until the room temperature rises to the thermostat setting. When the temperature in the room exceeds the thermostat setting, furnace output decreases due to negative feedback, which corrects for any excess of heat.

In the body, negative feedback systems actually signal satiety well before the physiological need is fully replenished (Adolph, 1980). At first, people eat and drink rapidly, but the rate of eating and drinking decreases quickly over the course of a meal (Spitzer & Rodin, 1981). As people digest food and water, the body displays an amazing aptitude to estimate how much of the food or water, when transformed and transplanted, is needed to gratify the underlying physiological need. During drinking, for example, the body continuously monitors the volume of fluid ingested on each swallow and uses that information to predict how much water will eventually make its way into the bloodstream and bodily cells. Understanding precisely how the body signals satiety constitutes the study of negative feedback systems.

MULTIPLE INPUTS/MULTIPLE OUTPUTS

Drive has multiple inputs, or means of activation. One can feel thirsty, for example, after sweating, eating salty foods, or donating blood; from electrical stimulation of a particular brain structure; or simply at a particular time of the day. In much the same way, drive has multiple outlets, or behavioral responses, that satisfy the drive. When cold, a person can put on a jacket, turn up the furnace, engage in exercise, or shiver. Each of these behaviors achieves the same end result—a raised body temperature. The basic idea is that drive can arise from a number of different sources (inputs), and it can be expressed in a number of different behavioral ways (outputs).

The convergence of multiple inputs with multiple outputs, shown in Figure 3.3, is actually what makes drive such an appealing motivational construct. In theoretical terms, drive is an *intervening variable,* one that integrates the relationships among several otherwise diverse input and output variables. Pain, as an intervening variable, for example, helps explain the motivational processes that occur immediately after, for instance, a hammer strikes the hand (Antecedent 1 in the figure), a hand touches a hot stove (Antecedent 2), or a bare foot scrapes across a nail (Antecedent 3) to the time that the person shakes his hand frantically (Consequence 1), pours cold water over his hand (Consequence 2), or hops around on one foot while holding the injured foot (Consequence 3). Drive, therefore, intervenes between states of deprivation (input stimuli) and restorative actions (output responses) being caused by an input that thus causes the output.

Consider the theoretical advantage of using drive as an intervening variable for connecting multiple inputs with multiple outputs. Imagine that the three inputs in Figure 3.3 were hours of food deprivation, percent of decrease in body weight, and the tempting smell of fresh popcorn. Now imagine that the three outputs were calories consumed, latency to

FIGURE 3.3 **Drive As an Intervening Variable**

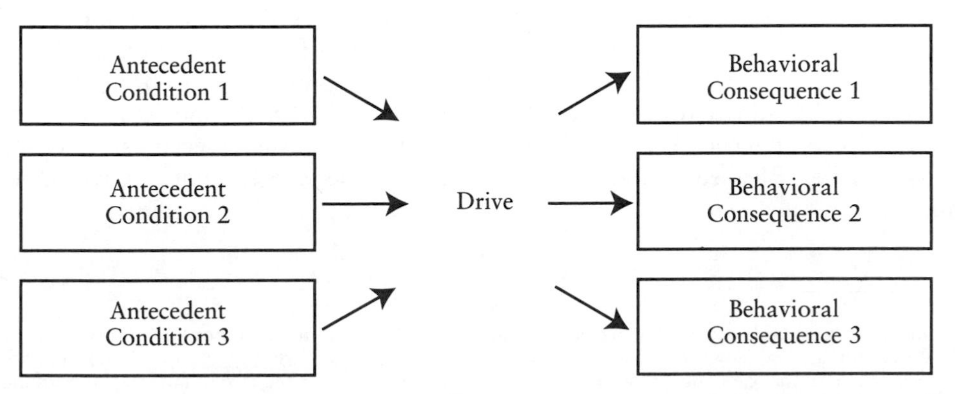

begin eating, and probability of eating lunch versus skipping it. Without using drive as an intervening variable, one would need to keep track of all the effects each input has on each output (e.g., how hours of deprivation affects amount eaten, latency to eat, and probability of lunching, and so on for all possible inputs). Using our intervening variable of hunger allows for a theoretical common ground in which the focus is on how each input affects hunger and how hunger affects each output. Thus, what becomes important to study is the intervening variable, not necessarily all the hundreds of individual inputs and outputs.[1]

INTRA-ORGANISMIC MECHANISMS

Intra-organismic regulatory mechanisms include all the biological systems that act in concert to activate, maintain, and terminate the physiological needs that underlie drive. Brain centers, the endocrine system, and bodily organs constitute the three main categories of intra-organismic regulating mechanisms. Intra-organismic mechanisms for hunger regulation, for example, include the hypothalamus (brain centers), glucose and insulin hormones (endocrine system), and the stomach and liver (bodily organs). Together, the hypothalamus, glucose, insulin, stomach, and liver (as well as additional intra-organismic mechanisms) create the bodily conditions of need (i.e., deprivation) and satiety (i.e., gratification) that activate, maintain, and terminate hunger.

Intra-organismic mechanisms take center stage in any analysis of physiological needs. It is difficult to really understand the role thirst and hunger, for example, play in motivation without first gaining an understanding of the basics of the brain, limbic system, neurotransmitters, hormones, and bodily organs. The specific intra-organismic mechanisms for each of the different physiological needs will be identified and discussed in greater detail under the section heading, "Physiological Regulation."

EXTRA-ORGANISMIC MECHANISMS

Extra-organismic mechanisms include all the nonbiological mechanisms that play a part in activating, maintaining, and terminating the psychological drive that regulates need-satisfying behaviors such as eating, drinking, and copulating. The four categories of extra-organismic mechanisms are cognitive, environmental, social, and cultural influences. For eating, extra-organismic influences include beliefs about calories and personal goals for losing weight (cognitive influences), the smell of food and the time of day (environmental influences), the presence of others and peer pressure to eat or not to eat (social influences), and sex roles and cultural ideals about desirable and undesirable body shapes (cultural influences). For each need, the extra-organismic mechanisms are different, as will be discussed in the pages that follow under the heading, "Environmental Influences."

---

[1] The intervening variable approach depicted in Figure 3.3 applies to all motives, not just to drive. The inputs and outputs for the need for achievement, for instance, could be optimal challenge, rapid feedback, and personal responsibility for one's outcomes (multiple inputs) and persistence in the face of failure, choice of moderately difficult undertakings, and entrepreneurship (multiple outputs).

PAIN

Pain is caused by tissue damage (Jessell & Kelly, 1991). Cavities, cuts and burns to the skin, uncomfortable chairs, sore muscles, very cold and very hot temperatures, and bee stings are examples of events that either damage our bodily tissues directly (bee stings) or signal that tissue damage has occurred (sore muscles).

Like thirst and hunger, the experience of pain is unpleasant and few people desire it. But pain is an adaptive motivational state in the sense of the adaptive, beneficial behavior to which it leads. It is a potent motivational experience in that it demands our attention, disrupts ongoing behavior, acts as a punisher to suppress the behavior that causes the pain, and negatively reinforces any behavior able to alleviate the pain. Because pain is so evolutionary primitive, the motivation to escape from and avoid pain are highly attention-getting motives that dominate consciousness. Further, pain is attention-getting because its occurrence is often less predictable than are the other physiological needs, such as thirst, hunger, and sex.

Pain motivates two types of behavior: escape and recuperation. As to escape behavior, pain ruptures whatever our ongoing behavior is with an attention-getting urge to escape (Eccleston & Crombez, 1999; Price, 1988). Such an urge arises in ways that are reactive. For instance, we want to pull our hand away from a thorn, and such an urge arises in ways that are proactive. For instance, with experience, we fear walking in the woods where the thorns are (to avoid pain-inflicting damage to ourselves). As to recuperation, pain can motivate passivity and defensive behaviors. The human pain victim typically slows down and seeks out conditions that allow rest, safety, nurturing, social support, bodily care, and suppressed activity (Bolles & Fanselow, 1980).

Physiological Regulation

At the behavioral level, to escape pain, we run inside the house on a cold day, tell the dentist to skip a procedure or two, take off tight shoes, and rush our hand back from the sink's freezing water. To avoid pain, we stay inside the house when it's cold, neglect to make that overdue dentist appointment, throw away ill-fitting shoes, and wait until we see some steam before putting our hands under the faucet. Intervening between these experiences and potential experiences of pain and our adaptive behavior, however, is the underlying physiological regulation of pain.

The peripheral nervous system has an extensive network of free nerve endings that extend throughout the skin and bodily tissues (Jessell & Kelly, 1991). When tissue damage occurs, these free nerve endings activate pain in a variety of ways, such as through the sensations of excessive temperature (hot coffee spill, cold ice cube), chemical agents (acids), direct pressure (tight shoes), and touch (pinprick). These nerve endings are typically stimulated directly, but they can also be activated by a more diffuse chemical release following the injury.

Two types of nerve fibers transmit pain information from the free nerve endings to the spinal cord and eventually to the brain. A-fibers are thick and coated with myelin. They send the very rapid neural sensations of sharp, prickling pain. C-fibers are thin and are not coated in myelin. They send the slow, long-lasting sensations associated with sore, aching, and chronic pain. A- and C-fibers extend up the spinal cord to three areas of the brain: reticular formation, which processes pain's arousal information; limbic system (e.g., hypothalamus), which processes pain's emotional information; and thalamus, which processes pain's experiential aspect. In other words, the tissue damage from a paper cut communicates pain's arousal (intensity), emotion (fear), and experience (hurt).

Pain Suppression Network

The perception of pain is only half of the story. Anyone who has had to suppress pain, as during a polite conversation or while driving down the interstate looking for a rest area, knows that the brain can suppress pain messages and feelings. Distraction can be an effective technique, at least when the pain is of moderately low intensity; pain at high intensity is just too difficult to ignore (McCaul & Mallott, 1984).

Just as A-fibers and C-fibers connect free nerve endings to the brain, A-fibers and C-fibers also project from the brain stem downwards to where the A- and C-fibers enter the spinal cord (Mayer, et al., 1971; Oliveras, et al., 1975). Once activated by endorphins, these brain stem projections can inhibit, even turn off, the incoming pain messages (Yaksh & Rudy, 1976). The threat to life, fear, and intense emotion, in general, constitute the small range of experience that leads the brain to release the endorphins needed to shut down the pain message (Bolles & Fanselow, 1980; Fanselow, 1985). Evidently, even pain takes a back seat when injured rats face a predator, like a cat (Lester & Fanselow, 1985), or war-injured humans engage in battle (Beecher, 1956).

Endorphins (e.g., B-endorphin) limit pain, even shut off pain to some degree, by binding to pain receptor sites in the brain. Pain information is delivered from the peripheral nervous system to the brain, but the pain is not processed and experienced when all available receptor sites are filled by endorphins (similar to not being able to find a parking place in a full lot). The brain manufactures endorphins in the pituitary gland and hypothalamus, and it releases them during times of stress and injury. Opiate drugs, such as morphine and heroin, work essentially the same way, except that endorphins are manufactured naturally by the brain, whereas opiates are given externally.

ENVIRONMENTAL INFLUENCES

Given exposure to the same noxious event, different people experience different sensations and depths of pain. It is extremely difficult to know whether two people actually experience different levels of pain at the physiological level. At the experiential level, however, hypnotized individuals report feeling less pain than individuals who were not hypnotized (Hilgard & Hilgard, 1975), athletes report feeling less pain than people who categorize themselves as not being athletic (Ryan & Kovacic, 1975), and women report feeling more pain than men (Noterman & Tophoff, 1975).

Memories relevant to pain are one way to explain individual differences in subjective intensity of experienced pain (see Figure 3.4). According to Howard Leventhal and David Everhart's (1979) model, pain-associated memories can reduce a person's current sensory

FIGURE 3.4 **Role of Memory in the Attenuation of Felt Pain**

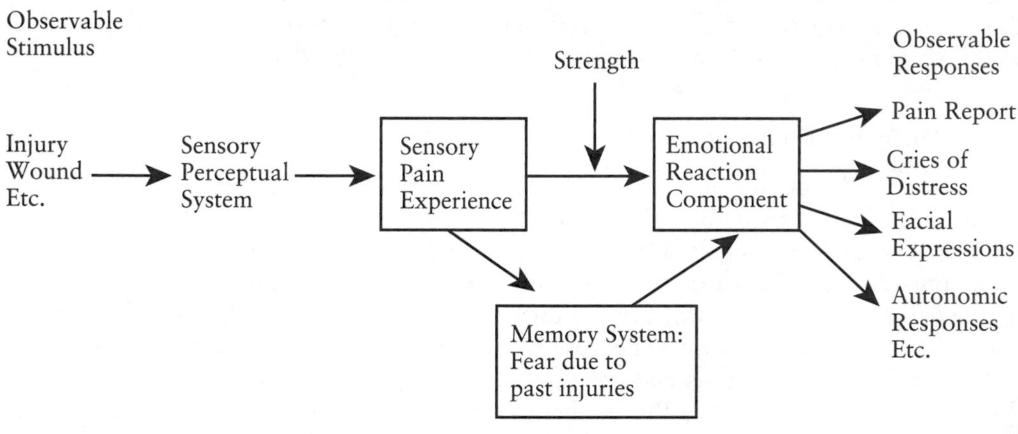

SOURCE: From "Emotion, Pain, and Physical Illness," by H. Leventhal and D. Everhart, *Emotions in Personality and Psychopathology* (pp. 263–299), C. E. Izard (Ed.), 1979, New York: Plenum.

pain experience. For instance, women who have given birth report less intense pain than women who have not yet given birth (Hapidou & deCatanzaro, 1992). Thus, not unlike endorphins, past memories related to pain-inflicting events can attenuate a current pain experience.

Overview

Pain is such a potent motive because of its intrinsic ability to grab, hold, and direct our attention (Eccleston & Crombez, 1999). It generates the urge to escape so that we will minimize the tissue damage presently occurring, and it creates a desire for passive, defensive behaviors so that we will want to recuperate, rest, and take care. Its motivation arises from an extensive network of free nerve endings that send pain information to the reticular formation, limbic system, and thalamus. Endorphins can moderate the felt pain by activating the pain suppression network, and memories of coping well with past injuries can attenuate (or exacerbate) the pain experienced.

THIRST

Our bodies are mostly water—about two-thirds. When our water volume falls by about 2%, we begin to feel thirsty. The body is continually losing water, as through perspiration, urination, exhalation, and even through bleeding, vomiting, and sneezing (i.e., multiple inputs). Loss of water, below an optimal homeostatic level, creates the physiological need that underlies thirst. Thirst is the consciously experienced motivational state that readies the body to perform behaviors necessary to replenish a water deficit.

Pain is obviously an emergency-ridden, physiological, need-based motivation. Our survival depends on adapting successfully to pain, so it has an evolutionary primacy in terms of grabbing attention. But thirst runs a close second behind pain. Without water to drink, each of us would die in about two days. If you have ever gone a full day without water, you know it too has an evolutionary primacy to grab attention.

Physiological Regulation

The water inside the human body lies in both intracellular and extracellular fluids. The intracellular fluid consists of all the water inside the cells (approximately 40% of body weight). The extracellular fluid (approximately 20% of body weight) consists of all the water outside the cells; it exists in blood plasma and interstitial fluid. Water is water no matter where it is in the body, but the differentiation is important because thirst arises from these two distinct sources. Because thirst arises from both intracellular and extracellular deficits, physiologists endorse the "double-depletion model" of thirst activation (Epstein, 1973). According to this model, osmometric thirst and volumetric thirst represent two separate means of physiologically regulating thirst. When the intracellular fluid needs replenishment, osmometric thirst arises. Cellular dehydration causes osmometric thirst, and cellular hydration stops it. When the extracellular fluid needs replenishment (e.g., after bleeding or vomiting), volumetric thirst arises. Hypovolemia (reduction of plasma volume) causes volumetric thirst, and hypervolemia stops it.

Thirst Activation

Consider the standard water deprivation study in which laboratory animals are deprived of water but not food for about 24 hours (Rolls, Wood, & Rolls, 1980). After depriving the animals of water, researchers selectively replace either the intracellular or the extracellular water (using special infusion techniques). The procedure yields three conditions: (1) 24-hour water deprivation followed by intracellular fluid replenishment; (2) 24-hour water deprivation followed by extracellular fluid replenishment; and (3) 24-hour water deprivation with no fluid replenishment. The amount of water drunk by animals in the third group (a control group) serves as a standard of normal thirst (indexed by drinking) following water deprivation. Rats that received replenishment of their extracellular fluids drank just a bit less than did the rats that received no replenishment at all. That is, they drank as if they were still very thirsty. Rats that received replenishment of their intracellular fluid drank much less. That is, they drank as if they were mostly full. These results suggest that osmometric thirst is the primary cause of thirst activation, whereas volumetric thirst is of secondary importance. Thirst comes mostly from dehydrated cells.

Thirst Satiety

When people drink, they do not drink continuously. Something alerts the body to quit drinking. The negative feedback system is important because the body must not only replenish its water deficits, but it must also prevent intoxication from drinking so much water that cellular dysfunction occurs and threatens death. And generally speaking, humans and animals have evolved hardy thirst-satiety abilities. Animals that are not water deprived do not really want to drink, and if forced to do so, they just let the water dribble out the side of their mouths without swallowing it (Williams & Teitelbaum, 1956). Humans, of course, often binge when drinking, but such drinking is regulated by factors other than water, such as taste or alcohol.

During drinking, water passes from the mouth and esophagus to the stomach and intestines and is then absorbed into the bloodstream. Through the process of osmosis, water eventually passes from the extracellular fluids into the intracellular fluids. The negative feedback mechanism for this satiety must therefore lie in one (or more) of these bodily sites: mouth, stomach, intestines, bloodstream, cells.

To locate thirst's negative feedback mechanism(s), physiologists devised a number of experiments. In one experiment, animals drank water, but the experimenters arranged for the water to pass through the mouth but not reach the stomach (or intestines, bloodstream, or cells; Blass & Hall, 1976). The animals, on average, drank four times their normal amount of water, but they did eventually stop drinking. Thus, water passing through the mouth does provide one means of thirst inhibition, albeit a weak one. Later research identified that the mouth's specific stop system was related to the number of swallows during drinking (Mook & Wagner, 1989). After many swallows (but not necessarily after one drinks a large volume of water), drinking stops.

Subsequent studies arranged for animals to drink so that water passed from the mouth to the stomach but not into the intestines, bloodstream, or cells (Hall, 1973). Animals receiving water into their mouths and stomachs drank twice as much as normal. Thus, the stomach, like the mouth, also has a thirst inhibitory mechanism, albeit another weak one. Other studies allowed animals to drink with water passing through the mouth, stomach, and intestines, and into the extracellular fluids (Mook & Kozub, 1968). The water the rats drank, however, was a salt solution. Drinking the salt solution allowed much water into the extracellular fluids but little into the intracellular fluids. (Following the principle of osmosis, salty water does not diffuse into intracellular areas.) These animals drank more than normal. Therefore, the cells themselves must also house a negative feedback mechanism. Evidently, multiple negative feedback systems exist—in the mouth, stomach, and cells. Water consumption does not fully alleviate thirst and stop drinking unless it eventually hydrates bodily cells (Mook, 1996).

Hypothalamus and Liver

The mouth, stomach, and cells coordinate thirst activation and satiety, but so do the liver, hypothalamus, and specific hormones. The brain (through the hypothalamus) monitors intracellular shrinkage (due to low-water levels) and releases a hormone into the blood plasma that sends a message to the liver to conserve its water reserves (by producing concentrated, rather than diluted, urine). While the hypothalamus is managing the involuntary behavior of the liver, it also creates the conscious psychological state of feeling thirsty that directs attention and behavior toward water-replenishing courses of action. It is in

FIGURE 3.5 **Relative Pleasantness of Four Taste Solutions**

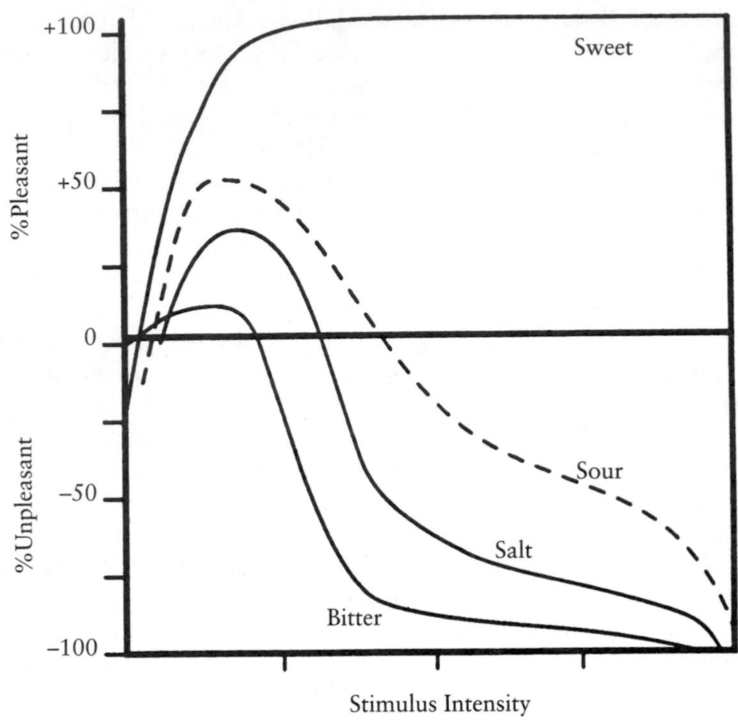

SOURCE: From "The Pleasures of Sensation," by C. Pfaffmann, 1960, *Psychological Review, 67,* pp. 253–268. Copyright 1960 by the American Psychological Association. Reprinted with permission.

the hypothalamus that the psychological experience of thirst originates and enters into consciousness.

ENVIRONMENTAL INFLUENCES

Three extra-organismic influences on drinking behavior are the perception of water availability, adherence to drinking schedules, and taste. Animals with water-plentiful environments drink less over the course of a day than do animals with water-restricted environments (Toates, 1979). Animals also acquire and closely adhere to drinking schedules, irrespective of their physiological need for water (Toates, 1979). The most important environmental influence for drinking, however, is taste (Pfaffmann, 1961, 1982).

Pure water is tasteless and, therefore, offers no incentive value above and beyond water replenishment (though water replenishment can, at times, be a potent incentive). When water is given a taste, drinking behavior changes in accordance with the incentive value of the fluid. The incentive values for four tastes appear in Figure 3.5: sweet, sour, salty, and bitter, represented at various stimulus intensities. Using tasteless (pure) water as a baseline (no pleasantness), any taste is slightly pleasant at a very low intensity. At more substantial intensities, sucrose-flavored (sweet) water is markedly more pleasant than is tasteless water. Tartartic acid (sour), salt, and quinine-flavored (bitter) water are all markedly more unpleasant than tasteless water.

When factors such as a sweet taste offer a high incentive value for drinking, human beings drink excessively and sometimes consume dangerously high amounts, biologically speaking (Rolls, Wood, & Rolls, 1980). People often drink soft drinks for their taste alone. Complications can emerge with water-based drinks that contain alcohol or caffeine. Alcohol and caffeine generate addictions, and both alcohol and caffeine, therefore, introduce a number of additional physiological processes that motivate people to drink to excess. Further, a number of social and cultural influences surround the drinking of alcoholic and caffeinated beverages that make drinking behavior more complex than thirst-regulated water consumption. Students on college campuses, for instance, binge in alcohol consumption quite often. Thus, drinking occurs for two reasons: water replenishment, which satisfies physiological needs, and pleasure, which involves reasons above and beyond thirst and physiological need.[2]

HUNGER

The physiological regulation of hunger is relatively more complex than for thirst. Water loss instigates thirst, and water replenishment satiates it. Hunger, then, might simply involve the cyclical loss and replenishment of food. Hunger, however, only partially follows a "depletion-repletion" model. There does exist a relationship between duration of food deprivation and hunger, and people do eat on the basis of deprivation. If this were not the case, people would not eat three meals a day. But hunger regulation is best understood not only as a function of short-term processes operating under homeostatic regulation (e.g., depletion and repletion of blood glucose and calories) but also as a function of long-term processes operating under metabolic regulation and stored energy (e.g., fat cells). Hunger and eating are further affected, and substantially so, by cognitive, social, and environmental influences, so much in fact that an understanding of hunger and eating requires not only short-term and long-term physiological models but cognitive-social-environmental models as well (Weingarten, 1985).

PHYSIOLOGICAL REGULATION

Two types of models occupy hunger researchers' attention. The first is a short-term model in which immediately available energy (blood glucose) is constantly monitored. Hunger arises in response to declining amounts of energy and terminates in response to energy replenishment. This model is known as the glucostatic hypothesis, and it does a good job accounting for the onset and termination of hunger and eating. The second model is a

---

[2] The relationship between taste and drinking behavior is made complicated by the fact that water deprivation affects the perception of the taste of water. Water becomes increasingly more hedonically positive (more rewarding) with increased deprivation, and water becomes increasingly more hedonically aversive with water satiation (Beck, 1979; Williams & Teitelbaum, 1956).

long-term one in which stored energy (fat mass) is available and is used as a resource for supplementing energy regulation. This model is known as the lipostatic model, and it does a good job showing how fat stores become integrated with other regulators of food intake, such as habits and social factors.

Before summarizing the glucostatic hypothesis and lipostatic model, consider hunger's intra-organismic mechanisms. Hunger arises from both brain and peripheral (nonbrain) bodily cues. These peripheral bodily cues include the mouth (Cabanac & Duclaux, 1970), stomach distentions (Deutsch, Young, & Kalogeris, 1978; McHugh & Moran, 1985), and body temperature (Brobeck, 1960). To exemplify the role of peripheral cues in hunger activation and satiation, consider the stomach. It empties itself at a calorie-constant rate (about 210 calories per hour), so appetite returns more quickly after a low-calorie than after a high-calorie meal (McHugh & Moran, 1985). During a meal, the stomach releases peptides such as CCK to reduce appetite (Woods, Seeley, Porte, & Schwartz, 1998). With a full stomach, people report no hunger; with a stomach that is 60% empty, people report a hint of hunger; and with a stomach that is 90% empty, people report maximum hunger, even though some food remains in the stomach (Sepple & Read, 1989).[3]

Brain signals are particularly important in hunger regulation (Wyrwicka, 1988). The lateral hypothalamus (LH) is the brain's feeding center partly because its stimulation causes extensive overeating and partly because its destruction will cause animals to stop eating and literally starve to death (Delgado & Anand, 1953). The LH manufactures appetite-boosting peptides called orexins (which is the Greek word for appetite; Yanagisawa, 1998). Orexins are powerful appetite boosters, and when injected into the brain of rats, the animals will eat three to six times more than control rats. Findings such as these are very exciting to drug researchers trying to find ways to stimulate appetite in humans, such as people going through chemotherapy (Woods, et al., 1998).

The ventromedial hypothalamus (VMH) is the brain's satiety center (i.e., a negative feedback system) because its surgical destruction will cause animals to become chronic overeaters such that they may double their body weight (Miller, 1960; Stevenson, 1969). The VMH houses receptors for leptin. Leptin (or hormone OB) is secreted by fat cells, circulates in the blood, and is transported to the VHM where its receptors monitor its presence and send out signals to reduce food intake, reduce glucose and insulin, and increase metabolic rate (Campfield, Smith, & Burn, 1996, 1997). Findings such as these are very exciting to drug researchers trying to find ways to reverse obesity in humans (Campfield, Smith, & Burn, 1998).

In brief, peripheral and brain areas coordinate to regulate hunger as follows: Deficits in one's energy balance—stored via glucose, fat, or both—send excitatory signals to the LH, which manufactures appetite-boosting peptides to create the psychological experience of hunger. Hungry people seek out and consume food. Once eating has begun, food

[3] Deutsch and Gonzalez (1980) further find that the stomach signals not only food volume information but food content information as well. This pair of researchers removed specific nutrients from an animal's food and found that the animal responded by eating foods that had those particular nutrients and refusing foods without those nutrients. Thus the stomach monitors food content and food volume, and both food content and food volume regulate hunger and its satiety.

interacts with receptors in the tongue, stomach, intestines, and liver. The detection, processing, and absorption of food sends satiety signals by way of the bloodstream and by way of afferent nerve fibers from the liver, stomach, and intestines. These signals accumulate and are processed in the VHM to bring a meal to its end. With the energy balance restored, the LH goes quiet, the VHM is stimulated, and hunger fades.

Glucostatic Hypothesis

The glucostatic hypothesis argues that blood-sugar levels are critical to hunger (Mayer, 1952, 1953). Cells require glucose to produce energy. When the cell's capacity for energy production drops, a physiological need for glucose arises that, in turn, sends a deficit signal to the LH, the brain center responsible for generating the psychological experience of appetite. In one study, animals received an intravenous injection of glucose, and researchers plotted the extent of subsequent neural firing in the hypothalamus. Activity in the LH increased, whereas activity in the VMH decreased (Anand, Chhina, & Singh, 1962). Hence, high blood glucose levels activate the VMH with a negative feedback signal, whereas low glucose levels activate the LH with a hunger signal.

When blood glucose drops, people begin to eat (Campfield, et al., 1996). The bodily organ that actually monitors level of blood glucose is the liver, and when blood glucose is at or above an optimal level, the liver communicates an inhibitory satiety signal to the hypothalamus (Russek, 1971; Schmitt, 1973). However, blood glucose is not the full story, as diabetics will tell you because they often have both high glucose and high hunger. While diabetics have high blood glucose, what they need (and don't have) is high *cellular* glucose. Diabetics need insulin because insulin (the hormone diabetics lack) increases cell membrane permeability so that glucose can flow freely from the bloodstream into the cells. Blood glucose can then become cellular glucose. Hence, the glucostatic hypothesis proposes the following: When deficient glucose exists, it is detected by the liver. The liver then sends an excitatory signal to the LH to stimulate appetite, motivate food-consuming behaviors, and increase plasma glucose (and cellular glucose when insulin is present). The liver detects and then signals satiety to the VMH.

Lipostatic Hypothesis

Like glucose, fat (adipose tissue) also produces energy. And like the body monitors its glucose levels rather precisely, it also monitors its fat cells rather precisely (Faust, Johnson, & Hirsch, 1977a, 1977b). According to the lipostatic (lipo = fatty; static = equilibrium) hypothesis, when the mass of fat stored drops below its homeostatic balance, adipose tissue secretes hormones into the bloodstream to stimulate food intake and promote weight gain motivation (Borecki, et al., 1995). When the mass of fat stored increases above its homeostatic balance, adipose tissue secretes hormones (e.g., leptin) into the bloodstream to reduce food intake and promote weight loss motivation (Schwartz & Seeley, 1997; Woods et al., 1998). Because fat stores are relatively stable and enduring sources of energy, the lipostatic hypothesis illustrates the body's neurohormonal system for smoothing out the otherwise short-term fluctuations in energy balance from blood glucose levels. The lipostatic hypothesis is also tied much more closely to enduring factors like genetics and metabolic rates.

A spin-off version of the lipostatic hypothesis is the set-point theory (Keesey, 1980; Keesey, et al., 1976; Keesey & Powley, 1975; Powley & Keesey, 1970). Set-point theory argues that each individual has a biologically determined body weight or fat thermostat that is set by genetics either at birth or shortly thereafter. Genetics create individual differences in the number of fat cells per person. In set-point theory, hunger activation and satiety depend on the size of one's fat cells, which vary over time. When fat cell size is reduced (e.g., through dieting), hunger appears and persists until feeding behavior allows the fat cells to return to their natural (set-point) size. Evidence for set-point theory comes mostly from research on obese individuals who participate in extensive weight-loss treatment programs. People can and do lose weight, but very few people can keep the weight from returning back to its original starting (set) point (Brownell, 1982).

Environmental Influences

The sight, smell, appearance, and taste of food; the time of day; and stress are all antecedents to eating behavior. Eating behavior increases significantly, for instance, when an individual confronts a variety of foods, a variety of nutrients, a variety of tastes, and particular shapes of food (Rolls, 1979; Rolls, Rowe, & Rolls, 1982). The mere availability of food variety encourages more eating than does a monotonous diet (Sclafani & Springer, 1976). Even when the individual has only one type of food (e.g., ice cream), variety in the number of flavors available increases food intake (Beatty, 1982). Food availability and large portion sizes also lead people to overeat (Hill & Peters, 1998).

Eating is often a social occasion. People eat more when they are in the presence of others (who are also eating) than when they are alone (Berry, Beatty, & Klesges, 1985; deCastro & Brewer, 1991). People who are trying to diet are also more likely to relapse when they are in the presence of others who are eating (Grilo, Shiffman, & Wing, 1989). One demonstration of this social facilitation effect involved an experiment with the help of college students. The students were asked to participate in an ice-cream tasting experiment. Half the students ate alone, whereas the other half ate in a group of three. Ice-cream eaters also had either one or three flavors from which to choose (a variety manipulation). Table 3.1 lays out the following results to the experiment: how much ice cream males and females ate (1) when alone versus with others and (2) when offered one versus three flavors. Both males and females ate more in the presence of others and in the presence of variety.

Situational pressure to eat or to diet serves as another environmental influence on eating behavior. Bingeing on food, for instance, is an acquired behavioral pattern under substantial social control (Crandall, 1988). It often occurs in small groups, such as athletic teams (Crago et al., 1985) and cheerleading squads (Squire, 1983), partly because small groups develop and enforce norms about what is appropriate behavior. Deviation from these norms typically results in some form of interpersonal rejection and a reduction in popularity. If eating is an important behavior for the group, then group pressure can become a more potent eating signal than one's physiology. Eating is often an important behavior in the lives of children, and children prefer the same foods eaten by

TABLE 3.1 **Ice-Cream Intake (in Grams) for Students Alone Versus in Group and With One Versus Three Flavors**

	Social setting			
	Alone		Three-person group	
	Number of flavors		Number of flavors	
	1	3	1	3
Males	113.8	211.1	245.6	215.6
Females	76.9	137.7	128.5	170.8

SOURCE: From "Sensory and Social Influences on Ice Cream Consumption by Males and Females in a Laboratory Setting," by S. L. Berry, W. W. Beatty, and R. C. Klesges, 1985, *Appetite, 6,* pp. 41–45.

those they admire (Birch & Fisher, 1996). In other words, extra-organismic influences add to, and even somewhat override, intra-organismic influences on hunger and eating.

Restraint-Release Situations

Much in the same way that social pressures can interfere with and override physiological regulation, dieting too can interfere with and override physiological guides. By dieting, the dieter attempts to bring eating behavior under cognitive, rather than under physiological, control (e.g., "I will eat this much at this time," rather than "I will eat when hungry"). More often than not, however, dieting paradoxically causes bingeing. The dieter becomes increasingly susceptible to disinhibition (or "restraint release"), especially under conditions of anxiety, stress, alcohol, depression, or exposure to high-calorie foods (Greeno & Wing, 1994; Polivy & Herman, 1983, 1985). One study, for example, found that people on a diet ate less ice cream than people not dieting, as you would expect, but dieters actually ate more than people not dieting when everyone first drank a 15-ounce milk shake. After the dieters drank the high-calorie food, they became increasingly vulnerable to bingeing (Herman, Polivy, & Esses, 1987), a phenomenon known as restraint release and a pattern of bingeing described as counterregulation (Polivy & Herman, 1985).

Counterregulation describes the paradoxical pattern displayed by dieters who eat very little when just nibbling but who eat very much after consuming a large, high-calorie "preload" (Herman & Mack, 1975; Polivy, 1976; Ruderman & Wilson, 1979; Spencer & Fremouw, 1979; Woody et al., 1981). Consuming high-calorie food is only one of many conditions that unleash dieters' bingeing. Depression also triggers a dieter's restraint release. For instance, depressed dieters typically gain weight, whereas people who are not dieting and are depressed typically lose weight (Polivy & Herman, 1976a). The same pattern holds for anxiety as anxious dieters eat more than anxious people not dieting (Baucom & Aiken, 1981). Conditions that threaten one's ego (e.g., failure at an easy task, making a speech before an evaluative audience) produce the same paradoxical effect in which restrained eaters eat more than do unrestrained eaters (Heatherton, Herman, & Polivy, 1991). Alcohol has this same restraint-release effect on dieters as well (Polivy & Herman, 1976b). Taken as a whole, research on social facilitation, social pressure, and restraint-release documents that eating behavior can and often does

Reversing Self-Regulation Failure

Question: Why would a person want to learn about the motivational states discussed in this chapter?

Answer: Because self-regulation failure has created a national epidemic of obesity.

Body weight and obesity are a lot like the weather: Everybody talks about it, but no one seems to do much about it. One reason people are talking so much about obesity is because it has become nothing less than a national epidemic in the United States and is threatening to become a global epidemic (WHO, 1998). Currently, 22.5% of the U.S. population is considered obese, and that compares to rates of 14.5% in 1980, 14.1% in 1974, and 12.8% in 1962 (Taubes, 1998). As you can see, the rates of obesity are rapidly rising. Fully 54% of U.S. adults are overweight (Hill & Peters, 1998). Half of us are overweight—not obese necessarily but getting there nonetheless. These numbers are based on the measure of body mass index (BMI), which is calculated by dividing the person's weight in kilograms by his height in meters squared. A BMI of greater than 25 is overweight; a BMI of greater than 30 is obese. By this measure, a 5 feet, 10 inch (1.78m) individual would be considered overweight at 175 pounds (80 kg) and obese at 210 pounds (95 kg).

A second reason people are talking so much about obesity is because it is linked to an increased risk of heart disease, diabetes, cancer, and premature death (Stevens, 1998). Unfortunately, little or no research supports the claim that weight loss produces health benefits (Blackburn, 1995). And the cure for obesity (i.e., weight loss) might very well be worse than the condition (Kassirer & Angell, 1998). Therefore, instead of concentrating on encouraging weight loss, most obesity researchers emphasize prevention (adults in their 20s and 30s often gain a lot of weight) and the cultivation of a healthier lifestyle that centers on exercise.

To prevent obesity, however, one has to know its origins (Jeffrey & Knauss, 1981; Rodin, 1982). Obesity, which is basically just a surplus of body fat, is a multi-

move away from physiological regulation and toward some type of nonphysiological regulation, such as social, cognitive, or emotional regulation (Polivy & Herman, 1985).

Cognitively Regulated Eating Style

As illustrated by the glucostatic and lipostatic hypotheses, the body defends its weight. Sometimes, however, people come to the conclusion that their physiologically regulated body weight does not measure up well to their personal or cultural aspirations. Rather like a civil war, people decide that it is time for the mind, or will, to begin the revolution to take over and regulate body weight. The revolt begins as cognitive controls try to supplant physiological controls. Successful dieting (in terms of weight loss goals) requires that the dieter first deaden her responsiveness to internal cues (e.g., feeling hungry or full) and second substitute cognitive controls for physiological ones (Heatherton, Polivy, & Herman, 1989). The problem, however, is that cognitive controls feature no negative feedback system. Dieters are faceted phenomenon that integrates both genetic (Foch & McClearn, 1980; Price, 1987; Stunkard, 1988) and environmental (Grilo & Pogue-Geile, 1991; Jeffrey & Knauss, 1981) causes and influences. Some environmental influences associated with obesity, for instance, include child-rearing (Birch, Zimmerman, & Hind, 1980) and child-feeding (Klesges et al., 1983) practices, low socioeconomic status (Sobal & Stunkard, 1989), high-fat content in the diet (Sclafani, 1980), lack of exercise (Stern & Lowney, 1986), and stress (Greeno & Wing, 1994). Clearly, genetic factors, such as metabolic efficiency, number of fat cells, liver disorders, and hypothalamic sensitivity (Hill, Pagliassotti, & Peters, 1994), are important as some bodies are genetically predisposed to hoard their fat resources more than other bodies.

But our collective genes have not changed substantially in the last quarter century in which the obesity rates have shot through the roof. The primary culprits are a culturally engineered environment that promotes overeating on the one hand and physical inactivity on the other hand (Hill & Peters, 1998). Environments encourage mass food intake largely through easily available food, large portion size of meals, and high-fat meals (Hill & Peters, 1998). Environments encourage physical inactivity through advances in transportation and technology (including television, computers, and electronic games). And unfortunately, increased food intake and decreased physical activity are inextricably linked, such that the heavier we get, the more bothersome physical exercise, even walking, becomes.

One optimistic finding is that intense physical activity can mitigate the detrimental effects of overeating and protect against weight gain (Birch et al., 1991). Thus, motivation seems centrally important in the effort to reverse the obesity epidemic as motivation is centrally important to beginning, maintaining, and increasing the severity of an exercise program.

therefore vulnerable to bingeing when situational events interfere with cognitive inhibitions (e.g., the presence of others, depression, anxiety, alcohol, intake of high-calorie preloads).[4]

SEX

In lower animals, sexual motivation and behavior occur only during the female's ovulation period (Parkes & Bruce, 1961). During ovulation, the female secretes a pheromone

[4] Restraint eating is problematic not only because it relies on cognitive rather than physiological cues for hunger and satiety but also because it drops the individual below set-point weight status (Lowe, 1993). The bingeing of restrained eaters can therefore be explained in part by cognitive restraint and its absence of negative feedback mechanisms and in part by the influence of low weight status. Self-imposed restraint is therefore a double blow against homeostatic eating behavior.

and its scent stimulates sexual advances from the male. For the male, injections of testosterone, a gonad hormone, can further increase his sexual behavior. Hence, in the lower animals, sex conforms to the cyclical physiological need and psychological drive process shown in Figure 3.2. Time passes, physiological need emerges and stimulates psychological drive, and its ensuing consummatory behavior satiates both the psychological drive and the physiological need. The biggest difference between sex and the other physiological needs is that sexual abstinence does not cause death like deprivation from water and food or the neglect of pain would.

The farther one goes up the evolutionary scale, the less physiological forces govern sexual motives. In human sexual motivation, physiological forces play an augmenting, rather than governing, role in sexual motivation. For humans, sexual incentives and forces in the environment, such as social, cultural, and evolutionary influences, are potent forces. Some cognitive forces, for instance, include beliefs of romantic love, expectations of romance, and sexual scripts (discussed later). Some social forces include judgments of physical attractiveness, peer promiscuity, and the social feelings of loneliness and love. Some cultural forces include religious and moral attitudes towards sex, cultural attitudes toward men and women, and gender role identification. Some evolutionary forces include fertility assessment, commitment seeking and avoidance, and parental certainty and investment. That being said, physiological influences do contribute to sexual motivation and behavior.

PHYSIOLOGICAL REGULATION

Human sexual behavior is influenced, but not determined, by hormones. The sex hormones are the androgens and estrogens. Though present in both sexes, androgens contribute to the sexual motivation of males, and estrogens contribute to the sexual motivation of females. Pharmacological drugs and surgical removal of androgens (primarily testosterone) and estrogens (primarily estradiol) suppress sexual motives for both males and females (Money et al., 1976). Hormones mostly promote the individual's responsiveness to external stimuli (e.g., a potential partner), though a host of nonhormonal factors (e.g., sight, smell, touch) also promote such responsiveness.[5]

Human sexual behavior is also influenced by sexual arousal. Hormones establish sexual arousal, but external factors are particularly important arousal triggers. Within the context of stimulation from a sexual partner (an obvious arousal trigger), people show a culturally universal four-phase sexual response cycle (Masters & Johnson, 1966). During the first phase, *excitation,* muscle tension and blood flow around the sexual organs increase. *Plateau,* the second phase, occurs when excitation is at its upper limit. The third phase, *orgasm,* starts with rapid breathing and a series of rhythmic contractions of the pelvic muscles and ends with an experience of pleasure, a feeling that emanates from re-

---

[5] In terms of brain structures, it is the hypothalamus—through its regulation of the hormonal (i.e., endocrine) system—that controls the release of androgens and estrogens into the bloodstream.The hypothalamus stimulates the (anterior) pituitary to release two executive hormones that regulate sexual motives: FSH (follicle-stimulating hormone), which activates sperm production in males and estrogen release in females, and LH (luteinizing hormone), which stimulates testosterone production in males and ovulation in females.

lease of muscle tension and blood swell but also partly from psychological intimacy. The fourth and final phase is *resolution.* In males, resolution is short-lived and quickly returns arousal to a preexcitatory phase. In females, resolution can continue for a longer time. If sexual stimulation continues, resolution can continue with multiple orgasms (the third and fourth phases overlap). If sexual stimulation ceases, resolution returns the female, like the male, to a preexcitatory phase.

ENVIRONMENTAL INFLUENCES

Visual Cues: Facial Metrics

Many stimuli arise from a sexual partner—chemical (smell), tactile, auditory, and visual. The physical attractiveness of a (potential) partner strongly affects human sexual motivation. Western cultures generally rate a slim body build for women as attractive (Singh, 1993a, 1993b). But standards of physical attractiveness vary from one culture to the next because these standards are mostly acquired through experience, cultural consensus, and socialization (Mahoney, 1983). These standards are "mostly" acquired through these influences because some physical characteristics are viewed as universally attractive, including health (e.g., clear skin; Symons, 1992), youthfulness (Cunningham, 1986), and those associated with greater reproductive value (Singh, 1993a).

Although men (and women) rate slim females as attractive, women's perceptions of male attractiveness generally have little consensus as to what body shapes or body parts are attractive (Beck, Ward-Hull, & McLear, 1976; Horvath, 1979, 1981; Lavrakas, 1975). The main predictor of women's rating of attractiveness in men's bodies is waist-to-hip ratio (WHR, a measure that ranges typically from 0.7 to 1.0; it is calculated via the narrowest circumference of the waist divided by the widest circumference of the hips/buttocks). Women rate moderately slim WHRs in males as most attractive, presumably because it reflects a positive health status (Singh, 1995).

While standards for bodily attractiveness vary by culture, each culture shows an impressive convergence in what facial characteristics are considered attractive and unattractive. The study of people's judgments of the attractiveness of facial characteristics is called *facial metrics* (Cunningham, 1986; Cunningham, Barbee, & Pike, 1990; Cunningham et al., 1995). Consider the face—and its facial-metric parameters—shown in Figure 3.6. The questions that link facial-metrics with the study of sexual motivation are, "On what dimensions do faces vary from each other, and which of those dimensions determine which faces are attractive and which are not?"

Faces vary considerably, and Figure 3.6 illustrates 24 different structural characteristics (e.g., eye size, mouth width, cheekbone prominence). Three categories explain which faces are judged attractive: neonatal features, sexual maturity features, and expressive features. Neonatal features correspond to those associated with the newborn infant, such as large eyes and a small nose, and are associated with attractive nonverbal messages of youth, openness and agreeableness (Berry & McArthur, 1985, 1986). Sexual-maturity features correspond to those associated with postpubescent status, such as prominent cheekbones and, for males, thick facial and eyebrow hair, and are associated with attractive nonverbal messages of strength, status, and competency (Keating, Mazur, & Segall,

FIGURE 3.6 **Male and Female Facial-Metric Parameters**

1, Length of face, distance from hairline to base of chin; 2, Width of face at cheekbones, distance between outer edges of cheekbones at most prominent point; 3, Width of face at mouth, distance between outer edges of cheeks at the level of the middle of the smile; 4, Height of forehead, distance from eyebrow to hairline; 5, Height of upper head, measured from pupil center to top of head estimated without hair; 6, Height of eyebrows, measured from pupil center to lower edge of eyebrow; 7, Height of eyes, distance from upper to lower edge of visible eye within eyelids at pupil center; 8, Width of eyes, inner corner to outer corner of eye; 9, Width of iris, measured diameter of eye; 10, Width of pupil, measured diameter of center of eye; 11, Standardized width of pupil, calculated as a ratio of the width of the pupil to the width of the iris (not shown); 12, Separation of eyes, distance between pupil centers; 13, Cheekbone width, an assessment of relative

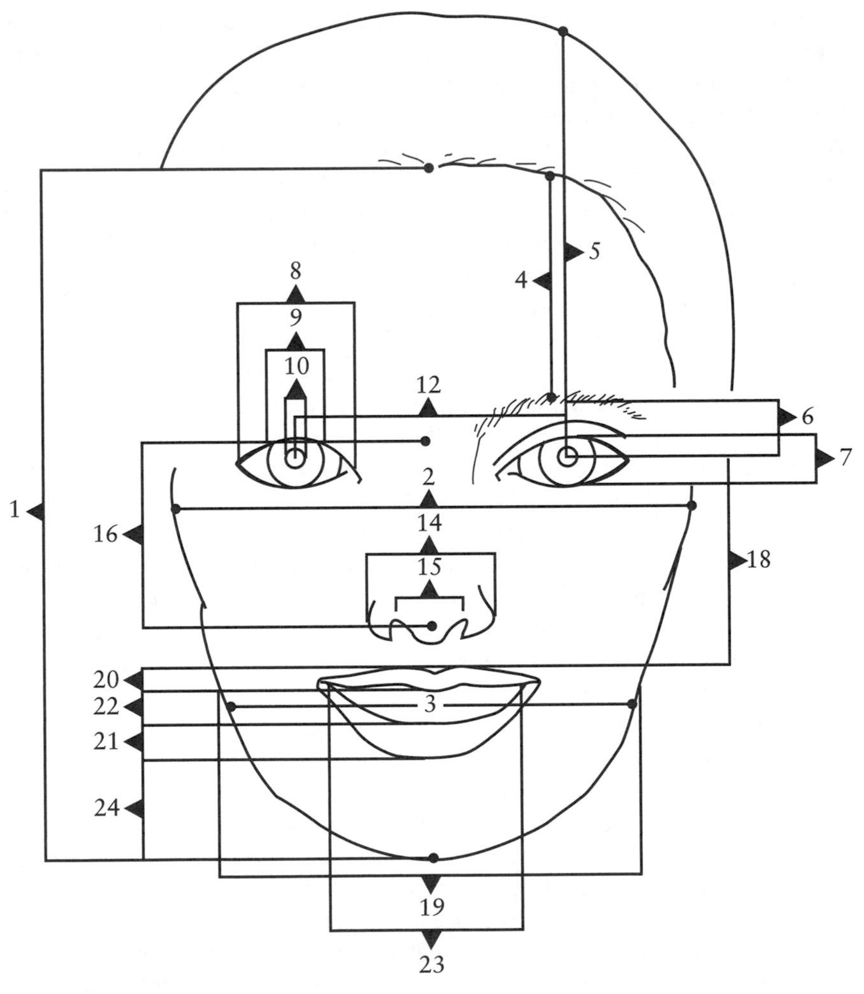

SOURCE: From "Measuring the Physical in Physical Attractiveness: Quasi-Experiments on the Sociobiology of Female Facial Beauty," by M. R. Cunningham, 1986, *Journal of Personality and Social Psychology, 50*, pp. 925–935. Copyright 1986 by the American Psychological Association. Reprinted with permission.

cheekbone prominence calculated as difference between the width of the face at the cheekbones and the width of the face at the mouth length of the face (not shown); 14, Nostril width, width of nose at outer edges of nostrils at widest point; 15, Nose tip width, width of protrusion at tip of nose, usually associated with crease from nostril; 16, Length of nose, measured from forehead bridge at level of upper edge of visible eye to nose tip; 17, Nose area, calculated as the product of the length of nose and width of nose at the tip length of the face (not shown); 18, Mid-face length, distance from pupil center to upper edge of upper lip, calculated by subtracting from the length of face the height of forehead, height of eyebrows, width of upper lip, height of smile, width of lower lip, and length of chin; 19, Width of cheeks, calculated as an assessment of facial roundness based on the measured width of face at mouth; 20, Thickness of upper lip, measured vertically at center; 21, Thickness of lower lip, measured vertically at center; 22, Height of smile, vertical distance between lips at center of smile; 23, Width of smile, distance between mouth inner corners; 24, Length of chin, distance from lower edge of lower lip to base of chin.

1981). Expressive features such as a wide smile/mouth and higher-set eyebrows are means to express positive emotions such as happiness and openness to potential mates (McGinley, McGinley, & Nicholas, 1978).

Facial-metrics research proceeds by showing dozens of different faces of men and women (via a slide projector) to a group of opposite-sex heterosexual individuals (or same-sex homosexual individuals; Donovan, Hill, & Jankowiak, 1989). The individuals judge each face on a variety of dimensions (e.g., how attractive and how desirous as a sexual partner), and the experimenters painstakingly measure each face on all the facial-metric dimensions listed in Figure 3.6. With these data in hand, the researchers investigate the correlations that emerge between attractiveness ratings and facial characteristics.

Facial metrics predict physical attractiveness ratings for the faces of women (Cunningham, 1986), and men (Cunningham, Barbee, & Pike, 1990), across different cultures (Cunningham et al., 1995), and across different age groups (Symons, 1992). For women's faces, the facial metrics associated with physical attractiveness are the neonatal features (large eyes, small nose, small chin), but sexual maturity (cheekbone prominence and thinness) and expressive characteristics (eyebrow height and smile height and width) are also important factors for physical attractiveness. For men's faces, the facial metrics associated with physical attractiveness are the sexual maturity features (thick eyebrows and prominent chin length), but expressive features (smile height and width) are somewhat important factors for physical attractiveness.

Sexual Scripts

The complexity of human sexuality requires that we add social, cultural, and developmental perspectives. For instance, the individual's socialization history leads to the creation of sexual scripts (Gagnon, 1974, 1977; Simon & Gagnon, 1986). A sexual script is one's mental representation of the step-by-step sequence of events that occur during a typical sexual episode. A sexual script, not unlike a movie script, includes specific actors, motives and feelings of those actors, and a set of appropriate verbal and nonverbal behaviors that should successfully conclude with sexual behavior (Gagnon, 1974). In its essence, the sexual script is the individual's story line of what a typical sexual encounter involves.

FIGURE 3.7 **Males' and Females' Sexual Response Cycles Paired With Adolescent Masturbation and Coitus**

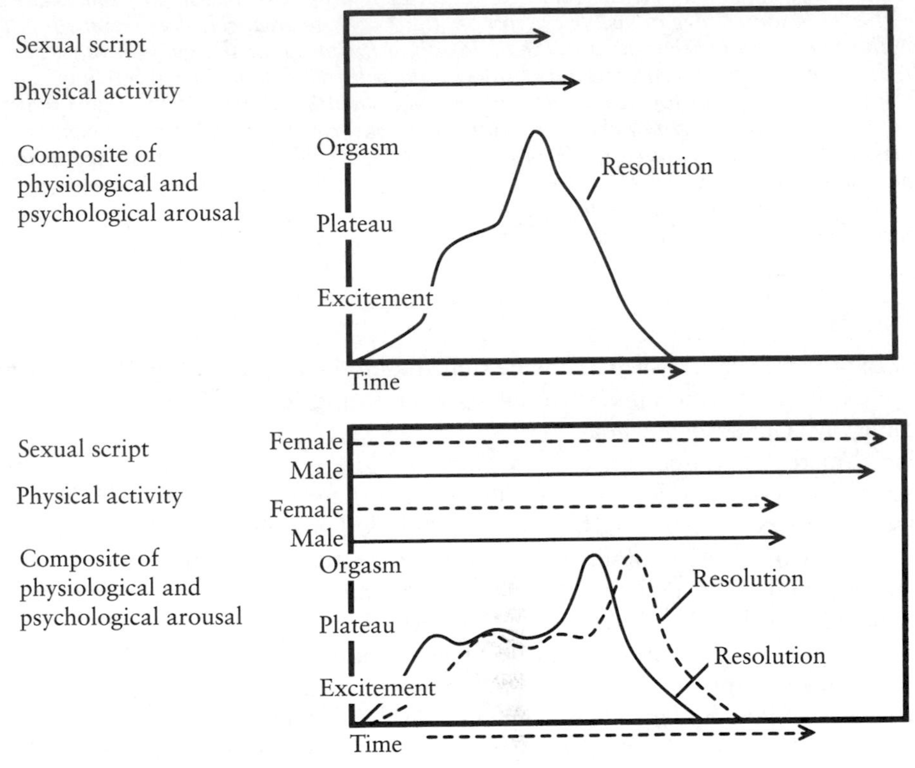

SOURCE: Adapted from "Scripts and the Coordination of Sexual Conduct," by H. Gagnon in *Nebraska Symposium on Motivation* (Vol. 21, pp. 27–59), J. K. Cole and R. Diensteiber (Eds.), 1974, Lincoln: University of Nebraska.

The initial basis of a sexual script is the culture-bound gender script one learns early in life. Children learn what boys do, what girls do, and how boys and girls behave together. Stereotypical gender-appropriate behavior is the crude beginning of a sexual script. Though the preadolescent does not yet have a sexual script, she does have a vast knowledge of gender-appropriate behaviors. With adolescence, masturbatory fantasies (in males, mostly) combine with gender roles in the emergence of a rudimentary sexual script. In masturbatory fantasies, the male coordinates physical activity with an ongoing sexual script that features actors, moral or not-so-moral motives and feelings, as well as nonsexual activities (e.g., walking on the beach). Panel A of Figure 3.7 shows the coordination of an emerging sexual script with self-stimulatory physical activity (Masters and Johnson's four-phase sexual response cycle discussed earlier). The young male learns to coordinate his sexual script to coincide with each of the four stages of excitement, plateau, orgasm, and resolution.

For females the coordination of sexual script and physical activity is more awkward because fewer females masturbate in early adolescence. Further, for females, the content of emerging sexual scripts contains little material that is sexual (from the male point of view). The sexual content of the female is more likely to include events such as falling in love (rather than participating in sex). Nonetheless, such events do contain romantic and anticipatory excitement (phase 1) and therefore allow the female a first means of coordinating imagined interpersonal behavior with sexual activity. Later in adolescence, females' sexual scripts conform more closely to the four-stage sexual response cycle.

With dating, both the male and female sexual scripts begin a process of transition from an independent, fantasy-based script to an interpersonal, team-like script. In petting, the young couple explores nonsexual behaviors that they have learned as appropriate from the culture. Each partner physically touches the dressed other. The behavior is exciting, but it does not produce orgasm. The excitement without orgasm leads the male to adjust his rudimentary sexual script to include an excitement phase that does not end with orgasm, and it leads the female to adjust her script to include the experience of arousal via activities instigated by the male. With repeated petting, both sexes master experiences of sexual excitement and gain the practice that will form the foundation for the general complexities of the coital situation (Gagnon, 1974). Later, there is practice in mutual disrobing, in learning the social skills to secure privacy, in focusing attention on the other, and so forth. At this stage, sexual performance is awkward, anxiety ridden, and frequently unsuccessful. Continued practice improves the couple's ability to coordinate their sexual scripts with each other's four-phased sexual response cycle (see panel B in Figure 3.7). Finally, workable sequences of behavior become conventionalized, and the couple's sexual scripts begin to have an adaptive, additive, and reeducative character (Simon & Gagnon, 1986).

Sexual Schemas

People differ in their cognitive representations of their sexual selves (Anderson & Cyranowski, 1994). Sexual self-schemas are cognitive generalizations about the sexual self that are derived from past experiences and manifest themselves in day-to-day thoughts and behaviors. Sexual schemas include both positive approach aspects as well as negative avoidance aspects. On the positive side, a person's sexual self includes an inclination to experience passionate romantic emotions and a behavioral openness to sexual participation. On the negative side, a person's sexual self includes a degree of embarrassment or conservatism that is frequently a deterrent to sexual romantic emotions and actions. Positive elements of sexual schemas promote sexual desire and the phases of the sexual response cycle; negative elements of sexual schemas inhibit sexual desire and the phases of the sexual response cycle (Anderson & Cyranowski, 1994).

Sexual Orientation

A key component of postpubescent sexual scripts is the establishment of sexual orientation, or one's preference for sexual partners of the same or other sex. Sexual orientation actually exists on a continuum, and about a third of all adolescents have participated in at

TABLE 3.2 **Gender Differences in Mate Preferences**

VARIABLES	MEN	WOMEN	F RATIO
Physical appearance			
Not good looking	3.41	4.42	172.39**
Age			
Older by five years	4.15	5.29	182.48**
Younger by five years	4.54	2.80	394.17**
Earning potential			
Not likely to hold a steady job	2.73	1.62	213.25**
Earns less	4.60	3.76	88.44**
Earns more	5.19	5.93	98.89**
More education	5.22	5.82	73.69**
Less education	4.67	4.08	39.00**
Other variables			
Married before	3.35	3.44	2.03
Has children	2.84	3.11	9.56*
Different religion	4.24	4.31	0.76
Different race	3.08	2.84	12.97**

SOURCE: From "Mate Selection Preferences: Gender Differences Examined in a National Sample," by S. Sprecher, Q. Sullivan, and E. Hatfield, 1994, *Journal of Personality and Social Psychology*, 66, pp. 1074–1080. Copyright 1994 by the American Psychological Association. Adapted with permission.

*p < .05, **p < .01.

least one homosexual act (with more boys than girls having done so; Money, 1988). The sexual orientation continuum extends from exclusively heterosexual through a bisexual orientation and continues to an exclusively homosexual orientation. Most adolescents rather routinely commit to a heterosexual orientation, but about 4% of males and 2% of females do not, and these percentages climb higher if one includes a bisexual orientation.

Though still far from conclusive, research suggests that sexual orientation is not a choice; it is something that happens to the adolescent rather than something that is more deliberate and results from soul-searching (Money, 1988). Homosexuality is not a recent cultural product, as many instances of homosexuality have been recorded in the history of many and widely different cultures (Money & Ehrhardt, 1972). Just as homosexuality seems to be something that happens to the individual during prenatal development, so too is heterosexuality. One way to understand sexual orientation is to try to understand why people are attracted to members of the opposite sex. But aside from the evolutionary explanation, it is not yet clear why people develop a heterosexual or homosexual orientation.

Part of the explanation for why some people develop a homosexual rather than heterosexual orientation is genetic (see the twin studies by Bailey & Pillard, 1991; Bailey et al., 1993), and part of the explanation is environmental. Unfortunately, this literature is characterized more by rejected hypotheses than by confirmed ones. For instance, there is little evidence to support the idea that homosexuality emanates from a domineering mother and weak father (Bell, Weinberg, & Hammersmith, 1981) or from exposure to an older same-sex seducer (Money, 1988). The most promising research frontiers in understanding sexual orientation are those in genetics (Bailey & Pillard, 1991; Hamer, et al., 1993) and in the prenatal hormonal environment (Berenbaum & Snyder, 1995; Kelly, 1991; Paul, 1993).

EVOLUTIONARY BASIS OF SEXUAL MOTIVATION

Sexual motivation and behavior have an obvious evolutionary function and basis. In an evolutionary analysis, men and women are hypothesized to have evolved distinct psychological mechanisms that underlie their sexual motivations and mating strategies (Buss & Schmitt, 1993). It is difficult to say with confidence whether men's and women's mating strategies and preferences are conscious or unconscious, but it is clear that distinct sexual/mating strategies do exist. Compared to women, men have shorter-term sexual motivations, impose less stringent standards, value cues of sexual accessibility such as youth and attractiveness, become jealous for different reasons, and value chastity in mates. Compared to men, women value signs of a man's resources (spends money, gives gifts, lives an extravagant lifestyle), social status and ambition, and promising career potential (Buss & Schmitt, 1993).

The essential differences between the sexes in mate-selection preferences appear in Table 3.2 (Sprecher, Sullivan, & Hatfield, 1994). The data in the table confirm that, essentially, men find youth and physical attractiveness important in selecting women partners, whereas women find earning potential important in selecting men partners. These data come from asking thousands of unmarried 19- to 35-year-old African-American (36%) and White (64%) men and women the following question: "How willing would you be to marry someone who . . . ," and then from asking each participant to respond on a scale ranging from 1 (not at all willing) to 7 (very willing). Mean scores for men and women for each item are organized into the categories of physical attractiveness, age, earning potential, and other variables. The F ratio is a statistical term, and any F ratio followed by an asterisk or two denotes a significant mean difference between men and women on that mate selection preference.

Although these conclusions are blatantly and undeniably sexist, they nonetheless represent the expressed preferences of men and women. Such preferences might not be consistent with cultural aspirations, but they are consistent with evolutionary aspirations. They are consistent with heterosexual aspirations as well. Some differences emerge when examining the mating preference of homosexuals (Bailey et al., 1994). Like heterosexual males, homosexual males rate the physical attractiveness of their partners as very important, but unlike heterosexual males, they do not show a strong preference for younger partners and are not as prone to sexual jealousy.

FAILURES TO SELF-REGULATE PHYSIOLOGICAL NEEDS

Trying to exert conscious mental control over our physiological needs often does more harm than good. Still, we try. People try to control their appetites—their hunger, their taste for chocolate, their weight, their drinking of alcohol and coffee, their sexual impulses, their chronic back pains, and the like. Such appetites can at times overwhelm us, and in this experience of being overwhelmed, we look for ways to override our physiological needs in favor of mental control. When mental states regulate physiological needs, self-regulation occurs; but when biological urges overwhelm mental control, self-regulation failure occurs (Baumeister, Heatherton, & Tice, 1994).

People fail at self-regulation for three primary reasons (Baumeister et al., 1994). First, people can lack standards, have inconsistent or conflicting standards, have unrealistic standards, or have inappropriate standards (Karoly, 1993). For instance, many people have extreme (unrealistic) standards for thinness or conflicting standards with the body type they are born with versus the body type they would like to have (Brownell, 1991).

Second, people fail at self-regulation because they fail to monitor what they are doing as they become distracted, preoccupied, overwhelmed, or intoxicated (Kirschenbaum, 1987). Alcohol, for instance, reduces self-awareness and self-monitoring, and intoxicated people become more likely to do things outside of their normal mental control (Hull, 1981).

Third, people lack the ability to make the self conform to the relevant standards as people may feel tired, exhausted, or stressed, or there may be times when they have difficulty keeping their impulses and desires in check, such as the desire to go to the bathroom. What all these mishaps have in common is a lack of control over one's attention. Mental control that focuses attention on standards, long-term goals, and on monitoring what one is doing generally leads to self-regulation successes (Baumeister, et al., 1994).

Eating Too Much

Eating is generally a pleasant task, and all goes well when people begin to eat when they feel hungry and quit when they feel satisfied. And most of the time people eat within reasonable boundaries, though they engage in an occasional splurge here and there. Still, people face a motivational conflict within eating—"I want to enjoy myself" (by eating tasty foods), versus "I want to avoid becoming overweight" (by eating too much).

This approach-avoidance dilemma most often goes awry and leads to eating problems such as bulimia and obesity when, paradoxically, people explicitly try to gain control over their eating, as through a diet. People try to gain mental control by exerting great effort in ignoring or denying their physiological hunger cues. Ignoring physiological cues becomes a primary explanation for self-regulation failure when the individual loses control over his attention. When attention is lost, people are vulnerable to eating with abandon. When diets are broken (e.g., at a social occasion, when emotionally upset), dieters are highly vulnerable to being overwhelmed by situational cues and by momentary impulses. And diets are difficult to maintain not only because food can be tempting, but one must eat to survive (i.e., it is unavoidable). When dieters lose control, the restraint-released eating often snowballs into a destructive binge that leaves them worse off than had they not dieted at all.

Drinking Too Much (alcohol)

The motivational problem underlying eating is very much the same problem underlying the drinking of alcohol, namely: "I want to enjoy myself and experience the desirable effects of alcohol" (by drinking), versus "I want to avoid the heavy drinking that brings with it the problems that attend drunkenness."

People overdo their drinking pretty much for the same reason they overdo their eating—namely, because they fail to self-regulate their attention when they become tired or when they experience an emotional upset of one kind or another, such as feeling stressed or overburdened or having self-esteem threatened.

Abstinence beliefs about alcohol consumption (zero-tolerance beliefs, such as "I'll make sure I don't drink too much by not drinking at all") can function much like dieting beliefs about food consumption. With their attention displaced (by emotional or social cues and obligations), people take a drink. Once a person has a drink, attentional shortcomings become increasingly evident, and people lose their ability to monitor both themselves and their surroundings. Drinkers are therefore likely to lose track of how much they have consumed, and it becomes increasingly likely that social cues will regulate their forthcoming drinking decisions. Because of alcohol's effect on attention and self-monitoring, people lose the negative feedback systems they need to stop drinking (e.g., "I am no longer thirsty"; "I've had my two-drink limit"; "I'll stop drinking when I can no longer remember my own name"). By ignoring or by being distracted away from physiological stop signals, drinking can snowball.

SUMMARY

Pain, thirst, hunger, and sex are four motivational states that arise from physiological needs. These needs can be organized into a continuum according to the relative degree of physiological versus environmental regulation. At the biological end of the continuum are pain and thirst, and at the environmental end of the continuum is sex, with hunger somewhere in between the two. This continuum is useful because other physiological needs not discussed in this chapter could be understood via their placement on the continuum. For instance, temperature regulation would be discussed toward the physiological end of the continuum, whereas aggression would be discussed toward the environmental end.

The anchor for the chapter was Hull's biologically based drive theory (Figure 3.2). According to drive theory, physiological deprivations and deficits give rise to bodily need states, which in turn give rise to a psychological drive, which motivates the consummatory behavior that results in drive reduction. Then, time goes by, the physiological deprivations recur, and the cyclical process repeats itself. In outlining the regulatory process for pain, thirst, hunger, and sex, the chapter introduced seven fundamental processes: need, drive, homeostasis, negative feedback, multiple inputs and outputs, negative feedback, intra-organismic variables, and extra-organismic variables.

The cause of pain is tissue damage. When tissue damage occurs, we become psychologically aware of pain as the body's pain receptors communicate pain's arousal, emotional, and experiential aspects through the spinal cord to the reticular formation, limbic system, and thalamus. Pain demands our immediate attention, disrupts ongoing behavior, acts as a punisher to suppress the behavior that caused it, and negatively reinforces any behavior able to alleviate it. Because pain is so evolutionarily primitive, it dominates our attention as it motivates two types of behavior: escape and recuperation. The function of escape and recuperative behaviors is to terminate the cause of pain, which is tissue damage. Like escape and recuperation, endorphins, when triggered in the brain by stress, can turn off pain through the pain suppression network.

Thirst activation and satiety is rather straightforward. Water depletion inside the cells (intracellular thirst) and water depletion outside the cells (extracellular thirst) activate thirst. Of the two, intracellular dehydration is the more critical thirst activator. Water restoration satiates thirst. Once initiated, drinking behavior continues until inhibited by separate negative feedback mechanisms in the mouth, stomach, and cells. These negative feedback systems prevent water intoxication, which can threaten homeostasis and physical well-being. Drinking behavior is influenced by extra-organismic variables, such as water availability and taste, which gives water added incentive value.

Hunger and eating involve a complex regulatory system of both short-term (glucostatic hypothesis) and long-term (lipostatic hypothesis, including set-point theory) regulation. According to the glucostatic hypothesis, glucose deficiency stimulates eating by activating the lateral hypothalamus, whereas glucose excess inhibits eating by activating the ventromedial hypothalamus. According to the lipostatic hypothesis, shrunken fat cells initiate hunger, whereas normal or larger fat cells inhibit it. Eating behavior is influenced by the sight, smell, and taste of food; time of day; stress; presence of others; and situational pressures such as conforming to a group norm. Environmental factors are sometimes such substantial contributors to eating that they sometimes interfere with physiological factors. Dieting, for instance, is the prototypical manifestation of the person's attempt to supplant involuntary physiological controls for eating with voluntary cognitive controls. Such a cognitively regulated eating style has implications associated with bingeing, restraint release, and obesity.

The physical characteristics of a potential sexual partner are among the most important determinants of sexual motivation. Attractive bodily characteristics are mostly culturally determined, but many facial characteristics are considered attractive across different cultures and ages, as shown by studies in facial metrics. Sexual scripts and sexual schemas add a distinct cognitive influence to sexual motivation that help bridge the gap between self-stimulatory sexual activity and interpersonal sexual behavior. Research on the determinants of sexual orientation is inconclusive, but it points toward the importance of genetics and prenatal development and away from environmental and cultural influences. Sexual motivation is regulated, in part, by evolutionary influences such that men and women inherit distinct preferences in their mating strategies.

Trying to exert conscious mental control over our physiological needs often does more harm than it does good. People fail to self-regulate their bodily appetites for three primary reasons. First, people lack standards or have inconsistent standards for what their base line for self-regulation should be (e.g., How much should I weigh?). Second, people fail because they neglect to monitor what they are doing, as they become distracted or preoccupied. Third, people fail at self-regulation when they lack the ability to make the self conform to the relevant standards they hold, as when they are tired, exhausted, or stressed. Generally speaking, studies of bingeing on food and alcohol show that people successfully regulate their physiological needs when they devote attention to standards and long-term goals and monitor what they do, whereas people fail when physiological needs dominate attention for one or more of the three reasons listed above (lack standards, fail to monitor their behavior, and forego the standards they have).

Recommended Readings

Pain

Eccleston, C., & Crombez, G. (1999). Pain demands attention: A cognitive-affective model of the interruptive fuction of pain. *Psychological Bulletin, 125,* 356-366.

Hapidou, E. G., & deCatanzaro, D. (1992). Responsiveness to laboratory pain in women as a function of age and childbirth pain experience. *Pain, 48,* 177–181.

Jessell, T. M., & Kelly, D. D. (1991). Pain and analgesia. In E. R. Kandel, J. H. Schwartz, & T. M. Jessell (Eds.), *Principles of neural science* (3rd ed., pp. 385–399). Norwalk, CT: Appleton and Lange.

Thirst

Blass, E. M., & Hall, W. G. (1976). Drinking termination: Interactions among hydrational, orogastric, and behavioral control in rats. *Psychological Review, 83,* 356–374.

Toates, F. M. (1979). Homeostasis and drinking. *Behavior and Brain Sciences, 2,* 95–102.

Hunger

Berry, S. L., Beatty, W. W., & Klesges, R. C. (1985). Sensory and social influences on ice cream consumption by males and females in a laboratory setting. *Appetite, 6,* 41–45.

Crandall, C. S. (1988). Social cognition of binge eating. *Journal of Personality and Social Psychology, 55,* 588–598.

Keesey, R. E., & Powley, T. L. (1975). Hypothalamic regulation of body weight. *American Scientist, 63,* 558–565.

Polivy, J., & Herman, C. P. (1985). Dieting and binging. *American Psychologist, 40,* 193–201.

Sepple, C. P., & Read, N. W. (1989). Gastrointestinal correlates of the development of hunger in man. *Appetite, 13,* 183–191.

Sex

Anderson, B. L., & Cyranowski, J. M. (1994). Women's sexual self-schema. *Journal of Personality and Social Psychology, 67,* 1079–1100.

Cunningham, M. R. (1986). Measuring the physical in physical attractiveness: Quasi-experiments on the sociobiology of female facial beauty. *Journal of Personality and Social Psychology, 50,* 925–935.

Gagnon, H. (1974). Scripts and the coordination of sexual conduct. In J. K. Cole & R. Dienstbier (Eds.), *Nebraska symposium on motivation* (Vol. 21, pp. 27–59). Lincoln: University of Nebraska Press.

4

ORGANISMIC PSYCHOLOGICAL NEEDS

Imagine visiting a lake at a campground or state park, for instance. As you lie on the shore soaking up the sun's rays, you notice a young girl playfully skipping stones across the water's surface. Before each toss, she studiously inspects piles of stones to find the flattest one. With stone in hand, she puts all her effort into the toss. Each time a rock skips according to plan, she smiles and her enthusiasm grows. Each dud brings a somber expression but also increased determination. At first, she tries only to make each stone skip once off the water's surface. She then uses three or four finely tuned techniques—one very long skip, short skips with many hops, and so forth. And she pretends to throw some stones like a baseball and others, the big and heavy ones, like hand grenades because these splashes look like explosions in her imagination. Despite her family's fish fry currently going on, her rock skipping continues.

The child is at play. For her, an urban child, the lake is a relatively novel setting. It allows her to use her imagination in a way that is different from every day. As she plays, she feels excited and entertained. Each rock and each toss provides her with a different, surprising result. Each attempt seems to challenge her skills. In tossing rocks and in using her imagination, she feels competent and she develops skills. Her growing sense of mastery fuels her enjoyment. From the perspective of the next two chapters, such behavior is more than frivolous play. It is integral to healthy development. The lake setting provides the child with an opportunity to develop skills, to feel competent and self-determining, and to learn to enjoy an activity solely for the experience and the positive emotion it provides.

Like play, sports, hobbies, school, work, and travel also offer opportunities for people to engage in environments capable of involving and satisfying their psychological needs. This chapter examines the motivational significance of three psychological needs: self-determination, competence, and relatedness. The conclusion offered is that when people find themselves in environments that support and nurture their psychological needs, then positive emotions and healthy development follow.

PSYCHOLOGICAL NEEDS

People and animals are inherently active. As children, we push and pull things; we shake, throw, carry, explore, and ask questions about the objects that surround us. As adults, we continue to explore and to play. We play games, solve mysteries, undertake challenges, pursue hobbies, surf the Web, build and organize, and do any number of activities because these activities are inherently interesting and enjoyable things to do. When an activity involves our needs, we feel interest; when an activity satisfies our needs, we feel enjoyment. So although we apparently engage in activities out of interest and enjoyment (i.e., "I play tennis because it's fun"), the underlying cause of engaging our environment to exercise, challenge, and develop our skills is psychological need involvement (one origin of interest) and psychological need satisfaction (one origin of enjoyment). Playing games, solving mysteries, and undertaking challenges are interesting and enjoyable things to do because they provide an arena for involving and satisfying the full range of our psychological needs.

Psychological needs are an important addition to our analysis of motivated behavior. As discussed in the last chapter, physiological needs for water, sugar, fat, and so on emanate from biological deficits. Physiological needs function to alert the person (via psychological drive) to the existence and intensity of biological emergencies. This sort of motivated behavior is essentially reactive, in the sense that its purpose is to react against and alleviate a deficit bodily condition. Psychological needs are of a qualitatively different nature. The energy generated by psychological needs is proactive. Organismic psychological needs arise and express themselves as motivation to promote 1) active engagement with the environment, 2) skill development, and 3) healthy development.

NEED STRUCTURE

There are many types of needs that exist, and these types can be organized within a need structure (recall Figure 3.1; see also Deci, 1980). Physiological needs are inherent within the workings of biological systems (chapter 3). Organismic psychological needs are inherent within the strivings of human nature and healthy development (discussed in detail in this chapter). Acquired social needs are internalized or learned from life experiences and our socialization histories (chapter 6).

The distinction between physiological and psychological needs is a relatively easy one to make, but the distinction between types of psychological needs is more subtle. Organismic psychological needs exist within human nature and are, therefore, innate in everyone. Three such organismic needs are self-determination, competence, and relatedness. Acquired social needs arise from our unique personal experiences and thus vary considerably from one person to the next. Four such acquired needs are achievement, affiliation, intimacy, and power.

ORGANISMIC APPROACH TO MOTIVATION

Organismic theories get their name from the term *organism,* an entity that is alive and in active exchange with its environment (Blasi, 1976). The survival of any organism depends on its environment because the environment offers resources like food, water, social support, and intellectual stimulation. And all organisms are equipped to initiate and engage in exchanges with their environment as all organisms possess skills and the motivation to exercise and develop those skills. Organismic theories of motivation take for granted that environments constantly change and, hence, organisms need flexibility to adjust to and accommodate those changes. Organisms also need environmental resources to grow and to actualize their latent potentials. To adapt, organisms must learn to substitute a new response for a previously successful but now outdated one (because the environment changed), and organisms must grow and develop so that new skills, new interests, and new ways of adjusting emerge. The whole focus concerns how organisms initiate interactions with the environment and how organisms adapt, change, and grow as a function of those environmental transactions.

The opposite of an organismic approach is a mechanistic one. In mechanistic theories, the environment acts on the person and the person reacts in a predictable manner. For instance, environments produce heat, and the person responds to this heat in a rather predictable and automatic way by sweating. Sweating leads to water loss, and when the biological systems detect the loss, thirst arises rather automatically (i.e., mechanistically). Chapter 3 discussed these biologically rooted needs. Subsequent chapters will discuss other relatively mechanistic motives (e.g., reinforcement in chapter 5; the TOTE unit in chapter 7). In each of these approaches, you will see that the person and the environment relate in a one-way relationship such that the environment acts and the person reacts.

Organismic theories reject such one-way portrayals and instead emphasize the person-environment dialectic (Deci & Ryan, 1991). In a dialectic, the environment acts on the person and the person acts on the environment. Both the person and the environment constantly change. Organismic theories of motivation emphasize both the person's (i.e., the organism's) intrinsic motivation to seek out and affect changes in the environment as well as the environment's capacity to generate in the person an extrinsic motivation to adjust to and accommodate to its demands (Deci & Ryan, 1985a). The outcome of the person-environment dialectic is an ever-changing synthesis in which the person's needs are fulfilled by the environment, and the environment produces in the person new forms of motivation.

As a point of illustration, consider the motivation of an athlete involved in competitive sports. Initially, a relatedness need might lead her to begin to participate in a team sport, and a competence need might lead her to be attracted to the challenge offered by the sport. Once she begins to compete, the competitive setting's emphasis on winning, however, produces in her an artificial or socially engineered "need" to win or, perhaps, to gain status and see her name praised in the local newspaper (Deci & Olson, 1989; Vallerand, Gauvin, & Halliwell, 1986). After some history of interpersonal competition, the athlete's sports motivation becomes a mixture of inherent psychological needs (i.e., relatedness, competence) and socially acquired desires to win and to impress others. Of course, if the environment emphasizes something other than winning, then the athlete will acquire (internalize) other motivations. Students in school are not much different from the athlete, as students enter schools with interests and curiosities, and schools create in students motivations to make good grades and to please teachers and admissions committees.

Two assumptions define an organismic approach to motivation:

1. Human beings are inherently active.
2. The principles of differentiation and integration guide development.

The organismic approach to motivation begins with the assumption that the organism is inherently active. Organismic psychological needs are the source of that inherent activity (Deci & Ryan, 1985a).

Differentiation and integration describe the two complementary developmental processes that underlie the organism's tendency to pursue a developmental trajectory of becoming more elaborate or complex (i.e., growing). Differentiation involves elaboration, the developmental tendency to grow in ways that are increasingly complex; integration involves organization, the developmental tendency toward coherence, wholeness, or unity (Deci & Ryan, 1991). Differentiation occurs because people are inherently active and because people are constantly engaging in complex environments. Inherently active people explore and discover new interests, seek out challenges, encounter new situations, and expand their capabilities. As a result, people differentiate themselves—their skills, interests, beliefs, values, career aspirations, etc.—in terms of complexity, which is another way of saying that people grow. Integration occurs as people refine their differentiated expanding complexity into a new synthesis. As people grow in complexity, they also tend to organize their ever-expanding interests and capacities with other aspects of the self (e.g., I am a traditional male who now wants to learn how to cook. How can I make sense of who I am? How can I integrate my old values with my new interest?).

Trees provide a metaphor for these differentiation and integration processes as they grow new leaves and branches where the sunlight is plentiful and they drop old leaves and branches where the sunlight becomes blocked. Like trees, differentiation and integration allow human beings to develop and grow in ways that can be characterized as an organized and adaptive complexity.

Organismic Psychological Needs

Consider why people wish to exercise or develop skills such as walking, reading, swimming, driving, making friends, and hundreds of other such competencies. In part, these competencies emerge maturationally, but they further emerge through motivated learning (Gibson, 1988; White, 1959). Innate organismic psychological needs provide the motivation that supports such learning (Deci & Ryan, 1985a; White, 1959). As illustrated in the chapter's opening example of the young girl skipping rocks into the lake, young children best illustrate how organismic psychological needs motivate the exercise and development of skills. Endlessly, young children motor about from one place to another without any apparent motivation other than to just do so and just do it better than they did it the time before (because of the need for competence). Further, children desire to experiment with the world on their own terms as they want to decide for themselves what to do, how to do it, when to do it, and whether to do it at all (because of the need for self-determination). And which activities, skills, and values children regard as important depends largely on the psychological need for relatedness as children willingly internalize only that which is also valued by those with whom they have a close, trusting relationship.

Collectively, the organismic psychological needs of self-determination, competence, and relatedness provide people with a natural motivation for learning, growing, and developing in a way that is healthy and for transforming the self (through differentiation and integration) from that which begins as simple, ineffective, and immature to that which is complex, effective, and mature (Ryan, 1995).

SELF-DETERMINATION

When deciding what to do and how to spend our time, we desire choice and decision-making flexibility. We want to be the one who decides what to do, when to do it, how to do it, and when to stop doing it. We want our choices to determine our actions, rather than have some other person or some environmental constraint force us into a particular course of action. We want our behavior connected to, rather than divorced from, our interests, preferences, wants, and desires. We want the freedom to construct goals for ourselves, and we want the freedom to decide for ourselves how to go about achieving that which is important to us. In other words, we have a need for self-determination.

Behavior is self-determined when our interests, preferences, and beliefs guide the decision in engaging or not engaging in a particular activity. We are not self-determining (i.e., our behaviors are determined by others) when some outside force pressures us to think, feel, or behave in particular ways (Deci, 1980). Formally, self-determination is the need to experience choice in the initiation and regulation of behavior, and it reflects the desire to have one's choices rather than environmental events determine one's actions (Deci & Ryan, 1985a).

Three experiential qualities work together to define the experience of self-determination: perceived locus of causality, perceived choice, and volition. Perceived locus of causality (PLOC) refers to an individual's understanding of the causal source of his motivated actions (Heider, 1958). PLOC exists on a continuum that ranges from internal to external. For instance, the reasons a person reads a book or mows the lawn exist either as something inside the self (internal PLOC) or as something external to the self, like other people or an attractive incentive (external PLOC). Perceived choice is a second quality within self-determination. We feel a sense of choice when we find ourselves in environments that provide us with decision-making flexibility that affords us with many opportunities to choose; and we feel only a sense of obligation when we find ourselves in environments that push us into an action by communicating a rigidity about how we should think, feel, and behave. For instance, when children are given options within their schoolwork (Cordova & Lepper, 1996), when nursing-home residents are given options in how to schedule their daily activities (Langer & Rodin, 1976), and when patients communicate with flexible, as opposed to authoritarian, doctors (Williams & Deci, 1996), the children, residents, and patients all feel that their behavior flows from a sense of choice. The third quality within self-determination is volition. Volition is a sense of an unpressured willingness to engage in an activity (Deci, Ryan, & Williams, 1995). It centers on how free versus coerced people feel while they are either doing what they want to do (e.g., playing, studying) or avoiding what they do not want to do (e.g., apologizing, smoking a cigarette). Volition is high when the person engages in an activity and feels free rather than pressured in engaging in that activity (Deci & Ryan, 1987; Ryan, Koestner, & Deci, 1991).

Some theorists use the terms "origins" and "pawns" to communicate the distinction between a person whose behavior emanates from an internal PLOC, a perception of choice, and a sense of volition (i.e., is self-determined) versus a person whose behavior emanates from an external PLOC, a perception of obligation, and a sense of being pressured (i.e., is not self-determined; deCharms, 1976, 1984; Ryan & Grolnick, 1986). Because people have a need for self-determination, they strive to be the causal agents of their behavior—to be origins. Origins "originate" their own intentional behavior. "Pawn,"a metaphor taken from the game of chess, is a term that tries to capture the experience we feel when powerful people push us around in much the same way that employers boss around their workers, military sergeants command privates, and parents order their children to behave. When people are treated as origins, they show active engagement and take personal responsibility for their goals and actions; when people are treated as pawns, they act in ways that are relatively passive and reactive and that show little personal responsibility for their goals and courses of action (Ryan & Grolnick, 1986). When treated as a pawn, play becomes work and leisure becomes obligation.

INVOLVING AND SATISFYING THE NEED FOR SELF-DETERMINATION

Environments, relationships, and social contexts vary in how much versus how little they support a person's need for self-determination. For instance, when the environment imposes a deadline, it interferes with self-determination, but when it provides choices, it supports self-determination. Relationships, too, can interfere with rather than support self-determination, as when a coach bosses athletes around (and undermines their self-determination) or when a close friend listens carefully and takes the time to understand your point of view (and supports your self-determination). Social contexts also vary in how much versus how little they support people's self-determination, as is illustrated when the military commands orders to its personnel, the church decides what parishioners should and should not do, or the day care goes out of its way to support children's interests and initiatives. When environments, relationships, and social contexts successfully involve and satisfy people's need for self-determination, these environments are referred to as autonomy-supportive environments; when environments, relationships, and social contexts frustrate, neglect, and interfere with people's need for self-determination, these environments are referred to as controlling environments (Deci & Ryan, 1987).

An autonomy-supportive environment gets its name by virtue of the fact that this type of environment finds ways to promote in people an internal PLOC, a perception of choice, and a sense of freedom and volition. A controlling environment (which promotes in people an external PLOC, a perception of obligation, and a sense of pressure) gets its name on the grounds that this type of environment works to "control" a person's behavior toward what an authority figure deems to be appropriate or desirable. As a point of illustration, each of the following elements of an environment, a relationship, or a social context has been studied in terms of how autonomy supportive (and self-determination promoting) versus controlling (and self-determination frustrating) they are: rewards (Lepper, Greene, & Nisbett, 1973), prizes (Harackiewicz, 1979), money (Deci, 1971), deadlines or time limits (Amabile, DeJong, & Lepper, 1976), surveillance (Pittman et al., 1980), threats (Deci & Cascio, 1972), evaluations (Benware & Deci, 1984), limits or rules (Koestner et al., 1984), interpersonal competition (Reeve & Deci, 1996), opportunities for choice (Zuckerman et al., 1978), families (Deci et al., 1993), classrooms (Deci, et al., 1981), athletic fields (Gould, et al., 1989), and work settings (Deci, Connell, & Ryan, 1989).

SUPPORTING AUTONOMY

A synonym for self-determination is autonomy. Therefore, an autonomy-supportive environment is one that involves, nurtures, and satisfies the need for self-determination. Autonomy-supportive environments encourage people to make their own choices, set their own goals, choose their own ways of achieving, solve problems in their own way, and basically pursue their own agendas. Autonomy-supportive environments are not, however, social contexts that can be characterized as laissez faire, permissive, neglecting, or indulging. Rather, when people work to create autonomy-supportive environments, they struggle diligently to identify and support the interests, needs, and strivings of others. Just how people go about the task of creating and establishing autonomy-supportive environments appears in Table 4.1, as it lists the four essential ingredients that combine to create an autonomy-supportive environment (adapted from Deci, 1995; Deci, Connell, & Ryan, 1989; Deci et al., 1994; Koestner et al., 1984; Reeve, 1996).

Autonomy-Supportive Environments Emphasize the Individual's Point of View

A prerequisite to supporting another person's self-determination is to identify that person's needs, interests, preferences, and aspirations. Once they have been identified, then one can begin to find ways to support and nurture these needs and preferences in ways

TABLE 4.1 **Four Elements of an Autonomy-Supportive Environment**

1. Emphasizes the individual's point of view.
2. Encourages choice and initiative.
3. Communicates rationale for social control. That is, communicates the rationale for any behavioral rules, limits, or constraints placed on the individual's plans and behaviors.
4. Uses a communication style rich in noncontrolling, positive feedback.

that cultivate an internal PLOC and sense of choice and volition. At the heart of an autonomy-supportive environment is a striving of one person to understand, acknowledge, truly appreciate and value, and respond to another person's perspective or point of view. To do so, for example, teachers, employers, coaches, therapists, parents, and others put the proverbial shoe on the other foot to identify and appreciate the perspective of their students, employees, athletes, clients, and children, respectively. One way an employer can begin to understand how employees' experience their jobs, for instance, is to spend time doing that job or at least carefully observing, listening, and responding to employees as they work. The employer-manager would soon understand what it feels like, for example, to answer the phone, listen to customer complaints, type memos, write reports, be frustrated by a lack of resources, participate in committee discussions, worry about child care, relate to difficult coworkers, manage an avalanche of deadlines, and so on. After taking the role of the employee, the manager would then be better able to identify the needs and feelings of the employees. She could then make decisions and provide a work environment that reflected not only the employer's perspective but also the employees' perspective. When employers identify workers' concerns in an emotionally meaningful way and when they foster a responsive working environment, they enable employees' work to take place in an air of trust, interest, and self-determined motivational strivings rather than in an air of suspicion, pressure, and conflict (Csikszentmihalyi & LeFevre, 1989; Deci, Connell, & Ryan, 1989).

Autonomy-Supportive Environments Encourage Choice and Initiative

As individuals identify the interests, needs, preferences, and feelings of others, they are better positioned to create for those people meaningful opportunities for choice, initiative, and self-reliance (McCombs & Pope, 1994). In a work setting, greater opportunities for choice occur when employees are given a variety of projects to pursue, flexibility in their schedules, information that enables them to make informed choices and decisions, options regarding coworker preferences for assignments, and options regarding particular tasks and the order of these tasks. Greater opportunities for initiative revolve around employees making decisions, setting priorities, diagnosing problems, and implementing their own ways of solving problems and overcoming the obstacles that arise. Greater opportunities for self-reliance occur as employees receive more time for (directed) independent work and greater personal responsibility for their own performance, production, and outcomes. This provision for choice, initiative, and self-reliance applies equally well to employers as it does to teachers, coaches, therapists, parents, and others (Deci & Ryan, 1987).

Autonomy-Supportive Environments Communicate the Rationale for Rules, Limits, or Constraints

Rules, limits, and constraints are a necessary and important part of the structure for any social context. The important point is not whether rules, constraints, and limits are necessary in the home, classroom, workplace, and gymnasium (because they are), but rather in how these elements of structure are used. One way to communicate rules, limits, and constraints is to rely on control and to essentially bypass people's need for self-determination; another way to communicate these same rules, limits, and constraints is to rely on information and to speak directly to people's need for self-determination (Ryan, Connell, & Grolnick, 1992). When the person communicating the rules, limits, and constraints relies on information (as opposed to control), he offers rationale for those limits (e.g., "The reason it is important to be on time is because . . . " or "The reason it is important that you take your medicine two times a day is because . . . "). In doing so, this person explains the importance and necessity of the constraints and articulates clearly and unambiguously the good reasons behind the rules and constraints (Deci & Ryan, 1985a; Koestner et al., 1984). Structure can, therefore, be minimal, optimal, or overbearing (i.e., laissez faire, autonomy supportive, or controlling). The logic in communicating the information-rich rationale for elements of structure is that the person being constrained or limited is more likely to internalize and voluntarily accept the rules, constraints, and limits ("That rule makes sense. I can now see its value. I therefore voluntarily accept it as my own.")

Autonomy-Supportive Environments Use a Communication Style Rich in Noncontrolling, Positive Feedback

At times people perform poorly, and at other times, they behave inappropriately. Autonomy-supportive environments treat poor performance and inappropriate behavior as problems to be solved rather than as targets for criticism (Deci, Connell, & Ryan, 1989). A noncontrolling communication style begins with resisting coercive, pressuring language, such as saying that the other person should, must, ought to, or has to do a certain thing (e.g., "Johnny, you should try harder," or "you must finish the project before four o'clock"). Instead of pressuring people into doing what they should or have to do, a noncontrolling communication style takes the other person's point of view and asks why the performance is poor or why the behavior is maladaptive. (For example, a coach might say to her athlete, "I've noticed that your scoring average has declined lately; do you know why this might be?") More often than not, the individual has some insight as to why performance is poor or behavior is maladaptive (e.g., insufficient resources, lack of training, the task seems pointless). A noncontrolling social context supports the individual with resources, training, and rationale regarding the importance of the task. When so supported, individuals can then diagnose the cause of their poor performance or misbehavior and then initiate their own solutions to the problems they face. As to positive feedback, an autonomy-supportive communication style resists critical negative feedback (e.g., "your workmanship is sloppy"), and instead makes an effort to identify points of improvement and progress (e.g., "I've noticed a new liveliness in your writing style lately," or "I've noticed that your running times were improving, but now they appear to have leveled off"). Noncontrolling communications

Your Interpersonal Motivating Style

Question: Why would a person want to learn about the motivational states discussed in this chapter?

Answer: To learn about his own interpersonal motivating style (and possibly even improve it).

What do you do when you try to motivate others? What do teachers do? What do parents do? What do work supervisors do? What do athletic coaches and personal trainers do? What do psychologists, clergy, military sergeants, and authors of self-help books do? Consider your own style. The following is one of the vignettes from the Problems in Schools questionnaire (Deci et al., 1981), a questionnaire frequently used to assess interpersonal motivation style (Deci et al., 1981; Flink, Boggiano, & Barrett, 1990; Reeve, Bolt, & Cai, 1999). Which of the four ways of solving the problem makes sense to you, and which ways do not make sense?

Jim is an average student who has been working at grade level. During the past two weeks, he has appeared listless and has not been participating during reading group. The work he does is accurate, but he has not been completing assignments. A phone conversation with his mother revealed no useful information. The most appropriate thing for Jim's teacher to do is:

1. Impress upon him the importance of finishing his assignments since he needs to learn this material for his own good.
2. Make him stay after school until the day's assignments are done.
3. Let him know that he doesn't have to finish all of his work now and see if she can help him work out the cause of the listlessness.

invite poor performers to initiate their own solutions; positive feedback informs poor performers of points of progress and achievement.

Autonomy-Supportive and Controlling Environments in Moment-to-Moment Interaction

The four characteristics of an autonomy-supportive environment listed in Table 4.1 outline general ways that one person facilitates in another person an internal PLOC and a sense of choice and volition. In addition, when people create autonomy-supportive environments for others, they typically do so by exhibiting characteristic moment-to-moment behaviors. Consider, for instance, the specific behaviors exhibited by autonomy-supportive tutors (as compared to controlling tutors) during a 20-minute teaching session (Deci et al., 1982). Using a two-group experimental design, the researchers told one group of tutors that their role was to help the learner learn. The researchers told the second group that it was their job and responsibility to make sure their learners performed up to high standards on a forthcoming test. The first group of tutors therefore taught in a way that supported the students' auton-

4. Patiently support the participation and work he does show.

The first two options express a relatively controlling style, while the last two options express a relatively autonomy-supportive style.

To get a concrete sense of what behaviors you rely on when motivating others, try the following exercise. Take on the role of a tutor. Try to teach someone how to learn a spreadsheet computer program, to drive a car, to play the piano, to paint with oils, to wash clothes, to say basic phrases in a foreign language, or to do just about any activity. The question soon becomes just what to say and what to do to motivate another person. People with a controlling style generally take charge and focus on getting the other person to behave in an expert way. People with an autonomy-supportive style generally take a student-centered approach and listen carefully to what the interests and needs of the student are as the student tries to learn.

Another exercise would be to watch from a distance as an expert provides instructions to a novice. For instance, watch a golf professional try to teach golf to someone or attend a local sporting event and watch the coach help his players during the game.

In doing one or more of these exercises, you can begin to learn about your own way of motivating others. One discovery you are likely to run into is just how difficult it can be to support the autonomy of another person. The benefits of doing so are many, but it is easier said than done when it comes to identifying a learner's perspective and finding ways to support that perspective.

omy, while the second group of tutors taught in a controlling way as they pressured the learners to focus on getting the right answers. The researchers videotaped each tutoring session and then compared the moment-to-moment teaching behaviors of the two types of teachers. Controlling tutors talked more, were more critical, used praise frequently, gave more directives and commands, invoked deadlines, and allowed their students less choice and autonomy. In contrast, autonomy-supportive tutors gave their students more choice, allowed them leeway to experiment with the learning materials, provided them with more time to work independently, came across as less demanding and controlling, promoted conceptual rather than factual understanding, and were rated as generally more likeable.

POSITIVE OUTCOMES FROM AUTONOMY-SUPPORTIVE ENVIRONMENTS

Whether an environment, relationship, or social context supports or frustrates a person's need for self-determination has strong implications for that person's motivation, productivity, development, and well-being (Deci, 1995; Deci & Ryan, 1987). People—including students, workers, athletes, clients, and patients—who feel self-determining (rather than controlled) show an impressive array of positive outcomes. How people benefit from having their need for self-determination involved and satisfied while engaged in an activity appears in the following list. The list shows one specific positive outcome (on the left-hand side) and one or two supportive and illustrative references (on the right-hand side) that the interested reader can pursue for additional information.

POSITIVE OUTCOME EXPERIENCED IN AN AUTONOMY-SUPPORTIVE ENVIRONMENT	SUPPORTIVE REFERENCE(S)
Improved performance	Miserandino, 1996; Boggiano et al., 1993
Higher achievement	Flink et al., 1990, 1992
Greater perceived competence	Ryan & Grolnick, 1986
Higher self-esteem	Deci, Schwartz, et al., 1981
Enhanced sense of self-worth	Ryan & Grolnick, 1986
Greater creativity	Amabile, 1985; Koestner et al., 1984
Enhanced conceptual learning	Benware & Deci, 1984; Boggiano et al., 1993
Greater flexibility in thinking	McGraw & McCullers, 1979
More active information processing	Grolnick & Ryan, 1987
Preference for optimal challenge	Shapira, 1976; Boggiano et al., 1988
Pleasure from optimal challenge	Harter, 1974, 1978b
Positive emotional tone	Patrick et al., 1993; Ryan & Connell, 1989
Stronger perceptions of control	Boggiano & Barrett, 1985
Greater trust in the relationship	Deci, Connell, & Ryan, 1989
Maintenance of behavioral change	Williams et al., 1996
Long-term retention	Ryan et al., 1997
Lower attrition; higher retention	Vallerand et al., 1997

This list of positive outcomes makes the case that empirical evidence supports the idea that people benefit when environments involve and satisfy people's need for self-determination. Each of these empirical studies employed one of two methodologies. In the first, researchers begin with a questionnaire to assess individual differences in how self-determined versus how controlled a person's motivation toward a particular activity is (Ryan & Connell, 1989). For instance, school-age children might be asked, "Why do you do your homework?" Self-determined reasons to this question would include "because doing homework is interesting or important" (i.e., something I want to do), whereas controlled reasons would include "because it's a requirement, or to make my parents proud" (i.e., something other people want me to do). Researchers then assess people's outcomes (e.g., performance, creativity, emotional tone). The consistent finding is that the quality of people's motivation (i.e., how self-determined their motivation is) predicts the quality of their interaction with that task, as shown in the list of positive outcomes above.

In the second methodology, researchers begin by experimentally manipulating how autonomy-supportive versus how controlling a particular social context is. For instance, children can be asked to read a particular text to see how interesting it is (autonomy-supportive manipulation) or told to read because they will be tested on the information (controlling manipulation). Researchers then assess the quality of people's motivation and performance under those conditions. The consistent finding is that people benefit when they have their autonomy supported and suffer when they are controlled. The two paragraphs that follow summarize a pair of experiments that represents each of these research methodologies.

In a study investigating how the quality of a person's motivation (self-determined versus controlled) affects his preference for optimal challenges versus easy successes, researchers showed participants seven versions of an interesting task, with each version differing only in how difficult it appeared to be (Shapira, 1976). The probabilities of successfully completing each version of the task ranged from .03 (an extremely hard task), through .18 (very hard), .34 (hard), .51 (moderately difficult), .66 (easy), .82 (very easy), to .97 (extremely easy). Each participant was simply asked to select his most preferred task to work on (and rank order his preferences on the remaining versions). Using random assignment, participants were either told or not told that they would receive money if they successfully completed the task. The dependent measure was that version of the task each person chose to work on (easy, optimally challenging, or hard). Results appear in Figure 4.1. When choice was controlled by the monetary incentive, people avoided anything challenging and selected the easiest version of the task (i.e., .82 level of

FIGURE 4.1 **Distribution of Participants' Choices of Which Level of Difficulty to Work On**

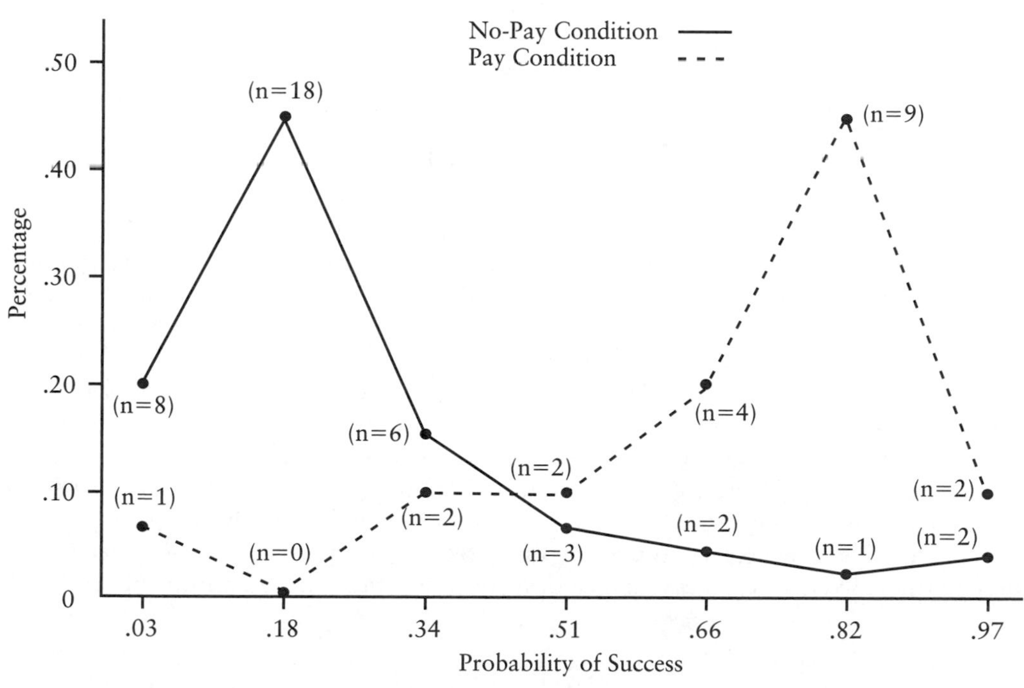

SOURCE: From "Expectancy Determinants of Intrinsically Motivated Behavior," by Z. Shapira, 1976, *Journal of Personality and Social Psychology, 34,* 1235–1244. Copyright 1976 by American Psychological Association. Reprinted with permission.

expected success). When free to choose out of interest and competence, people selected the optimally challenging version (i.e., .18 level of expected success). What this finding shows is that when people are free and self-determining, they will select tasks that allow them to pursue their interests and to exercise and develop their skills. But when people are controlled by environmental incentives, they will divorce their behavior from their interest and developmental opportunities.

In a study of how social contexts affect motivation and behavior, a group of researchers asked schoolchildren to paint an art collage under a barrage of imposed constraints, including instructions on not getting the colors all mixed up, washing out the brushes and wiping the brushes with a paper towel before switching to a new color of paint, and painting only on a small piece of the paper (Koestner et al., 1984). Half of the children painted under these controlling conditions. The other half of the children painted under autonomy-supportive conditions in which the rationale for each rule was communicated until the children understood why the constraints were important and worthwhile. After the children painted, the researchers measured the quality of their motivation and scored their artwork on various dimensions. Children who painted under autonomy-supportive conditions enjoyed the painting more, were more intrinsically motivated to paint, and produced artwork that was more creative and was judged to be of higher technical merit. What this finding shows is that when the social context supports people's need for self-determination, rather than frustrates this need, the quality of people's motivation and performance flourishes.

As a final example, consider one study that combined both research methodologies to test a motivational model of high-school dropouts (Vallerand et al., 1997). The motivational model on which the study was based appears in Figure 4.2. As shown on the left-hand side of the figure, the researchers began their study by interviewing the parents, teachers, and school administrators of high-school students to determine how autonomy-supportive versus controlling each person was. These measures provided an idea of how autonomy-supportive versus controlling a social world each high-school student lived in. These measures then predicted how much or how little perceived competence and perceived autonomy (i.e., self-determination) each student felt toward school. How competent and self-determining the student felt toward school then predicted the quality of her academic motivation. Self-determined academic motivation was assessed in terms of how self-determining versus controlling it was (e.g., "Why do you do your homework?"). Finally, how self-determined versus controlled each student's school-related motivation was predicted her intentions of dropping out of school as well as whether each student actually dropped out. These findings are important because they show that the more social agents neglect and frustrate people's need for self-determination (i.e., the less autonomy supportive they are), the less self-determining students feel. And when people feel relatively low levels of self-determination, the more likely it becomes that their development suffers (i.e., they drop out of school).

COMPETENCE

Everyone wants and strives to be competent. Everyone desires to interact effectively with their surroundings, and this desire for effectance extends into all aspects of every-

FIGURE 4.2 **Motivational Model of High-School Dropouts**

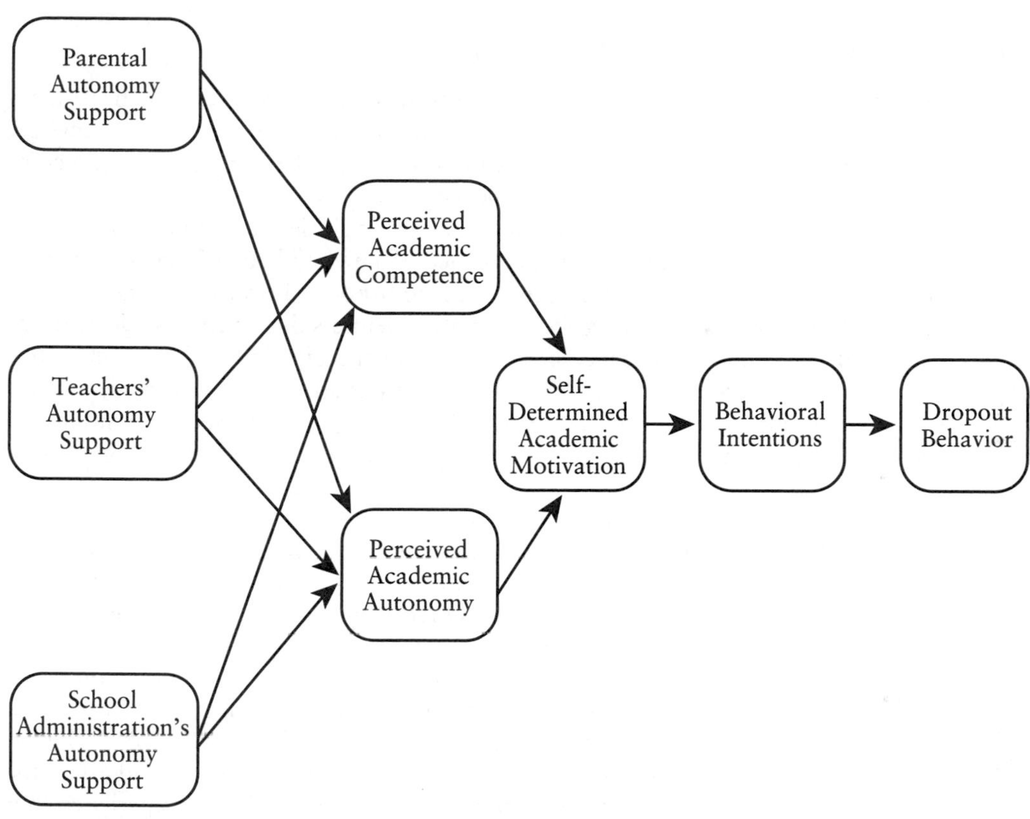

SOURCE: Adapted from "Self-Determination and Persistence in a Real-Life Setting: Toward a Motivational Model of High School Dropout," by R. J. Vallerand, M. S. Fortier, and F. Guay, 1997, *Journal of Personality and Social Psychology, 72,* 1161–1172. Copyright 1997 by American Psychological Association. Adapted with permission.

one's lives—in school, at work, in relationships, and during recreation and sports. Everyone wants to develop skills, and everyone wants to expand and improve on their capacities, talents, and potential. Everyone wants to advance and to make progress. When a person feels masterful and feels that he is making progress, he experiences some of his most positive and satisfying emotions. In other words, everyone has a need for competence.

Competence is a psychological need that provides an inherent source of motivation for seeking out and mastering optimal challenges. Optimal challenges are developmentally appropriate challenges, such that only some aspects of school, work, or sports successfully test a person's skills at exactly that point that is most appropriate for that person's current level of skill or talent. Defined formally, competence is the need to be effective in interactions with the environment, and it reflects the desire to exercise one's capacities and skills and, in doing so, to seek out and master optimal challenges (Deci & Ryan, 1985a).

COMPETENCE AS EFFECTANCE MOTIVATION

Infants engage in their environments with only the most basic of skills, such as sucking and grasping. Throughout early infancy, additional motor competencies emerge, including shaking, reaching, carrying, and tossing (Gibson, 1988). In late infancy, competencies emerge related to language and to locomotion. By early childhood, children engage in their environments with social skills and with abilities such as dressing, reading, and skipping rope. The same timely emergence of new skills continues throughout the school years and throughout adolescence and adulthood. In terms of the person's developing history, countless physical, social, and academic skills must emerge and undergo refinement if one is to engage in the environment effectively. To be effective, skills must not only emerge, they also must be exercised, stretched, improved, and refined. It is the need for competence that generates people's desire to seek out situations that allow them opportunities to exercise, stretch, improve, and refine personal skills and capacities.

When people exercise their skills, they produce effects on the environment. A responsive environment communicates the extent to which personal skills can or cannot alter the environment in a desired way. For example, exercising computer skills can produce an impressive document or a flurry of beeps and error messages. An entertainer, for instance, can tell a joke and hear the audience's laughter or cold silence. A gardener can plant and care for flowers and later watch them grow or wither. An animal trainer can instruct a dog to sit and watch as the dog either complies quickly or stares off into space. And a shot off the hands of a basketball player can bring the triumphant swish of the net or only the clank of the rim. The perception that a person can manipulate and effect the environment in ways that are consistent with personal intentions is the experience that cultivates a sense of competence.

Over time and across innumerable skill areas, an accumulated history of competent experiences aggregates into a personal belief that one does or does not possess the skills necessary to interact successfully (i.e., competently) with the environment. This accumulated sense of whether a person can (or cannot) interact effectively in the world constitutes "effectance motivation" (Harter, 1978a; White, 1959). The greater one's effectance motivation, the greater one's desire to seek out and approach situations that challenge existing skills.

Figure 4.3 illustrates Robert White's (1959) classic description of how effectance motivation energizes and directs (i.e., intrinsically motivates) behavior. Effectance motivation, which is the integration of the need for competence with one's history of producing effective changes on the environment, is the foundation for the desire to exercise skills and capacities. When skills are used, the ensuing behaviors produce changes in the environment, some of which are intentional and strategic while others are incidental and superfluous. Cooking a meal, for instance, produces food and feedback about personal culinary skills, but cooking also incidentally and accidentally raises the temperature in the room and invites people in other rooms to wander toward the kitchen. As people act on their

FIGURE 4.3 **Model of Effectance Motivation**

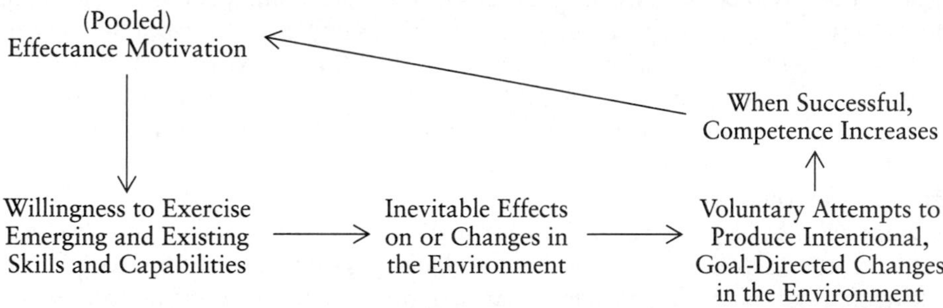

SOURCE: From *Motivating Others: Nurturing Inner Motivational Resources,* by J. Reeve, 1996. Needham Heights, MA: Allyn & Bacon. Copyright 1996 by Allyn & Bacon. Reprinted with permission.

environment, they learn the extent to which their skills influence their surroundings. Knowing whether and how their actions influence their environment, people then attempt to effect purposive, intentional, and goal-directed adjustments in their surroundings. Some of these intended adjustments are successful. And when skills successfully effect intentional change ("I meant to do that."), the need for competence is satisfied and one's generalized sense of effectance motivation increases. Each experience in the self-perception of competence increases the individual's accumulating reservoir of effectance motivation. Finally, as depicted in Figure 4.3, the greater one's pooled effectance motivation, the greater one's desire to seek out and master optimal challenges.

COMPETENCE AS A NEED

A portrayal of competence as a psychological need extends the concept of competence beyond that of a history of and a perception of successful environmental interactions. Competence as a need implies that people intentionally and voluntarily strive to master their environments and to control the outcomes that happen to them. It motivates people to pay attention to and learn about the contingencies that exist between their behavior and the environment's reactions and outcomes.

INVOLVING THE NEED FOR COMPETENCE: OPTIMAL CHALLENGE

The principal environmental condition that involves the need for competence is optimal challenge. The principal environmental condition that satisfies the need for competence is competence-affirming (i.e., positive) feedback.

Optimal Challenge and Flow

To determine the conditions that create enjoyment, Mihaly Csikszentmihalyi (1975, 1982, 1990) interviewed and studied hundreds of people he presumed knew what it felt like to have fun: rock climbers, surgeons, dancers, chess champions, basketball players, and others. Later, he studied more representative samples, including working professionals, high-school students, assembly-line workers, groups of the elderly, and people who generally sat at home and watched television. Irrespective of which sample he studied, Csikszentmihalyi found the essence of enjoyment could be traced to the "flow experience."

Flow is a state of concentration that involves a holistic absorption in an activity. In flow, action is effortless, and the performer focuses attention narrowly on a task that provides an optimal challenge to her current skills and abilities. Flow is such a pleasurable experience that the person often repeats the activity with the hope of experiencing flow again (Csikszentmihalyi & Nakamura, 1989). Maximal enjoyment with holistic involvement (i.e., flow) arises when the person perceives that the challenges offered by the task equal or match her task-related skills and competencies. That is, optimal challenge to the performer's current skill level causes flow.

The relationship between task challenge and personal skill is illustrated in Figure 4.4. The figure identifies the emotional consequences that arise from the different pairings of

FIGURE 4.4 **Model of Intrinsic Motivation and Flow**

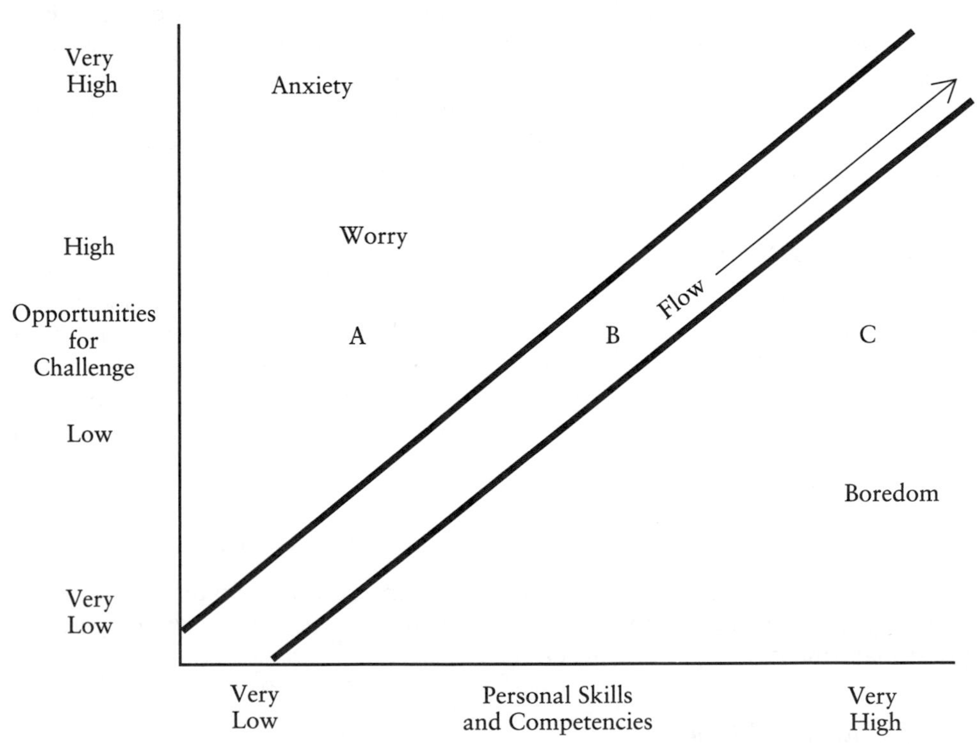

SOURCE: Adapted from *Beyond Boredom and Anxiety: The Experience of Flow in Work and Play,* by M. Csikszentmihalyi, 1975, San Francisco: Jossey-Bass.

challenge and skill. When challenge outweighs skill (skill is low; challenge is high), performers worry that the demands of the task will overwhelm their skills. Being overchallenged threatens competence, and that threat manifests itself emotionally as worry (if moderately overchallenged) or anxiety (if extremely overchallenged). When challenge matches skill (challenge and skill are both average or are both high), concentration, involvement, and enjoyment rise. When challenge and skill are perfectly matched, concentration, involvement, and enjoyment rise to their maximums to collectively produce the psychological experience of flow. When skill outweighs challenge (skill is high; challenge is low), task engagement is characterized by reduced concentration, minimal task involvement, and emotional boredom. Worry, anxiety, and boredom are all antithetical to flow.

Being overchallenged or overskilled produces emotional problems and suboptimal experience, but the worst profile of experience actually emanates from the pairing of low challenge and low skill (the lower left-hand corner of Figure 4.4). With both challenge and skill at low levels, literally all measures of emotion, motivation, and cognition are at their lowest levels—the person simply does not care about the task (Csikszentmihalyi, Rathunde, & Whalen, 1993). Flow is therefore a bit more complicated than just the balance of challenge and skill because balancing low skill and low challenge produces only apathy. A more accurate description of how challenge relates to skill is that flow emerges in those situations in which both challenge and skill are high or moderately high (Csikszentmihalyi & Csikszentmihalyi, 1988). With this qualification in mind, another way to look at Figure 4.4 is to divide it into four quadrants in which the upper-left quarter represents conditions for worry and anxiety, the lower-left quarter represents conditions for apathy, the lower-right quarter represents conditions for boredom, and the upper-right quarter represents conditions for flow.

The hypothetical case of three individuals, A, B, and C, also appears in Figure 4.4, as each individual performs a moderately difficult task. A, B, and C differ only in their levels of personal skill brought to the task. Person A will worry because his skills cannot match the demands and challenges of the task; person B will experience flow because his skills equally match with the demands and challenges of the task; and person C will be bored because her skills exceed the demands and challenges of the task. To alleviate worry, person A has two options: decrease task difficulty or increase personal skill. To alleviate boredom, person C has two options: increase task difficulty or decrease personal skill (through self-handicapping, for instance). To alter the challenge, persons A and C can manipulate task difficulty by solving easier or harder math problems, choosing an easier or harder jigsaw puzzle, or selecting a more or less proficient partner in an athletic contest. Persons A and C might also change the rules of the task by, for instance, solving the jigsaw puzzle with a partner or within a time limit, or allowing the baseball hitter additional or fewer strikes. As to manipulating skills, persons A and C can practice to increase skills or impose handicaps on skills to effectively decrease these manipulating skills, such as running a race with ankle weights or playing left-handed if one normally plays right-handed.

For a concrete example, consider three friends on a snow-skiing outing. Ski slopes offer different difficulty levels such that some slopes are relatively flat (beginner slopes), some are fairly steep (intermediate slopes), and others are downright death-defying (advanced slopes). If the skiers have different levels of skill, Figure 4.4 predicts that the emotional experience will vary for each skier on each slope. The novice skier will enjoy the beginner slopes but will experience mostly worry on the intermediate slopes and anxiety on the advanced slopes. Because the novice's skill level is so low, she might ski all day and experience only a hint of flow. The average skier will enjoy the intermediate slopes but will experience mostly boredom on the beginner slopes and worry on the advanced slopes. The professional will most likely enjoy the advanced slopes but will experience mostly mind-numbing boredom on the beginner slopes and some boredom on the intermediate slopes. Each skier, however, can experience flow on each slope by intentionally adjusting level of personal skill or level of slope difficulty. For example, a skier might increase skill by taking lessons and practicing or decrease skill by handicapping (i.e., using only one ski, using shorter skis, skiing backwards); the skier might increase skiing difficulty by confronting moguls or decrease skiing difficulty by going at a very slow speed. The fact that people can adjust both level of skill and level of task difficulty means that people can establish the conditions for optimal challenge.

The most important practical implication of flow theory is the following: Given optimal challenge—the appropriate balance of reasonably high skill and challenge—*any* activity can be enjoyed. Doing electrical work, writing papers, debating issues, sewing, analyzing a play, mowing the lawn, and other such activities do not necessarily make the top of most people's list of must-do, Saturday afternoon joys, but the balance of high skill with high challenge adds the spice of flow—concentration, absorption, enjoyment, and optimal experience. Consistent with the idea that optimal challenge gives rise to flow, Csikszentmihalyi found in a pair of studies that students enjoyed doing homework and working on part-time jobs more than they enjoyed viewing (challengeless) television programs (Csikszentmihalyi, Rathunde, & Whalen 1993). And people actually experienced flow more often at work than they did during leisure (Csikszentmihalyi, 1982). For these people, optimal challenge was more readily found in school and at work rather than in leisure.

Under some conditions, people actually enjoy being overchallenged (Stein et al., 1995). With very high challenge, people sometimes see in a task a potential for gain, growth, and personal improvement. The perception of improvement and progress can be enjoyable, at least until the hope for gain gives way to the reality of being overwhelmed. Also under other conditions, people sometimes enjoy very low levels of challenge (Stein et al., 1995). Generally speaking, people enjoy feedback that confirms they have a skill level that is above and beyond the challenge of the task. Easy success can generate some level of enjoyment, especially in the early stages of task engagement when performers harbor doubts as to how the performance will go. The quality of enjoyment that easy success breeds, however, is a defensive and relief-based type of enjoyment. This type of enjoyment might keep anxiety at bay, but it does little to nurture the psychological need for competence. Instead, it is success in the context of optimal challenge that generates sincere, competence, need-satisfying enjoyment (Clifford, 1990).

Interdependency Between Challenge and Feedback

Most everyone is challenged every day. In school, teachers put examinations in front of students. At work, projects and assignments test a person's writing, creativity, and teamwork skills. On the drive home, the interstate challenges a person's driving skills. If the car breaks down, a person's automotive repair skills are put to the test. In the gym, the proficiency of an opponent or the weight of a barbell challenges an individual's athletic skills. These situations, like those Csikszentmihalyi used to test his theory of flow, set the stage for challenge. But setting the stage for challenge is not the same thing as creating the psychological experience of being challenged. One additional ingredient still needs to be tossed into the equation—performance feedback. Confronting a test, project, or contest invites challenge, but a person does not experience challenge per se until she begins to perform and receive feedback. It is at that point—facing challenge and receiving performance feedback—that people report the psychological experience of being challenged (Reeve & Deci, 1996).

Error Tolerance, Failure Tolerance, and Risk Taking

The problem with optimal challenge, motivationally speaking, is that when people face moderately difficult tasks, they are as likely to experience failure and frustration as they are to experience success and enjoyment. In fact, one hallmark of optimal challenge is that success and failure are both likely. Thus, the dread of failure can diminish the competence need-involving qualities of optimal challenge. If intense, the dread of failure can motivate avoidance behaviors so that people go out of their way to escape from challenging tasks (Covington, 1984a, 1984b).

Before people will engage freely in and persevere at optimally challenging tasks, the social context must tolerate (and even value) failure and error making (i.e., adopt a performance climate rich in "failure tolerance" or "error tolerance"; Clifford, 1988, 1990). Optimal challenge implies that considerable error making is essential for optimizing motivation (Clifford, 1990). Error tolerance, failure tolerance, and risk taking rest on the belief that we learn more from failure than we do from success. Failure produces opportunities for learning because it has its constructive aspects when people identify its causes, try new strategies, seek advice and instruction, and so on. When our environment—in school, at work, and in sports—tolerates failure and sincerely values the contribution it can make to our learning and developing, then as performers, we experience an emotional green light for listening fully to the competence need and for the desire it generates in us to seek out and attempt to master optimal (rather than easy) challenges (Clifford, 1984, 1990).

Satisfying the Competence Need: Positive Feedback

Whether individuals perceive their performance to be competent or incompetent is often an ambiguous undertaking. To make such an evaluation, a performer needs feedback. Feedback comes from one (or more) of the following three sources: the task itself, comparisons of one's current performance with one's past performances, and the evaluations of others (Boggiano & Ruble, 1979; Dollinger & Thelen, 1978; Grolnick, Frodi, & Bridges, 1984; Koestner, Zuckerman, & Koestner, 1987; Schunk & Hanson, 1989).

In some tasks, competence feedback is inherent in the performance of the task itself, as in successfully logging onto the computer (or not) or in repairing a machine (or not). In most tasks, however, performance evaluation is more ambiguous than a right-versus-wrong performance outcome (for example, consider competence evaluations of social skills or artistic talents). In performances such as these, our own past performances and the evaluations of other people (rather than the task itself) supply the information necessary for making an inference of competence versus incompetence. As for our own past performances, the perception of progress is an important signal of competence (Schunk & Hanson, 1989), just as the perception of a lack of progress signals incompetence. As for the evaluation of other people, positive feedback bolsters perceptions of competence, whereas negative feedback deflates it (Anderson, Manoogian, & Reznick, 1976; Blank, Reis, & Jackson, 1984; Deci, 1971; Dollinger & Thelen, 1978; Vallerand & Reid, 1984). To convey a message of competence in one experiment, researchers gave participants bogus feedback such as, "You did better than the average student on these puzzles" (Harackiewicz, 1979). In another study, participants performed an unfamiliar task as experimenters offered praise ("It looks like you have a natural ability . . . and it shows in your performance") or criticism ("This is an easy task, but your improvement is quite slow"). Praise increased perceived competence, whereas criticism decreased it (Vallerand & Reid, 1984). In summary, performance feedback in its various forms—task-generated, self-generated, and other-generated—supplies the information individuals need to formulate a cognitive evaluation of their perceived level of competence.

The Pleasure of Optimal Challenge in the Context of Positive Feedback

To confirm that people do indeed derive pleasure from optimal challenge, Susan Harter (1974, 1978b) gave school-age children anagrams of different difficulty levels and monitored each student's expressed pleasure (through smiling) upon solving each anagram. (An anagram is a word or phrase such as *table,* with its letters rearranged to form another word or phrase, as in *bleat.)* In general, anagram-solving success produced greater smiling and higher enjoyment than did failure (Harter, 1974), suggesting that mastery in general gratifies the competence need. In addition, however, some anagrams were very easy (three letters), some were easy (four letters), others were moderately difficult (five letters), and still others were very hard (six letters). As the anagrams increased in difficulty, it took students longer and longer to solve them, as expected, but the critical measure in the study was expressed pleasure (through smiling) as a function of how difficult the solved anagram was (Harter, 1978b). A curvilinear inverted-U pattern emerged in which smiling was muted following success on the very easy problems, greatest following success on the moderately difficult problems, and only moderate following success on the easy and very hard problems. The central point is that children experience the greatest pleasure following success in the context of moderate challenge. In the words of the children, "The fives were just right. They were a challenge, but not too much challenge," and "I liked the hard ones because they gave you a sense of satisfaction, but the really hard ones were just too frustrating" (Harter, 1978b, p. 796).

RELATEDNESS

Everyone needs to belong. Everyone desires social interaction. All people want to form and maintain warm, close, affectionate relationships with others. Everyone wants people to understand who they are as individuals, and everyone wants to be accepted and to be valued. Everyone wants interactions to become relationships. And all people want relationships and attachments not only with individuals but with groups, organizations, and communities as well. When these relationships are reciprocal, such that people want not only to form social bonds but to be included in their relationships and groups, that is the most desired. Everyone wants others to be responsive to their needs. But when an individual feels ignored or neglected, she feels alone and alienated. In other words, people have a need for relatedness.

Relatedness is the need to establish close emotional bonds and attachments with other people, and it reflects the desire to be emotionally connected to and interpersonally involved in warm relationships (Baumeister & Leary, 1995; Fromm, 1956; Guisinger & Blatt, 1994; Ryan, 1991; Ryan & Powelson, 1991; Sullivan, 1953). Because we inherit an organismic need for relatedness, we gravitate toward people who we perceive are capable of satisfying our needs and we drift away from those who cannot or will not. And what people are essentially looking for within need-satisfying relationships is the opportunity to relate the self authentically to another person in a caring and emotionally meaningful way. Relatedness is an important motivational construct because people function better, are more resilient to stress, and report fewer psychological difficulties when their interpersonal relationships support their need for relatedness (Cohen, Sherrod, & Clark, 1986; Lepore, 1992; Ryan, Stiller, & Lynch, 1994; Sarason et al., 1991; Windle, 1992).

Because each of us has a need for relatedness, social bonds form easily (Baumeister & Leary, 1995). Given an opportunity to engage others in face-to-face interaction, people go out of their way to create relationships (Brewer, 1979). The emergence of friendships and alliances seems to require little more than proximity and spending time together (Wilder & Thompson, 1980). The more people interact and the more people spend time together, the more likely they are to form friendships. Once social bonds are formed, people are generally reluctant to break them. When we move, when we graduate from school, and when others take their leave of us, we resist the breakup of the relationship. We promise to write and to telephone, we cry, we exchange addresses and phone numbers, we plan an occasion to get together in the future, and so on.

INVOLVING THE NEED FOR RELATEDNESS: INTERACTION WITH OTHERS

Interaction with others is the primary condition that involves the relatedness need, at least to the extent that those interactions take place in an environment of warmth, care, and mutual concern. The act of starting a new relationship seems especially to involve the need for relatedness. Consider, for instance, the relatedness-involving potential of the following events, each of which promises an entry into new social relationships: first dates, falling in love, childbirth, fraternity or sorority pledging, and starting anew in school or in employment. Generally speaking, people seek emotionally positive interactions and interaction partners. And people want these interactions to occur within a context of a stable, long-term relationship rich in warmth, care, and mutual concern.

SATISFYING THE NEED FOR RELATEDNESS: PERCEPTION OF A SOCIAL BOND

Although frequent interaction is sufficient for involving the relatedness need, relatedness-need satisfaction requires the creation of a social bond between the self and another (or between self and group). To be satisfying, that social bond needs to be characterized by the perceptions that the other person (1) cares about the self's welfare and (2) likes the self (Baumeister & Leary, 1995). But more than caring and liking, the relationships that deeply satisfy the need for relatedness are those steeped in the knowledge that one's "true self"—one's "authentic self"—has been shown and deemed to be important in the eyes of another person (Deci & Ryan, 1995; Ryan, 1993).

Relationships that do not involve care, liking, acceptance, and valuing do not satisfy the need for relatedness. Researchers, for instance, routinely find that people who are lonely do not lack frequent social contact. Rather, they lack close, intimate relationships (Wheeler, Reis, & Nezlek, 1983). More often than not, quality is more important than quantity when it comes to relatedness and relationships (Carstensen, 1993). Similarly, marriages, which are clearly close relationships, are not always emotionally satisfying. Some marriages are full of conflict, stress, and criticism and basically make the other person's life more difficult than it otherwise would be. Alternatively, supportive marriages, those rich in mutual care and liking, are the emotionally satisfying relationships that lead people to feel happy (Coyne & DeLongis, 1986). Further, youths' relationships with their parents follow the same pattern in that to keep youths' depression at bay, parent-youth relationships not only need to exist but they also need to be supportive and nonproblematic (Carnelley, Pietromonaco, & Jaffe, 1994). Having one's relatedness need satisfied, as opposed to neglected, promotes vitality and well-being (Ryan & Lynch, 1989), and it lessens loneliness and depression (Pierce, Sarason, & Sarason, 1991; Windle, 1992).

Life lived in the absence of intimate social bonds—life lived without opportunities for involving and satisfying the need for relatedness—is life lived within a host of negative emotions, including sadness, depression, jealousy, and loneliness (Baumeister & Leary, 1995; Williams & Solano, 1983). Whereas quantity of relationships sufficiently involves the relatedness need, it takes quality relationships to satisfy it.

Communal Versus Exchange Relationships

We all involve ourselves in many different relationships. Some of these relationships are more need satisfying than others. The distinction between communal and exchange relationships captures the essence of relationships that do (communal) and do not (exchange) satisfy the relatedness need (Mills & Clark, 1982). Exchange relationships are those between acquaintances or between people who do business together. Communal relationships are those between persons who care about the welfare of the other, as exemplified by friendships, family, and romantic relationships.

What distinguishes exchange from communal relationships are the implicit rules that guide the giving and receiving of benefits, such as money, help, and emotional support (Clark, Mills, & Powell, 1986). Exchange partners give benefits with the expectation of receiving comparable benefits in the near future. In exchange relationships, no obligation exists between interactants to be concerned with the other person's needs or welfare. Communal partners give benefits in response to the other person's needs, or simply to please the other. The only obligation is to care for the needs of the other and to support her welfare. Only communal relationships satisfy the relatedness need.

In communal relationships, people monitor and keep track of the other's needs, regardless of any forthcoming opportunities for reciprocity or material gain (Clark, 1984; Clark & Mills, 1979; Clark, Mills, & Powell, 1986; Clark et al., 1987). For instance, people involved in communal (as compared to exchange) relationships frequently check up on the needs of the other (Clark, Mills, & Powell, 1986), resist keeping track (or score) of individual inputs into their joint projects (Clark, 1984), provide help when the other feels distressed (Clark et al., 1987), and experience tangible economic gifts as *detrimental* to how friendly, relaxed, fun, spontaneous, and smooth forthcoming interactions are (Clark & Mills, 1979). On this latter point, consider the emotional discomfort you might feel after providing a ride home to a close (communal) friend and, upon arrival, were handed ten dollars in payment of the favor (Mills & Clark, 1982).

Role of Relatedness in Internalization

Internalization refers to the process through which an individual transforms a formerly externally prescribed regulation or value into an internal one (Ryan, Rigby, & King, 1993). For instance, a person might internalize the value of education or internalize why brushing one's teeth is important. As a process, internalization reflects the individual's tendency to voluntarily adopt and integrate into the self the values and regulations of other people (or society).

Relatedness to others provides the social context in which internalization occurs (Goodenow, 1993; Grolnick, Deci & Ryan, 1997; Ryan & Powelson, 1991). When a person feels emotionally connected to and interpersonally involved with another, relatedness is high and internalization occurs willingly. When a person feels emotionally distant from and interpersonally neglected by another, relatedness is low and internalization takes place at a snail's pace, if at all. For instance, children who have a positive relationship with their parents will generally internalize their own parents' ways of thinking and behaving. Children with stormy relationships with their parents will generally reject their parents' ways of thinking and behaving and go in search of a value system elsewhere.

Relatedness does not make internalization automatic. Relatedness does not guarantee that internalization will occur. For internalization to occur, the individual must also see the value, meaning, and utility in other people's prescriptions (do X, believe Y) and proscriptions (don't do X, don't believe Y). To internalize a value or way of behaving, the person needs to understand why the value or way of acting has merit. ("Now why is it important that I brush my teeth?") Therefore, relatedness is a necessary (but not sufficient) condition for internalization and cultural transmission to occur. Internalization

FIGURE 4.5 **Engagement Model to Illustrate the Motivational Significance of Involvement, Structure, and Autonomy Support**

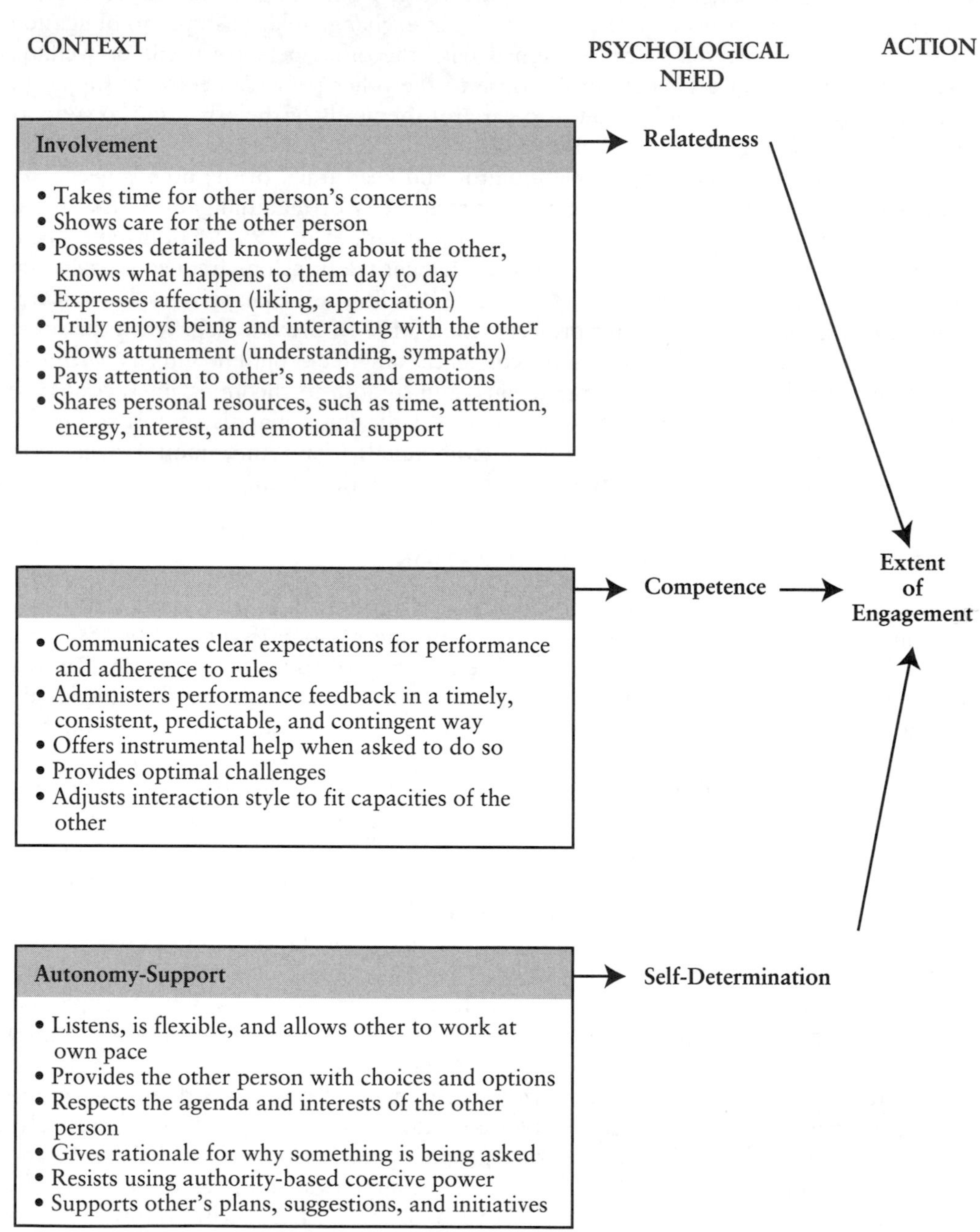

flourishes in relationships that provide a rich supply of (1) relatedness need satisfaction and (2) information-laden and psychologically satisfying rationale for making sense of the prescriptions and proscriptions.

PUTTING IT ALL TOGETHER: SOCIAL CONTEXTS THAT INVOLVE AND SATISFY ORGANISMIC PSYCHOLOGICAL NEEDS

Specific aspects of the social context are noteworthy in their capacity to involve and satisfy the organismic psychological needs. For illustration, Table 4.2 summarizes some prototypical events that reliably involve the needs of self-determination, competence, and relatedness as well as some prototypical events that reliably satisfy these three needs. When involved in activities that offer opportunities for choice and initiative, optimal challenge, and frequent social interaction, people typically experience need involvement and feel interested in what they do. When involved in activities that offer opportunities for autonomy-support, positive feedback, and communal relationships, people typically experience need satisfaction and feel enjoyment in what they do.

The motivational model of engagement (see Figure 4.5) illustrates the contribution that general aspects of the social context have for organismic psychological needs (Connell, 1990; Connell & Wellborn, 1991; Skinner & Belmont, 1993). Engagement is a term that captures the intensity and emotional quality people show when they initiate and carry out activities, such as learning in school or practicing skills in music or sports. When highly engaged, people behave in ways that are active and that allow them to express positive emotion; when highly disengaged, people behave in ways that are passive and that cause them to express negative emotion (Patrick, Skinner, & Connell, 1993). Jim Connell and Ellen Skinner explain the conditions under which people show high and low engagement by tracing the origin of engagement to the three organismic psychological needs. Specifically, they argue that (1) involvement enhances engagement because it involves and satisfies the need for relatedness, (2) structure enhances engagement because it involves and satisfies the need for competence, and (3) autonomy support enhances engagement because it involves and satisfies the need for self-determination.

Involvement refers to the quality of the interpersonal relationship between two people, such as a teacher and a student, and also to each person's willingness to dedicate psychological resources (e.g., time, interest, attention) to the other. The opposite of

Table 4.2 Factors That Involve and Satisfy Organismic Psychological Needs

Organismic psychological need	Involvement factors	Satisfaction factors
Self-determination	Choice, initiative	Autonomy-supportive environments
Competence	Optimal challenge	Positive feedback
Relatedness	Frequent social interaction	Communal relationships

involvement is rejection or neglect. The many ways involvement expresses itself is summarized in Figure 4.5, but some examples include expressing affection and truly enjoying time spent together (Connell, 1990; Connell & Wellborn, 1991; Grolnick & Ryan, 1989; Grolnick, Ryan, & Deci, 1991; Skinner & Belmont, 1993).

Structure refers to the amount and clarity of information one person, such as a teacher or coach, provides to another regarding the best ways to achieve desired skills and behavioral outcomes. The opposite of structure is chaos or confusion. The many ways structure expresses itself is summarized in Figure 4.5, but some examples include communicating clear expectations and providing optimal challenges.

Autonomy support refers to the amount of freedom one person gives to another so that he can find the means to connect his behavior to personal goals, interests, and values. The opposite of autonomy support is coercion or being controlled. How autonomy support expresses itself is summarized in Figure 4.5, but some examples include supporting the other person's initiative and providing choices and options (recall Table 4.1).

WHAT MAKES FOR A GOOD DAY?

To study day-to-day fluctuations in well-being, one group of researchers asked college students to keep a daily diary of their moods (joyful, angry) and well-being (vitality, symptomatology). The researchers predicted that good days are those in which one's organismic psychological needs are met (Sheldon, Ryan, & Reis, 1996). The results from this diary study showed that circumstances partly dictated when people had good days, as people had their best days on weekends, for instance. But people also had their best days when they experienced higher levels of daily competence and daily self-determination. (Unfortunately, the researchers did not include a measure of daily relatedness.) For instance, as people spent their days attending classes, talking with friends, and playing the cello, the more effective they felt (daily competence) and the more internal was their perceived locus of causality (daily autonomy) during these activities, the greater was their positive affect, vitality, and healthy well-being. These findings take on a special importance because they suggest that organismic psychological needs provide the "psychological nutriments" necessary for good days and positive well-being (Sheldon et al., 1998).

Consider an ordinary trip to the gym to exercise. Imagine at the end of the workout that you completed a questionnaire asking how enjoyable the hour was, why you came to exercise, how challenging the workout was and how much you improved, and what the quality of the social interaction was during the hour. Notice that these questions correspond to the psychological needs for self-determination, competence, and relatedness. One group of researchers did conduct this study, and they found that the greater was the experience of self-determination, competence, and relatedness, the greater was the exerciser's enjoyment (Ryan, et al., 1997). In contrast, people who exercised for other motives (appearance, body image) enjoyed the experience less and worked out for a briefer time. A study with the elderly in nursing homes found much the same result in that the more self-determining and interpersonally related residents felt each day, the greater was their vitality and well-being and the less was their distress (Kasser & Ryan, 1999).

One way people experience a good day is through a subjective experience of vitality. For instance, consider the following three sentences (Ryan & Frederick, 1997):

- I feel alive and vital.
- Sometimes I feel so alive I just want to burst.
- I feel energized.

When people have days that allow them to feel self-determining, competent, and interpersonally related, they are significantly more likely to agree with these statements (Kasser & Ryan, 1993, 1996; Sheldon et al., 1996).

SUMMARY

Two assumptions define an organismic approach to motivation: (1) People are inherently active, and (2) the principles of differentiation and integration guide developmental growth. Organismic theories get their name from the term "organism," an entity that is alive and in active exchange with its environment. The role of the organismic psychological needs is to generate the energy and desire that allows human beings to be inherently active and to seek out and interact with the need-involving and need-supporting qualities of the environment. Differentiation involves elaboration and growing in complexity. Integration involves a synthesis that refines the individual's emerging complexity into an organized and adaptive coherence. The picture that emerges in an organismic approach to motivation is that human beings possess a natural motivation to learn, grow, and develop in a way that is healthy and mature.

Self-determination is the need to experience choice in the initiation and regulation of one's behavior, and it reflects the desire to have personal choices, rather than environmental events, determine one's actions. When self-determined, behavior feels free, emanates from an internal perceived locus of causality, and carries with it a phenomenological tone of play, leisure, and positive emotion. The extent to which an individual is able to involve and satisfy her need for self-determination depends a good deal on how supportive and nurturing (i.e., autonomy supportive) versus neglecting and frustrating (i.e., controlling) the environment is perceived to be. Autonomy-supportive environments emphasize the individual's point of view, encourage choice and self-initiative, communicate the rationale for any behavioral controls, and rely on a communication style that is rich in noncontrolling, positive feedback. People whose behavior is self-determined, as opposed to controlled, show performance and achievement gains; experience high levels of perceived competence, self-worth, and self-esteem; solve problems in ways that are flexible, conceptual, and creative; prefer optimal challenges over easy successes; and experience task-related emotions such as interest and enjoyment rather than tension and pressure. In other words, people benefit when environments involve, satisfy, and support their need for self-determination.

Competence is the need to be effective in interactions with the environment. It reflects the desire to exercise one's capacities and skills and, in doing so, to seek out and master optimal challenges. The need for competence generates the motivation to want to develop, improve upon, and refine personal skills and talents. The principal environmental event that involves the competence need is optimal challenge. When challenge and skill are both relatively high, people experience flow, which is a psychological state characterized by maximal enjoyment, intense concentration, and full absorption in the task. The principal environmental event that satisfies the competence need is positive feedback. Performance feedback supplies the objective information performers need to construct a cognitive evaluation regarding the effectiveness of their skills.

Relatedness is the need to establish close emotional bonds and attachments with other people, and it reflects the desire to be emotionally connected to and interpersonally involved with others in warm, caring relationships. Mere interaction with others is a sufficient condition for involving the need for relatedness. To satisfy the relatedness need, however, a person needs to confirm that the emerging social bonds with other people are sincere and true. A communal relationship provides one example of the type of relationship that is capable of satisfying the relatedness need. Relationships that are not embedded within a context of liking and mutual care (i.e., exchange relationships) frustrate the relatedness need and leave people feeling distressed, sad, lonely, depressed, or jealous. Relatedness to others provides the social context that supports internalization, which is the process through which one person takes in and accepts as his or her own another person's belief, value, or way of behaving. When a person feels emotionally connected to and interpersonally involved with another, relatedness is high and internalization occurs willingly.

An engagement model of motivation (Figure 4.5) illustrates how general aspects of the social context successfully involve and satisfy (or neglect and frustrate) the organismic needs for self-determination, competence, and relatedness. Autonomy support facilitates the need for self-determination, structure facilitates the need for competence, and involvement facilitates the need for relatedness. Collectively, autonomy support, structure, and involvement are important because they provide the elements within any social context that support and nurture people's organismic psychological needs. When people have days in which experiences of psychological need involvement and satisfaction are plentiful, they have "a good day" in that they are more likely to experience positive affect, healthy well-being, and subjective vitality.

RECOMMENDED READINGS

Organismic Psychological Needs

Ryan, R. M. (1995). Psychological needs and the facilitation of integrative processes. *Journal of Personality, 63,* 397–427.

Sheldon, K. M., Ryan, R. M., & Reis, H. T. (1996). What makes for a good day? Competence and autonomy in the day and in the person. *Personality and Social Psychology Bulletin, 22,* 1270–1279.

Self-Determination

Deci, E. L., & Ryan, R. M. (1987). The support of autonomy and the control of behavior. *Journal of Personality and Social Psychology, 53,* 1024–1037.

Ryan, R. M., & Grolnick, W. S. (1986). Origins and pawns in the classroom: Self-report and projective assessments of individual differences in children's perceptions. *Journal of Personality and Social Psychology,* 50, 550–558.

Vallerand, R. J., Fortier, M. S., & Guay, F. (1997). Self-determination and persistence in a real-life setting: Toward a motivational model of high school dropout. *Journal of Personality and Social Psychology, 72,* 1161–1172.

Competence

Csikszentmihalyi, M. (1982). Toward a psychology of optimal experience. *Review of Personality and Social Psychology, 3,* 13–36.

Harter, S. (1978a). Effectance motivation reconsidered: Toward a developmental model. *Human Development, 21,* 34–64.

Harter, S. (1978b). Pleasure derived from optimal challenge and the effects of extrinsic rewards on children's difficulty level choices. *Child Development, 49,* 788–799.

Relatedness

Baumeister, R. F., & Leary, M. R. (1995). The need to belong: Desire for interpersonal attachments as a fundamental human motivation. *Psychological Bulletin, 117,* 497–529.

Kasser, V. G., & Ryan, R. M. (1999). The relation of psychological needs for autonomy and relatedness to vitality, well-being, and mortality in a nursing home. *Journal of Applied Social Psychology, 29,* 935–954.

Ryan, R. M., & Powelson, C. L. (1991). Autonomy and relatedness as fundamental to motivation and education. *Journal of Experimental Education, 60,* 49–66.

5

Intrinsic Motivation and Types of Extrinsic Motivation

Each year more than a half million Americans suffer injuries from automobile accidents, many of which cause fatalities. Fortunately, drivers and passengers have a way to drastically reduce their probability of suffering serious injuries; namely, by wearing seat belts. Despite, convincing data that seat belts save lives and despite our society's consensus that wearing a seat belt is a desirable behavior, all too many people still drive without buckling up. To reverse seat belt apathy, the government tried national advertising campaigns to encourage riders to buckle up. These educational campaigns failed miserably. One study, for instance, reported that a nationwide multimedia advertising campaign increased seat belt usage by 0.1% of drivers (Robertson et al., 1974). Promoters next tried to offer attractive incentives to riders who buckled up (Elman & Killebrew, 1978; Geller, Casali, & Johnson, 1980; Geller, et al., 1987). The logic behind incentive-based programs is that if people cannot find the motivation to buckle up within themselves, then perhaps the offer of an attractive incentive will give them the motivation they lack.

For instance, consider the seat-belt sweepstakes program tested at a Virginia university (Rudd & Geller, 1985). To conduct the sweepstakes, researchers placed posters like the one in Figure 5.1 on bulletin boards in campus classrooms and lecture halls. Campus radio stations also announced the seat-belt sweepstakes. In the conduct of the sweepstakes, campus police recorded all license-plate numbers of the drivers they saw wearing a (shoulder) seat belt. Those license-plate numbers were entered into a raffle of weekly prizes, which ranged in value from $20 to $450. To be eligible to win the prizes, drivers

FIGURE 5.1 **Campus Poster to Advertise Seat-Belt Sweepstakes**

SOURCE: From "A University-Based Incentive Program to Increase Safety Belt Use: Towards Cost-Effective Institutionalization," by J. R. Rudd and E. S. Geller, 1985, *Journal of Applied Behavior Analysis, 18,* pp. 215–226. Copyright 1985, *Journal of Applied Behavior Analysis*. Reprinted by permission.

therefore had to first engage in the desired behavior—wear a seat belt. During the three weeks of the sweepstakes, campus seat-belt usage doubled.

Offering an attractive incentive for compliant behavior represents one strategy of extrinsic motivation. A second strategy is to offer an aversive incentive. This strategy is different, but the logic is the same: If people cannot find the motivation to buckle up within themselves, then perhaps the threat of an aversive consequence will give them the motivation they lack. With seat-belt usage, the aversive stimulus is typically a harsh-sounding buzzer, bright or flashing panel light, or an ignition interlock system (Geller, Casali, & Johnson, 1980). All automobiles now offer at least one of these aversive stimuli, and the buzzer, light, or locking system continues until the driver complies and fastens the seat belt. Thus, people buckle up not in the name of saving their lives but simply to prevent or escape from something irritating. This kind of irritating incentive leads people to buckle up even better than the prospect of an attractive incentive (Geller, Casali, & Johnson, 1980).

The discussion throughout this chapter follows the spirit of the seat-belt sweepstakes and obnoxious buzzer studies by addressing the question of how external events generate motivational states. The introductory example featured seat-belt usage, but any number of other familiar incentive programs would present the same argument, programs such as frequent-flyer programs, token economies, academic honor rolls, perfect attendance certificates, pay-for-performance programs, end-of-the-year bonus checks, school grades, reading-incentive programs (e.g., Learn to Earn, Book It!), rebate credit cards, or frequent-usage cards that offer discounts issued by places such as restaurants and hotels. In each case, the logic is the same: Extrinsic incentives and rewards can control behavior. Because incentives and rewards exert such a strong and reliable effect on behavior, people working in applied settings have embraced extrinsic motivation as a motivational strategy for changing people's behavior.

Practically every environment we find ourselves in discriminates between desirable and undesirable behaviors. Further, practically every environment rewards us in one way or another for performing those desired behaviors and punishes us for performing those undesired behaviors. As a result, we generally follow our hedonistic tendencies (approach pleasure, avoid pain) and engage in those courses of action that we believe will produce reward and prevent punishment. Over time, we learn preferences for engaging in particular behaviors, such as buckling a seat belt, because those behaviors have a history with us for being associated with attractive consequences. It is not that we develop a desire to engage in any one particular behavior. Instead, what we want is to do whatever the environment will reward us for doing.

In the two previous chapters on needs, motivation arose from inner sources—physiological and psychological needs. These needs explained why people ate and drank, sought out optimal challenges and intimate relationships, and so on. To propose that people eat and drink and that people seek out challenges and relationships because of needs to do so, however, recognizes only half of the story. A person might also engage in these same behaviors because of an external reason to do so. Some examples of external events that create extrinsic motivation include money, grades, praise, the approval of others, advertising influences, social customs, laws and their consequences, and so on. A fruitful and comprehensive analysis of motivated behavior, according to the behavior theorists that will be introduced in this chapter (Baldwin & Baldwin, 1986; Skinner, 1938, 1953,

1986), requires that we add the analysis of how environmental incentives and consequences promote in us a sense of want and desire.

INTRINSIC AND EXTRINSIC MOTIVATIONS

Needs generate motivational states within us. Causal observation of day-to-day behavior, however, suggests that our needs are sometimes silent, or at least somewhere on the back burner of consciousness. In schools, students are sometimes apathetic and disinterested in engaging in the school's curriculum. At work, employees are sometimes listless and slow to apply themselves. In hospitals, patients sometimes feel little desire to exercise and are reluctant to take their medicines. Such observations suggest that people do not always generate their own motivation from within. Instead, people sometimes turn passive and look to the environment to supply motivation for them. In school, teachers see this lack of inner motivation, and they therefore use grades, stickers, praise, recess privileges, and threats of doom to motivate their students. At work, employers use paychecks, bonuses, surveillance, competitions, and threats of termination to motivate their employees. In the hospitals, doctors use orders, implicit threats, and appeals for pleasing loved ones to motivate their patients. Such are the external events that constitute the incentives and consequences that generate extrinsic motivational states.

Experience teaches us that there are two ways to enjoy an activity: intrinsically or extrinsically. Consider activities like playing the piano, using the computer, or reading a book. On the one hand, the pianist may become interested and begin to enjoy piano playing because it is an opportunity to involve and satisfy psychological needs. The musician plays the piano to have fun, to exercise and develop valued skills, and to feel free and self-entertained. On the other hand, the same piano-playing behavior can be enjoyed because it is an opportunity to make money, to win accolades and approval, and to earn a college scholarship. Any activity, in fact, can be approached with either an intrinsic or an extrinsic motivational orientation (Amabile, 1985; Pittman, Boggiano, & Ruble, 1983; Pittman, Emery, & Boggiano, 1982; Pittman & Heller, 1988; Ryan & Deci, 2000).

INTRINSIC MOTIVATION

Intrinsic motivation is the innate propensity to engage one's interests and to exercise one's capacities and, in doing so, to seek out and master optimal challenges (Deci & Ryan, 1985a). It emerges spontaneously from organismic psychological needs, personal curiosities, and innate strivings for growth. Because people have innate organismic psychological needs, they have within themselves the means to experience spontaneous satisfactions inherent in engaging interesting activities. It is within the experience of feeling competent and feeling self-determining that people experience intrinsic motivation. When people engage in tasks and feel competent and self-determining, they are experiencing intrinsic motivation as a natural motivational force that energizes behavior in the absence of extrinsic rewards and pressures. For instance, even without the assistance of rewards and pressures, interest can spark the desire to read a book, and competence can involve a person in a challenge for hours. Functionally, intrinsic motivation provides the innate motivation to engage the environment, pursue personal interests, and exert the effort necessary to exercise and develop skills and capabilities.

Extrinsic Motivation

Extrinsic motivation arises from environmental incentives and consequences. Whenever we act to gain a high academic grade, win a trophy, or beat a deadline, our behavior is extrinsically motivated (i.e., the motivation owes its origin to events present in the environment). When employees work hour after hour to earn a bonus, make a quota, or impress their peers, their behavior is extrinsically motivated. Extrinsic motivation arises from a sort of "Do this and you will get that" motivation, and it exists as an "in order to" motivation (as in, "Do this in order to get that"). It is an environmentally created reason to initiate or persist in an action. Extrinsic motivation is a means to an end—the means is the behavior and the end is some consequence. Children who study hard for school may do so out of a desire to make a good grade, earn a sticker, or please their parents. In these examples, the extrinsic motivation to work hard is socially engineered—the desired end is the grade, sticker, or approval, and working hard in school just happens to be the means by which the end is attained.

Often, intrinsically and extrinsically motivated behaviors look precisely the same. Just as the intrinsically motivated person reads a book, paints a picture, or goes to school or work, the extrinsically motivated person does so as well. Therefore, it is difficult to just observe someone and know whether she is intrinsically or extrinsically motivated. The essential difference between the two types of motivation lies in the source that energizes and directs the behavior. With intrinsically motivated behavior, the motivation emanates from organismic needs and spontaneous satisfaction the activity provides; with extrinsically motivated behavior, the motivation emanates from incentives and consequences made contingent on the observed behavior.

INCENTIVES AND CONSEQUENCES

The study of extrinsic motivation revolves around the language and perspective of operant conditioning. The term *operant conditioning* refers to the process by which a person learns how to operate effectively in the environment. Operating effectively in one's environment means learning and engaging in those behaviors that produce attractive consequences (e.g., gaining approval, earning money) and preventing unattractive consequences (e.g., being rejected, getting fired).

To communicate how incentives and consequences motivate behavior, proponents of operant conditioning (Baldwin & Baldwin, 1986) offer the following conceptualization of behavior:

$$S : R \rightarrow C$$

In this three-term model, *S, R,* and *C* stand for situational cue (i.e., incentive), behavioral response, and consequence, respectively. The colon between *S* and *R* shows that the situational cue sets the occasion for (but does not cause) the behavioral response. The arrow between *R* and *C* shows that the behavioral response causes a consequence (Baldwin & Baldwin, 1986). Having the attention of a group of friends (S), for instance, does not cause a storyteller to recite jokes (R), but the group does serve as a situational cue to set the occasion for storytelling (S : R). Once told, the jokes cause the friends' reactions (C), such that the telling of the jokes causes the audience's laugh or ridicule (R → C).

INCENTIVES

An incentive is an environmental event that attracts or repels a person toward or away from a particular course of action. Incentives always precede behavior (i.e., S : R), and, in doing so, they create in the person an expectation that attractive or unattractive consequences are forthcoming. Some positive incentives might include a smile, a green traffic light, the presence of friends and colleagues, an envelope that looks like it holds a check, and an icon at the bottom of a computer screen that reads "you have mail." Some negative incentives might include a grimace, a red traffic light or stop sign, the presence of enemies or competitors, an envelope that looks like junk mail, and a grinding noise from the computer that indicates it is about to crash.[1]

Incentives do not cause behavior. Instead, they affect the likelihood of whether or not a response will be initiated. The incentive is the situational cue that signals the likelihood that a behavior will or will not produce rewarding or punishing consequences, and this knowledge about a stimulus' incentive value is learned through experience. Car noises do not bring behavior-stopping fear to people until that noise has proven in the past to be a reliable predictor that disaster is right around the bend. Similarly, the sight of a particular person is not an attractive or aversive incentive until experience teaches us that this person probably brings ridicule and rejection (we learn that this person is an aversive incentive) or amusement and acceptance (we learn that this person is an attractive incentive). It is this learning process (this "conditioning") that shapes our goal-directed behavior, as positive incentives direct approach behavior while negative incentives direct avoidance behavior.

These examples might appear to confound what constitutes an incentive and what constitutes a consequence. Both are external events that direct behavior, but two important differences exist. Incentives differ from consequences on the basis of (1) when each occurs and (2) how it motivates behavior. Incentives always precede behavior (S : R), and incentives excite or inhibit the initiation of behavior. Consequences always follow behavior (R → C), and consequences increase or decrease the persistence (i.e., probability of recurrence) of behavior.

WHAT IS A REINFORCER?

From a practical point of view, defining a reinforcer is easy. It is any extrinsic event that increases behavior. From a theoretical point of view, however, the definition is more

[1] Though members of a culture share an understanding of which situational cues signal favorable and unfavorable events, it is still the case that each individual learns from his or her own unique history which events serve as positive incentives (signals of attractive events) and which events serve as negative incentives (signals of unattractive events).

difficult. Theoretically, a reinforcer must be defined in a manner that is independent from its effects on behavior. The problem with defining a reinforcer solely in terms of its effects on behavior is that its definition becomes circular: The cause produces the effect, but the effect justifies the cause (i.e., reinforcers produce behavior, but anything that increases behavior is a reinforcer). If the only way to identify a reinforcer is to actually give the reinforcer and wait to see if it increases behavior, then researchers and practitioners have no means of identifying a reinforcer before using it. The challenge is therefore to know ahead of time what reinforcer will work—that is, what will increase behavior (Timberlake & Farmer-Dougan, 1991). And the challenge is to explain why the reinforcer will work: Why would anyone expect this external event to increase another person's behavior? To get out of this circular quagmire, the researcher needs to select an extrinsic event never used before on a particular person (e.g., candy bar, field trip to the zoo) and know a priori whether it will or will not increase the sought-after desired behavior.

In the history of motivation research, each of the following noncircular definitions of what constitutes a positive reinforcer has been offered: (1) a stimulus that decreases drive (e.g., food increases behavior because it decreases hunger; Hull, 1943); (2) a stimulus that decreases arousal (e.g., a drug increases behavior because it tranquilizes anxiety; Berlyne, 1967); (3) a stimulus that increases arousal (e.g., a rock concert increases behavior because it stimulates and excites; Zuckerman, 1979); (4) an attractive environmental object (e.g., money increases behavior because people have learned the attractiveness of money; Skinner, 1938); (5) hedonically pleasurable brain stimulation (e.g., electrical stimulation of the medial forebrain bundle produces high rates of response because it is a pleasurable sensation; Olds, 1969); (6) the opportunity to perform a high-frequency behavior (e.g., opportunity to watch television increases one's willingness for chores; Premack, 1959); and (7) the opportunity to perform a prohibited behavior (e.g., talking is especially reinforcing after being made to keep quiet for a while; Timberlake, 1980; Timberlake & Allison, 1974). The advantage of these definitions of a reinforcer, as compared to the "anything that increases behavior" definition, is that the researcher, by knowing the stimulus's effect on one of the seven effects listed above, knows the stimulus will increase behavior. These alternative definitions have the virtue of being able to explain *why* the stimulus will increase behavior.

From a more practical perspective, consider one study that used various potential reinforcers to encourage an 8-year-old to wear an orthodontic device (Hall et al., 1972). The parents observed that the child had little intrinsic motivation to wear the device, so they sought to create in the child an extrinsic motivation to wear the gear. As shown in Figure 5.2, the parents kept track of the percentage of time their child wore the orthodontic device (five observations per day at random times, such as at breakfast, when leaving for school, just before bedtime). In the first week of observation (with no positive reinforcer), the child wore the device 25% of the time. The parents then began to praise the child each time they saw the orthodontic gear being worn. With praise, the child wore the gear 36% of the time. For the next two weeks, the parents administered a delayed monetary reward for wearing the orthodontic device. Each time the parents saw the child wearing the gear, they promised 25 cents at the end of the month. With money on the line, the child wore the gear 60% of the time. For a two-week period, the parents next administered an immediate, on-the-spot, 25-cent reward for any observed compliance. Wearing the gear zoomed to 97%. For the next five days, the child received no positive reinforcers for

FIGURE 5.2 Effect of Reinforcement on Use of Orthodontic Device

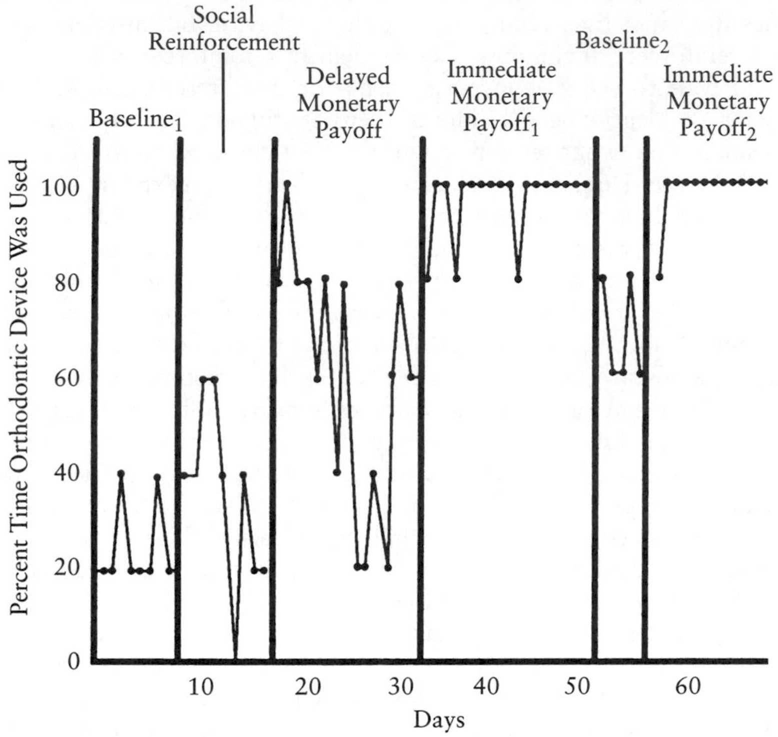

SOURCE: From "Modification of Behavior Problems in the Home With a Parent as Observer and Experimenter," by R. V. Hall, S. Axelrod, L. Tyler, E. Grief, F. C. Jones, and R. Robertson, 1972, *Journal of Applied Behavior Analysis, 5,* pp. 53–64. Copyright 1972 by the Journal of Applied Behavior Analysis. Reprinted with permission.

compliance. Wearing dropped to 64%. Finally, for two weeks, the parents reintroduced the immediate 25-cent reward, and the child's compliance returned to 100%.

This study highlights two important considerations in the attempt to understand the nature of reinforcers. First, reinforcers vary in their quality. In the preceding example, money worked better than praise. Second, the immediacy at which a reinforcer is delivered partly determines its effectiveness. Money given immediately was more effective than the same amount of money promised at some time in the future. In addition, four other characteristics determine what is or is not a reinforcer. First, a reinforcer can be effective for one person but not for another, suggesting that the person/reinforcer fit is as important as is any particular characteristic of the reinforcer per se. Attention and candy might prove effective for young children (and ineffective for adults), whereas a job promotion and stock options might prove effective for adults (and ineffective for young children). Second, the same reinforcer can be effective for a person at one time but ineffective at another time. A cup of coffee might increase behavior early in the morning, but it may prove ineffective several hours later. Third, reinforcers vary in their intensity. Money is typically an effective reinforcer but only if considered to exceed some threshold of intensity. If only a penny is given as a reinforcer, it is typically not effective as a reinforcer. Lastly, the rewards that administrators (e.g., parents, teachers, employers, therapists, coaches) expect to increase behavior often do not correspond to what their recipients actually find to be reinforcing (Green et al., 1988; Pace et al., 1985; Smith, Iwata, & Shore, 1995). For example, a parent might give a child a big hug, thinking the child highly values hugging, though the child might rather have a bowl of chocolate pudding. Thus, six considerations determine a positive reinforcer's effectiveness: (1) its quality; (2) its immediacy; (3) the person/reinforcer fit; (4) the recipient's need for that particular reward; (5) its intensity; and (6) the recipient's perceived value of the reinforcer.

CONSEQUENCES

There are two types of consequences: reinforcers and punishers. And there are two types of reinforcers (positive and negative) and two types of punishers (positive and negative).

Positive Reinforcers

A positive reinforcer is any environmental stimulus that, when presented, increases the probability that the behavior that produced this stimulus will recur in the future. Approval, paychecks, and trophies operate as positive reinforcers that occur after saying thank you, working a 40-hour week, and practicing athletic skills. What makes the approval, paycheck, or trophy a positive reinforcer is its capacity to increase the probability that the behaviors of being polite, working hard, or practicing for hours will recur in the future. That is, the person who receives the positive reinforcer becomes more likely to repeat the behavior than is the person who receives no such attractive consequence for the same behavior. Similarly, if giving a child a trophy for athletic participation increases the child's future athletic participation, then the trophy is a positive reinforcer. External consequences that most of us find rewarding (and therefore increase the probability of the behavior that produced these consequences) include money, praise, attention, grades, scholarships, approval, prizes, food, awards, trophies, public recognition, and privileges.

Negative Reinforcers

A negative reinforcer is any environmental stimulus that, when removed, increases the probability that the behavior that removed this stimulus will recur in the future. Like positive reinforcers, negative reinforcers increase the probability of behavior. Unlike positive reinforcers, negative reinforcers are aversive, irritating stimuli. The shrill ring of the alarm clock is an aversive, irritating stimulus. Stopping the ringing is negatively reinforcing when it increases the probability that the would-be sleeper gets out of bed. In the same way, medicine that removes headache pain is a negative reinforcer that increases the sufferer's willingness to take this same medicine in the future (i.e., removing pain negatively reinforces the act of taking headache medicine). Some external events that most of us find negatively reinforcing (and therefore increase the probability of the behavior that

FIGURE 5.3 **Front and Rear View of Person Wearing Postural Harness**

The front view in the upper sketch shows the signal component worn around the neck. A wire runs from the component, under the arm, and to the posture switch on the back, which is shown in the lower sketch. The posture switch is attached by the shoulder straps, which are adjusted for the desired posture. Outer garments are worn over the assembly and thereby conceal it from view.

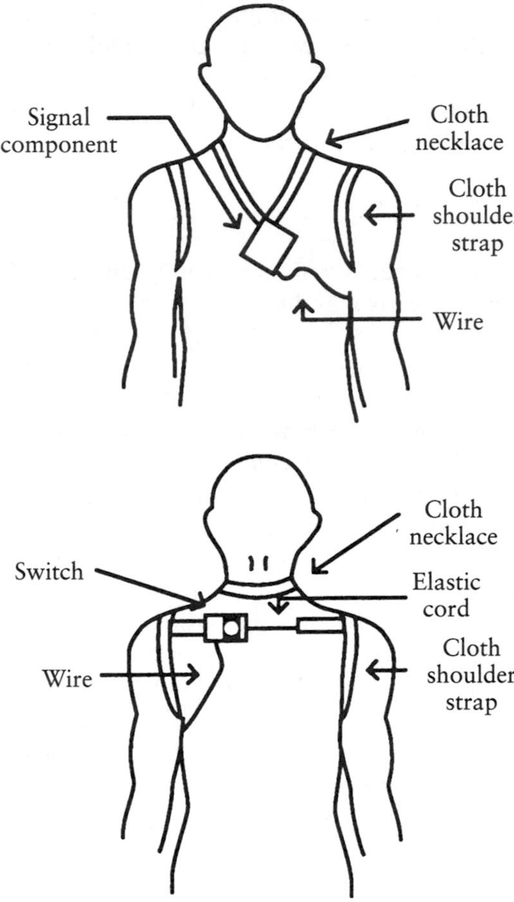

SOURCE: From "Behavioral Engineering: Postural Control by a Portable Operant Apparatus," by N. H. Azrin, H. Rubin, F. O'Brien, T. Ayllon, and D. Roll, 1968, *Journal of Applied Behavior Analysis, 2,* pp. 39–42. Copyright 1968 by the Journal of Applied Behavior Analysis. Reprinted with permission.

removed these events) include whining, crying, and nagging by a child, surveillance, deadlines or time limits, a pet's incessant meowing or barking, all sorts of pain, and worrisome noises that come from under the hood of our car.

It is relatively easy to visualize the approach behavior motivated by positive reinforcers. But a couple of examples will help illustrate how negative reinforcers motivate escape and avoidance behaviors. Escape removes a person from the aversive stimulus;

avoidance prevents the aversive stimulus from occurring in the first place (Iwata, 1987). Consider how people escape from the sound of the alarm clock by getting out of bed, escape from the car buzzer by buckling a seat belt, and escape from the whining child by leaving the room. Once we discover which behaviors are effective in removing us from the alarm, buzzer, or whining, we tend to repeat these same escape maneuvers when the alarm, buzzer, or whining return. To prevent the aversive stimuli from occurring in the first place, however, people learn to get out of bed early to avoid the alarm, to buckle up before starting the car to avoid the buzzer, and to stay away from the child to avoid hearing the whines. Escape behaviors are reactive; avoidance behaviors are proactive.

One illustration that nicely captures how a negative reinforcer motivates escape and avoidance behaviors is the wearing of a postural harness (Azrin et al., 1968), shown in Figure 5.3. An automated shoulder harness to discourage postural slouching sends off a 55-dB tone whenever slouching at the shoulders occurs. Slouching sets off the aversive tone. To escape it, the wearer must adjust his posture accordingly. Noise termination negatively reinforces the escape behavior of thrusting back the shoulder blades. To avoid hearing the tone, the wearer must maintain correct posture by keeping his shoulders thrust backward. The motivation stems not from wanting good posture but, rather, from not wanting to hear that irritating blast of noise. For all 25 adults using such a postural harness in one study, a marked improvement in posture occurred. The postural harness (like a crying baby or a yelling drill sergeant) communicates a nice metaphor for illustrating extrinsic motivation, as the source of motivation (the signal box and its 55-dB noisemaker) clearly lies outside the individual—literally on him rather than in him.

Punishers

A punisher is any environmental stimulus that, when presented, decreases the probability that the behavior that produced this stimulus will recur in the future. Criticism, jail terms, and public ridicule operate as punishers that occur after dressing sloppily, stealing another person's property, and endorsing antisocial attitudes. What makes the criticism, a jail term, or public ridicule a punisher is its capacity to decrease the probability that the behaviors of careless dressing, stealing property, and voicing antisocial attitudes in public will recur in the future (i.e., the person who receives the punisher is less likely to repeat the behavior than is the person who receives no such aversive consequence for doing the same thing). Similarly, if a dog bite makes it less likely that a person will pet a dog on his next encounter with a dog, then the bite is a punisher that suppresses dog petting. A traffic ticket for parking in a handicapped parking space, a reprimand for staying out past curfew, and a harsh look for suggesting intimate behaviors are examples of punishers if the parking, staying out late, and intimate suggestions are subsequently suppressed.

Some potential confusion exists in discriminating punishers from negative reinforcers because both are aversive stimuli, as when parents reprimand children for not cleaning their room. The reprimand is a punisher if its intent is to suppress behavior (e.g., suppress the child's cluttering of the room). The reprimand is a negative reinforcer, however, if the child cleans the room to escape from or avoid the reprimand before it occurs. Punishers decrease (undesirable) behavior; negative reinforcers increase (escape and avoidance) behavior.

FIGURE 5.4 **Valence of Consequence as Function of Stimulus Presentation or Removal**

	Valence of Consequence: Positive	Valence of Consequence: Negative
Stimulus Presented	Positive Reinforcement	Punishment
Stimulus Removed	Punishment	Negative Reinforcement

SOURCE: Based on *Behavior Modification in Applied Settings,* rev. ed., by A. E. Kazdin, 1980, Pacific Grove, CA: Dorsey Press. Copyright 1975 and 1980 by the Dorsey Press. Used with the permission of Brooks/Cole Publishing Corp., Pacific Grove, CA.

When most people think of punishers, what comes to mind are negative punishers. All negative punishers involve the administration of an aversive stimulus for suppressing future behavior. But there is a second type of punisher—a positive punisher. Positive punishers involve the removal of positive consequences for suppressing future behavior. Punishment via removal of positive consequences constitutes essentially a time-out from positive reinforcers. Examples include a suspended driver's license to suppress drunk driving, a toy being taken away from a child to suppress a temper tantrum, or a child being sent to bed without the privilege of watching a favorite television show. For reference, Figure 5.4 provides a matrix to organize the four behavioral consequences discussed. Consequences can be pleasant or aversive, and they can be given or removed. As summarized in Figure 5.4, giving a pleasant stimulus to increase behavior is a positive reinforcer, giving an aversive stimulus to decrease behavior is a negative punisher, removing a pleasant stimulus to decrease behavior is a positive punisher, and removing an aversive stimulus to increase behavior is a negative reinforcer.

HIDDEN COSTS OF REWARD

The research on intrinsic and extrinsic motivation began with an interesting and practical question: "If a person is involved in an intrinsically interesting activity and begins to receive an extrinsic reward for doing it, what happens to his or her intrinsic motivation for that activity?" (Deci & Ryan, 1985a, p. 43). For example, what happens to the motivation of the student who reads for the fun of it after she begins to receive money from her parents for reading? One might suppose that rewarding reading behavior with a monetary prize would add to the person's motivation. Common sense seems to argue that if a person enjoys reading and is also rewarded for it, then the intrinsic (enjoyment) and the extrinsic (money) motivations should sum to produce an increased motivation to read. And if you ask people to make predictions about what would happen to a person's motivation under these conditions, increased motivation is what most people will predict (Hom, 1994).

Increased motivation, however, does not always occur. Rather, the imposition of an extrinsic reward for an intrinsically interesting activity often undermines (has a negative effect on) future intrinsic motivation (Condry, 1977; Deci, Koestner, & Ryan, 1999a; Kohn, 1993; Lepper, Greene, & Nisbett, 1973). The reward's adverse effect on intrinsic motivation is termed the "hidden cost of reward" (Lepper & Greene, 1978) because our society typically regards rewards as positive and universally beneficial contributors to motivation (Boggiano, et al., 1987). People use rewards expecting to gain the benefit of increasing another person's behavior, but in doing so, they incur the hidden cost of undermining that person's intrinsic motivation toward the activity.

Extrinsic rewards can have positive effects on motivation and behavior, as discussed earlier with the seat belt, the straight posture, and the orthodontic gear examples. But extrinsic rewards and controls yield hidden costs as well. The concept of self-determination (chapter 4) provides one way for understanding the hidden costs of reward (Deci & Ryan, 1987). When experimental participants are paid (Deci, 1972), promised an award (Lepper, Greene, & Nisbett 1973), promised a toy (Lepper & Greene, 1975), threatened with a punisher (Deci & Casio, 1972), given a deadline (Amabile, DeJong, & Lepper, 1976), or watched over as they work (i.e., surveillance; Pittman et al., 1980), these participants gradually lose their perception of self-determination and show decreased intrinsic motivation. In other words, a person's perceived locus of causality (chapter 4) gradually becomes less internal and more external (deCharms, 1984). Basically, coercing individuals to engage in a task, even when using wonderfully attractive bribes like money, instigates a shift in their understanding of why they choose to engage in that task from one of self-determination to one of reward-determination, from origin to pawn, and from an internal to an external perceived locus of causality.

Early experiments by Mark Lepper and his colleagues nicely illustrate the hidden costs of extrinsic rewards (Greene & Lepper, 1974; Lepper & Greene, 1975, 1978; Lepper, Greene, & Nisbett, 1973). Preschool children with a high interest in drawing were grouped into one of three experimental conditions: expected reward, no reward, and unexpected reward. In the expected reward group (extrinsic motivational orientation), children were shown an extrinsic reward—an attractive Good Player certificate featuring the child's name and a big blue ribbon—and asked if they wanted to draw in order to win the reward. In the no reward group (intrinsic motivational orientation), children were simply asked if they wanted to draw. In the unexpected reward group, children were asked if they wanted to draw, but they unexpectedly received the Good Player certificate after drawing. One week later, the experimenters provided the children with another opportunity to draw at their choice. During this week, children who initially drew in order to win the certificate (expected reward group) spent significantly less time drawing than did children in the other two groups. In effect, children in the expected reward group lost their intrinsic interest in drawing. The no reward and unexpected reward groups showed no such interest decline. The interest maintenance of the unexpected reward group is important because it shows that the extrinsic motivational orientation (rather than the reward per se) was the causal agent that decreased the children's interest in drawing. It was not the reward that undermined interest, but rather, it was the "in order to" contingency between "what you do" and "what you get" that undermined self-determination and shifted perceived locus of causality from internal to external.

In interpreting these findings, one might feel a bit of skepticism and muse over the fact that the sample included preschoolers, the experimental task was drawing, and the reward was a certificate. Perhaps one might then conclude that the findings probably have little to do with more complex adult motivations. These findings, however, have been replicated using adults, using different tasks, and using different rewards (see Deci, Koestner, & Ryan, 1999a). In accepting the generality of the negative effects (i.e., "the hidden costs") of an extrinsic motivational orientation (Deci et al., 1999a; Deci & Ryan, 1985a; Kohn, 1993; Lepper & Greene, 1978; Rummel & Feinberg, 1988; Sutherland, 1993), one might turn the tables and ask whether rewards always decrease intrinsic motivation. This is precisely what psychologists questioned next. After three decades of research, the conclusion is that extrinsic rewards *do* generally undermine intrinsic motivation, but not always (Deci et al., 1999a; Eisenberger, Pierce, & Cameron, 1999; Rummel & Feinberg, 1988; Wiersma, 1992). In particular, two factors explain which rewards decrease intrinsic motivation: expectancy and tangibility.

HIDDEN COSTS OF EXPECTED AND TANGIBLE REWARDS

Expected Rewards

People typically engage in behaviors in order to receive a reward. And these people generally will engage in a particular behavior when they are aware of the reward to be received. If, however, the person engages in the behavior with no such knowledge of a reward yet still receives a reward once the task is completed, then the reward is an unexpected one. The earlier study with children drawing for Good Player certificates (Lepper et al., 1973) showed that reinforcers decrease intrinsic motivation only when the person expects that her task engagement will end with the receipt of a reward. The telltale sign that a person expects a reward for task participation is an if-then or in-order-to orientation, such as, "If I read this book, then I can watch TV." Expected rewards undermine intrinsic motivation, while unexpected rewards do not (Greene & Lepper, 1974; Orlick & Mosher, 1978; Pallak et al., 1982).

Tangible Rewards

A second factor in understanding which rewards undermine intrinisic motivation and which do not is the distinction between tangible and verbal rewards. Tangible rewards, such as money, awards, and food, tend to decrease intrinsic motivation, whereas verbal (i.e., intangible) rewards, such as praise, do not (Anderson, Manoogian, & Reznick, 1976; Blank, Reis, & Jackson, 1984; Cameron & Pierce, 1994; Deci, 1972; Dollinger & Thelen, 1978; Kast & Connor, 1988; Koestner, Zuckerman, & Koestner, 1987; Sansone, 1989; Swann & Pittman, 1977). In other words, rewards that one can see, touch, feel, and taste generally decrease intrinsic motivation, whereas verbal, symbolic, or abstract rewards do not.

IMPLICATIONS OF THE HIDDEN COSTS OF REWARDS

The above-described limiting factors regarding expectancy and tangibility suggest that rewards decrease intrinsic motivation only when they are expected or tangible. This conclusion is a sort of good news/bad news message. The good news is that extrinsic rewards can be used in a way that does not put intrinsic motivation at risk. The bad news is that our society so often relies on expected and tangible rewards to motivate others. Money, bonuses, paychecks, prizes, trophies, scholarships, privileges, grades, gold stars, awards, honor-roll lists, incentive plans, recognition, food, frequent-flyer miles, and so on are ubiquitous incentives and consequences in Western societies (Kohn, 1993). In practice, therefore, it is not so comforting to say that only expected and tangible extrinsic rewards will decrease intrinsic motivation because so many rewards are presented in an expected and tangible way.

Expected, tangible rewards also put more at risk than just intrinsic motivation (Condry, 1977, 1987; Deci & Ryan, 1987; Kohn, 1993). Extrinsic reinforcers not only decrease intrinsic motivation, they also interfere with both the process and quality of learning. During information processing, extrinsic rewards distract attention away from learning and toward its product (i.e., toward getting the reward). Rewards shift the learner's goals away from attaining mastery in favor of attaining extrinsic gain. Compared to those who are intrinsically motivated, extrinsically motivated individuals choose to engage in easy tasks because these tasks maximize the probability of a quick reward (Harter, 1978b; Pittman, Boggiano, & Ruble, 1983; Shapira, 1976). Extrinsically motivated learners are also more prone to a negative emotional tone (e.g., frustration; Garbarino, 1975) and less prone to positive emotion (e.g., enjoyment; Harter, 1978b; Ryan & Connell, 1989; Skinner & Belmont, 1993). Further, extrinsically motivated learners are relatively passive information processors (Benware & Deci, 1984).

Rewards interfere with the quality of learning by narrowing one's attention on focusing on rote factual information at the expense of conceptual understanding (Benware & Deci, 1984; Boggiano et al., 1993; Flink, Boggiano, & Barrett, 1990). Rewards further put at risk a learner's flexibility in her way of thinking and problem solving (as she tries to produce a right answer quickly rather than discover an optimal solution; McGraw & McCullers, 1979). Rewards also undermine creativity (Amabile, 1985; Amabile, Hennessey, & Grossman, 1986), as people are more creative when they draw and write out of interest than when they draw and write for rewards. And when rewards are involved, learners typically quit as soon as some reward criterion is attained (e.g., reading only the 100 pages required for the test). When rewards are not involved, learners generally persist until curiosity is satisfied, interest is exhausted, or mastery is attained (Condry, 1977; Condry & Chambers, 1978). Thus, not only is intrinsic motivation potentially at risk with the use of expected and tangible rewards, but the learning processes (e.g., attention, preference for challenge, emotional tone, active information processing, cognitive flexibility, and creativity) and the learning quality (e.g., conceptual understanding) are also at risk.

A final point is that rewards interfere with the development of self-regulation (Lepper, 1983; Ryan, 1993). When the social environment tells people what to do and also provides expected and tangible rewards for taking that action, people have little difficulty regulating their behavior in rewarding ways. But schools, families, places of work, and other settings often value self-regulation (i.e., initiative, autonomy, intrinsic motivation). Learning to depend on rewards can forestall the development of self-regulatory abilities.

POSITIVE NOTE ON EXTRINSIC MOTIVATION

In recognition of the fact that rewards sometimes undermine intrinsic motivation, interfere with learning, and forestall self-regulation, researchers have tried to use rewards in ways that minimize the detrimental effects of the rewards. One way to do this, as discussed earlier, is to use rewards that are unexpected and verbal (e.g., praise) and refrain from those that are expected and tangible (e.g., bribes). A second means is to limit the use of extrinsic motivators to tasks that have social importance but very little intrinsic appeal. That is, if a person has little or no intrinsic motivation to engage in a task in the first place, then intrinsic motivation is not likely to be put at risk by extrinsic rewards (because there is little or no intrinsic motivation present in the person to undermine).

To borrow a phrase from a popular movie, extrinsic motivators have their "dark side." But extrinsic motivators have their benefits as well. Rewards can make an otherwise uninteresting task seem suddenly worth pursuing. So long as the reward is attractive enough, rewarded individuals will engage in almost any task. Children will eagerly wash dishes if it means that doing so will gain them a new toy. This is typically not so with unrewarded children. Without a reward at stake, those dishes stay piled in the sink. The dishes remain unwashed because the person engages in the task only on the basis of its intrinsic appeal, which is quite low. Consider the value of extrinsic motivators in the following instances in which researchers used rewards to increase socially important but intrinsically uninteresting tasks:

- developing daily living skills, such as dressing (Pierce & Schreibman, 1994)
- teaching severely nearsighted children to wear contact lenses (Mathews et al., 1992)
- preventing drunk driving (Geller, Altomari, & Russ, 1984)
- eating foods that can inhibit seizures (Amari, Grace, & Fisher, 1995)
- participating in recycling (Brothers, 1994; Austira et al., 1993)
- motivating young children to start their homework (Miller & Kelley, 1994)
- teaching autistic children to initiate peer conversations (Krantz & McClannahan, 1993)
- preventing antisocial behaviors such as biting and poking (Fisher et al., 1993)

In each of these examples, an argument can be made that the society's concerns for promoting desirable behavior from its citizens outweighs the concerns for preserving or protecting the individual's intrinsic motivation. That is, the positive motivational effects of rewards (increase positive behavior) can outweigh their negative effects (undermine intrinsic motivation), at least under some conditions (when interest is already dismally low) and within one particular ideological way of thinking about motivation (e.g., acceptable in behaviorism, unacceptable in humanism).

Therefore, is it good to use extrinsic motivators when another person's intrinsic motivation is low? Not necessarily. Consider the following five reasons for not using extrinsic motivators for even intrinsically uninteresting endeavors (Kohn, 1993):

1. Extrinsic motivators still undermine the quality of performance and interfere with the process of learning.
2. Extrinsic motivators still undermine the individual's long-term capacity for autonomous self-regulation.
3. It is naive to presume that one person can predetermine what another will find intrinsically interesting or uninteresting.
4. Using rewards distracts attention away from asking the hard question of why ask another person to do an uninteresting task in the first place.
5. There are better ways to encourage participation than extrinsic bribery (e.g., consider autonomy-supportive environments).

When all is said and done, many people believe that extrinsic motivators simply carry too high a psychological cost in terms of intrinsic motivation, the process of learning, the quality of learning, and autonomous self-regulation. But such a conclusion turns out to be more of the beginning of the story on extrinsic motivators than it does the end of the story, as you will see in the next section on cognitive evaluation theory.

COGNITIVE EVALUATION THEORY

When people use external events as incentives and consequences, they generally seek to create in themselves or in others an extrinsic motivation for engaging in that activity. Much of the spirit behind the use of an extrinsic motivator is therefore to control behavior. Sometimes the attempt to control is obvious (e.g., using money to bribe a child to wear orthodontic gear; see Figure 5.2), but other times it is more seductive (e.g., giving free soft drinks at a bar to anyone agreeing to be a designated driver; Brigham, Maier, & Goodner, 1995). Thus, part of the purpose of implementing almost any extrinsic motivator is to control another person's behavior—that is, to increase some desirable behavior or to decrease some undesirable behavior. But there is a second purpose because incentives and consequences also provide feedback that informs the person about her competence at the task. Rewards such as money, awards, good grades, academic scholarships, and verbal praises not only function to increase behavior (i.e., control behavior), but they also function to communicate a message of a job well done (i.e., inform competence).

Cognitive evaluation theory asserts that *all* external events have both a controlling aspect and an informational aspect (Deci & Ryan, 1985a). The theory presumes that people have organismic needs for self-determination and competence (chapter 4) and that the external event's controlling aspect relates to the need for self-determination whereas its informational aspect relates to the need for competence. More formally, cognitive evaluation theory exists as a set of three propositions, which appear in Table 5.1.

TABLE 5.1 **Cognitive Evaluation Theory**

Proposition 1

External events relevant to the initiation and regulation of behavior will affect a person's intrinsic motivation to the extent that these events influence the perceived locus of causality (PLOC) for that behavior. Events that promote a more external PLOC will undermine intrinsic motivation, whereas those that promote a more internal PLOC will enhance intrinsic motivation.

Proposition 2

External events will affect a person's intrinsic motivation for an optimally challenging activity to the extent that these events influence the person's perceived competence within the context of some self-determination. Events that promote greater perceived competence will enhance intrinsic motivation, whereas those that diminish perceived competence will decrease intrinsic motivation.

Proposition 3

Events relevant to the initiation and regulation of behavior have three potential aspects, each with a functional significance. The informational aspect facilitates an internal PLOC and perceived competence, thus enhancing intrinsic motivation. The controlling aspect facilitates an external PLOC, thus undermining intrinsic motivation and promoting extrinsic compliance or defiance. The amotivating aspect facilitates perceived incompetence, thus undermining intrinsic motivation and promoting amotivation. The relative salience of these three aspects to a person determines the functional significance of the event.

SOURCE: From *Intrinsic Motivation and Self-Determination in Human Behavior*, by E. L. Deci and R. M. Ryan, 1985a, New York: Plenum.

Propositions 1 and 2 repeat two themes expressed in chapter 4. According to Proposition 1, external events that promote an internal perceived locus of causality (PLOC) promote intrinsic motivation because these events involve or satisfy the need for self-determination. External events that promote an external PLOC promote extrinsic motivation because these events neglect the need for self-determination and instead establish an if-then contingency between behavior consequence. Hence, the more an event is presented in a noncontrolling way, the more likely it is to promote self-determination, an internal PLOC, and intrinsic motivation; the more an event is presented in a controlling way, the more likely it is to undermine self-determination, promote an external PLOC, and increase extrinsic motivation.

According to Proposition 2, events that increase perceived competence promote intrinsic motivation, whereas events that decrease perceived competence undermine this motivation. Hence, the more an external event communicates positive effectance information, the more likely it is to satisfy the need for competence and increase intrinsic motivation; the more an external event communicates negative effectance information, the more likely it is to frustrate the need for competence and decrease intrinsic motivation. The contribution that the first two propositions offer for understanding the motivational significance of incentives and consequences is that they focus attention not only on how an extrinsic event affects behavior but, in addition, on how it affects people's organismic psychological needs.

Proposition 3 ties together the first two propositions into a full theoretical statement. According to Proposition 3, the relative salience of whether an event is mostly controlling or mostly informational determines its effects on intrinsic and extrinsic motivation. When an extrinsic event is presented in a relatively controlling way, it effectively undermines intrinsic motivation (via its effects on self-determination) and promotes extrinsic motivation. When an extrinsic event is presented in a relatively informational way, it effectively increases intrinsic motivation (via its effect on competence) rather than extrinsic motivation. It is in Proposition 3 that the usefulness of cognitive evaluation theory becomes apparent. The utility of cognitive evaluation theory is that the reader can use its propositions to predict the effect that any extrinsic event will have on intrinsic and extrinsic motivations.

Two Examples of Controlling and Informational Events: Praise and Competition

Any external event—for instance, praise, money, grades in school, a scholarship, surveillance, a deadline, or interpersonal competition—can be administered in a relatively controlling or relatively informational way. A supervisor using praise, for instance, might communicate in a controlling way, saying, "Excellent job, you did just as you should." The supervisor might, however, communicate in an informational way, saying, "Excellent job, your productivity increased by 10%." Tagging phrases such as "you should," "you must," "you have to," and "you ought to" onto the praise gives the feedback a tone of pressure (Ryan, 1982). In contrast, providing clear, specific, and competence-diagnosing feedback typically gives praise a highly informative function (Brophy, 1981). For example, the praise, "Excellent job, I noticed that you greeted the customer warmly and with a sincere tone in your voice," speaks informatively to an employee's sense of competence in a way that a simple and vague, "Excellent job," does not. The conclusion is that the motivational effect is not in the praise per se but is instead in the way a person administers the praise (Deci & Ryan, 1985a); is it used to control behavior or to inform competence (e.g, "Predicting How Any External Event Will Affect Motivation" box).

A second illustration of how the same external event can be experienced as either a relatively controlling or relatively informational event is interpersonal competition (Olson, 1985; Reeve & Deci, 1996). Under some conditions, people experience competition as a relatively controlling event. When the social context puts a good deal of pressure on winning (with its evaluative audience, coaches, peers, newspaper reporters, championship trophies, career implications), competitors usually compete with a sense of contingency, pressure, and a sense of doing the work for others. When experienced in such a controlling way, competition decreases intrinsic motivation because competitors care relatively little about the task itself and relatively much about the reward of winning (Deci, et al., 1981; Vallerand, Gauvin, & Halliwell, 1986). The point of the competition ceases to be about the game or sport but, instead, becomes about winning. But all competitions are not necessarily embedded in a controlling context, and sometimes competitors really do just play a game of basketball or a game of checkers, for instance. When the social context places little emphasis on winning (recreational competition, no audience present, no trophy or scholarship for winning, an autonomy-supportive versus controlling coach), then competition's informational aspect can emerge as relatively more salient. Through its outcome and through competitors' perceptions of making progress in their skills, competitive situations can provide a useful arena for sending a message of competence to competitors. As you might expect (based on Proposition 2 in cognitive evaluation theory), winning

Predicting How Any External Event Will Affect Motivation

Question: Why would a person want to learn about the motivational states discussed in this chapter?

Answer: So that he can predict, in advance and with high accuracy, what effect *any* external event will have on his motivation.

When teachers put stickers on children's homework, they hope that the stickers will motivate the child to work hard. When employers give end-of-the-year holiday bonuses to workers, they hope the money will motivate the workers to work hard.

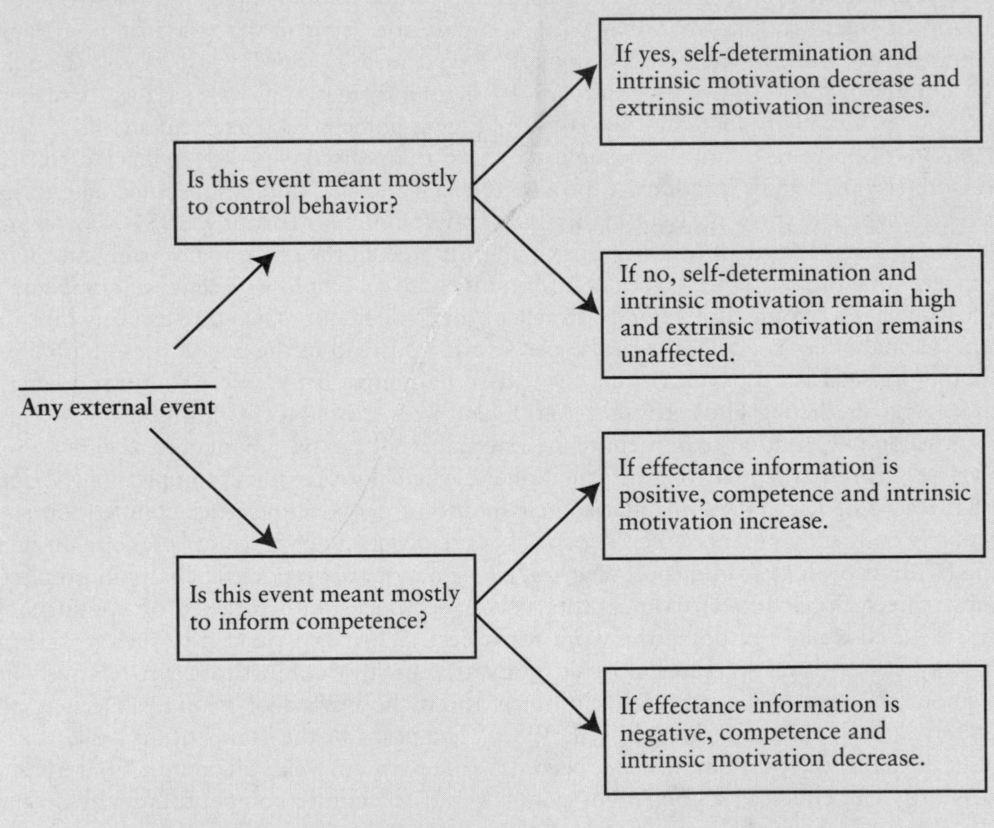

increases intrinsic motivation, while losing decreases it (Reeve, Olson, & Cole, 1985). It is, however, the perception of high competence, rather than the reward of winning per se, that increases intrinsic motivation (McAuley & Tammen, 1989). But when the interpersonal competition focuses highly on winning, then the message of high competence gets

And when street panhandlers wash the windows of a person's car, they hope that person will give them some money. People often use extrinsic motivators without really knowing what effect they will have on others. The logic is: since stickers, money, and favors are good, the person's motivation will probably respond in a positive way. But theories of motivation find that *how* something is given is at least as important as is *what* is given. A sincere pat on the back can enhance motivation even more than can a big fat check with a bunch of strings attached to it.

Understanding how any external event affects another person's motivation is the domain of cognitive evaluation theory. The theory can be articulated in the accompanying flow chart at left.

To make sense of the figure, first write in the blank line on the left of the figure any external event. A teacher, for instance, might be interested in the motivational effects of external events like grades, praise, tests, or deadlines. Next, working from left to right of the figure, determine the external event's functional significance. Is the external event being used to control behavior, or is it being used to inform competence? In particular, which of these two aspects is the relatively more salient one? Is the purpose behind the event (i.e., its "functional significance") mostly about control or mostly about communicating information?

If the external event is used largely to control behavior, then its motivational effect will be to decrease self-determination, decrease intrinsic motivation, and increase extrinsic motivation. If the external event is not used to control behavior, then it will not decrease self-determination, not decrease intrinsic motivation, and not increase extrinsic motivation. If the external event is used to inform competence and a job well done, then its motivational effect will be to increase competence and increase intrinsic motivation. When the external event communicates a job poorly done, however, its motivational effect will be to decrease competence and decrease intrinsic motivation.

Notice that in predicting how any external event will affect another person's motivation, the critical question is not what the external event is, but rather, how one person administers it to another.

overwhelmed by the message of pressure. In fact, winning in a controlling context does not increase intrinsic motivation because its controlling aspect is so detrimental to self-determination that the competence message loses its salience (Reeve & Deci, 1996). Thus, for intrinsic motivation to flourish, both competence and self-determination must be

TABLE 5.2 Motivational Effects of Rewards When Administered for Three Different Purposes

PURPOSE OF THE REWARD	DEFINITION, WITH AN EXAMPLE		Effects on* SD	C	IM	EM	ILLUSTRATIVE REFERENCE
Task-noncontingent	Reward given in exchange for mere participation, irrespective of what the person actually does.		o	o	o	o	Okano (1981)
	Example: Salary for spending time at the car dealership.						Harackiewicz (1979)
Task-contingent	Reward given in exchange for actually doing the task. *Example*: Paid money for each customer attended to.		↓	o	↓	↑	
Performance-contingent	Reward given in exchange for attaining a specified performance level. *Example*: Paid money for each $1,000 generated in sales.	compared to no reward at all:	↓	↑	↑↓**	↑	Ryan et al. (1983)
		compared to only positive feedback:	↓	o	↓	↑	Karniol and Ross (1977)

Notes: *SD = self-determination; C = competence; IM = intrinsic motivation; EM = extrinisic motivation; 0 = has no effect on; ↑ = increases; ↓ = decreases.
**The effect on a performance-contingent reward on intrinsic motivation depends on which of its aspects—controlling or informational—is more salient (see the text discussion).

high (Fisher, 1978), and for both competence and self-determination to be high, an external event must be presented in both a noncontrolling and informational way.

REWARD ADMINISTRATION

Cognitive evaluation theory makes it clear that the purpose for which an extrinsic motivator is given—to control behavior or to inform competence—determines its effects on motivation. Often, the purpose behind giving an incentive or consequence—why it is given in the first place—depends on the conditions under which it is given. Three different conditions under which people administer rewards to others are as categorized in Table 5.2: task-noncontingent, task-contingent, and performance-contingent (Deci & Ryan, 1985a; Deci et al., 1999a; Ryan et al., 1983). The table provides a definition for each type of reward administration, and it includes an illustrative example from one of the bastions of extrinsic motivators, the local car dealership giving rewards to its sales force. The right-hand side of the table shows how each type of reward effects perceived self-determination (SD), competence (C), intrinsic motivation (IM), and extrinsic motivation (EM). Lastly, the table includes supportive references for the reader for pursuing good examples of how each type of reward administration affects motivation.

Task-noncontingent rewards, which are given for mere presence or participation, affect neither perceived self-determination (they are not controlling) nor competence (they are not informative) and therefore affect neither intrinsic nor extrinsic motivation. These are rewards given with "no strings attached." Anytime a person receives a reward that is extraneous to doing the task at hand, the person receives a task-noncontingent reward, as might be the case when a friend brings you a soda as you work on a paper for class (i.e., the soda gift has nothing to do with whether you work on the paper or not).

Task-contingent rewards, which are given in exchange for doing what is asked, decrease perceived self-determination (they are controlling) and therefore decrease intrinsic motivation and increase extrinsic motivation. With task-contingent rewards, there is always a string attached (i.e., "If you do this, then I will reward you with that"). Perhaps your friend brings you a soda because you are working studiously on the paper. If you were not engaged in the paper or if you did not finish the paper, then you would not have received the soda (i.e., it is contingent on you doing the task).

Performance-contingent rewards, which are given for the quality of one's performance, generally decrease intrinsic motivation and increase extrinsic motivation. When compared to no rewards, performance-contingent rewards are both controlling and informational at the same time. Their effect, therefore, depends on which aspect (controlling or informational) of the performance-contingent reward is relatively more salient. When compared to positive feedback only, performance-contingent rewards undermine intrinsic motivation because performance contingency itself is experienced as controlling and thus undermines self-determination. Having a string attached to what you are asked to do, even if you do it really well, is controlling. For instance, perhaps your friend brings you a soda when you write at least 10 high-quality pages (i.e., the beverage is given contingent on attaining some performance criterion).

The utility in analyzing types of reward administration is the same lesson as expressed in cognitive evaluation theory; namely, the how and why behind the giving of the incentive or consequence is more important than what is actually given. In other words, *why* a person is given money, attention, or frequent-flyer miles is more important than *whether* that person receives either money, attention, or frequent-flyer miles.

SELF-DETERMINATION THEORY

One of the themes of motivation presented in chapter 1 was that motivation varies not only in intensity but also in its type. This chapter points out the utility in making the distinction between intrinsic and extrinsic motivations. In addition, types of extrinsic motivation exist (Rigby et al., 1992; Ryan & Deci, 2000).

Types of extrinsically motivated behaviors can be understood along the PLOC continuum, as some extrinsically motivated behaviors are clearly initiated out of an external PLOC and feature little or no self-determination (e.g., "I'm running laps around the track because the coach is yelling in my ear; if she were not here, I'd be gone"). Other extrinsically motivated behaviors are initiated out of an internal PLOC and feature a strong sense of self-determination (e.g., "I'm running laps around the track because I want to get in shape and become the best runner I can become"). The theory that explains types of extrinsic motivation is self-determination theory (Deci & Ryan, 1985a, 1991; Rigby et al., 1992).

The self-determination continuum of motivation appears in Figure 5.5. According to self-determination theory, distinct types of motivation exist and can be represented on a continuum that ranges from motivation that is not at all self-determined to motivation that is fully self-determined. On the far right-hand side, intrinsic motivation reflects the individual's full endorsement of self-determination and pertains to all those instances in which a person's organismic psychological needs generate a motivation to act. In the middle of the figure are four types of extrinsic motivation, which can be distinguished from one another on the basis of their degree of self-determination: external regulation (not at all self-determined), introjected regulation (somewhat self-determined), identified regulation (mostly self-determined), and integrated regulation (fully self-determined). On the left-hand side is amotivation, which literally means "without motivation," a state in which the person is neither intrinsically nor extrinsically motivated (e.g., a drop-out student, disillusioned athlete, or apathetic marriage partner who can find little or no value or interest in what the school, sport, or relationship has to offer).

Identifying types of motivation is important because the amount of self-determination within any motivational state has a substantial effect on what people feel, think, and do (Gottfried, 1985; Grolnick & Ryan, 1987; Ryan & Connell, 1989; Vallerand et al., 1992). For instance, school-age children were asked what motivated their academic behaviors (e.g., "Why do you try to do well in school?"), and researchers later assessed their school-related emotion, effort, and performance (Ryan & Connell, 1989). Students' reasons reflected various amounts of perceived self-determination that ranged from very little ("because it's the rule; I have to"), through a little self-determination ("because I would feel guilty if I didn't"), to much self-determination ("because it is important to me") to full self-determination ("because it's fun, I enjoy it"). The more self-determined students' motivations were, the more effort they put forth, and the more they achieved. Schoolchildren with little self-determination put forth minimal effort and achieved poorly.

These findings show the importance of making distinctions among types of extrinsic motivation, and they generalize not only to the students' motivation toward school but also to the efforts exerted by individuals in an alcohol-treatment program (Ryan et al., 1995), in a weight-loss program (Williams et al., 1996), in a relationship (Blais et al., 1990), in adhering to exercise (Ryan et al., 1997), in political participation (Koestner et al., 1996), and to religious participation (Ryan et al., 1993).

TYPES OF EXTRINSIC MOTIVATION

External Regulation

External regulation is the prototype of nonself-determined extrinsic motivation. For the person who is externally regulated, the presence versus absence of extrinsic motivators (e.g., rewards, threats) regulates the rise and fall of motivational states. A person who

FIGURE 5.5 **The Self-Determination Continuum Showing Types of Motivation With Their Regulatory Styles, Loci of Causality, and Corresponding Processes**

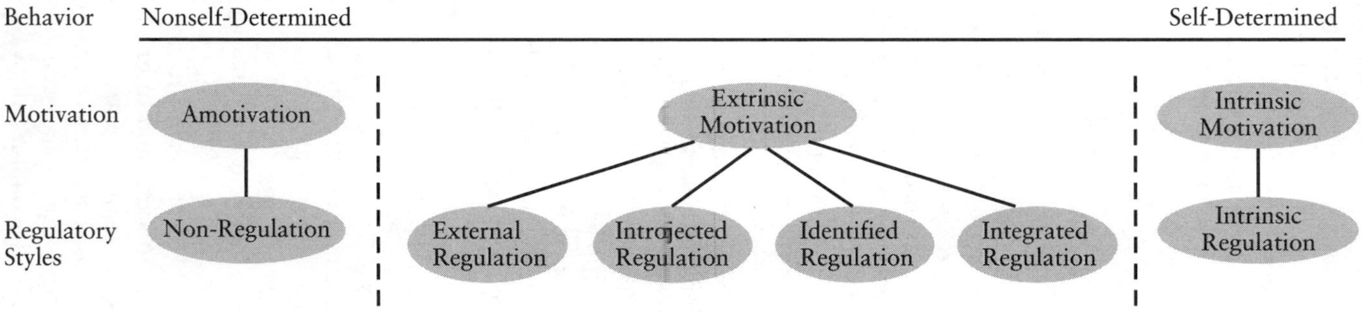

Behavior	Nonself-Determined					Self-Determined
Motivation	Amotivation	Extrinsic Motivation				Intrinsic Motivation
Regulatory Styles	Non-Regulation	External Regulation	Introjected Regulation	Identified Regulation	Integrated Regulation	Intrinsic Regulation
Perceived Locus of Causality	Impersonal	External	Somewhat External	Somewhat Internal	Internal	Internal
Relevant Regulatory Processes	Nonintentional, Nonvaluing, Incompetence, Lack of Control	Compliance, External Rewards and Punishments	Self-control, Ego-Involvement, Internal Rewards and Punishments	Personal Importance, Conscious Valuing	Congruence, Awareness, Synthesis With Self	Interest, Enjoyment, Inherent Satisfaction

SOURCE: Ryan, R. M., & Deci, E. L. (2000). Self-determination theory and the facilitation of intrinsic motivation, social development, and well-being. *American Psychologist, 55,* 68-78. Copyright 2000 by American Psychological Association. Reprinted by permission.

is externally regulated typically has a difficult time beginning a task unless there is some external prompt to do so. A student, for instance, begins to study only when a test is upcoming or begins to write a term paper only when the deadline nears. Without the test or the deadline, the student lacks the motivation necessary to study or to write. With external regulation, the person has not internalized a voluntary willingness to perform the activity for its own sake (i.e., to study, to write). With no internalization, the person simply waits for incentives and pressures in the environment to provide a reason to act. External regulation means that motivation is regulated by events external to the self.

Introjected Regulation

Introjected regulation involves taking in, but not truly accepting, other people's rules or demands for thinking, feeling, or behaving in a particular manner. Introjection represents a partial internalization of beliefs and is characterized by self- and other-approval-based pressures. In essence, the person, acting as a proxy for the external environment, emotionally rewards himself for performing other-defined good behavior and emotionally punishes himself for performing other-defined bad behavior. Therefore, internalization has occurred, but the internalization is kept at an arm's length, so to speak, instead of being really integrated into the self in an authentic and volitional way. With introjected regulation, the person carries the rules, commands, and standards of another person (or society in general) inside her head to such an extent that the internalized voice, not the self per se, generates the motivation to act. Notice, however, that introjected regulation does include the changing of internal structures because the behavior is regulated not by explicit external contingencies but rather by internalized representations of those contingencies (i.e., a parent's voice, cultural expectations). For instance, employees might come to work on time or may resist stealing office supplies not because they choose to be punctual or honest, but because being late or dishonest would produce the punishing feelings of guilt and shame, whereas being on time or honest would produce the positively reinforcing feelings of pride and approval. Introjected regulation means that motivation is regulated by a socially internalized voice.

Identified Regulation

Identified regulation represents mostly internalized extrinsic motivation. With identified regulation, the person voluntarily accepts the merits and utility of a belief or behavior because that way of thinking or behaving is seen by the self as important or useful. Thus, if a student comes to believe that extra work in mathematics is important (e.g., it has utility for a career in science) or if an athlete comes to believe that extra practice on the backhand is important (e.g., to becoming a professional tennis player, to keeping a college scholarship), the motivation to study and to practice are extrinsic but freely chosen. Extra work in mathematics or in tennis is extrinsic because these behaviors are instrumental to other aims (a career as a scientist or tennis pro), yet they are freely chosen because they are perceived to be useful and valuable for one's life. Exercise and cooperation provide two additional examples of ways for behaving that frequently arise out of identified regulation. Many people exercise religiously and cooperate freely with others not because they enjoy jogging or sharing, but because they value what such behaviors can do for them and for their relationships with others. Identified regulation, therefore, involves substantial internalization of societal norms, values, priorities, and habits to such an extent that they are integrated into and become a part of the self. Identified regulation means that motivation is regulated by values with which the self identifies.

At first glance, intrinsic motivation and identified extrinsic motivation seem similar because both feature high self-determination. But the distinction is that the regulatory process underlying identified regulation asks, "Is this activity *important*?" The regulatory process underlying intrinsic motivation asks, "Is this activity *enjoyable*?" (Deci, 1992a).

One practical implication of self-determination theory is that it highlights three different ways that exist in the attempt to motivate the self and others. The first two are extrinsic motivation (via the offering of incentives and consequences) and intrinsic motivation (via the involvement and satisfaction of organismic psychological needs). But identified regulation adds a third route to generate motivation in oneself and for others. (Introjected regulation would be a fourth means to generate motivation, but it is associated with poor adjustment and development and thus leaves little to recommend it; Ryan & Connell, 1989.) Hence, three reasons exist for engaging in a task:

1. The task is fun (intrinsic motivation).
2. The task produces an attractive consequence (extrinsic motivation).
3. The task is an important and personally useful thing to do (identified regulation).

Identified regulation gives practitioners (e.g., teachers, parents, managers) a useful alternative to extrinsic regulation on those tasks that are important but are not intrinsically motivating. For instance, on an uninteresting task, such as asking a child to rake the leaves, one might promise the child $5 (i.e., promote extrinsic motivation), or alternatively, one might have a conversation about why raking leaves is an important and useful thing to do (i.e., promote identified regulation). The benefit of identified regulation, as compared to external regulation, is that it avoids all the hidden costs of rewards. The reason identified regulation avoids the hidden costs of rewards is that it, like intrinsic motivation, preserves and supports the person's sense of self-determination (Deci, 1995; Deci & Ryan, 1991; Rigby et al., 1992).

Integrated Regulation

Integration constitutes the fourth type of extrinsic motivation (see Figure 5.5). It is the most self-determined type of extrinsic motivation. While internalization is the process of taking in a value or regulation, integration is the process through which individuals fully transform the values and regulations they take in into the self (Ryan & Deci, 2000). It is as much a developmental process as it is a type of motivation engendered by incentives and consequences, because it involves the self-examination necessary to bring new ways of thinking, feeling, and behaving into an unconflicted congruence with the self's preexisting ways of thinking, feeling, and behaving.

USING EXTERNAL EVENTS TO MOTIVATE PEOPLE

External events exert multiple effects on motivation. To facilitate a practical understanding of using external events to motivate people, consider the following list of examples of commonly used incentives, reinforcers, and punishers, as well as the common relationships in which incentives and consequences are exchanged:

Attractive Incentives
Grades
Promises
Prizes

Aversive Incentives
Threats or warnings
Scowled facial expressions
"No Parking" signs

Positive Reinforcers
Praise
Money
Stickers or gold stars

Negative Reinforcers
Deadlines
Surveillance
Yelling, crying, or screaming

Positive Punishers
Parking tickets
Ridicule or criticism
Spankings

Negative Punishers
Time-outs
Loss of a privilege
Being kicked off the team

Relationship
Coaches
Parents
Spouses

Social Context
Family atmosphere
Montessori school
Corporate culture

This list is, of course, not exhaustive. One can always come up with yet one more illustrative incentive or consequence. The thought of figuring out how many hundreds of different external events affect people's motivation soon becomes overwhelming. But the practitioner does not need an exhaustive list because the motivational significance of practically any extrinsic motivator can be understood through two general principles.

The first principle is to be aware of the characteristics of the incentive or consequence. There is nothing particularly noteworthy about any one incentive or consequence, such that money is not a universally better reinforcer than is praise. Instead, what matters in terms of motivation are the characteristics of the external event: its quality, immediacy of delivery, person/reinforcer fit, appeal to its recipient, intensity, salience, and extent to which it is expected and tangible. Focusing on these variables allows the practitioner to predict the effect of any extrinsic motivator on a person's behavior (e.g., behavior's intensity, latency, persistence, and probability of occurrence) and inner states (e.g., perceived locus of causality, organismic psychological needs, intrinsic and extrinsic motivations). The practitioner does not necessarily need to understand the motivational significance of money or trophies or corporal punishment, so much as she needs to understand how the characteristics of the external event affect motivation.

The second principle of application is to be aware of how the incentive or consequence is presented (recall the "Predicting How Any External Event Will Affect Motivation" box). In other words, what matters is what the external event means to the person—why is this incentive being offered? Why is this reinforcer being given? Why is punishment being handed down? Events whose purpose is to control behavior have predictable effects on behavior (positive incentives and reinforcers increase behavior; negative incentives and punishers decrease it). Events whose purpose is to inform competence have predictable effects on behavior (competence increases behavior; incompetence decreases it). These events affect underlying motivation as well, as controlling events affect perceived self-determination, intrinsic motivation, and extrinsic motivation while informational events affect perceived competence and intrinsic motivation. Again, the practitioner does not so much need to understand the motivational significance of praise, smiles, or parking tickets, so much as he needs to understand the purpose behind why, or reason for which, one person administers an external event to another.

SUMMARY

Extrinsic motivation arises from an environmentally created reason to initiate or persist in an action. External events generate extrinsic motivation to the extent that they establish a "means to an end" contingency in the person's mind, in which the means is the behavior and the end is some attractive consequence (or the prevention of an unattractive consequence). Thus, behavior is motivated in the pursuit of attractive consequences.

The study of extrinsic motivation revolves around the three central concepts of incentives, reinforcers, and punishers. An incentive is an environmental event that attracts or repels a person toward or away from a particular course of action. A positive reinforcer is any environmental event that, when presented, increases the probability that the behavior that produced this event will recur in the future. A negative reinforcer is any environmental event that, when removed, increases the probability that the behavior that removed this event will recur in the future. A positive punisher is any environmental event that, when removed, decreases the probability that the behavior that removed this event will recur in the future. A negative punisher is any environmental event that, when presented, decreases the probability that the behavior that produced this event will recur in the future.

The chief differences between consequences and incentives are (1) when each occurs and (2) what the extrinsic event is supposed to do. Incentives precede behavior and give rise to an expectation that attractive or unattractive consequences are forthcoming; they therefore excite or inhibit action. Consequences follow behavior and increase or decrease its future probability of occurrence.

While extrinsic events can have positive effects on motivation and behavior, they can also produce serious detrimental effects as captured in the phrase the "hidden costs of reward." Expected and tangible extrinsic reasons to engage in a task typically undermine motivation by decreasing self-determination. They also interfere with the learning process, the quality of learning, and the developing capacity for autonomous self-regulation.

Cognitive evaluation theory provides a way for predicting the effects that any extrinsic event will have on motivation. The theory explains how an extrinsic event (e.g., money, grade, deadline) affects intrinsic and extrinsic motivations, as mediated by the event's effect on the organismic psychological needs for competence and self-determination. When an extrinsic event is presented in a relatively controlling way (i.e., given to gain compliance), it undermines intrinsic motivation because of its detrimental effects on self-determination. When an extrinsic event is presented in a relatively informational way (i.e., given to communicate a message of a job well done), it increases intrinsic motivation because of its favorable effect on competence. Hence, whether an extrinsic event is motivationally beneficial or motivationally harmful depends on the relative salience of its controlling and informational aspects. Research on reward administration (i.e., task-noncontingent rewards, task-contingent rewards, performance-contingent rewards) highlights the importance of how (i.e., for what purpose) rewards are given to others.

Self-determination theory extends the distinction between intrinsic versus extrinsic motivation into a continuum of motivational states that exists along a continuum of self-determination. External regulation reflects the least self-determination type of extrinsic motivation and involves no internalization and high dependence on the presence of external events to generate (extrinsic) motivation. Introjected regulation reflects some self-determination because it involves an internalization (but not truly an acceptance) of social rules, limits, and ways of behaving. With introjected regulation, motivation appears as if the person were carrying others' rules and commands inside her head to such an extent that the internalized voice generates self-administered rewards and punishments. Identified regulation refers to authentically internalized extrinsic motivation. With identified regulation, the person volitionally accepts the merit or usefulness of an externally prescribed way of thinking or behaving. Identified regulation is carried out to accomplish extrinsic aims (get a job, improve one's health), but the person's willfulness (rather than the extrinsic event per se) generates the motivation to act. Integration is the most self-determined type of extrinsic motivation, and it involves the self-examination necessary to bring new ways of thinking, feeling, and behaving into congruence with the pre-existing ways. Lastly, intrinsic motivation represents the prototype of fully self-determined motivation. When intrinsically motivated, the person relies not on extrinsic incentives and consequences for motivation but, instead, on the organismic need-satisfying interest and enjoyment that participation in the activity brings.

RECOMMENDED READINGS

Extrinsic Motivation

Cameron, J., & Pierce, W. D. (1994). Reinforcement, reward, and intrinsic motivation: A meta-analysis. *Review of Educational Research, 64,* 363–423.

Elman, D., & Killebrew, T. J. (1978). Incentives and seat belts: Changing a resistant behavior through extrinsic motivation. *Journal of Applied Social Psychology, 8,* 73–83.

Hall, R. V., Axelrod, S., Tyler, L., Grief, E., Jones, F. C., & Robertson, R. (1972). Modification of behavior problems in the home with a parent as observer and experimenter. *Journal of Applied Behavior Analysis, 5,* 53–64.

Hidden Costs of Rewards

Amabile, T. M., DeJong, W., & Lepper, M. R. (1976). Effects of externally imposed deadlines on subsequent intrinsic motivation. *Journal of Personality and Social Psychology, 34,* 92–98.

Deci, E. L., Koestner, R., & Ryan, R. M. (1999). A meta-analytic review of experiments examining the effects of extrinsic rewards on intrinsic motivation. *Psychological Bulletin, 125,* 627–668.

Hom, H. L., Jr. (1994). Can you predict the overjustification effect? *Teaching of Psychology, 21,* 36–37.

Lepper, M. R., & Greene, D. (1975). Turning play into work: Effects of adult surveillance and extrinsic rewards on children's intrinsic motivation. *Journal of Personality and Social Psychology, 31,* 479–486.

Cognitive Evaluation Theory

Deci, E. L., & Ryan, R. M. (1980). The empirical exploration of intrinsic motivational processes. In L. Berkowitz (Ed.), *Advances in experimental social psychology* (Vol. 13, pp. 39–80). New York: Academic Press.

Koestner, R., Ryan, R. M., Bernieri, F., & Holt, K. (1984). Setting limits on children's behavior: The detrimental effects of controlling versus informational styles on intrinsic motivation. *Journal of Personality, 52,* 233–248.

Self-Determination Theory

Rigby, C. S., Deci, E. L., Patrick, B. P., & Ryan, R. M. (1992). Beyond the intrinsic-extrinsic dichotomy: Self-determination in motivation and learning. *Motivation and Emotion, 16,* 165–185.

Ryan, R. M., & Connell, J. P. (1989). Perceived locus of causality and internalization: Examining reasons for acting in two domains. *Journal of Personality and Social Psychology, 57,* 749–761.

Ryan, R. M., & Deci, E. L. (2000). Intrinsic and extrinsic motivations: Classic definitions and new directions. *Contemporary Educational Psychology, 25,* 54-67.

6

ACQUIRED SOCIAL NEEDS

Imagine you have been driving down the interstate for hours and the sun begins to set. The monotony grows. Your mind and imagination begin to wander. Glancing at the passing countryside, you see houses and farms. Horses run outside one farm, and you imagine what it would be like to race in the Kentucky Derby. You imagine going neck and neck with the best jockeys in the world. Of course, you win and the crowd goes wild. Having conquered the racing world, your thoughts turn to the examination you took before leaving town. You blew it, and that failure feedback gnaws at you, asking you to figure out ways to improve. You conclude that next time you will budget your time more efficiently. Hopeful in your plan, you begin to dream of the days when you will graduate and become a physician. You think about working in the laboratory, making important scientific advancements, and perhaps discovering the cure for cancer or AIDS. Yours will be a grand career.

The driving and monotony continue. A song on the radio reminds you that all your friends are 600 miles behind. You feel the loss, and the sense of separation reminds you of the trivial argument with your partner just before you left. You imagine all the things that you could do to make things right again—make a telephone call, send an apologetic e-mail, or, better yet, turn the car around and surprise your partner with an impromptu visit. As you pass a high school, you remember how comfortable it was to hang out with your high-school friends. It was the best of times, and you smile and laugh. Your laughing draws the attention of a passerby, and for a moment, you wonder what it would be like to get to know her and learn about her life and interests. What does she do? Where is she going? What does she believe? Who is she?

Still, the driving continues. A car zooms by at 90 miles per hour. For some reason, you feel that the other driver has somehow made you look bad, as he drives so fast and you so slow. And the way the driver darted in front of you seemed unnecessarily aggressive, in a posturing sort of way. Offended, you feel an impulse to yell at him and flash your bright lights in his rearview mirror. To restrain yourself, you mutter some tough-sounding name-calling, turn up your shirt collar, and put on your sunglasses to look cool. But since it is dark, you put the sunglasses away, and your thoughts wander to what it would be like to drive down the road in a convertible and to have people see you talking on a car phone. Maybe you could drive one of those high-sitting, all-terrain, superpowered vehicles. You like the thought of being rich and well respected and maybe thought of with a reputation of being a no-nonsense deal maker.

Fantasies of winning a race, doing well in competition, becoming a better student, and accomplishing something unique like a cure for a disease are achievement-related thoughts. Thoughts of separation and goals to make amends for a broken relationship, be with close friends, and establish new friendships are affiliation- and intimacy-related thoughts. Impulses of assertiveness and concerns over status and reputation arise from power-related thoughts. Generally, as the mind wanders, our needs have a way of working their way into consciousness to affect our thoughts, emotions, and desires.

ACQUIRED NEEDS

This chapter discusses two categories of acquired psychological needs: social needs and quasi-needs. None of us is born with psychological needs for achievement, power, money, a high grade-point average, or a new car that will impress our friends. Yet each of us develops many such strivings, at least to some degree. Personal experience, socialization opportunities and pressures, and our unique developmental history teach us to expect more positive emotional experiences in some situations than in other situations. Experiences teach us to associate positive emotional experience with some domains (e.g., opportunities for achievement, affiliation, intimacy, power), and the anticipation of a positive emotional experience in these domains leads us to organize our goals, plans, and lifestyle around these experiences. Over time, we acquire preferences for situations, hobbies, and careers that involve and satisfy the needs we acquire and value. Some of us learn to prefer situations that challenge us with explicit standards of excellence (i.e., achievement needs). Others learn to prefer situations that afford plentiful opportunities for relationships (i.e., affiliation and intimacy needs). Still others learn to prefer situations that allow them to capitalize on their reputation or to exercise influence over others (i.e., power needs).

People harbor a multitude of needs, some of which originate from inherited brain structures and evolutionary history to regulate bodily homeostasis (physiological needs), some of which are innate dispositions in the cerebral cortex to provide psychological nutriments for growth and healthy development (organismic psychological needs), some of which are dispositions we learn that lead us to prefer some aspects of the environment rather than other aspects (social needs), and some of which exist as situationally induced wants and desires (quasi-needs).

What is common among the needs discussed in this chapter—the social and quasi-needs—is that both have social origins. Social needs originate from preferences gained through experience, socialization, and development. These needs endure over time and exist within us as acquired individual differences and as part of our personality. Quasi-needs are more ephemeral, and include situationally induced wants, such as the immediate need for money, self-esteem, an umbrella when it rains, an item in a store window, marriage before the age of 30, and so on.

The needs analysis of motivation has now expanded to include three major types: physiological, psychological, and quasi. Table 6.1 summarizes the definitions for and the organizational structure among all the needs included in part I of this book. Recall from chapter 3 that the general definition of need is as follows: Any condition of the person that is essential and necessary for life and growth, such that its nurturance produces well-being, while its thwarting produces damage. Given that general definition, the table lists

Table 6.1 **Four Types of Needs and Their Definitions**

Type of need	Definition, with examples
Physiological	A biological condition within the organism orchestrating brain structures, hormones, and major organs to regulate and correct bodily imbalances that are essential and necessary for life, growth, and well-being. Examples of specific physiological needs include pain avoidance, thirst, hunger, and sex.
Psychological	
Organismic	An innate psychological process that generates the motivation organisms need to seek out interactions with their environment to gain those experiences essential and necessary for vitality, growth, and well-being. Examples of specific organismic psychological needs include self-determination, competence, and relatedness.
Social	An acquired psychological condition from one's socialization history that activates emotional and behavioral potentials in the presence of a need-relevant incentive. Examples of specific social psychological needs include achievement, affiliation, intimacy, and power.
Quasi	Ephemeral, situationally induced wants that create tense energy to engage in behavior capable of reducing the built-up tension. Examples of specific quasi-needs include the desire for money at the store, a Band-Aid after a cut, and an umbrella in the rain.

the specific needs that represent four need subcategories. Other specific needs exist and could be added to this list (Smith, 1992), but the table nonetheless provides a comprehensive summary of the types and categories of needs.

The emphasis in this chapter is on needs as acquired individual differences, that is, as personality characteristics. The set of needs most often studied as acquired individual differences are achievement, affiliation, intimacy, and power. This chapter traces the social origins of each of these needs and discusses how each need, once acquired, manifests itself in thought, emotion, action, and lifestyle. The analysis of social needs constitutes most of the chapter's content, but another class of more ephemeral needs also energizes and directs behavior—quasi-needs.

QUASI-NEEDS

Quasi-needs are situationally induced wants and desires that are not actually full-blown needs in the same sense that physiological, organismic, and social needs are. Quasi-needs are so called because they resemble true needs in some ways. For instance, they affect how we think, feel, and act (i.e., affect cognition, emotion, and behavior). A set of quasi-needs that commonly gains the attention of college students are those for money, a secure job, and a career plan that is capable of gaining the approval of one's parents. Day-to-day circumstances remind us of our needs for money, job, and approval, and events like shopping, job interviewing, and a visit home keep these situationally induced wants in the forefront of our attention. And these quasi-needs, more often than not, have a sense of urgency about them that can, at times, dominate consciousness and perhaps overwhelm other needs.

Quasi-needs originate from demands and pressures in the environment. Whenever a person satisfies a situational demand or pressure, the quasi-need fades away. When a bill arrives in the mail, we need money. After being rejected, we need self-esteem. During a downpour, we need an umbrella. Upon seeing an item in the store window, we need to possess it. As we age into our late 20s, we need to get married, and so on. Once we get the money, self-esteem, umbrella, item, or marriage, however, the situation is such that we no longer need more money, self-esteem, umbrellas, items, or marriage proposals. (Of course, some situational pressures can endure for a reasonably long period of time.) The fact that quasi-needs disappear once we get what we want, however, is the telltale sign that the need is not a full-blown need. It is not a condition that is essential and necessary for life, growth, and well-being. Rather, it is something we introject from the environment for a time and something that has more to do with the pressures in the environment than it does the needs of the individual. Any change to the environment leads to a corresponding change in our quasi-need (i.e., if it stops raining, our need for an umbrella fades).

Quasi-needs originate from situational events that promote a psychological context of tension, pressure, and urgency. Hence, quasi-needs are deficiency-oriented, situationally reactive need states. Quasi-needs are what we lack, yet need, from the environment in a rather urgent way. For example, when a situation pressures a person in one way or another, she may say she needs a vacation, needs to make a good grade on a test, needs to get a haircut, needs to find her lost car keys, needs a piece of paper to write on, needs a friend to talk to, needs to take a bath, needs to get a job, and so on in response to that situation. The strength of a quasi-need—its potency to gain attention and demand an action—is largely a function of how pressuring and demanding the environment is (e.g., "I just *have to* find my car keys!"). It is this situationally induced psychological context of tension, pressure, and urgency that supplies the motivation for the quasi-need.

ACQUIRING SOCIAL NEEDS

Humans acquire social needs through experience, development, and socialization. In an extensive investigation of how people acquire social needs, one group of researchers sought to determine the child-rearing antecedents of adult needs for achievement, affiliation, and power (McClelland & Pilon, 1983). The researchers initially scored the parental practices of mothers and fathers of 78 five-year-old boys and girls. When the children grew to the age of 31, the researchers assessed the social needs of each adult. Only a few child-rearing antecedents emerged as significant, but the few that did emerge illustrate some early origins of social needs. Adults high in the need for achievement generally had parents who used a strict feeding schedule and severe toilet training practices. Adults with high needs for affiliation generally had parents who used praise (rather than authority or coercion) as a socialization technique. Adults with high needs for power generally had parents who were permissive about sex and aggression (i.e., permissive about masturbation, fighting with siblings and parents).

The finding that few child-rearing experiences predict adult motives suggests that social needs are not set at an early age. In adulthood, social contexts shape the development and change of the social needs. For instance, some occupations are more congenial to achievement than are others because they provide opportunities for moderate challenges, independent work with personal responsibility, and rapid performance feedback. People in achievement-congenial occupations (e.g., entrepreneurs) show marked increases in their achievement strivings over the years compared to people in achievement-noncongenial occupations (e.g., nursing; Jenkins 1987). As to developing power strivings, workers in jobs that require assertiveness (e.g., sales) show increases in the need for power over the years (Veroff et al., 1980). Social contexts, like the family and work environments that surround us, therefore, exert an influence over the needs we acquire.

Once acquired, we experience social needs as emotional and behavioral potentials that are activated by particular situational incentives (Atkinson, 1982; McClelland, 1985). That is, when an incentive associated with a particular need is present (e.g., a date is an intimacy incentive, an inspirational speech is a power incentive), the person high in that particular social need experiences emotional and behavioral activation (i.e., feels hope, seeks interaction). Experience teaches each of us that we will acquire certain positive emotional reactions in response to some incentives rather than others. Generally speaking, the need-activating incentive for each social need is as follows (McClelland, 1985):

SOCIAL NEEDS	INCENTIVES THAT ACTIVATE EACH NEED'S EMOTIONAL AND BEHAVIOR POTENTIAL
Achievement	Doing something well to show personal competence
Affiliation	Opportunity to please others and gain their approval
Intimacy	Warm, secure relationship
Power	Having impact on others

HOW SOCIAL NEEDS MOTIVATE BEHAVIOR

Social needs arise and activate emotional and behavioral potential when need-satisfying incentives appear. For instance, depending on one's unique constellation of acquired needs, a school test might activate emotional fear and behavioral avoidance, whereas a school dance might activate emotional hope and behavioral approach. For another person who has a different constellation of acquired needs, the same test might bring emotional hope and behavioral approach, while the dance cues up only emotional fear and behavioral avoidance. With social needs, people react to events like tests and dances by learning the incentive value (positive or negative) of the objects around them. When these objects appear, they activate social needs, and people react through positive-negative emotions and through approach-avoidance behavior.

Social needs are mostly reactive in nature. They lie dormant within us until we encounter a potentially need-satisfying incentive that brings the social need to the front of our attention in terms of our thinking, feeling, and behaving. In addition, however, people also learn to anticipate the emergence of need-relevant incentives. People learn rather quickly that particular occupations, organizations, and recreational events, for example, are primarily opportunities for doing well and demonstrating personal competence, for pleasing others and gaining their approval, for participating in warm and secure relationships, or for having an impact on others. Thus, people gain and rely on personal knowledge of their social needs to gravitate toward environments that are capable of activating and satisfying their needs. The person high in achievement strivings might enter business to become an entrepreneur or a stockbroker, while the person high in power strivings might enter management, run for a local political office, or take up a hobby that offers opportunities for exerting influence over others.

ASSESSING SOCIAL NEEDS

Henry Murray, the pioneer investigator of the social needs, understood each personality as a unique constellation of social needs that energized and directed behavior toward satisfying the needs that were most central to that personality, or person (Murray, 1937, 1938). One person, for instance, might have a central need for achievement and, as a consequence, spend much time playing sports or pursuing an entrepreneurial business career. Another person might be low in this need but high in others, such as affiliation, and therefore spend much time building and repairing relationships. Murray sought to measure social needs in a multitude of ways because he believed that needs expressed themselves in many ways, as through strong emotional reactions, approach behavior, avoidance behavior, selective attention, and so forth. Murray used as many techniques as possible to measure human needs, for example: questionnaires, interviews, free association, dream analysis, diaries, autobiographical statements, observation of behavior in group settings, laboratory experiments, and reactions to frustration, music, and humor. Most importantly, he developed the Thematic Apperception Test (TAT; Murray, 1943; Morgan & Murray, 1935).

The TAT presents a set of pictures and asks the test taker to write a short story about the events portrayed in each picture (Bellak, 1993; Smith, 1992). *Thematic* refers to the content, or theme, expressed in each story (i.e., Does the narrative revolve around a theme of power?). *Apperception* refers to the human tendency to perceive more than is actually present in an object (to "apperceive"). A person's apperception fills in the picture's ambiguous aspects with personal interpretations to make sense of the picture (e.g., seeing a mushroom shape in a cloud). In taking the TAT, the test taker looks at a series of between 4 and 21 pictures one at a time. (Recently, researchers have substituted sentences for pictures (e.g., "Ann is sitting on a chair with a smile on her face"; Jenkins, 1987). With a narrative/story in hand, researchers interpret this story by using a scoring manual (for examples for achievement, see McClelland et al. 1958; for affiliation, see Heyns, Veroff, and Atkinson 1958; for intimacy, see McAdams 1980; for power, see Winter 1973; for additional social needs, see Smith 1992; and for clinical uses, see Bellak, 1993).

The TAT has been criticized on the basis of its poor reliability (Entwistle, 1972; Fineman, 1977). For instance, the TAT shows low reliability on several indices, including retest reliability, split-half reliability, equivalent forms, and internal consistency. TAT defenders acknowledge the TAT has low reliability, but they do not see this psychometric shortcoming as a stumbling block (Atkinson, Bongort, & Price, 1977; McClelland, 1980). After all, the test taker writes short stories for many different pictures (or sentences) that are meant to arouse different motives. Some scenes, for instance, typically arouse achievement themes (e.g., "At the end of the day, Mark is going back to the office"), whereas others arouse affiliation themes (e.g., "A young man is talking about something important with an older person"). When one considers that the TAT pictures constantly change, low reliability is to be expected because, by design, the test changes the stream of the test taker's imagination. The real test of the TAT's usefulness concerns its validity: Can the TAT predict how people behave (McClelland, 1980)? This chapter shows that it can.

In the attempt to measure social needs in a way that is reliable and more convenient to administer and score, researchers developed many self-report measures (Edwards, 1959; Gough, 1964; Hermans, 1970; Jackson, 1974; Lindgren, 1976; Mehrabian, 1968; Mehrabian & Bank, 1975). The self-report measure that is particularly reliable, valid, and well constructed is Jackson's measure (Anastasi, 1982; Clarke, 1973; Harper, 1975; Wortruba & Price, 1975). Like the TAT, Jackson's scales are based on Murray's theory of needs, and the scales have proven themselves useful as empirical measures of social needs (Costa & McCrae, 1988; Harackiewicz, Sansone, & Manderlink, 1985). Like the projective test of the TAT, Jackson's self-report measure of the social needs shows that it too can predict how people behave.

ACHIEVEMENT

The need for achievement is the desire to do well relative to a standard of excellence. It motivates people to seek "success in competition with a standard of excellence" (McClelland et al., 1953). Standard of excellence is, however, a broad term as standards of excellence encompass competitions with a task (e.g., solving a jigsaw puzzle, writing a persuasive essay); competitions with the self (e.g., running a race in a personal best time, improving one's GPA); or competitions against others (e.g., winning a competition, becoming the class valedictorian; Heckhausen, 1967). What all types of achievement situations have in common is that the person knows the forthcoming performance will produce an emotionally meaningful evaluation of personal competence. Standards of excellence activate the need for achievement because they provide a highly meaningful arena for evaluating one's level of competence.

When facing standards of excellence, people's emotional reactions vary. Individuals high in the need for achievement generally respond with approach-oriented emotions such as hope, pride, and anticipatory gratification. Individuals low in the need for achievement generally respond with avoidance-oriented emotions such as anxiety, defensiveness, and with a fear of failure. People's behavioral responses to standards of excellence also vary. When confronted with an opportunity for engaging in a task featuring a clear standard of excellence, people show differences in choice, latency, effort, persistence, and the willingness to take personal responsibility for the ensuing outcomes (Cooper, 1983). High-need achievers, compared to low-need achievers, choose moderately difficult to difficult versions of tasks instead of easy versions (Kuhl & Blankenship, 1979; Slade & Rush, 1991); quickly engage in achievement-related tasks rather than procrastinate or avoid them altogether (Blankenship, 1987); show more effort and better performance on moderately difficult tasks because pride energizes high-need achievers, whereas fear debilitates low achievers (Karabenick & Yousseff, 1968; Raynor & Entin, 1982); persist more in the face of difficulty and failure on moderately difficult tasks (Feather, 1961, 1963); and take a personal responsibility for successes and failures rather than seeking help or advice from others (Weiner, 1980).

ORIGINS OF THE NEED FOR ACHIEVEMENT

As discussed earlier in this chapter, researchers set out decades ago on a journey to discover the roots of children's needs for achievement in parenting style and in social learning opportunities. The hope was to explain the social determinants of the high- versus low-need achiever's personality. As research progressed, it became increasingly clear that the need for achievement was a multifaceted phenomenon steeped not in a single trait but in a host of social, cognitive, and developmental processes.

Socialization Influences

Part of the development of strong and resilient achievement strivings revolves around socialization influences (Heckhausen, 1967; McClelland & Pilon, 1983). Children develop relatively strong achievement strivings when their parents provide the following:

independence training (e.g., self-reliance, autonomy), high performance aspirations, realistic standards of excellence (Rosen & D'Andrade, 1959; Winterbottom, 1958), high ability self-concepts (e.g., "This task will be easy for you"), a positive value for achievement-related pursuits (Eccles-Parsons, Adler, & Kaczala, 1982), explicit standards for excellence (Trudewind, 1982), a home environment rich in stimulation potential (e.g., books to read), a wide scope of experience such as traveling, and exposure to children's readers rich in achievement imagery (e.g., *The Little Engine That Could;* deCharms & Moeller, 1962). In the end, however, this effort to identify the childhood socialization practices of high-need achievers was only partly successful, largely because longitudinal findings began to show that achievement strivings change a great deal from childhood to adulthood and that adult achievement strivings were mostly unreliable from one decade to the next (Jenkins, 1987; Maehr & Kleiber, 1980).

Cognitive Influences

Many researchers gave up on the idea that people internalize an achievement-related personality. Instead, these researchers turned their attention to the cognitive underpinnings of an achievement-based way of thinking (Ames & Ames, 1984). Some ways of thinking are more achievement-related than are others—namely, perceptions of high ability, adoption of a mastery orientation, high expectations for success, strong valuing of achievement, and an optimistic attributional style. Perceptions of high ability facilitate both task persistence (Felson, 1984; Phillips, 1984) and competent performance (Hansford & Hattie, 1982; Marsh, 1990). A mastery orientation (compared to a helpless orientation, discussed in chapter 8) leads people to choose moderately difficult tasks and to respond to difficulty by increasing rather than decreasing effort (Dweck, 1986, 1999; Elliot & Dweck, 1988). Expectations for success breed approach-oriented behaviors such as seeking out optimal challenges (Eccles, 1984a) and performing well (Eccles, 1984b; Volmer, 1986). Valuing achievement in a particular domain predicts persistence in that domain (Eccles, 1984b; Ethington, 1991). An optimistic attributional style (attributing success to the self but failure to an outside cause, discussed in chapter 9) fosters positive emotions like hope and pride following successes and keeps negative emotions like fear and anxiety at bay (Weiner, 1985, 1986). Thus, when conditions in the home, school, gymnasium, workplace, and therapeutic setting promote high ability beliefs, a mastery orientation, expectations for success, a valuing of achievement, and an optimistic attributional style, these conditions provide the cognitive soil for cultivating an achievement way of thinking and behaving.

Developmental Influences

The identification of cognitive influences on achievement behavior led researchers to study how these ways of thinking develop over a person's life span (Heckhausen, 1982; Parsons & Ruble, 1977; Ruble et al., 1992; Stipek, 1984; Weiner, 1979). One such framework is that of Deborah Stipek (1984), who outlined the developmental course of achievement-related beliefs, values, and emotions.

Achievement-related beliefs, values, and emotions all show predictable developmental patterns. Young children are notorious amateurs in estimating their actual abilities.

They hold unrealistically high ability beliefs (Nicholls, 1979; Stipek, 1984), do not lower their ability beliefs following failure (Parsons & Ruble, 1977), and ignore their poor performance in relation to their peers (Ruble, Parsons, & Ross, 1976). During middle childhood, however, children increasingly pay attention to peer performance comparisons, and by late childhood, they rely on the full gamut of information to construct relatively realistic ability beliefs: self-evaluations, peer evaluations, teacher evaluations, and parental evaluations (Felson, 1984; Nicholls, 1978, 1979; Rosenholtz & Rosenholtz, 1981; Ruble et al., 1992; Stipek, 1984). As to values, young children value the approval of others very much, but they care very little about achievement per se (Stipek, 1984). Achievement-related values are learned over time as children learn to place a high or low value on achievement, mostly from their parents (Eccles-Parsons, Adler & Kaczala, 1982), and later on, achievement in specific domains, such as their occupational endeavors (Waterman, 1988). As to emotions, children are not born with pride or shame. Neither pride nor shame is an innate emotion. Instead, pride emerges as a social construction from a developmental history of success episodes ending in mastery; shame emerges as a social construction from a developmental history of failure episodes ending in ridicule (Stipek, 1983).

ATKINSON'S MODEL

Two theoretical approaches dominate the understanding of achievement motivation: classical and contemporary (Elliot, 1997). The classical view is Atkinson's model of achievement behavior, which includes the dynamics-of-action model. The contemporary view is a cognitive approach that centers on the goals people adopt in achievement situations.

Each approach will be discussed in turn, but what is common between the approaches is that both share the same portrayal of achievement motivation as an inherent struggle of approach versus avoidance. All of us experience standards of excellence as a two-edged sword; part of us feels excitement and hope and anticipates the pride of a job well done, yet another part of us feels anxiety and fear and anticipates the shame of possible humiliation. Thus, achievement behavior exists as a sort of balance between the emotions and beliefs underlying the tendency to approach success versus the emotions and beliefs underlying the tendency to avoid failure.

John Atkinson (1957, 1964) argued that the need for achievement only partly predicts achievement behavior. Achievement behavior depends not only on the individual's need for achievement but also on her probability of success at a task and her incentive value for succeeding at that task. For Atkinson, probability of success and incentive value for succeeding were situationally determined. That is, some tasks had high probabilities for success, whereas others had low probabilities for success. Some tasks offered greater incentive for success than did others. For instance, consider the classes you are presently taking. Each course has its own probability of success (e.g., a senior-level advanced calculus course is generally harder than is an introductory-level physical education class) and its own incentive value for success (e.g., doing well in a course in your major is generally valued more than doing well in a course outside of your major).

Atkinson's theory features four variables: achievement behavior and its three predictors—need for achievement, probability of success, and incentive for success. Achievement behavior is defined as the tendency to approach success, abbreviated as *Ts*. The three determining factors of *Ts* are (1) the strength of a person's need for achievement (Ms, motive to succeed), (2) the strength of the perceived probability of success (Ps), and (3) the incentive value of success at that particular activity (Is). Atkinson's model is expressed in the following formula:

$$Ts = Ms \times Ps \times Is$$

Tendency to Approach Success

The first variable in the equation, *Ms*, corresponds to the person's score on the TAT and represents the strength of that person's need for achievement. The variable *Ps* is estimated from the perceived difficulty of the task and from the person's perceived ability at that task. The variable *Is* is equal to 1 − Ps. If the probability of success is .25, the incentive for success at that task would be .75 (1.00 − .25). Consider an example of two teammates on a high-school wrestling team who differ in their level of need for achievement and in their weekly opponent. One wrestler, who has a strong need for achievement motive (TAT score = 8), is scheduled to wrestle last year's state champion (Ps = .1) and consequently has a strong incentive to beat the champ (Is = 1 − Ps = .9). The second wrestler, who has a weaker need for achievement (TAT score = 1), is scheduled to wrestle an opponent who is his equal (Ps = .5) and consequently has a moderate incentive to succeed (Is = .5). The first wrestler's tendency to approach success (Ts) is 0.72 (8 × .9 × .1), and the second's Ts is 0.25 (1 × .5 × .5). If the two teammates had equal achievement strivings—TAT score = 1 for both wrestlers—Atkinson's theory predicts the greater achievement motivation for the second wrestler (Ts = .25 versus Ts = .09) because optimal challenge (Ps = .5) provides the richest motivational combination of expectancy of success and incentive for success.

Tendency to Avoid Failure

Just as people face standards of excellence with a need for achievement (Ms) so too do they harbor a motive to avoid failure (Atkinson, 1957, 1964). The tendency to avoid failure motivates the individual to defend against the loss of self-esteem, the loss of social respect, and the fear of embarrassment (Birney, Burdick, & Teevan, 1969). Atkinson measured *Maf* with the Test Anxiety Questionnaire (TAQ; Sarason, 1977), a 23-item self-report questionnaire with questions such as, "During tests, I find myself thinking of the consequences of failing," to assess anxiety-based avoidance motivations such as evaluation apprehension and fear of failure. The tendency to avoid failure, abbreviated *Taf,* is calculated with a formula that parallels that for Ts:

$$Taf = Maf \times Pf \times If$$

The variable *Maf* represents the motive to avoid failure (as scored by the TAQ), *Pf* represents the probability of failure (which, by definition, is 1 − Ps), and *If* represents the negative incentive value for failure (If = 1 − Pf). Thus, if an individual has a moderate motive to avoid failure (Maf = 5), the tendency to avoid failure on a difficult task (Pf = .9) can be calculated as 0.45 (Maf × Pf × If, which = 5 × .9 × .1 = 0.45).

Combined Approach and Avoidance Tendencies

Atkinson conceptualized *Ms* as a force within the person that prefers and seeks out achievement situations and *Maf* as a force within the person that escapes from (or is anxious and uncomfortable regarding) achievement situations. Thus, to engage in any achievement task is to enter into a risk-taking dilemma in which the person struggles to find a balance between the attraction of pride, hope, and social respect versus the repulsion of shame, fear, and social humiliation. When *Ts* is greater than *Taf,* the person approaches the opportunity to test personal competence against the standard of excellence, but when *Taf* is greater than *Ts*, the person avoids the opportunity. Atkinson's complete formula for predicting the tendency to achieve (Ta) and hence for displaying achievement-related behaviors (i.e., choice, latency, effort, persistence) is as follows:

$$\text{Ta} = \text{Ts} - \text{Taf} = (\text{Ms} \times \text{Ps} \times \text{Is}) - (\text{Maf} \times \text{Pf} \times \text{If})$$

Although the model can appear to be overwhelming at first, in actuality one needs to know only three variables: the individual's approach motive (Ms), the individual's avoidance motive (Maf), and probability of success (Ps) on the task at hand. Notice that *Is, Pf,* and *If* are all calculated solely from the value of *Ps.*

If you work through a couple of examples, you will find two general principles that underlie the numerical value for *Ta*. First, *Ta* is highest when *Ts* is greater than *Taf* and lowest when *Taf* is greater than *Ts* (a personality factor). Second, *Ta* is highest when *Ps* equals .5 and lowest when *Ps* is around .9 (task is too easy to generate an incentive value for succeeding) or .1 (task is too difficult to be motivating). To make sense of how the numbers fit together to predict approach versus avoidance behavior, consider the hesitant child trying to decide if he wants to take a chance and ride the huge horse at the city's petting zoo. If *Ms* equals 2, *Maf* equals 5, and *Ps* equals .2, then Ta would equal an avoidance-biased number (i.e., negative number) of − .48 because of the following formula:

$$\text{Ta} = [(2 \times .2 \times .8) - (5 \times .8 \times .2)]$$

Achievement for the Future

Not all achievement situations are alike, as some have implications that affect one's future achievement efforts, whereas others have implications only for the present (Raynor, 1969, 1970, 1974). For example, a track athlete tries to win a race not only to experience the pride of a moment's accomplishment, but a win in today's race might lead to invitations to other important track meets, such as qualifying for the state championships or gaining a college scholarship. "Future achievement orientation" refers to an individual's psychological distance from a long-term achievement goal (e.g., winning the state championship). The importance of future achievement orientation is that, other things being equal, any achievement goal perceived far away in time receives less approach-versus-avoidance weight than does a goal in the very near future. Thus, achievement behavior is a function of not only *Ms, Ps, Is, Maf, Pf,* and *If,* but also whether the present achievement will lead toward some future achievement. From this point of view, achievement behavior is a series of steps in a path, and those achievement situations that are psychologically near have more impact on *Ta* than those that are psychologically far (Gjesme, 1981).

DYNAMICS-OF-ACTION MODEL

In the dynamics-of-action model, achievement behavior occurs within a stream of behavior (Atkinson & Birch, 1970, 1974, 1978). The stream of behavior is determined largely by three forces: instigation, inhibition, and consummation. *Instigation* causes a rise in approach tendencies and occurs by confronting environmental stimuli associated with past reward (i.e., anything that cultivates an increased hope for success). Instigation is the same as *Ts*. *Inhibition* causes a rise in avoidance tendencies and occurs by confronting environmental stimuli associated with past punishment (i.e., anything that cultivates an increased fear of failure). Inhibition is the same as *Taf*. Therefore, instigation and inhibition are contemporary terms for *Ts* and *Taf*. The one new variable in the dynamics-of-action model is consummation. *Consummation* refers to the fact that performing an activity brings about its own cessation (e.g., running, eating). Adding consummatory forces allows achievement behavior to be understood as dynamic (changing over time) instead of episodic or static. For instance, your achievement strivings in this particular school class change as the class progresses and as you study more hours, attend more classes, and receive more feedback about your class performances.

The four panels in Figure 6.1 portray achievement behaviors over time (Blankenship, 1987). Each panel shows the individual's behavioral preference for an achievement task (a task that arouses hope for success and fear of failure) and for a nonachievement task (an emotionally neutral task). The four panels correspond to four imaginary people with different levels of instigative and inhibitory forces. Panel 1 shows behavior with high instigation and low inhibition (Ms > Maf); panel 2 shows behavior with high levels of both instigation and inhibition (Ms = Maf, and both are high); panel 3 shows behavior with low levels of both instigation and inhibition (Ms = Maf, and both are low); and panel 4 shows behavior with low instigation and high inhibition (Ms < Maf).

Notice that all four individuals, represented in each panel of the figure, begin interacting with the nonachievement-related activity (e.g., watching television), and the question is, how much time passes until each person starts to engage the achievement task (e.g., studying)? The (i.e., high need for achievement) individual in panel 1 shows the shortest latency for engaging the achievement task (i.e., the quickest achievement behavior), while the (low need for achievement) individual in panel 4 shows the longest latency for engaging the achievement task. Once achievement behavior has begun, it tends to consume itself, and the individual will eventually return to the nonachievement-related task, which over time will also consume itself (i.e., you can only watch so much television). The motive profiles *(Ms* in relation to *Maf)* explain not only latency to initiate achievement behavior but also its persistence, once begun. The most important messages

FIGURE 6.1 **Streams of Behavior for People High and Low in *Ms* and *Maf***

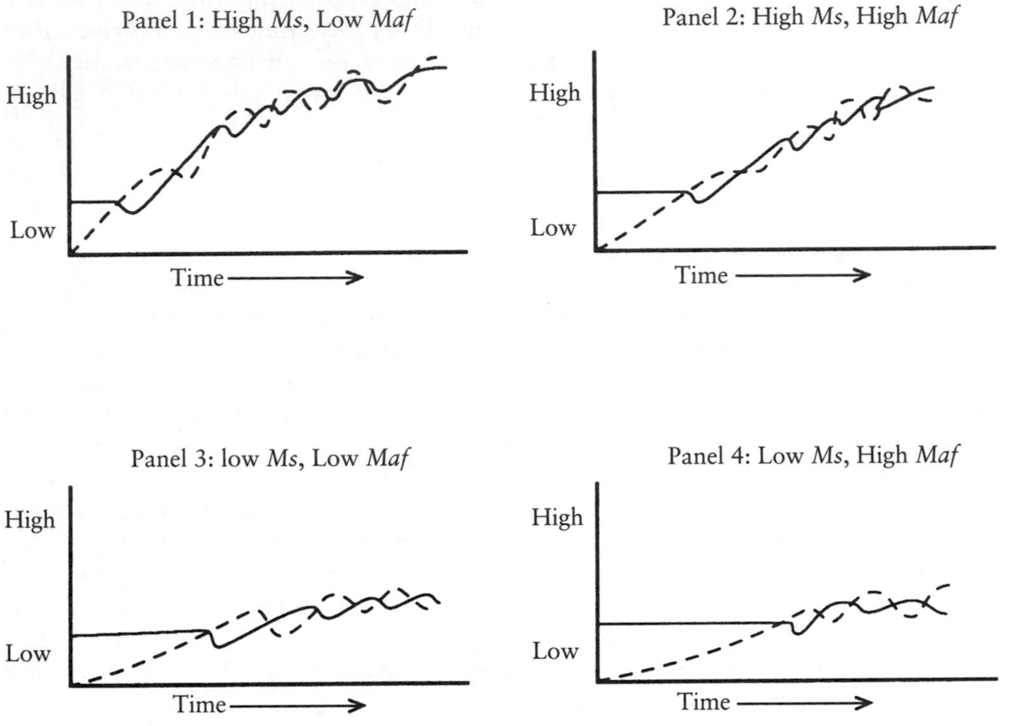

SOURCE: From "A Computer-Based Measure of Resultant Achievement Motivation," by V. Blankenship, 1987, *Journal of Personality and Social Psychology, 53,* pp. 361–372. Copyright 1987 by the American Psychological Association. Adapted with permission.

Note: Dashed line represents tendency strength to engage the achievement-related task; solid line represents tendency strength of nonachievement task.

communicated in Figure 6.1 are the ideas that (1) latency to initiate an achievement task varies with motive strengths, (i.e., a quick latency is associated with a high *Ms)*, (2) persistence on an achievement task varies with motive strengths (i.e., long persistence is associated with a low *Maf)*, and (3) tendencies to pursue achievement and nonachievement tasks rise because of facilitating incentives and fall because of inhibitory fears and consummatory forces.

CONDITIONS THAT INVOLVE AND SATISFY THE NEED FOR ACHIEVEMENT

Three situations are particularly noteworthy for their ability to involve and satisfy the need for achievement: moderately difficult tasks, competition, and entrepreneurship (McClelland, 1985).

Moderately Difficult Tasks

High-need achievers (Ms > Maf) outperform low-need achievers (Maf > Ms) on intermediately difficult tasks. High-need achievers do not, however, outperform low-need achievers on easy or difficult tasks (Karabenick & Yousseff, 1968; Raynor & Entin, 1982). Performance on a moderately difficult task activates in the high achiever a set of positive emotional and cognitive incentives not socialized into the low achiever. Emotionally, moderately difficult tasks provide an arena for best testing skills and therefore optimally cultivating emotions like pride and satisfaction. Cognitively, moderately difficult tasks provide an arena for best diagnosing one's level of ability. The stronger a person's need for achievement, the stronger the tendency to seek information about her abilities (Trope, 1975, 1983). Hence, moderately challenging tasks provide a mixture of pride from success and the ability to properly diagnose important abilities, a mixture that high-need achievers find more motivating than do low achievers.

Competition

Interpersonal competition captures much of the risk-taking dilemma involved in achievement settings. It generally promotes positive emotion, approach behavior, and improved performance in high-need achievers but negative emotion, avoidance behaviors, and debilitated performance in low-need achievers (Covington & Omelich, 1984; Epstein & Harackiewicz, 1992; Ryan & Lakie, 1965; Tauer & Harackiewicz, 1999). Consider that high-need achievers in general seek diagnostic ability information (Trope, 1975), seek opportunities for testing their skills (Epstein & Harackiewicz, 1992; Harackiewicz, Sansone, & Manderlink, 1985), value competence for its own sake (Harackiewicz & Manderlink, 1984), are attracted to activities that allow for self-evaluation (Kuhl, 1978), and enjoy opportunities that demonstrate or prove their ability (Harackiewicz & Elliot, 1993). Competition often offers all these attributes and is therefore attractive to high-need achievers (Harackiewicz & Elliot, 1993). For low-need achievers, competition's inherent evaluative pressures outweigh these potential benefits (Epstein & Harackiewicz, 1992).

Entrepreneurship

David McClelland (1965, 1987) finds that high-need achievers often display the behavioral pattern of entrepreneurship. He assessed the need for achievement in a group of college students and then waited 14 years to check their occupational choices. Each occupation was classified as either entrepreneurial (e.g., founder of own business, sales, stockbroker) or not entrepreneurial (e.g., office manager, service personnel). Results confirmed that most entrepreneurs were high-need achievers in college, while most low-need achievers were not entrepreneurs. Entrepreneurship appeals to the high-need achiever because it requires taking moderate risks and assuming responsibility for one's successes and failures. Entrepreneurship also provides concrete, rapid performance feedback (e.g., profits and losses and moment-to-moment results as from the business or stock market) to generate emotions like pride and satisfaction and to diagnose one's competence on a continual basis. Beyond entrepreneurship, high-need achievers prefer just about any occupation that offers challenge, personal responsibility, and rapid performance feedback (Jenkins, 1987). The high-need achievers consider these aspects of work combined define an explicit standard of excellence for the worker in which to best diagnose skills, abilities, and rates of improvement, which are the conditions known to involve and satisfy the need for achievement (Atkinson, 1981; Jenkins, 1987; McClelland, 1961, 1980; Trope & Brickman, 1975).

ACHIEVEMENT GOALS

Atkinson's model treats achievement behavior as a choice: Should a person accept and approach the standard of excellence, or should he reject and avoid it? The model seeks to understand whether a person will approach success or avoid failure, and if so, with what intensity, latency, and persistence. Contemporary researchers, however, have become increasingly interested in *why* a person shows achievement behavior, not so much in whether achievement behavior occurs, but why. (For what reason does it occur?) So often people are asked, or even required, to approach a standard of excellence put before them by someone else, as happens at school, at work, in sports, and so on. In this sort of setting, contemporary achievement motivation researchers seek to understand why people adopt one type of achievement goal over another type.

The two main achievement goals are performance goals and mastery goals. With performance goals, the person seeks to demonstrate or prove competence; with mastery goals, the person seeks to develop or improve competence (Ames & Archer, 1988; Dweck, 1986, 1990; Nichols, 1984; Spence & Helmreich, 1983). Performance goals generally cultivate a norm-based evaluation of one's competence, and these goals focus the performer's attention on the demonstration of ability relative to that of others. Achievement in the context of a performance goal means doing better than others. Mastery goals generally cultivate a self-based (or task-based) evaluation of one's competence, and these goals focus the performer's attention on developing competence and mastering the task. Achievement in the context of a mastery goal means making progress.

The distinction between performance and mastery goals is important because the adoption of mastery goals in an achievement context (e.g., in school, at work, in sports) is associated with positive and productive ways of thinking, feeling, and behaving, whereas the adoption of performance goals in an achievement context is associated with relatively negative and unproductive ways of thinking, feeling, and behaving (Dweck, 1999; Dweck & Leggett, 1988; Harackiewicz & Elliot, 1993; Spence & Helmreich, 1983). The endorsement of mastery goals instead of performance goals cultivates in a performer a self-regulated type of learning in which she exercises control over her way of thinking, feeling, and acting while learning, acquiring, and refining knowledge and skill. When people adopt mastery goals, compared to when they adopt performance goals, they usually do the following: persist longer at the task (Elliot & Dweck, 1988), prefer challenging tasks they can learn from rather than easy tasks on which they can demonstrate high ability (Ames & Archer, 1988; Elliot & Dweck, 1988), use conceptually based learning strategies such as relating information to existing knowledge rather than superficial learning strategies such as memorizing (Meece et al., 1988; Nolen, 1988), increase effort in the face of difficulty rather than turn passive or quit (Elliot & Dweck, 1988), are less susceptible to learned helplessness deficits (Stipek, & Kowalski, 1989), are more likely to be intrinsically rather than extrinsically motivated (Heyman & Dweck, 1992), and are more likely to ask for help and information from others that will allow them to continue working on their own (Newman, 1991).

Educational psychologists find the concept of achievement goals to be helpful in understanding students' achievement motivation (Ames & Archer, 1988). Part of the reasons achievement goals appeal to educators is that teachers exert a relatively strong influence over the types of achievement goals students adopt. For instance, in one study with elementary-grade children, students were asked to agree or disagree with questions assessing the extent to which their teachers promoted mastery goals ("The teacher pays attention to whether I am improving," and "Making mistakes is part of learning") or performance goals ("I work hard to get a high grade," and "Students feel bad when they do not do as well as others"). The researchers then assessed students' learning strategies, willingness to be challenged, and attitude toward the class. Students with mastery goals, compared to students with performance goals, used relatively sophisticated rather than superficial learning strategies, were attracted to challenge rather than threatened by it, and enjoyed the class more (Ames & Archer, 1988). This pattern of findings by using grades for students and salaries for workers helps explains why people with mastery goals outperform people with performance goals (Spence & Helreich, 1983). Overall, how students with mastery goals and how students with performance goals differently construe the classroom climate is summarized in Table 6.2.

TABLE 6.2 **Manifestations of Mastery and Performance Goals in the Classroom Context**

CLIMATE DIMENSION	MASTERY GOAL	PERFORMANCE GOAL
Success defined as . . .	Improvement, progress	High grades, high normative performance
Value placed on . . .	Effort, learning	Normatively high ability
Reasons for satisfaction . . .	Working hard, challenge	Doing better than others
Teacher oriented toward . . .	How students are learning	How students are performing
Views errors or mistakes as . . .	Part of learning	Anxiety eliciting
Focus of attention	Process of learning	Own performance relative to others' performance
Reasons for effort	Learning something new	High grades, performing better than others
Evaluation criteria	Absolute progress	Normative

SOURCE: From "Achievement Goals in the Classroom: Students' Learning Strategies and Motivation Processes," by C. Ames and J. Archer, 1988, *Journal of Educational Psychology, 80*, pp. 260–267.

Note: The table can be interpreted by selecting one classroom climate dimension of interest and then reading across the row for how students with mastery goals rate—what they believe, what they are likely to say—on that dimension and then for how students with performance goals rate on that dimension.

FIGURE 6.2 **Antecedents and Consequences of the Three Achievement Goals**

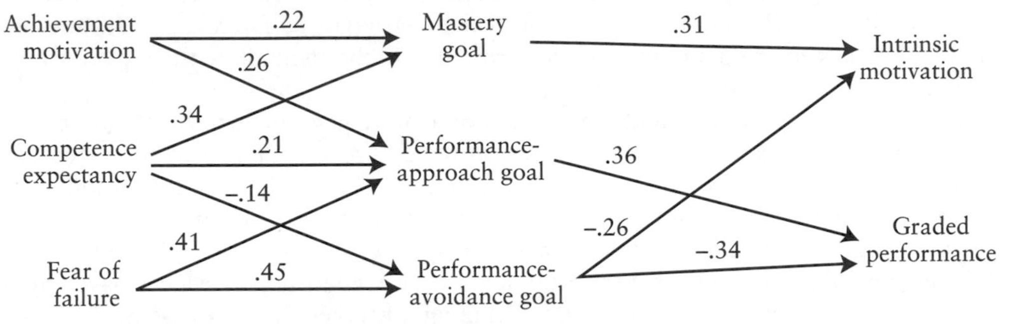

SOURCE: From "A Hierarchical Model of Approach and Avoidance Achievement Motivation," by A. J. Elliot and M. A. Church, 1997, *Journal of Personality and Social Psychology, 72,* pp. 218–232. Copyright 1997, American Psychological Association. Reprinted with permission.

INTEGRATING CLASSICAL AND CONTEMPORARY APPROACHES TO ACHIEVEMENT MOTIVATION

Recently an effort to integrate the classical and contemporary approaches to achievement motivation has gained acceptance largely because it combines the valuable features of both approaches into a single comprehensive model (Elliot, 1997). In the integrated model, two different types of achievement performance goals exist: performance-approach and performance-avoidance. Performance-approach goals emanate from a person's need for achievement, the tendency to approach success. Performance-avoidance goals emanate from a person's fear of failure, the tendency to avoid failure.

The overlap within the classical and contemporary approaches occurs within the relationship between Ms, Maf, and Ps and the types of goals the person adopts. People high in the need for achievement tend to adopt performance-approach goals, people high in the fear of failure tend to adopt performance-avoidance goals, and people with high competency expectancies tend to adopt mastery goals. The classical achievement motivation constructs (Ms, Maf, and Ps) serve as antecedent conditions that influence the specific type of goals the person takes in a given achievement setting. For instance, the relationships between Ms, Maf, and Ps to the three types of achievement goals appears in Figure 6.2. The figure shows the results from an actual study (Elliot & Church, 1997) that found that the need for achievement served as an antecedent for adopting mastery and performance-approach goals, the fear of failure served as an antecedent for adopting performance-approach and performance-avoidance goals (i.e., performance goals in general), and competency expectancies served as an antecedent for adopting mastery and performance-approach goals and for rejecting performance-avoidance goals (notice the negative sign for − .14). Further, once these types of achievement goals were adopted, mastery goals increased intrinsic motivation, whereas performance-avoidance goals decreased it; performance-approach goals increased performance, whereas performance-avoidance goals decreased it (Elliot & Church, 1997). To communicate a better

TABLE 6.3 **Two Items From Each Scale of the *Achievement Goals Scale***

MASTERY GOAL
1. I desire to completely master the material presented in this class.
2. In a class like this, I prefer course material that really challenges me so I can learn new things.
PERFORMANCE-APPROACH GOAL
1. My goal in this class is to get a better grade than most of the students.
2. I want to do well in this class to show my ability to my family, friends, advisors, and others.
PERFORMANCE-AVOIDANCE GOAL
1. I just want to avoid doing poorly in this class.
2. My fear of performing poorly in this class is often what motivates me.

SOURCE: From "Approach and Avoidance Motivation and Achievement Goals," by A. J. Elliot, 1999, *Educational Psychologist, 34,* pp. 169–189.

understanding of just what performance-approach and performance-avoidance goals are, sample items from the Achievement Goal Questionnaire (Elliot & Church, 1997) appear in Table 6.3.

Integrating the classical and contemporary approaches to achievement motivation overcomes the shortcomings of each approach (Elliot, 1997). The problem with the classical approach is that general personality dispositions (Ms, Maf) do a poor job predicting achievement behavior in a specific setting. In other words, general personality factors are not necessarily the regulators of achievement behavior in specific life domains like school, sports, and work. The problem with the contemporary approach is that a person is potentially left wondering where these different types of goal orientations come from in the first place. In other words, if you know a basketball player has a performance-approach goal (e.g., to have the highest scoring average on the team), the question remains as to why he adopted that particular achievement goal rather than another. Together, the two theories can predict achievement behavior in specific situations (using achievement goals) and can explain from where these goals arise (using personality dispositions and competence perceptions).

How the classical and contemporary approaches have been integrated can be illustrated through a second reading of Figure 6.2. It models the developmental relationships between personality factors and specific achievement goals:

Ms → performance-approach goals

Maf → performance-avoidance goals

competence perceptions → mastery goals

The left-hand side of the figure shows that achievement-related motives (Ms, Maf) prompt the person to adopt one type of goal over another. The right-hand side shows that it is the type of achievement goal (rather than Ms, Maf, Ps, per se) that constitutes the direct predictor of important, situation-specific, achievement-related outcomes (which, in this particular study, were intrinsic motivation and quality of performance).

Reducing Achievement Anxiety

Question: Why would a person want to learn about the motivational states discussed in this chapter?

Answer: So that he can reduce personal anxiety experienced in achievement situations.

How much anxiety do you feel while taking tests in school, while competing in athletics, while making a presentation at work, or while working on a project such as building or repairing something? Whenever we face a standard of excellence, especially when we feel we are being evaluated by others during the performance, we feel some mixture between enthusiasm and a desire to participate and anxiety and a desire to avoid it all. The athlete running a race, for example, is both eager to test her skills and hesitant to embarrass herself.

The easiest way to reduce anxiety in achievement settings is to change the content of your thoughts. Just before running the race, for instance, an eager runner thinks, "I want to accomplish something special today," while the anxious runner thinks, "I'm afraid I'll do something wrong" (Schmalt, 1999). Notice that these thoughts mirror the performance-approach and performance-avoidance goals listed in Table 6.3. To the extent that the runner (or test taker, conference presenter, etc.) could change his performance goal from one of avoidance to one of approach, he would significantly decrease felt anxiety. And performance would improve as well.

Can control over achievement anxiety really be that simple, that straightforward—change your goals and you change your anxiety? The answer to that is no, for two reasons. First, changing the way you think is not as easy as it might first sound. Thoughts are often deeply rooted. Second, achievement situations themselves generate some anxiety—time deadlines, presence of an audience, task

Avoidance Motivation and Well-Being

So far the discussion on achievement motivation has focused attention mostly on the "approach" side of achievement. But the fear of failure drives people to regulate their behavior in all sorts of ways that interfere with performance, persistence, and emotionality (Birney et al., 1969; Elliot & Sheldon, 1997; Schmalt, 1982). That is, the fear of failure (Maf) prompts people to adopt performance-avoidance goals, such as trying to avoid performing poorly, and these avoidance-oriented goals lead people to underperform, quit quickly, and lose interest in whatever they are doing, whether the task is solving anagrams (Roney, Higgins, & Shah, 1995) or performing in school (Elliot & Church, 1997; Elliot & Harackiewicz, 1996).

Such a relationship (fear of failure → adoption of performance-avoidance goals → maladjusted coping style in achievement settings) has important implications for personal adjustment and mental health. One team of researchers measured college students' fears of failure and the extent to which they endorsed performance-avoidance goals. The researchers then assessed the students on a host of well-being measures, such as self-esteem, difficulty, and so on. And our own dispositional neuroticism (emotional instability) directly contributes to felt anxiety.

But achievement anxiety comes in two forms: cognitive worry and physiological "hyperemotionality" (i.e., arousal). The good news is that physiological hyperemotionality does not undermine performance in achievement settings, only cognitive worry does (Elliot & McGregor, 1999). The primary cause of worry in achievement settings are performance avoidance goals. That is, the roots of worry are performance-avoidance goals like, "I just want to avoid making a mistake." So in a sense, these avoidance goals are that straightforward. In trying to reduce worry-based anxiety, some good advice is to change performance-avoidance goals into performance-approach (or mastery) goals. The arousal-based anxiety may remain (e.g., you may still feel nervous or pumped up standing in front of an evaluative audience), but the worry-based anxiety that really debilitates performance will fade.

The preceding advice is precisely the procedure used in experiments on how achievement goals affect motivation, anxiety, and performance. One group of participants is randomly given a performance-approach goal, "Demonstrate you have high ability." A second group of participants is randomly given a performance-avoidance goal, "Don't do worse than others." The first group experiences less anxiety than does the second group (Elliot, 1999; Elliot & Harackiewicz, 1996; Elliot & McGregor, 1999). Experiments such as these make it clear that experimenters can change the contents of our thoughts. To reduce personal anxiety experienced in achievement situations, one has merely to do the same and change the contents of one's own thoughts and goals.

personal control, vitality, life satisfaction, and subjective well-being. The more each student feared failure, the more likely he would adopt performance-avoidance goals. And the more avoidance goals each student harbored, the poorer his well-being was on all five of these measures (Elliot & Sheldon, 1997). The primary reason well-being suffered was that in trying so hard to avoid poor performances, students regulated their day-to-day behavior in ways that produced dissatisfaction, much negative affect, and little enjoyment or sense of fulfillment.

A follow-up investigation by these same researchers showed that additional dispositional characteristics predispose people to adopt performance-avoidance goals, personality factors such as neuroticism and the belief that one has poor life skills (e.g., social skills, time management; Elliot, Sheldon, & Church, 1997). People high in the fear of failure, high in neuroticism, and low in life-skill competence tended to adopt performance-avoidance goals. For instance, some common performance-avoidance goals might be to avoid procrastination, avoid being a boor at parties, avoid being a follower, avoid being lonely, and avoid smoking or drinking. Trying to avoid doing something turns out to be a hard thing to do, relative to trying to do something (e.g., work more efficiently, be friendly at parties, take a leadership role). When people pursue avoidance goals, they generally perceive that they make little progress in the effort, and it is this perception of a lack of progress that leads to dissatisfaction, negative affectivity, and diminished interest. Such motivational and emotional states, when experienced over time, chip away at and eventually undermine subjective well-being (e.g., self-esteem, personal control, vitality, life satisfaction).

This line of research is particularly important because it shows rather convincingly that mastery goals are not necessarily more productive goal orientations than are performance goals. Instead, the pursuit of approach-oriented goals—be they mastery or performance goals—produces a self-regulatory style that is more positive and productive than the pursuit of performance-avoidance goals. Both mastery and performance-approach goals facilitate achievement and positive life outcomes, whereas performance-avoidance goals undermine them.

AFFILIATION AND INTIMACY

In its early study, the need for affiliation was conceptualized as, "establishing, maintaining, or restoring a positive, affective relationship with another person or persons" (Atkinson, Heyns, & Veroff, 1954). According to this definition, the need for affiliation is not the same construct as extraversion, friendliness, or sociability. In fact, the early investigators noted that persons high in the need for affiliation were often less popular than persons low in affiliation strivings (Atkinson, Heyns, & Veroff, 1954; Crowne & Marlowe, 1964; Shipley & Veroff, 1952). Rather than being rooted in extraversion and popularity, the need for affiliation is rooted in a fear of interpersonal rejection (Heckhausen, 1980). People with high-need affiliation interact with others to avoid negative emotions, such as fear of disapproval and loneliness, and typically experience much anxiety in their relationships. As they try to calm their anxieties, these high-need people monitor whether others disapprove of them and spend time seeking reassurance from others, a pattern of behavior that, unfortunately, tends to make them rather unpopular, as they come to be seen as "needy." The need for affiliation then can be thought of as the need for approval, acceptance, and security in interpersonal relations.

The more contemporary view of affiliation strivings recognizes its two facets: the need for approval and the need for intimacy. This dual view of affiliation strivings answers the criticism that the former conceptualization was too heavy on rejection anxiety and too light on affiliation interest, the more positive aspect of the need for affiliation (Boyatzis, 1973; McAdams, 1980).

The call for a more positive conceptualization of affiliation strivings that focused on intimacy motivation was answered by giving attention to the social motive for engaging in warm, close, positive interpersonal relations that hold little fear of rejection (McAdams, 1980, 1982a, 1982b; McAdams & Constantian, 1983; McAdams, Healy, & Kraus, 1984). The intimacy motive reflects a concern for the quality of one's social involvement. It is not so much the need to be with others as it is a willingness to "experience a warm, close, and communicative exchange with another person" (McAdams, 1980).

TABLE 6.4 **Profile of High Intimacy Motivation**

CATEGORY	DESCRIPTION
Thoughts	Of friends, of relationships
TAT Themes	Relationships produce positive affect, reciprocal dialogue between two people, expression of relationship commitment and union, and expression of interpersonal harmony
Interaction Style	Self-disclosure Intense listening habits Many conversations
Autobiography	Themes of love and dialogue are mentioned as personally significant life experiences
Peer Rating	Individual is judged to be warm, loving, sincere, nondominant
Memory	Enhanced recall with stories involving themes of interpersonal interactions

A profile of how the need for intimacy expresses itself appears in Table 6.4. An individual with a high need for intimacy thinks frequently about friends and relationships; writes imaginative stories about positive affect-laden relationships; engages in self-disclosure, intense listening, and frequent conversations; identifies love and dialogue as especially meaningful life experiences; is rated by others as warm, loving, sincere, and nondominant; and tends to remember episodes involving interpersonal interactions.

The full picture of affiliation strivings includes a theoretical conceptualization that includes both its positive aspects—the need to engage in warm, close, positive relations—and its negative aspects—the anxious need to establish, maintain, and restore interpersonal relations. These positive and negative aspects affect the extent to which people live happy, well-adjusted lives. One group of researchers, for instance, assessed young adults' needs for affiliation and intimacy (with the TAT) and found that after two decades, the men with high needs for intimacy were happier—better adjusted in work and marriage—than the men with low needs for intimacy (McAdams & Vaillant, 1982). An energizing growth quality exists within the need for intimacy.

CONDITIONS THAT INVOLVE AND SATISFY THE NEEDS FOR AFFILIATION AND INTIMACY

The principal condition that involves the need for affiliation is the deprivation of the opportunity for social interaction (McClelland, 1985). Conditions such as loneliness, rejection, and separation raise people's desires, or social needs, to be with others. Hence, the need for affiliation expresses itself as a deficiency-oriented motive (the deficiency is a lack of social interaction). In contrast, the desires, or social needs, for intimacy arise from opportunities for interpersonal caring and concern, warmth and commitment, emotional connectedness, reciprocal dialogue, congeniality, and love (McAdams, 1980). The need for intimacy expresses itself as a growth-oriented motive (the growth opportunity is enriching one's relationships). In the words of Abraham Maslow (1987), involvement and satisfaction of the need for affiliation revolves around "deprivation-love," whereas involvement and satisfaction of the need for intimacy revolves around "being-love."

Fear and Anxiety

Social isolation and fear-arousing conditions are two situations that increase a person's desire to affiliate with others (Baumeister & Leary, 1995; Schachter, 1959). Under conditions of isolation and fear, people report being jittery and tense, feeling as if they are suffering and are in pain, and seeing themselves as going to pieces. To reduce such anxiety and fear, humans typically adopt the strategy of seeking out others (Rofé, 1984). When afraid, people desire to affiliate for emotional support and to see how others handle the emotions they feel from the fear object. For example, imagine camping out in the wilderness and hearing a sudden loud noise in the middle of the night. The sudden, unexplained noise might produce fear. While feeling fear and anxiety, people seek out others, partly to see if others seem as afraid and partly to gain emotional and physical support. Having other people around while anxious is comforting, but our confidants can be practical allies as well, at least to the extent that they can help us clarify the threatening situation, provide coping strategies, and help carry out our coping attempts (Kirkpatrick & Shaver, 1988; Kulik, Mahler, & Earnest, 1994).

Stanley Schachter (1959) tested the fear-affiliation relationship. He created two experimental conditions, one of high anxiety and one of low anxiety. All participants were told that they were about to receive some electric shocks (the fear object). The experimenter told participants in the high-anxiety group that they were going to receive intense shocks: "These shocks will hurt, they will be painful." The experimenter told participants in the low-anxiety group that they were going to receive very mild shocks that "will not in any way be painful" and would feel more like a tickle than a shock. The experimenter announced that there would first be a 10-minute wait, and he asked participants if they preferred to wait alone, with another participant, or did not care one way or the other. Of course, no one was ever shocked. As to the findings, most high-anxiety participants wanted to wait with another person, whereas most low-anxiety participants preferred to wait alone or did not care one way or the other. A second investigation found that anxious people's desires to affiliate applied only to those instances in which each person was anxious for the same reason (i.e., they faced the same threat). Hence, the old adage "misery loves company" must be qualified as "misery loves miserable company." The popularity of mutual support groups, for example, for alcoholics, unwed mothers, patients suffering a particular illness, and people facing particular adjustment problems, provides some confirming testimony to the human tendency to seek out others with similar problems or conditions when troubled or anxious.

Embarrassment

Whereas anxiety increases affiliation strivings, embarrassment decreases them. Imagine a study in which one group of participants were told they would be asked to disclose their innermost private feelings, personal inadequacies, and fears to strangers while their truthfulness was monitored by a lie detector (Teichman, 1973). Participants in a second group were told they were to engage in normal, natural conversation on enjoyable topics. In addition to this high- versus low-anxiety manipulation, the study added a high- versus low-embarrassment manipulation. Participants in the high-embarrassment group were asked to use objects of oral gratification such as baby bottles, pacifiers, breast shields, and lollipops, so the experimenter could ostensibly determine their physiological responsiveness to oral gratification. Participants in the low-embarrassment group were given essentially the same story, except the objects of oral gratification were neutral and not embarrassing, such as whistles and balloons. When made to feel anxious, people generally preferred to wait with another person (as was found in the previous study), but when made to feel embarrassed, fewer people wanted to wait with another person. Thus, anxiety increased, while embarrassment decreased, affiliation strivings.

Development of Interpersonal Relationships

In an apparent effort to initiate new friendships, people with a high need for intimacy typically join more social groups, spend more of their time interacting with others, and when friendships are started, form more stable, long-lasting relationships than do persons with a low need for intimacy (McAdams & Losoff, 1984). As relationships develop, high-need intimacy individuals come to know more personal information and history about their friends (McAdams & Losoff, 1984; McAdams, Healy, & Krause, 1984). And they report being more and more satisfied as their relationships progress, whereas individuals with a low need for intimacy report being less and less satisfied with their developing relationships (Eidelson, 1980). Individuals with a high need for intimacy perceive the tightening bonds of friendship as satisfying, whereas those with a low-need intimacy perceive the tightening bonds of friendship as stifling and as an entrapment.

Maintaining Interpersonal Networks

Once a relationship has been established, individuals with a high need for affiliation strive to maintain those relationships by making more telephone calls, writing more letters, and paying more visits to their friends than do those with a low need for affiliation (Lansing & Heyns, 1959). Those with a high need for intimacy also spend more time in telephone conversations (Boyatzis, 1972) and more time writing letters and participating in face-to-face conversations, compared to those with a low need for intimacy (McAdams & Constantian, 1983).

One study asked persons with high and low needs for intimacy to keep a logbook over a two-month period on which they were to record 10 twenty-minute friendship episodes (McAdams, Healy, & Krause, 1984). Those with a high need for intimacy reported more dyadic (versus larger group) friendship episodes, more self-disclosure, more listening, and more trust and concern for the well-being of their friends. Such a finding underscores the high-intimacy-need person's want of a warm and personal (i.e., intimate) friendship pattern. Even when thinking and talking about strangers, high-intimacy-need persons treat others differently from low-intimacy-need persons in that they use more positive adjectives when describing others and they avoid talking about others in negative terms (McClelland, et al., 1982).

High-intimacy-need persons laugh, smile, and make eye contact with others during interaction more frequently than do low-intimacy-need persons (McAdams, Jackson, &

Kirshnit, 1984). Such laughing, smiling, and eye contact behaviors lead others to rate high-intimacy-need persons as relatively warm, sincere, and loving human beings (McAdams & Losoff, 1984).

Gender moderates the relationship between the need for affiliation and its satisfaction. Both high-need-for-affiliation boys and girls report wishing to be with their friends, but girls actually spend more time with their friends than boys. Hence, high-need-for-affiliation girls generally report a positive day-to-day mood, whereas high-need-for-affiliation boys generally report a negative (need-frustrated) day-to-day mood (Wong & Csikszentmihalyi, 1991).

Satisfying the Needs for Affiliation and Intimacy

Because it is largely a deficit-oriented motive, the need for affiliation, when satisfied, brings out emotions like relief rather than joy. When interacting with others, people high in the need for affiliation go out of their way to avoid conflict (Exline, 1962), avoid competitive situations (Terhune, 1968), are unselfish and cooperative (McAdams, 1980), avoid talking about others in a negative way (McClelland, 1985), and resist making imposing demands on others (McAdams & Powers, 1981). High-need-for-affiliation individuals prefer careers that provide positive relationships and support for others (the helping professions; Sid & Lindgren, 1981), and they perform especially well under conditions that support their need to be accepted and included (McKeachie, et al., 1966). When told that others will be evaluating them, high-need-for-affiliation people experience relatively high levels of anxiety via a fear of rejection (Byrne, 1961). Social acceptance, approval, and reassurance then constitute need-satisfying conditions for people high in the need for affiliation.

Because it is largely a growth-oriented motive, people satisfy the need for intimacy through achieving closeness and warmth in a relationship. Hence, people high in the need for intimacy more frequently touch others (in a nonthreatening way; McAdams & Powers, 1981), successfully cultivate deeper and more meaningful relationships (McAdams & Losoff, 1984), find satisfaction in listening and in self-disclosure (McAdams, Healey, & Krause, 1984), and look, laugh, and smile more during interaction (McAdams, Jackson, & Kirshnit, 1984). Participating in a warm, close, reciprocal, and enduring relationship then constitutes the need-satisfying condition for people high in the need for intimacy.

POWER

The essence of the need for power is a desire to make the material and social world conform to one's personal image or plan for it (Winter & Stewart, 1978). People high in the need for power desire to have "impact, control, or influence over another person, group, or the world at large" (Winter, 1973). *Impact* allows power-needing individuals to initiate and establish power, *control* allows for power to be maintained, and *influence* allows them to expand or restore power.

Such power strivings often center around a need for dominance, reputation, status, or position. High-need-for-power individuals seek to become (and stay) leaders, and they interact with others with a forceful, take-charge style. When asked to recall the peak experiences in their lives, for instance, individuals high in the need for power report life events associated with strong positive emotions that occurred as a result of their impact on others, such as being elected to a leadership position or receiving applause from an audience (McAdams, 1982b).

David Winter (1973) provides two scenarios that illustrate power strivings. In the first scenario, research participants watched a film of an authority figure giving an influential speech (John F. Kennedy's presidential inaugural address), and in the second scenario, another set of participants watched a hypnotist ordering students to behave in particular ways as an audience watched. After having his participants view one of these two scenarios, Winter asked each group to complete a TAT, and he scored the resulting protocols for the arousal of power strivings. As expected, these groups scored higher in power strivings (by writing stories rich in power-related imagery) than did a comparison group who did not view the film or hypnosis session (Winter, 1973).

Others have performed experiments that essentially replicated this procedure, but in addition to measuring power strivings, they added measures of mood and physiological arousal (Steele, 1977). As high-need-for-power individuals listened to inspirational speeches, their moods became significantly more lively and energetic and their physiological arousal (measured by epinephrine, or adrenaline) showed a striking increase. Based on these findings, the opportunity to involve one's power strivings fills the power-needing individual with a vigor that can be measured via fantasy, mood, and psychophysiological activation (Steele, 1977).

CONDITIONS THAT INVOLVE AND SATISFY THE NEED FOR POWER

Four conditions are noteworthy in their capacity for involving and satisfying the need for power: leadership, aggressiveness, influential occupations, and prestige possessions.

Leadership

People with a high need for power seek recognition in groups and find ways for making themselves visible to others, apparently in an effort to attain influence (Winter, 1973). Power-seeking college students, for example, write more letters to the university newspaper, and power-seeking adults willingly take risks in achieving public visibility (McClelland & Teague, 1975; McClelland & Watson, 1973). They are also more likely to put in hours at a public radio station, presumably in pursuit of an impact on an audience of listeners (Sonnenfield, 1974, cited in McClelland, 1985). They argue more frequently with their professors, and they show an eagerness in getting their points across in the classroom (Veroff, 1957). In selecting their friends and coworkers, power-striving individuals generally prefer others who are not well known and are thus in a position to be led (Fodor & Farrow, 1979; Winter, 1973). When hanging out with their friends, they prefer small groups over dyads, and they utilize an interpersonal orientation that takes on more of a tone of influence and organization than it does one of intimacy (McAdams, Healey, & Krause, 1984).

In dating relationships, high-need-for-power men generally fare poorly (Stewart & Rubin, 1976). And they fare no better in marriage, as they generally make poor husbands, at least from the spouse's point of view (McClelland et al., 1978). In both dating and marriage, high-need-for-power women do not suffer the same poor outcomes that men do, apparently because they resist using interpersonal relationships as an arena for satisfying their power needs (Winter, 1988).

To test the influence of the need for power on tendencies toward leadership, experimenters arranged to have a group of strangers interact with each other for a short time (after completing the TAT to identify each individual's need for power; Fodor & Smith, 1982; Jones, 1969, cited in McClelland, 1985; Winter & Stewart, 1978). Power-seeking individuals talked more and were judged to have exerted more influence. However, the power-seeking individuals were not the best liked, nor were they judged to have contributed the most to getting the job done or for coming to a satisfactory conclusion. In fact, groups that had high-need-for-power leaders were the ones that produced the poorest decisions. These groups exchanged less information, considered few alternative strategies, and reached poorer final decisions than did groups with a leader low in the need for power. These findings suggest that power-seeking leaders attempt to make others follow their personal plan, even though their assertiveness and leadership style is often detrimental to group functioning.

Aggressiveness

If the need for power revolves around desires for impact, control, and influence over others, aggression ought to be a means for both involving and satisfying power needs. To some extent, the relationship between the need for power and aggression holds true, as men high in power strivings get into more arguments and participate more frequently in competitive sports (McClelland, 1975; Winter, 1973). However, the relationship between the need for power and aggression is diluted because society largely controls and inhibits people's acts of overt aggression. For this reason, aggressive manifestations of the need for power largely express themselves as impulses to (rather than actual acts of) aggression. Males and females with high needs for power report significantly more impulses to act aggressively (McClelland, 1975). When asked, "Have you ever felt like carrying out the following: yelling at someone in traffic, throwing things around the room, destroying furniture or breaking glassware, or insulting clerks in stores?" individuals high in the need for power report significantly more impulses to carry out these acts (Boyatzis, 1973). When asked if they had carried out such behaviors, those with a high need for power did not actually act on their impulses any more or less than did those with a low need for power.

Societal inhibitions and restraints largely constrain the power-seeking person's expression of aggression, but when societal inhibitions are forgone, high-need-for-power men are more aggressive than low-need-for-power men (McClelland, 1975; McClelland, et al., 1972; Winter, 1973). Alcohol is one socially acceptable means of gaining a release from societal inhibitions, and power-seeking men do indeed act relatively more aggressively after drinking (McClelland et al., 1972). Alcohol likely contributes to individuals' aggressiveness, however, by making them feel more powerful. Similarly, because men get feelings of power from drinking, men with the highest need for power drink the most (McClelland et al., 1972). This research suggests that people can not only increase power through reputation, prestige, and leadership, but they can also create the perception and the feeling of increased power through strategies such as drinking alcohol, risk-taking, gesturing and posturing, using abusive language, using drugs, and driving very fast. When life becomes stressful and frustrating, high-need-for-power individuals sometimes seek alcohol as a means for inflating their sense of control (Cooper et al., 1995). Similarly, power-seeking men, but not power-seeking women, frequently respond to stress and setbacks by inflicting abuse on their intimates (Mason & Blankenship, 1987).

Influential Occupations

People high in the need for power are attracted to occupations such as business executives, teachers or professors, psychologists, journalists, clerics, and international diplomats (Winter, 1973). Each of these occupations shares a common denominator in that the person in the occupational role is in the position to direct the behavior of other people in accordance with some preconceived plan (Winter & Stewart, 1978). People in some of these professions speak to and influence audiences (teachers, journalists, clergy), others have inside information they use to influence others (psychologists, diplomats), and others have a professional status that allows them to tell others what to do (business executives). Further, these careers equip the individual with the rewards and punishments necessary for sanctioning the behavior of others. The teacher, cleric, and diplomat, for instance, all have the means for rewarding and punishing other people's compliance or disobedience (through grades, heavenly rewards, and deal making). The journalist can sanction the behavior of others through editorial means. The business executive administers orders and employee schedules and enforces these orders and schedules through salaries and wages, bonuses, and job security. Thus, people can involve and satisfy their power strivings through the job they choose.

Prestige Possessions

People high in the need for power tend to amass a collection of symbols of power, or "prestige possessions" (Winter, 1973). Among college students, individuals high in the need for power are more likely than others to possess a car, wine glasses, a television set, a stereo, wall hangings, carpeted floor, and so on. They are also more likely to put their name on their dormitory room door. Older, power-seeking individuals are more likely to own a rifle or pistol, a convertible car, or a truck that exudes status, power, or both (McClelland, 1975).

LEADERSHIP MOTIVE PATTERN

A special variant of the need for power is the leadership motive pattern (McClelland, 1975, 1985; McClelland & Burnham, 1976; Spangler & House, 1991). Leadership motivation consists of a threefold pattern of needs: (1) above-average need for power, (2) below-average need for intimacy/affiliation, and (3) above-average activity inhibition (operationally determined by the number of times the word "not" appears in a TAT protocol, usually signifying inhibition of action; McClelland, 1982). Thus, the leadership motive pattern features individuals who desire to exercise influence, are not concerned with being liked, and are well controlled. For instance, the stereotypical military commander or traditional father figure fits this leadership motive pattern rather well.

Such a constellation of high power, low affiliation, and self-control/inhibition generally results in effective leaders and managers (Spangler & House, 1991). The characteristics of an internally controlling style (i.e., high activity inhibition) are important because managers who are high in power, low in affiliation, and high in inhibition are generally productive, successful, and rated high by workers (McClelland & Burnham, 1976). In contrast, managers who are high in power, low in affiliation, but low in inhibition are often unproductive, unsuccessful, and rated low by workers. Apparently, an internally controlling style leads power-striving managers to internalize characteristics associated with effective management: respect for institutional authority, discipline, self-control, and a concern for just rewards (McClelland, 1975, 1985).

Effectiveness of U.S. Presidents

The leadership motive provides a framework for assessing the effectiveness of U.S. presidents (Spangler & House, 1991; Winter, 1973, 1987). Winter coded the thematic content of each president's inaugural address for the social needs of achievement, affiliation, and power and used these scores to predict presidential effectiveness. Presidents generally considered strong by historians—Kennedy, Truman, Wilson, and both Roosevelts—scored relatively high on power needs and relatively low on affiliation needs.

The following five variables defined presidential effectiveness: direct presidential actions (e.g., entering and avoiding war), perceived greatness by others, performance on social issues, performance on economic issues, and international relations. To assess each president's needs for power, affiliation, and activity inhibition, the researchers coded their inaugural speeches, presidential letters, and other speeches. The leadership motive pattern of high power, low affiliation, and high inhibition correlated significantly with all five measures of effectiveness. Apparently, when the United States elects a candidate with personal dispositions consistent with the leadership motive pattern, the nation is electing someone into office who will probably perform quite well, given the demands and challenges of the office.

The leadership motive pattern also predicts when leaders will engage in war and when leaders will pursue peace (Winter, 1993). Of course, war has many nonpsychological causes, but on the psychological side, historical research shows that when leaders express a motive profile of high power and low affiliation, the probability of subsequent war increases. Using British history, British-German World War I communications, and U.S.-Soviet communications during the Cuban Missile Crisis as his database, Winter found that the motive patterns expressed in speeches predicted forthcoming war-versus-peace decisions. When power imagery rose, war became a historically more likely event. When power imagery fell, war was less likely and ongoing wars tended to end. When affiliation imagery rose, war became a historically less likely event. When affiliation imagery fell, war was more likely to begin (Winter, 1993).

SUMMARY

Acquired psychological needs include both quasi-needs and social needs. Quasi-needs are situationally induced wants and desires, such as wanting a high grade-point average or needing money. Such situational pressures produce a psychological context of tension and urgency that generates an ephemeral motivation for interacting with the environment. Social needs are more enduring. They arise from the individual's personal experiences and unique developmental, cognitive, and socialization histories. Once acquired, social needs act as emotional and behavioral potentials activated by situational incentives. For achievement, the need-activating incentive is doing something well to show personal competence. For affiliation, the need-activating incentive is an opportunity to please others and gain their approval. For the intimacy need, the need-activating incentive is a warm, secure relationship. For power, the need-activating incentive is having impact on others.

The need for achievement is the desire to do well relative to a standard of excellence. When facing standards of excellence, people's emotional reactions vary. Individuals high in the need for achievement generally respond with approach-oriented emotions (e.g., hope) and behaviors, whereas individuals low in the need for achievement and high in the fear of failure generally respond with avoidance-oriented emotions (e.g., anxiety) and behaviors. In terms of specific approach-avoidance behavioral differences, high-need achievers, compared to low-need achievers, choose moderately difficult tasks, quickly engage in achievement-related tasks, put forth more effort and perform better on moderately difficult tasks, persist in the face of difficulty and failure, and take a personal responsibility for successes and failures.

According to Atkinson's classical model of achievement, behavioral approach versus avoidance is a multiplicative function of the individual's needs for achievement, probability of success, and incentive for success (i.e., $Ts = Ms \times Ps \times Is$), as well as the individual's fear of failure, probability of failure, and incentive to avoid failure (i.e., $Taf = Maf \times Pf \times If$). This formula predicts approach versus avoidance behaviors rather well in situations such as performance on moderately difficult tasks, interpersonal competition, and entrepreneurship.

Achievement goals explain why a person shows achievement behaviors, and three types of achievement goals exist: performance-approach, performance-avoidance, and mastery. In general, high need for achievement predicts the adoption of performance-approach goals, high fear of failure predicts the adoption of performance-avoidance goals, and high competency expectancies on the task at hand predict mastery goals. Mastery and performance-approach goals are generally associated with achievement and positive outcomes, whereas performance-avoidance goals are not.

Affiliation strivings have two facets: the need for affiliation (rejection anxiety) and the need for intimacy (affiliation interest). The need for affiliation involves establishing, maintaining, and restoring relationships with others, mostly to escape from and to avoid negative emotions such as disapproval and loneliness. The need for intimacy is the social motive for engaging in warm, close, positive interpersonal relationships that produce positive emotions and hold little threat of rejection. Depriving people of the opportunity for social interaction is the principal condition that involves the need for affiliation, and social acceptance, approval, and reassurance constitute its need-satisfying conditions.

Engaging in, developing, and maintaining warm, close relationships involve the need for intimacy, and individuals with high intimacy needs are more likely to join social groups, spend time interacting with others, and form stable, long-lasting relationships that are characterized by self-disclosure and positive affect expressed through looking, laughing, and smiling. Participating in these warm, reciprocal, and enduring relationships constitutes the condition that satisfies the need for intimacy.

The need for power is the desire for making the material and social world conform to one's personal image for it. High-need-for-power individuals strive for leadership and recognition in small groups, experience frequent impulses of aggression, prefer influential occupations, and amass prestige possessions. A special variant of the need for power is the leadership motive pattern, which consists of the threefold pattern of needs involving (1) above average need for power, (2) below average need for intimacy, and (3) above average activity inhibition. Leaders, managers in the workplace, and presidents in U. S. history who possess constellations of needs consistent with the leadership motive pattern generally perform well and are rated by others as effective.

RECOMMENDED READINGS

Need for Achievement

Atkinson, J. W. (1964). A theory of achievement motivation. *An introduction to motivation* (240–268). Princeton, NJ: D. Van Nostrand.

Elliot, A. J. (1999). Approach and avoidance motivation and achievement goals. *Educational Psychologist, 34,* 169–189.

Elliot, A. J., & Church, M. A. (1997). A hierarchical model of approach and avoidance achievement motivation. *Journal of Personality and Social Psychology, 72,* 218–232.

Elliot, A. J., & Sheldon, K. M. (1997). Avoidance achievement motivation: A personal goals analysis. *Journal of Personality and Social Psychology, 72,* 218–232.

McClelland, D. C. (1965). Achievement and entrepreneurship: A longitudinal study. *Journal of Personality and Social Psychology, 1,* 389–392.

Needs of Affiliation and Intimacy

Lansing, J. B., & Heyns, R. W. (1959). Need affiliation and frequency of four types of communication. *Journal of Abnormal and Social Psychology, 58,* 365–372.

McAdams, D. P., Jackson, R. J., & Kirshnit, C. (1984). Looking, laughing, and smiling in dyads as a function of intimacy motivation and reciprocity. *Journal of Personality, 52,* 261–273.

McAdams, D. P., & Losoff, M. (1984). Friendship motivation in fourth and sixth graders: A thematic analysis. *Journal of Social and Personal Relations, 1,* 11–27.

Need for Power

Spangler, W. D., & House, R. J. (1991). Presidential effectiveness and the leadership motive profile. *Journal of Personality and Social Psychology, 60,* 439–455.

Steele, R. S. (1977). Power motivation, activation, and inspirational speeches. *Journal of Personality, 45,* 53–64.

Winter, D. G. (1988). The power motive in women—and men. *Journal of Personality and Social Psychology, 54,* 510–519.

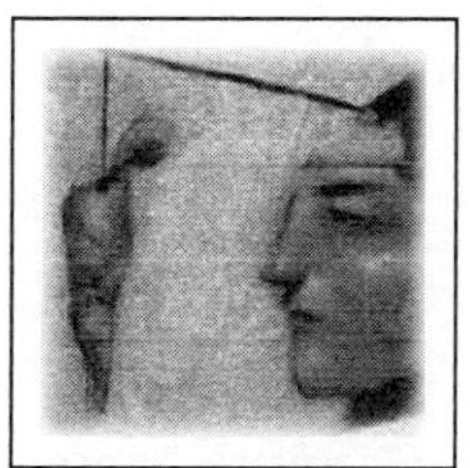

II

Cognition

7

Plans and Goals

You have heard the expression, "Mirrors don't lie." Lately, your mirror has been saying you have added a few pounds. It is time, you decide, to lose 10 pounds and get back on the road to physical fitness. You want to take action, but how? When? What?

Jogging seems sensible, so you start. At first, jogging is new, even fun, as you enjoy the outdoors and sense of accomplishment. A week goes by, but you do not lose much weight. You begin to wonder how much exercise is enough exercise. Another week goes by and the pressures of everyday living increase and distract your attention away from exercise. Each day you find it more difficult to mobilize the effort and find the time to exercise. After a month of lackluster progress, jogging is history.

Months later, strolling through a used bookstore, you happen across the book *Aerobics* (Cooper, 1968). You still think exercising and getting into shape are important, so you flip through its pages. Its critical feature is a point system. Page after page, the book lists several different aerobic activities, such as running, swimming, and cycling. For each exercise, the system lists a distance, a performance time, and a number of aerobic points earned for that particular distance and time. For example, under running, joggers who run one mile in 8 minutes or less earn 5 aerobic points. Under cycling, cyclists who bike for 2.5 miles in 12 minutes or less earn 5 aerobic points. A few pages later, the book provides a personal progress chart with space for writing in the date, the exercise, its distance and duration, number of points earned, and cumulative points earned for each week. According to *Aerobics,* a person needs to earn 30 aerobic points per week to increase physical fitness and to decrease weight.

You have a goal. No longer are you going to just "do your best"; you are now going to earn 30 aerobic points per week. You start the week bent on earning 30 points, but your body protests that 20 is enough. Because you cannot quite earn 30 points, you find yourself devising point-increasing strategies (e.g., exercise in the morning). By the end of the third week, you earn the 30 points and feel the warm glow of accomplishment. After a month, you boldly decide to try for 40 points per week. You now have a new goal. It will take more effort, more persistence, and perhaps a new and improved exercise strategy. But because you achieved your earlier goal and because your stamina has increased, you feel up to the lifestyle change. Eagerness has replaced apathy.

This chapter asks how and why mental events such as goals mobilize effort and increase commitment to a long-term course of action. How do mental events lead us to envision the possibilities for our future, and how do mental events help us develop the plans and intentions we need to bring those possibilities to fruition? This chapter discusses plans and goals as ways of thinking that have motivational properties. The first part of the chapter focuses on making plans and goals, while the second half focuses on formulating intentions for actually carrying out those plans and goals. Chapters 8 through 10 will discuss other ways of thinking that are also capable of energizing and directing behavior—expectancies (chapter 8), attributions and values (chapter 9), and the self (chapter 10). The nature of cognition will first be considered.

NATURE OF COGNITION

A cognitive perspective on motivation focuses on mental processes (thoughts) as causal determinants to action (Gollwitzer & Bargh, 1996). Among the more heavily researched motivational agents in the cognition → action sequence are the following: plans (Miller, Galanter, & Pribram, 1960), goals (Locke & Latham, 1990), implementation intentions (Gollwitzer, 1999), implicit theories (Dweck, 1999), dissonance (Harmon-Jones & Mills, 1999), appraisals (Lazarus, 1991a), schemas (Ortony, Clore, & Collins, 1988), mental simulations (Taylor et al., 1998), expectancies (Peterson, Maier, & Seligman, 1993), self-efficacy (Bandura, 1986), attributions (Weiner, 1986), values (Brophy, 1999), and the self-concept (Markus & Nurius, 1986).

A typical sequence of events within a cognitive analysis of motivation appears in Figure 7.1. Events in the external environment affect the senses and supply information to be processed and interpreted by the brain. Seeing a friend beckoning us or hearing the telephone ring initiates active information processing. Such sensory information is attended to, transformed, organized, elaborated on, and held in mind while relevant information is retrieved from memory to assist in the information-processing flow. Based on our understanding of the meaning and personal significance of the information processed, we build up expectancies (e.g., of what our friend wants to talk about), construct goals (e.g., to persuade our friend to join us for lunch), formulate plans (e.g., of what to talk about), and so forth. These cognitive constructions direct behavior toward a particular course of action that reflects the content of our thoughts (e.g., goals lead to goal-directed behaviors). Once the behavioral activity is carried out, outcomes occur (e.g., success, failure, improvement, rejection) that are attended to, appraised, and explained. These behavioral outcomes add further to the active information-processing flow and, hence, contribute to the ongoing cognitive regulation of behavior.

The concern of cognitive psychology is twofold. First, cognitive psychology is the study of how people understand the world in which they live, as indicated on the left-hand side of Figure 7.1 (sensory experience affects information processing; Anderson, 1995a, 1995b; Neisser, 1967). Second, cognitive psychology is the study of how people use thoughts to regulate behavior and adapt successfully to the environment (cognitive constructions affect action; Wittrock, 1992). Motivational psychologists attend to this second concern—how thoughts guide action. From a motivational point of view, cognition can function as a "spring to action," a moving force that energizes and directs action in purposive ways (Ames & Ames, 1984).

FIGURE 7.1 **Sequence of Events in the Cognitive View of Behavior**

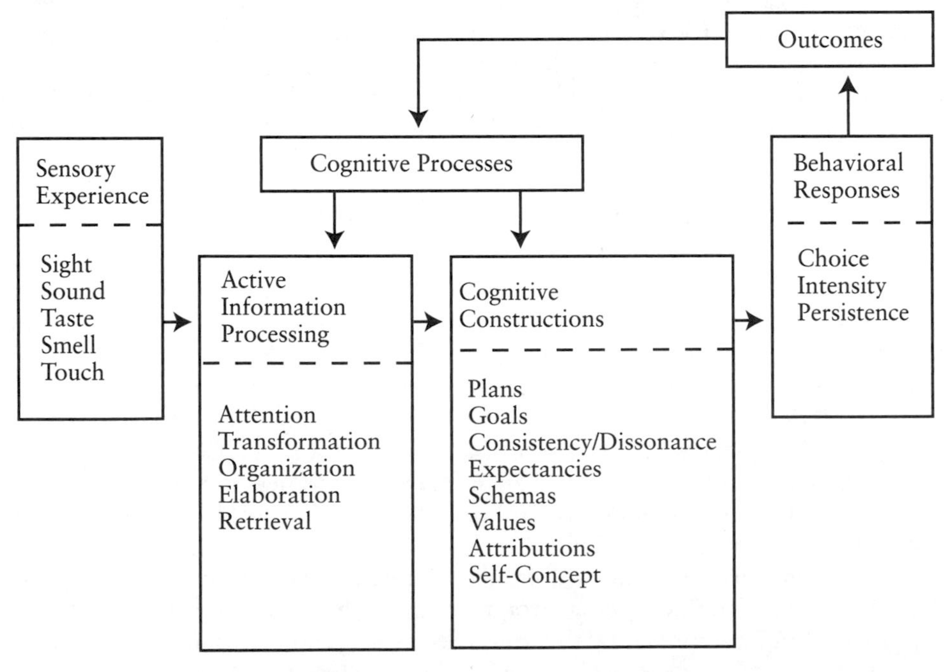

PIONEER THEORISTS IN THE COGNITIVE APPROACH TO MOTIVATION

This chapter illustrates how plans and goals function as springs to action. First, however, a little history might help. Two pioneers in the cognitive understanding of motivation were Edward Tolman and Kurt Lewin.

Tolman

Tolman was an early- to mid-1900s behaviorist whose observations led him to conclude that behavior "reeks of purpose." Tolman (1925, 1932, 1959) actually meant that behavior was perpetually goal directed and that people were always approaching or avoiding goal objects. For instance, people drive to particular places, and librarians search for particular books. Once the goal is attained, behavior ceases. Hence, behavior is fundamentally purposive. In addition, behavior exudes knowledge (cognition). To attain goals, people depend heavily on hypotheses and expectations. The librarian's book searches, for instance, are entrenched in hypotheses/expectations because librarians know where to look and know what they will find when they look there (Tolman, 1938; Tolman, Ritchie, & Kalish, 1946a, 1946b).

Tolman's terms for purpose and cognition were demand and expectation, respectively. *Demands* arose from bodily needs (e.g., hunger, thirst, sex, sleep, pain), so purpose therefore constituted the desire to obtain an environmental object capable of satisfying the bodily demand (food, water). Behavior reeked with purpose because people always had bodily demands to satisfy. *Expectations* arose as people searched for demand-satisfying objects. Cognition was the person's acquired "cognitive map" of "what leads to what" in the environment. Environmental searches for demand-satisfying objects were not random but instead were constantly informed by expectations.

As an illustration, consider how you learned your way around campus. First, you learned the general location of a major building, such as a dormitory. Then you learned what buildings are near that building, perhaps the student union and the administration building. You learned these things simply through repetition and by becoming familiar with your new surroundings. Soon, you developed a cognitive map of the campus—the distances and directions of certain locations, such as the athletic fields, library, parking lots, and cafeteria. Most of what you learned occurred because demands arose (e.g., need to register for classes, need to find a cup of coffee) that initiated search behavior. If you have no need to find the biology lab, for example, you probably have never learned where it is. Thus, purpose drives the searching, which is instrumental in improving your cognition. Notice how much of our behavior is guided by demand and expectations and by purpose and cognition.

Tolman's Influence on Contemporary Motivation Theory

In Tolman's era, the dominant learning theories were stimulus-response (S-R) conceptualizations (Hull, 1943; Guthrie, 1959). In contrast, Tolman advocated mental events as intervening variables between S and R. Tolman showed how expectancies are acquired and how expectancies, once acquired, motivate behavior. In doing so, Tolman formulated and popularized the cognitive approach to motivation and behavior. Throughout part 2 of this book, the reader should not lose sight of Tolman's intervening-variable approach in which mental events (not environmental stimuli) motivate action:

$$S \rightarrow \text{cognitive event} \rightarrow R$$

This model is the basis for many cognitive interpretations of motivation. The primary variable that changes from one cognitive theory to the next is the cognitive event that is being studied as the agent of motivation, as the spring to action (plans, goals, expectations, self-concept, etc.).

Lewin

Like Tolman, Lewin's (1935) cognitive understanding of motivation portrayed the individual as a goal-seeking organism. The person was always approaching or avoiding something. What made the person approach or avoid was a need. Needs originated not only from bodily demands but also from psychological demands. ("I need to do well on this test today!") Needs produced *intentions*. Thus, for example, a need for a new pair of shoes produced an intent to go to the shoe store to buy them. Once an intention was formulated, tension remained until that intention was fulfilled through consummatory action. Thus, for Lewin, needs created intentions, intentions produced tensions, and tensions motivated approach and avoidance consummatory behavior:

$$\text{need} \rightarrow \text{intention} \rightarrow \text{tension} \rightarrow \text{approach and avoidance}$$

Lewin's cognitive construct was valence. *Valence* referred to the positive or negative value environmental objects had on an individual. Attractive and tension-reducing objects acquired positive valence; threatening and tension-producing objects acquired negative valence. Notice that a goal object becomes attractive in proportion to one's need for it (Biner & Hua, 1995; Biner et al., 1995; Biner et al., 1998). Hence, motivation unfolds as a continuous and perpetually repeating cycle of the following formula for finding positively valenced goal objects capable of quieting the need:

$$\text{need} \rightarrow \text{intention} \rightarrow \text{tension} \rightarrow \text{goal-directed search}$$

Consider the motivational dynamics—the intentions and valences—of the child who peers into the store window and eyes a wished-for toy. The sight of the toy arouses a toy-desiring need, which both arouses an intention to approach the toy and which gives the toy a positive valence. The intention stirs the child to restlessness (i.e., a state of tension). The child then engages in a great deal of cognitive activity (e.g., expectancies, problem solving) to figure out a means for satisfying the toy-possessing need. The motivational force will continue until the need for the toy is satisfied.

Lewin's Influence on Contemporary Motivation Theory

For Lewin, individuals locomote through a psychological space, pushed by intentions and pulled by environmental valences. Lewin conceptualized human beings as bodies in motion that moved in certain directions because of pushing internal forces and pulling environmental forces. Traditional theorists (including Tolman) emphasized the long developmental learning history of individuals that created relatively enduring motivations (e.g., long-term goals). Lewin, on the other hand, emphasized the here-and-now influences underlying contemporaneous and situation-specific motivations and behaviors (Jones, 1985). Thus, the study of motivation was expanded to include analyses of the motivations that arose as one peers longingly into store windows and as one madly panics and problem solves to beat a five o'clock deadline.

PLANS

The contemporary cognitive study of motivation began when a trio of psychologists, George Miller, Eugene Galanter, and Karl Pribram, investigated how plans motivate behavior (1960). According to the trio, people have mental representations of the ideal states of their behavior, environmental objects, and events. In other words, people, for instance, have in mind what an ideal tennis serve looks like (ideal behavior), what an ideal birthday gift would be (ideal environmental object), and what constitutes an ideal night on the town (ideal event). People are also aware of the present state of their behavior, environment, and events. That is, people have the knowledge of their current tennis serve (present behavior), gift (present object), and evening itinerary (present event).

Any mismatch perceived between one's present state and one's ideal state instigates an experience of "incongruity," which has motivational properties. Suffering incongruity, people formulate a plan of action to remove it (Miller, Galanter, & Pribum, 1960; Newell, Shaw, & Simon, 1958). To do so, people develop a plan of action to progress their present state toward the ideal. The incongruity acts as the motivational "spring to action" (provides energy), and the plan is the cognitive means for advancing the present state toward the ideal state (provides direction).

The cognitive mechanism by which plans energize and direct behavior is the test-operate-test-exit (TOTE) model, as illustrated in Figure 7.2 (Miller, Galanter, & Pribram, 1960). *Test* means to compare the present state against the ideal. A mismatch between the two (incongruity) springs the individual into action. That is, the mismatch motivates the individual to *operate* on the environment via a planned sequence of action. After a period of action, the person again *tests* the present state against the ideal. Given incongruity, the person continues to *operate* on the environment (T-O-T-O-T-O, and so on). As long as the incongruity persists, action ("operate") continues. If and whenever the present matches the ideal, the person *exits* the plan.

Consider the following example of the TOTE model. A painter takes an easel to a waterfall, paints the scenery, compares the canvas to the waterfall, and notices that the two are quite dissimilar. Because the canvas does not yet show a satisfactory representation of the waterfall, the painter operates on the painting to reflect on the canvas the ideal picture in her mind. The painter continually compares (tests) the painting on the canvas to its ideal in her mind. As long as incongruity persists, the painting continues (T-O-T-O-T-O, and so on). Only when the actual and ideal paintings match does the painter exit the plan and cease to

FIGURE 7.2 **Schematic of the TOTE Model**

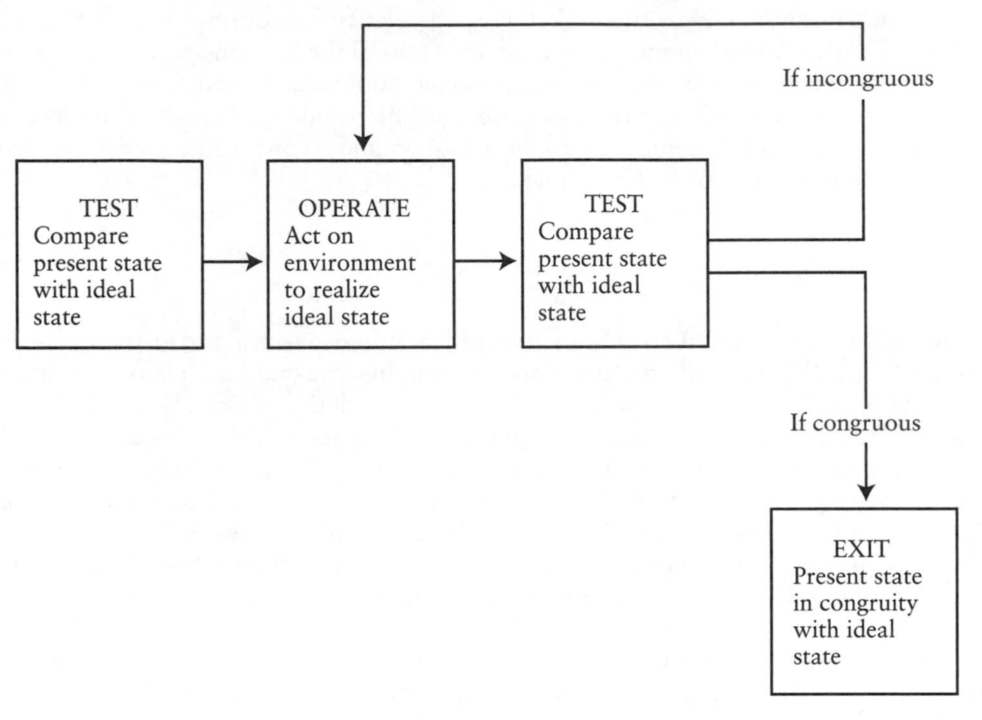

paint. The ever-repeated process of comparing the present versus the ideal, followed by incongruity-reducing behavioral adjustments, is a common feature of everyday life.

CORRECTIVE MOTIVATION

The plan → action sequence portrays individuals as (1) detecting present-ideal inconsistencies, (2) generating a plan to eliminate the incongruity, (3) instigating plan-regulated behavior, and (4) monitoring feedback as to the extent of any remaining present-ideal incongruity. Most contemporary researchers (Campion & Lord, 1982; Carver & Scheier, 1981, 1982, 1990), however, no longer view plans as so fixed, static, and mechanical. Rather, plans are adjustable and subject to frequent revision. Given an incongruity between present and ideal, the individual's plan is as likely to change and undergo modification as is his behavior. The emphasis on modifiable plans is important because it presents human beings as active decision makers who choose which process to follow: (a) act to achieve the ideal state or (b) change and revise an ineffective plan (Carver & Scheier, 1981, 1982). From this point of view, any present-ideal incongruity does not instigate an automatic discrepancy-motivated action sequence. Rather, incongruity gives rise to a more generalized "corrective motivation" (Campion & Lord, 1982).

Corrective motivation activates a decision-making process in which the individual considers many ways for reducing the present-ideal incongruity: Change the plan, change behavior (increase effort), or withdraw from the plan altogether. That is, plan-directed behavior is a dynamic, flexible process in which corrective motivation energizes the individual to pursue the most adaptive course.

Corrective motivation also involves emotional processes (Carver & Scheier, 1990). When people progress toward their ideal states at rates equal to their expectations, they feel little emotion. When people progress toward their ideal states at slower than expected rates, however, the persistent and salient discrepancy produces negative emotions such as anxiety, frustration, or despair. When people progress toward their ideal states at faster than expected rates, discrepancy reduction produces positive emotions such as enthusiasm, hope, excitement, and joy (Carver & Scheier, 1990).

When a person realizes that a present state-ideal state incongruity exists, devising a good plan for removing or reducing this incongruity is only half of the battle. Actually carrying out the plan is the other half because people all too often encounter problems (e.g., situational constraints, personal inadequacies) while trying to translate their plans into action. After discussing the motivational significance of goals, this chapter in the section "Implementation Intentions" will return to the sticky issue of enacting plans and achieving goals.

DISCREPANCY

The idea of incongruity as a motivational principle caught on. The awareness that a difference exists between present state and ideal state gave life to plans and to generalized corrective motivation. But the more cognitive psychologists worked with present state versus ideal state mismatches, the more they came to see "discrepancy" as a core motivational construct. Consider the following illustrations of everyday life that can be understood as examples of discrepancy. In each example, discrepancy is represented by the arrow between the present state and the ideal state:

PRESENT STATE ◄──────►	IDEAL STATE
The job you have	The job you want
How skillful you are	How skillful the guy on television is
Being behind in a contest	Being ahead in the contest
Current quality of a relationship	How good the relationship could be
GPA you currently have	GPA needed to make the Dean's List
Feeling lonely	Being socially engaged
Feeling thirsty	Feeling sated
Stuck in traffic	Driving without interference
Messy, cluttered desktop	Clean, well-organized desktop
Suffering headache pain	Not suffering headache pain
Excluded from a club	Included as a club member
Making $6 an hour	Making $10 an hour
Having 200 more miles to drive	Being there
10 laps to run around the track	No more laps to run
260 unread pages in this book	No more unread pages

The discrepancy list represents 15 ways for saying essentially the same thing. In these and all other instances of discrepancy, the person envisions possible circumstances that are different from present circumstances. The awareness of the mismatch between "that which presently is" and "that which is desired" creates a sense of incongruity that produces motivational consequences. Therefore, when people ask themselves, "What can I do to increase motivation?" those who study discrepancy-based motivation have a very practical answer: Basically, create an ideal state in your mind, or more precisely, create a present state-ideal state discrepancy.

GOALS

A goal is whatever an individual is striving to accomplish (Locke et al., 1981). When people strive to earn $100, make a 4.0 GPA, sell 100 boxes of Girl Scout cookies, or go undefeated in an athletic season, they engage in goal-directed behavior. Like plans, goals generate motivation by focusing people's attention on the discrepancy (or incongruity) between their present level of accomplishment (no boxes of cookies sold) and their ideal level of accomplishment (100 boxes sold at the end of the month). Researchers refer to this discrepancy between present and ideal accomplishments as a "goal-performance discrepancy" (Locke & Latham, 1990).

There are two types of goal-performance discrepancies (Bandura, 1990). The first is *discrepancy reduction,* which is based on discrepancy-detecting feedback. Some aspect of the environment (e.g., a boss, scholarship, athletic opponent) provides feedback that informs the person of differences between current performance and an ideal level of accomplishment. For instance, at work, the supervisor might tell the salesperson that 10 sales are not enough; 15 sales are needed. Likewise, a student might read in a brochure that his 2.0 GPA is not enough for scholarship eligibility; a 3.0 GPA is needed. Environmental feedback communicates that a performance-goal discrepancy exists and energized and directed behavior is needed to pull the performance up to the goal level.

The second type of goal-performance discrepancy is *discrepancy creation* that is based on a "feed-forward" system, in which the person proactively sets a future, higher goal. The person deliberately sets a higher goal and does not require feedback from a boss or a scholarship to impose it. For instance, the salesperson might, for whatever reason, decide to try for 15 sales in one week instead of the usual 10, and the student might decide to try for a 3.0 GPA. Thus, the person creates a new, higher goal to pursue.

Two important distinctions between discrepancy reduction and discrepancy creation exist: (1) Discrepancy reduction corresponds to plan-based corrective motivation (discussed in the previous section), whereas discrepancy creation corresponds to goal-setting motivation (discussed in the present section); and (2) discrepancy reduction is reactive, deficiency overcoming, and revolves around a feedback system, whereas discrepancy creation is proactive, growth pursuing, and revolves around a "feed-forward" system. As you will see, goal setting is first and foremost a discrepancy-creating process (Bandura, 1990).

PERFORMANCE

Generally speaking, people with goals outperform people without goals (Locke & Latham, 1990). And generally speaking, the same person performs better when she has a goal than when she does not have a goal.

Consider one study in which elementary-grade students performed sit-ups for 2 minutes (Weinberg et al., 1988). Some students set a goal for themselves as to how many sit-ups they would accomplish during the 2 minutes (goal-setting group), while others simply completed sit-ups without a predetermined goal (no-goal group). After 2 minutes of exercise, the goal-setting students finished significantly more sit-ups than did the no-goal students. In effect, the presence of a goal motivated exercisers more than did the absence of a goal. The same result can be found in any number of other studies, as people with goals outperform people without goals, such as in trying to lift weights, learn text information, sell products, shoot archery, conserve natural resources, tolerate pain, study for tests, and lose weight (see Locke & Latham's [1986] Table 2.5, which lists 88 different tasks).

In addition to the mere presence of goals, the type of goals one sets is also important. Goals vary in how difficult and in how specific they are. Goal difficulty refers to how hard a goal is to accomplish. As goals increase in difficulty, performance increases in a linear fashion (Locke & Latham, 1990; Mento, Steel, & Karren, 1987; Tubbs, 1986). Relative to goals such as scoring 80 on a test, running a mile in 10 minutes, and making one new friend, more difficult goals would be scoring 90 on a test, running a mile in 8 minutes, and making three new friends. The more difficult the goal, the more it energizes the performer.

Goal specificity refers to how clearly a goal informs the performer precisely what he is to do. Telling a performer to "do your best" sounds like goal setting, but it is actually only an ambiguous statement that does not make clear precisely what the person is to do (Locke & Latham, 1990). On the other hand, telling a writer to have a first draft in 1 week, a revised draft in 2 weeks, and a final manuscript in 3 weeks specifies more precisely what the writer is to do. The effect that goal specificity has on performance is to reduce its variability. Giving a group of performers a vague goal (e.g., "work quickly" or "read a lot of pages") produces a relatively wide range of performances compared to giving a group of performers a specific goal (e.g., "complete the task in the next 3 minutes" or "read 100 pages"), which produces a relatively narrow range of performances (Locke, et al., 1989).

Which Goals Facilitate Performance?

Goals do not always enhance performance. Only those goals that are difficult and specific facilitate performance (Locke et al., 1981). The reason difficult, specific goals increase performance is a motivational reason. Difficult goals energize the performer, specific goals direct her toward a particular course of action (Earley, Wojnaroski, & Prest, 1987). Therefore, goals need to be difficult to create energy, and goals need to be specific to focus direction.

Why Do Difficult, Specific Goals Facilitate Performance?

Difficult goals energize behavior, which is to say that they increase effort and persistence. Output of effort is directly proportional to the perceived demands of the task (Bassett, 1979; Locke & Latham, 1990). The harder the goal, the greater the effort expended in accomplishing it (Earley, Wojnaroski, & Prest, 1987; Bandura & Cervone, 1983, 1986). Goals increase persistence because effort continues until the goal is reached (LaPorte & Nath, 1976; Latham & Locke, 1975). The athlete trying for 45 sit-ups, for example, keeps performing sit-up after sit-up until all 45 are done. Goals also decrease the probability that the performer will be distracted away from the task or will give up prematurely (LaPorte & Nath, 1976). With a goal in mind, performers quit the task when the goal is accomplished, not when they get bored, frustrated, tired, or distracted.

Specific goals direct attention and strategic planning. Specific goals focus the individual's attention toward the task at hand and therefore away from tasks that are incidental (Kahneman, 1973; Locke & Bryan, 1969; Rothkopf & Billington, 1979). Goals tell the performer where to concentrate and what specifically to do (Klein, Whitener, & Ilgen, 1990; Latham, Mitchell, & Dossett, 1978; Locke et al., 1989). In studies with students reading texts, for instance, readers with specific goals spent significantly more time looking at their text during a study session than did readers with ambiguous goals, who were more likely to let their eyes wander around the room (Locke & Bryan, 1969; Rothkopf & Billington, 1979). Specific goals also prompt performers to plan a strategic course of action (Latham & Baldes, 1975; Terborg, 1976). With a specific goal in mind, a performer who is unable to accomplish a goal on a first attempt will tend to drop that strategy and revise it by creating a new and improved strategy (Earley & Perry, 1987; Earley, Wojnaroski, & Prest, 1987).

Goals generate motivation, but motivation is only one of the causes underlying performance. Performance also depends on factors that are not motivational, such as ability, training, coaching, and resources (Locke & Latham, 1984). Because these factors also contribute to the quality of performance, no one-to-one correspondence exists between goals and performance. Thus, if two performers have comparable ability, training, coaching, and resources, then performers with difficult and specific goals will likely outperform performers without such goals. This is an important practical point because when difficult, specific goals fail to enhance performance, one might be well advised to focus on factors that are not motivational and that relate to increasing ability (via instruction, practice, role models, videotaped-performance feedback) or resources (via supplying equipment, books, tutors, computers, money).

Importance of Feedback

Difficult, specific goals enhance performance by energizing effort and persistence and by directing attention and strategy. One additional variable is crucial in making goal setting effective: feedback (Erez, 1977). Goal setting translates into increased performance only in the context of timely feedback that documents the performer's progress in relation to the goal (Locke et al., 1981). In other words, a performer needs both a goal *and* performance feedback to maximize performance (Bandura & Cervone, 1983; Becker, 1978; Erez, 1977; Strang, Lawrence, & Fowler, 1978; Tubbs, 1986).

Without feedback, performance can be emotionally unimportant and uninvolving. A runner can have a goal to run a mile in 6 minutes, a dieter can have a goal to lose 10 pounds, and a student can have a goal of mastering a subject matter. But if the runner, dieter, and student never gain access to a stopwatch, scale, or examination, respectively, then all the running, dieting, and studying have no way for informing the performer of her progress made toward goal attainment.

The combination of goals with feedback produces an emotionally meaningful mixture: Goal attainment breeds emotional satisfaction, while goal failure breeds emotional dissatisfaction (Bandura, 1991). Felt satisfaction contributes favorably to the discrepancy-creating process, while felt dissatisfaction contributes favorably to the discrepancy-reducing process. When feedback shows the individual that he is performing at or above goal level, the individual feels satisfied and competent, competent enough perhaps to create a higher, more difficult goal (the discrepancy-creation process; Wood, Bandura, & Bailey, 1990). When performance feedback shows the individual that he is performing below goal level, the individual feels dissatisfied and becomes keenly aware of the goal-performance discrepancy, enough perhaps to marshal greater efforts in eliminating the goal-performance incongruity (the discrepancy-reduction process; Bandura & Cervone, 1983, 1986). Feedback therefore provides the emotional punch that brings the goal-setting process to life within experiences of felt satisfaction and felt dissatisfaction.

GOAL ACCEPTANCE

In addition to goals needing to be (1) difficult and specific, and (2) paired with performance feedback, a third condition is necessary before goals translate into performance gains: goal acceptance (Erez & Kanfer, 1983). Goal acceptance involves the person's decision either to accept or reject the goal and varies on a continuum from total acceptance to total rejection (Erez & Zidon, 1984). Only internalized (i.e., accepted) goals improve performance (Erez, Earley, & Hulin, 1985).

If the person accepts a performance goal, a positive relationship exists between task difficulty and performance, such that as goal difficulty increases, performance increases as well (Erez & Zidon, 1984). If the goal is rejected, a negative relationship actually exists between task difficulty and performance, such that as goal difficulty increases, performance declines. With difficult but rejected goals, the person generally puts forth little or no effort. Four factors determine whether a goal will be accepted or rejected:

- Perceived difficulty
- Participation in the goal-setting process
- Credibility of the person assigning the goal
- Extrinsic incentives

Goal acceptance is inversely related to goal difficulty. Before a person accepts a goal, she evaluates its level of difficulty. Easy goals generally breed goal acceptance, whereas difficult goals breed goal rejection (Erez, Earley, & Hulin, 1985). When a parent tells his child to bring home all A-level grades, for instance, the child evaluates the likelihood of attaining such a goal before accepting it. As the goal changes from C-level grades ("that's reasonable; I'll try") to a B-level grades ("that will take my best effort; I'll probably try") and perhaps finally to A-level grades ("that's impossible; I won't even try"), the child's willingness to accept the parent's goal decreases accordingly.

Participation in the goal-setting process refers to how much say the performer has in the goal she is to pursue. If the performer sets the goal herself, it is readily accepted. However, goals often originate in the minds of a teacher, manager, parent, coach, friend, priest, or society in general. With an external goal origin, an interpersonal negotiation process ensues in which the performer's goal acceptance versus rejection is at stake. In general, performers reject assigned goals that others try to force on them (Latham & Yukl, 1975), but they accept assigned goals when others listen carefully to their point of view and also provide a clear rationale for the goal (Latham, Erez, & Locke, 1988; Latham & Saari, 1979).

Credibility of the person assigning the goal refers to how trustworthy, supportive, knowledgeable, and likeable the performer perceives this person to be. A person with little credibility comes across as authoritarian, manipulative, and pejorative when assigning goals. All other things being equal, performers are more likely to accept and internalize goals assigned to them by credible others, as opposed to suspicious or manipulative others (Locke & Latham, 1990; Oldham, 1975).

When extrinsic incentives and rewards are contingent on goal attainment, a performer's goal acceptance increases in proportion to the perceived benefits of attaining the goal (Locke & Latham, 1990). Incentives such as money, public recognition, scholarships, and the like add to a performer's willingness to accept a goal regardless of its difficulty, its origin, or the credibility of the person assigning the goal.

Overall, then, goal acceptance is highest when goals are perceived to be easy or moderately difficult, are self-set (or are at least negotiated to the performer's satisfaction), are assigned by credible and trustworthy others, and are associated with personal benefit. When these conditions are met, goal acceptance sets the stage for productive goal-directed performance.

LONG-TERM GOAL SETTING

Short-Term and Long-Term Goals

A student who wants to become a doctor or an athlete who wants to win an Olympic event exemplify individuals involved in long-term goal setting. To accomplish a distant goal, the performer first has to attain several requisite short-term goals. Would-be doctors first have to make a high GPA as undergraduates, get accepted into a medical school, raise a great deal of money, probably move to a different city, graduate from medical school, complete an internship, join a hospital or partnership, and so forth, all before they can begin their careers as doctors. Thus, goals can be short term (read this chapter), intermediate (read this book), long term (make a "B" in this course), or a series of short-term goals linked together into one long-term goal (first read chapter 1, then read chapter 2, etc., on the way to making a "B" in this course). No significant difference in performance emerges among performers with short-term, long-term, or a mixture of short- and long-term goals (Hall &

Byrne, 1988; Weinberg, Bruya, & Jackson, 1985; Weinberg et al., 1988). People with short-term goals in mind, therefore, perform about the same as do people with long-term goals (though both outperform people with no goals).

Instead of affecting performance per se, goal proximity affects persistence and intrinsic motivation. As for persistence, many would-be doctors and Olympians forfeit their long-term goals because of a lack of positive reinforcements along the way. During all those years of studying and practicing, the goal of actually being a doctor or Olympian never materialize. Because the long-term goal striver receives insufficient opportunities for performance feedback and positive reinforcement, she might benefit from setting a series of short-term goals that chain together to eventually end in the long-term target goal. Transforming one long-term goal into a series of short-term goals yields two benefits. First, short-term goals provide repeated opportunities for reinforcement following goal attainment that long-term goals cannot provide. Positive reinforcement for short-term goal attainment generally increases the individual's commitment to the long-term goal (Latham, Mitchell, & Dossett, 1978). Second, short-term goals provide repeated opportunities for relevant performance feedback that allows the performer to evaluate performance as being at, above, or below the goal. An athlete trying for a long-term goal such as winning the state championship receives little day-to-day feedback as compared to the athlete trying for a short-term goal such as winning a contest each week or running more miles in 1 week than in a past week's performance.

Goal-Setting and Intrinsic Motivation

Several researchers assessed the impact of goal setting on intrinsic motivation (Bandura & Schunk, 1981; Harackiewicz & Manderlink, 1984; Mossholder, 1980; Vallerand, Deci, & Ryan, 1985). In one study, participants worked on an interesting puzzle, and goal-setting participants performed better than no-goal participants (Mossholder, 1980). This performance boost from goal setting is a reliable finding; however, the goal-setting participants also showed significantly less intrinsic motivation for the activity than did the no-goal participants. Thus, goal setting increased performance, but it also decreased intrinsic motivation.

Two later experiments had performers complete an enjoyable task with either (1) several short-term goals, (2) one long-term goal, or (3) no goals ("do your best"), and intrinsic motivation was assessed after participation. Short-term goals enhanced performance, while long-term goals enhanced intrinsic motivation (Manderlink & Harackiewicz, 1984). When the task was an uninteresting one, results were somewhat different, as short-term goals increased both performance and intrinsic motivation (Bandura & Schunk, 1981).

These contradictory findings suggest that the performer's initial level of intrinsic motivation toward the task is the key variable determining how goal setting affects intrinsic motivation (Vallerand, Deci, & Ryan, 1985). On uninteresting tasks, short-term goals enhance intrinsic motivation by creating a means for enhancing the performer's sense of competence (following progress toward goal attainment). Short-term goals create opportunities for positive feedback, and the experience of making progress enhances perceptions of competence, which enhances intrinsic motivation (Vallerand, Deci, & Ryan, 1985). On interesting tasks, only long-term goals facilitate intrinsic motivation. For the highly interested

FIGURE 7.3 **A Long-Term Goal as a Complex Cognitive Structure**

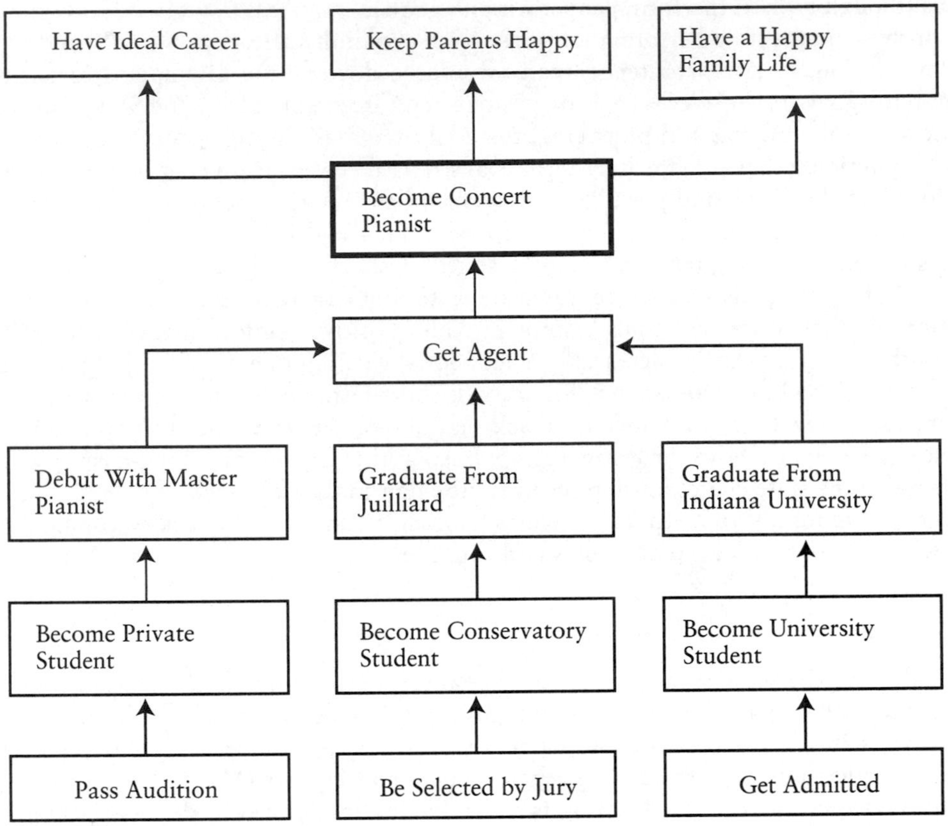

SOURCE: From "A Computer Model of Affective Reactions to Goal-Relevant Events," by S. B. Ravlin, 1987, in an unpublished master's thesis, University of Illinois-Urbana-Champaign. As cited in *The Cognitive Structure of Emotions,* A. Ortony, G. L. Clore, and A. Collins (Eds.), 1998. Cambridge: Cambridge University Press.

performer, short-term goals are experienced as superfluous, intrusive, and controlling. People who enjoy an activity typically already feel competent at that task, so their sense of competence is not in question and does not benefit much from goal-setting feedback. Hence, the only effect a short-term goal can have on an interesting task is a negative one. Generally speaking, people prefer to pursue long-term goals in their own way, and this explains why long-term goals can increase intrinsic motivation (through self-determination; Manderlink & Harackiewicz, 1984; Vallerand, Deci, & Ryan, 1985).

Goals as Complex Cognitive Structures

Goals can be thought of as specific targets, such as losing 5 pounds, finding a job, or making 10 consecutive free throws. Sometimes, however, goals cannot be identified so categorically. It is typically more accurate to think of goals as cognitive lattice structures (Ortony, Clore, & Collins, 1988). Figure 7.3, for example, represents an aspiring concert pianist's cognitive goal lattice (Ravlin, 1987). At the top of the lattice are the pianist's most abstract (and long-term) aspirations, and at the bottom are the most concrete (and short-term) aspirations. Each aspiration is interconnected with each other in the sense that each shares in the musician's overall (long-term) goal of becoming a concert pianist. Further, each aspiration is connected in a causal flow in which the achievement of one goal increases the probability of attaining another, whereas the failure to achieve one goal decreases the probability of attaining another.

CRITICISMS

Goal setting has its advantages, but it also has its cautions and pitfalls (Locke & Latham, 1984). There are generally two cautions and three concerns associated with goal setting, discussed in the following paragraphs.

Goal-setting theory (Locke & Latham, 1990) developed within the fields of business, management, the world of work, productivity, sales, and the bottom line (profit). Goal-setting theory is therefore more about enhancing performance (worker output) than it is about enhancing motivation per se. The following is the first caution associated with goal setting: The purpose of goal setting is to enhance performance, not necessarily motivation. The second caution is that goal setting works best when tasks are relatively uninteresting and require only a straightforward procedure (Wood, Mento, & Locke, 1987), as shown with tasks such as adding numbers (Bandura & Schunk, 1981), typing (Latham & Yukl, 1976), proofreading (Huber, 1985), assembling nuts and bolts (Mossholder, 1980), and sit-ups (Weinberg, Bruya, & Jackson, 1985). Goal setting aids performance on uninteresting, straightforward tasks by generating motivation that the task itself cannot generate (e.g., through challenge, feedback). On tasks that are inherently interesting and require creativity or problem solving, goal setting does not enhance performance (Earley, Connolly, & Ekegren, 1989). In fact, on interesting, problem-solving tasks, goal setting generally undermines both performance (Bandura & Wood, 1989; McGraw, 1978) and intrinsic motivation (Mossholder, 1980; Vallerand, Deci, & Ryan, 1985). The fact that goal setting concerns the quantity of performance, not its quality, is the second caution (Deci, 1992a).

Three concerns are associated with goal setting: increasing stress, creating opportunities for failure, and putting intrinsic motivation at risk. The logic behind goal setting is to increase performance demands so the performer's effort, persistence, attention, and strategic planning improve from lackluster to intense. Sometimes, however, overly challenging goals ask performers to put forth a level of effort, persistence, attention, and planning that exceeds their capabilities. These challenging goals can stress performers (concern one; Csikszentmihalyi, 1990; Lazarus, 1991a). These goals can also create an explicit, objective performance standard and therefore advance the possibility of failure and negative feedback (concern two). Failure feedback yields consequences that are emotional (e.g., feelings of inadequacy), social (e.g., loss of respect), and tangible (e.g., financial). The third concern is that goals, like any other external event, can be administered to performers in ways that are controlling and intrusive and thus can undermine intrinsic motivation by interfering with self-determination (Harackiewicz & Manderlink, 1984; Mossholder,

TABLE 7.1 A Sample of One Individual's Personal Strivings

1. Become a stronger teacher
2. Have a better attitude
3. Become more independent
4. Stay healthy
5. Lose weight
6. Have more money
7. Remain calm
8. Find a decent partner
9. Become better at my job
10. Finish school
11. Become more open-minded
12. Travel more often
13. Not be so mean
14. Eat healthier foods
15. Go to church more often

Note: To produce these personal strivings, 15 blank lines were listed down the left-hand side of the page, which began with the following instructions:

> A personal striving is an objective that you are typically trying to accomplish or attain. Personal strivings can be either positive or negative. In other words, a personal striving can be an objective that you typically approach and strive to attain, or it can be an objective that you typically strive to avoid. For instance, a striving you might approach and strive to attain might be "Be a fun person to be around." A striving you might strive to avoid might be "Quit smoking cigarettes."

1980; Vallerand, Deci, & Ryan 1985). When presented in a controlling way, goals put intrinsic motivation at risk (concern three). These cautions and concerns limit the practical application of goal setting.

PERSONAL STRIVINGS

Personal strivings are "what a person is typically or characteristically trying to do" (Emmons, 1989). These strivings represent what an individual is characteristically aiming to accomplish in his day-to-day behavior and over the course of his life (Emmons, 1986, 1996). Personal strivings are not goals per se but, instead, exist as superordinate aspects of the self that organize and integrate the many different goals a person seeks. Thus, personal strivings reflect general personality dispositions, whereas goals reflect situationally specific objectives. For instance, a person striving "to be physically attractive" might express that striving in (1) a school-specific goal to dress in the current fashion, (2) a gym-specific goal to exercise, or (3) a store-specific goal to purchase a magazine with tips on how to be physically attractive.

To provide a concrete illustration of personal strivings, one person's actual self-reported strivings appear in Table 7.1. This woman's strivings are organized around concerns about profession (becoming a teacher, performing better at work, finishing school),

personality (being more independent, being more open-minded), relationships (finding a partner, not being so mean), emotion regulation (improving attitude, remaining calm), and personal well-being (being healthy, losing weight, having more money, traveling more, eating better, going to church more often).

Once a person has committed to a personal striving, the striving motivates behavior through a discrepancy-reduction process (Emmons, 1996). That is, with a valued striving in mind, the person acts to reduce any perceived discrepancy between the desired state (the personal striving) and the person's present behavior. The personal striving-inspired goal gives the person something to try to accomplish, and it also frames present-day behavior in a context of making progress (or not) toward fulfilling that striving. For instance, the personal striving (in Table 7.1) to travel more might create the goal of going to Ireland in the summer, and it also serves as a standard by which behavior can be evaluated. (For example, "Did I travel anywhere new this year?")

Personal strivings also allow people to appraise the events in their lives as significant or not (Emmons, 1991). For instance, for the aforementioned person with a personal striving to travel more, events such as taking a foreign language class, meeting people from another country, and reading the international section of the newspaper all have a measure of significance that the same events do not have for a person with no such personal striving.

Personal Strivings and Subjective Well-Being

One reason personal strivings are important for understanding motivation is that they reveal and organize a person's goal system, as previously discussed. A second reason personal strivings are important relates to their effects on emotional processes and on subjective well-being. Personal strivings foreshadow a person's emotional well-being and his long-term positive and negative affect. More specifically, the content of a person's personal strivings predicts long-term emotional well-being versus distress.

In general, the more people organize their personal strivings around intimacy themes, the more positive is their long-term well-being; whereas the more people organize their strivings around achievement and power, the more they expose themselves to experiences of negative affect and distress (Emmons, 1991, 1996). In addition, the more people organize their personal strivings around autonomously and intrinsically motivated themes, the more positive is their long-term well-being in terms of life satisfaction, vitality, and self-actualization; whereas controlled and extrinsically motivated strivings expose their creators to psychological distress (Kasser & Ryan, 1993; Sheldon & Kasser, 1994). In the same spirit, the more people organize their personal strivings around approaching desired states ("spend time with friends"), the more positive is their long-term well-being; whereas the more people organize their strivings around avoiding aversive states ("don't be lonely"), the more they make themselves vulnerable to negative moods, lessened life satisfaction, and greater anxiety (Emmons, 1996).[1]

---

[1]It might be instructive for the reader to evaluate the personal strivings listed in Table 7.1 along these three dimensions of intimacy, autonomy, and approach-oriented. Once done, some confident predictions can be offered about this person's long-term affect and well-being.

Subjective well-being does not follow from attaining goals (i.e., from gaining popularity, having money, winning awards). Rather, subjective well-being comes from the content of what one is trying to do (Emmons, 1996; Sheldon & Kasser, 1994). When people strive for intimacy, autonomy, and appetitive aspirations, people are able to create a meaning in their lives that fosters positive affect and subjective well-being. When people strive for power, for cultural ideals, and to avoid aversion, people divorce their strivings from personal meaning in such a way that leads to negative affect, alienation, and subjective distress. Subjective well-being is more about what one is striving for than about what one can actually attain.

IMPLICIT THEORIES

Generally speaking, the way people think about their personal qualities can be characterized in one of two ways (Dweck, 1999). Personal qualities are resources such as intelligence, personality, and motivation. Some people see personal qualities as fixed and enduring characteristics. Other people, in contrast, see personal qualities as malleable characteristics that can be increased with effort. The first implicit theory applies to "entity theorists," who are people that believe they (and others) are endowed with fixed, enduring qualities. The thinking is "you either have it, or you don't" in that some people are smart and motivated while other people are not. The second implicit theory applies to "incremental theorists," who are people that believe they (and others) are endowed with malleable, changing qualities. The thinking is "the more you try and the more you learn, the better you get" in that all people can become smarter and more motivated, at least in proportion to their effort.

As an illustration, consider whether you agree or disagree with the following statements (Dweck, 1999):

- Your intelligence is something about you that you cannot change very much.
- You can learn new things, but you cannot really change your basic intelligence.
- You can always greatly change how intelligent you are.
- No matter who you are, you can change your intelligence a lot.

Entity theorists will generally agree with the first two statements but disagree with the last two. Entity theorists believe people have a fixed amount of intelligence, personality, and motivation. In other words, characteristics exist as entities or traits that dwell within the person. Incremental theorists will generally agree with the last two statements but disagree with the first two. Incremental theorists believe personal qualities are something that people cultivate through effort and learning. While they realize that some people are high while other people are low in these qualities, incremental theorists believe that instruction, guidance, effort, learning, and experience increase and improve these qualities.

Implicit theories guide the type of goals people pursue, especially in achievement situations (Dweck, 1999; Dweck & Elliot, 1983; Elliot & Dweck, 1988). Entity theorists generally adopt performance (or, performance-oriented) goals. People who adopt performance goals are concerned with looking smart and with not looking dumb. That is, they are concerned with performing well, especially while others are watching. The goal is therefore to use performance to prove that one has much of a desirable characteristic (i.e., intelligence). Incremental theorists generally adopt learning goals. People who adopt learning goals are concerned with learning new skills, mastering new tasks, and understanding new things. That is, they are concerned with learning as much as they can. The goal is therefore to use task engagements to improve—to get smarter by learning something new or important.

Both types of goals—performance goals and learning goals—are common in the culture and can encourage achievement (Elliot & Church, 1997; Harackiewicz, et al., 1997). But typically, social settings like the workplace, sports field, and classroom pit these two goals against one another and ask (force) workers, athletes, and students to pick one goal as more important than the other. People are often asked to choose between courses of action that allow them to (1) look smart and competent but at the sacrifice of learning something new versus (2) learn something new, useful, or important but at the sacrifice of looking smart or competent. For instance, when college students select "elective" courses, they sometimes choose a course in which they can be assured of doing well, looking smart, avoiding errors, and impressing others, or they sometimes choose a course in which they hope will teach them something new, provide opportunities to learn, and an arena to grow their skills. When given such a choice (at school, at work, in sports, etc.), about half of the population will, on average, select a performance goal while the other half will select a learning goal.

Different Implicit Theories Mean Different Achievement Goals

When entity and incremental theorists face achievement situations, do they prefer different achievement goals? This is an important question because the type of achievement goal one pursues (performance versus learning) predicts that person's subsequent motivation, emotion, and performance (Ames & Archer, 1988; Stipek & Kowalski, 1989).

A series of studies with elementary-school (Bandura & Dweck, 1981), middle-school (Dweck & Leggett, 1988), and college (Mueller & Dweck, 1997) students assessed students' entity and incremental theories, using questions based on Dweck's (1999) four statements on intelligence (listed previously). The researchers then asked the students to choose between tasks that were either (1) easy enough so mistakes would not be committed or (2) hard, new, and different—confusion and mistakes could occur, but the student would probably learn something new and useful. The more students endorsed an entity theory (i.e., agreed with the first two statements), the more they chose the performance opportunity (1). The more students endorsed an incremental theory (i.e., agreed with the last two statements), the more they chose the learning opportunity (2).

Therefore, implicit theories—entity or incremental—predict the type of achievement goal the individual chooses to pursue—performance or learning. But do implicit theories cause achievement goal choices? To answer this question of causation, what needs to be demonstrated is that implicit theories can be experimentally manipulated, and once manipulated, they will predict people's achievement goal choices (Dweck, 1999). To experimentally manipulate implicit theories of self, researchers asked students to read

Setting Goals and Implementing Action

Question: Why would a person want to learn about the motivational states discussed in this chapter?

Answer: To translate the goals sought into effective action.

What would you like to accomplish? Would you like to increase the number of friends you have? increase your GPA? decrease your weight? One means for attaining the objectives you seek is goal setting. Effective goal setting entails following and then implementing the following sequential procedures:

1. Identify the objective to be accomplished. State the goal in numerical terms, if possible.
2. Specify how performance will be measured or assessed.
3. Define goal difficulty.
4. Clarify goal specificity.
5. Specify when performance will be measured to test for goal attainment.

For instance, consider the goal of getting in shape. In numerical terms, getting in shape could be represented by earning aerobic points through jogging (to continue the example introduced in the beginning of the chapter). A difficult goal would be to earn 30 points per week, and the goal setter must therefore calculate how far and in what amount of time to run (e.g., one 8-minute mile earns 5 points; that repeated for 6 days will earn 30 aerobic points: $1 \times 5 \times 6 = 30$). To clarify goal specificity, the goal setter might decide to run 1 mile a day, in 8 minutes or less, each day of the week, except for Wednesday. To specify when performance will be assessed, the goal

informative, entertaining articles that provided rather convincing (and true) evidence to support either an entity or an incremental theory of intelligence. Participants were randomly assigned to read either the entity-touting or the incremental-touting articles. All participants were then given a choice between a performance-goal task (easy enough to avoid mistakes) and a learning-goal task (hard, but one could learn something new). Students who read the passage supporting an entity view of intelligence were significantly more likely to pursue the performance-goal task, whereas students who read the passage supporting an incremental view of intelligence were significantly more likely to pursue the learning-goal task. Thus, implicit theories are malleable and can be changed, and implicit theories cause people to pursue either performance or learning goals.

Meaning of Effort

For an entity theorist, the meaning of effort is "the more you try, the dumber you therefore must be." High effort means low ability. It is, in fact, evidence that the performer lacks ability. For an incremental theorist, the meaning of effort is that it is a tool, the setter might decide to earn 30 aerobic points in each of the four weeks in March. At the end of each week, the test will be to earn 30 aerobic points, and at the end of the month, the test will be to earn 120 aerobic points.

Identifying the goal gets you halfway home. The other half is to specify the necessary implementation intentions, as in:

1. Getting started
2. Persisting, even in the face of difficulties
3. Resuming, even after disruptions

Getting started means specifying when, where, how, and for how long all this jogging will occur. The jogger might decide, for instance, to run at 4:00 each afternoon at the university's gym, on a treadmill, and for 15 minutes each day, including a warm-up and cool-down. An implementation intention for persistence and resumption of jogging might anticipate when exams and papers are due during the semester with an intention of forgoing exercise when feeling overwhelmed and doubling up the following day.

Given these goal-setting procedures and the forethought to formulate implementation intentions, the would-be jogger has both a goal and a plan of action. Of course, this is just one example, and you might be surprised by how readily these procedures generalize to other domains that might be more important to you and to the objectives you seek.

means by which people turn on and take advantage of their skills and abilities. High effort means the unleashing of ability. Consider the following:

> You see a puzzle in a science magazine and it's labeled "Test your IQ!" You work on it for a very long time, get confused, start over and over, and finally make progress, but very slowly, until you solve it. How do you feel? Do you feel sort of dumb because it required so much effort? Or, do you feel smart because you worked hard and mastered it? (Dweck, 1999).

The self's interpretation of the meaning of effort is most important in a motivational analysis of behavior when the individual faces a difficult task (Dweck, 1999). What one needs when facing a difficult task is high effort. But marshaling forth high effort possesses a motivational dilemma for the entity theorist. High effort is needed, but high effort is that which signals low ability, which is precisely the sort of thing an entity theorist wants most to avoid. Entity theorists do not really believe that high effort will be effective, even on difficult tasks. So on difficult endeavors, they tend to adopt maladaptive motivational patterns by (1) withholding effort, (2) engaging in self-handicapping, (3) failing to value effort, and (4) never really understanding or appreciating what effort expenditures can do for them in life (Dweck, 1999; Stipek & Gralinski, 1996; Zuckerman, Kieffer, & Knee, 1998). Incremental theorists, however, do understand the utility of effort—effort is that which becomes learning. Incremental theorists experience no conflict between the effort challenging tasks require and their willingness to roll up their sleeves and engage in persistent and effortful work.

IMPLEMENTATION INTENTIONS

Goal setting seems so promising, so ripe with potential, as a motivational intervention strategy for helping people accomplish the sort of things they wish to accomplish (see the "Setting Goals and Implementing Action" box). The self-help books that dominate the shelves of the larger bookstores seem to agree with the preceding sentence, as they advise readers to set goals and to focus their full attention on these goals. If you want to make better grades, lose 10 pounds, save a wad of money, or be successful in love and work, then you must visualize the goal you want and think frequently about it. In other words, identify your goal—focus on it, visualize it, see you with the goal in hand. Only then can you make things come true. Unfortunately, motivational processes are not that simple.

FOCUS ON GOAL PROCESS OVER GOAL CONTENT

Consider a series of studies designed explicitly to test the "visualize success" advice (Taylor, et al., 1998). In these studies, participants either (1) focused on the goal they wished to attain, (2) focused on the process of how to attain the goal, or (3) did not focus on anything in particular (a control group). Focusing on one's goal generally interfered with goal attainment. Focusing on how to accomplish one's goal, however, did facilitate eventual goal attainment. These data are important because (1) they draw out the distinction between the content of a goal (what one is striving for) and the process of goal striving (the means one uses to attain the goal), and (2) once a goal has been set, it does not inevitably and automatically translate itself into effective performance.

Mental Simulations of Goal Process

Salespeople know the following trick well: Ask someone to imagine having and using an item, and that person will become significantly more likely to later actually go out of her way to have and use that item (as in "Just imagine sitting in this beauty, driving it home, and parking this fine machine right in front of your home—can't you just see your neighbor turning green?"). In an experimental demonstration of what salespeople already know, researchers asked members of a community to imagine owning and using a cable-television service (Gregory, Cialdini, & Carpenter, 1982). Compared to nonvisualizers in a control group, those who worked through the mental simulation of using the service were indeed significantly more likely to subscribe. In mental simulations, people run through a set of events in their mind's eye such that they see events unfold in specific and concrete ways—ways that seem quite real to the imagination (Taylor et al., 1998). One benefit of engaging in mental simulations, compared to actually carrying out goal-directed action, is the flexibility one gains in trying out many different solutions to a problem to see which might work best.

Mental simulations are not fantasies of success or episodes of wishful thinking. Drawing out the difference between the content of a goal and the process for attaining that goal is an important distinction because visualizing fantasies of success (i.e., wishful thinking as in "the power of positive thinking") do not produce productive behavior (Oettingen, 1996). Instead of focusing on outcomes (i.e., on goal content), mental simulations focus on planning and problem solving, and this effort does produce productive goal-directed action. How about trying out a mock experiment for yourself? Imagine hearing one of the two following instructions (Pham & Taylor, 1999):

Outcome-Simulation Exercise

> In this exercise, you will be asked to visualize yourself getting a high grade on your psychology midterm and asked to imagine how you would feel. It is very important that you see yourself getting a high grade on the psychology midterm and have that picture in your mind.

Process-Simulation Exercise

> In this exercise, you will be asked to visualize yourself studying for the midterm in such a way that would lead you to obtain a high grade on the midterm. As of today and for the remaining days before the midterm, imagine how you would study to get a high grade on your psychology midterm. It is very important that you see yourself actually studying and have that picture in your mind.

The first set of instructions basically asked students to rehearse experiencing the joy of success, while the second set of instructions basically asked students to engage in planning and problem solving. Compared to a control group, students who engaged in the outcome-simulation exercise actually studied less and made poorer scores on the test, whereas students who engaged in the process-simulation exercise studied more and made better test scores. Focusing on success might have the virtue of cultivating a hopeful feeling, but it is not the way to promote productive goal-striving behavior. To facilitate action, people need to mentally simulate a goal process—the means by which they will accomplish the objective they seek.

FORMULATING IMPLEMENTATION INTENTIONS

When people fail to realize the goals they set for themselves, part of the problem can be explained by how people set goals (i.e., Is the goal difficult? specific? accepted? paired with feedback?). The other part of the problem in translating goals into effective performance is simply people's failure to act on the goals they set for themselves (Orbell & Sheeran, 1998).

Imagine that you have set a goal, such as making a 4.0 GPA, reading a book, losing 5 pounds, or saving $100 this month. How do you bridge the gap between goal and action? Should you focus on the content of the goal (visualize the slim, rich, well-read you) or on the means by which it is to be accomplished (the steps that one needs to take)? Should you spend time planning how to attain your goal, or would planning just be a waste of time and what you should really do is just get started? As discussed above with process-oriented mental simulations, planning how to attain a goal turns out to be an integral part of the goal-performance relationship (Gollwitzer, 1996, 1999). Planning how to carry out a goal helps the performer overcome the inevitable volitional problems associated with goal-directed behavior. Once a goal is set and committed to, the following volitional problems emerge:

- getting started, despite a multitude of daily distractions
- persisting, in spite of difficulties and setbacks
- resuming, once a disruption occurs

Planning how to carry out a goal involves deciding on *when, where, how,* and for *how long* one is to act. For example, in forming implementation intentions for goal-directed behavior, the performer decides to do X when situation Y is encountered (Gollwitzer, 1996). In planning an implementation intention, an anticipated future encounter ("When I encounter situation Y, . . .") is linked to specific goal-directed behavior (". . . I intend to do X").

The study of implementation intentions is the study of how goals, once set, are effectively acted on (Gollwitzer & Moskowitz, 1996). Implementation intentions are an important part of understanding motivation because it is one thing to set a goal, yet another to actually accomplish it. To set and attain a goal, one needs solutions to the sort of volitional problems listed above. All goals take time, but time has a way of opening the door to distractions, difficulties, and interruptions. The act of setting implementation intentions is the effort in closing the door on volitional problems. In effect, implementation intentions buffer performers against falling prey to volitional problems.

In the first experiment on implementation intentions, experimenters asked college students going home for the Christmas holidays how they planned to spend their time and what they wanted to get done (e.g., write a paper, read a book, solve a family conflict; Gollwitzer & Brandstatter, 1997). The experimenters asked half of the students to form implementation intentions for their goal by asking them to pick a specific time and a specific place in which those would be carried out. The other half of the students were not asked to specify a time and a place for their goal-directed behavior. When students returned, a majority of students in the implementation intentions group had indeed attained their goal, while only a minority of students in the control group had attained their goal. Plus, the more difficult the goal was to accomplish (i.e., writing a paper is a more difficult goal than going snow skiing), the more important the forming of implementation intentions were to completion rates (Gollwitzer & Brandstatter, 1997).

The motivational effect of an implementation intention is to link goal-directed behavior to a situational cue (i.e., to a time and place) so that goal-directed behavior is carried out automatically, without conscious deliberation or decision making. With an implementation intention in mind, the presence of the cue facilitates the goal-direction action being implemented swiftly and effortlessly. In other words, once an intention is formed (e.g., From December 27 through 29, I go to the university library and write a 10-page paper on topic X by working from 1:00 until 5:00 each afternoon), the mere presence of the anticipated situational cue (December 27 rolls around) automatically initiates goal-directed action. When no such intention is formed, the person's good intention to write the paper may suffer the same fate as a typical New Year's resolution.

Implementation intentions facilitate goal-directed behavior in two ways: getting started and finishing up. Getting started with goal-directed behavior is a problem when people let good opportunities to pursue their goals pass by. (For example, "I had all day to read the chapter, but I just never sat down and read it.") Finishing up is a problem when people get interrupted, distracted, and face difficulties. (For example, "I started to read the chapter, but then the phone rang and I never did get back to the book.")

GOAL PURSUIT: GETTING STARTED

Some people exercise every day at a certain time in the afternoon; some people read steadily and persistently when they are in the library; some people always stop completely at stop signs; and some people go to church each Sunday. Frequent and consistent pairings of particular situations with particular behaviors lead to strong links between the situation and the behavior. Creating an implementation intention for a new behavior in a new situation is essentially this same effect (Gollwitzer, 1996). Implementation intentions set up environment-behavior contingencies that lead to automatic, environmental control of behavior: "Implementation intentions create instant habits" (Gollwitzer, 1999).

Deciding in advance when and where a person will enact her goal-directed behavior facilitates getting started. Women who wrote down when and where they would conduct a breast self-examination actually did so 100% of the time during the next month, whereas women who simply had the goal of conducting a breast self-examination did so only 53% of the time (Orbell, Hodgkins, & Sheeran, 1997). Similar results occurred when these same procedures were carried out with the goals of eating healthy foods (Verplanken & Faes, 1999), taking vitamin pills (Sheeran & Orbell, in press), and resuming an active lifestyle following surgery (Orbell & Sheeran, 1999). These studies make it clear that attaining goals requires not only effective goal setting but also a pre-action period in which one decides when, where, and how that goal will be implemented.

One reason people fail to act on their goal-directed action occurs when the situational opportunity presents itself (e.g., the regular time of day to exercise has arrived), but the person experiences doubt about the goal's feasibility (Is this goal attainable?) or desirability (Is this goal worth doing?). When the goal-relevant situational cue presents itself, people who formulated a preexisting implementation intention think about how to carry out that goal. However, people who did not formulate such an intention tend to think about whether the goal-directed behavior is feasible or desirable. For instance, a group of college students who had set a goal for themselves to switch their majors were divided into two groups, the first of which formed implementation intentions of how and when to do this, and the second of which did not. Following the forming (or not forming) of the intention to carry out the goal, the students with the implementation intentions spent their time thinking about implementation issues—when, where, and how to change majors, whereas the students without the intentions spent their time thinking about the value of the majors under consideration and the wisdom of their decision to switch (Taylor & Gollwitzer, 1995). This result is important because it shows that implementation intentions, once set, protect the person from returning to the pre-goal-setting stage (Should I set this goal for myself?) and instead focus attention on getting started.

GOAL PURSUIT: PERSISTING AND FINISHING

Once started in the pursuit of a goal, people often face tasks that were more difficult than they expected. And they encounter distractions and demands on their time, and they also get interrupted and face the prospect of getting started all over again. But implementation intentions, once set, facilitate persistence during ongoing goal pursuit.

Implementation intentions facilitate persistence by helping people anticipate a forthcoming difficulty and form an intention of what they will do once the difficulty comes their way. For instance, a jogger trying to run four laps around the track can anticipate feeling exhausted after two laps and can then decide to make an intentional effort to run with extra effort for the 100 yards immediately following the two-lap, halfway mark. Thus, the implementation decision cues up a mobilization of effort just about the time the task difficulty begins to rise. Readied, therefore, the runner can counteract and overcome the difficulty.

Implementation intentions create a type of close-mindedness that narrows one's field of attention to include goal-directed action but to exclude distractions. For instance, students were placed in front of a computer terminal and asked to solve a series of attention-demanding mathematical problems while distracting video clips of award-winning television commercials played at random times on a television monitor mounted just above the computer screen. Some of the students were asked to form an implementation intention (i.e., as soon as the commercial came on, students told themselves to ignore it), while others were not. Students who formed the implementation intention prior to solving the mathematics problems solved more problems than did students who did not form the distraction-inhibiting intention (Schaal & Gollwitzer, 1999).

Implementation intentions also help people finish up uncompleted goals. Workers who began to write a letter of correspondence were interrupted by an experimenter, and half of the workers were then asked to form an implementation intention while the other half were not. When the two groups of workers returned to their desks, the workers with an intention to finish the letters upon their return (implementation intention) were indeed more likely to complete their unfinished business than were the writers who were similarly interrupted but who did not harbor an implementation intention to cope with the interruption (Posel, 1994).

Whether the problem is getting started or finishing up, taking the time necessary to plan how, when, where, and for how long one will carry out goal-directed behavior improves the performer's chance of realizing the goal. Of course, setting the goal is a crucial part of the goal-performance relationship, but the addition of implementation intentions helps close the gap that often exists between setting a goal and actually carrying it out. Implementation intentions narrow this gap because they effectively delegate the control of goal-directed action to merely encountering anticipated situational cues. When situational cues are encountered, conscious deliberation and decision making are not needed because action occurs automatically.

SUMMARY

The cognitive perspective on motivation focuses on mental processes as causal determinants to action. Thus, the cognitive study of motivation concerns itself with the cognition → action sequence. This chapter discusses the motivational significance of two elements in the cognition → action sequence: plans and goals. Both concepts rely on discrepancy as the driving motivational force to action. Cognitive discrepancies explain motivation by highlighting how mismatches between the person's present state and the person's envisioned ideal state energize and direct action.

People are routinely aware of the present state of their behavior, their environment, and the status of events in their lives. People also routinely envision ideal states for these same behaviors, environments, and events. When a present-state-versus-ideal-state mismatch exists, incongruity (or discrepancy) produces a general corrective motivation that gives rise to plan-directed behavior capable of reducing (or removing) the discrepancy. For instance, a student might say, "I have not read any pages in this book, but I would ideally like to have read 100 pages by now, so I think I'll make a plan to read the 100 pages tonight." When discrepancies generate corrective motivation, people either generate a plan that will advance their present behavior up to its ideal or they revise the plans to reverse the ideal state down to something closer to the present state. Corrective motivation also has emotional implications, as people who make slower than expected progress toward their plans experience negative emotions, whereas people who make faster than expected progress experience positive emotions.

Goals are objectives people strive to accomplish. Two types of goal-performance discrepancies exist: discrepancy reduction and discrepancy creation. Discrepancy reduction captures the essence of plans, whereas discrepancy creation captures the essence of goals and the goal-setting process. Goals that are both difficult and specific generally improve performance, and they do so by producing motivational effects: Difficult goals mobilize effort and increase persistence, while specific goals direct attention and promote strategic planning. Two conditions are necessary before goals will enhance performance: feedback and goal acceptance. With feedback, a performer can evaluate her performance as being at, above, or below the level of the goal standard. Performing below goal level generates dissatisfaction that underlies a desire to improve; performing above goal level generates satisfaction that underlies a willingness to set more difficult goals in the future. Goal acceptance refers to the process in which the performer accepts another person's assigned goal as his own.

Personal strivings constitute the superordinate goals people try to accomplish. Personal strivings are important not only because they reveal and organize a person's underlying goal system, but also because they foreshadow a person's emotional well-being. Research on personal strivings makes the case that subjective well-being is more about what one strives for than it is about what one actually obtains in life. For example, well-being is highest when personal strivings revolve around themes of intimacy, autonomy, and approaching desired states.

Implicit theories reveal whether people think their personal qualities are fixed and enduring (entity theorists) or are malleable and can be increased (incremental theorists).

Implicit theorists are important because they predict the type of goals people choose to pursue. Entity theorists generally adopt performance goals, whereas incremental theorists generally adopt learning goals. Entity and incremental theorists also interpret the meaning of effort differently. Entity theorists generally believe that high effort means low ability: "The more you try, the dumber you must be." Incremental theorists generally believe that effort is the means by which learning occurs and skills develop. When facing difficult tasks that require a relatively high effort, incremental theorists show the relatively more adaptive motivational style in that they understand the utility of effort and show a willingness to roll up their sleeves and engage in persistent and effortful work.

Once a goal has been set, it does not inevitably and automatically translate itself into effective performance largely because people have trouble getting started and because people have trouble persisting and finishing. In the effort to translate their goals into action, performers benefit from mental simulations and implementation intentions. Mental simulations help goal-directed action by focusing performers on the process of goal attainment—on envisioning how they will solve problems and on what courses of action will be most beneficial. Implementation intentions specify a plan as to when, where, how, and for how long one is to act. People who set implementation intentions are significantly more likely to attain or complete their goals than are people who do not set implementation intentions in advance of their goal-directed action. Implementations have positive effects on goal striving by helping performers overcome the volitional problems associated with getting started, persisting in the face of difficulties, and resuming goal-direction action once interrupted. These intentions essentially delegate the control of goal-directed action to merely encountering anticipated situational cues. (For example, "When I encounter situation X, I will do Y.")

RECOMMENDED READINGS

Plans

Campion, M. A., & Lord, R. G. (1982). A control systems conceptualization of the goal-setting and changing process. *Organizational Behavior and Human Performance, 30,* 265–287.

Goals

Dweck, C. S. (1991). Self-theories and goals: Their role in motivation, personality, and development. In R. Dienstbier (Ed.), *Nebraska symposium on motivation* (pp. 199–235). Lincoln: University of Nebraska Press.

Dweck, C. S., & Leggett, E. L. (1988). A social-cognitive approach to personality and motivation. *Psychological Review, 95,* 256–273.

Earley, P. C., Wojnaroski, P., & Prest, W. (1987). Task planning and energy expended: Exploration of how goals influence performance. *Journal of Applied Psychology, 72,* 107–113.

Elliot, A. J., & Dweck, C. S. (1988). Goals: An approach to motivation and achievement. *Journal of Personality and Social Psychology, 54,* 5–12.

Emmons, R. A. (1986). Personal strivings: An approach to personality and subjective well-being. *Journal of Personality and Social Psychology,* 51, 1058–1068.

Emmons, R. A. (1991). Personal strivings, daily life events, and psychological and physical well-being. *Journal of Personality*, *59*, 453–472.

Erez, M., Earley, P. C., & Hulin, C. L. (1985). The impact of participation on goal acceptance and performance: A two-step model. *Academy of Management Journal*, *28*, 50–66.

Locke, E. A., Shaw, K. N., Saari, L. M., & Latham, G. P. (1981). Goal setting and task performance: 1969–1980. *Psychological Bulletin*, *90*, 125–152.

Tubbs, M. E. (1986). Goal setting: A meta-analytic examination of the empirical evidence. *Journal of Applied Psychology*, *71*, 474–483.

Implementation Intentions

Gollwitzer, P. M. (1999). Implementation intentions: Strong effects of simple plans. *American Psychologist*, *54*, 493–503.

Gollwitzer, P. M., & Brandstatter, V. (1997). Implementation intentions and effective goal pursuit. *Journal of Personality and Social Psychology*, *73*, 186–199.

Taylor, S. E., Pham, L. B., Rivkin, I. D., & Armor, D. A. (1998). Harnessing the imagination: Mental simulation, self-regulation, and coping. *American Psychologist*, *53*, 429–439.

8

Expectancies

What does the future have in store? Will you graduate from college? Will next semester's classes be interesting? Will you pass this course? Will you find this eighth chapter interesting? Do you expect this chapter to address topics that are important to you, or will this chapter present only that which is dry, confusing, and irrelevant? This winter, will you catch the flu? When you apply for your next job, will you get it? Will you fall in love? Will you fall out of love? If you were to go on a blind date or to meet your mate's parents, would these strangers like you? Will you find someone to share your life with, as in marriage? When you drive to school or work tomorrow, will you get stuck in traffic? get a ticket? have a flat tire? When you turn the car's ignition key, will the car start on the first try? Will you live to see your 50th birthday?

How able are you to cope with what the future has in store? Do you have what it takes to graduate? In this course, questions will be asked, tests will be given, and papers will be due. How competent will your performances be? If you bomb the first exam, would you be able to mount a comeback and still do well in the course? Can you use a computer to write a term paper? What would happen if you tried to surf the Internet? surf a wave on the ocean? In relationships, can you make another person laugh? Can you cheer up your friends when they feel depressed? Can you defuse arguments? Could you be the life of a party? If a bully insults and pesters you, could you handle the situation? Can you run three miles without stopping to rest? How about one mile? Could you hit a golf ball on your first try? Could you hit the golf ball if an audience were watching?

Our expectancies of what will happen and our expectancies of how well we can cope with what happens have important motivational implications. Imagine how motivationally problematic your college experience would be if you expected not to graduate, not to pass a particular course, not to get a job after graduation, and not to understand the professor and if you expected your classes to be dull. Imagine how motivationally problematic your interpersonal relationships would be if you expected others not to like you, not to care about your welfare, or to express only hostility. What if you expected that everyone you met would reject you? Imagine how motivationally problematic your athletic participation would be if you expected only to fail and to embarrass yourself in front of others. Imagine how difficult it would be to muster the motivation to run three miles if you knew beforehand that you could not do so.

MOTIVATION TO EXERCISE PERSONAL CONTROL

The theme throughout this chapter features the motivation to exercise personal control over one's fate. To some extent, environments are predictable, and to some extent, people are able to figure out how to exert control over those aspects of the environment that they can predict. In predicting what will happen and in trying to influence what happens, people try to make desirable outcomes more likely and undesirable outcomes less likely. By exercising personal control in this way, people attempt to improve their lives and the lives of others.

The desire to exercise personal control is predicated on a person's belief that they have the power to produce results. When people believe they "have what it takes" to influence their environment and that the environments they are in will be responsive to their influence attempts, they will indeed try to make things happen for the better (i.e., try to exercise personal control). The strength with which people try to exercise personal control can be traced to the strengths of their expectancies. Expectancy is a subjective prediction of how likely it is that an event will occur. That event can be an outcome (e.g., losing 10 pounds) or a course of action that brings the outcome to pass (e.g., exercising enough to lose 10 pounds). When politicians enter an election or athletes enter a competition, they appraise the likelihood that they will win. Before people leap across a creek or tell a risqué joke, they appraise the likelihood of landing on solid ground. In anticipating events and outcomes, people rely on their past experiences to make forecasts about what the future holds and how they will be able to cope with what is to come.

Two Kinds of Expectancy

Two types of expectancies exist: efficacy expectations and outcome expectations (Bandura, 1977, 1986, 1997; Heckhausen, 1977; Peterson, Maier, & Seligman, 1993).

An efficacy expectation (see Figure 8.1) is a judgment of one's capacity to execute a particular act or course of action. An outcome expectation (see Figure 8.1) is a judgment that a given action, once performed, will cause a particular outcome. Efficacy expectations estimate the likelihood that an individual can behave in a particular way; outcome expectations estimate how likely it is that certain consequences will follow once that behavior is enacted.

Efficacy and outcome expectations are separate, causal determinants to the initiation and regulation of behavior (Bandura, 1991). Consider the different expectancies that might run through your mind when you go to the gym to run on a treadmill. The extent to which you begin to exercise and keep exercising depends on (1) your efficacy expectation that you can successfully run without having your lungs collapse and (2) your expectation that the running, once enacted, will produce certain physical, psychological, emotional, and social benefits.

While efficacy and outcome expectations are conceptually distinct from one another, engagement in action (influenced by efficacy expectations) is causally prior to, and therefore affects, one's outcomes. Therefore, high efficacy expectations can bias outcome expectations. For example, the surgeon's expectancy that an operation will produce certain benefits (outcome expectancy) depends, in part, on her strong confidence that she can perform the surgery with excellence (efficacy expectancy). If the surgeon sees herself as inefficacious, how could she expect any personal control over the surgery's outcome? But efficacy expectations affect outcome expectancies only in part because outcome expectancies are influenced by a host of additional factors as well (e.g., all those factors that are extraneous to the individual, such as equipment, help from others, and so on).

Both efficacy and outcome expectations must be reasonably high before behavior becomes energetic and directed. Thus, an analysis of efficacy and outcome expectancies allows us to understand people's reluctance to engage in activities such as public speaking, dating, athletics, and job interviews. To address a group, date, compete, or interview, the person must not only be confident in his efficacy to execute these behaviors but he must also be reasonably assured that an effective performance will pay off (i.e., will lead to desired outcomes). Take away either of these positive forecasts and reluctance and avoidance become logical ways of acting.

EFFICACY EXPECTATIONS

Efficacy expectations concern how confident the individual is of her ability to execute a specific act or a sequence of action. Generally speaking, the more people expect that they can adequately perform an action, the more willing they are to put forth effort and persist in facing difficulties when activities require such action (Bandura, 1989; Bandura & Cervone, 1983; Weinberg, Gould, & Jackson, 1979). In contrast, when people expect that they cannot adequately perform the required task, they are not willing to engage in activities requiring such behavior. Instead, they slacken their effort, prematurely settle for mediocre outcomes, and quit in the face of obstacles (Bandura, 1989).

Efficacy expectations do not just occur out of the blue; they have causes. Efficacy expectations arise from (1) one's personal history in trying to execute that particular

FIGURE 8.1 **Two Kinds of Expectancy: Efficacy and Outcome**

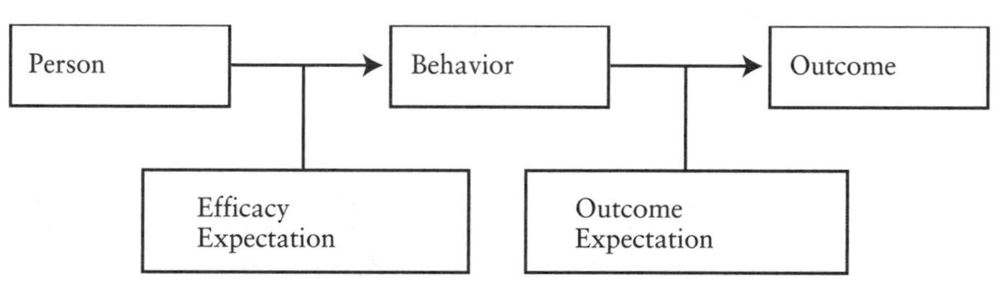

behavior, (2) observations of others as those others execute the behavior, (3) verbal persuasions (pep talks) from others, and (4) physiological states such as a racing heart versus a calm one.

Personal Behavior History

Personal history in trying to execute a particular course of action provides the performer with firsthand efficacy information (Bandura, Reese, & Adams, 1982). Performances judged as competent raise future efficacy expectations, whereas performances judged as incompetent lower these expectations. For instance, if a person prepares to ride a bicycle, her expectancy of being able to actually do it grows out of a personal history of cycling. How important any one behavioral enactment is to future efficacy expectations depends on the strength of the performer's preexisting expectation. Once one's personal behavior history has produced a strong expectation of efficacy, an occasional incompetent enactment will not change efficacy expectation much (or an occasional competent enactment will not raise an efficacy expectation much if it is preceded by a history of repeated incompetent experiences). If the performer is less experienced (i.e., lacks a behavioral history), however, each new competent or incompetent enactment will have greater effect on future efficacy expectations. Of the four sources of efficacy expectations, personal history is the most influential (Bandura, 1986).

Vicarious Experience

Seeing others perform masterfully raises an observer's own efficacy expectation (Bandura et al., 1980; Kazdin, 1979). Seeing others perform the same behavior permits a social comparison. (In other words, "If they can do it, so can I.") Of course, vicarious experience works the other way as well. Observing someone perform the same behavior incompetently lowers our own efficacy expectation. (In other words, "If they can't do it, what makes me think I can?"; Brown & Inouye, 1978.) The extent to which a model's enactment affects our own efficacy expectation depends on two factors. First, the greater the similarity between the model and the observer, the greater the impact the model's behavior will have on the observer's expectation (Schunk, 1989a). Second, the less experienced the observer is at the behavior (a novice), the greater the impact of the vicarious experience (Schunk, 1989b). Thus, vicarious experience is a potent source of efficacy expectations for relatively inexperienced observers who watch similar others perform.

Verbal Persuasion

Coaches, parents, teachers, employers, therapists, peers, spouses, friends, audiences, clergy, authors of self-help books, infomercials, inspirational posters, happy-face stickers, and songs on the radio often attempt to convince us that we can competently execute a given action—despite our entrenched inefficacy—if we will just simply try. Effective pep talks persuade the performer to focus more on potentials and personal strengths and less on deficiencies and personal weaknesses. Pep talks shift a performer's attention from sources of inefficacy to sources of efficacy. But verbal persuasion goes only so far if it is contradicted by direct experience. Its effectiveness is limited by the boundaries of the possible (in the mind of the performer) and depends on the credibility, expertise, and trustworthiness of the persuader. Individuals also give themselves pep talks, usually in the form of self-instruction, that can boost efficacy expectations (Schunk & Cox, 1986). The importance of verbal persuasions can be found in (1) providing the performer with enough of a temporary efficacy boost to generate the motivation necessary for another try (Schunk, 1991) and (2) counteracting the occasional setback that might otherwise cultivate sufficient doubt to halt task persistence (Schunk, 1992). Verbal persuasion is the third most influential source of efficacy expectations (Schunk, 1989a).

Physiological State

Fatigue, pain, muscle tension, mental confusion, and trembling hands are physiological cues that the demands of the task currently exceed the performer's ability (Taylor et al., 1985). An abnormal physiological state is a private, yet attention-getting, message that contributes to expectations of inefficacy. An absence of tension, fear, and stress, on the other hand, heightens efficacy expectations by providing firsthand bodily feedback that one can indeed cope adequately with task demands (Bandura & Adams, 1977). The causal direction between efficacy and physiological arousal is bidirectional: Inefficacy heightens arousal and heightened arousal feeds perceived inefficacy (Bandura et al., 1988). Physiology communicates efficacy information mostly when initial efficacy is uncertain (one is performing a task for the first time). When efficacy expectations are relatively certain, people sometimes discount, or even reinterpret, their physiological cues (Carver & Blaney, 1977). Like vicarious experience and verbal persuasion, physiological states are not as potent cues to future efficacy beliefs as is one's personal behavior history.

OUTCOME EXPECTATIONS

Whereas efficacy expectations involve the person's judgment of how masterfully he can execute a particular course of action, outcome expectations involve the judgment of whether that course of action will produce a desirable outcome. The essence of an outcome expectation is captured in questions such as, After I perform behavior X adequately, will I get outcome Y? Once I run a mile every day this week, will I lose two pounds? After I muster the courage to ask him to the dance, will he reject me? Whereas efficacy expectations pertain to the first parts of these three questions, outcome expectations pertain to the last parts of these questions.

All other things being equal (efficacy, needs, incentives), high effort and strong persistence are more likely in those outcomes for which individuals estimate a high probability of attainment; that is, they have an optimistic outcome expectancy. There are four determinants of outcome expectancies: (1) personal outcome history, (2) task difficulty, (3) social comparison information, and (4) personality.

Personal Outcome History

As individuals involve themselves in varying tasks, they invariably assess whether their task engagements produce mostly successes or mostly failures. These appraisals can be subjective (doing better than thought, therefore, succeeding) or more typically, objective (winning a prize, therefore, succeeding). To understand how individuals use success/failure experiences (i.e., personal outcome history) to construct future outcome expectancies, consider the example shown in Figure 8.2 (Feather, 1966). Participants worked on a

FIGURE 8.2 **Relationship Between Performance Feedback and Outcome Expectations**

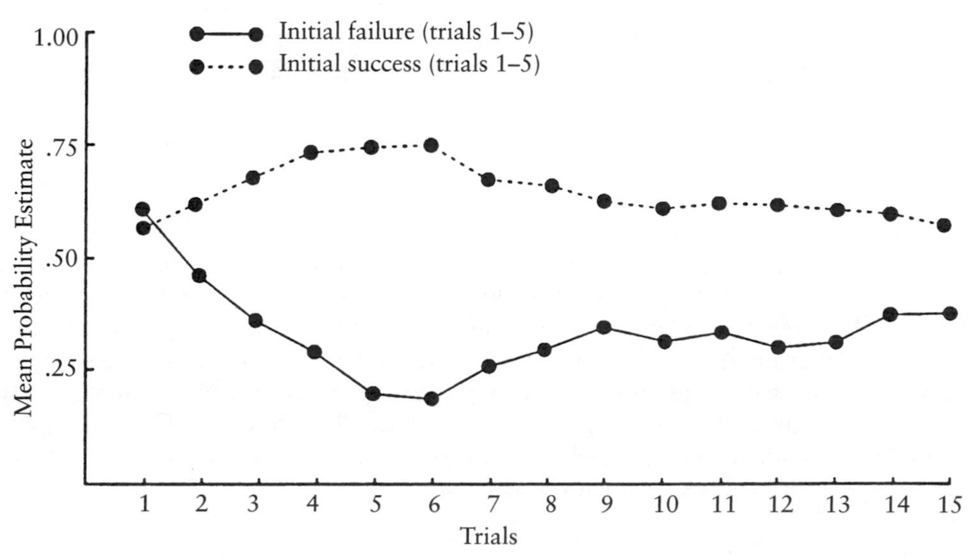

SOURCE: From "Effects of Prior Success and Failure on Expectations of Success and Subsequent Failure," by N.T. Feather, 1966, *Journal of Personality and Social Psychology, 3*, pp. 287–298. Copyright 1966 by the American Psychological Association. Reprinted with permission.

series of 15 anagrams in which the first 5 anagrams were either very difficult or very easy. Thus, half of the participants were set up for initial failure, whereas the other half were set up for initial success. On trials 6 through 15, all participants worked on the same set of anagrams, all of which were of the same moderate difficulty. As illustrated, expectations of success in trials 6 through 15 were significantly biased by the initial personal outcome history. Success feedback on trials 1 through 5 positively biased the later outcome expectancies, while initial failure outcomes negatively biased subsequent outcome expectancies (Feather, 1966; Feather & Saville, 1967). These data are especially noteworthy because participants in the initial failure and initial success groups actually performed about the same on trials 6 through 15. Therefore, what differed was not their ability, but their personal outcome history.

Social Comparison Information

People form outcome expectancies based on their observations of the outcomes others receive on the same tasks (DeVillis, DeVillis, & McCauley, 1978). As we watch others experience outcomes, we revise our own outcome expectancies in the direction of the outcomes we see others receive. Even if a performer does not see one's success/failure outcome directly, that performer is often aware of some group norm of how people in the past have either generally succeeded or generally failed at the task. For example, a college student who enrolls in a particular course is often aware of the outcomes experienced by previous students in that class. The student consequently does not enter the course naively. Rather, she enters the class with an outcome expectation that coincides with the typical outcomes others have previously attained. (That is, "This has been an easy course for others in the past, so I expect to earn a high grade.") Similarly, if an athletic team plays a team that everyone else has previously defeated, the team will expect a victory. (That is, "Everyone else has defeated this team, so we probably will too.")

Task Difficulty

Task difficulty appraisals depend on the specific salient characteristics of the task. Thus, for instance, the hiker notices the very steep cliff, the programmer scans the complex computer program, and the student flips through a 500-page book with dense figures and charts. The steepness of the rock, the complexity of the program, and the length of the book are all evaluated as difficult task characteristics. In contrast, the hiker may notice a gently sloping hill, the programmer may scan a basic computer program, and the student may flip through a three-page article (easy task characteristics). Generally speaking, difficult task characteristics yield low expectancies of success, whereas easy task characteristics yield high expectancies of success.

Personality

The final determinant of an outcome expectancy is the individual's personality. Need for achievement, for instance, predisposes people to overestimate their chances for success prior to task participation (Weiner, 1974). High-need achievers generally have overly optimistic outcome expectations, whereas low-need achievers generally have relatively pessimistic outcome expectancies (they underestimate their chances for success). The same pattern holds for individuals with high and low self-esteem (McFarlin & Blascovich, 1981), as high self-esteem individuals harbor significantly more optimistic outcome expectancies than do low self-esteem individuals. Similarly, research on an individual difference referred to as explanatory style (the habitual way people explain life's outcomes; discussed in chapter 9) shows that attributional optimists (optimistic explanatory style) expect their futures to hold mostly good outcomes, whereas attributional pessimists (pessimistic explanatory style) expect their futures to hold mostly bad outcomes (Scheier & Carver, 1985).

The variables that affect the acquisition and change of both efficacy and outcome expectations are summarized in Table 8.1. Besides just categorizing the set of causal determinants of efficacy and outcome expectations, the table has a second purpose. It suggests separate therapeutic strategies for designing motivational interventions for persons with low expectations. Personal behavior history, vicarious experience, verbal persuasion, and regulating physiological states are promising routes in altering efficacy expectations. To alter outcome expectations, attention is best directed toward personal outcome history, social comparison information, perceptions of task difficulty, and personality differences. For the person interested in changing efficacy or outcome expectancies in the self or in others, Table 8.1 shows the means for doing so.

SELF-EFFICACY

Efficacy expectations center on questions such as the following: Can I perform well on this particular task? If things start to go wrong during my performance, do I have the resources within me to cope successfully and turn things around for the better? But efficacy expectations and self-efficacy are not the same thing. Self-efficacy is more than a collection of behavior-specific efficacy expectations, as self-efficacy is a generative capacity in which the individual organizes and orchestrates his skills to cope with the demands and circumstances of a task. It is the capacity to use resources well under diverse circumstances. Formally, self-efficacy is defined as one's judgment of how well (or poorly) one will cope with a situation, given the skills one possesses and the circumstances one faces (Bandura, 1986, 1993, 1997).

TABLE 8.1 **Sources of Efficacy and Outcome Expectations**

SOURCES OF EFFICACY EXPECTATIONS	SOURCES OF OUTCOME EXPECTATIONS
Personal behavior history	Personal outcome history
Vicarious experience	Social comparison information
Verbal persuasion	Task difficulty
Abnormal physiological state	Personality

Self-efficacy is not the same construct as "ability." Competent functioning requires not only possessing skills (i.e., ability), but also the capacity to translate those skills into effective performance, especially under trying circumstances. A snow skier might have wondrous slalom, mogul, and downhill racing skills but still perform dismally if the wind blows, the snow ices, or the slopes are crowded with clumsy skiers who keep falling. Self-efficacy is the generative capacity that enables the performer to improvise in ways that best translate personal abilities into effective performance. It is just as important a determinant of performance as is ability because performance situations often are stressful, ambiguous, and unpredictable, and as one performs, circumstances always change.

"Perceived self-efficacy is not a measure of the skills one has but a belief about what one can do under different sets of conditions with whatever skills one possesses" (Bandura, 1997). Consider that most of us can drive a car rather well on the interstate as most of us rate very high on abilities such as steering, braking, negotiating traffic, reciting traffic laws, and finding our destinations. But self-efficacy becomes important when circumstances rise to test our abilities, as when driving in an unreliable car on an unfamiliar road with poorly marked streets, during a heavy snowstorm, or as monster trucks whiz by splashing slush that covers the windshield. Even highly skilled drivers sometimes perform dismally because circumstances change in stressful and overwhelming ways. Under trying circumstances, the driver must have what it takes to keep arousal in check, to think clearly in deciding between options, to avoid perils, and to perhaps negotiate or show leadership in enlisting the assistance of the passenger. The same self-efficacy analysis applies to academic test taking (Bandura, et al., 1988), athletic performance (Feltz, 1992), self-defense (Ozer & Bandura, 1990), gender role conduct (Bussey & Bandura, 1999), health-promoting behaviors (Bandura, 1998), and collective agency for solving social problems (Bandura, 1997).

The opposite of efficacy is doubt. For the driver who doubts his abilities, surprises, setbacks, and difficulties create anxiety (Bandura, 1988), confusion (Wood & Bandura, 1989), negative expectations (Bandura, 1983), and aversive physiological arousal and bodily tension (Bandura et al., 1985). Imagine the unfolding of events that might occur when the self-doubt of an otherwise skilled driver comes face to face with surprises, setbacks, and difficulties. Perhaps an unexpected storm begins (surprise), or the windshield wipers fail (setback), or ice forms on the road (difficulty). Under such trying conditions, doubt can interfere with effective thinking, planning, and decision making to cause anxiety, confusion, arousal, tension, and distress that can spiral performance toward disaster. Of course, surprises, setbacks, and difficulties may not produce poor performance, just as skill, talent, and ability may not produce excellent performance. Rather, extent of self-efficacy (versus self-doubt) determines the extent to which a performer copes successfully when skills and abilities are stressed.

Consider the more extended example of trying to present oneself as socially competent as during a job interview, auditioning for a play, or going on a first date. In a self-efficacy analysis, the skills involved in interviewing, auditioning, and dating and the situational demands placed on the performer are complex and multidimensional. The following list describes an adolescent on a first date (Rose & Frieze, 1989) by listing some task demands (left) as well as the skills needed to successfully cope with those demands (right).

Dating demands	Dating skills
Ask for the date	Assertiveness
Make a plan to do something interesting	Creativity
Arrive on time at date's house	Punctuality
Relate warmly to parents or roommates	Sociability
Joke, laugh, and talk	Sense of humor
Impress date	Salesmanship
Be polite	Social etiquette
Understand how other feels	Empathy
Be responsive to the other's needs	Perspective taking
Kiss goodnight	Romance

As the adolescent contemplates the date, she asks what specific events will take place. What skills will be needed to perform well? If things go unexpectedly wrong, can she make the necessary corrective adjustments? How does she expect to feel during the date and during each specific event? In this hypothetical situation, the adolescent expects that the overall task at hand will require a dozen or so skills, such as assertiveness, sociability, and so on. The adolescent also has some expectation of how effectively she can execute each of these skills, and those expectancies might range from woefully incompetent to highly competent. These expectations of anticipated performance effectiveness represent the heart and soul of self-efficacy beliefs: Just how competent will I be when the situation calls for me to be assertive? When I try to be assertive, will I feel mostly confidence and hope or mostly doubt and fear? Are my skills hardy enough to get the evening back on track if things go wrong (e.g., parents turn out to be very difficult to relate to)? Just how much social anxiety the adolescent feels can be predicted by a self-efficacy analysis of her perceived efficacy expectations in each of the 10 task-related demands.

Self-Efficacy Effects on Behavior

Once formed, self-efficacy expectations exert diverse effects on motivational aspects of behavior (Bandura, 1986, 1996, 1997). Self-efficacy beliefs affect (1) choice of activities and selection of environments, (2) extent of effort and persistence put forth during performance, (3) the quality of thinking and decision making during performance, and (4) emotional reactions, especially those related to stress and anxiety.

Choice

People continually make choices about what activities and what environments to pursue. In general, people seek out and approach with excitement those activities and situations that they feel capable of adjusting to or handling, while people shun and actively avoid those activities and situations that they see as likely to overwhelm their coping capacities (Bandura, 1977, 1989). In a self-efficacy analysis, a person will often avoid choices of tasks and environments as a self-protective act for guarding against the possibility of being overwhelmed by the demands and challenges of the task. If the student expects a math class or a foreign language class to be overwhelming, confusing, and frustrating, doubt overwhelms efficacy and produces avoidance decisions, such as withdrawing from class discussions or not enrolling in the class in the first place. The same doubt-plagued avoidance choices apply to social opportunities, sports or music, and organizations and careers.

Avoidance choices exert a profound, detrimental, long-term effect on development (Bandura, 1986). Weak self-efficacy beliefs set the stage for people to shun participating in activities and therefore contribute to arrested developmental potentials (Holahan & Holahan, 1987). When people shun an activity out of doubt over personal competence, they participate in the self-destructive process of retarding their own development. Further, the more they avoid such activities, the more entrenched self-doubt becomes because doubters never get the chance to prove themselves wrong. Tragically, such a pattern of avoidance progressively narrows people's ranges of activities and settings (Bandura, 1982; Betz & Hackett, 1986; Hackett, 1985).

Effort and Persistence

As people perform, self-efficacy beliefs influence how much effort they exert as well as how long they put forth that effort in the face of adversity (Bandura, 1989). Strong self-efficacy beliefs produce persistent coping efforts aimed at overcoming setbacks and difficulties (Salomon, 1984). The doubt from weak self-efficacy beliefs, on the other hand, leads people to slacken their efforts when they encounter difficulties or give up altogether (Bandura & Cervone, 1983; Weinberg, Gould, & Jackson, 1979). Self-doubt also leads performers to settle prematurely on mediocre solutions.

In trying to master complex activities, learning is always fraught with difficulties, obstacles, setbacks, frustrations, rejections, and inequalities, at least to a degree. Self-efficacy plays a pivotal role in facilitating effort and persistence not because it silences self-doubt following failure and rejection (because these are expected, normal emotional reactions), but because self-efficacy leads to a *quick recovery* of self-assurance following such setbacks (Bandura, 1986). Using examples of persistent writers, scientists, and athletes, Albert Bandura argues that it is the resiliency of self-efficacy in the face of being pounded by uninterrupted failure that provides the motivational support necessary in continuing the persistent effort needed for competent functioning and the development of expertise (Bandura, 1989).

Thinking and Decision Making

People who believe strongly in their efficacy for solving problems remain remarkably efficient in their analytic thinking during stressful episodes, whereas people who doubt their problem-solving capacities think erratically (Bandura & Wood, 1989; Wood & Bandura, 1989). To perform their best, people must first use memories of past events to predict the most effective course of action, they must then analyze feedback to assess and to reassess the merit of their plans and strategies, and they must then reflect upon performance, remembering which courses of action were effective and which were not. A strong sense of efficacy allows the performer to remain task focused, even in the face of situational stress and problem-solving dead ends. In contrast, self-doubt distracts decision makers away from such task-focused thinking as attention shifts to the deficiencies of the self and the overwhelming demands of the task. In short, doubt deteriorates, whereas efficacy buffers, the quality of a performer's thinking and decision making during a performance.

Emotional Reactions

Before performers begin an activity, they typically spend time thinking about how they will perform. Persons with a strong sense of efficacy attend to the demands and challenges of the task, visualize competent scenarios for forthcoming behaviors, and react to task challenges and feedback with enthusiastic effort, optimism, and interest. Persons with a weak sense of efficacy, however, dwell on personal deficiencies, visualize the formidable obstacles they face, and react to challenges and feedback with pessimism, anxiety, and depression (Bandura, 1986). Once performance begins and things start to go awry, strong self-efficacy beliefs keep anxiety at bay. People who doubt their efficacy, however, are quickly threatened by difficulties, react to setbacks with distress, and see their attention drift toward personal deficiencies and the potential consequences of failure.

Life in general brings any number of potentially threatening events (e.g., examinations, public performances), and perceived self-efficacy plays a central role in determining how much stress and anxiety such events bring to any individual performer. Rather than existing as a fixed property of events, "threat" always depends on the relationship a person has to the task (Folkman & Lazarus, 1985; Lazarus & Folkman, 1984). Knowing that one's coping abilities cannot handle an event's perceived demands conjures up thoughts of disaster, emotional arousal, and feelings of distress and anxiety (Bandura, 1983; Bandura, Reese, & Adams, 1982; Bandura et al., 1985; Lazarus, 1991a). More optimistically, when people plagued with self-doubt undergo therapy-like conditions to enhance their coping capabilities, the intimidating event that once conjured up such an avalanche of doubt, dread, and distress no longer does so (Bandura & Adams, 1977; Bandura et al., 1980; Bandura, Reese, & Adams, 1982; Ozer & Bandura, 1990). As self-efficacy increases, fear and anxiety slip away. Self-efficacy researchers go so far as to say that the root cause of anxiety is low self-efficacy (Bandura, 1983, 1988).

EMPOWERMENT

Two practical points about self-efficacy are important to highlight. First, self-efficacy beliefs come from personal behavior history, vicarious experiences, verbal persuasion, and physiological states (e.g., Table 8.1). What makes this a practical point is that it means high self-efficacy beliefs can be acquired and changed. Second, the level of self-efficacy predicts ways of behaving that can be called "competent functioning" or "personal empowerment" (e.g., overcoming avoidance-based fears, putting forth high effort, persisting in the face of adversity, thinking clearly and exercising control during performance). Thus, once enhanced, self-efficacy expectations provide the cognitive foundation underlying personal empowerment.

Empowerment involves possessing the knowledge, skills, and beliefs that allow people to exert control over their lives. One example of self-efficacy as empowerment can be found in learning to defend oneself against intimidation and threats from abusive others (Ozer & Bandura, 1990). When threatened, people typically feel anxious, stressed, vulnerable, at risk, and in danger. To empower oneself, people need more than just skills and the knowledge of what to do. People also need self-efficacy beliefs so they can (1) translate their knowledge and skills into effective performance when threatened and (2) exert control over intrusive negative thoughts. In one study, researchers trained a group of women over a 5-week period in self-defense and emotion-management skills. The researchers first asked the women to watch expert models defend themselves against assailants (using vicarious experience) and then asked the women to master the modeled behavior while hearing support and encouragement from peers (using verbal persuasion) during simulated attacks (Ozer & Bandura, 1990). With each successive week, women's self-efficacy beliefs to control interpersonal threats and intrusive negative thinking soared. Once empowered, the women felt less vulnerable and began to engage in activities that were once thought to be too risky (e.g., outdoor exercise and recreation, travel to different parts of town, evening social events). In other words, empowerment occurred as efficacy and engagement replaced doubt and avoidance.

One of the women voiced her empowerment by saying, "I feel freer and more capable than ever. I now make choices about what I will or won't do based on whether or not I want to, not whether or not it is frightening to me" (Ozer & Bandura, 1990). Understandably, the reader might wonder whether the women's increased confidence led them to behaving recklessly and being put in harm's way. This did not happen. Instead, the women's generalized avoidance was replaced by flexible, adaptive, confident behavior. Such a program would seemingly be effective in practically any activities that people avoided out of a fear of having their skills overwhelmed by situational challenges and demands.

LEARNED HELPLESSNESS

As efficacy expectancies underlie self-efficacy, outcome expectancies underlie learned helplessness. When people engage in a task, they typically know what outcome is at stake. They also have a sense of how controllable versus uncontrollable that outcome is. With controllable outcomes, a one-to-one relationship exists between behavior (what a person does) and outcomes (what happens to that person). With uncontrollable outcomes, a random relationship exists between behavior and outcomes. (For example, "I have no idea what effect, if any, my behavior will have on what happens to me.")

When people expect desired outcomes (e.g., making friends, getting a job) or undesired outcomes (e.g., preventing illness, being fired from a job) are independent of their behavior, they start to develop a "learned helplessness" over attaining those outcomes. Learned helplessness is the psychological state that results when an individual expects that life's outcomes are uncontrollable (Mikulincer, 1994; Seligman, 1975).

Consider the following experiment with three groups of dogs that were administered either (1) inescapable shock, (2) escapable shock, or (3) no shock (control group) (Seligman & Maier, 1967). Dogs in the two shock groups were placed into a sling and given mild 5-second electric shocks once a day for 64 days. In the inescapable shock group, the shocks occurred randomly, and no response could terminate the shock.

Whether the dog barked, howled, or thrashed about frantically, the shock continued for its full 5 seconds. In other words, the shock was inescapable. In the escapable shock group, the dogs could terminate the shock. If the dog pressed a button mounted on the wall (placed just in front of their snouts), the shock stopped. The dogs therefore had a response available to escape the shock—push the button. In the no-shock control group, dogs were placed into a sling but received no shocks.

Exposure to inescapable shock, escapable shock, or no shock constituted the first phase (the learning phase) of the two-phase experiment. In the second phase (the test phase), the dogs in each group were all treated the same. Each dog was placed into a shuttle box in which its two compartments were separated by a wall partition of elbow height. The two compartments were the same size and similar in most respects, except the first compartment had a grid floor through which a mild electrical shock could be delivered while the second compartment was safe from shock. To illustrate the procedure, the top half of Figure 8.3 (a) shows a dog in the sling (phase 1 of the experiment), and the lower half of the figure (b) shows the dog in the shuttle box (phase 2 of the experiment; Carlson, 1988). On each trial during phase 2, the dogs were placed into the grid floor compartment and a mild shock was delivered. The onset of this shock was always preceded by a signal (a dimming of the light on the wall). After the lights were dimmed, the electric shock followed 10 seconds thereafter. If the dog jumped over the partition, it escaped the shock. If the dog failed to jump over the partition within 10 seconds, the electric shock started and continued for either a minute or until the dog jumped over the partition.

A summary of the study's procedure and results appears in Table 8.2 (Seligman & Maier, 1967). The dogs in both the escapable shock and no shock groups quickly learned how to escape the shock in the shuttle box. When shocked, these dogs ran about frantically at first and rather accidentally climbed, fell, scrambled, or jumped over the barrier. That is, through trial and error, the dogs learned that if they somehow overstepped the barrier, they could escape the shock. After only a few trials, these dogs jumped over the barrier to safety as soon as the warning light dimmed.

TABLE 8.2 **Results of a Prototypical Learned Helplessness Study**

EXPERIMENTAL CONDITION	PHASE 1	PHASE 2	RESULTS
Inescapable Shock	Received shock, no coping response could terminate the shock	Received an escapable shock	Failed to escape from the shock
Escapable Shock	Received shock, pressing nose against button could terminate shock	Received an escapable shock	Quickly learned to escape shock by jumping over barrier
Control, No Shock	Received no shocks	Received an escapable shock	Quickly learned to escape shock by jumping over barrier

FIGURE 8.3 **Apparatus for Seligman and Maier Experiment on Learned Helplessness**

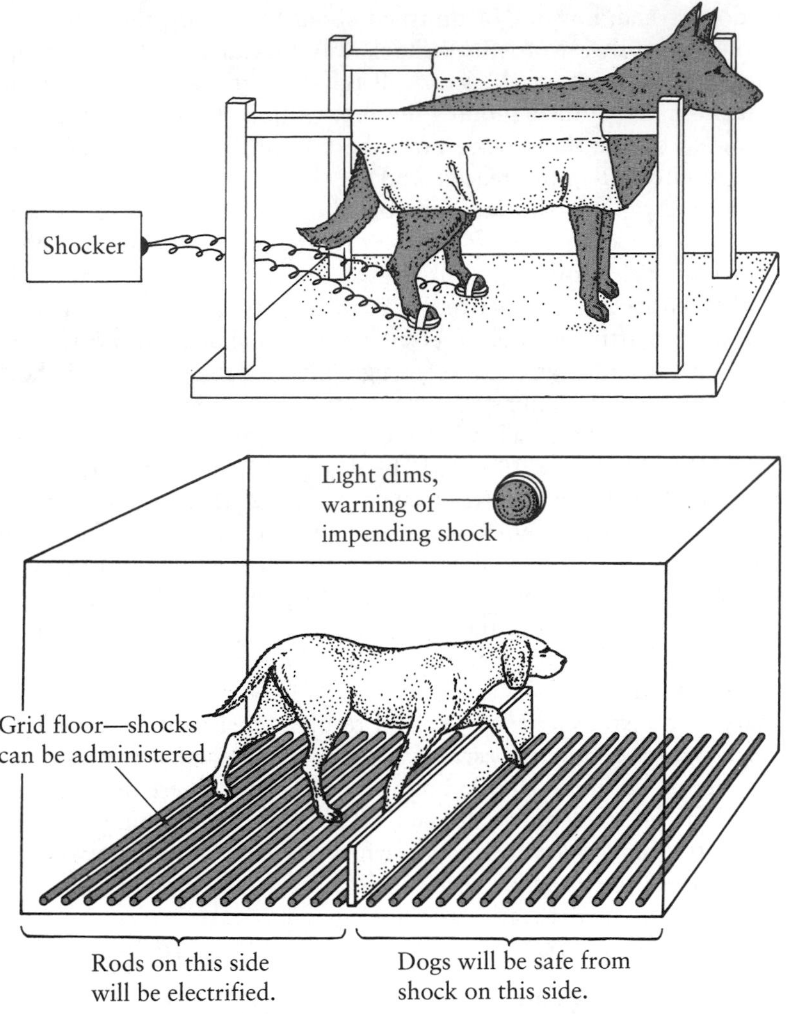

SOURCE: From *Discovering Psychology,* by N.C. Carlson, 1988. Boston: Allyn & Bacon. Copyright 1988 by Allyn & Bacon. Adapted with permission.

The dogs in the inescapable shock group behaved very differently. When shocked, these dogs at first behaved as the other dogs did by running about frantically and howling. However, unlike the dogs in the other two groups, these dogs soon stopped running around and, instead, whimpered until the trial (and shock) terminated. After only a few trials, these dogs gave up trying to escape and passively accepted the shock. On subsequent trials, the dogs failed to make any escape movements at all. What these dogs learned in the sling—the onset, duration, intensity, and termination of the shock (in phase 1) were all beyond their control—had a carry-over effect in the shuttle box: The dogs perceived that escape was beyond their control.

The startling generalization that emerged from this study is that whenever animals are placed in a situation in which they perceive they have little or no control, they develop the expectation that their future actions will have little or no effect on what happens to them. This learned expectation that one's voluntary behavior will not effect desired outcomes is the heart of learned helplessness.

APPLICATIONS TO HUMANS

The early experiments on learned helplessness used animals as research participants mostly because the uncontrollable events used in these studies included traumatic events, such as electric shock. Later studies found ways to test the extent to which helplessness applied to humans (Diener & Dweck, 1978, 1980; Dweck, 1975; Hiroto, 1974; Hiroto & Seligman, 1975; Mikulincer, 1994; Peterson, Maier, & Seligman, 1993). In Donald Hiroto's (1974) experiment, irritating noise constituted the aversive, traumatic stimulus event. College students participated by wearing a set of earphones capable of sending a blast of noise. For the inescapable noise group, the noise was programmed to be random. The blast of the noise was therefore uncontrollable, as terminating the noise was independent of whatever actions the participant tried. Those in the escapable noise group could terminate the loud noise by manipulating a lever (a toggle switch) from one side to the other. For the no-noise control group, participants wore the headphones but heard no noise. In the second phase of the study, all participants heard escapable noise bursts. The results with humans paralleled the results with dogs in that participants in the inescapable noise group sat passively and were unwilling to attempt an escape, whereas participants in the escapable and no-noise groups learned quickly to escape the noise (by operating the lever). Humans too learned helplessness.

To demonstrate how learned helplessness operates, try to solve problems that vary in how controllable they are: Can you solve academic problems? relationship problems? financial problems? health problems? Looking at the sequence of four cards shown in Figure 8.4, consider an experiment in which the participant's task is to figure out which feature the experimenter is looking for—triangle or square, dot or star, shaded or not. A series of 10 cards appear and the participant's task is to identify which feature is being tracked. On the first card, he simply guesses "left" or "right," and the experimenter replies "correct" or "incorrect." The same procedure occurs for the following nine cards. For instance, a person who is tracking the hypothesis of "square" would choose right, right, left, and right (in the four cards shown in Figure 8.4).

Now imagine that in one condition, the experimenter (or a computer program) provided authentic feedback such that the participant could, with concentration and effort, use the feedback to figure out the answer to the problem. In other words, the problem is controllable, at least with concentration and effort. In a second condition, however, the feedback was random and bogus. With random feedback, the participant could try all the hypotheses in the world and only gain a sense of confusion and frustration for the effort. After 10 of these problems, the second phase of the study begins as all participants (in both conditions) are asked to solve solvable, moderately difficult problems (e.g., multiplication problems, six-letter anagrams). The consistent finding is that people exposed to solvable problems in the first phase of the study solve significantly more problems in the second phase than do people exposed to unsolvable problems (random feedback) in the first phase (Diener & Dweck, 1978). It is not so much how smart and clever the participant is that matters most; instead, it

FIGURE 8.4 **Sample of a Problem Used in Learned Helplessness Studies With Humans**

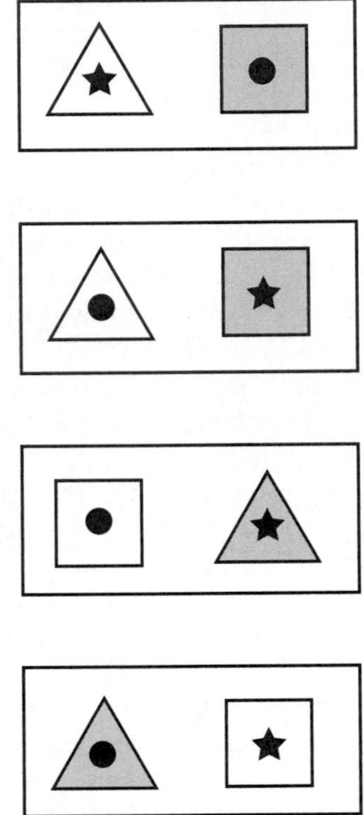

SOURCE: From "An Analysis of Learned Helplessness: Continuous Changes in Performance, Strategy, and Achievement Cognitions Following Failure," by C. I. Diener and C. S. Dweck, 1978, *Journal of Personality and Social Psychology, 36,* pp. 451–462. Copyright 1978 by the American Psychological Association. Reprinted with permission.

is how responsive and controllable is the environment in which one attempts to solve problems.

COMPONENTS

Learned helplessness theory relies on three fundamental components to explain the motivational dynamics that occur whenever experience leads people to expect that the events in their lives will be beyond their personal control. Those three components are contingency, cognition, and behavior (Peterson, Maier, & Seligman, 1993).

Contingency

Contingency refers to the relationship between a person's behavior and the environment's outcomes. The environment can be the home, classroom, workplace, sports field, interpersonal relationship, psychology laboratory, and so on. Contingency exists on a continuum that ranges from outcomes that occur on a random, noncontingent basis (i.e., uncontrollable outcomes) to outcomes that occur in perfect synchronization with a person's voluntary behavior (i.e., controllable outcomes). That is, how contingent any one environment is can be scored from 0 (features uncontrollable outcomes) to 1 (features controllable outcomes).

Take a moment to ask yourself what your own experiences have taught you about contingency in the following situations: getting a traffic ticket, getting a job in your hometown, winning a tennis match against a rival, winning the state lottery, catching the flu during winter, getting cancer from smoking cigarettes, gaining weight, and graduating from college. To characterize the contingency inherent in each of these situations, ask yourself the following: "To what extent does the average person's voluntary, strategic behavior influence the outcomes that occur in these settings?" That is, how much influence does voluntary coping behavior (from people in general, not from you in particular) exert on avoiding a traffic ticket, avoiding the flu, getting a job, winning a contest, winning the lottery, escaping cancer, preventing weight gain, and obtaining a college degree? Contingency will vary across these eight situations in that some are highly controllable outcomes, some are highly uncontrollable, and some are in between controllable and uncontrollable.

Cognition

A good deal of cognitive intervention takes place between the actual, objective environmental contingencies that exist in the world and a person's subjective understanding of personal control in such environments. Mental events dilute the relationship between objective contingencies and subjective understandings of personal control, and these events therefore create some margin of error between objective truth and subjective understanding.

Three cognitive elements are particularly important: biases, such as the "illusion of control" (discussed in chapter 9); attributions, or explanations of why we think we do or do not have control (chapter 9); and expectancies, which are the subjective personal control beliefs we carry over from past experiences to generalize as relevant to our current situations. To illustrate the importance of cognition, ask two people who experience the same environmental contingency why they avoided a traffic ticket, avoided the flu, got a job, and so on. People's outcome beliefs (and hence their replies to your question) stem not only from the objective information about the world but also from each person's unique biases, attributions, and expectancies. Hence, to understand learned helplessness, we need to pay attention not only to objective environmental contingencies (how controllable outcomes really are) but also to subjective personal control beliefs (how controllable the person thinks those outcomes are).

Behavior

Just as contingency exists on a continuum, coping behavior to prevent or avoid outcomes also exists on a continuum. In a traumatic event, people's voluntary coping behavior varies from passive to active.

Coping responses can be lethargic and passive, or coping responses can be active and assertive. Lethargy, passivity, and giving up typify a listless, demoralized effort that characterizes the behavior of the helpless individual (recall the passive behavior of the dogs in the inescapable shock group). Alertness, activity, and assertiveness characterize people who are not helpless (who have some expectation of control). To illustrate passive behavior as a component of learned helplessness, consider once again the situations listed earlier (driving on the highway, job hunting, competing against an opponent). Consider your own passive-to-active coping behaviors in the face of such situations and potential outcomes. The job hunter who quits reading newspaper advertisements, revising her résumé, telephoning prospective employers, and rising early and enthusiastically in the morning to look for a job manifests the listless coping behavior that characterizes helplessness.

EFFECTS

Learned helplessness occurs when people expect that their voluntary behavior will produce little or no effect on the outcomes they strive to attain or avoid. How learned helplessness generates passivity is through three kinds of deficits: motivational, learning, and emotional (Alloy & Seligman, 1979). Collectively, this set of expectancy-induced deficits causes passive, helpless behavior.

Motivational Deficits

Motivational deficits consist of a decreased willingness to try. Motivational deficits become apparent when a person's willingness to emit voluntary coping responses decreases or disappears altogether. Typically, when people care about an outcome and when the environment is at least somewhat responsive in delivering those outcomes, they act enthusiastically and assertively in bringing about those outcomes. For instance, at the beginning of a season, an athlete might practice diligently and persistently, but after a series of athletic defeats (victory becomes an uncontrollable outcome), willingness to practice wanes. The athlete begins to wonder if the time spent practicing is worth it. In the learned helplessness experiment described in the preceding paragraphs, the experimenters asked participants why they did not try to terminate an unpleasant noise in the second phase of the study (Thornton & Jacobs, 1971). Approximately 60% of the participants (from the inescapable noise group) reported that they felt little control over the noise so did not see the point in trying to terminate the noise This verbalization of "why try?" characterizes the motivational deficit in learned helplessness.

Learning Deficits

Learning deficits consist of an acquired pessimistic set that interferes with the ability to learn new response-outcome contingencies. Over time, exposure to uncontrollable environments cultivates an expectancy in which people believe that outcomes are generally independent of their actions. Once expectancies take on a pessimistic tone, the person has a very difficult time learning that a new response can effect outcomes. This pessimistic set essentially interferes with, or retards, the learning of future response-outcome contingencies (Alloy & Seligman, 1979).

When students first learn the results from learned helplessness experiments, they frequently wonder why dogs or humans in the inescapable groups do not learn in the second phase of the experiment that jumping over the barrier or flipping the lever terminates the shock or noise blast. Consider, however, what the subjects learn during the first phase of the earphone session with the inescapable noise. The first time they hear the noise, they flinch and jump, and the second time, they manipulate the lever or shift their weight from side to side. Perhaps they perceive that on some trials turning their heads or shifting their weight coincides with the turning off of the noise. But on later trials, they again turn their heads or shift their weight, but the noise persists for its programmed and uncontrollable 5 seconds. Gradually, they learn that no response turns off the noise in a reliable way. They try everything, but nothing works. Consequently, when they enter the second phase of the experiment and happen to move the now working lever, any positive outcome (turning off the noise) will appear to be a "successful accident" and unworthy of being tried again (as were head turning, weight shifting, and so forth in the first phase of the study). Compared to the participants in the escapable noise and control groups who are quick to learn which response works, participants in the inescapable noise groups still do not believe that any response works. Because they expect no response to work, participants in the inescapable noise groups have an unusually difficult time learning a new coping response.

Emotional Deficits

Emotional deficits consist of affective disruptions in which lethargic, depressive emotional reactions occur in situations that call for active, assertive emotion. In the face of trauma, the typical human response is one of highly mobilized emotion (e.g., fear, anger, assertiveness, frustration). When afraid, people struggle vigorously to overcome, escape, counteract, or do whatever is necessary to cope effectively. Over time, however, an unrelenting onslaught of environmental unresponsiveness leads people to view coping as futile. Once fear-mobilized emotionality is believed to be unproductive, depression-related emotionality takes its place. Once the person becomes fully convinced that there is nothing that can be done to escape the trauma, the resulting expectation makes energy-mobilizing emotions less likely and makes energy-depleting emotions (e.g., listlessness, apathy, depression) more likely.

Sudden Death

One catastrophic affective consequence of helplessness is sudden death, which is a death brought on by a psychological rather than by a physiological cause. Sudden death is most likely whenever an animal (1) perceives a strong threat to life, (2) gives up attempts to escape from the threat and accepts its fate, and (3) goes into a depressed, quiescent state stemming from hopelessness (Richter, 1957).

Consider the experiment in which one group of wild rats was placed into a vat of 3-foot-deep warm water. These rats swam for some 60 hours (swimming for survival and struggling for escape) or until they drowned from exhaustion (the experimenter had a submerged net that would catch them before they drowned). In a second group, the experimenter first held the wild rats in his gloved hand until each rat stopped struggling, which lasted on average about 30 minutes. Once the rats had stopped struggling, they were placed into the same 3-foot-deep, warm water vat. These rats swam excitedly for only a few minutes and then drowned, sinking with little struggle (again, there was a protective net to catch them). In a third group, the experimenter held the wild rats in his gloved hand until each stopped struggling, just as in the second group. After the rats stopped struggling, however, they were set free on the ground. Later, the experimenter again held the rats until they stopped struggling and then set them free again. He repeated this process a third time. Finally, these rats were placed into the water. He expected these rats would maintain a strong expectation or hope of escaping because their coping efforts had indeed set them free in the past. The rats in this third group behaved just as did the rats in the first group. Reflecting a high hope for eventual escape, they swam about excitedly for literally as long as they physically could.

While these sudden-death findings might turn the reader's stomach, they do nonetheless suggest profound implications. Consider, for instance, that susceptibility to death during bereavement following the loss of one's spouse is 40% greater than expected without bereavement (Parkes, Benjamin, & Fitzgerald, 1969). Helplessness also relates to susceptibility to cancer (Schmale & Iker, 1966), as psychological helplessness suppresses the cells in the human immune system that otherwise fight off foreign invaders, such as natural killer cells and T lymphocytes (Sklar & Anisman, 1979; Visintainer, Volpicelli, & Seligman, 1982). Sudden death does not have to be a product of such extremities as captured by a predator, bereavement, or cancer, however, as shown in the following study. This study divided elderly nursing-home residents into two groups (after matching the residents on physical health status; Langer & Rodin, 1976; Rodin & Langer, 1977). The experimental (high-control) group of residents received enhanced control over their daily lives by planning their schedules, taking responsibility to care for room plants, and so forth. The low-control group of residents had a schedule assigned to them, were given a plant but told that the nurse, not they, would care for it, and so on. A year and a half later, significantly more low-control residents had died than had high-control residents.

EXPLAINING WHY HELPLESSNESS OCCURS

Do Motivational, Learning, and Emotional Deficits Occur Because of Exposure to Trauma?

Helplessness results from the individuals' learned expectations that their responses are independent of desired outcomes (Peterson, Maier, & Seligman 1993). The cause of learned helplessness is therefore a cognitive one—an expectation of response-outcome independence. One might reasonably argue, however, that helplessness deficits are a function of physical trauma rather than psychological expectation. Put another way, traumatic experience might produce dramatic physical changes, and these physical changes might in turn produce motivational, learning, and emotional deficits. After all, participants in learned helplessness are usually subjected to trauma, electric shocks, noise blasts, migraine headaches, unsolvable problems, vats of water, and so forth.

Researchers addressed this criticism through a strategic experimental design, referred to as triadic (Weiss, 1972). To illustrate the triadic design, consider the arrangement of three rats (one rat in controllable shock, one rat in uncontrollable shock, and one rat in the control [no shock] group) participating in a learned helplessness study (see Figure 8.5). All three rats participated in the first phase of the experiment simultaneously. Notice also that each rat has both a paddle wheel placed in front of it and a wire attached to its tail. The rat on the left (subject to escapable shock) has a small current of electricity sent to its tail; to terminate the shock the rat must rotate the paddle wheel. The turning of the wheel terminates the shock. The rat in the middle (subject to inescapable shock) has the same current of electricity sent to its tail, but it cannot terminate the shock by rotating the wheel. This rat's wheel does not work, and this rat therefore has no response that will terminate its shock. The shock is terminated only if the rat on the left rotates its paddle wheel. The rats are "yoked"

FIGURE 8.5 **Triadic Design in Learned Helplessness Experiment**

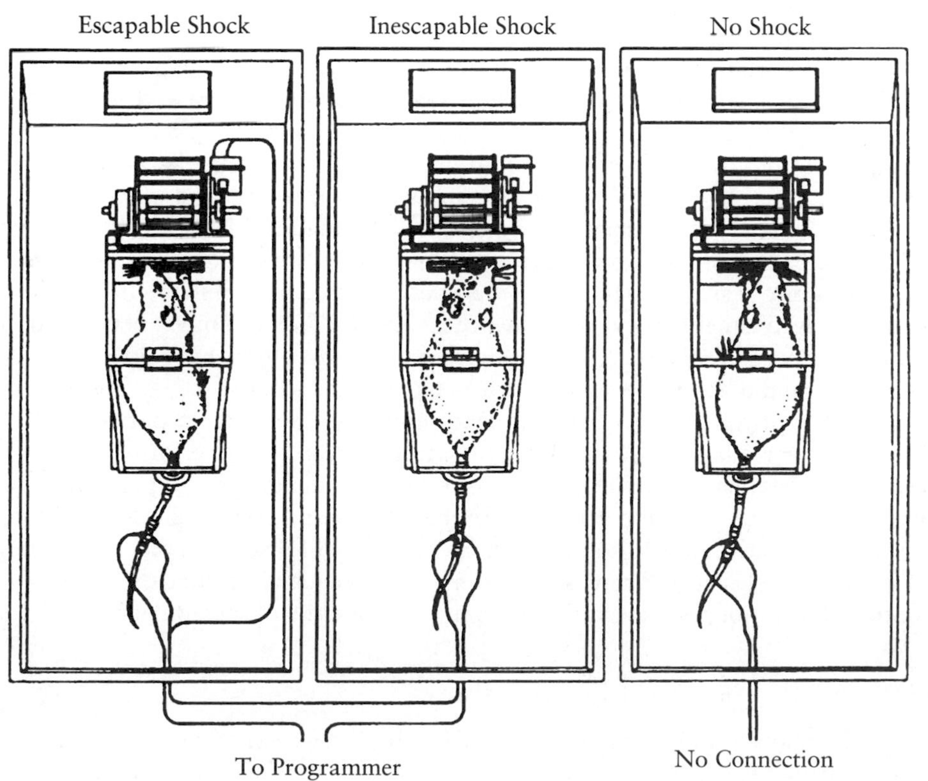

SOURCE: From "Psychological Factors in Stress and Disease," by J.M. Weiss, 1972, *Scientific American, 226,* pp. 104–113. Copyright 1972 by Scientific American. Adapted with permission from the illustration by Eric Mose.

together. Yoking is important because it ensures that both rats receive exactly the same number and duration of electric shocks (i.e., the same traumatic experience). The control rat on the right, however, has a wire attached to its tail, but no current passes through it, so the rat never gets shocked. Results in the triadic design are the same as in the earlier studies (e.g., Figure 8.3). It is a learned expectancy, not the physical trauma itself, that produces helplessness.

Do Deficits Occur Because of Perceived Failure?

A second concern in interpreting learned helplessness research is whether helplessness deficits arise from the expectation of uncontrollability or from the experience of failure. Many of the studies with humans use an unsolvable anagram task to induce helplessness (Dweck, 1975; Hiroto & Seligman, 1975; Mikulincer, 1988). Participants are given a series of either solvable (e.g., PAPYH = HAPPY) or unsolvable (e.g., PAPYT = ?) anagrams in the first phase of the experiment. In the second phase, all participants are given a series of solvable anagrams. The typical finding is that participants given the unsolvable anagrams in the first phase solve fewer anagrams in the second phase than do participants given the solvable anagrams in the first phase (a learned helplessness effect).

In these studies, it is not possible to tell whether it is an expectation of uncontrollability or an expectation of failure that degrades performance. Perhaps, the participants given the unsolvable anagrams developed a sense of incompetence and, therefore, quit. (Alternatively, the participants given the solvable anagrams might develop a sense of mastery and try harder.) To address this confusion, researchers designed an experiment with independent variables of prior exposure to uncontrollability and prior exposure to success-failure feedback (Winefield, Barnett, & Tiggemann, 1985). Half of the participants received an escapable noise blast in the first phase, while the other half received an inescapable noise blast (to manipulate expectations of controllability). In addition, participants received either success performance feedback ("You did much better than others had done"), failure feedback ("You did much worse than others have done"), or neutral feedback ("You did about the same as others have done"). In the second phase of the experiment, all participants were asked to learn how to escape from a potentially controllable noise. Controllability of the outcome affected subsequent performance more than success-failure feedback. In fact, there was a slight tendency for the participants in the failure group to outperform participants in the success and control groups. Failure actually provided positive motivation (a phenomenon we will discuss in the next section under "Reactance Theory"). From such results, the conclusion is that the expectation of uncontrollability, not the expectation of failure, caused the observed deficits.

Do Deficits Occur Because of Unpredictability?

A methodological problem in most learned helplessness experiments with humans is that uncontrollable events are also unpredictable events (Winefield, 1982). An outcome (e.g., shock, noise, natural disaster) is unpredictable when it is independent of all forecasting stimuli. What is needed for seeing if uncontrollability, unpredictability or both produce helplessness is an experiment in which an outcome's uncontrollability and unpredictability are experimentally manipulated and separated. Unfortunately, it is exceptionally difficult to arrange an outcome that is controllable yet unpredictable. In fact, the task of disentangling the effects of uncontrollability and unpredictability is "next to logically impossible" (Seligman, 1975).

But psychologists are a creative and persistent bunch. One group of researchers tested the effect of predictability on learned helplessness deficits using the following four experimental conditions (Tiggemann & Winefield, 1987): controllable-predictable (C-P), uncontrollable-unpredictable (UC-UP), uncontrollable predictable (UC-P), and a no-treatment (NT) control group. (The experimenters could not come up with a controllable-unpredictable condition.) In the first phase of the experiment, all participants sat at a computer terminal and understood that from time to time a buzzer would come on. Participants were to try to find a way to stop the buzzer, using a switch in front of them. The buzzer was either predictable or random, and the buzzer was either controllable or uncontrollable, depending on the experimental condition. Learned helplessness deficits emerged (in the second phase) only for the participants in the UC-UP condition. Participants in the UC-P condition learned to terminate the buzzer much as did the participants in the C-P and NT conditions. Predictability does therefore mitigate the learned helplessness deficit. A second study confirmed these results, showing that both controllability and predictability are necessary for producing helplessness (Burger & Arkin, 1980). Thus, uncontrollability is a necessary, but not a sufficient, condition for inducing learned helplessness deficits. For sufficiency, uncontrollability must coincide with unpredictability.

Relationship Between Helplessness and Depression

Some clinical psychologists view learned helplessness as a model of naturally occurring unipolar depression (Rosenhan & Seligman, 1984; Seligman, 1975). Learned helplessness and depression are similar in that the same expectations cause both: The individual expects that bad events will occur, and there is nothing she can do to prevent their occurrence (Rosenhan & Seligman, 1984). Learned helplessness and depression also share common symptoms (passivity, low self-esteem, loss of appetite) and therapeutic intervention strategies (time, cognitive behavior modification). Where the two differ is that depression is a broader concept than is helplessness, as depression includes biochemical, somatic, psychodynamic, emotional, and cognitive causes and symptoms that are not necessarily associated with learned helplessness. Learned helplessness is therefore a model of one type of naturally occurring unipolar depression.

Using the learned helplessness model to understand the etiology of unipolar depression touched off a flurry of research that brought both strong criticism (Costello, 1978; Depue & Monroe, 1978) and strong support (Seligman, 1975). One of the most exciting findings to emerge is that depressed individuals sometimes see the events in their lives as less controllable than do individuals who are not depressed. Such a finding led researchers to wonder whether the depressive tendency of individuals to see their worlds as uncontrollable might be the core cause of unipolar depression. Perhaps the root of depression lies in a depressed individual's inability to recognize that he has more control over his life outcomes than he knows.

Depressed college students and students who were not depressed (as assessed by a questionnaire) performed a task in which they pushed a button on some trials and did not push it on other trials (Alloy & Abramson, 1979). With a button push, a green light sometimes came on. The point of the study was for the participant to estimate what proportion of time the green light came on. The experimenters controlled the light—whether it came on and when it came on. For one group, the green light came on 75% of the time and only when the button was pressed. This was the high-control group. For a second group, the green light came on when the button was pressed 75% of the time, but the light also came on 50% of the time when no button was pushed. This was the low-control group. In a final group, the green light came on when the button was pressed 75% of the time, but it also came on 75% of the time when the participants did not push the button. This was the no-control group (because the light came on at the same rate regardless of the participant's button pressing).

Results were most surprising (see Figure 8.6). The depressed individuals accurately judged how much control they had over each situation, as did the individuals who were not depressed except in one condition, namely in the no-control situation (Alloy & Abramson, 1979). The depressed individuals accurately judged that they had no control in this condition. The individuals not depressed were the ones who misperceived how much control they had—they overestimated their perceived control.

FIGURE 8.6 **Perceived Control for Depressed Individuals Versus Individuals Who Are Not Depressed**

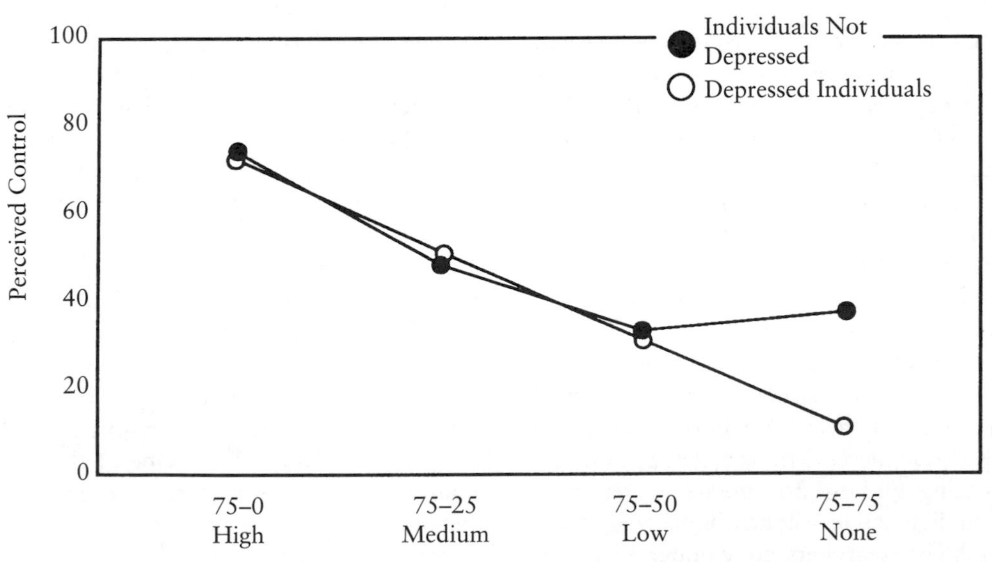

SOURCE: From "Judgments of Contingency in Depressed and Nondepressed Students: Sadder but Wiser?" by L.B. Alloy and L.T. Abramson, 1979, *Journal of Experimental Psychology: General, 108,* pp. 441–485. Copyright 1979 by the American Psychological Association. Adapted with permission.

A second study tested the idea that people who are not depressed have an "illusion of control" (Alloy & Abramson, 1982). An illusion of control is evident whenever individuals overestimate the extent of control over events (Langer, 1975). In the experiment's first phase, participants completed a button-pressing task and were told that a buzzer noise was either controllable or uncontrollable. In the second phase, participants either succeeded (won money for each trial they exerted control over) or failed (lost money for each trial they did not control). In actuality, outcomes in the second phase occurred randomly so that the participant had no control over her outcomes whatsoever. The experiment tested the judgments of control after success and failure feedback of the depressed individuals versus the judgments of the people who were not depressed. Results appear in Figure 8.7. Depressed individuals in all groups and individuals not depressed in the controllable-noise groups accurately judged the extent of their control over the win-and-lose problems. The interesting group was the individuals who were not depressed who received positive feedback over the uncontrollable noise outcomes. When they won on an uncontrollable task, these individuals showed a strong illusion of control.

The most interesting conclusion to draw from Lauren Alloy and Lyn Abramson's (1979, 1982) research is that depressed people are not more prone to learned helplessness

FIGURE 8.7 **Perceived Control for Depressed Individuals and Individuals Not Depressed After Winning and Losing**

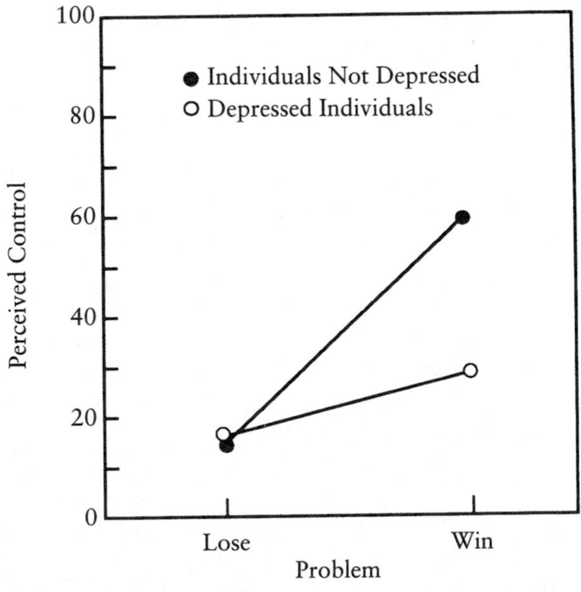

SOURCE: From "Judgments of Contingency in Depressed and Nondepressed Students: Sadder but Wiser?" by L.B. Alloy and L. T. Abramson, 1979, *Journal of Experimental Psychology: General, 108,* pp. 441–485. Copyright 1979 by the American Psychological Association. Adapted with permission.

Is Personal Control Always Good?

Question: Why would a person want to learn about the motivational states discussed in this chapter?

Answer: Because we live in the age of personal control, which leads one to wonder, "Is personal control always good?"

We live in the age of personal control. Indeed, the title of two books referred to in this chapter are Albert Bandura's (1997) *Self-Efficacy: The Exercise of Control,* and Christopher Peterson's, Steven Maier's, and Martin Seligman's (1993) *Learned Helplessness: A Theory for the Age of Personal Control.* In chapter 11, two more books will be featured: Ellen Skinner's, Malanie Zimmer-Gembeck's, and Jim Connell's (1998) *Individual Differences and the Development of Perceived Control,* and Jerry Burger's (1992) *Desire for Control: Personality, Social, and Clinical Perspectives.* This is indeed the age of personal control. But is the seeking and gaining of personal control really all it's cracked up to be? Is more always better?

Generally speaking, people love control. Most of us overestimate how much control we have in any given situation, are optimistic about our ability to achieve control in the situations we face, believe we have more skill and greater ability than we actually have, and underestimate how vulnerable we are to overpowering circumstances (Lewinsohn, et al., 1980; Seligman, 1991; Taylor & Brown, 1988, 1994; Weinstein, 1984, 1993). And generally speaking, people benefit from their perceptions of control. Compared to people who feel little control in life, people who feel in control experience psychological health and physical well-being (Bandura, 1997; Rodin & Langer, 1977; Seligman, 1991). The conclusion of the matter seems to be the following: Having control is good, and the more control you have, the better (Evans, Shapiro, & Lewis, 1993; Shapiro, Schwartz, & Astin, 1996; Thompson, 1981).

This near-worship of control, however, presumes that the world is a controllable place. Sometimes people unrealistically desire control, sometimes people's skills and abilities are not up to par, and sometimes people find themselves in unpredictable, uncontrollable situations. Control for all situations seems a bit delusional. Desiring too much control (i.e., a "control freak"), trying to master uncontrollable problems, and trying to predict random events can lead to anxiety, depression, and physical illness (e.g., cardiovascular hyperactivity, immuno-suppression; Shapiro et al., 1993). Hence, how much control a person wants should match up well with how much control an environment or situation actually affords.

deficits. Rather, it is the individuals who are not depressed who sometimes believe they have more personal control than they actually have (Taylor & Brown, 1988, 1994). Though the conclusion might sound startling, depressed persons' memories for the positive and negative events in their lives are balanced and equal, whereas the memories of the persons not depressed harbor biases for recalling more of the positive events (Sanz, 1996). While people often misjudge the control they have over the events in their lives

Consider the figure below. People possess psychological control factors, which is another way of saying that people harbor personal control beliefs (e.g., self-efficacy, mastery motivation). People bring these psychological factors into situations that vary in how controllable and predictable they are. Some situations match the person's control beliefs and others mismatch these beliefs. People-environment matches, rather than personal control beliefs per se, predict positive well-being and physical health outcomes. And people-environment mismatches, rather than personal vulnerability beliefs, predict physical illness and mental irregulation. The two-part conclusion seems to be that (1) people can sometimes want too much control for their own good, and (2) control is adaptive and beneficial when environments are controllable but is maladaptive when environments offer little opportunity for control (Shapiro et al., 1993).

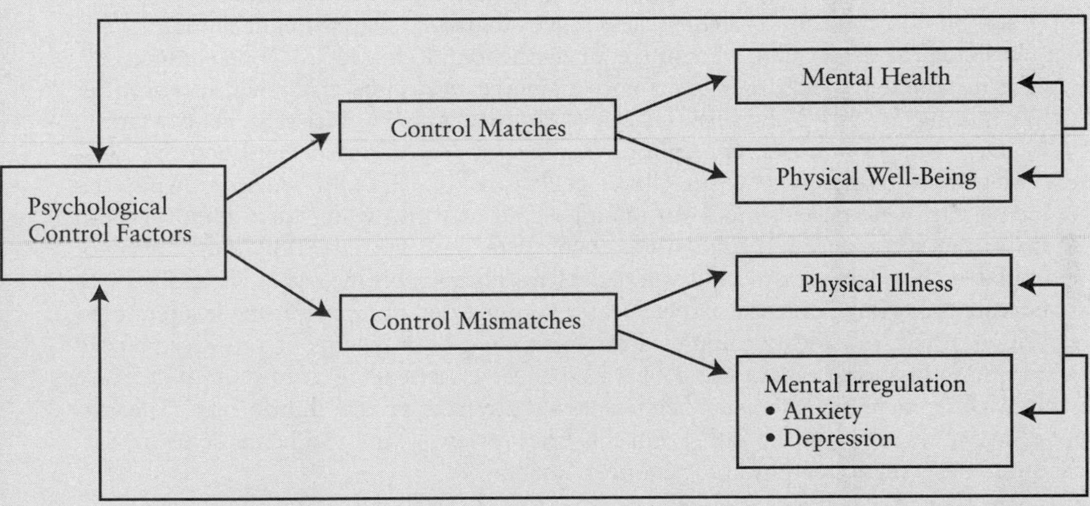

SOURCE: Adapted from "Controlling Ourselves, Controlling Our World: Psychology's Role in Understanding Positive and Negative Consequences of Seeking and Gaining Control," by D.H. Shapiro Jr., C.E. Schwartz, and J.A. Astin, 1996, *American Psychologist*, *51*, pp. 1213–1230. Copyright 1996 by the American Psychological Association. Adapted with permission.

(Abramson & Alloy, 1980; Alloy & Abramson, 1979, 1982; Langer, 1975; Nisbett & Ross, 1980), most of the misjudging is done by individuals not depressed.[1]

[1]The discussion on the interrelationships among depression, learned helplessness, and the illusion of control continues in chapter 9 by adding the attributional perspective to the analysis.

Criticisms and Alternative Explanations

The learned helplessness model is not without its critics (Costello, 1978; Weiss, Glazer, & Pohorecky, 1976; Wortman & Brehm, 1975). One alternative explanation for the fact that people give up in the face of uncontrollable outcomes is that people are actually motivated to remain passive. People are motivated to be passive if they sense that active responding will only make matters worse (Wortman & Brehm, 1975). In the face of a hurricane (an uncontrollable, unpredictable event), for example, it is possible that people are passive and helpless because they believe that negative outcomes will be more likely when they respond compared to when they do not respond. If this is the case, passivity is actually an enlightened strategic coping response that minimizes the trauma incurred. For a second example, imagine the socially anxious person who does not voluntarily engage in social interaction because of a belief that she will only make matters worse by initiating conversations. Perhaps this person is correct. By intentionally not initiating interactions, the anxious person may very well avoid making circumstances worse (by keeping secret her lack of social skill). Thus, looked at in a different light, passivity can be, in some circumstances, a strategic coping response rather than a motivational deficit.

A second interpretation of helplessness argues that helplessness might fundamentally be a physiological, rather than a cognitive, phenomenon (Weiss, 1972). When animals experience inescapable shock, they experience a significant decline in the neurotransmitter norepinephrine (Weiss, 1972, Weiss, Glazer, & Pohorecky, 1976; Weiss, Stone, & Harrell, 1970). Depletion of brain norepinephrine has been repeatedly associated with helplessness and giving-up responses (Weiss, Glazer, & Pohorecky, 1976). In one of Jay Weiss' experiments, rats were placed into a vat of either cold or warm water for 6 minutes. Both groups of rats were placed in equal amounts of water, and the extent of control was not manipulated. But exposure to cold water depletes norepinephrine, whereas exposure to warm water does not. Thus, the experimenter manipulated norepinephrine level, not expectations of control. Thirty minutes after swimming, both groups of rats were placed into a shuttle box. The rats in the cold water (those experiencing a substantial decrease in brain norepinephrine) showed helplessness-like effects in the shuttle box. The rats placed in the warm water did not. From this brief review, a case can be made for understanding helplessness as a physiological phenomenon.

Learned Laziness

When thinking about uncontrollable events, the outcomes that come to mind are typically aversive ones—shocks, loud noises, migraine headaches, accidents, impossible problems, family deaths, and other causes of uncontrollable and unpredictable grief. But the phenomenon of learned laziness questions whether any uncontrollable event—aversive or pleasant—produces helplessness deficits (Engberg et al., 1972). That is, do people who receive uncontrollable rewards also show motivational, learning, and emotional deficits?

To test this idea, experimenters placed pigeons in one of three experimental groups. Some were trained so that they received a reward for each appropriate response (industrious group). Other pigeons received the same rewards as the first group, but their rewards were independent of their behavior (learned-laziness group). The third group received no training in the first phase of the experiment (control group). In the second phase, all pigeons performed the same task in which they had to learn to attain a reward. The experiment measured how many trials it took each pigeon to learn the behavior necessary to get the food reward. The pigeons in the learned-laziness group learned the slowest, while the pigeons in the industrious condition learned the fastest. When rewards were free and pigeons had little reason to work for them, their capacity to learn was significantly retarded (i.e., a helplessness-based learning deficit).

Consider some speculative illustrations. Children who are showered with attention, toys, and treats may begin to develop learned laziness. If rewards are given randomly and with no correspondence to their behavior, then children may adopt a "so-why-try?" orientation in initiating effort to obtain rewards on tasks such as homework, chores, yard work, or cleaning their rooms. Spoiled children know that they will still get attention and toys whether or not they do their homework, do their chores, do yard work, or clean their rooms. A second (equally speculative) illustration might apply to people who are very attractive, very competent, or very intelligent. Very attractive people get free and continual attention and praise from others. Attention and praise often come independent of any behavioral effort on their part. ("People notice and like me whether or not I'm polite, whether or not I cheat on examinations, whether or not I . . .") If very attractive people perceive that rewards are independent of their behavior, then they might seemingly ask, "Why try?" (Why work for attention? Why work to be accepted? Why be polite?) No matter what they do, other people reward them.

REACTANCE THEORY

Why do people sometimes do precisely the opposite of what they are told to do? Why do people sometimes resist another person's well-intended favor? Why does propaganda often backfire? These are the questions posed by reactance theorists (Brehm, 1966; Brehm & Brehm, 1981). Any instruction, any favor, any advice, no matter how well intended, has the potential to interfere with people's expected freedoms in making up their own minds. When children do precisely what they were told not to do, when gift recipients are more resentful than thankful, and when the targets of propaganda do the opposite of the source's intention, each performs a countermaneuver aimed at reestablishing a threatened sense of freedom. The term reactance refers to the psychological and behavioral attempt at reestablishing ("reacting" against) an eliminated or threatened freedom.

REACTANCE AND HELPLESSNESS

A threat to personal freedom often coincides with the perception of an uncontrollable outcome. Reactance theory predicts that people experience reactance only if they expect to have some control over what happens to them. And people react to a loss of control by becoming more active, even hostile and aggressive. Both reactance and learned helplessness theories therefore focus on how people react to uncontrollable outcomes. But the two theories suggest that human beings act in very different ways when exposed to uncontrollable outcomes. Recognizing this discrepancy, Camille Wortman and Jack Brehm

(1975) proposed an integrative model of reactance and learned helplessness, which is shown in Figure 8.8.

If a person expects to be able to control important outcomes, exposure to uncontrollable outcomes arouses reactance (Wortman & Brehm, 1975). Thus, in the first few trials in a learned helplessness experiment, the person or animal should show vigorous opposition to the uncontrollable environment. Recall that the dogs in the inescapable shock group in the learned helplessness studies first howled, kicked, and generally thrashed about for several trials before eventually becoming helpless. The two lines graphed between points A and B in Figure 8.8 represent reactance responses. These active, assertive coping efforts usually pay off in life as they enable people and animals to reestablish their lost sense of control. Over time, however, if the environment continues to be uncontrollable, people eventually learn that all attempts at control are futile. Once a person becomes fully convinced that reactance behaviors exert little or no

FIGURE 8.8 **Integrative Model of Reactance and Learned Helplessness**

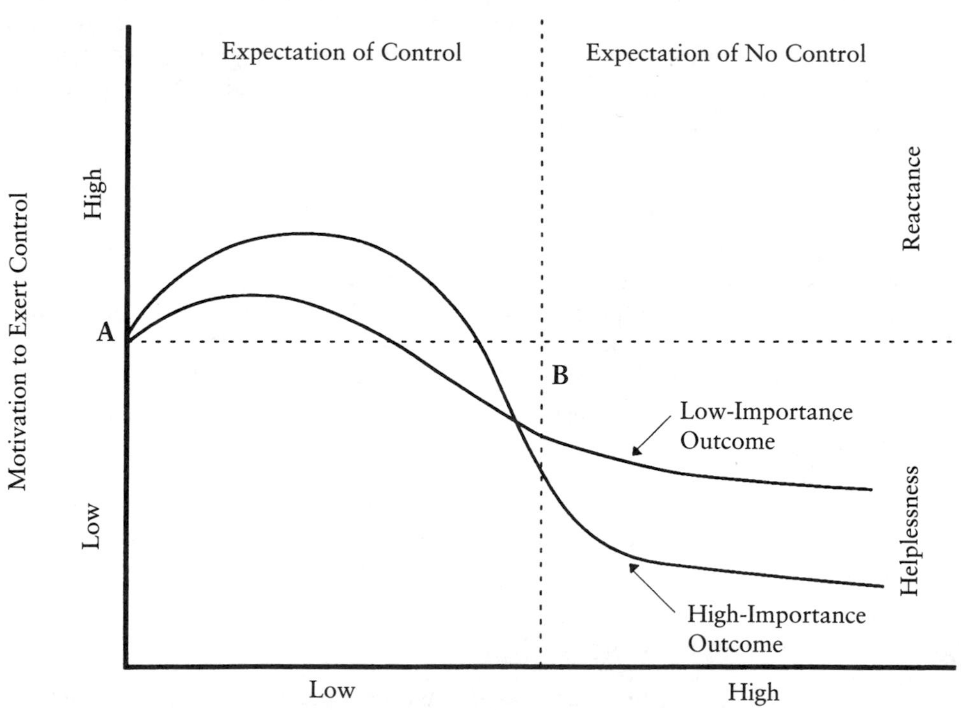

SOURCE: From "Responses to Uncontrollable Outcomes: An Integration of Reactance Theory and the Learned Helplessness Model," by C. B. Wortman and J. W. Brehm, 1975, in L. Berkowitz (Ed.), *Advances in Experimental Social Psychology* (Vol. 8, pp. 277–336): New York: Academic Press.

influence over the uncontrollable situation, he shows the passivity of helplessness. The lines graphed to the right of point B represent helplessness responses.

The critical difference in predicting whether an individual will show reactance or helplessness is the perceived status of the uncontrollable outcome. As long as the person perceives that coping behavior can effect outcomes, reactance behaviors persist. It is only after the person perceives a response-outcome independence (i.e., the unequivocal loss of a behavioral freedom) that he slips into helplessness. The critical information needed to interpret the relationships depicted in Figure 8.8 appears at the top of the figure, labeled "Expectation of Control" and "Expectation of No Control." Expectations of control foster reactance; expectations of no control foster helplessness.

Notice also that the figure shows two curved lines, one denoting the relationship between perceived control and motivation for a low-importance outcome and the other depicting the same relationship for a high-importance outcome. Reactance and helpless responses are exaggerated on those outcomes that the person most cares about and values, while reactance and helplessness are muted on low-importance outcomes (and may be zero for outcomes that have no importance to the person whatsoever; Mikulincer, 1986).

As an illustration of reactance and helplessness responses, consider the following experiment (Mikulincer, 1988). One group of undergraduates worked on one unsolvable problem, a second group worked on a series of four unsolvable problems, and a third group did not work on any problems (control group). Mario Mikulincer reasoned that exposure to one unsolvable problem would produce reactance and actually improve performance, while repeated exposure to unsolvable problems would produce helplessness and impair performance. In the second phase of the experiment, all participants worked on the same set of solvable problems. As predicted, participants that were given one unsolvable problem performed the best, participants that were given four unsolvable problems performed the worst, and participants that were not given any problems performed in between these two groups. This finding provides strong support for the ideas that (1) both reactance and helplessness arise from outcome expectancies; (2) reactance is rooted in perceived control, while helplessness is rooted in its absence; (3) a reactance response precedes a helplessness response; and (4) reactance enhances performance whereas helplessness undermines it.

SUMMARY

The motivation to exercise personal control over one's fate emanates from the expectations people harbor as to how much or how little power they have in producing desired effects and in preventing undesired effects. As people try to control the events they face, they learn expectancies. These learned expectancies then affect the person's motivation in exerting control over future events. Expectancies come in two types: efficacy and outcome. Efficacy expectations are forecasts about one's capacity to execute competently a particular course of action. (For example, "Can I perform some feat well?") Outcome expectancies are forecasts that a particular outcome will be achieved (or prevented) once a given action is adequately executed. (For example, "Assuming that I can perform the feat well, will I then win the prize?") If voluntary coping behavior is to be initiated and if it is to persist, both efficacy and outcome expectancies must be reasonably high.

Self-efficacy is the individual's belief that he "has what it takes" to marshal together the resources needed to cope effectively with the diverse and potentially overwhelming demands of a situation. The practical lesson that emerges from the study of self-efficacy is that competent performance requires not only physical, cognitive, social, and behavioral skills (ability), but also the generative capacity to orchestrate and manage those skills into effective performance. People have high self-efficacy when they believe that they can cope effectively, even when they face circumstances that are difficult and unpredictable. People have low self-efficacy when they worry about and expect to be overwhelmed during their performances. Of course, everyone experiences some worry, anxiety, and self-doubt, but self-efficacy beliefs reduce the worry, anxiety, and doubt that might otherwise interfere with and undermine skillful performance.

Self-efficacy arises from (1) personal behavior history of trying to execute that particular course of action in the past, (2) observations of similar others as they execute the same behavior, (3) verbal persuasions (or pep talks) from others, and (4) physiological states such as an abnormally fast versus calm heartbeat. Once formed, self-efficacy effects the performer's (1) choice of activities and selection of environments (approach versus avoidance), (2) extent of effort and persistence, (3) the quality of thinking and decision making, and (4) emotional reactions, especially those related to stress and anxiety. Because self-efficacy beliefs can be acquired and because self-efficacy beliefs enable such productive ways of thinking, feeling, and behaving, self-efficacy serves as a model for personal empowerment. People who participate in therapy-like conditions to build stronger and more resilient self-efficacy beliefs respond by showing flexible, adaptive, and confident engagements with the world.

Learned helplessness is the psychological state that results when an individual expects that events in her life are uncontrollable. More generally, learned helplessness theory relies on three fundamental components in explaining helplessness effects: contingency, cognition, and behavior. Contingency refers to the objective relationship between a person's behavior and the environment's positive or negative outcomes. Cognition includes all those mental processes (e.g., biases, attributions, expectancies) that the individual relies on to translate objective environmental contingencies into subjective personal control beliefs. Behavior refers to the person's voluntary coping behavior, and it varies along a continuum that extends from active and energetic to passive and withdrawing. Once it occurs, helplessness produces profound disruptions in motivation, learning, and emotion. The motivational deficit is a decreased willingness to engage in voluntary coping responses; the cognitive deficit is a pessimistic learning set that interferes with learning future response-outcome contingencies; and the emotional deficit involves the emergence of energy-depleting emotions such as depression to replace energy-mobilizing emotions such as frustration.

Reactance theory, like the learned helplessness model, seeks to understand how people react to uncontrollable life events. According to reactance theory, an individual's initial reaction to uncontrollable outcomes is typically an assertive, energy-mobilizing psychological and behavioral attempt in reestablishing control over the environment. A model for integrating learned helplessness and reactance research findings shows that people experience reactance when they expect high control over outcomes but experience helplessness when they expect low control over these outcomes. In short, expectations of controllability foster reactance, while expectations of uncontrollability foster helplessness.

RECOMMENDED READINGS

Self-Efficacy

Bandura, A. (1988). Self-efficacy conception of anxiety. *Anxiety Research, 1,* 77–98.

Bandura, A. (1989). Human agency in social cognitive theory. *American Psychologist, 44,* 1175–1184.

Bandura, A. (1991). Self-regulation of motivation through anticipatory and self-regulatory mechanisms. In R. A. Dienstbier (Ed.), *Nebraska Symposium on Motivation: Perspectives on motivation* (Vol. 38, pp. 69–164). Lincoln: University of Nebraska Press.

Bandura, A. (1993). Perceived self-efficacy in cognitive development and functioning. *Educational Psychologist, 28,* 117–148.

Bandura, A., Pastorelli, C., Barbaranelli, C., & Caprara, G. V. (1999). Self-efficacy pathways to depression. *Journal of Personality and Social Psychology, 76,* 258–269.

Ozer, E. M., & Bandura, A. (1990). Mechanisms governing empowerment effects: A self-efficacy analysis. *Journal of Personality and Social Psychology, 58,* 472–486.

Schunk, D. H. (1989). Self-efficacy and achievement behaviors. *Educational Psychology Review, 1,* 173–208.

Zimmerman, B. J., & Ringle, J. (1981). Effect of model persistence and statements of confidence on children's self-efficacy and problem-solving. *Journal of Educational Psychology, 73,* 485–493.

Learned Helplessness

Alloy, L. B., & Abramson, L. V. (1982). Learned helplessness, depression, and the illusion of control. *Journal of Personality and Social Psychology, 42,* 1114–1126.

Brown, I., Jr., & Inouye, D. K. (1978). Learned helplessness through modeling: The role of perceived similarity in competence. *Journal of Personality and Social Psychology, 36,* 900–908.

Mikulincer, M. (1986). Motivational involvement and learned helplessness: The behavioral effects of the importance of uncontrollable events. *Journal of Social and Clinical Psychology, 4,* 402–422.

Reactance

Mikulincer, M. (1988). The relationship of probability of success and performance following unsolvable problems: Reactance and helplessness effects. *Motivation and Emotion, 12,* 139–153.

Wortman, C. B., & Brehm, J. W. (1975). Responses to uncontrollable outcomes: An integration of reactance theory and the learned helplessness model. In L. Berkowitz (Ed.), *Advances in experimental social psychology* (Vol. 8, pp. 277–336). New York: Academic Press.

9

Attributions and Values

Imagine that spring has finally arrived. The melting of the snow and the greening of the grass mean one thing to you: It is tennis season. You and your roommate are doubles partners on the university's tennis team—both of you are talented and equally skilled.

As the season begins, you both hold conservative expectations of winning. For the first match, you both estimate your chances of winning at 50/50. The first match comes and goes, and you win a close one. Reviewing the match that evening, you figure the better team won and high ability caused the day's success. Your partner, however, is not so sure and suggests that a fortuitous run of good and timely breaks caused the victory. Reflecting on the victory, you feel pride, while your partner feels only relief.

The second match comes and goes, but this time, alas, your team takes a loss. This time you are sure the outcome was a fluke—the lucky breaks you needed at critical points in the match just never materialized. Your partner, once again, is not so sure. From your partner's point of view, the loss occurred because both of you are out of shape and lacked the needed stamina. Reflecting on the loss, your partner feels shame at being unprepared.

Today is the third match, and the pre-match conversation turns to your chances of winning. You are confident and predict a victory; your partner is not and predicts a loss. You cannot wait to play, while your partner has little difficulty concentrating on the biology textbook. Your partner's pessimism surprises you, and you wonder what happened to the earlier confidence and enthusiasm. After all, the two of you clearly earned your victory, and the loss was a fluke. Your partner explains the outcomes differently; the victory was the fluke, while the loss stemmed from incompetence.

The attributions people make—the reasons they use to explain why they succeeded or failed—have motivational significance. As was true for the tennis players, the attributions we make affect our expectancies for the future, our feelings of pride and shame, and our eagerness to put forth effort. Even when people experience identical outcomes, as the tennis players did, different attributions produce different cognitive, emotional, and motivational consequences.

ATTRIBUTIONS

The principal assumption of attribution theory is that people seek to discover why they or others experienced a particular outcome (Heider, 1958; Jones & Davis, 1965; Kelley, 1967, 1973; Weiner, 1980, 1985, 1986). We seek to understand the causes behind our successes or failures, our triumphs or tragedies, our social inclusions or rejections. Following life's outcomes, we might ask the following questions: Why did I fail that chemistry examination? Why did the Yankees win the World Series? Why did Suzy drop out of school? Why is that person poor? Why did Bush lose the 1992 presidential election? Why didn't Frank return my telephone call?

Some outcomes require little explanation. If a person expects a particular outcome to occur and it does indeed occur, why labor through a causal attributional analysis? If, for example, you expect the four o'clock bus to be on time and the bus is actually on time, then why spend cognitive effort trying to figure out why this favorable turn of events came to fruition? Success when success was expected and failure when failure was expected are predicted outcomes that fail to instigate attributional analysis. Unexpected outcomes, on the other hand, grab our attention (Pyszczynski & Greenberg, 1981). We search to discover their cause. Failure when success was expected or success when failure was expected are unexpected outcomes that beg for explanation: Why is the bus not here at 4:00? Why did the underdog politician win? Why did I fail the test? Why was I passed over for my sure-thing promotion? And why did she reject my innocent invitation?

In addition to unexpected outcomes, people also search to explain outcomes that are particularly negative (Bohner et al., 1988; Wong & Weiner, 1981) or important (Berscheid et al., 1976). Causal analysis occurs following those outcomes that are unexpected, negative, and important (Abele, 1985; Weiner 1985) Thus, the search for a causal attribution is most likely following an important and unexpected failure, such as failing a relatively easy course you need to pass to graduate (Gendolla, 1997).

People make attributions for two principal reasons. First, people just want to know why important and unexpected failures happen. Second, people use the information they gain from attributional searches to improve their lives and how they interact with the environment (Weiner, 1985). The student who fails an examination, for instance, and analyzes the cause better positions herself to do better the next time than does the student who does not seek to explain the failure. If the first student blames the failure on her lackluster effort, she is likely to take the steps necessary to remedy that underlying cause. The second student, in contrast, may well repeat the earlier failure.

ATTRIBUTIONS TO EXPLAIN OUTCOMES

A causal attribution explains why a particular outcome occurred (Weiner, 1985, 1986). The causal attribution is the reason a person provides for explaining why he won or lost, was accepted or rejected, was rewarded or punished. The interpretation that a person accepted an invitation for a date because the person asking for the date is such a charming person specifies an outcome (the date was accepted) and its causal attribution (because the person is so charming). Similarly, the interpretation that a person lost the 100-yard dash because she did not try very hard specifies an outcome (she lost) and its causal attribution (because effort was low). Of course, a dozen rival attributions are possible for explaining why a person accepted the date and why she lost the race, but attribution theory focuses on the individual's attribution and, once made, how it affects subsequent motivation and emotion (Weiner, 1986).

Think about a recent outcome you experienced in your own life, and take a moment to brainstorm reasons why it happened. You will probably think of many different and possible reasons. Consider an athlete who lost an important contest. Her defeat might be attributed to a lack of ability, lack of effort, the proficiency of an opponent, fatigue, biased referees, an injury, an ineffective strategy, lazy teammates, a hostile crowd, equipment failure, an incompetent coach, or just plain bad luck. Perhaps in considering your outcome, you thought of additional attributions beyond the dozen listed here, attributions such as intelligence, cleverness, physical attractiveness, mood, illness, the weather, a personality characteristic, the daily horoscope, biorhythms, hindrance, or bias of others.

In explaining your outcome, you probably experienced another attributional phenomena, namely economy (or simplicity) of causal analysis (Weiner, 1985). While dozens of attributions are possible, the most salient and frequently made attributions are ability and effort, at least in achievement situations (i.e., high ability and hard work generally cause success; low ability and lackluster effort cause failure; Weiner, 1985). While ability and effort are highly common attributions, many others are both possible and popular. Therefore, researchers organize all possible attributions into three primary causal dimensions, as discussed in the following section.[1]

---

[1]Some people prefer to use a single attribution in explaining any given outcome (Fiske & Taylor, 1984; Nisbett & Ross, 1980). Others prefer to use a complex array of attributions in explaining a single outcome, especially when the outcome has considerable personal significance, such as a marital separation (Fletcher, 1983). But just how many attributions a person uses in explaining a single outcome varies from one person to the next as an individual difference characteristic (Fletcher, et al., 1986).

CAUSAL DIMENSIONS

The array of viable causes for explaining any one outcome begins with the distinction between those causes located inside the person (e.g., personality, intelligence, skill, effort, strategy, and physical beauty) and those located in the environment (e.g., weather, influence of another person, or difficulty of the task). The internal-external (or person-environment) attributional dimension is referred to as locus. Locus means location, as in whether the cause is located in the person or in the environment.

Causes also vary in their consistency, or stability, which is the second causal dimension. Some attributions are relatively enduring and long lasting (e.g., intelligence, skill, and personality), while others are ephemeral and fluctuate from time to time (e.g., mood, effort, luck, and the weather). Causal attributions that are consistent across time and situations are stable causes, whereas attributions that change over time and across situations are unstable causes (Weiner et al., 1971; Weiner, 1986).

A third attributional dimension, controllability, distinguishes between controllable and uncontrollable causes (Weiner, 1979, 1986). Examples of controllable causes include effort and strategy, while examples of uncontrollable causes include the weather, the proficiency of an opponent, equipment failure, and the help, hindrance, or bias of others (e.g., teammates, teachers, referees). Notice, however, that whether or not a cause is controllable depends largely on individual interpretations, as ability or an injury might be a controllable cause to one person yet be an uncontrollable cause to another.

Therefore, the threefold classification scheme for causal attributions is as follows:

Locus	Internal versus external
Stability	Stable versus unstable
Controllability	Controllable versus uncontrollable

Two benefits and one caution emerge from this three-dimensional classification scheme of attributional dimensions. The first benefit is that any one attribution can be categorized as a type of attribution. For instance, *mood* is an internal-unstable-uncontrollable attribution. Similarly, *strategy* is an internal-unstable-controllable attribution. The second benefit is that these dimensions reveal the common denominator among otherwise diverse attributions. For instance, ability, intelligence, physical attractiveness, and personality all share a common classification (internal-stable-uncontrollable). It is this common denominator that motivation psychologists use for predicting the effects an attribution will have on motivation and emotion. The focus therefore shifts from understanding the motivational significance of specific attributions (e.g., ability) to understanding how causal dimensions of attributions affect motivation, emotion, and behavior (i.e., stable attributions have this effect, controllable attributions have that effect, and internal-stable-uncontrollable attributions have this other effect). The caution is that two different people might classify the same attribution in different ways. For instance, one person might see mood as a stable cause, while another might see it as unstable. Or ability might be seen as either a controllable or an uncontrollable cause.

ATTRIBUTIONAL ERRORS AND BIASES

Attributional decision making generally proceeds via logical information processing. After witnessing a car wreck, for example, we scan for possible causes—the slippery road, obstructions in the road, foul weather, selfish drivers, dense traffic, and so forth—and choose the attribution (or attributions) that best fit the observed evidence. One of the more interesting aspects of the attributional process, however, is that biases creep in and cloud what would otherwise be rational information processing (Harvey & Weary, 1981). In other words, if you provide people with sufficient information for making accurate causal attributions, people all too often arrive at the wrong answers (Funder, 1987). Those wrong answers are predictable, however, because the following errors and biases pervade the attributional process.

Attributional Errors

Two common attributional errors are the *fundamental attribution error* and the *actor-observer error.* When we explain other people's outcomes, we rely heavily on internal factors such as their personality characteristics. (For instance, "He won because he is so talented.") The tendency to use internal factors in explaining another person's outcomes is so pervasive that it constitutes the fundamental attribution error (Ross, 1977). Think about the last time one of your friends was late in meeting you for an appointment. You were probably more willing to think that your friend was late because of some personality factor (e.g., irresponsibility, laziness) rather than some external situational factor (e.g., traffic, unexpected telephone call). The fundamental attribution error applies also to positive characteristics, as when we attribute the salesperson's polite smiling to his personality rather than to a situational factor. This error is reversible. When we are instructed to pay close attention to how the situation influences one's behavior, we are as likely to attribute the person's outcomes to an external, as to an internal, factor (Quattrone, 1982). Hence, the fundamental attribution error emanates from a perceptual, not a motivational, bias.

After witnessing the same outcome, actors and observers tend to make different attributions. According to actor-observer error (Jones & Nisbett, 1971), individuals explain their own outcomes with external causes but explain the outcomes of others with internal causes (Eisen, 1979; Monson & Snyder, 1977; Taylor & Fiske, 1978). Inevitably, the actor and observer have different perspectives (Jones & Nisbett, 1972). Suppose, for example, that a person stumbles and trips over an ill-positioned chair. This person will tend to explain the trip on the basis of the intrusive chair (external cause), while an observer will tend to explain this person's stumble on the basis of his clumsiness (internal cause). Each explains the event using whatever evidence is most salient. This error too is reversible (Gould & Sigall, 1977). For instance, therapists working with alcoholics find their patients more willing to take personal responsibility for their drinking behavior after watching a videotape of their intoxicated behavior (Dworetzky, 1988). Watching oneself on a videotape essentially gives the actor the perspective of the observer, and when the actor gains the same visual perspective as an observer, the actor-observer error fades away (Storms, 1973). Thus, both the fundamental attribution error and the actor-observer error are perceptual, rather than motivational, phenomena.

Motivational Biases

A third attributional shortcoming is the *self-serving bias* (Arkin, Cooper, & Kolditz, 1980; Miller & Ross, 1975; Zuckerman, 1979): People typically attribute their successes to internal causes but attribute their failures to external causes. Unlike the previous two errors, the self-serving bias is a motivational phenomenon (Zuckerman, 1979). For example, in sports, competitors make more internal attributions for success (ability, effort) than they do for failure (Gill, Ruder, & Gross, 1982; Iso-Ahola, 1977; Lau & Russell, 1980; Riess & Taylor, 1984; Riordan, Thomas, & James, 1985; Spink, 1978). The self-serving bias also underlies coaches' explanations for winning and losing (Lau & Russell, 1980). Coaches explain victories by talking about their players' abilities or heroic efforts, but they explain defeats by talking about unexpected injuries or bad luck. The self-serving bias operates in other areas (Van Der Plight & Eiser, 1983). Successful business-people generally believe, for instance, that they are rich because of their personal ability rather than because of their privileged status, good luck, or convenient circumstances (O'Malley & Becker, 1984).

As a motivational phenomenon, the self-serving bias has its roots in the desire to protect self-esteem (Dunning, Leuenberger, & Sherman, 1995; Greenberg, Pyszcynski, & Solomon, 1982). To the extent that performers see success as internally caused and see failure as externally caused, they maintain a positive self-concept. Consider the destructive consequences to self-esteem if a performer were to internalize failures but externalize successes. For instance, attributing negative outcomes (failures) to personal deficiencies has been linked to depression (Peterson & Seligman, 1984). The self-serving bias therefore serves as a motivational buffer against feelings of unworthiness, apathy, and despair (Abramson, Seligman, & Teasdale, 1978).

Because people generally spend a great deal of effort in maintaining a positive view of the self, the self-serving bias has a near-ubiquitous status (Kunda, 1990). When people are asked to describe an effective leader, for instance, they typically describe someone who sounds just like themselves—friendly people say leaders need to be friendly, while ambitious people say leaders need to be ambitious (Dunning, Perie, & Story, 1991). When college professors judge the quality of their work, 94% describe themselves as "above average," which of course cannot possibly be true (Cross, 1977). The ubiquitousness of the self-serving bias shines through in just about any domain that allows room for subjective interpretation (Dunning, 1993; Dunning, Meyerowitz, & Holzberg, 1989).

PERSONAL CONTROL BELIEFS

Personal control beliefs reflect the degree to which an individual believes she causes desirable outcomes and prevents aversive ones (Peterson, Maier, & Seligman, 1993). When personal control beliefs are strong and resilient, the individual perceives a strong causal link between actions and outcomes. When personal control beliefs are weak and fragile, the individual perceives that personal initiatives and actions produce little effect on what happens. Whether people develop mastery-oriented or helpless-oriented personal control beliefs can be explained, in part, by their explanatory styles.

Explanatory Style

Explanatory style is a relatively stable, cognitively based personality variable that reflects the way people explain the reasons bad events happen to them (Peterson & Barrett, 1987; Peterson & Seligman, 1984). Bad events happen to everyone, but people explain these setbacks with attributions that vary in their locus, stability, and controllability. An *optimistic explanatory style* manifests itself as the tendency to explain bad events with attributions that are external, unstable, and controllable. (For example, "I lost the contest because my coach called the wrong plays.") A *pessimistic explanatory style* manifests itself as the tendency to explain bad events with attributions that are internal, stable, and uncontrollable. (For example, "I lost the contest because I'm physically uncoordinated.")

To understand the effect of explanatory style, imagine looking for a job, unsuccessfully, for several weeks. Reflecting back on the weeks, what would you say is the major cause of this misfortune? Once you identify that cause, rate it on the following three questions (Seligman et al., 1979):

1. Is the cause of your unsuccessful job search due to something about you or something about other people or circumstances?
2. In the future when looking for a job, will this cause again be present?
3. Is the cause something that you can do something about, or is this cause something over which you have little or no control?

These three questions pertain to the attributional dimensions of locus, stability, and controllability, respectively. These questions, based on the Attributional Style Scale (Seligman et al., 1979; also see the Attributional Style Questionnaire, Peterson et al., 1982; Peterson & Villanova, 1988), produce a three-dimensional profile of the person's attributional style. People with an optimistic explanatory style will explain bad events with external, unstable, and controllable causes. (For example, "It's just a bad job market at the moment.") People with a pessimistic explanatory style will explain bad events with internal, stable, and uncontrollable causes. (For example, "I'm an unqualified applicant.")

Pessimistic Explanatory Style

Academic failures, poor physical health, and subpar job performance are common. They happen to us all. Some of us react to such failures by trying even harder; others react by giving up. A pessimistic explanatory style predisposes people toward the latter response—giving up—in times of failure and setbacks. Consider the following three examples involving academic failure, health problems, and poor job performance that illustrate how a pessimistic explanatory style deflates motivation and cues up negative emotion.

Disappointing grades, uncompleted assignments, confusing and misplaced textbooks, writer's block, locked library doors, unintelligible lectures, and unprepared presentations are part of all academic careers, at least from time to time. When a student with a pessimistic style faces such educational frustrations and failures, she typically responds with a passive, fatalistic coping style (Peterson & Barrett, 1987). To document that pessimistic students act in passive, fatalistic manners, researchers measured how frequently each student sought out academic advising during the year and how well

TABLE 9.1 **Correlation Between Pessimistic Explanatory Style and Poor Physical Health**

POOR HEALTH: AGE	R
30	.04
35	.03
40	.13
45	.37****
50	.18*
55	.22**
60	.25***

N (sample size) = 99; r = coefficient of partial correlation
*p < .10; **p < .05; ***p < .01; ****p < .001.
SOURCE: From "Pessimistic Explanatory Style Is a Risk Factor for Physical Illness: A Thirty-Five Year Longitudinal Study," by C. Peterson, M. E. P. Seligman, and G. E. Vaillant, 1988, *Journal of Personality and Social Psychology, 55,* pp. 23–27. Copyright 1988 by American Psychological Association. Adapted with permission.

they performed in school. Attributional pessimists tended not to go to an advisor, and avoiding one's advisor, in turn, predicted making poor grades (Peterson & Barrett, 1987).

To link pessimistic explanatory style to physical health outcomes, researchers studied 99 college graduates over a four-decade period (Peterson, Seligman, & Vaillant, 1988). Each person, starting at the age of 25, completed a survey to assess explanatory style, and the researchers rated health status at five-year intervals. The correlation between pessimistic explanatory style and poor physical health appears in Table 9.1. Pessimistic explanatory style correlated significantly with poor physical health starting at age 45, and that relationship remained significant through the age of 60. When attributional pessimism leads people to react to life's setbacks in a passive, fatalistic manner, it eventually takes its toll on physical health.

As to job performance, one vocation with more than its share of frustrations, failures, and rejections is selling life insurance because only a small percentage of potential clients ever buy a policy. One pair of researchers assessed life insurance agents' explanatory styles and recorded which agents performed well or poorly and which agents stayed on the job or quit (Seligman & Schulman, 1986). The attributionally pessimistic agents were more likely to quit. Among the attributional pessimists who persevered, they performed significantly worse than did their more optimistic peers.

Overall, the pessimistic explanatory style is associated with academic failure (Peterson & Barrett, 1987), social distress (Sacks & Bugental, 1987), physical illness (Peterson, Seligman, & Vaillant, 1988), impaired job performance (Seligman & Schulman, 1986), depression (Beck, 1976), and even electoral defeat in presidential elections (Zullow et al., 1988). Individuals with a pessimistic explanatory style generally make lower grades in college, speak less with nonresponsive (uncontrollable) partners, quit work, suffer depressions, and consider suicide. Care must be exercised in interpreting these correlational data, however, as it certainly could be the case that poor grades, nonresponsive partners, and difficulties at work lead individuals toward adopting a pessimistic style. Thus, one can say that a pessimistic style and mental and physical well-being correlate negatively, but one cannot say assertively that a pessimistic style causes mental and physical distress. Researchers continue to investigate the causal status of a pessimistic explanatory style in coping with life's setbacks (Peterson, Maier, & Seligman, 1993).

Optimistic Explanatory Style

The illusion of control is an attributional phenomenon that, over time, fosters an optimistic explanatory style. People with an optimistic explanatory style tend to take substantial credit for their successes but accept little or no blame for their failures. As you might expect, depressed individuals rarely have an optimistic style, as they tend not to make self-serving attributions (Alloy & Abramson, 1982) and are not vulnerable to the illusion of control (Alloy & Abramson, 1979).

Equipped with a hardy self-serving bias for fueling an optimistic explanatory style, people readily ignore negative self-related information, impose distorting filters on incoming information, and interpret positive and negative outcomes in self-protecting ways. Attributing failure to an external cause allows the individual to discount the self-related meaning of the failure. In the same spirit, negative life outcomes are blamed on others, bad luck, and the environment in general. Externalizing failure therefore immunizes the individual against any detrimental effect of failure. Over time, a history of internalizing successes and externalizing failures breeds an enduring belief that one has more control over fate than is actually the case, even if what is needed is a full repertoire of excuses, denials, and self-deceptions (Lazarus, 1983; Sackeim, 1983; Tennen & Affleck, 1987).

In one sense, an optimistic explanatory style is delusional, and the extent to which people endorse a self-serving bias and optimistic explanatory style does indeed correlate with narcissism (John & Robins, 1994). Narcissists hold a grandiose sense of self-importance, tend to exaggerate their talents and achievements, and expect to be recognized as superior without commensurate achievements (Kohut, 1971; Millon, 1990). Because they harbor an inflated sense of self-importance and superior competence, narcissists are particularly prone to the self-serving bias (Westen, 1990). But most of us are not narcissists. For most of us (depressives and narcissists aside), an optimistic explanatory style is functionally an asset, because a "mentally healthy person appears to have the enviable capacity to distort reality in a direction that enhances self-esteem, maintains beliefs in personal efficacy, and promotes an optimistic view of the future" (Taylor & Brown, 1988).

MASTERY VERSUS HELPLESS MOTIVATIONAL ORIENTATIONS

Over time, people learn to view failure in different ways. A *mastery motivational orientation* refers to a hardy, resistant portrayal of the self during encounters of failure. The individual with a mastery motivational orientation responds to failure by remaining task-focused and by being bent on achieving mastery in spite of difficulties and setbacks (Diener & Dweck, 1978, 1980). A *helpless motivational orientation* refers to a fragile view of the self during encounters of failure. The individual with a helpless motivational orientation responds to failure by giving up and withdrawing, acting as if the situation were out of her control (Dweck, 1975; Dweck & Repucci, 1973).

Most people perform well and stay task-focused when working on easy problems and when performing well. When tasks turn difficult and challenging, however, the motivational significance of mastery versus helpless motivational orientation becomes clear. Mastery-oriented persons seize challenges and become energized by setbacks. Helpless-oriented persons shy away from challenges, fall apart in the face of setbacks, and begin to question and then outright doubt their ability. On those occasions in which success feedback slips into failure feedback, mastery-oriented individuals increase their efforts and change their strategies (Diener & Dweck, 1978, 1980). Under these same conditions, helpless-oriented individuals condemn their abilities and lose hope for any future successes (Dweck, 1975; Dweck & Repucci, 1973).

The different reactions to failure feedback for mastery-oriented and failure-oriented performers emanate from a different meaning of failure (Dweck, 1999). Mastery-oriented individuals do not see failure as an indictment of the self. Instead, these individuals, during setbacks and failures, might say things like, "The harder it gets, the harder I need to try"; "I love a challenge"; and "Mistakes are our friend." Failure feedback is, generally speaking, just information. Because mastery-oriented persons recognize that failure feedback is telling them they need more effort and more resources, these individuals typically perform better and more enthusiastically in the face of failure. Helpless-oriented individuals see failure as an indictment of the self. They see failure as a sign of personal inadequacy, one that in turn leads them toward a state of despair. Perhaps the reader might think the term "helpless" is a bit strong, but research by Carol Dweck (1975) suggests that it is not. When failure rears its ugly head, helpless-oriented people might start to say things like, "I'm no good at things like this" and "I guess I'm not very smart." In other words, they denigrate their abilities and even their self-worth (Diener & Dweck, 1978). Their emotions quickly turn negative, and they start to show unusual ways for dealing with their rising anxiety and doubt, such as acting silly or trying to change the task or its rules (Diener & Dweck, 1978). Their problem-solving strategies collapse into simply making wild guesses or picking answers for random reasons. The self-denigration, negative mood, and immature strategies signal the presence of helplessness, but the telltale sign of helplessness is how quickly and how emphatically the performer gives up (Dweck, 1999).

Even in the face of success, differences emerge between mastery-oriented and helpless-oriented individuals. After experiencing a series of successes, helpless-oriented children (1) underestimated the number of times that they succeeded, (2) resisted attributing their successes to ability, and (3) did not expect their success to continue in the future (Diener & Dweck, 1980). In other words, helpless-oriented performers find reasons to discount, deny, or otherwise excuse their successes.

The attributional significance of mastery versus helpless motivational orientations revolves around people's causal explanation for failure. Helpless-oriented performers rely on stable-uncontrollable attributions for explaining failure (i.e., a pessimistic explanatory style). Specifically, they blame their failures on low ability. Mastery-oriented performers rely on unstable-controllable attributions to explain their failures (i.e., an optimistic explanatory style). They commonly find fault in their efforts or strategies (not in their abilities). In sum, during failure feedback, helpless-oriented children focus on why they are failing (low ability), whereas mastery-oriented children focus on how they can remedy the failure (effort, strategy; Diener & Dweck, 1978).

Learned Helplessness

The original explanation for learned helplessness proposed that people show motivational, learning, and emotional deficits to the extent that they realize their voluntary behavior has little or no effect on the outcomes they seek to obtain or avoid (chapter 8; Peterson, Maier, & Seligman, 1993; Seligman, 1975). In other words, perceived uncontrollability caused helplessness. Attribution research, however, discovered that people do not *always* develop helplessness after learning there is little they can do about aversive events (Tennen & Eller, 1977). In the attributional analysis of learned helplessness, the causal attribution individuals make following a bad event is an additional crucial determinant of their expectations for future uncontrollability and helplessness.

The perception that the world is a nonresponsive, uncontrollable place (response-outcome noncontingencies) is the first causal element of helplessness. A second causal element is the individual's pessimistic analysis of the cause of the noncontingency (Abramson, Seligman, & Teasdale, 1978; Peterson et al., 1993). For helplessness to occur, individuals must (1) perceive the world as nonresponsive and uncontrollable and (2) believe they lack the capacity to overcome the nonresponsive, uncontrollable world. The person who sees the world as a nonresponsive, uncontrollable place but believes future control will be possible does not develop helplessness. Under these conditions, reactance is actually more likely to occur than is helplessness. It is only when expectancies turn pessimistic that people experience helplessness (Wortman & Brehm, 1975). Hence, the individual's pessimistic causal analysis of why outcomes are uncontrollable is just as important a determinant to learned helplessness as is the experience of uncontrollability itself.

Reformulated Model of Learned Helplessness

In the reformulated model of learned helplessness (Abramson et al., 1978), internal, stable, and uncontrollable attributions for explaining a lack of personal control put people at risk of learned helplessness. For example, suppose a job applicant's phone calls to a prospective employer are not returned for a week (an unresponsive environment). The applicant who attributes the unreturned calls to an internal-stable-uncontrollable cause (e.g., lacking talent) stands most at risk of reacting in a passive, listless manner. If the job applicant attributes the same unreturned calls to an external-unstable-controllable cause (e.g., the employer has a very busy schedule), then she is likely to respond in an assertive, active manner.

What the reformulated (attributional) model adds to the original (nonattributional) model of learned helplessness is that, given uncontrollable events, people think the world is an uncontrollable place but question whether this lack of control is their fault. People also question whether this lack of control will continue in the future and whether anything can be done to overcome or reverse it. External-unstable-controllable attributions for a lack of control send the message that failures and setbacks are surmountable, and the appropriate response is therefore assertive, energy-mobilizing coping. Internal-stable-uncontrollable attributions send the message that failures and setbacks are insurmountable, and the appropriate response therefore is to give up and accept one's soured fate.

DEPRESSION

Learned helplessness can be viewed as a model of environmentally created unipolar depression (Seligman, 1975). Helpless people, like depressed people, tend to view an aversive situation as an uncontrollable event produced by internal-stable-uncontrollable causes. Just as perceived uncontrollability contributes to helplessness, perceived loss of control over important life events contributes to depression. From an attributional perspective, learned helplessness and depression share a common etiology: negative personal control beliefs that emanate from a pessimistic attributional style.

Everybody experiences negative life outcomes. But not everyone is depressed. Following setbacks, failures, and rejections, depressed people tend to make either internal or internal-stable attributions (Rizley, 1978; Seligman et al., 1979). Depressed people also attribute the good things that happen to them pessimistically, believing that external-unstable causes produce positive outcomes. Thus, depressed people generally hold a lopsided view of positive and negative outcomes that is a bit on the dark side: Failures are self-inflicted; successes are excused away (Seligman et al., 1979).

It is the mixture between bad events and a pessimistic style for both bad and good events that opens the doors to unipolar depression. In general, research supports the covariation between attributional style and depression (Abramson, Metalsky, & Alloy, 1989; Brewin, 1985; Robins, 1988; Sweeney, Anderson, & Bailey, 1986). To say that attributions cause depression, however, is too strong a statement to make, given the current understanding of how attributions affect mental health. Saying that a pessimistic explanatory style causes depression is an overstatement because depression follows not only from pessimism but also from bad and traumatic events. Therefore, the safest conclusion to draw is that a pessimistic attributional style makes the individual more vulnerable to depression (Peterson & Seligman, 1984).

ATTRIBUTIONAL RETRAINING

People learn attributions. Through experience, people learn to interpret the causal structure of the world. In time, people learn to make sense of academic failure, interpersonal rejection, financial loss, unreturned phone calls, disappointing performances, automobile accidents, and so on. The conclusions we come to in interpreting the causal structure of our environmental interactions produce habitual ways of thinking, and when our habitual ways for explaining life's outcomes become pessimistic, we become vulnerable to academic listlessness, poor health, poor job performance, learned helplessness, and depression.

If people learn pessimistic attributions, then people should be able to learn optimistic attributions as well. This possibility is the cornerstone belief on which attributional retraining procedures are based. Because attributional styles are learned ways of thinking, the reformulated (attributional) model of learned helplessness proposes that helplessness is both *preventable* (Altmaier & Happ, 1985; Hirt & Genshaft, 1981; Jones, Nation, & Massad, 1977) and *reversible* (Klein & Seligman, 1976; Miller & Norman, 1981; Orbach & Hadas, 1982). Though still somewhat preliminary in its endorsement, clinical psychology sees attributional retraining as a promising cognitive approach to therapeutic intervention in helplessness-related emotional and behavioral problems (Cotton, 1981;

Forsterling, 1985; Peterson, Maier, & Seligman, 1993). Thus far, attributional retraining has been moderately effective in the treatment of unipolar depression (Person & Rao, 1985; Seligman et al., 1988), interpersonal aggression (Hudley & Graham, 1993), and poor academic performance (Wilson & Linville, 1982).

PREVENTING HELPLESSNESS

To prevent helplessness, one must understand its causes: (1) a belief that one's behavior has little or no influence over one's fate and (2) a pessimistic explanatory style. These causes suggest two strategies for heading off helplessness and preventing it. The first is to change the responsiveness of the environment from uncontrollable to controllable. The second is to immunize the individual against helplessness by developing an a priori optimistic explanatory style.

Change Environment From Nonresponsive to Responsive

Sometimes people feel helpless because their environments at home, at work, in school, in relationships, and on the athletic field are truly outside their realm of influence and control. In such situations, the problem is in the environment (e.g., discrimination), not in the person. Hence, the person's efforts are best directed not so much at changing attributions and personal control beliefs as they are at changing either the environment itself or one's way of interacting with it.

Responses to nature (e.g., hurricanes) and circumstances (e.g., cars that will not start) are difficult to change, except by moving to a new location, purchasing a new car, and taking other such measures. That said, the vast majority of environments are at least somewhat controllable. Conflicts do not have to escalate into aggression; sales pitches do not have to end with a door closed in the face; athletic competitions do not have to end in defeat; and people do not have to be lonely or unpopular. The controllability of almost any situation can be improved by enhancing the skillfulness of one's coping by brushing up on social skills, developing a social support network, refining communication skills, developing new athletic techniques, getting advice from a coach or an instruction book, or improving personal hygiene. In the same spirit, the controllability of almost any situation can be improved by enhancing the responsiveness of other people—the extent to which they harbor prejudices, are flexible and understanding, are willing to cooperate, and so on. Environments can be changed or restructured through negotiation, bargaining, confrontation, help-seeking, perspective taking and sharing, coalition formation, and the like. In these examples, it is not the individual's pessimism that underlies vulnerability to helplessness. Rather, the uncontrollability is quite real, and one's attention is best directed at changing the environment either directly (by changing its response-outcome contingencies) or indirectly (by changing how one interacts and copes with it).

Immunization

Even if the environment is at least partly responsive and controllable, people still sometimes react to failures and frustrations in helpless ways. A pessimistic explanatory style leaves people vulnerable to helplessness even in potentially controllable environments.

People who are attributionally optimistic, however, are somewhat immunized against the potentially demoralizing effects of life's failures (Seligman, 1991).

Immunization is an attempt to prevent helplessness before it occurs (Jones, Nation, & Massad, 1977; Seligman & Maier, 1967; Ramirez, Maldonado, & Markus, 1992). It is a developmental process in which the person is exposed to small doses of failure that are quickly followed up by experiences of control and mastery over the environment. The experiences of control and mastery are made possible by prearranging (1) training and coaching that enables the person to cope successfully with the failure and be ready to remedy it the next time, and (2) cognitive intervention that enables the person to interpret obstacles and setbacks in an optimistic way (identity external-unstable-controllable causes). Therefore, immunization is part prior experience (remedying failure by learning how to overcome it) and part attributional reinterpretation (reinterpreting the meaning of failure via an optimistic explanatory style).

One focus of immunization is therefore to foster strong and resilient personal control beliefs that prevent the initial onset of learned helplessness. This approach to immunization encourages people to see productive connections between their behaviors and their outcomes (Klein & Seligman, 1976). The second focus of immunization is to foster an optimistic explanatory style that prevents the onset of learned helplessness in the context of failure. This approach to immunization encourages people to see the situationally specific and external causes of failure as well as its internal causes (Ramirez, Maldonado, & Markus, 1992). Providing people with failure-remedying experiences and with optimistic attribution interpretations does indeed immunize them against the detrimental effects of uncontrollable environments (Altmaier & Happ, 1985; Eckelman & Dyck, 1979; Hirt & Genshaft, 1981; Jones, Nation, & Massad, 1977; Ramirez, Maldonado, & Markus, 1992; Thornton & Powell, 1974).

REVERSING HELPLESSNESS

Preventing helplessness is a noble undertaking. What if the person is already suffering helplessness, however? Once learned helplessness is entrenched, attributional retraining programs act as therapeutic attempts in reversing it. To reverse helplessness, research suggests a two-part retraining strategy: (1) Extend the range of possible attributions for explaining the lack of control and (2) persuade the person to exchange the original pessimistic attribution for a more optimistic one (Peterson et al., 1993).

Extend the Range of Possible Attributions

The first step in the attempt to reverse helplessness is to extend the range of attributions that can conceivably explain the setback or failure. For instance, in the face of a frustrating turn of events (e.g., having a job application rejected), applicants might pessimistically conclude that they just do not have what it takes to get a good job. Given such a pessimistic attribution (internal-stable-uncontrollable), a friend (or therapist) might suggest to the job applicant that he should consider alternative, yet equally valid, rival attributions, such as a lack of relevant experience, lack of preparation, ineffective interview strategy, tough economy, high odds against any single applicant getting a job with an average of 100 applicants per job opening (high task difficulty), and so on. Notice that most of these alternative attributions are unstable and controllable (e.g., experience, preparation, interview strategy). Notice also that each is just as viable an explanation for the negative outcome as is the internal-stable-uncontrollable one made by the person feeling helpless. Attributional retraining is not an effort to trick someone into thinking something she does not believe; rather, it is the effort to overcome the person's unnecessarily narrow (and pessimistic) way of thinking.

In his cognitive therapy of depression, Aaron Beck (1967, 1984) documents that depressed people often jump to self-depreciating thoughts on the basis of a single fact (a process referred to as "arbitrary inference"). An effective means for countering arbitrary inference is to encourage the individual to extend the limited range of possible attributions for a setback. It is not that the helpless or depressed person's attribution is wrong. Rather, his attribution is just unnecessarily limited. Adding rival attributions that are unstable and controllable has a way of opening doors of hope to the prospect that the world can, potentially, be a controllable place.

Change Unnecessarily Pessimistic Attributions

The fundamental objective in attributional retraining is encouraging a person to rethink the merits of unstable-controllable attributions following a setback. Stable-uncontrollable attributions lead to the conclusion that the setback is part of a permanent, irreversible condition. Unstable-controllable attributions, on the other hand, lead to the conclusion that a setback is a temporary, reversible condition. Thus, a primary goal in attributional retraining programs is to alter the individual's perception of why failure occurred (Andrews & Debus, 1978; Dweck, 1975; Zoeller, Mahoney, & Weiner, 1983).

One likely attribution for failure is, of course, a lack of ability (stable-uncontrollable), but ability attributions leave the person wondering, why try in the first place? Fortunately, other attributions are equally valid, including lack of effort (Dweck, 1975), lack of an effective strategy (Anderson & Jennings, 1980), and lack of experience (Wilson & Linville, 1982). Each of the attributions of effort, strategy, and experience are unstable and under volitional control. Failure therefore loses its stigma as an insurmountable, uncontrollable obstacle. Changing one's attribution for failure from low ability to poor effort, ineffective strategy, or insufficient experience does indeed enhance both performance and persistence (Anderson & Jennings, 1980; Dweck, 1975; Wilson & Linville, 1982).

Consider one attributional retraining study (Wilson & Linville, 1982). College freshmen, whose fall semester's work was worse than they expected, were asked why they performed so poorly. Most students attributed their perceived failure to a lack of academic ability. Timothy Wilson and Patricia Linville reasoned that many of these students were at risk of dropping out of college (because a stable-uncontrollable cause of failure could be expected to persist throughout their college careers). Recognizing this vulnerability to dropping out, half of the students were placed in an experimental group and shown real data supporting the fact that most students attain higher grades as they progress through college. These students watched testimonial videotapes of juniors and seniors who confirmed their own steady year-by-year academic improvement. The other half of the students (the control group) received no such attributional retraining information. One year later, students in the control group showed no increase in their grade-point averages, and 25% of these students did indeed drop out of college. The attributionally retrained students (the experimental group), on the other hand, showed a significant improvement in their grade-point averages, and only 5% of these students dropped out. Explaining academic failure with an unstable-controllable cause (e.g., gaining needed experience, learning how the system works, becoming familiar with resources such as the library) improved both performance (GPA) and persistence (dropout rate).

Friedrich Forsterling (1985) reviewed the procedures used in 15 different attributional retraining studies and concluded that researchers accomplish attributional retraining in one of three ways: persuasion, behavior modification, and information. Each method has proved successful, but it remains an open question whether one technique works better than another. The three methods are defined as follows:

1. *Persuasion.* The person performs a task while an expert/therapist verbalizes the desired attribution (Zoeller, Mahoney, & Weiner, 1983). Following failure, the therapist argues for the validity of the desired (unstable-controllable) attribution.
2. *Behavior modification.* The person performs a task and offers his attribution to explain the outcome. The therapist encourages the performer to verbalize a range of attributions, and desired attributions are reinforced, while undesired attributions are ignored. Following failure, the therapist verbally and nonverbally reinforces only those attributions that are unstable-controllable (Andrews & Debus, 1978).
3. *Information.* Before the person performs a task (hence before any pessimistic attribution has a chance to be voiced), the therapist offers information about likely causes of the outcomes to come. Preperformance information can open the door to optimistic attributions that might otherwise be ignored (as in the earlier example with at-risk college students; Wilson & Linville, 1982, 1985).

EMOTION

During success and failure, while being included and rejected, and in the face of triumph and tragedy, people respond emotionally. Following positive outcomes, people generally feel happy, and following negative outcomes, people generally feel sad or frustrated. Irrespective of the underlying causes to these outcomes, people feel joy and distress during and after the benefit and harm (Weiner, 1986). Attribution theory, however, proposes that in addition to these primary, outcome-generated emotional reactions, people explain why they succeeded or failed. Once explained, new emotions surface.

In his attributional theory of emotion, Bernard Weiner (1985, 1986) refers to the outcome-dependent emotional reaction as a "primary appraisal of the outcome." Basic emotions of happy and sad simply follow good and bad outcomes (Weiner, Russell, & Learman, 1978, 1979). Attributions constitute a "secondary appraisal of the outcome." They differentiate the general happy-sad initial emotional reaction into specific secondary emotions. The sequence of events in Weiner's attribution theory of emotion appears in Figure 9.1.

FIGURE 9.1 **Attributional Theory of Emotion**

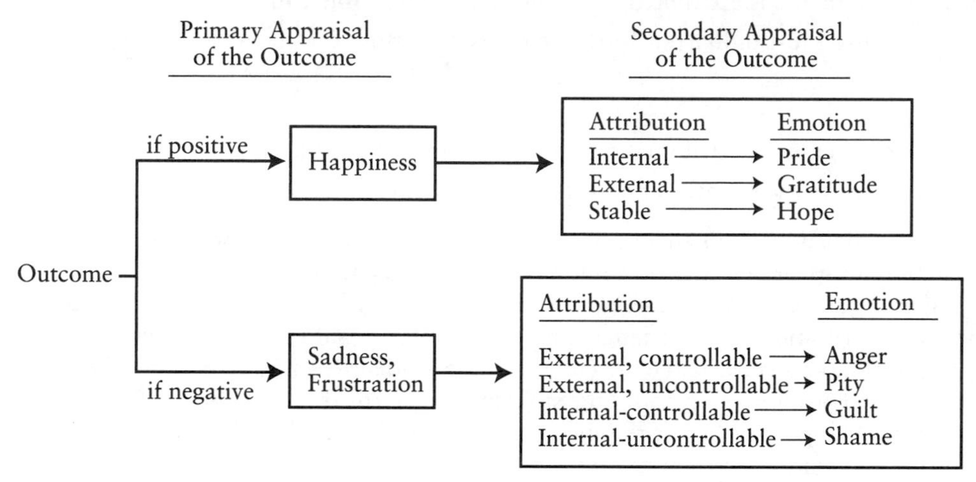

As depicted in Figure 9.1, seven emotions occur in reliable ways as a function of the attributional information-processing flow (Weiner, 1985, 1986). The attributional roots to the seven emotions are as follows:

Pride

A positive outcome is attributed to an internal cause, such as the self.
"I succeeded because of my outstanding ability."

Gratitude

A positive outcome is attributed to an external cause, such as another person.
"I succeeded because of all the help from my teammates."

Hope

A positive outcome is attributed to a stable cause.
"Because I am athletic, I will always do well in sports."

Anger

A negative outcome is attributed to an external-controllable cause.
"I lost because my opponent cheated."

Pity (or Sympathy)

A negative outcome is attributed to an external-uncontrollable cause.
"She has trouble reading because she was born with dyslexia."

Guilt

A negative outcome is attributed to an internal-controllable cause.
"I lost because I just didn't put forth the necessary effort."

Shame

A negative outcome is attributed to an internal-uncontrollable cause.
"I failed because I was born without any physical coordination whatsoever."

Notice that in each of these seven emotions (three positive, four negative), the attributional analysis of why the outcome came to pass is causally prior to the specific emotion. For instance, the fundamental assertion of an attributional analysis of emotion is that if the attribution was to change, then the emotion would change as well (i.e., change the attribution and you change the emotion). If a student feels pride because she feels her work won her a scholarship and if the student then learns the causal role played by someone's strong support of her at the meeting in which the scholarship decision was made, then the experienced emotion flows from pride into gratitude.

CRITICISMS

Attribution theory has its critics. Richard Nisbett and Timothy Wilson (1977) present two attention-getting criticisms. First, they argue that people do not routinely make attributions in explaining the events and outcomes in their lives. Rather, what people mostly think about is the consequence or implication of the outcome. That is, people's attention is more likely focused on the outcome's consequence than on its causes. For instance, after being rejected for a job, applicants worry more about what they will do without a job (consequences) than why they were rejected (attributions).

These critics argue that psychologists often artificially force attributions on their research participants by asking questions such as, "How important was your ability in determining your outcome?" People readily answer such questions, but it remains a fair question to ask whether people spontaneously ask themselves how important their ability was in determining why they succeeded or failed. This first criticism is that people just do not think all that much about attributions of ability, effort, task difficulty, and luck. Attribution theorists counter such criticisms by conceding that people do not always generate attributions. Rather, attribution theorists argue that people mostly make attributions following unexpected, negative, and important outcomes. Thus, attributions occur only some of the time.

Second, Nisbett and Wilson (1977) report that there is little evidence for the proposition that attributions produce any direct effect on behavior. In fact, the two critics report an inability to find *any* evidence in the research literature that attributions influence behavior. This second criticism is especially disturbing in light of the fact that psychology often defines itself as "the scientific study of behavior." Several attribution theorists have responded to the Nisbett and Wilson analysis (Smith & Miller, 1978), but this criticism remains valid. If attributions do not influence behavior, it seems reasonable (even crucial) to ask, "What do attributions influence?" The answer is that instead of exerting a direct effect on behavior, attributions affect the information-processing flow. By affecting the content of thought, attributions affect cognitive, motivational, and emotional processes. This chapter identified some of these processes—personal control beliefs, explanatory style, learned helplessness, depression, and emotion, for instance. These processes, rather than attributions per se, then affect behavior.

VALUES

In everyday conversation, values refer to principles or standards that the culture esteems (e.g., family values). In a motivational analysis, the term *value* refers to the usefulness or importance associated with an environmental object (Wigfield & Eccles, 2000). Values have motivational significance because they create a varying degree of anticipated satisfaction associated with the full range of objects in one's environment. That is, when a person faces an array of choices regarding what to do in a particular circumstance (which class to take, which product to buy, which person to date), the person makes a prognosis of anticipated satisfaction for each possible course of action. Hence, value expresses anticipated satisfaction toward something (Vroom, 1964).

An object has positive value when a person prefers attaining it to not attaining it; an object has negative value when a person prefers not attaining it to attaining it.[2] Because environmental objects vary in how attractive people perceive these objects to be, people harbor preferences in how to organize their behavior and how much investment to make in a course of action (Brophy, 1999; Feather, 1995). Values therefore create in the person an inclination to approach and interact with that object. Value strength—how intense the person's valuing of that object is—predicts that person's invested effort, persistence, choices, and emotional reactions (Feather, 1992, 1995; Wigfield & Eccles, 2000).

Value is expressed on a scale ranging from –10 to +10. Hedonic value is expressed in the + or – sign, and value strength is expressed in the low versus high magnitude of the number. When a child is at school, for instance, she is surrounded by objects that vary in value and that can be expressed as follows: recess, +9; best friend Cindy, +10; teacher, +5; principal, –1; reading time, –2; spelling bee, –10; art, +2; and dodgeball, –4.

Though understanding value is a relatively straightforward endeavor, there are many determinants in whether an objective is positively or negatively valued (Eccles et al., 1983; Ortony, Clore, & Collins, 1988; Wigfield & Eccles, 1992). First, an object can have *intrinsic* value derived from pleasure gained in the mere performance of the activity, as in the inherent enjoyment found in play, leisure, hobbies, and recreation. Second, an object can have a *difficulty* value stemming from the pleasure gained from succeeding at a skill-demanding activity, such as climbing Mount Everest or becoming the class valedictorian. Third, an object can have *utility* value from pleasure gained in accomplishing a task necessary in obtaining a larger future goal, such as passing a driver's license test or securing a job interview to launch a new career. Fourth, an object can

[2]Synonyms for value include *attractiveness, desirability,* or *subjective appeal.*

Moralization of Values

Question: Why would a person want to learn about the motivational states discussed in this chapter?
Answer: To learn how to become a vegetarian, for instance.

Why do people become vegetarians? If you asked people why they became vegetarians, they would give you all sorts of reasons. But two reasons would leap out as particularly important (Rozin, Markwith, & Stoess, 1997). First, people become vegetarians for health reasons. For instance, vegetarians will agree with statements like, "A diet containing meat is not as healthy as a vegetarian diet" (Rozin et al., 1997). This is a cognitive-rational sort of valuing. Second, people become vegetarians for moral reasons. For instance, vegetarians will agree with statements like, "I resist eating meat because it requires the killing of animals" (Rozin et al., 1997). This is an emotional-moral sort of valuing.

How a value might become moralized can be illustrated through the everyday process in which a person watches a television documentary or reads a newspaper article about how animals are slaughtered for human food. If the viewer or reader thinks killing animals is immoral, then vegetarianism is likely to become moralized. Moralization is the process through which an initial preference is converted into a heartfelt value (Rozin, 1999). When values become moralized, they are internalized into the person's self-definition, become highly resistant to change, show strong durability in time, and enable people to resist value-contradicting behaviors (e.g., eating meat; Rozin, 1999). But how does a preference to avoid eating meat become a moralized value to avoid eating meat? The chief way is through the recruitment of the disgust emotion.

have *extrinsic* value gained from the pleasure derived from rewards, such as a paycheck, sticker, or trophy. Fifth, an object can have *attainment* value from self-concept affirmation, such as playing a game of football to affirm one's identity as an athlete. Finally, an object can have *cultural* value that stems from being esteemed by the society, such as honor felt after enlisting in the armed forces or helping a person in need. Thus, value simply refers to how worthwhile we perceive any environmental object to be. But that object attains its value in the following ways: through its inherent enjoyment, by being difficult to attain, by being instrumental to some other end, by being a means to extrinsic rewards, by affirming our self-view, or by being esteemed by the culture.

EXPECTANCY × VALUE THEORY

According to expectancy × value theory, the motivation to approach or to avoid an object or event is the product of two factors: expectancy and value (Eccles et al., 1983; Wigfield, 1994; Wigfield & Eccles, 2000). The multiplicative product of these two terms is called *force*, and it represents the person's desire to approach or avoid the object or event.

Disgust is an innate emotion in which people perceive the object as being contaminated and associated with feelings of revulsion and nausea (Izard, 1991). Such objects are easy to dislike. Therefore, to the extent that a would-be vegetarian pairs eating meat with the disgust emotion, she is well on the way to becoming a practicing vegetarian. Once done, novice vegetarians often justify the moralized value by adding cognitive-rational reasons such as taste (dislike the taste of meat), ecology (a waste of resources to eat animal products), a social status (like the idea of being a vegetarian; Rozin et al., 1997). Moralized values can further expand from the individual to the cultural level as individuals recruit social support (e.g., family members) and public institutional support (e.g., government, church, schools).

Vegetarianism is but one example of the process of moralization. Cigarette smoking is another (Rozin & Singh, 1999). What was once a preference to smoke or not has recently become a heinous and intentional act at directly harming innocent bystanders. People with moralized values against secondhand smoke not only think smoking is disgusting, but they often can list additional reasons for supporting their moralized value, such as smoking is linked to cancer, heart disease, bad breath, wrinkled skin, stained teeth, environmental pollution, and litter (from cigarette butts) (Rozin & Singh, 1999). Some additional behaviors that have gone from being preferences to being downright morally criminal acts include attitudes toward slavery, eating high-fat foods (e.g., doughnuts), abortion, opiate drug usage, alcohol intoxication, and sunbathing (at least in some people's minds). In all these examples, the recruitment of disgust is the trigger that allows a preference to become a valve.

Expectancy

In the expectancy × value framework, *expectancy* is equivalent to *outcome expectancy* or to *expectancy for success.* It is expressed on a scale of probability (p) from 0 to 1, in which 1 represents a strong outcome expectancy, while 0 represents doubt that the behavior will produce the outcome. The expectancy for success associated with an object is essentially the chances one has in obtaining an outcome if a certain course of action is taken. A student, for instance, has expectancies for success of making a high grade for each course he is enrolled in (e.g., history, p[success] = .90; calculus, p[s] = .85) and expectancies for success associated with each store to visit in buying a pair of shoes (e.g., at the shoe store in the mall, p[s] = .70; at Wal-Mart, p[s] = .20).

Value

In the expectancy × value framework, *value* is the person's subjective attraction to (or repulsion from) an environmental object. As discussed above, value is expressed on a scale from −10 (extremely repulsive) to + 10 (extremely attractive).

Table 9.2 Expectancy × Value Framework Applied to Pursuing a Career

CAREER	EXPECTANCY	VALUE	(E × V) FORCE
Physician	.40	+7	+2.80
Teacher	.70	+5	+3.50
Astronaut	.01	+10	+0.10
Volunteer aide	.95	–1	–0.95
Politician	.25	–6	–1.50
Professional athlete	.10	+9	+0.90
Executive secretary	.45	–4	–1.80
Factory worker	.75	+4	+3.00
Nurse	.45	+7	+3.15

Expectancy = 0 to 1; value = –10 to +10.

Force

Expectancies and values combine to produce *force*, which is a motivational tendency to approach or avoid an object, situation, or event (Vroom, 1964). Intensity of force is a multiplicative product of expectancy and value, such that force = expectancy × value.

The greater the expectation of success multiplied by the positive value of obtaining the outcome, the more energetic the motivation to approach that object or event will be. The large positive product of E × V communicates intense approach motivation. The lower the expectation of success multiplied by the negative value of the goal object, the more energetic the motivation to avoid that object or event will be. The large negative product of E × V communicates intense avoidance motivation. If either expectancy or value is zero, force will be zero. For a person who has no expectancy of success (E = 0) or who has only a neutral value for the environmental object (V = 0), then force to approach or avoid will be zero. The expectancy × value = force conceptualization predicts approach/avoidance behavior rather well (Feather & Newton, 1982; Mitchell, 1974; Schwab, Olian-Gottleib, & Heneman, 1979; Wigfield & Eccles, 2000).

As an illustration of how the expectancy × value framework applies to a motivational analysis of action, consider the motivational quandary of the high-school student contemplating a career decision (see Table 9.2). Each career option can be assigned both an expectation for success as well as a value. The expectation represents the student's probability of attaining that vocation. The value represents the student's estimate of how useful and satisfying such a vocation would be (based on its intrinsic, difficulty, instrumental, extrinsic, attainment, and cultural values). Because each career option can be assigned an expectancy (of success) and a value, the student's motivation (force) to pursue each career can be calculated. The careers of teaching (3.50) and nursing (3.15) have relatively high forces, while the careers of being an executive secretary (−1.80) and politician (−1.50) have relatively low forces. Table 9.2 illustrates a fundamental proposition of

TABLE 9.3 **Expectancy × Value Framework Applied to Choosing a Date**

POTENTIAL DATE	EXPECTANCY	VALUE	(E × V) FORCE
Jamar Jackson	.40	+7	+2.80
Kurt Zoeller	.70	+5	+3.50
Billy Ray Johnson	.01	+10	+0.10
James Hatcher	.95	–1	–0.95

Expectancy = 0 to 1; value = –10 to +10.

the expectancy × value framework, namely that for an individual to be energized to pursue a goal, both expectancy of success and value must be relatively high. If only expectancy is high (volunteer aid, factory worker) or if only value is high (astronaut, professional athlete), the tendency to approach that goal remains relatively low.

A second example occurs for a young woman deciding on whom to invite to the school dance. She considers four potential dates (see Table 9.3). According to the expectancy × value formula, the woman will probably ask Kurt Zoeller to the dance because he is the date associated with the greatest force (approach motivation). Billy Ray Johnson is highly valued as a potential date, but he is not asked because of the woman's expectancy that he would not accept. James Hatcher is expected to accept the invitation (E is high), but he is not invited because of his relatively low value (V is low). Jamar Jackson is seen as a reasonably attractive second choice.

Notice that the *E* and *V* numbers associated with the four potential dates (Table 9.3) are the same as the numbers associated with the first four potential careers (Table 9.2). The idea of using the same numbers and just switching the environmental object under consideration is meant to communicate that the E × V decision-making process is the same for any sort of environmental object, whether the person is deciding to approach or avoid careers, dates, college majors, headache medicines, athletic endeavors, or political candidates.

ATTRIBUTION-CAUSED CHANGES IN EXPECTANCY AND VALUE

According to expectancy × value theory, a person's motivation to approach or avoid a particular goal is a product of the expectancy of success and the value assigned to that particular goal. Attribution theory provides a cognitive mechanism by which expectancies and values change over time. Consider the example shown in Table 9.4 for a high-school junior contemplating a list of courses for the coming semester. The left side of the table lists the student's first semester expectancies of passing each course and his subjective value for each course. Given *E* and *V*, the force to approach or to avoid each course can be calculated (expectancy × value = force). The center columns list hypothetical, semester-ending outcomes (pass or fail) for each course along with the student's attributions and their consequences. The right side lists the student's (new) second semester expectancies and values. Given the new *E*s and *V*s, the table lists a revised force for approaching each course. Change in force from one semester to the next occurs because of attribution-caused changes in expectancy and value.

TABLE 9.4 **Integration of Attribution and Expectancy × Value Theories**

	Before first semester						Between first semester and second semester		
CLASS	EXPECTANCY AT TIME 1	VALUE AT TIME 1	FORCE E × V	OUTCOME (GRADE)	ATTRIBUTION CATEGORY	ATTRIBUTION CONSEQUENCES	EXPECTANCY AT TIME 2	VALUE AT TIME 2	FORCE E × V
English	.8	6	4.8	Success	High ability	Expectancy: Increases Value: Increases	1.0	8	8.0
Art	1.0	4	4.0	Failure	Low ability	Expectancy: Decreases Value: Decreases	.8	2	1.6
Science	.4	9	3.6	Failure	Low effort	Expectancy: No change Value: Decreases	.4	7	2.8
Spanish	.7	4	2.8	Success	High effort	Expectancy: No change Value: Increases	.7	6	4.2
History	.7	2	1.4	Success	Low task difficulty	Expectancy: Increases Value: No change	.9	2	1.8
Physical Education	1.0	1	1.0	Success	Good luck	Expectancy: No change Value: No change	1.0	1	1.0
Mathematics	.3	2	0.6	Failure	Bad luck	Expectancy: No change Value: No change	.3	2	0.6

The attributional dimension of stability explains how and when expectancies change over time. According to Weiner's expectancy principle (1985) and its corollaries, expectancy changes as follows:

Expectancy Principle

Changes in expectancy of success following an outcome are influenced by the perceived stability of the cause of the event.

Corollary 1

If the outcome of an event is ascribed to a stable cause, then that outcome will be anticipated with increased certainty or with an increased expectancy in the future.

Corollary 2

If the outcome of an event is ascribed to an unstable cause, then the certainty or expectancy of that outcome may be unchanged or the future may be anticipated to be different from the past.

Following an outcome, an attribution to a stable cause increases the person's expectancy that the same outcome will recur. Unstable attributions leave expectancies unchanged because the cause of the outcome fluctuates and cannot be expected to recur. For instance, failure ascribed to bad luck (an unstable cause) leaves the performer with little reason to believe that failure will recur. If the bad luck is unstable, the failure outcome should also be unstable.

The attributional dimension of locus explains how and when values change (Weiner, 1974, 1986). Internal attributions (e.g., ability, effort) produce pride following success and shame following failure. These emotions in turn affect the individual's perceived value of a particular activity. Following pride, the individual values the activity more. Following shame, the individual values the activity less. External attributions leave value unaffected because the cause of the outcome lies outside the self.

Continuing the example summarized in Table 9.4, the student is expected in the first semester (left-hand side of the table) to approach (i.e., study for, attend, read the text) the courses with the highest forces (English, art) and to avoid the courses with the lowest forces (physical education, mathematics). By semester's end, the student succeeds in some courses and fails in others. (Succeeding and failing are subjectively defined; failing could be a grade of F or making any grade under an A.) Because grades are important events, the student assesses why each success or failure occurred. Suppose the student explains success in English by high ability, success in Spanish by effort, success in history by how easy it was, and success in physical education by good luck. Similarly, suppose the student explains failures in art by low ability, science by low effort, and mathematics by bad luck. Each attribution affects the student's future expectancies and values via the attributional dimensions of locus and stability.

The specific effect of each of the seven attributions appears on the right-hand side of Table 9.4. Notice what happens to the student's expectancy and value for each course as the second semester begins. Success attributed to internal and stable reasons (e.g., ability) increases both expectancy for success and the value of each course, respectively. Failure attributed to internal and stable causes, however, decreases expectancy for success and the value of each course. Success and failure attributed to external and unstable reasons (e.g., luck) affects neither subsequent expectancy for success nor value of that course. Notice that the student now has a different arrangement of forces for approaching each of the seven courses for the second semester (because E and V have changed for each course). English and Spanish now rank first and second in force.

Longitudinal research designs study real-world changes in expectancies and values by following mathematics students from the fifth through the twelfth grades (Eccles et al., 1983; Eccles & Wigfield, 1995; Wigfield, 1994). Recall that objects (math) acquire value in six different ways—intrinsic, difficulty, utility, extrinsic, attainment, and cultural. Therefore, changes in acquired values for math change as children's perceptions of math's intrinsic, difficulty, utility, extrinsic, attainment, and cultural value changes. Young children do not make many distinctions in the source of value, as intrinsic and utility explain which children value mathematics. As children make the transition from elementary to middle school, most students show a dropoff in their valuing of math, as it typically loses some of its intrinsic appeal and perceived utility for their lives. As children advance through high school, the additional sources of value—difficulty, extrinsic, attainment, and cultural—emerge and combine with intrinsic appeal and perceived utility to provide potential sources of value for math. Following these developmental changes in children's value is important because changes in expectancies and values (force) predict students' intentions to continue taking more math courses (choice, persistence) and students' grades in the math courses they take (performance).

SUMMARY

The principal assumption of attribution theory is that people actively seek to discover why they unexpectedly succeeded or failed at an important life event. Dozens of attributions are possible for explaining why any one particular outcome occurred (e.g., ability, effort). Instead of examining the motivational significance of specific attributions, attribution researchers generally study causal dimensions for understanding how attributions affect thinking, feeling, and wanting. The three attributional dimensions that categorize practically all possible attributions are locus (internal versus external), stability, and controllability.

Attributions are subject to errors and biases. Two noteworthy errors are the fundamental attribution error (overestimating the importance of internal or personality factors) and the actor-observer error (actors explain their behavior as externally caused but other people's behavior as internally caused). One noteworthy bias is the self-serving bias. It has roots in the desire to protect self-esteem and grows out of the illusion of control as people find ways for excusing away their failures as accidents (i.e., they externalize failure) and for taking credit for their successes (i.e., they internalize success).

Attribution theory offers a cognitive model for explaining a lengthy array of emotional and motivational processes, including explanatory style, personal control beliefs, learned helplessness, depression, emotion, expectancies, and values. Explanatory style is a relatively stable personality characteristic that reflects the way people explain the reasons bad events happen to them. An optimistic explanatory style manifests itself in the tendency to explain setbacks with external-unstable-controllable attributions; a pessimistic explanatory style manifests itself in the tendency to explain setbacks with internal-stable-uncontrollable attributions. The pessimistic explanatory style is associated with academic failure, social distress, physical illness, impaired job performance, and depression. Personal control beliefs revolve around mastery versus helpless motivational orientations. A mastery motivational orientation refers to a hardy, resistant portrayal of the self during encounters with failure. A helpless motivational orientation refers to a fragile view of the self during encounters with failure. Helpless-oriented individuals rely on internal-stable-uncontrollable attributions for explaining their failures (low ability), and they are therefore more likely than mastery-oriented individuals to denigrate themselves, experience negative emotions, fall back on immature problem-solving strategies, and quickly and emphatically give up.

In the reformulated model of learned helplessness, internal-stable-uncontrollable attributions for setbacks put people at risk of learned helplessness. For learned helplessness to occur, individuals must not only perceive the world as a nonresponsive and uncontrollable place (as discussed in chapter 8) but also believe that they lack the capacity to overcome the nonresponsive, uncontrollable aspects of their world. Hence, the individual's pessimistic attributional analysis of why outcomes are uncontrollable is just as important a determinant to learned helplessness as is the experience of uncontrollability itself. Research in attributional retraining shows that helplessness is both preventable and reversible. Learned helplessness deficits can be prevented by changing the environment from a nonresponsive to a responsive one and by immunizing the person in how to cope with uncontrollability before it occurs. Learned helplessness deficits can be reversed by extending the range of possible attributions for uncontrollable events and by changing unnecessarily pessimistic attributions into more optimistic ones.

Attribution theory is susceptible to two major criticisms. First, people do not spontaneously make attributions in explaining their life outcomes; instead, they pay more attention to the consequences and implications of what happens to them. Second, attributions do not directly affect behavior. Instead, attributions affect behavior only indirectly through their effects on cognitive, motivational, and emotional processes.

Value refers to the usefulness or importance of an environmental object. Values generate motivation by creating a level of anticipated satisfaction toward the various objects in one's environment. Expectancy × value theory proposes that the motivation to approach or avoid an object or event (called "force") is the product of expectancy (E) that an action will successfully produce a desired outcome and value (V), which is the anticipated satisfaction associated with that outcome. The expectancy × value framework applies best to those situations in which an individual must choose between competing events or objects, such as choosing among career options, choosing among various people to date, or choosing to take more math courses while in school.

RECOMMENDED READINGS

Attributions

Abramson, L. Y., Seligman, M. E. P., & Teasdale, J. (1978). Learned helplessness in humans: Critique and reformulation. *Journal of Abnormal Psychology, 87,* 49–74.

Anderson, C. A., & Jennings, D. L. (1980). When experiences of failure promote expectations of success: The impact of attributing failure to ineffective strategies. *Journal of Personality, 48,* 393–407.

Diener, C. I., & Dweck, C. S. (1978). An analysis of learned helplessness: Continuous changes in performance, strategy, and achievement cognitions following failure. *Journal of Personality and Social Psychology, 36,* 451–462.

Diener, C. I., & Dweck, C. S. (1980). An analysis of learned helplessness: II. The processing of success. *Journal of Personality and Social Psychology, 39,* 940–952.

Greenberg, J., Pyszcynski, T., & Solomon, S. (1982). The self-serving attributional bias: Beyond self-presentation. *Journal of Experimental Social Psychology, 18,* 56–67.

Peterson, C., Seligman, M. E. P., & Vaillant, G. E. (1988). Pessimistic explanatory style is a risk factor for physical illness: A thirty-five year longitudinal study. *Journal of Personality and Social Psychology, 55,* 23–27.

Taylor, S. E., & Brown, J. D. (1988). Illusion and well-being: A social psychological perspective on mental health. *Psychological Bulletin, 103,* 193–210.

Weiner, B. (1979). A theory of motivation for some classroom experiences. *Journal of Educational Psychology, 71,* 3–25.

Weiner, B. (1985). An attributional theory of achievement motivation and emotion. *Psychological Review, 92,* 548–573.

Values

Brophy, J. (1999). Toward a model of the value aspects of motivation in education: Developing appreciation for particular learning domains and activities. *Educational Psychologist, 34,* 75–85.

Rozin, P. (1999). The process of moralization. *Psychological Science, 10,* 218–221.

Rozin, P., Markwith, M., & Stoess, C. (1997). Moralization and becoming a vegetarian: The transformation of preferences into values and the recruitment of disgust. *Psychological Science, 8,* 67–73.

Wigfield, A. (1994). Expectancy-value theory of achievement motivation: A developmental perspective. *Educational Psychology Review, 6,* 49-78.

Wigfield, A., and Eccles, J. S. (2000). Expectancy-value theory of achievement motivation. *Contemporary Educational Psychology, 25,* 68-81.

10

The Self and Its Strivings

How have you been lately? Reflecting back on the last month, how many days have been happy ones? At school or work, how lively and satisfied have you felt? How about your relationships? Are they providing you with experiences that are energizing and fulfilling, or have they left you feeling mostly bland or frustrated? In the spirit of these questions, consider whether you agree or disagree with each of the following statements:

1. Many of my personal qualities trouble me enough that I wish I could change them.
2. I feel isolated and frustrated in interpersonal relationships.
3. When making important decisions, I rely on the judgments of others.
4. Often I am unable to change or improve my circumstances.
5. My life lacks meaning or purpose.
6. I have a sense of personal stagnation that often leaves me bored.

These six statements represent dimensions of psychological well-being. These dimensions are the following, in order: *self-acceptance,* or positive evaluations of oneself; *positive interpersonal relations,* or close, warm relationships with others; *autonomy,* or self-determination; *environmental mastery,* or the capacity to manage challenges and circumstances effectively; *purpose in life,* or the conviction that life offers meaning; and *personal growth,* or a sense of possessing a forward-moving developmental trajectory (Ryff, 1989, 1995; Ryff & Keyes, 1995). Your response on each of these dimensions reflects a distinct contour of self-functioning and psychological well-being. To be well psychologically is to possess positive self-regard, positive relationships with others, autonomy, environmental mastery, sense of purpose, and a trajectory of growth (Ryff, 1995). Pursuing these qualities is the province of the self. And your answers to these questions reveal how well or how poorly the self is doing its job.

THE SELF

In a motivational analysis of the self and its strivings, three problems take center stage: (1) defining or creating the self; (2) relating the self to society; and (3) discovering and developing personal potential (Baumeister, 1987). In the quest to define or create the self, we wonder about who we are, how others see us, how similar or different we are from others, and whether we can become the person we want to be. In the quest to relate the self to society, we contemplate how we want to relate to others, what place we wish to occupy in the social world, and what societal roles are (and are not) available to us. In the quest to discover and develop the self, we explore what does and does not interest us, we strive to create meaning and to discover our talents and exercise our skills, and we develop some skills and relationships while we ignore others.

Defining or creating the self shows how *self-concept* energizes and directs behavior. Some aspects of self-definition are simply ascribed to us (e.g., gender). Other aspects, however, must be gained through achievement and acts of choice (e.g., career, friends, values), which makes our struggle to define and create the self a motivational struggle.

Relating the self to society shows how *identity* energizes and directs behavior. In some respects, society is rigid in the roles it encourages or even allows individuals to pursue. In other respects, society is flexible in that it gives the individual some choice and responsibility in determining one's relationships to others (e.g., partners) and to society (e.g., careers). These acts of choice and internalization of responsibility make the struggle to relate the self to society a motivational struggle.

Discovering and developing the potential of the self is also a motivational struggle, one that reflects *agency*. Agency means that an agent (the self) has the power to act. It reveals the motivation that is inherent within the self, and hence, agency communicates an impulse to action that originates from within the person rather than from within the environment or culture. Thus, the self possesses a natural motivational force for developing from within toward a greater complexity and also toward a sense of coherency.

Self-Functioning and the Problem With Self-Esteem

Before discussing self-concept, identity, and agency, it will be helpful to pause and challenge a cornerstone belief that many people endorse: Namely, the best way to increase another person's motivation is to increase his self-esteem. Teachers, employers, and coaches consistently and enthusiastically say the way to motivate students, workers, and athletes is to increase their self-esteem. Make them feel good about who they are, and then watch as all sorts of wonderful things unfold.

Increasing self-esteem is a fine objective, and it seems silly to argue against promoting self-esteem in others. The problem with boosting self-esteem as a motivational intervention, however, is that "there are almost no findings that self-esteem causes anything at all. Rather, self-esteem is caused by a whole panoply of successes and failures. . . . What needs improving is not self-esteem but improvement of our skills [for dealing] with the world" (Seligman, quoted in Azar, 1994). In the same spirit, one pair of researchers concluded that self-esteem "is mainly a consequence of cumulative achievement-related successes and failures and that it does not have a significant impact on later achievement" (Helmke & van Aken, 1995). These same researchers went on to argue the merits of a "skill-development model" as the best way to build strong and resilient self-concepts in elementary grade children. The critical point to notice in these two quotations is the direction of the causal effect between self-esteem and achievement/productivity: Increases in self-esteem do not produce corresponding increases in achievement; rather, increases in achievement produce corresponding increases in self-esteem (Byrne, 1984, 1986, 1996; Harter, 1993; Helmke & van Aken, 1995; Marsh, 1990; Scheier & Kraut, 1979; Shaalvik & Hagtvet, 1990). Therefore, changes in self-esteem do not cause subsequent changes in achievement, but rather, changes in achievement cause subsequent changes in self-esteem.

Low self-esteem is no bargain. People low in self-esteem tend to suffer unusually high levels of anxiety. Some people argue that the chief benefit of high self-esteem is that it buffers the self against anxiety (Greenberg et al., 1992; Solomon, Greenberg, & Pyszczynski, 1991). Thus, low self-esteem leaves the person vulnerable to the suffrages of anxiety. But just because low self-esteem is bad does not mean that attempts to inflate self-esteem are good. In fact, inflated self-esteem has a dark side. People with an inflated self-view are significantly more prone to aggression and acts of violence when their favorable self-view is threatened (Baumeister, Smart, & Boden, 1996). For instance, when people with very high self-esteem perceive they have just been publicly ridiculed, they become unusually prone to acts of retaliatory aggression. For these two reasons—gains in self-esteem do not cause anything good, and threats to an inflated self-view is a prelude to violence—the crusade to boost self-esteem is overrated.

Self-esteem is an end product of the self's adaptive and productive functioning. It is much like happiness in that trying to be happy does not get you very far. Rather, happiness is a by-product of life's satisfactions, triumphs, and positive relationships (Izard, 1991). Likewise, self-esteem is a by-product of successfully measuring up to personal aspirations and to culturally mandated norms (Josephs, Markus, & Tafarodi, 1992). The same holds true for the six aspects of psychological well-being introduced earlier—self-acceptance, positive interpersonal relationships, autonomy, environmental mastery, purpose in life, and personal growth. Each is largely a by-product of other pursuits. This chapter is about those "other pursuits." The motivationally significant pursuits of the self are (1) defining or creating the self (self-concept), (2) relating the self to society (identity), and (3) discovering and developing the self's potential (agency).

SELF-CONCEPT

Self-concepts are individuals' mental representations of themselves. Just as people have mental representations of other people (what teenagers are like), places (sights to see in Chicago), and events (the happenings during Mardi Gras), people also have mental representations of themselves. To construct a self-concept, people attend to the feedback they receive in their day-to-day affairs that reveals their personal attributes, characteristics, and preferences. Most of the information people use to construct and define the self comes from specific life experiences, such as the following:

- During the group discussion, I felt uncomfortable and self-conscious.
- On the school field trip to the zoo, I did not talk very much.
- At lunch, I avoided sitting and hanging out with others.

People do not remember their thousands of individual life experiences. Rather, people aggregate their experiences into general conclusions. Over time, people translate their multitude of specific experiences into a general representation of the self (e.g., person A perceives herself as being mostly shy). It is this general conclusion (being shy), rather than the specific experiences (in the preceding list), that people readily remember and use as building blocks for constructing and defining the self-concept (Markus, 1977).

SELF-SCHEMAS

Self-schemas are cognitive generalizations about the self that are domain specific and are learned from past experiences (Markus, 1977, 1983). The earlier generalization of being shy exemplifies a self-schema. Being shy is both domain-specific (interpersonal style) and learned from past experiences (during group discussions, field trips, lunchroom conversations).

In athletics, a high-school student constructs a domain-specific self-schema by looking back on the week's experiences and recalling his last-place finish in a 100-meter dash, his abandonment of a mile run because of exhaustion, and his repeated crashes into the high jump bar at the track meet. In a different domain such as school, however, the same student might recall scoring well on a test, answering all the questions the teacher asked, and having a poem accepted for a school publication. Eventually, if the experiences in athletics and if the experiences in the classroom are consistent and frequent enough, the student will generalize a self that is, for the most part, incompetent in athletics but skillful in school. These generalizations (athletically being inept; intellectually being smart) constitute additional self-schemas (like the being shy self-schema mentioned earlier in the domain of interpersonal relationships).

The self-concept is a collection of domain-specific self-schemas. Which self-schemas are involved in the definition of the self-concept are those life domains that are most important to the person (Markus, 1977). The major life domains in early childhood, for instance, typically include cognitive competence, physical competence, peer acceptance, and behavioral conduct (Harter & Park, 1984). In adolescence, the major life domains generally include scholastic competence, athletic competence, physical appearance, peer acceptance, close friendships, romantic appeal, and behavioral conduct or morality (Harter,

1990). By college, the major life domains include scholastic competence, intellectual ability, creativity, job competence, athletic competence, physical appearance, peer acceptance, close friendships, romantic relationships, relationships with parents, morality, and sense of humor (Harter, 1990; Neemann & Harter, 1986). What this litany of major life domains shows is the general variety and range of self-schemas any one person is likely to possess at different stages in his life cycle. The specific life domains vary from one person to the next, but these domains illustrate the typical age-related structure of the self-concept (Harter, 1988; Kihlstrom & Cantor, 1984; Markus & Sentisk, 1982; Scheier & Carver, 1988).

Motivational Properties of Self-Schemas

Self-schemas generate motivation in two ways. First, self-schemas, once formed, direct an individual to behave in ways that make possible social feedback that is consistent with the established self-schemas. If that social feedback is inconsistent with the established self-schema, however, a motivational tension arises. The basic idea behind the motivation for self-schema consistency is that if a person is told she is introverted when she believes she is extraverted, that contradictory feedback generates a motivational tension. The tension motivates the self to restore consistency. For instance, in response to feedback that another person sees the woman as an introvert, a tension arises that creates a desire on the woman's part to prove to that other person that she is actually an extravert. Therefore, people behave in self-schema-consistent ways to prevent feeling the aversive motivational tension in the first place.

Second, self-schemas generate motivation to move the present self toward a desired future self. Much like goal setting's discrepancy-creating process (chapter 7), an ideal possible self initiates goal-directed behavior. Thus, the student who wants to become an actor initiates whatever actions seem necessary for advancing the self from being a student to becoming an actor. Seeking ideal possible selves is a fundamentally different motivational process than is striving to maintain a consistent self-view. Seeking possible selves is a goal-setting process (chapter 7) that invites self-concept change, whereas seeking a consistent self-view is a verification process that preserves self-concept stability.

Consistent Self

Once an individual establishes a well-articulated self-schema in a particular domain, he generally acts to preserve that self-view. Once established, self-schemas become increasingly resistant to contradictory information (Markus, 1977, 1983). People preserve a consistent self by actively seeking out information consistent with their self-concept and by ignoring information that contradicts their self-view (Swann, 1983, 1985; Tesser, 1987). It is psychologically disturbing to believe one thing is true about the self yet be told that the reverse is actually the case. Imagine the turmoil of the career politician who loses a local election or the turmoil of the star athlete who does not get drafted into the professional ranks. Inconsistency and contradiction generate an emotional discomfort that signals that consistency needs to be restored. It is this negative affective state that produces the motivation to seek self-confirmatory, and to avoid self-disconfirmatory, information and feedback.

To ensure that other people see us as we see ourselves, we adopt self-presentational signs and symbols. Through external appearances, we announce our self-view (i.e., our self-schemas) to others. Examples of such external appearances include the appearances we convey in our physical selves through clothes, dieting and weightlifting, and cosmetic surgery and in our physical possessions through room fixtures and arrangements and the kinds of cars we drive. For instance, the person wearing a Green Bay Packers jacket sends messages to others that might convey a sports enthusiast and an athlete.

Further, in the name of self-schema preservation, we intentionally choose to interact with others who treat us in ways that are consistent with our self-view, and we intentionally avoid others who treat us in ways that are inconsistent with our self-view (Robinson & Smith-Lovin, 1992). By choosing friends who confirm our self-view and by keeping our distance from those who contradict that self-view, we make self-confirmatory feedback more likely and we make self-disconfirmatory feedback less likely.

Despite preventive efforts, self-discrepant feedback does sometimes occur (as it did for the career politician and star athlete). The first line of defense in the effort to maintain a consistent self is to distort that information until it loses its status as discrepant information. In the face of discrepant self-schema feedback, the individual may ask if the feedback is valid, if the source of the feedback is trustworthy, and how important or relevant this feedback is (Crary, 1966; Markus, 1977; Swann, 1983). For example, a student with a self-view of being intelligent but who fails a college course might discredit that feedback by arguing against (1) its validity (i.e., the student scored as unintelligent because she was just too busy to focus), (2) the professor's judgment (i.e., the student felt her professor was a nitwit), and (3) its importance or relevance (i.e., the student feels it is not what she knows, but who she knows that is important). People also counter disconfirming feedback with compensatory self-inflation (Greenberg & Pyszczynski, 1985) and with compensatory self-affirmation (Steele, 1988). The effectiveness of these defense mechanisms depends on whether convincing counter-examples are readily available for reinforcing the preexisting self-views (Eisenstadt & Leippe, 1994). All these means for maintaining self-concept consistency have in common the marshaling forward of counter-examples and counter-explanations that essentially discredit the otherwise self-discrepant feedback.

In those domains in which experience is relatively rich and consistent, self-schemas are relatively stable; in those domains in which experience is sparse or contradictory, self-schemas exist in a state of flux and therefore are susceptible to change (Swann, 1983, 1985). An individual's confidence that his self-schema is valid and true constitutes "self-concept certainty" (Harris & Snyder, 1986). In effect, self-concept certainty anchors stable self-schemas. When self-concept certainty is high, discrepant feedback rarely changes a self-schema but rather leads only to a slight lowering of self-schema certainty (Swann, 1983). When self-concept certainty is low, discrepant feedback can instigate self-schema change. Conflict between an uncertain self-schema and discrepant feedback instigates a "crisis self-verification" (Swann, 1983): How does one verify the accuracy of her self-view, given contradictory feedback? People resolve the self-verification crisis by seeking

FIGURE 10.1 **Process of Self-Verification and Self-Concept Change**

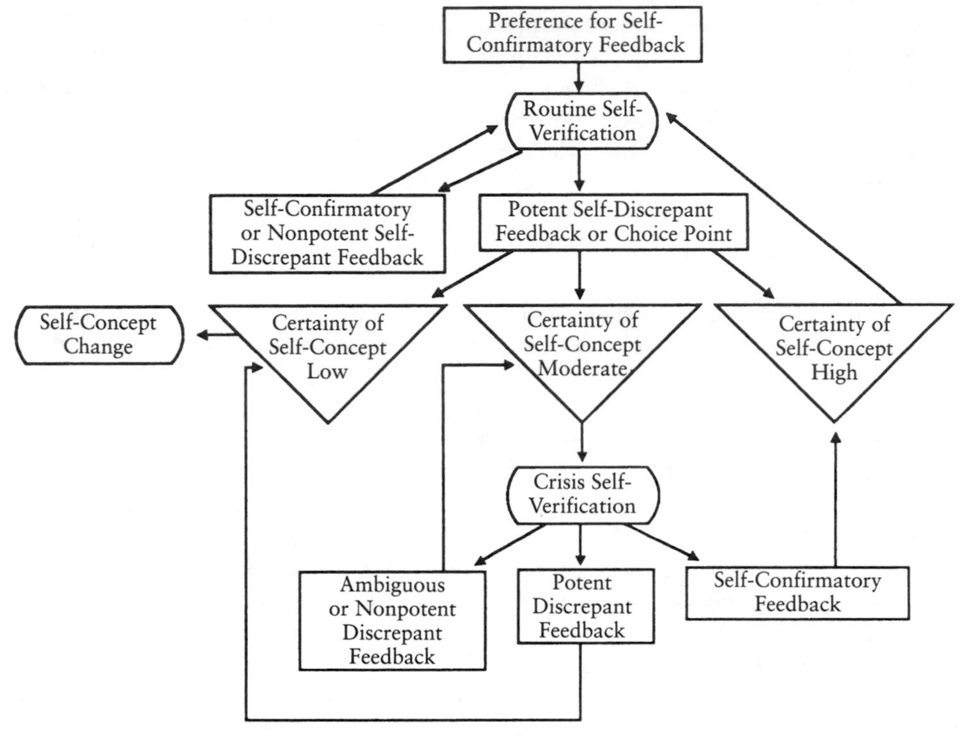

SOURCE: From "Bringing Social Reality Into Harmony With Self," by W. B. Swann Jr., 1983, in J. Suls and A. Greenwald (Eds.), *Psychological Perspectives on the Self* (Vol. 2, pp. 33–66). Hillsdale, NJ: Lawrence Erlbaum.

out additional domain-relevant feedback (Swann, 1983), a sort of "best two out of three to break the tie" approach for figuring out who they are.

The self-verification process is illustrated in Figure 10.1. Individuals start with a representation of self (a self-schema) and a preference for self-confirmatory feedback that leads to routine self-verification behaviors in everyday life. Social feedback, however, is not always self-confirming and in fact can be mildly self-disconfirmatory (i.e., nonpotent self-discrepant feedback in Figure 10.1) or even strongly self-disconfirmatory (potent self-discrepant feedback in Figure 10.1; Swann, 1983). People handle mild self-discrepant information rather well (Swann & Hill, 1982), as discussed earlier with the marshaling forward of counter-evidence. Mild self-discrepant feedback is therefore rather easily integrated into routine self-verification. The effect of strong disconfirming feedback on self-schema change, however, is not so easily integrated and depends on self-concept certainty. When self-concept certainty is low, potent feedback can overwhelm preexisting self-schemas and instigate either self-concept change or the crisis self-verification process.

When self-concept certainty is high, however, potent feedback is evaluated as only one piece of information in the context of a lifetime of historical information. (For example, "I was outgoing this time, but I was not outgoing on 100 occasions in the past; therefore, I still think I am shy, all things considered."

Before self-schemas change, (1) self-concept certainty must be relatively low and (2) self-discrepant feedback must be unambiguous, potent, and consistent—that is, difficult to discredit (Swann, 1983, 1985, 1987). The fact that social feedback can change a self-schema leads to a portrait of the self that is, in part, an architect of its own design (via self-verification processes) and a consequence of the feedback of others and the social world (McNulty & Swann, 1994).

Possible Selves

Self-schemas sometimes change in response to social feedback. But self-schemas change by a second, more proactive and intentional way as well. Self-schema change can occur through a deliberate effort to advance the present self toward a desired future possible self. Possible selves represent individuals' ideas of what they would like to become, what they might become, and what they are afraid of becoming (Markus & Nurius, 1986). Some hoped-for selves might include, for instance, the successful self, the creative self, the rich self, the thin self, or the popular self; some feared selves might include the unemployed self, the disabled self, the overweight self, or the rejected self.

Possible selves are mostly social in their origin, as the individual observes others and makes an inference of becoming a desired self based on the success of a similar other in obtaining that desired-self image (Markus & Nurius, 1986). For instance, a child might watch performers in a musical and aspire to be a singer. Possible selves do not always arise from our observations of positive models, though, as a person might read in the newspaper of massive job layoffs and imply that she too could become unemployed.

The self-schemas discussed in the previous section represent the past and present self. Possible selves represent the future, desired self (or the future, dreaded self). The motivational function of a possible self operates just like that of a goal. A possible self provides the individual with an attractive incentive for which to strive. A possible self can therefore act as a potent impetus for action by energizing effort and persistence and by directing attention and strategic planning (see chapter 7).

Possible selves add an important piece of the puzzle in understanding how the self develops. Possible selves are essentially mental representations of attributes, characteristics, and abilities that the self does not yet possess. (For example, "I would like to become a physician, though I don't know much about human anatomy or surgical techniques.") When the self does not have the evidence or feedback to confirm the emerging possible self, one of two outcomes follows (Markus, Cross, & Wurf, 1990). On the one hand, an absence of supportive evidence (or the presence of disconfirming feedback) will lead the self to reject and abandon the possible self. On the other hand, the possible self can energize and direct action so that the attributes, characteristics, and abilities of the self eventually materialize (Cross & Markus, 1994; Nurius, 1991; Oyserman & Markus, 1990). Thus, the possible self's motivational role is to link the present self with ways to become the possible self. Hence, an individual pursuing a possible self relies little on the present self-schema and much on the hoped-for self, possibly asking the following questions: If I am going to become my possible self, then how should I behave? What activities should I pursue? What education do I need? (Cantor, et al., 1986; Markus & Nurius, 1986; Markus & Wurf, 1987).

The notion of possible selves portrays the self as a dynamic entity with a past, present, and future (Cantor et al., 1986; Day et al., 1994). The individual without a possible self in a particular domain lacks an important cognitive basis for developing and using abilities in that domain (Cross & Markus, 1994). An individual who can envision a possible self in the domain, however, engenders feelings of competence and acts to attain the future view of self (Cross & Markus, 1994; Markus, Cross, & Wurf, 1990). Perhaps, the reader can look back at his or her own effort devoted to college courses and ask the following: To what extent did a possible self relate to each course I completed or dropped, each book I have or have not read, and each lecture I attended or skipped? The presence of a possible self creates a proactive motivation to develop the self in goal-directed ways.

IDENTITY

A second major aspect of self is identity. Identity is the means by which the self relates to society, and it captures the essence of who one is within a cultural context (Deaux et al., 1995; Gecas & Burke, 1995). Of course, people have unique personality traits and strivings, but people also are members of social and cultural groups. Within a cultural context, people assume roles that provide a basis for social identity. For instance, five broad parameters of social identity include (with illustrative roles in parentheses) the following: relationships (friend, grandfather), vocations (musician, salesperson), political affiliations (Republican, liberal), stigma groups (smoker, homeless person), and ethnic groups (Catholic, Southerner; Deaux et al., 1995). In addition to inhabiting roles within these broad parameters, people further find themselves in a host of additional roles, such as student, mother, jogger, and poet. Through identity, these roles have motivational properties.

ROLES

A role consists of cultural expectations for behavior from persons who hold a particular social position (Gross, Mason, & McEachern, 1958). Each of us holds a number of different social positions (roles), and which role we inhabit at any given time depends on the situation we are in and the people with whom we are interacting. For instance, in a college classroom, you probably assume the role of student as you interact with other students and with a professor. When you leave the classroom and go to your job at the psychology clinic, you might assume the role of counselor as you interact with clients. At home, you might assume the role of mother or father who interacts with a daughter.

While assuming one role rather than another, people change how they act—the topic of their conversation, the vocabulary they use, the tone of their voice, and so forth. Behavior varies to such an extent from one role to the next that it makes sense to speak of a set of identities rather than identity. Individuals have many identities, and they present to others the particular identity that is most appropriate for the situation. For instance, if you telephone an office, the person who answers your call is likely assuming a role of a secretary, a receptionist, or a salesperson. Figuring out who you are places a burden on the person answering the phone, and figuring out who the person answering the phone is places a burden on you. Perhaps that sounds silly, but deciding what to say and what to do is actually quite difficult when the identities of the self and others remain in question. Knowing what roles the self and others hold in a given situation tells interactants which behaviors and which ways of interacting are most and least appropriate (Foote, 1951).

Sociologists refer to this process of figuring out roles as the "definition of the situation" (Goffman, 1959; Gonas, 1977). Whenever people participate socially, their first task is to define the roles for the self and for others. Once done, social interaction can proceed to the extent that both interactants agree on their identities and on the definition of the situation.

AFFECT CONTROL THEORY

According to affect control theory (Heise, 1979, 1985; MacKinnon, 1994; Smith-Lovin & Heise, 1988), people act differently from one situation to the next because they inhabit different identities. In affect control theory, the multitude of possible identities anyone is likely to inhabit is reduced to a numerical rating along three dimensions known as EPA: evaluation (E; level of goodness), potency (P; level of powerfulness), and activity (A; level of liveliness; Osgood, May, & Miron, 1975; Osgood, Suci, & Tannenbaum, 1957). For instance, how good, how powerful, and how lively is a teacher? a lawyer? a drug addict? The important point is that one does not need to keep track of a hundred different identities; instead, one needs only to know the "EPA profile" of the identity one inhabits in order to understand identity-motivated action.

EPA scores generally range from –4 to +4 and are described as follows: evaluation—bad to good; potency—weak to strong; and activity—quiet to lively. The numbers 0 to 4 describe the extent of that goodness and badness, weakness and strength, quietness and liveliness. Ratings are defined as follows: 0 is "neutral," 1 is "slightly," 2 is "quite," 4 is "extremely," and 4 is "infinitely."

According to U.S. citizens (the reference culture that decides how good, how powerful, and how active various identities are), the EPA profile for a teacher is 1.5, 1.4, and −0.6. That is, teachers are considered slightly to quite good, slightly powerful, and slightly quiet. The EPA profile for a lawyer is 1.0, 1.7, and 0.2 (someone who is slightly good, quite powerful, and neither lively nor quiet). The EPA profile for a drug addict is −2.0, −1.7, and 0.7 (someone who is quite bad, quite weak, and slightly lively). Consider the EPA (evaluation, potency, and activity) profiles for these additional identities:

Alcoholic	−1.6,	−1.6,	−0.5	Musician	1.3,	0.4,	0.3
Baby	2.5,	−2.3,	2.3	Newcomer	0.9,	0.8,	0.2
Beggar	−1.0,	−2.1,	−1.3	Slob	−1.6,	−1.3,	−0.2
Criminal	−1.8,	−0.3,	1.1	Superstar	−1.0,	2.0,	1.8
Daughter	1.5,	−0.3,	1.2	Teammate	1.4,	1.2,	1.4

Trying to represent an identity by a three-dimensional profile might at first appear cumbersome, but once you get the hang of it, there is much to gain. EPA numerical profiles express a culturally agreed-upon common ground (how good, how powerful, and how active) for understanding any and all possible identities within that culture.

Like identities, the cultural meaning of behaviors and emotions can be expressed in EPA profiles. That is, any action a person takes and any emotion a person expresses can be understood in terms of its cultural meaning—its goodness, its potency, and its liveliness. To "assault" someone is extremely bad, slightly powerful, and quite active (EPA = −3.0, 1.2, 2.0). To "hug" someone is quite good, quite powerful, but not too lively (EPA = 2.3, 1.9, −0.2). The EPA profiles for five behaviors (on the left of the following list) and for five emotions (on the right of the following list) are as follows:

Amuse	1.9,	1.3,	1.3	Anger	−0.8,	0.2,	0.7
Command	−0.3,	2.0,	1.0	Disgust	−1.1,	−0.3,	0.2
Double-cross	−2.5,	0.1,	1.0	Fear	−0.8,	−0.9,	−0.2
Flee	−0.2,	−0.6,	1.3	Happiness	1.6,	0.9,	1.3
Work	0.1,	1.0,	0.5	Sadness	−1.3,	−1.1,	−1.0

These EPA profiles come from multiple data collections in which members of the U.S. culture rated the goodness, potency, and liveliness of many identities, behaviors, and emotions (Heise, 1991). Current EPA profile "dictionaries" exist not only for the U.S. culture but also for those in China, Japan, Canada, and Germany.

Terminology and Dynamics

Affect control theory labels the culturally defined meaning of its various identities as *fundamental sentiments,* which are the EPA profiles for any one particular identity. When identities participate in social interaction, the behaviors and emotions that occur create a *transient impression* of who the person is. Thus, if a teacher (EPA = 1.5, 1.4, −0.6, which is the culture's fundamental sentiment for a teacher) coerces (EPA = −1.0, 1.4, 0.0) a student, the teacher's act of coercing creates a transient impression of who the teacher is: Is this person a teacher (someone with an EPA = 1.5, 1.4, −0.6), or is this person one who coerces (someone with an EPA = −1.0, 1.4, 0.0)? The discrepancy between a culturally defined identity and a behaviorally implied identity creates a motivational state referred to as a *deflection.* Deflections range from nonexistent (identity-confirming behavior) to very large (identity-violating behavior). When they occur, deflections motivate behavior (MacKinnon, 1994) and, once energized, direct behavior in ways that restore the original, culturally defined fundamental sentiment (Smith-Lovin, 1990; Smith-Lovin & Heise, 1988). In affect control theory, deflection is the principal motivational construct.

The affect control principle is basically the following: People behave in ways that minimize affective deflection (MacKinnon, 1994). That is, people create new events (behavior) to maintain old meanings (identity). Deflection acts much the same as does the self-schema consistency process discussed earlier. To minimize affective deflection, people act in ways that maintain their identities and restore those identities when deflections arise (i.e., the consistent self). The following then is the vocabulary of affect control theory: fundamental sentiments, transient impressions, deflection, identity-confirming behaviors, and identity-restoring behaviors. These five constructs are the basis of the following principles:

1. *Fundamental sentiments:* Society defines the fundamental sentiments associated with each of its identities (a teacher is seen by the culture as somewhat nice, somewhat strong, and neither active nor passive).
2. *Transient impressions:* Social interactions create transient impressions of who the person is (a student brings the teacher an apple; this implies that the teacher is someone who is very nice, rather than only somewhat nice).
3. *Deflections:* Discrepancies between fundamental sentiments and transient impressions create deflections (a teacher's identity suggests that she is somewhat nice, but the student's gift suggests that she is instead very nice). A deflection is, essentially, a disruption in the meaning of one's identity.
4. *Identity-confirming behaviors:* People behave as the culture expects a person in that role-identity to behave (a person with an identity corresponding to an EPA profile of 2, 2, 1 engages in behaviors that correspond to an EPA profile of 2, 2, 1).
5. *Identity-restoring behaviors:* Whenever social interaction creates a discrepancy, people use a variety of means (discussed shortly) to remove the deflection and to restore their identity.

ENERGY AND DIRECTION

You may be wondering what EPA profiles have to do with understanding motivation and emotion. The direction for behavior and emotion comes from fundamental sentiments. The energy for (the intensity of) behavior and emotion comes from deflection. Thus, in affect control theory, motivation and emotion produce (1) identity-confirming (i.e., fundamental sentiment-confirming) behaviors and (2) identity-restoring behaviors.

Identity-Confirming Behaviors

Human beings possess a wide range of potential behaviors, but only a subset of those behaviors are appropriate and expected in any one particular setting. Precisely which behaviors and emotions are most appropriate is determined by the identity the person inhabits. That is, for a friend (EPA = 3.0, 1.5, 0.6), the behaviors that are most appropriate are those the culture assigns a similar EPA profile—help (2.2, 1.5, 0.3) and laugh (2.2, 0.8, 1.0). The numbers 2.2, 1.5, 0.3 and 2.2, 0.8, 1.0 are a little bit different from 3.0, 1.5, 0.6 (the EPA profile for a friend), but the point is that the behaviors of help and laugh have EPA profiles that are closer to the EPA profile for friend than are other possible behaviors. Hence, help and laugh are behaviors that are most consistent with someone occupying the identity of friend. For a pest (EPA = −1.8, −0.5, 1.7), however, the behaviors that are most appropriate are disrespect (−2.1, −0.2, 1.1) and annoy (−1.6, 0.0, 1.2). When the cultural meaning of an identity matches the cultural meaning of one's behavior, identity confirmation occurs, the person experiences little affective deflection, and the theory uses constructs like deflection and EPA profiles to illustrate how and why people behave in identity-maintaining ways.

The essence of affect control theory's behavioral predictions in regard to identity-confirming behavior is as follows: Nice identities lead people to behave in nice ways, powerful identities lead people to behave in powerful ways, passive identities lead people to

Reversing Negative Self-Views

Question: Why would a person want to learn about the motivational states discussed in this chapter?
Answer: To ready oneself to help others reverse negative self-views.

People generally respond to social feedback in two ways (Swann & Schroeder, 1995). First, people generally prefer positive feedback. People like praise and adoration, and when they hear praise, it just feels good. But people also desire self-verifying feedback. People want to hear the truth about themselves. For instance, suppose you and a friend are ice skating together. Your friend watches as you stumble around and, as you slip over to the balcony, makes a remark implying you are a klutz. While praise would have sounded good, people with negative self-views ("I'm a clumsy skater") truly want evaluations that confirm and validate their self-view.

People desire verification of their negative self-views, and to get it, they embrace confirming feedback, reject disconfirming feedback, and surround themselves with friends and associates who can act as accomplices in maintaining that negative self-view. In fact, it might be no accident that one reason you are this person's friend is precisely because you are the sort of person who would say something like klutz.

Self-verification is a ubiquitous motivation within the strivings of the self-concept. Males and females equally seek self-verification, and self-verification operates in all domains—intelligence, sociability, athleticism, dominance, depression, and so on (Swann, 1997). But self-verification does not mean "negative feedback" because people with favorable self-views also seek verification of their goodness. It is just hard to notice self-verification among people with positive self-views because self-enhancement and self-verification feedback will sound just the same (i.e., praise). The motive for self-verification becomes apparent when the person's self-view is negative because self-enhancement (praise) will sound very different from self-verification (criticism; Robinson & Smith-Lovin, 1992).

This chapter provides reasons why and ways in which people seek self-verification (e.g., the self-verification crisis in Figure 10.1, selective interaction, the consistent self). But what can a person do to reverse a negative self-view in another person (or in oneself)? To start with, such a self-appointed therapist would not want to make the mistake of underestimating the strength of the motivation to self-verify. Praising someone with a negative self-view leads rather predictably to a reaction along the lines of the following: "I like the favorable evaluation, but I am not sure that it is

behave in passive ways, and so on. Affect control theory is an identity-maintenance theory (Robinson & Smith-Lovin, 1992).

Identity-Restoring Behaviors

When situational events cause deflection from one's identity, the individual initiates restorative actions to bring affectively disturbing events back in line with his established correct. It sounds good, but . . ." (Swann, Stein-Seroussi & Giesler, 1992). Therefore, people generally do not embrace such doubtful feedback. Also, when a person with a negative self-view hears enhancing feedback (e.g., compliment, praise), she may very well be motivated to act in a way that proves the validity of the negative self-view (Robinson & Smith-Lovin, 1992). For instance, Marsha Linehan (1997) uses this logic for explaining the reasons a therapist's verbal affirmation is routinely unsuccessful in the attempts to change the negative self-views of drug abusers.

Figure 10.1 suggests the possible strategy of working to undermine the person's self-concept certainty (instead of working on the person's self-schema directly). But the most fruitful advice is first to make sure that the negative self-view is incorrect. When people who see themselves as clumsy, stupid, unworthy, and incompetent are in fact incorrect and are overly self-defensive, then a couple of strategies exist to help reconstruct an unnecessarily negative self-view.

One strategy that creates some potential room for self-concept change is to present extreme self-verification feedback. For instance, Bill Swann (1997) provides the example of suggesting to a generally unassertive person that he is a "complete doormat." The hope is that the person with a "generally unassertive" self-view will behaviorally resist the identity (e.g., will counter-argue, will show rebuttal "signs and symbols" of who they are). But the most promising strategy for creating potential room for self-concept change is to gain the self-enhancing support of key interaction partners, such as friends, lovers, relatives, and coworkers. Negative self-views are stabilized by being surrounded by interaction partners that provide negative feedback (e.g., being called a klutz). There is, in addition, some truth to the notion that women with low self-esteem marry men who are highly negative and abusive toward them (Buckner & Swann, 1995). Changing a negative self-view therefore involves changing the social feedback one receives day after day. And social interaction partners are the richest source of that social feedback (Swann & Predmore, 1985). Hence, gaining the cooperation and support of the person's key interaction partners is pivotal if one is to reverse a negative self-view. From this point-of-view, "self-views are not merely psychological structures that exist inside of people, as their hearts, lungs, or livers do; rather, through people's interactions, their self-views become externalized into the social worlds that they construct around themselves" (Swann, 1997).

identity (or with his "fundamental sentiments"). Consider the EPA of a mother (2.7, 1.6, 1.0) versus the EPA of a mother who scolds her child (−1.4, 0.9, 1.0). The changes in EPA profile numbers are generated by a computer program[1] (Heise, 1991). A mother

[1]The affect control theory computer program is available at the following Internet address:
www.indiana.edu/ ~ socpsy/ACT/interact.

who scolds her child becomes less good (2.7 drops to −1.4) and somewhat less powerful (1.6 drops to 0.9). To restore the culturally understood meaning of mother (E = 2.7; P = 1.6), she needs either to perform a good and powerful behavior or to express a good and powerful emotion. Thus, the mother who scolds her child needs subsequently to cuddle (1.7, 1.0, −0.7) or otherwise show she is pleased (1.5, 0.8, 0.8) with her child.

As this example shows, there are two primary ways people restore a deflected identity: through strategic emotion displays and through selective interaction. Consider first how people use strategic emotion displays to restore their identities (Robinson, Smith-Lovin, & Tsoudis, 1994). A teacher who ignores a student can help restore his "overall nice person" image with the student by looking sorrowful, which sends an identity-restoring message that expresses regret. Emotion displays create transient impressions, and these transient impressions act as identity cues such that good people who act bad should show sorrow if they are truly good people (just as bad people who act bad should show no such sorrow if they are truly bad people). If a good person commits a bad act and does not show remorse, an observer is left to wonder whether that person really is a good person or not.

Using post-behavioral displays of emotion to draw inferences about people's identity or character plays itself out over and over again in the drama of the courtroom. Jurors often must infer the underlying character of a stranger who allegedly committed some deviant act. The juror must decide whether this is a good person who got involved in an unfortunate accident or a bad person who committed some heinous crime (Robinson et al., 1994). The answer to the character question lies in the person's publicly expressed emotion display. Good people should display deep remorse following a deviant act (because the identity-behavior deflection should be very high), whereas bad people should display little post-behavior remorse (because the identity-behavior deflection would be too low to generate an identity-restoring emotional display). Notice here that the behavior is known, the emotion is observed, and the underlying identity is the only unknown. The mental calculus is to use the behavior and emotion in figuring out what the underlying character of the defendant must be. This is precisely why affect control theory uses all those EPA profile numbers.

Consider also how people restore their identities by selectively choosing those with whom they do and do not want to interact (Robinson & Smith-Lovin, 1992). In selective interaction, people seek those interaction partners they think are most likely to confirm, or verify, their identities and avoid those interaction partners they think are most likely to disconfirm their identities (McNulty & Swann, 1994; Robinson & Smith-Lovin, 1992; Swann, 1987, 1990; Swann, Hixon, & De La Ronde, 1992). Individuals who have a positive identity seek interaction partners (including friends, roommates, tutors, teachers, spouses, teammates, and so on) who will treat them in a positive way. Individuals with negative identities seek interaction partners who will treat them in a negative way. Similarly, individuals with powerful identities seek interaction partners who will treat them in a power-confirming way. That is, as a rule, people seek out interaction partners who confirm their identities, irrespective of whether or not that identity is a culturally valued one (Swann, Pelham, & Krull, 1989). You might wonder how this can be and why this is. The answer lies in the identity negotiation process in which people use social interactions to maintain, verify, and restore their identities (Swann, 1987).

Why People Self-Verify

The self prefers feedback that confirms or verifies its self-schemas and social identities. Self-verification theory (Swann, 1983, 1990, 1992a) assumes that the key to smooth interpersonal relationships is the individual's ability to recognize how other people and society in general perceive the self. The self notices how others respond to it and internalizes these social and cultural responses into a self-concept and into a sense of identity. Stable self-concepts and identities play such a central role in the self's negotiation of social reality that the self comes to prefer social feedback that confirms its self-schemas and identities (Swann, 1992a, 1992b). People with positive self-views prefer to hang out with friends who augment positive feedback and buffer negative feedback; people with negative self-views prefer to hang out with friends who buffer positive feedback and augment negative feedback (Robinson & Smith-Lovin, 1992; Swann, 1992a, 1992b; Swann, et al., 1990; Swann, Pelham, & Krull, 1989; Swann, Wenzlaff, & Tafarodi, 1992).

People prefer self-verification feedback for both cognitive and pragmatic reasons. On the cognitive side, people self-verify because they seek to know themselves (to be true to oneself). On the pragmatic side, people self-verify because they wish to avoid interactions that might be fraught with misunderstandings and unrealistic expectations and performance demands; they seek interaction partners who know what to expect from them and therefore ensure smooth interactions (Swann, 1992a).

AGENCY

The self presented thus far has been a highly cognitive and social one. But the self goes deeper than just cognitive structures and social relationships (Ryan, 1993). Within the self is an intrinsic motivation that gives it an agency quality. This section presents a view of self "as action and development from within, as innate processes and motivations" (Deci & Ryan, 1991).

The self does not enter into the world tabula rasa—an empty slate—awaiting life experiences to endow it with a self-concept and cultural identities. Rather, the newborn possesses a rudimentary self characterized by inherent needs, developmental processes, preferences, and capacities for interacting with the environment. As the newborn taps into her inborn capacities (e.g., walking, talking, intrinsic motivation), the self begins the lifelong process of discovering, developing, and fulfilling her potential. In doing so, the self begins to advance away from heteronomy (a dependence on others) and toward autonomy (a reliance on self; Ryan, 1993).

SELF AS ACTION AND DEVELOPMENT FROM WITHIN

Chapter 4 discussed the organismic psychological needs of self-determination, competence, and relatedness—needs that provide a natural motivational force to foster agency (i.e., initiative, action). Intrinsic motivation is inseparably coordinated with the active nature of the developing self (Deci & Ryan, 1991). It is the source of motivation underlying agency as it spontaneously energizes people to pursue their interests, seek out environmental challenges, exercise their skills, and develop their talents.

Differentiation and Integration

Differentiation and integration are two processes inherent within agency that guide development. Differentiation expands and elaborates the self into an ever-increasing complexity. Integration synthesizes that emerging complexity into a coherent whole, thereby preserving a sense of a single, cohesive self.

Differentiation proceeds as the individual exercises existing interests, preferences, and capacities in such a way that a relatively general and undifferentiated self becomes specialized into several life domains. For an illustration, consider your own history in which you learned that not all computers are alike, not all sports are alike, not all politicians are alike, not all relationships are alike, and not all religions are alike. Minimal differentiation manifests itself in simplicity in which the person has only a unidimensional understanding of a particular domain of knowledge; rich differentiation manifests itself in understanding fine discriminations and unique aspects of a particular life domain. Intrinsic motivation, interests, and preferences motivate the self to interact with the world in such a way that sets the stage for the self to differentiate into an ever-increasing complexity (e.g., the child with an interest in model airplanes skims through catalogues, attends club meetings, talks with peers about model building, subscribes to a topical magazine, experiments with new materials and with various construction techniques, and basically develops specialized skills while learning).

Differentiation does not expand the complexity of the self unabated. Rather, there exists a synthetic tendency to integrate the self's emerging complexity into a single sense of self, into a coherent unity. Integration is an organizational process that brings the self's differentiated parts together. Integration occurs as the self's individual parts (i.e., self-schemas, identities, interests, and so on) are successfully interrelated and organized as mutually complementary. One example of the interplay between differentiation and integration can be found in a study that asked young and old adults to list their possible selves and also what actions they took to realize them (Cross & Markus, 1991). The younger adults listed many more possible selves (showing strong differentiation), while the older adults took more actions to realize specific possible selves (showing more integration). Thus, younger adults explored and experimented with many possible selves, while the older adults, who had completed this experimental and expansive process, focused on a more cohesive, well-defined self (integration).

The notions of agency (via intrinsic motivation), differentiation, and integration argue that the self possesses innate aspects. Psychological needs and developmental processes provide a starting point for the development of the self. As individuals mature, they gain increasing contact with the social context, and some of these aspects of the social world become assimilated and integrated into the self-system. The motivational portrayal of self-development therefore argues strongly against the idea that the self is merely a passive recipient of the social world's feedback (self-schemas) and identities (places in the social order). An understanding of the developing self therefore begins by adopting the frame of reference of the individual rather than that of the society (Deci & Ryan, 1991; Ryan, 1993). The need for relatedness, however, keeps the individual close to societal concerns and regulations, and the self therefore develops both toward autonomy as well as toward an internalization of society's values and concerns.

Internalization

With its inherent needs and emerging interests, preferences, potentials, and capacities, the self is poised to grow, develop, and differentiate. But behaviors, emotions, and ways of thinking originate not only within the self but also within the social context and society. As a person plays, studies, works, performs, and interacts with others, these other people request that this person comply with particular ways of behaving, feeling, and thinking. Thus, intentional acts (i.e., agency) sometimes arise from the self, but intentional acts also sometimes arise from the guidance and recommendations of others. Hence, all intentional acts involve some degree of involvement of the self (Deci & Ryan, 1985a, 1991), and the process through which individuals take in and accept as their own an externally prescribed way of thinking, feeling, or behaving is referred to as *internalization* (Ryan & Connell, 1989; Ryan, Rigby, & King, 1993). Internalization refers to the process through which an individual transforms a formerly externally prescribed way of behaving or valuing into an internal one (Ryan et al., 1993).

Internalization is an outcome of organismic integration, as it occurs from the individual's desire to achieve meaningful relationships with friends, parents, teachers, coaches, employers, clergy, family, and others (via the relatedness need) and to interact effectively with the social world (via the competence need). Through internalization, external ways of thinking, feeling, and behaving become represented as internal ways of thinking, feeling, and behaving. Such internalization has adaptive interpersonal value for the self, as it promotes greater unity between the self and society, such as in the close relationships between parent and child, teacher and student, and so on (Ryan, 1993).

The contribution of agency to portray the self as action and development from within is to recognize that (1) human beings possess a core self, one energized by innate motivation and directed by the inherent processes of differentiation and integration, and (2) not all self-structures are equally authentic; while some reflect the core self, others reflect and reproduce the society (Deci, et al., 1994; Deci & Ryan, 1985a, 1991; Ryan, 1991, 1993; Ryan & Connell, 1989).

COGNITIVE DISSONANCE

Most people harbor a rather favorable view of themselves. Most people see themselves as competent, moral, and reasonable. Such a self-view is represented cognitively as a set of beliefs about the self. Sometimes, however, people engage in behavior that leaves them feeling stupid, immoral, and unreasonable. For instance, people smoke cigarettes, litter, tell white lies, neglect to recycle, fail to wear condoms during sex, drive their cars recklessly, skip classes, act rudely toward strangers, and engage in other such hypocritical conduct. When beliefs about who the self is and what the self does are inconsistent (i.e., believing one thing, yet actually behaving in the opposite way), people experience a psychologically uncomfortable state referred to as "cognitive dissonance" (Aronson, 1969, 1992, 1999; Festinger, 1957; Gerard, 1992; Harmon-Jones & Mills, 1999).

Two beliefs are consonant when one belief follows from the other (being a moral person and telling the truth); two beliefs are dissonant when the opposite of one belief follows from the other (being a moral person but lying). Just how psychologically uncomfortable dissonance is depends on its magnitude. When intense and uncomfortable enough, dissonance takes on motivational properties, and the person begins to seek ways to eliminate, or at least reduce, the dissonance.

Imagine the following scenario of a woman whose sense of self includes pro-environmental beliefs. She believes in clean water, clean air, clean land, energy conservation, and nature preservation. And she believes that polluted air, polluted land, energy consumption, and overdevelopment are immoral and unreasonable. Her pro-environmental beliefs are all consonant with one another (i.e., believing in clear water is consistent with believing in nature preservation). But suppose she reads an article in the newspaper that says that automobile exhaust fumes are rapidly and irreversibly depleting the ozone layer. Further, according to the article, used automobile tires are littering the rivers and crowding the landfills. Suppose further that this environmentalist drives her car to work every day, and she needs her car for many additional purposes as well. She loves the environment, but she needs her environment-destroying car. She believes one thing, but she does another. Believing one thing and doing another has an air of hypocrisy, and it is this experience of hypocrisy between self and action that causes dissonance (Aronson, 1999; Fried & Aronson, 1995).

The experience of dissonance is psychologically aversive (Elliot & Devine, 1994). People seek to reduce the feeling of discomfort. They do so in one of four ways[2] (Festinger, 1957; Harmon-Jones & Mills, 1999; Simon, Greenberg, & Brehm, 1995):

- Remove the dissonant belief
- Reduce the importance of the dissonant belief
- Add new consonant belief
- Increase the importance of the consonant belief

Our environmentalist, for instance, might (1) quit driving her car and start riding a bicycle, or she might come to believe that volcano ash, not automobile exhaust, is responsible for the hole in the ozone layer (thereby removing the dissonant belief); (2) trivialize her immoral or unreasonable act of driving by justifying that her driving to work will have no impact on the global condition, especially when considering how much worse pollution is at the factories and refineries (thereby reducing the importance of the dissonant belief; Simon, Greenberg, & Brehm, 1995); (3) read articles that reassure her that science is hard at work and will soon solve the pollution problem, or she might think of how truly enjoyable and useful it is to drive her car (thereby adding a new consonant belief, or two); or (4) think to herself that car exhaust proves that the city needs more bike trails, and the government needs emission-control device laws for all automobiles (thereby increasing the importance of the consonant belief). How resistant to change these beliefs are depends on (1) how close to reality they are (e.g., Will science really find a solution?), (2) how important or central they are to one's view of the self (Simon et al., 1995; Thibodeau & Aronson, 1992), and (3) how much pain and cost must be endured

---

[2] This list of four dissonance-reducing behaviors is not comprehensive. For instance, another way people reduce dissonance is by adding an irrelevant belief, which is another way of saying that people rationalize what they do.

(e.g., How painful will it be to quit driving a car?). Therefore, reality, importance, and personal costs work to support one's current beliefs, while dissonance stirs up a belief system that puts pressure on those ways of thinking and those ways of behaving that are least resistant to change. It is a psychological competition—reality versus dissonance—with motivational implications.

DISSONANCE-AROUSING SITUATIONS

Human beings frequently encounter information that is dissonant with their beliefs and values, and they sometimes engage in behavior that is dissonant with their beliefs and values. Four specific situations and ways of behaving illustrate dissonance-arousing circumstances: choice, insufficient justification, effort justification, and new information. In reading through the paragraphs that follow, notice how circumstantial information and little-justified ways of behaving generate the dissonance motivation that pressures people to change their attitudes, beliefs, or values.

Choice

People often choose between alternatives. In some cases, the choice between alternatives is easy, as the merits of one alternative far outweigh the merits of its rival. In other cases, the choice is not so easy, as both alternatives offer a number of advantages and disadvantages. If a person is choosing between apartments, this person must consider that one might be in a convenient location but expensive while the other might be in an inconvenient location but inexpensive. Once such a difficult choice is made, people experience dissonance. After a decision, the negative aspects of the chosen alternative and the positive aspects of the rejected alternative are dissonant with the choice just made. In other words, as soon as the choice for one apartment is made, the decision maker must face the facts that the chosen apartment has a small kitchen and that the other apartment was cheaper. Given dissonance (or "post-decision regret"), the person engages in cognitive work to manipulate the relative desirability of the two alternatives. Dissonance is resolved by viewing the chosen alternative more positively and the rejected alternative more negatively (Brehm, 1956; Gilovich, Medvec, & Chen, 1995; Knox & Inkster, 1968; Younger, Walker, & Arrowood, 1977).

To illustrate the fact that people do indeed reduce dissonance by appreciating their choice and depreciating rejected alternatives, simply ask a person both *before* and *after* acting on a difficult choice the following question: "How sure are you that your choice is the correct one?" Whether the choice involves deciding between restaurants, classes, or marriage partners, post-choice decision makers are invariably more confident in the wisdom of their choices than are those still in the decision process. Post-choice individuals engage in dissonance-motivated cognitive work to value their chosen alternative and to devalue their rejected alternative.[3]

---

[3] A good illustration of this phenomenon is the often heard (yet absurd) quote from a person looking back on life, "If I had to live my life over again, I wouldn't change a thing—not where I lived, what school I attended, who I married, which career I pursued, nor anything I said or did."

Insufficient Justification

Insufficient justification addresses how people explain their actions for which they have little or no external prompting. For example, people might ask themselves why they donated money to a charity or why they stopped to pick up litter.

In one experiment, researchers asked participants to engage in a terribly dull and pointless task (Festinger & Carlsmith, 1959). Afterwards, an experimenter asked each participant to tell the next hour's participants that the task was really quite entertaining. Half of the first participants received $1 for the telling (insufficient justification for lying), while the other half received $20 (sufficient justification for lying). After the participants complied (and they all did), a different experimenter asked each participant to rate how interesting the task was. Deceivers with insufficient justification ($1) reported liking the task significantly more than deceivers with sufficient justification ($20). Those paid the larger amount had little dissonance to wrestle with. ("I know why I lied—to earn the big bucks!") Those paid a measly dollar, however, had to wrestle the dissonance brought on by deceiving another without good reason. ("I don't know why I lied.") With $20 worth of sufficient justification to back up an initial attitude of a boring task, there is little reason to change one's attitude toward the task. With $1 worth of insufficient justification, however, there exists good reason for changing one's attitude toward a greater liking of the task by actually thinking the task was not as boring as once first thought.

Effort Justification

During initiation rituals in the military, fraternities, sororities, athletic teams, neighborhood gangs, and other groups, recruits often exert great effort and perform extreme behaviors that must later be justified. Consider the Army private who parachutes out of an airplane as part of boot-camp training. For novice recruits, parachuting is extreme behavior. To justify why they would put their lives on the line like this, privates typically endorse a rather extreme liking for the behavior. Extreme behaviors breed extreme beliefs: "If I did *that,* then I must really *love* this place!"

Dissonance theory proposes that the attractiveness of a task increases as a direct function of the magnitude of effort expended to complete it. In an experiment, researchers asked college-age women to join a weekly discussion group on the topic of the psychology of sex (Aronson & Mills, 1959). The women underwent either a mild initiation ritual (recite aloud a list of sexual but not obscene words) or a severe initiation ritual (recite aloud a list of obscene words from sexually explicit novels). After completing one initiation ritual or the other, all women participated in a rather dull discussion on an unrelated topic and then rated how interesting that second discussion was. Women in the severe initiation group reported significantly more interest in the discussion than did women in the mild initiation group. Other researchers have found essentially the same result in similar studies (Beauvois & Joule, 1996; Rosenfeld, Giacalone, & Tedeschi, 1984): People who engage in extreme and otherwise unreasonable behavior need extreme values for justifying their otherwise dissonance-arousing behavior (Aronson, 1988).

New Information

As you listen to the radio, watch television, attend lectures, and interact with others, you are exposed to opportunities that might contradict your beliefs. One group of researchers followed the Seekers, a cult-like group convinced that their city and the entire western coast of the Americas would be destroyed by a great flood on a specific day (Festinger, Riecken, & Schachter, 1956, 1958). The specific day of cataclysm came and passed rather uneventfully, so the Seekers found their cherished belief of doom unequivocally disconfirmed. Given belief disconfirmation, what were the dissonance-suffering Seekers to do?

Some Seekers did reject their belief and dropped out of the group. Other Seekers, however, were more rationalizing than rational. They saw the disconfirmation as a test of their commitment to the cause and responded with strong, persistent attempts at proselytizing. By proselytizing to gain new members, the latter group of Seekers attempted to resolve their dissonance by adding new consonant beliefs (i.e., other people who would agree with and support their beliefs).

Motivational Processes Underlying Cognitive Dissonance

People engage in all sorts of behavior that suggests that, given this particular behavior, they must be incompetent, immoral, or unreasonable. Inconsistency between what one believes (being competent) and what one does (acting incompetently) creates the cognitive inconsistency that is dissonance. Being psychologically uncomfortable, people implement various strategies for reducing dissonance (as discussed earlier: remove the dissonant belief, add new consonant belief, etc.). By changing the number of consonant or dissonant cognitions or by changing the level of importance attached to consonant or dissonant cognitions, people reduce, and sometimes even eliminate, dissonance.

But what precisely is the nature of the motivation underlying cognitive dissonance? Several researchers have attempted to pinpoint the nature of dissonance motivation. Some found that one's hypocritical behavior must produce aversive consequences before it produces dissonance (Goethals, Cooper, & Naficy, 1979; Johnson, Kelly, & LeBlanc, 1995). That is, not only does a person litter or drive his car to work, but he also must believe that this littering and driving produces a measure of harm. Another group of researchers found that cognitive dissonance produces a physiological (autonomic nervous system) arousal (Croyle & Cooper, 1983; Elkin & Leippe, 1986; Fazio & Cooper, 1983; Losch & Cacioppo, 1990; Zanna & Cooper, 1976). That is, believing one thing but doing another is physiologically arousing. Still other researchers found that dissonance produces a negative emotional state, one that operated not at a physiological level but instead at a psychological level (Burris, Harmon-Jones, & Tarpley, 1997; Elliot & Devine, 1994). For instance, when college students were asked to write an essay about the merits of a tuition increase (they believed one thing, yet wrote an essay for its opposite), they reported feeling relatively high levels of psychological discomfort (i.e., feeling uncomfortable, uneasy, and bothered; Elliot & Devine, 1994).

All three of these reasons—aversive consequences, physiological arousal, and psychological arousal—have been criticized as incomplete explanations of dissonance motivation

FIGURE 10.2 **Dissonance Processes**

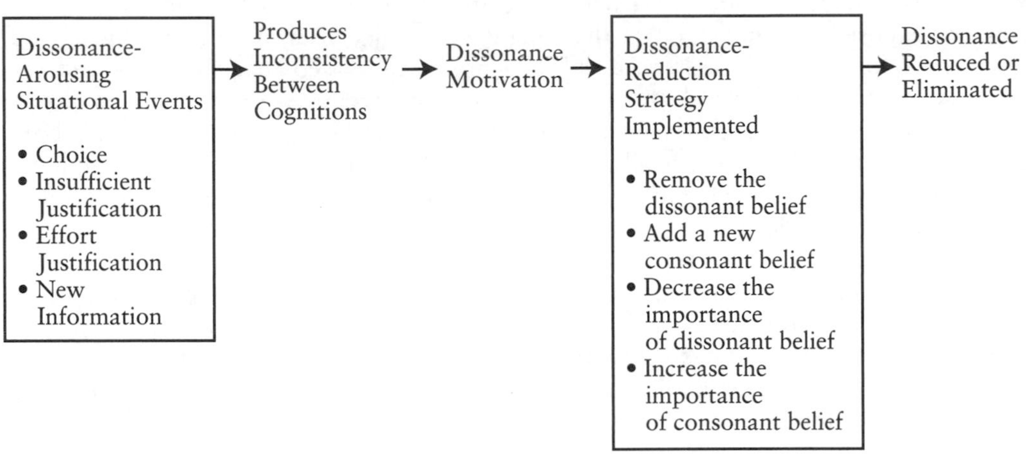

(Harmon-Jones & Mills, 1999). The struggle to pinpoint the precise nature of dissonance motivation is important, however, because it seeks to reveal precisely what is happening in the time between the onset of dissonance and the implementation of a dissonance-reduction strategy. Pinpointing the precise nature of dissonance motivation will allow an understanding of why people change their ways of thinking and believing—because of perceived aversive consequences, negative physiological arousal, or negative emotional arousal (Gerard, 1992; White & Gerard, 1983).

As the debate continues in trying to understand the precise nature of dissonance motivation (Harmon-Jones & Mills, 1999), the sequence of events depicted in Figure 10.2 explains most of the data. With cognitive consistency (what one believes is the same as what one does), action flows from the self in ways that are effective and nonconflicting. When people encounter information that is inconsistent with their self-view, negative emotion is aroused because one is left unsure of what to think or how to act. As one thinks about the self and as one prepares for future action, dissonance generates a negative emotional state that interferes with effective and smooth action. Feeling uncomfortable puts pressure on people's ways of thinking and behaving. In general, it is easier to engage in cognitive work and just change one's belief (believing that smoking will not kill you because you feel you will probably die of some freak accident before the cancer has a chance to set in). However, some beliefs are very important to the self, and dissonance is more likely to put pressure on people's behavior (feeling that you are *really* pro-environment and that you will stop driving your car or at least drive it less often). Therefore, dissonance as a motivational state revolves mostly around eliminating a rather ephemeral negative emotional state so that thinking and behaving can proceed in ways that are effective, smooth, and nonconflicting (Jones & Gerard, 1967; Gerard, 1992; Harmon-Jones, 1999).

Most dissonance researchers portray dissonance motivation through the analogy of pain—the person changes beliefs or behaviors in order to eliminate the aversive, persistent, and uncomfortable experience. But this characterization of dissonance as an aversive motivational state is not all gloom and doom. Dissonance can be used to accomplish wonderfully productive social goals. For instance, using a dissonance framework, researchers have been successful in changing people's attitudes and behaviors toward pro-social causes such as using condoms during sex (Aronson, Fried, & Stone, 1991), conserving natural resources (e.g., water; Dickerson, et al., 1992), and reducing prejudice (Leippe & Eisenstadt, 1994). In this latter experiment, researchers asked White college students to write a counter-attitudinal essay endorsing a university scholarship policy that favored African-American students at some cost to White students. After writing the pro-African-American essay, researchers measured and found that White students had significantly changed their attitudes in a direction that was more favorable toward African Americans. Writing the essay (believing one thing, but doing its opposite) put pressure on White students' beliefs. Because they could not undo their behavior (i.e., writing the essay), they changed (undid) their attitudes.

The findings from this study, like many others, allows dissonance theory to be summarized succinctly in the following phrase: "Saying, or doing, is believing." Such is one way to change people's attitudes toward pro-social causes. For instance, if you join your friend while she walks in the multiple sclerosis walk-a-thon, your attitude toward patients with multiple sclerosis will probably start to change for the better (i.e., add new consonant belief to justify the effort).

SELF-PERCEPTION THEORY

An alternative interpretation of cognitive dissonance is that people do not develop and change their beliefs in response to a negative emotional state born in cognitive contradiction (i.e., dissonance) but, rather, from self-observations of their behavior. For example, we eat squid for whatever reason (maybe we did not know it was squid because the restaurant referred to it as calamari) and after doing so presume that since we ate squid, we must therefore like it. Acquiring or changing attitudes via self-observations of one's own behavior is the basic tenet to self-perception theory (Bem, 1967, 1972; Bem & McConnell, 1970).

Both cognitive dissonance theory and self-perception theory revolve around the tenet that "saying, or doing, is believing." The difference between the two theories is that cognitive dissonance theory argues that beliefs change because of negative affect from cognitive inconsistencies, whereas self-perception theory argues that we simply believe whatever we do and say.

The dissonance versus self-perception debate generated a great deal of research (Elliot & Devine, 1994; Fazio, Zanna, & Cooper, 1977, 1979; Ronis & Greenwald, 1979; Ross & Shulman, 1973; Snyder & Ebbesen, 1972; Zanna & Cooper, 1976). The conclusion was that both cognitive dissonance and self-perception theories are correct, but the two theories apply best to a different set of circumstances. Self-perception theory is more applicable to situations in which people's beliefs are initially vague, ambiguous, and weak.

In such cases, people do indeed draw inferences from their behavior. For example, suppose you go to the supermarket to buy hand lotion but have little or no brand preference. After you pick brand X instead of brand Y, by chance or because of a coupon or because it cost less, the next time you tend to buy the same lotion because you bought it the first time, you must then, therefore, prefer that brand. On the other hand, dissonance theory applies best to situations in which people's beliefs are initially clear, salient, and strong. In those cases, people do indeed experience negative emotion following counter-attitudinal behavior.

SUMMARY

Three basic problems occupy the self: defining and creating the self, relating the self to society, and discovering and developing its potential. This chapter presented these problems as self-concept (defining the self), identity (relating the self to society), and agency (developing personal potential). The notions of self-concept, identity, and agency tell the story of how the self generates motivation by highlighting the self's cognitive structures, social relationships, and strivings from within.

Self-schemas are cognitive generalizations about the self that are domain specific and are learned from past experience. The self-concept is a collection of domain-specific self-schemas (e.g., how people mentally represent their personal characteristics in domains such as cognitive competence and interpersonal relationships). Self-schemas generate motivation in two ways: the consistent self and the possible self. For the consistent self, self-schemas direct behavior to confirm the self-view and to prevent episodes that generate feedback that might disconfirm that self-view. In other words, behavior is used to verify one's self-concept. For the possible self, the individual observes others and forecasts a view of the future self that the person would very much like to become. Possible selves generate a proactive source of motivation for developing and growing toward particular goals or aspirations.

Identity is the means by which the self relates to society, and it captures the essence of who the self is within a cultural context. Affect control theory explains how identities motivate behavior such that cultural values (how good, how powerful, how active) direct behavior, while affective deflections (between fundamental sentiments and transient impressions) energize behavior. Once people assume social roles (e.g., mother, bully), their identities direct their behaviors in ways that express the role-identity's cultural value. Thus, a physician is helpful and kind, rather than hostile or cruel, because these behaviors exemplify the identity of doctor. When identities act in identity-confirming ways, social interactions flow smoothly. When identities act in identity-conflicting ways, however, affective deflection occurs. Deflection is a motivational force that energizes identity-restoring courses of action, such as strategic emotion display and selective interaction.

The self also possesses motivation of its own, or agency. Its activity emerges spontaneously from intrinsic motivation, and its development proceeds through the processes of differentiation and integration. Intrinsic motivation, which is inherent within psychological needs, energizes the self to exercise and develop its inherent capabilities. Differentiation occurs as the self exercises interests, preferences, and capacities in such a way that a relatively general self becomes differentiated into specific domains. Integration of the self occurs as these differentiated parts are brought together into a sense of unity. The process is a dynamic one in which intrinsic motivation, differentiation, integration, and internalization of social experience all contribute to the ongoing development and growth of the self.

Cognitive dissonance theory focuses on the motivational implications of attitude-behavior contradictions and of hypocrisy. Its basic tenets are that people dislike inconsistency, that the experience of dissonance is psychologically aversive, and that people seek to reduce dissonance by striving to maintain consistency in their thoughts, beliefs, attitudes, opinions, values, and behaviors. Four common dissonance-arousing situations include making a choice, insufficient justification, effort justification, and new information. These situations all lead people into self-observations of believing one thing but actually doing its opposite. Once aroused, dissonance motivates people to change their beliefs or behaviors much in the same way that pain motivates people to take action. Dissonance motivation, when intense enough to motivate the person to action, gives rise to one or more of the following four dissonance-reducing coping strategies: Remove the dissonant belief, reduce the importance of the dissonant belief, add a new consonant belief, or increase the importance of the consonant belief. Changing one's belief is the most common way of reducing dissonance (e.g., "Saying, or doing, is believing"). But some beliefs are important to the self, and this sense of self-definition puts pressure on people to change their behaviors in ways that will be consistent with that self-view (e.g., either changing one's self-view of being an environmentalist or discontinue driving one's air-polluting automobile).

RECOMMENDED READINGS

Self-Functioning

Baumeister, R. F. (1987). How the self became a problem: A psychological review of historical research. *Journal of Personality and Social Psychology, 52,* 163–176.

Ryff, C. D. (1989). Happiness is everything, or is it? Explorations on the meaning of psychological well-being. *Journal of Personality and Social Psychology, 57,* 1069–1081.

Self-Concept

Markus, H. (1977). Self-schemata and processing information about the self. *Journal of Personality and Social Psychology, 35,* 63–78.

Markus, H., & Nurius, P. (1986). Possible selves. *American Psychologist, 41,* 954–969.

Swann, W. B., Jr. (1987). Identity negotiation: Where two roads meet. *Journal of Personality and Social Psychology, 53,* 1038–1051.

Identity

MacKinnon, N. J. (1994). Affect control theory. In *Symbolic interactionism as affect control* (Chapter 2, pp. 15–40). Albany, NY: SUNY Press.

Robinson, D. T., & Smith-Lovin, L. (1992). Selective interaction as a strategy for identity maintenance: An affect control model. *Social Psychology Quarterly, 55,* 12–28.

Smith-Lovin, L. (1991). An affect control view of cognition and emotion. In J. A. Howard and P. L. Callero (Eds.), *The self-society dynamic: Cognition, emotion, and action* (pp. 143–169). New York: Cambridge University Press.

Agency

Deci, E. L., & Ryan, R. M. (1991). A motivational approach to self: Integration in personality. In R. Dienstbier (Ed.), *Nebraska symposium on motivation: Perspectives on motivation* (Vol. 38, pp. 237–288). Lincoln: University of Nebraska.

Ryan, R. M. (1993). Agency and organization: Intrinsic motivation, autonomy, and the self in psychological development. In J. E. Jacobs (Ed.), *Nebraska symposium on motivation: Perspectives on motivation* (Vol. 40, pp. 1–56). Lincoln: University of Nebraska.

Cognitive Dissonance

Aronson, E. (1992). The return of the oppressed: Dissonance theory makes a comeback. *Psychological Inquiry, 3,* 303–311.

Gerard, H. (1992). Dissonance theory: A cognitive psychology with an engine. *Psychological Inquiry, 3,* 323–327.

Goethals, G. R., Cooper, J., & Naficy, A. (1979). Role of foreseen, foreseeable, and unforeseeable consequences in the arousal of cognitive dissonance. *Journal of Personality and Social Psychology, 37,* 1179–1185.

Harmon-Jones, E., & Mills, J. (1999). An introduction to cognitive dissonance theory and an overview of current perspectives on the theory. In *Cognitive dissonance: Progress on a pivotal theory in social psychology* (Chapter 1, pp. 3–21). Washington, DC: American Psychological Association.

Leippe, M. R., & Eisenstadt, D. (1994). Generalization of dissonance reduction: Decreasing prejudice through induced compliance. *Journal of Personality and Social Psychology*, 67, 395–413.

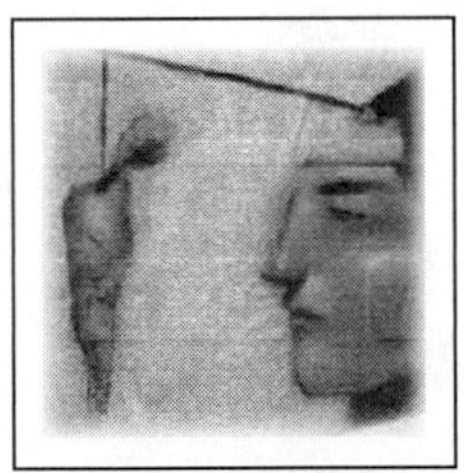

III

Individual Differences

11

Personality Characteristics

Want to jump out of an airplane? How about a spin on a motorcycle? What would you think about traveling to a foreign country and trying to learn how to converse in a foreign language? How about driving in downtown Chicago during rush hour? Would you want to go to a party in which you know most people will behave in ways that are spontaneous? How appealing or how aversive do situations like public speaking, college exams, competitive sports, surfing the Internet, and getting to know strangers sound?

Any situation imaginable provides some measure of stimulation that affects felt arousal, and any situation provides some measure of controllability that affects perceived control. All situations vary in how stimulating and how controllable they are. Of particular importance to the present chapter, individuals too harbor personality dispositions that affect how they respond to the levels of stimulation and controllability within these situations. The theme that runs throughout this chapter is that each of us possesses a cluster of personality characteristics that influences how we feel and how we perform in monotonous versus stimulating situations and in uncontrollable versus controllable situations.

Some people prefer highly arousing situations, while others prefer less arousing ones, and some people perceive and desire a great deal of control over what happens, while others let things happen. Thus, given the situations we find ourselves in, individual differences in arousal and control are important variables in explaining some of why a person performs well or poorly, why emotionality is positive or negative, and why functioning is optimal or unproductive. The personality characteristics presented in this chapter—extraversion, sensation seeking, affect intensity, perceived control, and desire for control—explain why different people have different motivational and emotional states even when they are in the same situation.

One important caution applies throughout the chapter: When the discussion refers to specific individual differences, the reader should remember that relatively few people are at either extreme of the characteristics. A few people are sensation seekers, and a few people are sensation avoiders, but most people are somewhere in the middle, as shown graphically in the top half of Figure 11.1. As illustrated, when a large number of people take the Sensation-Seeking Scale (SSS), about 15% score between 15 and 21, the high end of the SSS. About 15% score between 0 to 7, the low end of the SSS, which identifies sensation avoiders. About 70% of people, however, score between 7 and 15 (the middle) and are therefore identified as neither sensation seekers nor sensation avoiders. Also, beware of typologies, shown in the lower part of Figure 11.1. Typologies categorize people as one type of personality or the other (e.g., as a sensation seeker or as a sensation avoider). In doing so, typologies oversimplify the contribution of personality processes in motivation. Instead, personality characteristics exist within everyone, and this chapter approaches these characteristics as a continuum in which some people score relatively lower or higher than do other people.

AROUSAL

Arousal represents a variety of processes that govern alertness, wakefulness, and activation (Anderson, 1990). These processes are cortical, behavioral, and autonomic mechanisms. Thus, the activity of the brain (cortical), skeletal muscular system (behavioral), and autonomic nervous system (autonomic) together give meaning to the general motivational construct of arousal. Three principles explain arousal's contribution to motivation:

1. Arousal level is mostly a function of how stimulating the environment is.
2. People engage in behavior to increase or decrease their level of arousal.
3. When underaroused, increases in environmental stimulation are pleasurable while decreases are aversive; when overaroused, increases in stimulation are aversive while decreases are pleasurable.

These three principles can be organized together into the so-called "inverted-U" relationship between arousal and performance/well-being (see Figure 11.2). As you will see,

FIGURE 11.1 Individual Differences as Understood Within a Normal Distribution or as a Typology

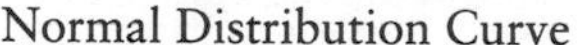

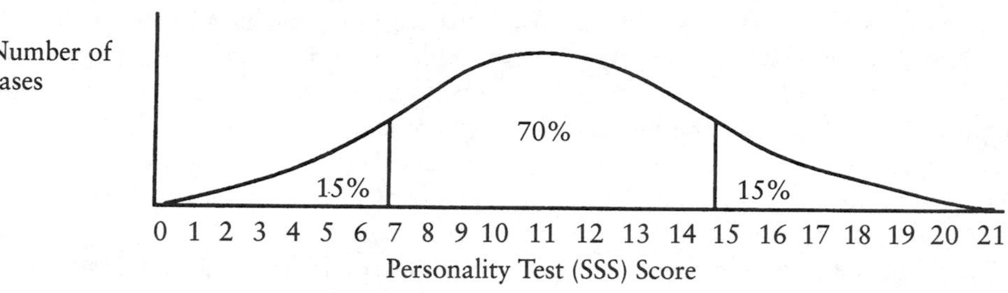

Typology

People are either:

Sensation Seekers (50%)	Sensation Avoiders (50%)

the inverted-U curve, first introduced by Robert Yerkes and John Dodson (1908), helps explain the relationship between felt arousal and ensuing motivational and emotional states (Berlyne, 1967; Duffy, 1957; Hebb, 1955; Lindsley, 1957; Malmo, 1959).

PERFORMANCE AND EMOTION

Arousal and Performance

The inverted-U curve illustrates that a low level of arousal produces relatively poor performance (lower left). As arousal level increases from low to moderate, the intensity and the quality of performance improves. As arousal level continues to increase from moderate to high, performance quality and efficiency (but not intensity) decrease (lower right). Thus, optimal performance is a function of being aroused but not too aroused. To make sense of the arousal-performance relationship, recall your personal performance efficiency while doing something important—public speaking, competing in athletics, or job interviewing, for instance. When nonchalant and underaroused or when anxious and

FIGURE 11.2 **The Inverted-U Curve: Relationship Between Arousal Level and Performance/Well-Being**

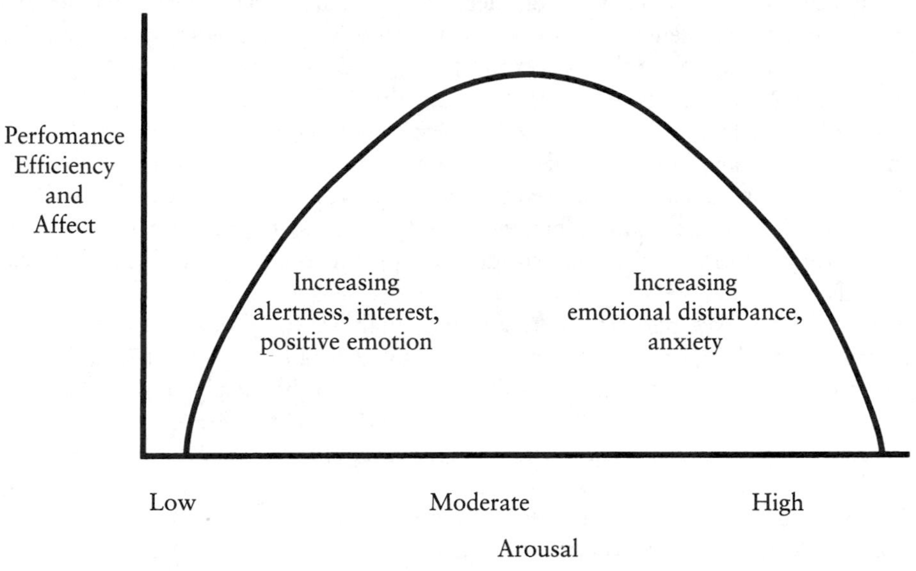

SOURCE: From "Drive and the C. N. S.—Conceptual Nervous System," by D. O. Hebb, 1955, *Psychological Review, 62,* pp. 245–254.

overaroused, performance tends to suffer. When moderately aroused—alert but not tense—performance tends to be optimal.

Arousal and Emotion

A moderate level of arousal coincides with the experience of pleasure (Berlyne, 1967). Low stimulation produces boredom and restlessness; high stimulation produces tension and stress. Both boredom and stress are aversive experiences, and people strive to escape from each. When underaroused and experiencing negative affect, a person will seek out activities that offer increased stimulation, opportunities for exploring something new, and perhaps even risk taking. On the other hand, when arousal is greater than optimal, a person will avoid and is repulsed by further increases in environmental stimulation. When overaroused, increased stimulation, novelty, and risk create negative affect—stress, frustration, and hassle. Overaroused people find themselves attracted to an environmental calm—a vacation, a casual reading of the newspaper, or going for a quiet walk. Thus, the inverted-U curve predicts when increases and decreases in stimulation will lead to positive affect and approach behavior and when they will lead to negative affect and avoidance.

Insufficient Stimulation and Underarousal

Sensory deprivation research illustrates the psychological consequences of being underaroused (Bexton, Heron, & Scott, 1954; Heron, 1957; Zubek, 1969). Sensory deprivation refers to an individual's sensory and emotional experience in a rigidly unchanging environment. In his studies, Woodburn Heron (1957) paid male college students a substantial amount of money per day to lie on a comfortable bed for as many days as they cared to stay (see Figure 11.3). The participant's task was simply to stay in the unchanging environment, with time out for meals and visits to the restroom. To restrict sensory information from touch, participants wore cotton gloves with long cardboard forearm cuffs. They wore a special translucent visor that restricted their visual information. To restrict auditory information, an air conditioner purred out a steady hum that masked most sounds.

Even on the first day, participants reported an inability to think clearly. In the first few hours, participants thought about their work, personal problems, movies, and other experiences. As the hours passed, many reported experiencing blank periods (running out of things to think of), and others just let their minds wander. Nearly everyone reported dreams and visions while awake, and hallucinations were common. As part of the study, the sensory-deprived men took a series of arithmetic, anagram, and word association tests after 12, 24, and 48 hours of deprivation. As the sensory deprivation continued, performance on simple math problems depreciated quickly. After the second day, basic mathematic computations (e.g., 16×65) were too difficult to solve. Participants also became increasingly irritable. In fact, Heron found it difficult to keep his irritated participants in the experiment for more than two or three days, despite the large financial incentive for staying.

Sensory deprivation studies underscore the fact that the brain and nervous system prefer a continual and moderate level of arousal generated by environmental stimulation. Imagine the emotional experiences of zoo animals in cages, inmates in prison cells, the elderly in nursing homes, political prisoners in solitary confinement, long-term patients in hospital wards, and students enduring monotonous lectures. Each experiences some measure of unvarying stimulation. But human beings are not simply passive recipients of whatever stimulation the environment offers. When understimulated, people rely on various cognitive and behavioral means for increasing arousal level (e.g., mental imagery, social interaction). That is, human beings have motives for counteracting insufficient stimulation and underarousal.

Excessive Stimulation and Overarousal

Life is stressful. Stress comes from major events, such as divorce, physical injury, and unemployment (Holmes & Rahe, 1967; Iversen & Sabroe, 1989); from daily hassles, such as misplacing or losing things and getting stuck in traffic (DeLongis, Folkman, & Lazarus, 1988; Lazarus & DeLongis, 1983); and from chronic circumstances, such as inadequate child care, overcrowding, or repetitious relationship difficulties (DeLongis et al., 1982; Eckenrode, 1984). Major life events jolt the body's nervous and endocrine systems, whereas daily hassles and chronic circumstances produce a cumulative taxing effect on bodily systems.

FIGURE 11.3 **Sensory Deprivation Chamber**

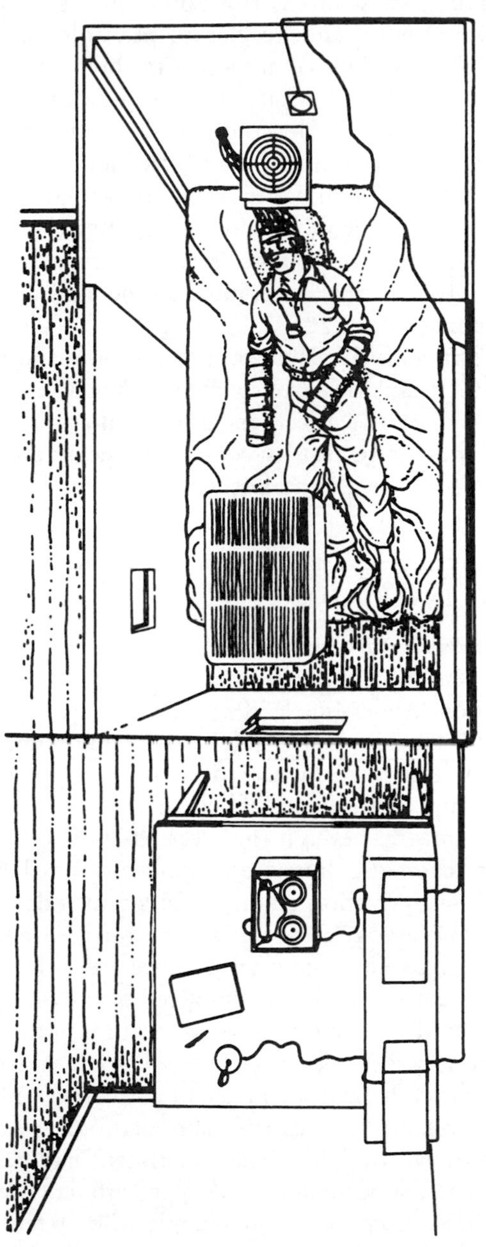

SOURCE: From "The Pathology of Boredom," by W. Heron, 1957, *Scientific American, 196,* pp. 52–56. Copyright 1957 by Scientific American. Adapted with permission from the illustration by Eric Mose.

In the absence of major events, daily hassles, troubling circumstances, our emotional state, thinking efficiency, and physiological functioning are basically at their normal, baseline levels. Overstimulating, stressful environments, on the other hand, upset emotion states, impair cognitive activity, and accelerate physiological processes. Emotional disruption manifests itself in feelings of anxiety, irritability, and anger (Horowitz et al., 1980). Cognitive disruption manifests itself in confusion, forgetfulness, and impaired concentration (Broadbent et al., 1982). Physiological disruption manifests itself in sympathetic nervous system hyperactivity, as through high blood pressure (Seyle, 1956). As a case in point, imagine that your term paper is due in two hours and is nowhere near its completion. Your amiability is probably decidedly negative (few overly stressed individuals smile, laugh, and tell jokes), your mental efficiency is probably disturbed (not being able to think straight), and your heart rate, muscle tone, and vulnerability to a headache are probably high and rising.

Because stress and strain are aversive ways of thinking and feeling, people generally want to escape from overstimulating environments. When unable to do so, daily functioning is characterized by negative affect, cognitive confusion, performance impairment, and health problems. Fortunately, just as we harbor motives to counteract insufficient stimulation and underarousal, we also harbor motives to counteract excessive stimulation and overarousal.

CREDIBILITY OF THE INVERTED-U HYPOTHESIS

The validity of the inverted-U curve (see Figure 11.2) is not without debate. Rob Neiss (1988) levied four criticisms against the hypothesis, only two of which are really relevant to motivation and emotion (Anderson, 1990). Neiss' first criticism is that the inverted-U curve is descriptive rather than explanatory. That is, the hypothesis summarizes the relationship between arousal and performance/affect, but it stops short of explaining *how* arousal facilitates or impairs performance/affect.

Neiss' second criticism is that even if the inverted-U hypothesis is true, it is still trivial. In other words, the inverted-U hypothesis applies only when arousal levels are extreme, such as in sensory-deprivation studies. Neiss concludes that the inverted-U hypothesis does not apply to everyday affairs in which arousal level changes relatively little. Others, however, disagree. To illustrate how the inverted-U hypothesis applies to mundane changes in arousal, college students completed a pair of vocabulary tests under a condition of leisure and under a condition of stress (time pressure; Revelle, Amaral, & Turriff, 1976). In addition, before taking the tests, all students took either a 200-mg caffeine pill (equivalent to the caffeine in two cups of coffee) or a placebo pill (no caffeine). The purpose of the time pressure and caffeine manipulations was to create the sort of high stimulation that occurs in everyday life. The experiment had one more important variable: Each student completed a personality survey to differentiate introverts (people who are chronically overaroused) from extraverts (people who are chronically underaroused). Based on the inverted-U hypothesis, the experimenters predicted that (1) overaroused introverts would perform well when relaxed but poorly when stimulated, whereas (2) underaroused extraverts would perform poorly when relaxed but well when stimulated. Results confirmed the predictions. The experiment is important because it shows that the

FIGURE 11.4 **Three Ways to Regulate Arousal**

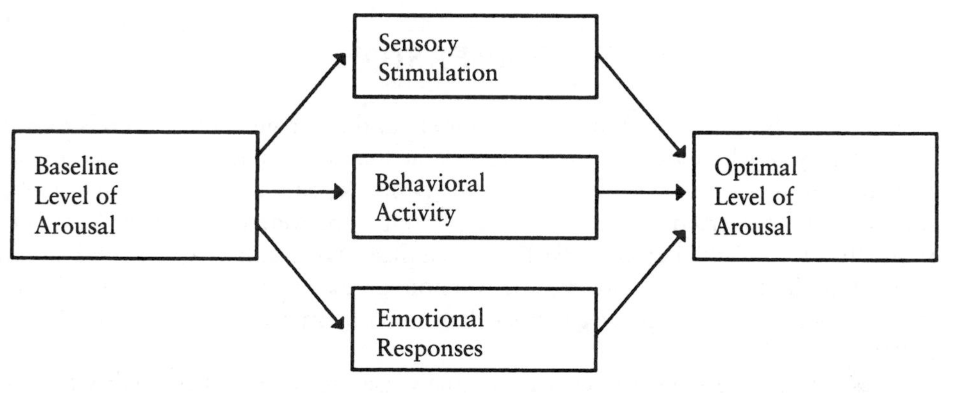

SOURCE: From "Affect Intensity as an Individual Difference Characteristic: A Review," by R. J. Larsen and E. Diener, 1987, *Journal of Research in Personality, 21*, pp. 1–39. Reprinted with permission.

inverted-U hypothesis applies nicely to everyday sources of stimulation—caffeine and time pressure.

INDIVIDUAL DIFFERENCES IN THE PREFERENCE FOR AROUSAL

Human beings differ in their genetic baseline level of arousal and in their reactivity to intense environmental stimuli. Baseline level of arousal is arousal level without external stimulation. Reactivity is one's arousal reaction when exposed to external stimulation.

To illustrate how individual differences in the preference for arousal lead to differences in self-regulation, consider Figure 11.4. Extraverts, sensation seekers, and affect-intense individuals possess three modes of affect regulation (Larsen & Diener, 1987). One means of arousal increase is to seek stimulating sensory experience. For example, sensation seekers tend to seek out drugs, alcohol, sex, and unusual activities. A second means is to engage in stimulating behavior. For example, extraverts tend to socialize with friends, accept dares, and play practical jokes. A third means of arousal increase is emotional hyperreactivity. For example, the affect-intense individual increases arousal through exaggerated emotional reactions to everyday situations.

From this point of view, sensory stimulation, impulsive behavior, and emotional hyperreactivity are all means of regulating arousal (Derryberry & Rothbart, 1988). The preference for shocking art (sensory stimulation), going to parties (extraverted behavior), and overreacting to a compliment (emotional responsiveness) are strategic means for augmenting arousal. The preference for soothing art (sensory avoidance), vacationing in solitude (introverted behavior), and a nonchalant reaction to a compliment (emotional unresponsiveness) are strategic means for attenuating arousal.

EXTRAVERSION

One personality characteristic important in understanding arousal regulation is extraversion. Personality psychologists generally agree that the introversion-extraversion characteristic is hereditary, meaning that differences in people's genes are largely responsible for introverted and extraverted tendencies (Eaves, Eysenck, & Martin, 1989; Pedersen et al., 1988; Shields, 1976; Viken et al., 1994). For instance, twins reared apart score similarly in terms of their disposition toward introversion or extraversion, suggesting that extraversion is based more on genetic factors than it is on environmental factors (Pedersen et al., 1988).

In assessing extraversion, researchers routinely use the Eysenck Personality Inventory (EPI; Eysenck & Eysenck, 1968), a self-report questionnaire with such questions as: Do you stop and think things over before doing anything? Can you easily get some life into a rather dull party? Extraverts are generally impulsive and sociable, compared to introverts. Figure 11.5 shows the sub-traits that make up the super-trait of extraversion (Eysenck, 1986).

To understand how extraversion relates to arousal, consider that inborn genetic differences produce physiological differences between individuals in the ascending reticular activating system (ARAS). The ARAS is the brain structure responsible for diffuse cortical arousal in response to external stimulation (Eysenck, 1967; Eysenck & Eysenck, 1969, 1985). Extraverts are characterized by ARAS insensitivity to low levels of stimulation and ARAS reactivity to high levels of stimulation. In other words, extraverts need strong

FIGURE 11.5 **Traits That Define Extraversion**

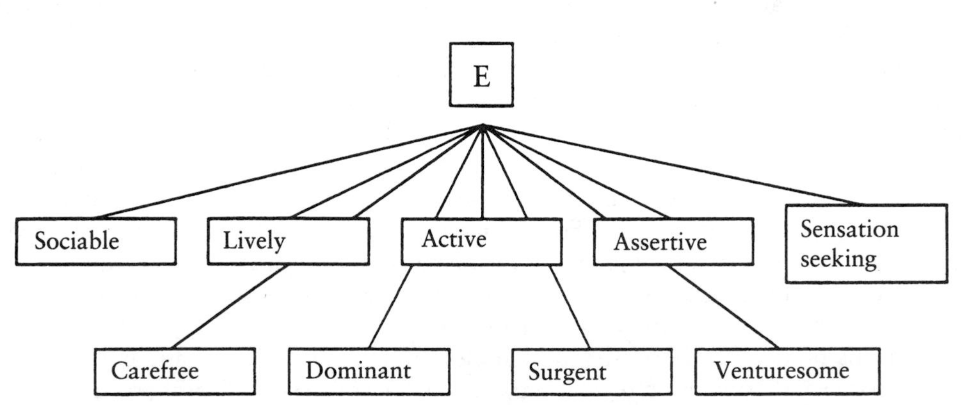

SOURCE: From "Can Personality Study Ever Be Scientific?" by H. J. Eysenck, 1986, *Journal of Social Behavior and Personality, 1,* pp. 3–19. Reprinted with permission.

external stimuli to arouse their ARAS. Introverts are characterized by ARAS sensitivity to low levels of stimulation and ARAS reactivity (intolerance) to high stimulation. They need only milder external stimuli to arouse their ARAS.

The basic tenets of Eysenck's neurophysiological theory of extraversion appear in Figure 11.6 (Gale & Edwards, 1986). The ARAS mediates arousal level (A). The ARAS and neocortex have reciprocal relations in which each can excite or inhibit the other (B). Sense organs send axons into both the ARAS and cortex (C). There is an optimal level of arousal for the ARAS (D). Extraverts genetically inherit a below-optimum level of arousal, whereas introverts inherit an above-optimum level of arousal (E). Lastly, extraverts behave to

FIGURE 11.6 **Neurophysiological Basis of Extraversion-Introversion in Eysenck's Theory**

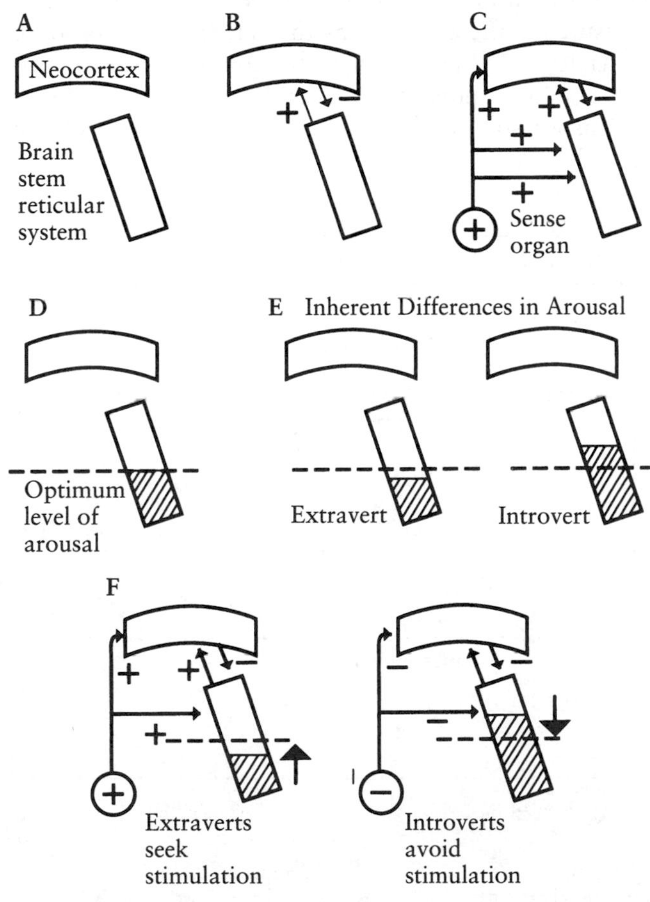

SOURCE: From "Individual Differences," by A. Gale and J. A. Edwards, 1986, in M. G. H. Coles, E. Donchin, and S. W. Proges (Eds.), *Psychophysiology: Systems, Processes, and Applications* (pp. 431–507). New York: The Guilford Press. Adapted with permission.

increase external stimulation (by seeking stimulation), whereas introverts behave to decrease external stimulation (by avoiding stimulation; F).

Introverts attain optimal levels of arousal at relatively low levels of stimulation and therefore shun strong stimulation. Extraverts attain optimal levels of arousal at relatively high levels of stimulation and therefore seek out strong forms of stimulation (Derryberry & Rothbart, 1988). Figure 11.7 graphically illustrates the relationship between external stimulation and hedonic tone for introverts, extraverts, and the average population that is somewhere between an introvert and an extravert. Introverts attain optimal levels of arousal at relatively low levels of external stimulation (OL_I); the average population attains optimal levels of arousal at moderate levels of stimulation (OL_P); and extraverts attain optimal levels of arousal at high levels of external stimulation (OL_E; Derryberry & Rothbart, 1988).

Psychophysiological and pharmacological studies support the basic idea of Eysenck's ARAS arousal theory of extraversion. In most, but not all, situations, introverts show greater cortical (as measured in the brain by the electroencephalograph, EEG) and skin conductance (as measured in the fingertips by the galvanic skin response, GSR) reactivity than do extraverts (Gale, 1973, 1983). One situation, for instance, involved placing introverts and extraverts in a soundproof room and asking them to look at a black visual field (to minimize sensory stimulation) while the experimenter obtained EEG records (Gale, Coles, & Blaydon, 1969). In such a setting, introverts showed greater cortical

FIGURE 11.7 **Relationship Between External Stimulation and Hedonic Tone for Introverts, Extraverts, and the Average Population That Is Somewhere in Between**

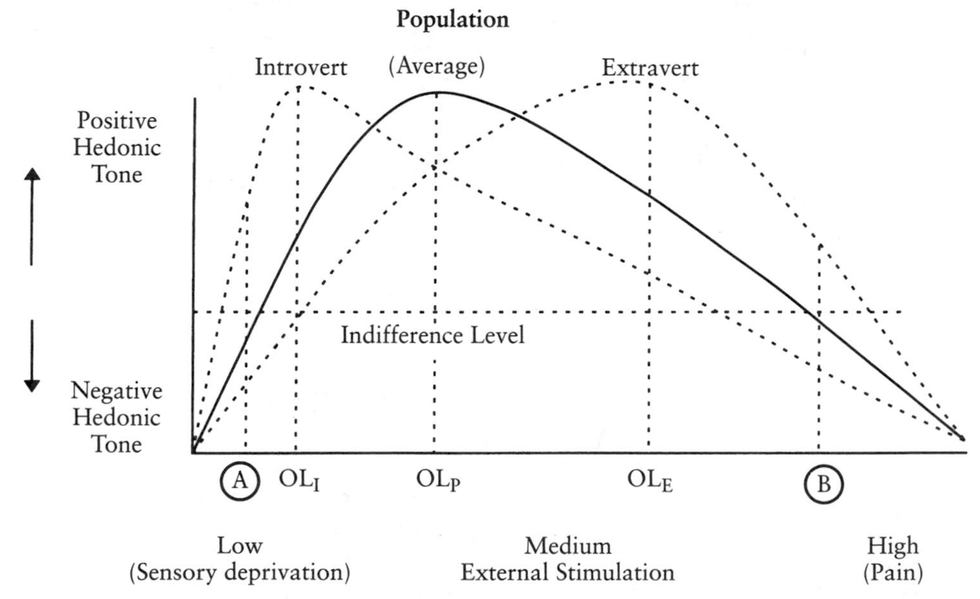

Source: From *Experiments With Drugs: Studies in the Relation Between Personality, Learning, Theory, and Drug Action* by H. J. Eysenck, 1963, New York: Pergamon Press.

arousal than did extraverts. Drugs also affect extraverts and introverts differently. Because introverts are inherently more aroused than extraverts, introverts are less affected by sedatives and depressants than are extraverts. Introverts feel and function better after taking a depressant (i.e., after an arousal decrease); extraverts feel and function better after taking a stimulant (i.e., after an arousal increase).

Because introverts prefer lower levels of external stimulation, they tolerate monotony relatively well and thus typically outperform extraverts in tasks of vigilance. In low-stimulation tasks, extraverts are more susceptible to performance impairments from boredom. Extraverts, on the other hand, show a greater social intelligence, as they are better able to relate to people and anticipate their social responses. Extraverts are also generally happier, as they report more positive affect and more pleasant day-to-day moods than introverts (Costa & McCrae, 1980; Emmons & Diener, 1986; Larsen & Ketelaar, 1991; Watson et al., 1992; Williams, 1990). Extraverts are generally the happier bunch because (1) they are more likely to engage in frequent social interaction (Watson et al., 1992) and (2) they engage in a more active lifestyle that revolves around positive-affect-inducing events such as dating, partying, and social drinking (Larsen & Ketelaar, 1991).

SENSATION SEEKING

Like extraversion, sensation seeking is based on the ability to arouse. A high sensation seeker prefers a continual external supply of brain stimulation, becomes bored with routine, and is continually in search of ways to increase arousal through exciting experiences. A low sensation seeker prefers less brain stimulation and tolerates routine relatively well. In general, the sensation-seeking construct pertains to the extent to which a person's central nervous system (brain and spinal cord) requires change and variability, as sensation seekers prefer to change activities, change television channels, change drugs, change sexual partners, and so on (Zuckerman, 1994).

Sensation seeking is a trait defined as "the seeking of varied, novel, complex, and intense sensations and experiences, and the willingness to take physical, social, legal, and financial risks for the sake of such experience" (Zuckerman, 1994). Marvin Zuckerman (1994) uses the example of driving very fast after heavy drinking to illustrate a sensation seeker's willingness to take physical risks (injure self or others), social risks (being exposed as a drunk driver), legal risks (being arrested and jailed), and financial risks (being fired from work). Such risks are the price sensation seekers are willing to take to receive the sensations and experiences they seek.

Sensation seeking exists as a set of interrelated components (like extraversion; see Figure 11.5). Table 11.1 lists the four components of sensation seeking with a sample item to represent each scale of the Sensation Seeking Scale (SSS). Each item on the SSS asks the test taker to identify which of two situations or activities is the more preferred (Zuckerman, 1978, 1994). One alternative is a high-stimulation activity (A alternative), while the second is a low-stimulation activity (B alternative).

Thrill and adventure seeking (TAS) is the desire to engage in physical risk taking. These activities include outdoor, noncompetitive activities that involve danger, personal

TABLE 11.1 **Sample Items From the Sensation Seeking Scale (SSS)**

Directions: For each sentence pair, pick the one option that is most true for you.

Thrill and Adventure Seeking (TAS)
A. I sometimes like to do things that are a little frightening.
B. A sensible person avoids activities that are dangerous.

Experience Seeking (ES)
A. I would like to hitchhike across the country.
B. Hitchhiking is too dangerous a way to travel.

Disinhibition (Dis)
A. Keeping the drinks full is the key to a good party.
B. Heavy drinking usually ruins a party because some people get loud and boisterous.

Boredom Susceptibility (BS)
A. I get bored seeing the same old faces.
B. I like the comfortable familiarity of everyday friends.

SOURCE: From "Sensation Seeking," by M. Zuckerman, 1978, in H. London and J. E. Exner Jr. (Eds.), *Dimensions of Personality* (pp. 487–559), New York: John Wiley & Sons, Inc. Copyright 1978. Reprinted with permission of John Wiley & Sons, Inc.

challenge, and risk, such as flying, parachute jumping, scuba diving, motorcycle riding, speeding in a car, and mountain climbing. *Experience seeking (ES)* is the desire to pursue new experiences through the mind and senses. Art, music, travel, and certain types of drugs express the pursuit of experience through the senses, whereas a spontaneous, nonconforming lifestyle, especially with unusual people, typifies experience seeking through the mind. *Disinhibition (Dis)* is a desire to disinhibit oneself in social situations in the pursuit of pleasure. The use of alcohol as a means of disinhibition and participation in gambling, sexual variety, and wild parties characterizes disinhibition. *Boredom susceptibility (BS)* is an aversion to any type of routine—monotony in work, repetition of experience, or exposure to boring people. When circumstances are unchanging, the boredom-susceptible person becomes restless and intolerant (Zuckerman, 1978).

Sensation seeking and extraversion correlate only weakly with one another (Zuckerman, 1979a). Though both traits have their roots in the search for stimulating environments, Marvin Zuckerman (1994) illustrates the difference between the two constructs. Extraverts enjoy sociability and hence the company of many people, but sensation seekers are more interested in the stimulation value other people offer. Instead of sociability, the sensation seeker is interested in (1) the search for new experience, (2) risk taking, and (3) unusual activities.

SEARCH FOR NEW EXPERIENCES

The sensation seeker continually searches for novel experiences—spicy foods (Terasaki & Imada, 1988), switching television programs (Schierman & Rowland, 1985), listening to music with some punch (Litle & Zuckerman, 1986), and so on. One manifestation of the search for new experiences is sex. Compared to sensation avoiders, sensation seekers report a greater frequency and variety (number of partners) in sexual activity

TABLE 11.2 **Correlations Between SSS, Sexual Activity, and Drug Use**

	Males (N = 38)				Females (N = 60)			
SSS SCALE	SEXUAL ACTIVITY	NUMBER OF SEX PARTNERS	DRUG USE	ALCOHOL USE	SEXUAL ACTIVITY	NUMBER OF SEX PARTNERS	DRUG USE	ALCOHOL USE
TAS	.44**	.47**	.42**	.39*	.16	.20	.28*	.15
ES	.37*	.35**	.47**	.10	.32*	.28*	.55**	.26*
Dis	.33*	.42**	.08	.47**	.43**	.29*	.43**	.43**
BS	.36*	.25*	.34*	–.09	.29*	.20	.32*	.12

*p < .05; **p < .01; N=sample size

SOURCE: From "What Is the Sensation Seeker? Personality Trait and Experience Correlates of the Sensation Seeking Scale," by M. Zuckerman, R. N. Bone, R. Neary, D. Mangelsdorff, and B. Brustman, 1972, *Journal of Clinical Counseling Psychology, 39,* pp. 308–321. Copyright 1972 by American Psychological Association. Adapted with permission.

(Zuckerman et al., 1972; Zuckerman, Tushup, & Finner, 1976). Sensation seekers report that less of a relationship and less emotional involvement are necessary prerequisites for participation in sexual relations than do sensation avoiders (Hendrick & Hendrick, 1987; Zuckerman, Tushup, & Finner, 1976). Further, as parents, high sensation seekers set more permissive standards for their children's sexual activity (Zuckerman, Tushup, & Finner, 1976).

Drugs can also provide the means for a quick arousal elevation. Drugs open the door to new experiences (hallucinations), release inhibitions against risky behavior, and serve as an escape from boredom. Through any or all of these means of altering experiences, drug use functions as a form of sensation seeking (Zuckerman, 1978, 1994; Zuckerman et al., 1972). To substantiate these claims, Zuckerman and his colleagues (1972) asked college students to complete the SSS and a questionnaire on the variety of drug use and frequency of alcohol use. Table 11.2 lists the correlations between the SSS and the questionnaire on drug and alcohol use (as well as sexual frequency and variety). Several scales correlated with alcohol and drug use, especially for males.

The search for new experiences extends into deviance such as vandalism, aggression, stealing, and criminality (Newcomb & McGee, 1991; White, Labourvie, & Bates, 1985). The effect on drug use of sensation seeking explains the relationship between sensation seeking and adolescent deviance, as sensation seeking predicts drug use and drug use predicts general deviance (Newcomb & McGee, 1991). Such a finding suggests the interesting intervention strategy for preventing adult deviance—providing adolescents high in sensation seeking with substitutes for the excitement of illicit drugs (Zuckerman, 1979).

RISK TAKING

No one particularly likes risk per se, which is essentially the perception of the probability that a behavior will produce aversive consequences. The risks related to sensation seeking involve those that are physical, social, legal, or financial. It is not that sensation seekers are attracted to such risks; rather, sensation seekers see sensations and experiences being worth these risks, whereas sensation avoiders do not. Thus, "risk accepting" seems to be a more appropriate term than does "risk taking."

High sensation seekers voluntarily engage in physically risky hobbies, such as motorcycling (Brown et al., 1974), parachuting and skydiving (Hymbaugh & Garrett, 1974), adventuresome travel (Jacobs & Koeppel, 1974), immigration (Winchie & Carment, 1988), cigarette smoking (Zuckerman, Ball, & Black, 1990), downhill skiing (Calhoon, 1988), and gambling (Kuhlman, 1975). In contrast, low sensation seekers show phobic-like reactivity to risky sources of stimulation such as snakes, heights, and darkness (Mellstrom, Cicala, & Zuckerman, 1976). Gambling illustrates some of the sensation seekers' motivation for risk taking, as excitement, rather than money, motivates most people's gambling (Anderson & Brown, 1984). Sensation seekers like the large increase in heart rate they experience by placing a wager, and they are willing to place large wagers to get large heart-rate spikes (Anderson & Brown, 1984).

Sensation seekers' risk taking manifests itself in many areas of life, such as in criminal behavior (shoplifting, selling drugs), minor violations (traffic offenses), finances (gambling, risky businesses), and sports (parachuting; Horvath & Zuckerman, 1993). Fast driving, for instance, offers potential physical, social, legal, and financial risks. Compared to sensation avoiders, sensation seekers report driving fast (well over the posted speed limit) under normal conditions (Arnett, 1991; Clement & Jonah, 1984; Zuckerman & Neeb, 1980), and they do not perceive tailgating (driving close behind the car in front) as risky or as physiologically upsetting (Heino, van der Molen, & Wilde, 1992, as reported in Zuckerman, 1994).

Volunteering for Unusual Activities

Suppose several experimenters visited your psychology class to recruit volunteers for their experiments in learning, social psychology, sleep research, sensory deprivation, ESP, hypnosis, and drug research. For which experiments would you be most willing to participate? If you are a high sensation seeker, you would be just as willing as a sensation avoider to volunteer for the usual experiments (e.g., learning, social psychology), but you would be significantly more willing to volunteer for the unusual experiments, such as hypnosis and drug research (Trice & Ogdon, 1986; Zuckerman, 1978).

U.S. Army personnel had a chance to volunteer for a high-risk or low-risk activity (or neither) after filling out the SSS questionnaire (Jobe, Holgate, & Sorapanshy, 1983). The high-risk activity involved setting off a dynamite explosive, while the low-risk activity involved filling out personality questionnaires. Sensation seekers volunteered more frequently for the high-risk activity. Sensation seekers and avoiders did not differ in how frequently they volunteered for the low-risk activity, thereby confirming that sensation seekers volunteer for risky activities, not just any activities.

Biological Basis

The sensation seeker in not chronically underaroused. Instead, he seeks out and is excited by intense sources of stimulation (Zuckerman, 1994). For example, sensation seekers prefer stimuli that cause a sudden orientation reaction (Neary & Zuckerman, 1976), a rapid, 5- to 10-second drop in heart rate and a tensing of the musculature—a physiological jolt to the ANS upon encountering novel, complex, or personally significant stimuli. The sensation seekers' preferences for stimuli that produce orienting reactions help explain why they prefer, and actively seek out, activities like motorcycle riding, parachuting, and streaking (Zuckerman, 1994).

Biochemical events in the brain determine how people react to environmental stimulation, so researchers have investigated the linkages between the sensation-seeking trait and biochemical events in the brain. The most reliable finding is that sensation seekers have low levels of monoamine oxidase (MAO; Schooler et al. 1978). MAO is a limbic system enzyme involved in breaking down brain neurotransmitters such as dopamine and serotonin. Dopamine contributes to the experiences of reward toward biologically significant events such as food and sex and therefore facilitates approach behaviors (Stellar & Stellar, 1985). Serotonin contributes to a biological inhibition, or to the physiological stop system, in the brain and therefore inhibits approach behaviors (Panksepp, 1982). Sensation seekers tend to have relatively high levels of dopamine; hence, their biochemistry favors approach over inhibition (Zuckerman, 1994). Though the neurobiological basis of sensation seeking is not perfectly clear (Zuckerman, 1994), three conclusions have emerged: (1) Sensation seekers have low levels of MAO; (2) MAO enzymes regulate, in part, brain availability of dopamine, serotonin, and other biochemical agents; and (3) brain dopamine regulates approach tendencies, whereas brain serotonin inhibits it. There is also indirect evidence that sensation seeking has a genetic basis (Zuckerman, Buchsbaum, & Murphy, 1980).

AFFECT INTENSITY

Affect intensity is a third individual difference related to arousal regulation, as it concerns people's emotional abilities to be aroused. Affect intensity is defined in terms of the strength with which individuals typically experience their emotions (Larsen & Diener, 1987). Affect-intense individuals experience their emotions strongly and show emotional reactivity and variability across many different emotion-eliciting situations. Affect-stable individuals experience their emotions only mildly and show only minor fluctuations in their emotional reactions from moment to moment or day to day.

Affect intensity is significantly correlated with extraversion (Diener et al., 1985) and with activity level, the ability to be aroused, and emotionality (Larsen & Diener, 1987). Affect intensity is not correlated, however, with any of the sensation-seeking scales (Larsen, Diener, & Emmons, 1986).

Researchers measure affect intensity with a self-report questionnaire that includes items such as the following: When I feel happy, it is a strong type of exuberance; when I am nervous, I get shaky all over (Larsen & Diener, 1987). Originally, researchers assessed affect intensity in an interesting, although laborious, way (Larsen, 1988). Over a period of 80 to 90 consecutive days, respondents completed a daily-mood questionnaire that featured positive (e.g., happy, joyful) and negative (e.g., depressed, worried) mood words. To compute affect intensity, the individual's daily score on the negative mood words was totaled and

FIGURE 11.8 **Daily Mood Reports Graphed Over 80 Consecutive Days**

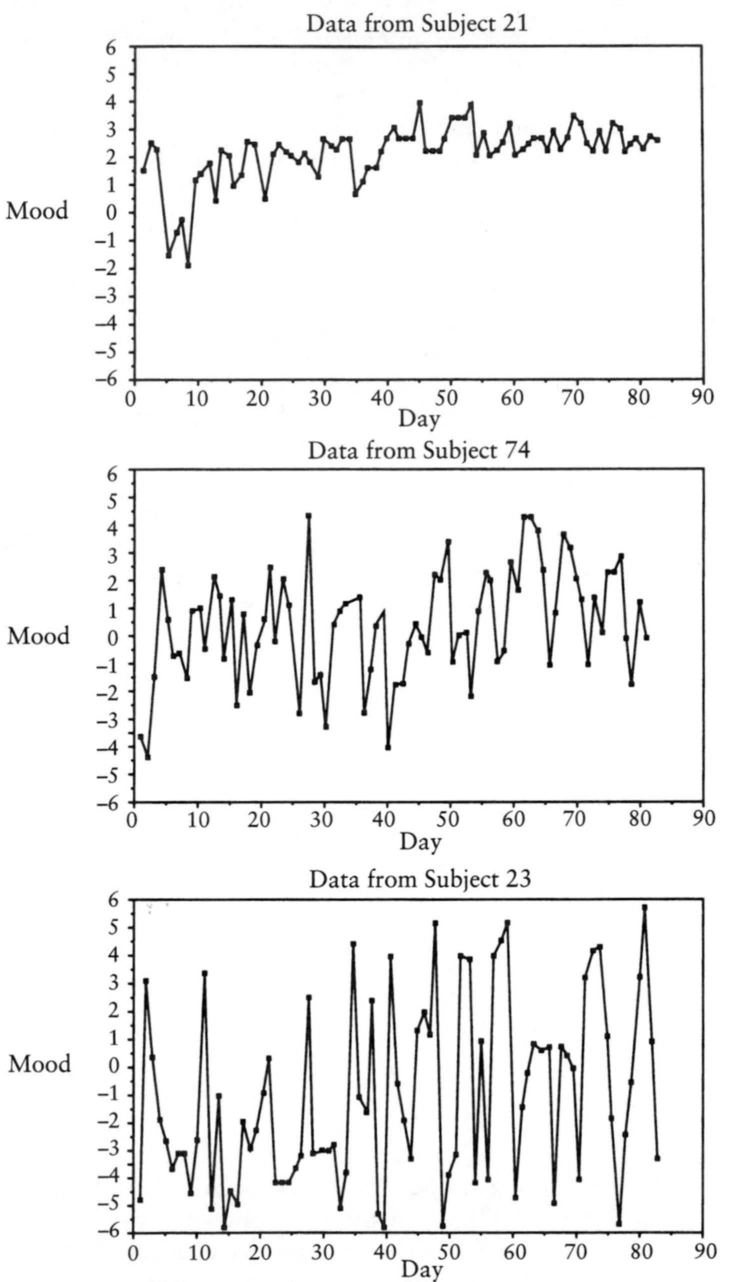

SOURCE: From "Individual Differences in Affect Intensity," by R. J. Larsen, 1988, paper presented at the annual meeting of the Motivation and Emotion Conference at Nags Head, NC.

FIGURE 11.9 **Affective Reactions to Good and Bad Events by Affect-Intense and Affect-Stable Individuals**

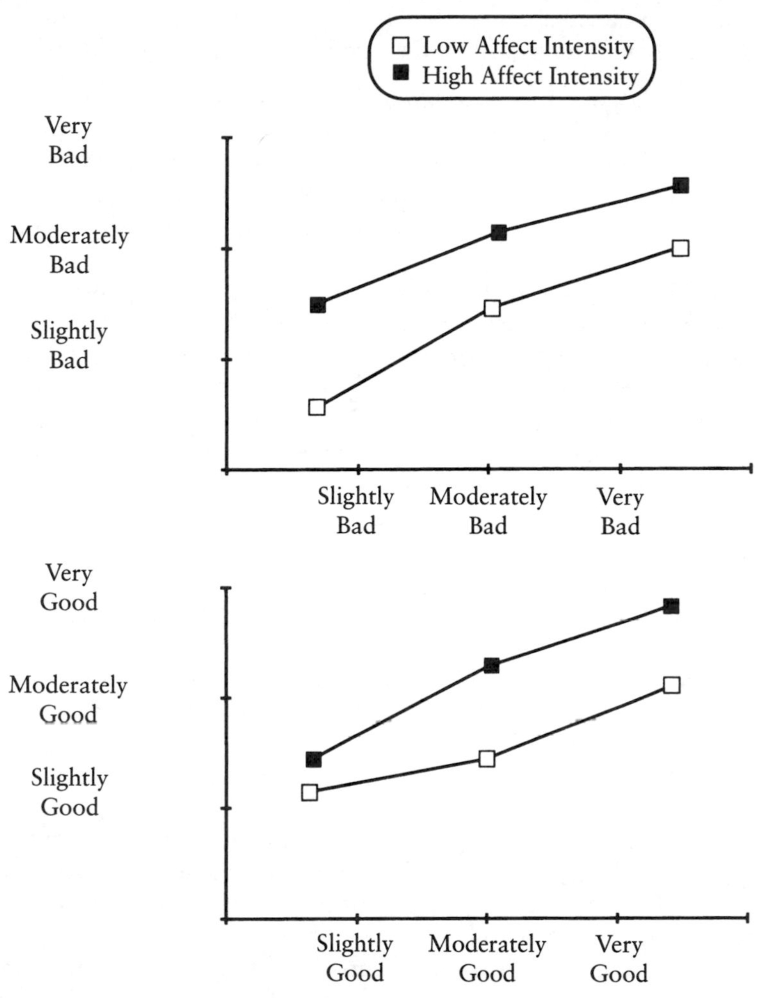

SOURCE: From "Affect Intensity and Reactions to Daily Life Events," by R. J. Larsen, E. Diener, and R. A. Emmons, 1987, *Journal of Personality and Social Psychology, 51,* pp. 803–814. Copyright 1987 by American Psychological Association. Adapted with permission.

subtracted from the daily score on the positive mood words total to yield a daily mood. On each consecutive day, the overall daily mood score was plotted on a graph. A daily-mood graph for three different people in the experiment appears in Figure 11.8. The daily mood of the affect-intense individual (subject 23) rises and falls rather substantially, whereas the mood of the affect-stable individual (subject 21) hovers continuously around neutral. How much the person's daily mood score deviated from neutral (0) defined her affect intensity.

Arousal and Stress

Question: Why would a person want to learn about the motivational states discussed in this chapter?

Answer: To see how biology affects the psychology of arousal and stress.

Arousal and stress are two motivationally based responses to stimulating, demanding environments. Environmental stimulation and challenge require adaptive responses from the body, and it, in turn, produces the biological underpinnings of what people experience as felt arousal and felt stress. Arousal is mostly a function of how stimulating the environment is; stress is mostly a function of how demanding and controllable the environment is.

The sympathetic-adrenal-medullary system generates the body's acute, short-lived response to stimulating, stressful environments. When stimulation is high, the sympathetic-adrenal-medullary system activates the sympathetic nervous system to expend energy (as in the fight-or-flight response). When stimulation is low, the system activates the parasympathetic nervous system to conserve energy (as in resting and digesting food). One motivationally important event in the activation of the sympathetic nervous system is the release of epinephrine (or adrenaline), which is the catecholamine responsible for increasing heart rate, blood pressure, and respiration rate. It is the elevated versus suppressed state of bodily activation that people experience as felt arousal.

The pituitary-adrenocortical system generates the body's chronic, long-lived response to stimulating, stressful environments. When demands and challenges are high, the adrenal gland secretes corticosteroids, the most motivationally important of which is cortisol. Unlike epinephrine, which is released by the sympathetic-

For purposes of illustration, imagine that each of the following events, some good and some bad, recently happened to you: You won a scholarship you desperately needed or received a letter from a long-lost friend (positive life events); your automobile had a flat tire or you saw your ex-boyfriend/girlfriend with a new flame (negative life events; Larsen, Diener, & Emmons, 1987). Suppose further that you were asked to rate precisely how good or how bad each event was immediately after it occurred. For example, how good did you feel when you received a letter from your long-lost friend? How bad did you feel when your tire went flat? Figure 11.9 shows how affect-intense and affect-stable individuals reacted to events classified by objective people who rated these events as "slightly good," "moderately good," or "very good" and to events classified as "slightly bad," "moderately bad," or "very bad." Affect-intense individuals reacted more positively to all categories of good events, and they reacted more negatively to all categories of bad events. In other words, whereas an affect-stable individual feels slightly good about receiving a letter in the mail, an affect-intense individual feels moderately or very good about the same event. Affect-intense individuals therefore augment (intensify) the emotional effects of an event.

adrenal-medullary system in seconds, cortisol is released by the pituitary-adrenocortical system in minutes and hours following exposure to a stressing event. As long as the person experiences stress, cortisol continues to be released; to the extent that the person is coping successfully with the stressing event, cortisol is then suppressed. Therefore, the psychological experience that produces elevated versus suppressed cortisol is the perception of low versus high control over the stressing event. The suppression of cortisol is central to effective coping because elevated cortisol decreases intellectual functioning, alters metabolism, diminishes the immune response, reduces the body's response to infection, and suppresses the reproductive process. For instance, when cortisol is high, people's ability to solve intellectual problems is significantly impaired (Kirschbaum et al., 1986). But increased perceived competence at a task suppresses cortisol (Booth et al., 1989). Thus, perceived control works as an antidote to cortisol.

The individual differences discussed in this chapter help explain why some people experience enhanced performance and positive emotion in sympathetic-activating environments (i.e., extraverts, sensation seekers, and affect-intense individuals) and why others experience enhanced performance and positive emotion in parasympathetic-activating environments (i.e., introverts, sensation avoiders, and affect-stable individuals). Individual differences also help explain why demanding environments sometimes overwhelm and stress the individual performer (i.e., low perceived control, low desire for control) and why others are able to cope with, and even thrive in, demanding, challenging environments (i.e., high perceived control, high desire for control).

Originally, researchers presumed that affect-intense individuals were physiologically underaroused, relative to their affect-stable counterparts (Larsen, Diener, & Emmons, 1986). Follow-up research, however, found that affect-intense individuals were neither less chronically aroused than their affect-stable counterparts nor experienced greater arousal spikes in arousal-generating situations (Blascovich et al., 1992). Instead of differing at the physiological level, affect-intense individuals are more psychologically sensitive to changes in arousal than affect-stable individuals. It is almost as if affect-intense persons have a highly sensitive "arousal thermostat" that monitors their arousal increases, whereas affect-stable individuals have a relatively dull thermostat (Blascovich et al., 1992).

While extraverts and sensation seekers seek out stimulating and novel activities for increasing their arousal upward to an optimal level, affect-intense individuals use emotional reactivity to do much the same thing (Larsen & Diener, 1987). Affect-intense individuals seek out and prefer opportunities for rich emotional arousal, whereas affect-stable individuals avoid emotional situations (Basso, Schefft, & Hoffmann, 1994; Larsen, Diener, & Cropanzano, 1987).

INDIVIDUAL DIFFERENCES IN PERSONAL CONTROL BELIEFS

Many personality characteristics could be included in the category of personal control beliefs, including locus of control (Findley & Cooper, 1983; Levenson, 1981; Rotter, 1966), perceived control (Skinner, 1985), causality orientations (Deci & Ryan, 1985b), mastery versus helpless orientations (Diener & Dweck, 1978, 1980), explanatory style (Peterson & Seligman, 1984), desire for control (Burger, 1992), type A behavior pattern (Strube et al., 1987), self-esteem (Janis & Field, 1959), self-efficacy (Bandura, 1986; Berry & West, 1993), and personal strivings (Emmons, 1996; Emmons & McAdams, 1991). Two of these personality characteristics, however, adequately capture most of the spirit of control beliefs: perceived control and desire for control. Perceived control concerns differences in people's preperformance expectancies of possessing the needed capacity and strategies for producing outcomes (Skinner, Zimmer-Gembeck, & Connell, 1998). Desire for control concerns the extent to which people strive to make their own decisions, influence others, assume leadership roles, and enter situations in overly prepared ways (Burger, Oakman, & Bullard, 1983).

PERCEIVED CONTROL

Perceived control refers to the beliefs and expectations a person holds that she can interact with the environment in ways that produce desired outcomes and prevent undesired outcomes (Skinner, 1995; Skinner, Zimmer-Gembeck, & Connell, 1998). In order to perceive that one has control over a given situation, one first needs to be convinced that the self is capable of obtaining the desired outcomes available. In addition, one must also perceive that the situation in which she attempts to exercise control over is at least somewhat predictable and responsive. Unstructured situations, because they are unpredictable and unresponsive, undermine perceived control.

Research on learned helplessness (chapter 8) shows that as people find themselves in unpredictable, unresponsive environments, they learn that their actions and efforts are futile. But the reverse is not necessarily true. That is, when environments are predictable and responsive—at least to a degree—people do not necessarily put forth strong efforts in exerting control over their outcomes. This is true because even structured situations can be difficult to control, as is often the case in education, sports, relationships, and at work. When some barrier like task difficulty separates the person from attractive outcomes (e.g., good grades, fame, marriage, promotion), individual differences in perceptions of control intervene, explaining when and why people willingly put forth efforts necessary to controlling their fate.

The relationships among perceived control, effort, and performance outcomes appear in the top half of Figure 11.10 (Skinner, 1995). Perceived control beliefs predict how much effort a person is willing to exert. Instead of using *effort,* the figure uses the more general term *engagement,* which includes not only expenditure of effort but also how positive versus negative one's emotional tone is during the expenditure of effort. Engagement, in turn, affects quality of performance. As discussed in chapter 9, people

FIGURE 11.10 Model of How Perceived Control Regulates Engagement, Outcomes, and Postperformance Perceptions of Control

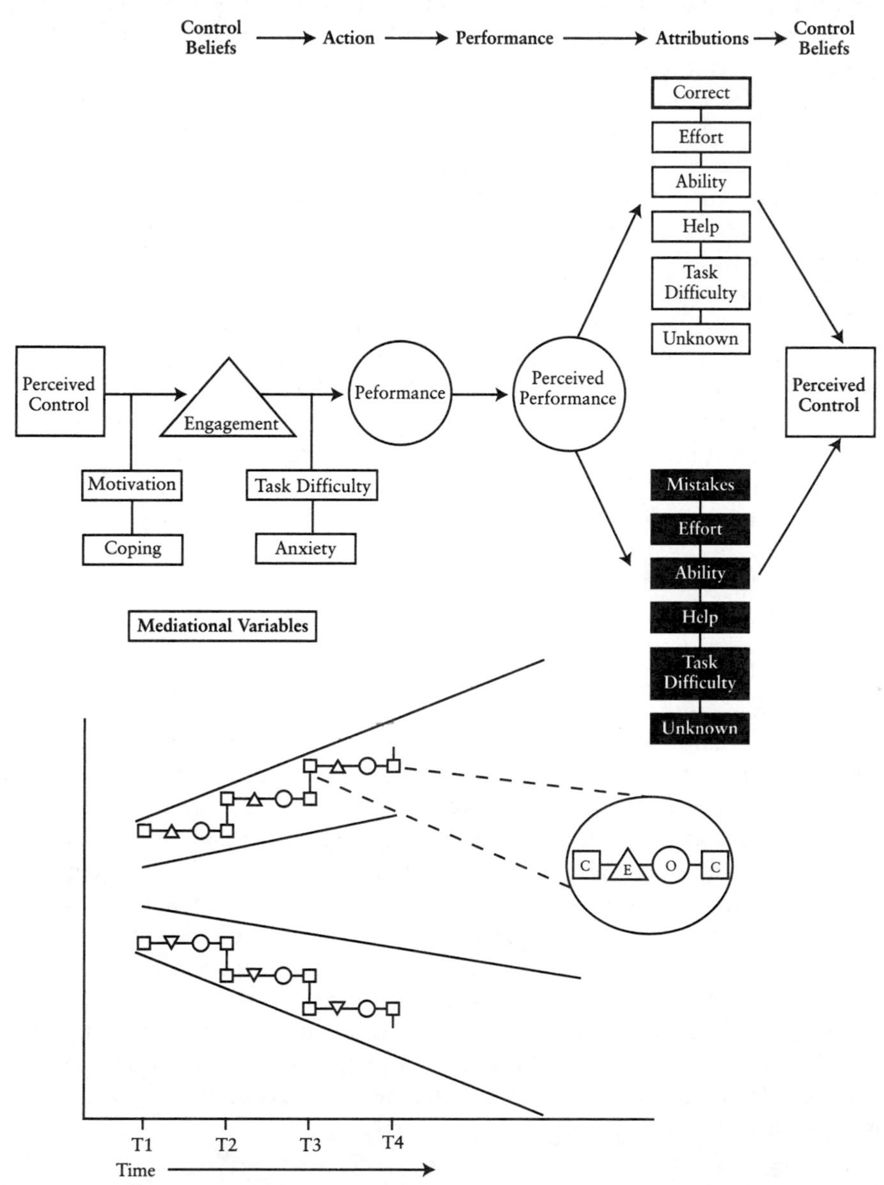

SOURCE: Top half of figure: From "Perceived Control, Effort, and Academic Performance: Interindividual, Intraindividual, and Multivariate Time-Series Analyses," by B. Schmitz and E. Skinner, 1993, *Journal of Personality and Social Psychology, 64,* pp. 1010–1028. Lower half of figure: From "Development and Perceived Control: A Dynamic Model of Action in Context," by E. Skinner, 1991, in M. Gunnar and L. A. Sroufe (Eds.), *Minnesota Symposium on Child Development* (Vol. 23), Hillsdale, NJ: Lawrence Erlbaum.

make attributions for explaining the underlying causes of why they succeeded or failed. These attributions, in turn, influence changes in perceptions of control (which determine subsequent engagement, etc.).

When a person with relatively high perceived control faces a reasonably structured situation, he seeks out and selects relatively challenging tasks, sets relatively high goals, and generates sophisticated plans about how to succeed and what to do when progress is slow. With this forethought, a person with high perceived control initiates action, exerts effort, focuses concentration, and persists in the face of difficulty. During performance, the high-perceived-control-individual keeps her plans and strategies in mind, maintains positive emotional states, monitors problem-solving strategies, and generates and monitors feedback to adjust or improve relevant skills. Such an engaged focus on the task generally leads to strong performance and makes control over desirable and undesirable outcomes possible. In contrast, when a person with relatively low perceived control faces the same reasonably structured situation, he seeks out and selects relatively easy tasks, sets lower and vaguer goals, and generates simple plans with few fallback strategies. With this forethought, a person with low perceived control is more impoverished. If things go wrong, concentration is likely to wander, confidence is quick to drop, and attention often turns to ruminating over why the task is so difficult. As effort decreases and cognitive and emotional engagement decline, discouragement and passivity set in, and performance suffers accordingly. Over time, such events lead people to become more pessimistic, to reduce their expectations of future control, and to quit making plans and strategies to prevent such a recurrence.

This course of events depicts the self-confirming cycle that characterizes the relationship between perceived control, engagement, and performance outcomes, as depicted in the lower half of Figure 11.10. When two people enter a potentially controllable, but somewhat difficult, situation with different perceptions of control, the self-confirming cycle can magnify initial preperformance differences. People with high perceptions of control are more likely to put forth a higher quality task engagement and are therefore more likely to succeed in attaining desired outcomes. Attained outcomes affect postperformance perceptions of control. And upon engaging the difficult task on a second occasion, these postperformance perceptions of control for the first task engagement become preperformance perceptions of control for the second task engagement.

Notice in the figure how perceptions of control increase from one task engagement to the next. Increases in perceived control occur in proportion to successfully attaining outcomes. People with low perceptions of control put forth a lower quality engagement and are therefore more likely to fail in attaining desired outcomes and in preventing undesired outcomes. Unattained outcomes lower postperformance perceptions of control. Over time (after T4 [time 4] in Figure 11.10), initial differences in perceptions of control magnify to be substantial differences in perceptions of control.

ORIGINS

To assess individual differences in perceptions of control, researchers use questionnaires written for elementary-grade children that contain the following items (Skinner, Chapman, & Baltes, 1988):

- If you decide to sit yourself down and learn something really hard, can you learn it?
- Let's say that you want to get all the problems (like in spelling) right. Can you do that?
- I'll bet you don't like to get bad grades. Can you do anything to keep from getting any?
- Let's say: You decide that you're not going to get any problems wrong (like on a math or spelling paper). Can you do it?

From these items, perceived control appears to be conceptually similar to related constructs, such as perceived competence, self-efficacy, and perceived ability. One difference, however, is that perceived control functions as the antecedent foundation on which beliefs such as competence, efficacy, and ability are constructed. For instance, perceived control bolsters perceived competence, and perceived competence predicts performance outcomes, such as preference for challenge and positive emotionality (Boggiano, Main, & Katz, 1993). Perceived control is, therefore, a necessary forerunner for constructing beliefs about one's competence, efficacy, and ability. A second difference between perceived control and these other constructs is that perceived control beliefs can emanate from any capacity, not just from one's own competence, efficacy, or ability. For instance, an athlete might perceive high control because of a capacity to solicit help and assistance from the coach, from teammates, or from the heavens. The belief that one has high control over outcomes therefore means that one has control over whatever it is that controls the outcomes—self, teammates, luck, or the heavens—one desires to attain.

One source from which perceived control beliefs originate is a person's performance outcomes (Skinner et al., 1998). More precisely, a reciprocal link exists between a person's performance outcomes and the perceptions of control that person holds (Philips & Zimmerman, 1990; Stipek, 1980, 1984). Such a relationship might suggest that perceived control is just a substitute concept for one's level of task-related ability. But perceived control beliefs are not the same as perceived ability beliefs because perceived control is much more of a motivational construct. Perceived control beliefs predict effort expenditures and performance outcomes, even after controlling the person's level of ability (Schmitz & Skinner, 1993).

A second source from which perceived control beliefs originate is the social context in which engagement takes place (Skinner et al., 1998). From a developmental point of view, perceived control beliefs originate in children from within a context of interpersonal relationships. Under the guidance and watchful eye of parents, teachers, tutors, coaches, and others, children learn how much effect, if any, their actions have on their outcomes. Children develop relatively strong perceived control beliefs when those they learn from provide stimulating environments (Bradley & Caldwell, 1979; Nowick & Schneewind, 1982); consistent, sensitive, and responsive feedback (Hokoda & Fincham, 1995; Skinner, 1986); guidance on problem-solving tasks (Hokoda & Fincham, 1995; Nolen-Hoeksema, et al., 1995); and less intrusion, criticism, and punishment (Grolnick & Ryan, 1989; Grolnick, Ryan, & Deci, 1991). When adults provide stimulation, sensitivity, teaching, and autonomy support, they provide children with the structured, contingency-rich environments that help to cultivate opportunities for control and mastery.

When providing control-building structure, adults directly model, explain, coach, and teach children. These adults explain problem-solving strategies, communicate clear expectancies, help children regulate their emotions, give insight on repairing or preventing negative outcomes, and administer consequences in ways that are consistent, predictable, and contingent on the child's actions (Connell, 1990; Connell & Wellborn, 1991; Skinner & Belmont, 1993). Overall, what adults are doing when they provide children with structure is (1) providing information about the pathways children can take in achieving desired outcomes and (2) providing support and guidance for pursuing these pathways (Connell & Wellborn, 1991; Skinner, 1991, 1995; Skinner et al., 1998).

Theories that focus on the development of strong and resilient perceived control beliefs clearly and rightfully argue for the primacy of providing children with the sort of environmental and interpersonal structures in which they can encounter optimal challenges, build and diagnose skills, and use feedback to improve. Structure can be provided in ways that are cold, critical, hostile, and inappropriate or in ways that are warm, supportive, caring, and appropriate, a dimension of interpersonal relationships referred to as *sensitivity* (Ainsworth, 1979) or as *involvement* (Connell & Wellborn, 1991; Grolnick et al., 1991; Skinner, 1991, 1995, Skinner et al., 1998). When adults provide high involvement, they relate to children in ways that can be characterized as caring, benevolent, warm, and emotionally supportive[1] (Beyer, 1995; Estrada, Arsenio, Hess, & Holloway, 1987; Hokoda & Fincham, 1995; Nolen-Hoeksema et al., 1995). Involvement is an especially important contributor to perceived control beliefs when children are young (Skinner, 1986). As children age, however, involvement becomes less dominant, and the provision of structure becomes increasingly important (Skinner et al., 1998).

SELF-CONFIRMING CYCLES OF ENGAGED AND DISAFFECTED ACTION

Engagement exists along a continuum that ranges from disaffection to engagement (Skinner & Belmont, 1993; Wellborn, 1991). It captures the intensity and emotional quality of a person's participation during somewhat difficult undertakings (Connell & Wellborn, 1991; Skinner, 1991). When highly engaged, people exert strong and persistent effort and express positive emotion; when disaffected, people behave passively and express negative emotion (Patrick, Skinner, & Connell, 1993). Sample items from a measure for assessing student engagement in the classroom appears in Table 11.3.

Once perceived control beliefs are formed, they influence the individual's subsequent engagement, emotion, coping, and challenge-seeking (Boggiano et al., 1993; Skinner, 1995; Skinner et al., 1998). And this relationship between perceived control and engagement is especially important when tasks are challenging and difficult. People with high perceived control show relatively high effort, concentrate and pay attention, persist in the face of failure, maintain interest and curiosity in the task, and maintain optimism for

[1]During face-to-face interaction, involvement expresses itself when adults dedicate resources to children (e.g., give their time, attention), enjoy spending time with children, pay attention to the children's needs, express affection toward the children, communicate detailed knowledge about the children, and generally take time for the children's concerns (Connell, 1990; Connell & Wellborn, 1991; Grolnick & Ryan, 1989; Grolnick et al., 1991; Skinner & Belmont, 1993).

TABLE 11.3 **Sample Items From a Teacher-Generated Measure of Student Engagement in the Classroom**

BEHAVIORAL ENGAGEMENT		
In my class, this student . . .	works as hard as he/she can.	(+)
	does just enough to get by.	(–)
	comes unprepared.	(–)
When we start something new in class, this student . . .	participates in discussions.	(+)
	doesn't pay attention.	(–)
	thinks about other things.	(–)
EMOTIONAL ENGAGEMENT		
When we start something new in class, this student . . .	is relaxed.	(+)
	is bored.	(–)
In my class, this student . . .	is happy.	(+)
	is enthusiastic.	(+)
	is anxious.	(–)
	is angry.	(–)
When working on class work in my class, this student appears . . .	involved.	(+)
	worried.	(–)
	frustrated.	(–)

SOURCE: From *Engaged and Disaffected Action: The Conceptualization and Measurement of Motivation in the Academic Domain,* by J. G. Wellborn, an unpublished doctoral dissertation, University of Rochester.

future positive outcomes. People with low perceived control show relatively low effort, doubt their capacities, tend to give up in the face of challenge or failure, become discouraged quickly, are prone to passivity, anxiety, and even anger, and appear to simply go through the motions of participating (Skinner et al., 1998).

Such patterns of engagement versus disaffection are important in their own right, but they are also important because they predict the outcomes people attain. Attained outcomes, in turn, effect performers' postperformance perceptions of control. Hence, engaged effort produces the positive outcomes and postperformance perceptions of high control that produced the engaged effort in the first place. Disaffection (i.e., going through the motions) produces the negative outcomes and postperformance perceptions of low control that produced the disaffected effort in the first place.

One group of researchers tested over a four-month period the validity of these self-confirming cycles by asking grade-school children to complete short questionnaires (Schmitz & Skinner, 1993). The researchers assessed the children's expected control, extent of engagement, perceived task difficulty, actual performance, perceived performance, attributions for success and failure, and estimates of future control. On each graded assignment, the researchers examined the following relationships: (1) effects of preperformance expected control on subsequent engagement, (2) effects of engagement on actual performance, (3) effects of performance outcome on subsequent attributions, and (4) effects of attributions on subsequent expectations of control. The researchers then, using a sophisticated statistical technique called time-series analysis, aggregated the multiple-task engagements of each child into a developmental model to test the extent to which postperformance control beliefs served as preperformance control beliefs the next time the same activity was encountered. The researchers confirmed the validity of each of the links (1 through 4 above), and they also confirmed how the cyclical pattern becomes magnified over time through the self-confirming cycle depicted in Figure 11.10 (Schmitz & Skinner, 1993).

DESIRE FOR CONTROL

Desire for control (DC) reflects the extent to which individuals are motivated in establishing control over the events in their lives (Burger, 1992; Burger & Cooper, 1979). High-DC individuals approach situations by asking themselves whether they will be able to control what happens. They are not content to take whatever life throws their way but instead are motivated to influence life and what happens (Burger, 1992). High-DC persons prefer making their own decisions, prepare for situations in advance, avoid dependence on others, and assume leadership roles in group settings. Low-DC persons tend to avoid responsibilities and feel comfortable having others make decisions for them (Burger, 1992; Burger & Cooper, 1979). They prefer to take life as they find it, to wing it.

The scale to assess the desire for control is the DC scale (Burger, 1992; Burger & Cooper, 1979). Three typical items from the DC scale are the following:

- I prefer a job where I have a lot of control over what I do and when I do it.
- I like to get a good idea of what a job is all about before I begin.
- I am careful to check everything on an automobile before I leave for a long trip.

What makes the desire for control different from perceived control (discussed earlier) is that high-desire-for-control individuals want control over their fates irrespective of how much control they currently have and irrespective of how structured or responsive the situation appears to be. Desire for control relates to a variety of experiences and behaviors that are fundamental to personal control beliefs, including learned helplessness, depression, illusion of control, hypnosis, achievement, perceived crowding, stress and coping, interpersonal style with friends, health habits, and even an elderly person's choice of a place to die—in control at home or managed by others in a hospital (Burger, 1984, 1992; Burger & Arkin, 1980; Burger & Cooper, 1979; Burger, Oakman, & Bullard, 1983; Burger & Schnerring, 1982; Smith et al., 1984). The common links between desire for control and these behavioral manifestations of personal control are the high desire to establish control and to restore control when it is threatened or lost.

ESTABLISHMENT OF CONTROL

Control is often an issue in our daily conversations and interactions with others. To establish some measure of control over interpersonal conversations (what will be talked about, what attitudes the persons in the conversations hold, what plans will be made), high-DC individuals speak loudly, explosively, and rapidly; they respond quickly to questions and comments; and they interrupt and talk over their partners (Dembroski, MacDougall, & Musante, 1984). High-DC persons also tend to end conversations when they want to, usually after having finished what they wanted to say or after having successfully persuaded the other person of the correctness of the high-DC individual's viewpoint (i.e., after establishing control; Burger, 1990, 1992).

Desiring control is adaptive and productive when situations are controllable. Often, however, high-DC individuals want and expect control over events when, in fact, their outcomes are determined by chance. For example, many gambling opportunities such as slot machines, lottery games, bingo, roulette, and coin tosses are determined by chance. These games are known as "games of chance." Nonetheless, high-DC individuals tend to perceive that they can control such outcomes through personal effort. The *desire* for control feeds into the *illusion* of control (Burger, 1986, 1992).

Consider the following experimental demonstration: Participants signed up for a gambling experiment, received 50 poker chips, and bet whether a pair of thrown dice would add to a specific number between 2 and 12. For one group (the "bet-before" group), the experimenter picked a number, asked the participants to make a bet, and then had the participants try to roll that number to win. In the "bet-after" group, the participants first rolled the dice while the number was hidden under a cup; after the roll, the participants made bets. The logic of the first condition (bet-before) is that it sets up in the gambler's mind an illusion of control—basically, if a person knows what number he is trying to roll, then the way he rolls the dice might matter and therefore affect his control. Of course, this is an absurd assumption because the rolling of dice is an act of chance. But high-DC individuals in the bet-before group wagered significantly more chips than did participants in any of the other three groups (high-DC, bet-after; low-DC, bet-before; low DC, bet after) (Burger & Cooper, 1979). The magnitude of the bets served as an expression of the high-DC, bet-before individuals' personal control beliefs.

Achievement situations provide another illustration of high-DC individuals' desires to establish control (Burger, 1985). High-DC individuals typically interpret a difficult task as a challenge to their ability to control. Thus, when confronted with a difficult task, the high-DC individual should persist longer than the low-DC individual. To give up on a difficult task is to admit that the task is beyond personal control. To test this idea, Jerry Burger gave students a series of insoluble puzzles and observed how long the high- and low-DC individuals persisted. As predicted, high-DC individuals persisted longer at the puzzles than did the low-DC individuals.

The means by which high-DC individuals attempt to exert control in achievement situations extend beyond just sheer persistence. Burger (1985) proposed a four-step model to illustrate the multidimensional nature of the high-DC individual's quest to establish control in achievement situations (see Figure 11.11). High-DC persons select hard tasks because they generally have high aspirations and standards, put forth unusually high effort when challenged, persist at difficult tasks and are slow to give up and move on, and make self-serving and control-enhancing attributions such as taking credit for success while attributing failure to an unstable cause (Burger, 1985, 1992).

FIGURE 11.11 **Influence of Desire for Control During Achievement-Related Performance**

	Aspiration Level	Response to Challenge	Persistence	Attributions for Success and Failure
High DC Compared with Low DC	Select harder tasks; set goals more realistically	React with greater effort	Work at difficult task longer	More likely to attribute success to self and failure to unstable source
High DC Benefit	Higher goals are achieved	Difficult tasks are completed	Difficult tasks are completed	Motivation level remains high
High DC Liability	May attempt goals too difficult	May develop performance-inhibiting reactions	May invest too much effort	May develop an illusion of control

SOURCE: From "Desire for Control and Achievement-Related Behaviors," by J. M. Burger, 1985, *Journal of Personality and Social Psychology, 48*, pp. 1520–1533. Copyright 1985 by American Psychological Association. Adapted with permission.

The desire for control is generally a positive resource in achievement situations. But Figure 11.11 also outlines the desire for control's counterproductive side during achievement-related behavior. Because high-DC individuals strongly desire control, they sometimes attempt overly difficult goals, exhibit a hostile reactance effect with failure, persist too long on tasks that cannot be solved, and develop an illusion of control. What these data show is that the desire for control leads people to overestimate how well they will perform, to overinvest their energies, to persist too long on difficult tasks, and to interpret success and failure feedback in ways that feed an illusion of control.

LOSS OF CONTROL

People sometimes face situations where little control is possible. In circumstances such as overcrowding, military life, nursing homes, hospitals, prison, and living next door to an offensive dump, little control is possible. Such situations present an obvious plight for the high-DC individual. When their control is threatened or lost altogether, high-DC individuals exhibit distinct reactions, such as distress, anxiety, depression, dominance behavior, and assertive coping (Burger, 1992).

Visiting the dentist's office is one of these low-control situations (Law, Logan, & Baron, 1994). When people with a high DC visit the dentist, the idea of another person

Table 11.4 **Crowding and Discomfort Ratings for High- and Low-Desire-for-Control (DC) Individuals in High and Low Crowding**

	High crowding (6 persons)		Low crowding (3 persons)	
Rating scale	High DC	Low DC	High DC	Low DC
Crowding	6.2	4.9	4.8	3.6
Discomfort	5.6	4.2	4.0	3.2

The higher the number, the more crowding and discomfort on a 9-point scale.

Source: From "Desire for Control and the Perception of Crowding," by J. M. Burger, J. A. Oakman, and N. G. Bullard, 1983, *Personality and Social Psychology Bulletin, 9,* pp. 475–479. Copyright 1983. Reprinted with permission of Sage Publications.

using tools on their teeth causes unusually high levels of anxiety, anticipated pain, and distress. Interestingly, a 20-minute stress-inoculation training session immediately before the dental visit can give high-DC individuals the control-coping strategies and responses they desire (Law, Logan, & Baron, 1994). Anxiety, pain, and distress motivate the high-DC individual to want to gain control, and when control-establishing coping responses are discovered, the anxiety, pain, and distress fade away.

Crowding is another low-control situation. Crowding, defined by the number of people per square foot, undermines control because one cannot move about freely (Stokols, 1972). Having a lot of other people around, as in dense traffic, overpopulated sidewalks, and long supermarket checkout lines, interferes with anyone's ability to get things done. High-DC individuals are more vulnerable to perceptions of being crowded, and they therefore try to avoid such distressing situations (Burger, 1992). In an experiment, college students worked on a series of mathematical puzzles for 20 minutes in a six-foot-by-six-foot room (Burger, Oakman, & Bullard, 1983). Each student worked on problems and traveled from one side of the room to the other to accomplish the task. The small room had either three (low-crowding condition) or six (high-crowding condition) participants working individually on the problems at the same time. After the participants moved through either a crowded (six person) or not as crowded (three person) environment and solved as many problems as they could, the experimenters asked participants to report how much crowding and discomfort they felt during the 20 minutes. Results of this experiment appear in Table 11.4. High-DC individuals reported more crowding and greater discomfort than low-DC individuals in both the high and low crowded environments.[2]

Consider the implications for the high-DC individual in situations in which her desire for control exceeds her ability to exert control, such as being in the military, being in a hospital, being in prison, living in a nursing home, and living adjacent to a noisy airport. Wondering what effect such low-control environments have on high-DC individuals, Jerry Burger and Robert Arkin (1980) asked high- and low-DC individuals to participate in a

[2]Notice also the similarity between the high-DC individual's felt stress in the three-person room and the low-DC individual's felt stress in the six-person room. The high-DC individual's felt stress in low crowding was as high as the low-DC individual's felt stress in high crowding.

typical learned-helplessness experiment in which they were exposed to harsh, uncontrollable, and unpredictable noise. Compared to low-DC persons, high-DC persons reported higher levels of post-task depression. When people desire control but the environment refuses to afford it, the person becomes vulnerable to learned helplessness and depression. Further, the magnitude of the helplessness and depression vary with how important control is for that person in that situation (Mikulincer, 1986).

SUMMARY

Studying personality in motivation returns the discussion to a series of questions raised in chapter 1: For which motives are there individual differences? How do such motivational differences between people arise? And what are the implications of such individual motivational differences? This chapter identified three personality characteristics related to arousal and two characteristics related to control. It outlined how these personality differences arise, and it pointed out the implications of such personality characteristics for motivation and everyday life (e.g., task preferences, career choices).

Three arousal-based personality characteristics include extraversion, sensation seeking, and affect intensity. Extraversion is a super-trait that includes several sub-traits, including sociability, activity level, and impulsiveness. Differences in introversion-extraversion stem from physiological differences in the ascending reticular activating system (ARAS). Because of a chronically underaroused ARAS, extraverts need strong external stimulation in reaching an optimal level. Introverts, because of a chronically overaroused ARAS, need and prefer less intense external stimulation. These genetic differences lead extraverts to seek out stimulating social activity and lead introverts to seek opportunities to exercise more restrained, inhibited behavior.

Sensation seeking is the need for varied, novel, complex, and intense sensations and the willingness to take physical, social, legal, and financial risks for the sake of such experiences. Sensation seeking is a super-trait that organizes the four individual characteristics of thrill and adventure seeking, experience seeking, disinhibition, and boredom susceptibility. Sensation seekers (1) seek new experiences, as in sex and drugs; (2) engage in risk-taking behavior, as in gambling; and (3) volunteer for unusual activities, such as experiments on hypnosis. Psychophysiological, biochemical, and pharmacological studies generally support Zuckerman's conceptualization of the sensation-seeking construct as a physiologically based personality characteristic.

Affect intensity represents the strength with which individuals typically experience their emotions. Affect-intense individuals experience emotions strongly and show emotional hyperactivity in emotion-eliciting situations. Affect-stable individuals experience their emotions only mildly and show only minor fluctuations in their emotional reactions. To increase their otherwise low levels of arousal upward, affect-intense individuals exaggerate their emotionality by responding in emotionally intense ways to the positive and negative events in their lives.

Perceived control concerns the capacity to initiate and regulate the behavior needed to gain desirable outcomes and to prevent undesirable ones. When perceived control is strong, people engage in tasks with active coping and positive emotion, and this on-task engagement increases the probability that these people will attain the outcomes they seek. But when perceived control is weak, people engage in tasks in only halfhearted ways as they show passivity and negative emotion. This disaffection, in turn, decreases the probability that they will attain the outcomes they seek. Thus, by affecting engagement, perceived control beliefs initiate a self-confirming cycle in which people with high perceived control initiate the effort that produces the positive outcomes that, in turn, increases subsequent perceptions of high control. From a developmental point of view, children learn strong perceived control beliefs when the people who teach them provide learning environments characterized by both high structure and high involvement. Structure is especially important because it provides children with the information they need for discovering the pathways of control necessary for achieving their desired outcomes.

Desire for control reflects the extent to which people are motivated to control the events in their lives. High-DC individuals approach situations by wanting to control what happens to them. The two common links between the desire for control and control-involving life situations, such as interpersonal interactions, achievement behavior, health, hypnosis, and crowding, are the high-DC individuals' striving to (1) establish control and (2) restore control when lost or threatened. To establish control, high-DC individuals embrace high standards and aspirations, put forth high effort when challenged, overly persist at difficult tasks, and interpret success/failure feedback in a self-serving and control-enhancing way. When control is threatened or lost, as in visiting the dentist or entering a crowded room, high-DC individuals exhibit distinct reactions such as distress, anxiety, depression, dominance, and assertive coping.

RECOMMENDED READINGS

Personality Characteristics in the Preference for Arousal

Anderson, K. J. (1990). Arousal and the inverted-U hypothesis: A critique of Neiss's Reconceptualizing arousal. *Psychological Bulletin, 107,* 96–100.

Heron, W. (1957). The pathology of boredom. *Scientific American, 196,* 52–56.

Larsen, R. J., & Diener, E. (1987). Affect intensity as an individual difference characteristic: A review. *Journal of Research in Personality, 21,* 1–39.

Wilson, G. (1978). Introversion/Extraversion. In H. London & J. E. Exner Jr. (Eds.), *Dimensions of personality* (pp. 217–261). New York: John Wiley.

Zuckerman, M. (1978). Sensation seeking. In H. London & J. E. Exner Jr. (Eds.), *Dimensions of personality* (pp. 487–559). New York: John Wiley.

Zuckerman, M., Bone, R. N., Neary, R., Mangelsdorff, D., & Brustman, B. (1972). What is the sensation seeker? Personality trait and experience correlates of the Sensation Seeking Scale. *Journal of Clinical and Counseling Psychology, 39,* 308–321.

Personal Control Beliefs in Personality

Boggiano, A. K., Main, D. S., & Katz, P. A. (1988). Children's preference for challenge: The role of perceived competence and control. *Journal of Personality and Social Psychology, 54,* 134–141.

Burger, J. M. (1985). Desire for control and achievement-related behaviors. *Journal of Personality and Social Psychology, 53,* 1520–1533.

Hokoda, A., & Fincham, F. D. (1995). Origins of children's helpless and mastery achievement patterns in the family. *Journal of Educational Psychology, 87,* 375–385.

Law, A., Logan, H., & Baron, R. S. (1994). Desire for control, felt control, and stress inoculation training during dental treatment. *Journal of Personality and Social Psychology, 67,* 926–936.

Schmitz, B., & Skinner, E. A. (1993). Perceived control, effort, and academic performance: Interindividual, intraindividual, and multivariate time-series analyses. *Journal of Personality and Social Psychology, 64*, 1010–1028.

Skinner, E. A., Wellborn, J. G., & Connell, J. P. (1990). What it takes to do well in school and whether I've got it: The role of perceived control in children's engagement and school achievement. *Journal of Educational Psychology, 82*, 22–32.

12

Growth Motivation

Temperament predisposes a person to act in ways that are guided by genetics and biology. But cultures sometimes have other ideas about how a person should behave—for instance, by having standards of being extraverted and emotionally intense (exciting and entertaining). When biological disposition contradicts socialization preference, a problem surfaces: What happens when an experience feels right and natural, but the culture devalues anyone who gravitates toward that experience? And what happens when members of the culture reject their inner nature and try to substitute a more socially acceptable style in its place? All might be well. The individual accommodates and adjusts to the culture. Humanistic psychology, however, disagrees. It argues that rejecting nature in favor of social priorities puts personal growth and psychological well-being at risk.

Imagine yourself in the following experiment (Ford, 1991a): The experiment begins by asking you to self-report your temperament, using questionnaires such as those discussed in chapter 11 for extraversion, sensation-seeking, and affect intensity. The experimenter also asks for permission to send identical questionnaires to one of your parents (i.e., your primary caretaker), asking him or her to complete each in terms of how you behaved during the preschool ages of 3 to 5 years (old enough for temperament to express itself, young enough to precede heavy socialization). The study's prediction is that adults who express something other than their childhood temperament will show maladjustment.

To index maladjustment, the experimenter also asks you to complete questionnaire measures of anxiety, depression, hostility, feelings of inadequacy, and physical/somatic troubles. To test the humanistic hypothesis, the experimenter computes a discrepancy score of the difference between your expressed temperament as an adult (how extraverted, how sensation seeking, how emotionally intense) and your parent's rating of your temperament as a child. Results showed the greater the discrepancy, the greater the adult's maladjustment. People who were pressured—willingly or unwillingly—into acting in ways that contradicted their biologically based temperaments encountered problems. These findings introduce the theme of this chapter: "If this essential core (inner nature) of the person is frustrated, denied, or suppressed, sickness results" (Maslow, 1968). To Abraham Maslow's theme, we can add its logical complement: If this essential core is nurtured, appreciated, and supported, health results.

HOLISM

Human motives can be understood from many different perspectives, ranging from the most objective viewpoints of objectivism (Diserens, 1925), behaviorism (Watson, 1919), and logical positivism (Bergmann & Spence, 1941) to the most subjective viewpoints of existentialism (May, 1961), gestalt psychology (Goldstein, 1939; Perls, 1969), and holism (Aristotle, *On the Soul*). Along with existentialism and gestalt psychology, holism asserts that a human being is best understood as an integrated, organized whole rather than as a series of differentiated parts. It is the whole organism that is motivated rather than just some part of the organism, such as the stomach or brain. In holism, any event that affects one system affects the entire person. To borrow a phrase from Maslow, it is John Smith who desires food, not John Smith's stomach. Therefore, in modern parlance, holism sees little value in a "bottom-up" approach (i.e., focus on specific, individual motives, one at a time, and in relative isolation from one another) and, instead, prefers a "top-down" approach (i.e., focus on general, all-encompassing motives, seeing how the master motives govern the more specific ones).

Holism derives its name from "whole" or "wholeness" and therefore concerns itself with the study of what is healthy, or unbroken. In contrast, a broken view of personality emphasizes human beings as fragmented sets of structures or forces that oppose one another. For instance, a broken view speaks of the conflict between an ideal self and an actual self, or the conflict between the biological desire for food and the social demand for a slim figure. In psychoanalytic theory, a broken self manifests itself in a sort of psychological competition among the three personality structures of id, ego, and superego. In contrast, humanism identifies strongly with the holistic perspective, as it stresses "top-down" master motives, such as the self and its strivings toward fulfillment.

In a nutshell, humanistic psychology is about discovering human potential and encouraging its development. To accomplish this, the humanistic perspective concerns strivings (1) toward growth and self-realization and (2) away from facade, self-concealment, and the pleasing and fulfilling of the expectations of others (Rogers, 1966). In every page authored by humanistic thinkers, the reader can hear a commitment to growth as the ultimate motivational force. The first half of this chapter presents the ideas of Maslow and Carl Rogers to provide a sense of how human potential is discovered and nurtured. The second half of the chapter takes a step back from these ideas to see how well they stand up to the rigors of empirical test.

SELF-ACTUALIZATION

Self-actualization is the process of developing in a way that leaves behind infantile heteronomy—dependence on others—defensiveness, cruelty, and timidity and moves toward autonomous self-regulation, realistic appraisals, compassion toward others, and the courage to create and to explore. It is "an underlying flow of movement toward constructive fulfillment of its inherent possibilities" (Rogers, 1980). It refers to an ever-fuller realization of one's talents, capacities, and potentialities (Maslow, 1987). Such a flowing process cultivates a climate for optimal psychological growth and healthy development. It also cultivates a climate for progress toward being a fully functioning human being.

The two fundamental directions for healthy growth are autonomy and openness to experience. *Autonomy* means moving away from heteronomy and toward an ever-increasing capacity to depend on one's self and to regulate one's own behavior (Deci & Ryan, 1991). *Openness* means a way of receiving information and feelings such that neither is repressed, ignored, filtered, nor distorted by wishes, fear, or past experiences (Mittelman, 1991).

HIERARCHY OF HUMAN NEEDS

The cornerstone of Maslow's understanding of motivation is the proposition that human beings possess needs at the organismic level. Maslow proposed that one cluster of interrelated needs—those toward growth—govern and organize all other needs into a hierarchy featuring five clusters that range from relatively potent survival needs to relatively weak growth needs. The arrangement of these needs, Maslow felt, was best communicated visually by a hierarchy, as illustrated in Figure 12.1. The first set of needs contains those physiological needs necessary for bodily homeostasis, quiescence, and survival. All the other needs in the hierarchy (safety and security, love and belongingness, esteem, and self-actualization) are psychological needs.

The hierarchical presentation conveys three fundamental themes about the nature of human needs (Maslow, 1943, 1987).

FIGURE 12.1 **Maslow's Need Hierarchy**

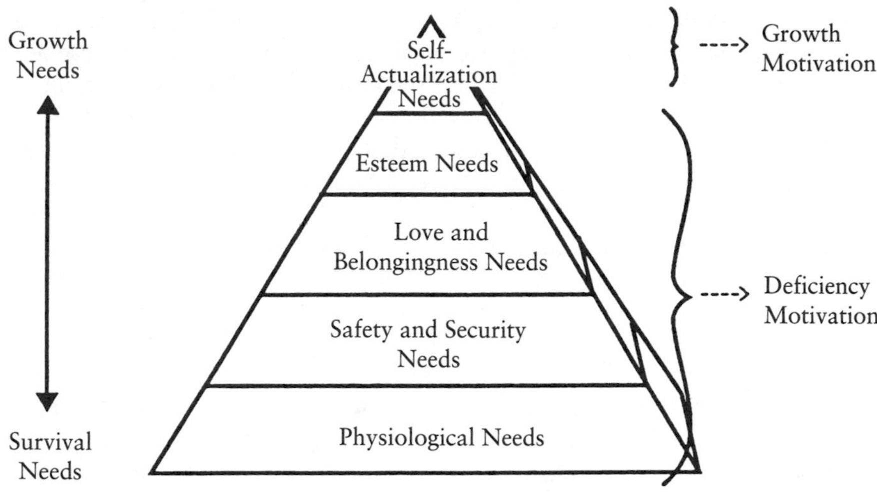

1. Needs arrange themselves in the hierarchy according to potency or strength.
2. The lower the need is in the hierarchy, the sooner it appears in development.
3. Needs in the hierarchy are fulfilled sequentially, from lowest to highest, from the base of the pyramid to its apex.

The first theme communicated by the hierarchical organization is that the physiological needs (at the bottom of the hierarchy) dominate as the strongest motives, whereas the self-actualization needs (at the top) are the weakest motives. Self-actualization needs are quiet urges that are often confused and easily overlooked in day-to-day affairs. The second theme communicates that the lower needs (e.g., safety and security) characterize needs typical of nonhuman animals and of children, whereas the higher needs (e.g., esteem) are uniquely human and pertain to adults. Notice that this developmental principle applies to both phylogenetic (species—from simple species to complex ones) and ontological (individual—from infancy to adulthood) development. Third, the hierarchical organization stipulates that before people seek esteem and peer respect, they must first have physiological, safety, and belongingness needs sufficiently gratified. Satisfying lower needs is a prerequisite to satisfying higher needs.

Deficiency Needs

Physiological disturbances and needs for safety, belongingness, and esteem are collectively referred to as *deficiency needs*. Deficiency needs are like vitamins; we need them because their absence inhibits growth and development. For Maslow, human beings are constantly wanting and rarely reaching a state of satisfaction, except for only a brief time. When one set of needs is fulfilled, however, it typically gives rise to another set of needs. The physiological needs, for example, dominate consciousness until these needs have been gratified and then allows the next, higher cluster of needs to emerge. Once emerged, the safety and security needs then dominate consciousness and occupy the individual's attention. Thus, gratification of hunger, thirst, and sleep, for instance, not only submerge these needs, but in effect, their gratification opens the door for the individual's desire for a predictable, orderly, and safe environment.

An interesting point made by Maslow was that the presence of any of the deficiency needs indicated that the individual was in a state of deprivation, whether that state of deprivation involved food, job security, group membership, or social status. Maslow (1971) characterized such deprivation as human sickness, a term he used to connote a failure to move toward growth and actualization.

Growth Needs

Given satisfaction, rather than deprivation, of the deficiency needs, growth needs surface and render the person restless and discontent. The person no longer feels hungry, insecure, isolated, or inferior, but he instead feels a need to fulfill personal potential by becoming that person he is specifically suited to be. Self-actualization is the desire to become more of what one is and to become everything that one is capable of becoming: "A musician must make music, an artist must paint, a poet must write, if he is to be ultimately happy. What a man can be, he must be. This need we may call self-actualization" (Maslow, 1943). Putting the sexist language aside for the moment, it is a bit difficult to pinpoint precisely what self-actualization needs are and are not. One can understand physiological needs by thinking of hunger and thirst, but self-actualization is a more abstruse term. It is actually a master motive that coalesces 17 "metaneeds" (or higher-order needs; see Table 12.1). One good way to discover just what self-actualization needs are is to pay attention to each metaneed's pathogenic deprivation state (listed on the right-hand side of Table 12.1). For instance, in monitoring these deprivation states during conversation (or counseling), one can hear human sickness in the man who speculates that his wife could easily find another, equally good mate (see number 7 in the table) or who seems only to be going through the motions at work (see number 6) or who has not developed any new interest in years (see number 13).

Research on the Need Hierarchy

Maslow's need hierarchy (see Table 12.1) has been embraced as a modus operandi in education, business, management, the workplace, psychotherapy, and the health professions of medicine, nursing, and geriatrics (Cox, 1987). While the professions have been eager to embrace the need hierarchy, the empirical evidence testing its validity has been much more cautious. Despite its popularity, research has actually found very little empirical support for the need hierarchy (Wahba & Bridwell, 1976).

One research strategy investigates changes in motivation related to age (Goebel & Brown, 1981). According to Maslow, the young tend to be occupied with physiological and safety needs, while adults tend to be occupied with esteem and actualization needs, generally speaking. Goebel and Brown (1981) had children, adolescents, young adults,

TABLE 12.1 **Maslow's Metaneeds and Their Pathogenic Deprivations**

METANEED	PATHOGENIC DEPRIVATION
1. Truth	Dishonesty
2. Goodness	Evil
3. Beauty	Ugliness
4. Unity, wholeness	Chaos, atomism, loss of connectedness
5. Dichotomy transcendence	Black and white dichotomies, loss of gradations
6. Aliveness, process orientation	Deadness, mechanizing of life
7. Uniqueness	Sameness, uniformity, interchangeability
8. Perfection, necessity	Imperfection, sloppiness, poor workmanship
9. Completion, finality	Incompleteness
10. Justice	Injustice
11. Order	Lawlessness, chaos, breakdown of authority
12. Simplicity	Confusing complexity, disconnectedness
13. Richness, totality, comprehensiveness	Poverty, constricture
14. Effortfulness	Effortlessness
15. Playfulness	Humorlessness
16. Self-sufficiency	Contingency, occasionalism
17. Meaningfulness	Meaninglessness

SOURCE: From "A Theory of Metamotivation," by Abraham Maslow, 1971, *The Farther Reaches of Human Nature* (pp. 290–340), New York. Copyright 1971 by Bertha G. Maslow. Used with permission of Viking Penguin, a division of Penguin Books USA Inc.

middle-aged adults, and older adults complete the Life Motivation Scale (LMS); one of the items of the scale appears in the upper part of Table 12.2. Results appear in the lower part of the same table. Looking across each row, children rated the physiological needs as more important than did the other four groups, just as Maslow would predict. However, for safety, older adults rated these needs as most important. For belongingness, all age groups (except maybe children) rated these needs as equally important. For esteem, adolescents rated these needs as more important than did the other age groups. Self-actualization is ranked highest by the young adults and middle-aged adults and ranked lowest by the children and older adults.

A second research strategy tests the hierarchy's validity using the rank order method (Blai, 1964; Goodman, 1968; Mathes, 1981). In this methodology, participants rank the needs in the order of desirability or importance. In general, the way people rank the needs does not conform to Maslow's predicted order; for instance, a group of adult service workers ranked safety/security needs as most important and esteem needs as least important (Blai, 1964). In a study with college students, young adults ranked the needs they could most stand to have unmet (i.e., do without). College students' priorities were as follows, in order from least important to most important: esteem needs, security needs, self-actualization needs, belongingness needs, and physical needs (Mathes, 1991).

TABLE 12.2 **Life Motivation Scale Items and Rated Responses**

Directions: Rank in order the five statements listed below in terms of how important each is to you.

_______ I like doing things that make other people look up to me. (Esteem)
_______ I like doing things with my family and friends. (Belongingness)
_______ I like doing things that fill my physical needs. (Physiological)
_______ I like doing things that let me develop my talents or interests. (Self-Actualization)
_______ I like doing things that are planned ahead. (Safety)

NEED HIERARCHY	CHILDREN (N =22)	ADOLESCENTS (N = 21)	YOUNG ADULTS (N = 24)	(MIDDLE ADULTS (N = 22)	OLDER ADULTS (N = 22)
Physiological	22.59	14.24	14.50	13.14	14.82
Safety/security	19.77	19.14	19.25	20.00	22.50
Belongingness	29.68	32.14	34.21	33.14	33.73
Esteem	17.50	19.33	13.63	15.73	15.36
Self-actualization	20.50	25.14	28.60	27.91	23.59

SOURCE: From "Age Differences in Motivation Related to Maslow's Need Hierarchy," by B. L. Goebel and D. R. Brown, 1981, *Developmental Psychology, 17*, pp. 809–815. Copyright 1981 by American Psychological Association. Adapted with permission.

Admittedly, these data involve only self-reports of needs (rather than actually experiencing deprivation directly), but overall, the pattern of findings casts considerable doubt on the hierarchy's validity. The one finding that is supported by empirical research is the conceptualization of a dual-level (rather than a five-level) hierarchy. In a dual-level hierarchy, the only distinction is between deficiency and growth needs (Wahba & Bridwell, 1976). In the studies just reviewed, a difference does emerge between *deficiency* and *growth* needs. Thus, the conclusion from research on Maslow's need hierarchy is to (1) reject the five-level hierarchy; (2) collapse the physiological, safety, belongingness, and esteem needs into the single category of deficiency needs; and (3) embrace a simplified, two-level hierarchy distinguishing only between deficiency and growth needs.

ENCOURAGING SELF-ACTUALIZATION

Maslow estimated that less than 1% of the population ever reached self-actualization. Because the self-actualization needs were supposedly innate, one is left wondering why everyone does not ultimately self-actualize. In some cases, Maslow reasoned, people fail to reach their potential because of a nonsupportive environment (e.g., not enough food or shelter to gratify basic needs). In other cases, the person was responsible for her own lack of growth (i.e., each of us fears our own potential, which Maslow termed the "Jonah complex"). Maslow recognized the contradiction between his proposition that self-actualization was innate (and therefore operative in all human beings) and his observation that few among us actually gratify self-actualization needs. Ever the counselor and

TABLE 12.3 **Eight Behaviors That Encourage Self-Actualization**

1. See life as a series of choices, forever a choice toward progression and growth versus regression and fear. The progression-growth choice is a movement toward self-actualization, whereas the regression-fear choice is a movement away from self-actualization.
2. Dare to be different, unpopular, nonconformist.
3. Set up conditions to make peak experiences more likely. Get rid of false notions and illusions. Find out what you are not good at, and learn what your potential is by learning what your potentials are not.
4. Identify defenses and find the courage to give them up.
5. Be honest rather than not, especially when in doubt. Take responsibility for your choices and the consequences of those choices.
6. Let the self emerge. Perceive within yourself and see and hear the innate impulse voices. Shut out the noises of the world.
7. Experience fully, vividly, selflessly with full concentration and total absorption. Experience without self-consciousness, defenses, or shyness.
8. Use your intelligence to work toward doing well the thing one wants to do well, be it the work of physician, parent, pianist, scholar, or athlete.

clinician, Maslow (1971) therefore offered several everyday behaviors for encouraging self-actualization, as listed in Table 12.3.

Maslow also stressed that people could not directly bring about peak experiences in their lives (Hardeman, 1979). Instead, peak experiences were more of a by-product of psychological health. By making growth choices, by being honest, by identifying and giving up defenses, and by experiencing life situations fully (i.e., the behaviors listed in Table 12.3), people can make peak experiences more likely. But that is not the same as saying that people can create a peak experience directly.

One prescription for setting up conditions that make peak experiences probable can be found in Csikszentmihalyi's (1990) flow model (see chapter 4), which identifies the pairing of the level of challenge with the level of skill to generate the flow experience. A second prescription would be to move toward being more spontaneous, original, and open to experience. Being given the opportunity to act in a creative way in one endeavor frequently enhances creativity on a second endeavor (Conti, Amabile, & Pollak, 1995). Imagine, for instance, getting ready to begin task B, but first doing task A. On task B, your creativity, intrinsic motivation, and conceptual understanding would all be enhanced by the prior creative experience. In short, creative activity produces a spillover effect that cultivates further spontaneity, creativity, and an eagerness to gain more information (Conti, Amabile, & Pollak, 1995).

In addition to his advice (i.e., Table 12.3), Maslow stressed the important role of relationships—beautiful, intimate, and fulfilling relationships rather than the all-too-common superficial ones—as the soil for cultivating peak experiences (Hardeman, 1979). Setting up conditions to foster peak experiences often means involving oneself in relationships that are open and mutually supportive of each person's autonomy and potential.

ACTUALIZING TENDENCY

Humanistic psychology's emphasis on holism and self-actualization can be represented by Carl Rogers' oft-cited quotation: "The organism has one basic tendency and striving—to actualize, maintain, and enhance the experiencing self" (1951). Fulfillment of physiological needs maintains and enhances the organism, as does the fulfillment of needs for belongingness and social status. Further, a motive like curiosity enhances and actualizes the person via greater complexity and understanding. Overall, Rogers (1959, 1963) recognized the existence of specific human motives and even the existence of clusters of needs (e.g., Figure 12.1), but he emphatically stressed the holistic proposition that all human needs serve the collective purpose of maintaining, enhancing, and actualizing the person.

Rogers, like Maslow, believed that the actualizing tendency was innate, a continual presence that guides the individual toward genetically determined potentials. This forward-moving pattern of development was characterized by "struggle and pain," and Rogers offered the following illustration for communicating the self-actualizing tendency's path toward development and growth. The 9-month-old infant has the genetic potential to walk but must struggle to advance from crawling to walking to make those first steps. Such a struggle inevitably includes episodes of falling and feeling frustrated, hurt, and disappointed. Despite the struggle and pain, the child persists toward walking and away from crawling. The pain and disappointment undermine the child's motivation to walk, but the actualization tendency, "the forward thrust of life," supports the child ever forward. The actualizing tendency is the source of that energy that motivates development "toward autonomy and away from heteronomy" (Rogers, 1959).

All experiences within the struggle and pain of actualizing are evaluated in accordance with an "organismic valuation process," an innate capability for judging whether a specific experience promotes or reverses growth. Experiences perceived as maintaining or enhancing the person are positively valued. Such growth-promoting experiences are subsequently approached. Experiences perceived as regressive are valued negatively. Such growth-blocking experiences are subsequently avoided. In effect, the organismic valuation process provides a feedback system that allows the individual to coordinate life experiences in accordance with the actualization tendency. The actualizing tendency guides the individual in undertaking new and challenging experiences, and the organismic valuation process provides the interpretive information needed for deciding whether the new undertaking is growth-promoting or not.

EMERGENCE OF THE SELF

The actualizing tendency characterizes the individual as a whole. With the emergence of the self, a person grows in complexity, and the organismic valuation process begins to apply not only to the organism as a whole but also to the self in particular. The most important motivational implication of the emergence of the self is that the actualizing tendency begins to express itself in part toward that portion of the organism conceptualized as the self. This means that the individual gains a second major motivational force in addition to the actualizing tendency, namely the self-actualizing tendency. Notice that actualization and self-actualization are not the same thing (Ford, 1991b), as the actualizing tendency and the self-actualizing tendency can work at odds with one another, as discussed in the next section.

The emergence of the self prompts the emergence of the need for positive regard. Positive regard includes approval, acceptance, and love from others. The need for positive regard is of special significance because it makes the individual sensitive to the feedback of others (criticisms and praises). Other people (and their attitudes, evaluations, and perspectives) assume a greater importance in one's life. Over time, evaluating the self from other people's points of view becomes a rather automated process. By attending to the criticisms and praises of others, the individual internalizes societal feedback. The person's sense of self then becomes an increasing reflection of other people's perspectives.

Conditions of Worth

Soon after birth, children begin to learn the "conditions of worth" on which their behavior and personal characteristics (the self) are judged as either positive and worthy of acceptance or negative and worthy of rejection. Eventually, because the need for positive regard sensitizes the individual to attend to the acceptances and rejections of others, the child internalizes parental conditions of worth into the self structure. Throughout development, the self structure expands beyond parental conditions of worth to include societal conditions of worth as well. By adulthood, the individual learns from parents, friends, teachers, clergy, spouses, coaches, employers, and others what behaviors and which characteristics are good and bad, right and wrong, desirable and undesirable.

According to Rogers (1959), all of us live in two worlds—the inner world of the organismic valuing process and the outer world of conditions of worth. As a consequence of internalizing conditions of worth, acquired conditions of worth substitute, and largely replace, the innate organismic valuation process. When governed by conditions of worth, individuals necessarily divorce themselves from their inherent means of coordinating experience with the actualizing tendency. No longer is experience judged in accordance with the innate organismic valuation process. Rogers viewed the child's movement toward socialized conditions of worth and away from organismic valuation as antithetical to the development of the actualizing tendency. When the developing individual adheres to conditions of worth, he moves farther away from an inherent ability to make the behavioral choices necessary to actualize the self.[1] The overall process and consequences of adherence to either the organismic valuation process or socialized conditions of worth are summarized in Figure 12.2.

The way not to interfere with organismic valuation is to provide "unconditional positive regard," rather than the "conditional positive regard" that emanates from conditions of worth. If given unconditional positive regard, a child has no need to internalize societal

[1] At this point, the reader might have already recalled the experiment at the beginning of the chapter. Ford's study was designed, in fact, as an explicit test of Rogers' ideas presented here (and in Figure 12.2).

FIGURE 12.2 **Rogerian Model of the Process of Self-Actualization**

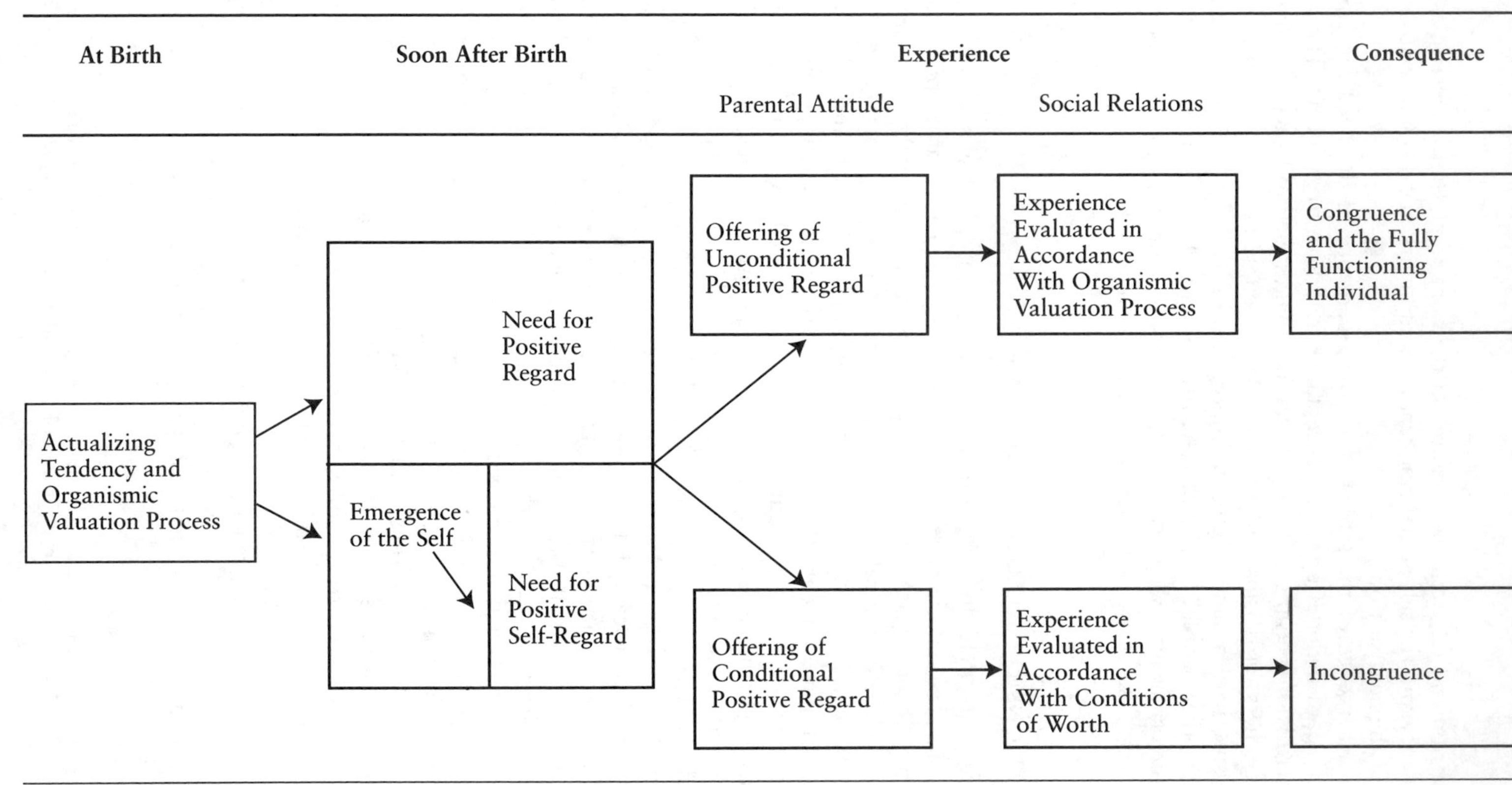

conditions of worth. Experiences are judged as valuable to the extent that they enhance oneself. A condition of worth arises, however, when the positive regard of another person is conditional—depends on something or on some way of behaving. Here, experiences are judged as valuable to the extent that they are approved of by others. If parents approve of, love, and accept their child for who she naturally is rather than for who the parents wish her to be, then the child and the child's self-structure will be a relatively transparent representation of her inherent preferences, talents, capacities, and potentialities.

In the absence of salient conditions of worth, there exists no conflict between the actualizing tendency and the self-actualizing tendency, and the two motivational tendencies remain unified (Rogers, 1959). Internalized conditions of self-worth, however, create the potential for motivational conflict. With conditional self-regard, conflict between the actualizing and self-actualizing tendencies creates a tension and internal confusion since some aspects of behavior are regulated by the actualizing tendency, while other aspects of behavior are regulated by the self-actualizing tendency (Ford, 1991b; Rogers, 1959). Self-actualization, when evaluated and directed via conditions of worth rather than organismic valuation, can paradoxically lead a person to develop in a way that is incongruent, conflicting, and maladaptive (Ford, 1991b). Thus, self-actualization does not necessarily lead to and result in health and growth. Sometimes the pursuit of self-actualization leads to and results in maladjustment, as when conditions of worth define and direct self-actualization processes. Health and growth occur only when the actualizing tendency and the self-actualizing tendency are in synchronization and when all experiences are evaluated internally within the framework of organismic valuation.

Parents, for instance, are placed in difficult positions when their child expresses a somewhat socially undesirable characteristic, such as shyness, moodiness or irritability, or an explosive temper. Socially appropriate conditional positive regard implies rejection and retraining for the child's temperament, in the name of promoting social inclusion and popularity. But unconditional positive regard implies acceptance of and support for the child's natural temperament. The difficult position the parents face manifests itself in the dilemma of avoiding psychological costs (e.g., depression) versus avoiding social costs (e.g., peer rejection) to the developing child.

CONGRUENCE

Congruence and incongruence describe the extent to which the individual denies and rejects (incongruence) or accepts (congruence) the full range of his personal characteristics, abilities, desires, and beliefs. Psychological incongruence is essentially the extent of discrepancy or difference between "the self as perceived and the actual experience of the organism" (Rogers, 1959). The individual might perceive himself as having one set of characteristics and one set of feelings but then publicly express a different set of characteristics and a different set of feelings. Independence between experience and expression reveals incongruence; overlap between experience and expression reveals congruence.

When people move toward identifying with external conditions of worth, they adopt facades. A facade is essentially the social mask a person wears, and it relates to ways of behaving that have little to do with inner guides and much to do with a front for hiding behind (Rogers, 1961). Consider the unauthentic smile. People vary in their extraversion and sociability, yet culture varies little in its preferences for people who are outgoing and entertaining. Hence, introverts often find themselves wearing the facade of the unauthentic smile. Consider the consequence of wearing a sociability facade on a regular basis (e.g., at a social gathering; Ford, 1995). Relying on social facades predicts proneness to maladjustment, including high anxiety, depression, low self-assertiveness, and both a history and an expectation of negative experience in social interaction. Adopting socially desirable facades carries its psychological costs.

FULLY FUNCTIONING INDIVIDUAL

The fully functioning individual allows the full range of her experiences to nurture the actualizing tendency. When fully functioning, the individual lives in close and confident relationship to the organismic valuation process, trusting that inner direction. Further, the fully functioning individual spontaneously communicates inner impulses both verbally and nonverbally. To characterize the moment-to-moment experience of the fully functioning individual, Figure 12.3 illustrates the sequential process of a motive's emergence, acceptance, and unedited expression.

GROWTH-SEEKING VERSUS VALIDATION-SEEKING

When people identify with and internalize societal conditions of worth, they do more than just adopt socially desirable facades. A quasi-need emerges. The quasi-need (see chapter 6) emerges to the extent that the individual *needs* social approval—directly or symbolically—during social interaction. That is, valuing oneself along the lines of societal conditions of worth leads people into processes of validation-seeking. In seeking validation, people often strive to attain external symbols of achievement and peer acceptance, and they routinely view other people—their peers, employers, teachers, and romantic partners—as possible sources of external validation (Dykman, 1998).

Validation-seeking individuals strive to prove their self-worth, competence, and likeability. Seeking validation leads to a pattern of thinking in which difficult or challenging situations are seen as tests or measurements of one's self-worth, competence, or likeability. In particular, outcomes from interpersonal interactions come to be seen as judgments about, or yardsticks by which to measure, one's personal worth, competence, or likeability. Positive outcomes generally leave the validation-seeking individual feeling rather

FIGURE 12.3 **Fully Functioning as the Emergence, Acceptance, and Expression of a Motive**

Emergence		Acceptance		Expression
Onset of innate desire, impulse, or motive	→	Desire, impulse, or motive is accepted "as is" into consciousness	→	Unedited communication of desire, impulse, or motive

validated. The adjustment problems surface following negative outcomes because these problems imply a lack of personal worth, competence, or likeability.

In contrast to validation-seeking individuals, growth-seeking individuals center their personal strivings around learning, improving, and reaching personal potential. Seeking growth leads one to adopt a pattern of thinking in which difficult or challenging situations are seen as opportunities for personal growth, learning, or self-improvement. As with validation-seeking individuals, positive outcomes from interpersonal interaction (e.g., social inclusion, interpersonal acceptance, athletic or academic successes) generally leave the growth-seeking individual feeling validated as well because the growth-seeking individual experiences a sense of progress in growing, learning, or improving. Unlike validation-seeking individuals, however, negative interpersonal outcomes (e.g., exclusion, rejection, failure) fail to usher in adjustment problems because negative outcomes simply identify and communicate information about life areas that are in need of improvement.

The Goal Orientation Inventory (GOI; Dykman, 1998) measures validation-seeking and growth-seeking strivings as relatively enduring personality characteristics. As a way of illustration, the first two items listed below are from the GOI's Validation-Seeking scale, whereas the last two items are from the inventory's Growth-Seeking scale. In responding to each question, the respondent is asked to agree or disagree on whether the item describes how she thinks and acts in general (Dykman, 1998):

Validation-Seeking Items

1. Instead of just enjoying activities and social interactions, most situations to me feel like a major test of my basic worth, competence, or likeability.
2. I feel like I'm constantly trying to prove that I'm as competent as the people around me.

Growth-Seeking Items

3. Personal growth is more important to me than protecting myself from my fears.
4. I look upon difficult life situations knowing that I can accept failure or rejection as long as I learn and grow from the experience.

This distinction between personal striving for validation versus growth is important because it predicts vulnerability to losing one's sense of worth. For instance, the more people strive for validation, the more likely they are to suffer high anxiety during social interaction, high social anxiety in general, high fear of failure, low self-esteem, poor task persistence, and high depression (see Table 12.4). In contrast, the more people strive for growth, the more likely they are to experience low interaction anxiety, low social anxiety, low fear of failure, high self-esteem, high task persistence, and low depression (see Table 12.4). All of the outcomes listed in Table 12.4 are important life outcomes, but researchers pay special attention to the relationship between validation-seeking and depression because seeking validation is associated with a fragile and contingent self-worth that could leave a person vulnerable to being overwhelmed by each rejection or failure (Dykman, 1998). On a cheerier note, seeking validation versus

Perfectionism as Conditions of Worth

Question: Why would a person want to learn about the motivational states discussed in this chapter?

Answer: Because concepts like "conditions of worth" invite the individual to examine the origin and quality of his own beliefs about self.

Nowhere in the industrialized world is the suicide rate higher for young men than it is in New Zealand. The everyday cultural expectations these men face stresses inflated standards of masculinity, unrealistic self-reliance, total emotional control, and unbound excellence in school and sports. From a humanistic perspective, these young men are asked to internalize conditions of worth characterized by perfectionism. The psychological costs of perfectionism become apparent when the individual experiences stressful and negative life events and is prone to depression, thoughts of suicide, and, to the extreme, acts of suicide (Blatt, 1995).

High personal standards are not all bad, however. These standards often precede positive achievement strivings and good work habits (Frost, et al., 1990). In "normal perfectionism," people remain capable of experiencing pleasure and satisfaction in their work (Hamachek, 1978; Timpe, 1989). But perfectionism, like ice cream, comes in flavors, including "self-oriented perfectionism" and "socially prescribed perfectionism" (Hewitt & Platt, 1991a, 1991b).

Self-oriented perfectionism features exceedingly high, self-imposed, unrealistic standards that are paired with extreme self-criticism and an unwillingness to accept failure and personal flaws. When the self-oriented perfectionist does experience failure, self-criticism and depression are likely aftershocks. Socially prescribed perfectionism is rooted in one's belief that other people hold exaggerated and unrealistic expectations for the self that are difficult, if not impossible, to meet—yet must be met if one is to gain acceptance and approval (Hewitt & Platt, 1991a, 1991b). Unfortunately, because these extremely high standards are imposed upon the self, a person experiences them as uncontrollable and hence produce aftershocks in the form of anxiety, helplessness, and hopelessness—affects associated with depression and thoughts of suicide (Blatt, 1995).

growth relates to self-actualization, as growth-seeking individuals are more likely (than validation-seeking individuals) to view themselves as being highly time competent (i.e., living in the present) and inner directed (i.e., guiding behavior according to one's own principles; see Table 12.4).

This distinction between validation-seeking and growth-seeking personal strivings is another way of expressing Maslow's distinction between deficiency and growth needs. Seeking validation is the pursuit of continually trying to restore one's deficiency needs, at least at the interpersonal level, whereas seeking growth is the pursuit of looking for opportunities to realize one's growth potential.

The distinction between validation-seeking and growth-seeking also expresses Rogers' distinction between conditional positive regard and unconditional positive regard. Seeking

When relationships (as with parents and teachers) are supportive and nurturing, both self-oriented and socially prescribed dimensions of perfectionism can facilitate constructive strivings (Nystul, 1984). When relationships are not supportive and when life experiences result in episodes of failure, however, perfectionism often collapses into "neurotic perfectionism" (Hamachek, 1978), which essentially is the intense need to avoid failure. With neurotic perfectionism, no performance is good enough, and even well-done jobs can yield little or no satisfaction. Deep feelings of inferiority throw the individual into an endless cycle of self-defeating, excessive striving accompanied by self-criticism, self-attack, and intense negative feelings. In general, neurotic perfectionism is associated with a wide range of psychopathology—depression (Hewitt & Dyck, 1986; LaPointe & Crandell, 1980), suicide (Adkins & Parker, 1995; Delisle, 1986; Shaffer, 1977), and eating disorders (Brouwers & Wiggum, 1993; Druss & Silverman, 1979; Katzman & Wolchik, 1984).

Neurotic perfectionism grows out of childhood experiences with disapproving parents whose love is conditional on how well the child performs and behaves (Hamachek, 1978). Rather than providing unconditional positive regard, these parents constantly urge their child to do better. The child never feels satisfied because his performances and behaviors never hit his parents' moving target of being good enough to gain approval and love. To the extent that such conditions of worth are internalized, the individual uses self-criticism and withdrawal of self-love as personal punishments. The result is an intense pressure for perfectionism and a constant quest to avoid mistakes. The internalized voice keeps saying, "If I try a little harder, if I do a little better, if I become perfect, my parents will love me" (Hollender, 1965). All too often, the harsh, judgmental relationship the child has with her parents is internalized as a self-critical voice. Such a relationship is the antithesis of unconditional positive regard, and such a voice is the antithesis of organismic valuing.

validation is a striving that grows out of parent-child interactions characterized by critical, conditional, and perfectionistic parenting, whereas seeking growth is a striving that grows out of parent-child interactions characterized by supportive, nonjudgmental, and acceptance parenting (Blatt, 1995; Dykman, 1998).

CAUSALITY ORIENTATIONS

People vary in their understandings of the forces that cause their behavior. Some people adopt a general orientation that their behavior is caused primarily by inner guides and self-determined forces; others adopt a general orientation that their behavior is caused

TABLE 12.4 **Correlations Between the Goal Orientation Inventory (GOI) and Related Personality Measures**

PERSONALITY MEASURE	VALIDATION-SEEKING SCALE OF THE GOI	GROWTH-SEEKING SCALE OF THE GOI
Interaction anxiety	.46**	–.48**
Social anxiety	.42**	–.41**
Fear of failure	.50**	–.48**
Self-esteem	.59**	–.56**
Task persistence	.40**	–.55**
Depression	.38**	–.36**
Self-actualization		
Time competence scale	–.51**	.20*
Inner directedness scale	–.56**	.31**

*p < .05; **p < .01. *N* ranged from 101 to 251 for each correlation reported above.

NOTE: The personality scale for each measure listed above was as follows: Interaction anxiety, Interaction Anxiousness Scale (Leary, 1983); social anxiety, Social Anxiety Subscale of the Self-Consciousness Scale (Fenigstein, Scheier, & Buss, 1975); fear of failure, Fear of Failure Scale (Dykman, 1998); self-esteem, Rosenberg's Self-Esteem Scale (Rosenberg, 1965); task persistence, Hope Scale (Snyder et al., 1991); depression, Beck Depression Inventory (Beck et al., 1979); and self-actualization, Personality Orientation Inventory (Shostrom, 1964, 1974).

primarily by social guides and environmental incentives. To the extent that individuals rely on internal guides (e.g., needs, interests), individuals have an "autonomy causality orientation." To the extent that individuals rely on external guides (e.g., social cues), they have a "control causality orientation."

The autonomy orientation involves a high degree of experienced choices with respect to the initiation and regulation of behavior (Deci & Ryan, 1985b). When autonomy-oriented, people's behavior proceeds with a full sense of volition and an internal locus of causality. Needs, interests, and personally valued goals initiate the person's behavior, and needs, interests, and goals regulate her decision in persisting or quitting. Behavior follows spontaneously from inner guides; for example, decisions pertaining to choices of majors to pursue in college and choices of careers to pursue represent expressions of personal needs, interests, and goals. External factors such as salary and status are not irrelevant to these decisions, but autonomy-oriented individuals pay closer attention to their needs and feelings than they do environmental contingencies and pressures.

The control orientation involves a relative insensitivity to inner guides, as control-oriented individuals prefer to pay closer attention to behavioral incentives, cues, and pressures that exist either in the environment or inside themselves (Deci & Ryan, 1985b). When control-oriented, people make decisions in response to the presence and quality of incentives, such as extrinsic rewards or concerns over attaining some outcome, such as pleasing others. A central ingredient in the determination of control-oriented people's ways of thinking, feeling, and behaving is a sense of pressure. Behavior occurs in response to feelings of tension and in compliance to what is demanded and reflects a sense of needing to behave in a certain manner and behaving in a certain manner because it is what should be done. Environmental factors such as pay and status are very important. When researchers ask control-oriented individuals what they aspire to, their goals are more likely to center around financial and material success (Kasser & Ryan, 1993).

Religion provides one example of the difference between autonomy-oriented and control-oriented ways of thinking, feeling, and behaving (Ryan, Rigby, & King, 1993). Based on their experiences, some people commit to religious beliefs and behaviors with a relatively extrinsic orientation (attending church services because that is what has to be done), whereas others commit to religious beliefs and behaviors with an intrinsic orientation (attending church services because of a choice; Donahue, 1985). Education and pro-social behavior provide additional examples of the differences between autonomy-oriented and control-oriented ways of thinking, feeling, and behaving, as some people study and help others for extrinsic reasons, whereas others study and help for intrinsic reasons (Ryan & Connell, 1989).

The General Causality Orientations Scale (Deci & Ryan, 1985b) measures causality orientations by presenting a series of 12 vignettes (short stories). Each vignette presents a situation and lists responses to that situation, one of which is autonomy-oriented and the other of which is control-oriented. (A third scale to assess the impersonal orientation is not discussed here.) For instance, one of the vignettes presents the following situation:

> You have been offered a new position in a company where you have worked for some time. The first question that is likely to come to mind is:
>
> I wonder if the new work will be interesting? (Autonomy)
>
> Will I make more at this position? (Control)

Causality orientations reflect self-determination in personality. Hence, self-determination theory explains the origins and dynamics of causality orientations (chapter 5; Deci & Ryan, 1985a). The autonomy-oriented personality is characterized by intrinsic motivation and identified regulation, as the forces that cause behavior are personal needs and interests (intrinsic motivation), as well as beliefs and values that have been integrated into the self (identified regulation). The control-oriented personality is characterized by extrinsic motivation and introjected regulation, as the forces that cause behavior are environmental rewards and constraints (extrinsic motivation), and beliefs and values that have been forced onto the self (introjected regulation). Because of its close relationship to self-determination in personality, the autonomy orientation, like self-determination in general, correlates positively with measures of positive functioning, such as self-actualization, ego development, self-esteem, openness to experience, and acceptance of one's true feelings (Deci & Ryan, 1985b; Koestner, Bernieri, & Zuckerman, 1992; Scherhorn & Grunert, 1988).

Attitude-Behavior Consistency and Inconsistency

Because autonomy-oriented people pay closer attention to needs and feelings than they do to external contingencies, they are able to maintain a high degree of consistency and harmony among their needs, thoughts, feelings, and behaviors. By contrast, control-oriented individuals are more alert to external contingencies and to internal imperatives than they are to their own needs and feelings. The consequence is a lack of consistency or harmony among needs, thoughts, feelings, and behaviors. Hence, control-oriented individuals are more affected by social persuasions, such as advertising appeals (Scherhorn & Grunert, 1988; Zuckerman, Gioioso, & Tellini, 1988).

Attitude-behavior consistency and inconsistency are expressed in several ways. In a typical intrinsic motivation study, for instance, people are asked to engage in a task that they find interesting or uninteresting and that is or is not associated with some external incentive such as a reward. Autonomy-oriented individuals engage in the task according to how interesting they find it to be. Control-oriented individuals engage in the task when offered an incentive but do not engage in the task when no incentive is offered. Hence, autonomy-oriented persons follow their interests closely, whereas control-oriented persons behave in ways that do not correlate with their (intrinsic) interests (Koestner, Bernieri, & Zuckerman, 1992).

In another study, researchers assessed college students on conscientiousness (how dependable, organized, and hard-working they were) and then presented an opportunity for testing that trait. The researchers gave the students a questionnaire and asked them to return the completed questionnaire one week later. All students agreed to return the questionnaire, but external factors also affected people's conscientious behavior, such as the weather, how much they liked the experimenter, whether they get paid for doing so, and so on. The autonomy-oriented students who were high in conscientiousness generally returned their questionnaires, whereas those low in conscientiousness did not. Knowing whether the control-oriented students were conscientious or not did not predict their questionnaire-returning behavior (i.e., they did not behave in a way that was consistent with their personalities; Koestner, Bernieri, & Zuckerman, 1992).

Maintenance of Behavior Change

When people seek to change their behavior, they typically rely on either internal guides (goals) or external guides (rules) to do so. To lose weight, for instance, people can rely on inner guides (i.e., "I believe it's the best way to help myself") or on outer guides (i.e., "I want others to see that I am really trying to lose weight"; Williams et al., 1996). While involved in a weight-loss program, people can generally rely on both internal and external support for assistance and motivation for changing their behavior. After the program ends, however, people lose much of their external support (the staff, the structure of the program) for changing their behavior. These researchers therefore reasoned that the more autonomy oriented the participants were, the more likely it was that they would stay in the program from one week to the next, lose weight during the program, and, most importantly, maintain their weight loss after the program ended (i.e., maintain the behavior change).

How autonomy-oriented individuals succeeded in maintaining their behavior change appears in Figure 12.4 (Williams et al., 1996). The more autonomy oriented the participants were (and the more autonomy supportive the staff-patient interactions were), the more these participants relied on relatively autonomous reasons for losing weight. Rooting weight loss motivation in autonomous reasons promoted week-to-week attendance. And the more frequently they attended meetings, the more successful they were in losing weight and maintaining that weight loss. Overall, the figure shows that the autonomy-causality orientation promoted self-determination in the personality (autonomous reasons

Figure 12.4 **Model of Self-Determined Weight Loss**

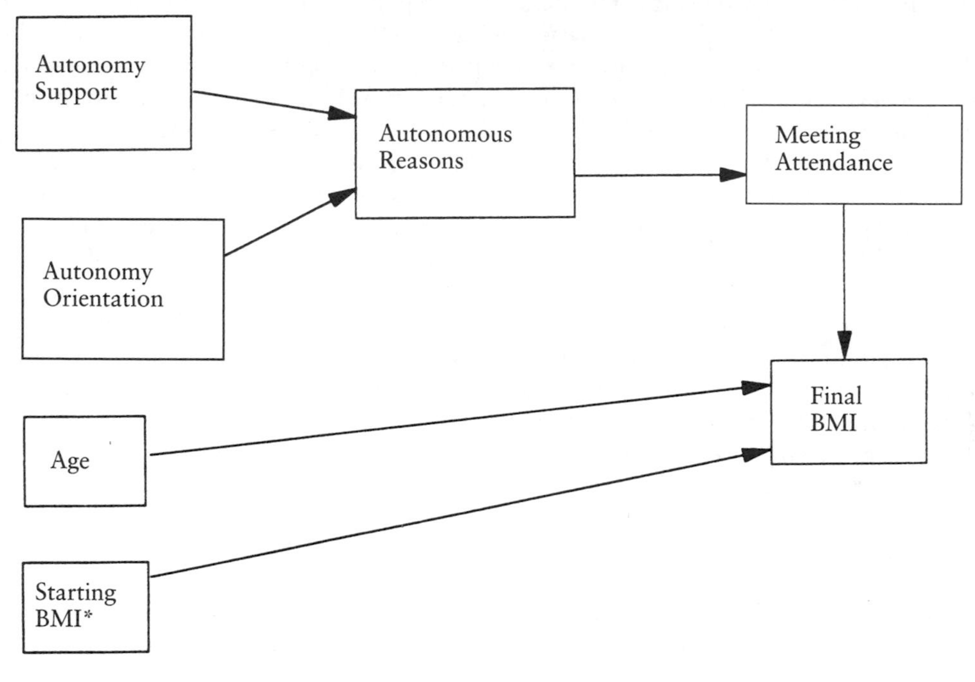

* Body Mass Index

Source: From "Motivational Predictors of Weight Loss and Weight-Loss Maintenance," by G. C. Williams, V. M. Grow, E. R. Freedman, R. M. Ryan, and E. L. Deci, 1996, *Journal of Personality and Social Psychology, 70,* pp. 115–126. Copyright 1996 by American Psychological Association. Adapted with permission.

for behaving), and self-determined reasons for acting led to the volitional behaviors (attendance) necessary for maintaining that behavior change in the future.

HOW INTERPERSONAL RELATIONSHIPS SUPPORT THE ACTUALIZING TENDENCY

The extent to which individuals develop toward congruence and adjustment depends greatly on the quality of their interpersonal relationships. At one extreme, relationships take on a controlling tone as others force their agendas on other people, pushing these other people toward heteronomy and a commitment to conditions of worth. Such relationships oppress the actualizing tendency. At the other extreme, relationships take on a supportive tone as they promote self-determination by affording people the opportunity and flexibility necessary to move from heteronomy toward autonomy. Such relationships nurture the actualizing tendency.

In humanistic therapy, for example, a client moves toward health and psychological congruence when his therapist brings the following characteristics into the relationship: warmth, genuineness, empathy, interpersonal acceptance, and confirmation of the other person's capacity for self-determination (Kramer, 1995; Rogers, 1973, 1980, 1995). *Warmth* essentially means caring for and enjoying spending time with the other person. *Genuineness* acknowledges that each person must be fully present in and open to the relationship's here and now, offering no pretense of emotional distance and no professional facade of being a therapist, or "the expert." Genuineness means authenticity. *Empathy* relates to listening to and hearing all the messages the other is sending and also truly understanding and willingly adopting the other's perspective on experience. Empathy occurs as one person gains the capacity to enter into the private perceptual world of the other and becomes thoroughly at home in that world. *Interpersonal acceptance* means that each person in the relationship experiences a basic acceptance and trust from the other (unconditional positive regard); that is, each person honors and prizes the uniqueness of the other without imposing conditions or contingencies. Finally, *confirmation of the other person's capacity for self-determination* acknowledges that the other person is capable and competent and possesses an inherently positive developmental direction. These five characteristics reflect the quality of interpersonal relationships.

HELPING OTHERS

Interpersonal relationships become constructive, helpful relationships when one person, by virtue of her contact with another, becomes better informed, more mature, more open to experience, and better integrated (Rogers, 1995). In trying to communicate how interpersonal relationships become helpful (growth-promoting) relationships, Rogers (1995) offers the following four insights:

> 1. In my relationships with persons, I have found that it does not help, in the long run, to act as though I were something that I am not.

Here, Rogers presents the antithesis of conditional positive regard and conditions of worth. The goal in helping is not to manipulate the other into conforming to conditions of worth, but instead, it is to understand. The facade of being loving or polite or interested does not help the other person if the helper actually feels hostile or critical or bored. This was Rogers' first insight into helping others.

> 2. I have found it effective, in my dealings with people, to be acceptant of myself.

Self-acceptance sets the stage for the interpersonal climate between two people to move past the superficial and into the real. Rogers considered it a "very paradoxical thing" that the more willing the helper is to be herself and the less willing she is to try to manipulate the other person, "the more change seems to be stirred up" (Rogers, 1995).

> 3. I have found it of enormous value when I can permit myself to understand another person.

Typically, when we interact with people who hold different opinions (e.g., on the death penalty), different ideologies (e.g., how to best discipline our children), and different conclusions (e.g., whether a person is inadequate as a human being), we counterargue and debate the other's opinion, ideology, or conclusion from our own perspective. Rogers argued that such an orientation forces us to pay more attention to our own frame of reference than we pay to the other person's frame of reference. To help, one must instead identify with the other person's frame of reference and understand why he believes and feels whatever it is he believes and feels.

> 4. The more I am able to understand myself and others, the more I accept myself and others, the more I am open to the realities of life, the less I find myself wishing to rush in.

Helping, in the humanistic tradition, does not involve an expert rushing in to solve the problem, to fix things, to advise people, or to mold and manipulate them in some way. Instead, helping involves letting the other person discover and then be herself. This last insight communicates the antithesis of conditions of worth.

FREEDOM TO LEARN

Rogers continually lamented contemporary educational practices. He did not like the idea of a "teacher" because he felt that the only learning that really mattered was self-initiated (actualizing tendency-initiated) learning (Rogers, 1969). As a teacher looking back at the results of his own efforts, Rogers felt that he was responsible for more damage than good. Little of consequence occurs when a teacher gives out heaps of information for students to digest. Instead of "teacher," Rogers preferred "facilitator," a term that describes the classroom leader as one who creates and supports an atmosphere conducive to students' learning. Learning does not follow teaching. Rather, learning follows having one's interests identified, facilitated, and supported. Self-discovery and self-evaluation are of prime importance, while criticisms and evaluation by teachers are inconsequential or harmful. Thus, education is not something a teacher can give to (or force on) a student. Rather, education must be acquired by the student through an investment of his energies and interests.[2]

In practice, humanistic education typically manifests itself in three themes (Allender & Silberman, 1979):

- The facilitator (i.e., teacher) functions as a structuring agent in an open classroom.
- Students learn cooperatively and in a context of the peer group.
- Students take responsibility for initiating their own learning.

A facilitator relies on setting up learning centers or stations in the classroom to encourage students' choices and initiatives, and the facilitator focuses most of her attention on identifying and supporting students' needs, desires, and interests (McCombs & Pope, 1994). Peer-based cooperative learning facilitates individual learning by allowing students

---

[2] On this point and for example, golfer Ben Hogan, in a Rogerian spirit, gave the following reply to answer why he had not written another instructional book: "Golf is a game that cannot be taught; it must be learned."

to communicate their ideas to others as well as to learn from the feedback, modeling, and insight of their peers (Johnson & Johnson, 1985). Personal responsibility for learning moves students out of the role of passive receivers of knowledge and into the role of active learners who construct their own understandings. When classrooms support students' initiatives, students gain academic confidence, show greater mastery motivation, and participate more actively in the classroom (deCharms, 1976; Ryan & Grolnick, 1986).

Self-Definition and Social Definition

Self-definition and social definition are personality processes related to how individuals conceptualize who they are (Jenkins, 1996; Stewart, 1992; Stewart & Winter, 1974). Socially defined individuals accept external definitions of who they are. External definitions pressure socially defined individuals to identify with stereotypical identities and ways of behaving that are appropriate for their social group. Self-defined individuals resist these external definitions and instead favor internal definitions of the self.

Self-definition and social definition processes are particularly instructive in the developing identities of women (Jenkins, 1996). Compared to their socially defined counterparts, self-defined women are more autonomous and independent in their interpersonal relationships (they depend less on others) and social roles (they may prefer nontraditional occupations). They take decisive and successful goal-directed actions, as in occupational decisions and strategies for career development. They organize their goals around their self-determined aspirations, including family goals such as the decision to get married and the decision to have children. They are also less invested in so-called traditional roles, such as wife and mother.

Socially defined women prefer to work with and depend on others (Jenkins, 1996). They prefer traditional female roles both at home and at work. They are typically willing to compromise in terms of their plans, college-degree aspirations, career persistence, and relationships in general. Decisions and experience flow not from the self but, instead, from the social support of others and the beliefs, abilities, and aspirations of those others. And by depending on others, socially defined married women hope for husbands who can provide them with a life that is stimulating and challenging.

Self-definition and social-definition processes represent two ways for self-actualization to proceed, the first of which represents authentic self-actualization, while the second of which represents commitment to conditions of worth. These ways of actualizing the self affect the ways people think and behave, the decisions they make (e.g., career choices), the ways they relate to social pressures, and the interpersonal adjustments they voluntarily make to achieve the social/occupational outcomes they desire.

Personal Autonomy Versus Social Compliance: The Fundamental Antithesis

One index of healthy psychosocial development is the extent to which the individual accepts social conventions, accommodates the self to the society, internalizes cultural values, cooperates with others, shows respect for others, and so on. What motivates the willingness to accommodate the self to others is the need for relatedness (Goodenow,

1993; Ryan & Powelson, 1991). Interpersonally, relatedness (chapter 4) refers to the quality of the relationship between socializer and socializee. When one person feels emotionally connected to, interpersonally involved with, liked by, respected by, and valued by another person, relatedness is high and internalization occurs willingly (Ryan & Powelson, 1991).

But relatedness can come with a price—a hidden agenda in which one person asks for compliance from the other before granting love or approval (Gruen, 1976). Conditions of worth, for instance, essentially mean that the other person's (or society's) love, approval, care, and emotional connectedness are contingent on compliance with socialization standards and norms. Maladjustment under such conditions is not always transparent, as the compliant individual might be held up as an exemplary "good boy," for instance. The maladjustment becomes clearer when socializing agents—family, school, church, coworkers, culture—begin to supply contradictory values and contradictory conditions of worth. Facing contradictory conditions of worth, the self has a difficult time regulating its behavior in ways that gain widespread approval and relatedness. It is hard to comply with a moving target.

The humanistic perspective argues that there is another agent that capably guides development—namely the actualizing tendency. And the humanistic perspective argues that there is another type of relatedness between people besides a conformity-demanding conditional positive regard—namely, the unconditional acceptance and support between people (Hodgins, Koestner, & Duncan, 1996; Ryan, 1993). Consider relatedness in both childhood and adult development. The quality of relatedness in early attachments (infant and caretaker) depends on how sensitive and responsive caregivers are to the infant's needs and initiatives. The quality of relatedness in adult relationships depends on the mutuality of autonomy and involves an openness to each other's selves. In both childhood and adulthood, relatedness requires understanding, accepting, and supporting the self as it expresses itself freely. Chapter 4 referred to this way of relating as "autonomy support" and documented several positive adaptive outcomes that emanate from autonomy-supportive relationships, including greater perceived competence, enhanced sense of self-worth and self-esteem, greater creativity, positive emotional tone, maintenance of behavioral change, and interpersonal relationships based on trust.

Autonomy is *not* independence, and autonomy is *not* interpersonal detachment (Ryan, 1993). Independence involves not relying on others for need fulfillment; detachment involves breaking ties with others. Neither fosters the self's autonomy (Ryan, 1991, 1993; Ryan & Lynch, 1989). In fact, adolescents who detach themselves from their family become increasingly susceptible to conformity and decreasingly capable of mature relationships with others. The paradoxical conclusion that emerged from Mary Ainsworth's classic program of research on infant attachment was that infants who received warm, need-satisfying, responsive, sensitive care from mothers did not become dependent or needy; instead, nurturance enabled and even liberated the child's autonomy (Ainsworth, 1989). Relationships rich in relatedness paradoxically facilitate autonomy (Hodgins et al., 1996). In contrast, when others provide contingent conditions of worth, people often forgo autonomy in order to preserve relatedness. In optimal development, neither autonomy nor relatedness is forgone (Ryan, 1993).

THE PROBLEM OF EVIL

Do we as a society dare trust a person to be self-determining? Freedom and self-determination are fine if human nature is benevolent, cooperative, and warmhearted. But what if human nature is malevolent, selfish, and aggressive? What if human nature is evil, or at least partly evil?

Recently, humanistic thinkers have become willing to wrestle with the nature of evil (Goldberg, 1995; Klose, 1995). The discussion typically takes one of two forms. On the one hand, the discussion asks *how much* of human nature is evil? This question asks, "If family, political, economic, and social institutions and systems were benevolent and growth-promoting, then would human evil be reduced to zero or would some residual ferociousness remain?" (Maslow, 1987). On the other hand, the discussion of the problem of evil tries to understand evildoers (e.g., murderers, rapists) who confess to enjoying what they do and express a willingness to continue doing such acts whenever an unpunished possibility presents itself (Goldberg, 1995).

Evil is the deliberate, voluntary, intentional infliction of painful suffering on another person without respect for his humanity or personhood. Rogers' conviction was that evil was not inherent in human nature. He argued that if caretakers provided enough nurturance and acceptance and if they established a genuine connectedness with those they cared for, then people would inevitably choose good over evil (Rogers, 1982).

According to Rogers, human beings behave malevolently only to the extent that they have been injured or damaged by their experience. Violence often reflects relationships of power and control rather than autonomy and support (Muehlenhard & Kimes, 1999). Other humanists see more ambiguity in human nature and assume that benevolence and malevolence are part of everyone, as are the impulses to do good or evil. In this view, under one set of social conditions, the actualizing tendency pairs itself with life-affirming values and adopts constructive ways for relating and behaving; but under another set of conditions, the actualizing tendency pairs itself with malicious values and leads to cruelty and destructive behavior (May, 1982). Thus, a person needs a value system (principles of law, standards of right and wrong) to support the organismic valuation process. If adults (parents) do not provide a child or adolescent with such, then that child will grab a value system wherever it is available, be it among equally confused peers on the street, the college fraternity world, or Wall Street (Maslow, 1971). In this view, the actualization tendency and organismic valuation process need a benevolent and supportive value system. If a society cannot provide such a benevolent value system for all its members, then it must build safeguards into its social systems to uphold compassionate behavior and to renounce cruelty (Bandura, 1999)

When people *desire* to act in ways that promote evil, they possess a malevolent personality (Goldberg, 1995). The descent into a malevolent personality is a slippery course of choices and developmental progressions (as determined by insights gained through clinical practice, Fromm, 1964; Goldberg, 1995; and through experimental research, Baumeister & Campbell, 1999). Evil develops or evolves (Stuab, 1999). First, the self is a child of scorn. Adults shame the child such that the child comes to the conclusion that she is flawed and incompetent as a human being. Second, the self incubates a negative self-view. To hide from her shame, the child comes to prefer lies and self-deceit over the critical self-examination that makes self-correction possible. Third, a transition occurs from being a victim to becoming a perpetrator. Insensitivity and disregard for others manifest themselves in the attempt to blame others for personal inadequacies and life failures. Fourth, the self initiates experimental malevolence. In manipulating others and in carrying out acts of cruelty, the self relies on denial, rationalization, lying, pretense of goodness, and blaming others. Finally, there is the forging of the malevolent personality through a rigid refusal to engage in critical self-examination. The self becomes unwilling to examine itself (e.g., scapegoating is used as a strategy for sacrificing others to preserve one's own self-image; Baumeister, Smart, & Boden, 1996). The malevolent personality often possesses superior physical, social, or intellectual skills with which to intimidate others, and success in intimidation fosters the self-aggrandizement that counteracts the need for self-examination. In short, adult self-aggrandizement vanquishes childhood shame (Goldberg, 1995).

It is difficult to determine whether or not evil is inherent in human nature. Within a supportive interpersonal climate, people's choices move them in the direction of greater socialization, improved relationships, and toward what is healthy and benevolent (Rogers, 1982). Therefore, as murder, war, and prejudice continue, the culprit might not be the evil in human nature but, alternatively, the sickness in culture. But culture is not the "bad guy" here, as cultures can promote either health and well-being *or* sickness and psychopathology, depending on the decisions of its individual members (May, 1982). As long as society offers people choices, the possibility remains that its members will internalize a pathological value system that makes possible the descent into evil and the forging of a malevolent personality. Perhaps human nature is not evil, and perhaps cultures are not evil. Rather, the capacity for choice allows people to internalize and to resist the value system opportunities—both benevolent and malevolent—that come their way.[3]

CRITICISMS

After spending a few hours reading either Maslow or Rogers, it will be difficult for you not to feel good and optimistic about yourself and about human beings in general. For instance, if you read any one of the 15 chapters in Rogers' (1980) *A Way of Being*, you will more than likely experience a moving sense of personal enrichment. Still, one must square the optimism of humanism with the reality of observation and wonder if it is not overly naive to conceptualize human nature as intrinsically good. If human nature is something to be nurtured rather than constrained, then one must explain why hatred, prejudice,

---

[3] A final question asks whether human evil can be healed. One constant in humanistic thinking is that it never condemns without an affirmation of hope. But the malevolent personality is a tough one. Four reasons exist in explaining the difficulty in healing evil: (1) the malevolent personality's closed nature (unwillingness to engage in critical self-examination), (2) the rarity of the malevolent personality's genuine motivation to change, (3) the odds against the malevolent personality finding those supportive conditions in which motivation for personal change can take root and fulfill itself, and (4) the strong influence of the individual's choice to change or not to change (Klose, 1995).

crime, exploitation, and war persist throughout human history without interruption (Geller, 1982). Perhaps people are not so intrinsically honorable and trustworthy. Perhaps people have within themselves not only positive human potentialities but also the potential to destroy themselves and others (Baumeister & Campbell, 1999; May, 1982; Staub, 1999). One can image the potentially adverse consequences of a parent or a government that presupposes benevolent inner guides and therefore allows a permissive environment for misbehaving children or citizens (Bandura, 1999). It seems that the humanistic view emphasizes only one part, although an important part, of human nature.

A second criticism is that both Maslow and Rogers use a full range of vague and ill-defined constructs. It is difficult to pinpoint precisely what an "organismic valuation process" and a "fully functioning individual" are, for example. Any theoretical construct that evades a precise operational definition must remain scientifically dubious. For this reason, humanistic views on motivation have been harshly criticized (Daniels, 1988; Neher, 1991). The critics essentially recommend we drop these quasi-scientific concepts. But there is a middle ground that recognizes the relative infancy or newness of humanistic study (O'Hara, 1989). So far in humanistic psychology's balance between method and topic, topic gets more attention, emphasis, and celebration than does method. As humanistic psychology matures, its study is slowly but surely leaving behind armchair speculation in favor of a more scientific understanding of the origins, dynamics, and consequences of human potentiality.

"Feelingism" is a third criticism (Rowan, 1987). Humanism sometimes presents feelings as "the royal road to the true self" (to twist a Freudian phrase), such that feelings provide markers for identifying the inner guides of the actualizing tendency and organismic valuation process. "Feelingism" becomes a problem, however, when humanists afford feelings a conceptual status above all other aspects of experience, such as thinking, imagining, and so forth. This criticism is not so much against humanism per se as it is a branch or version of humanistic psychology, especially that practiced by some clinicians practicing group therapy.

A fourth criticism questions how one is to know what is *really* wanted or needed by the actualizing tendency (Geller, 1982). For example, if a person is 100% confident that abortion is bad, wrong, and something to be refused, then how is that person to know for sure that such a preference is a product of the organismic valuation process rather than an internalized product of societal conditions of worth? Knowledge of right and wrong can be difficult to trace back to the origins of its true source. If standards of right and wrong are introjected from infancy, a person can be self-deceived into thinking their preference is their own rather than their parents' preference.

A fifth criticism is that humanistic psychology is a bit single-minded in its focus on the individual. In other words, it relatively neglects or underappreciates the contribution of social, economic, political, and sociological forces on personal development (Greening, 1995). In its eagerness to promote individual potential, humanistic study often "fails to acknowledge that our sense of personal autonomy, our sense of identity, our sense of stable personality, our sense of personhood itself comes to us from outside" (O'Hara, 1989). Detaching the self from (as opposed to integrating the self with) society's shared values and beliefs potentially exacts some serious costs on the individual, such as becoming increasingly vulnerable to suicide (Durkheim, 1951). Like inherited potentials, social forces too contribute to people's senses of autonomy, identity, and personality, and these social forces do so in a way that is necessary, healthy, and productive. This criticism asserts that society and the standards of others are not necessarily a pair of corrupt bogeymen that seek to pollute the self. More and more, humanistic thinking studies (1) how society contributes to self-actualization and (2) how the self-actualizing individual, in turn, becomes an advocate for transforming the society at large into one capable of encouraging actualization goals for others (Bugental, 1970; Rogers, 1980).

SUMMARY

Humanistic psychology identifies strongly with the holistic perspective and, in doing so, stresses the notions of inherent potentialities, the self, and strivings toward realization and fulfillment. In practice, humanistic psychology is about identifying and developing human potential.

For Maslow, self-actualization referred to the full realization and use of one's talents, capacities, and potentialities. Driving the process of self-actualization were five sets of hierarchically arranged urges or basic needs at the organismic level—physiological, safety, belongingness, esteem, and self-actualization. Despite its intuitive appeal and its comfortable fit with common sense, research finds little support for the hierarchy. One finding that does gain empirical support, however, is the distinction between deficiency and growth needs. Maslow offered a number of specific behaviors the person could engage in to encourage progress toward self-actualization (see Table 12.3), and he further emphasized the role that intimate relationships contribute to self-actualization.

For Rogers, one fundamental need—the actualizing tendency—subsumed and coordinated all other motives for achieving organismic maintenance, enhancement, and actualization. With the emergence of the self, the actualizing tendency differentiates part of its motivational force into the need for self-actualization. With socialization, children learn societal conditions of worth on which their behavior and personal characteristics are judged as either positive and valued or negative and rejected. As a consequence, all of us begin to live in two worlds—the inner world of the organismic valuation process and the outer world of conditions of worth. When people move away from organismic valuing and toward identifying with external conditions of worth, they adopt facades and become willing to reject or deny personal characteristics, preferences, and beliefs. The terms "congruence" and "incongruence" described the extent to which an individual denies and rejects personal qualities (incongruence) or accepts the full range of his personal characteristics and desires (congruence). The congruent, fully functioning individual lives in close proximity to the actualizing tendency and therefore experiences a marked sense of freedom, spontaneity, and growth.

A strong commitment to societal conditions of worth leads people into a process of seeking validation from others. In social interaction, validation-seeking individuals strive to prove their self-worth, competence, and likeability. In contrast, growth-seeking individuals center their strivings around learning, improving, and reaching personal potential. The distinction between the two is important for two reasons. First, validation-seeking individuals are more vulnerable to losing their sense of self-worth and to experiencing anxiety and depression. Second, the distinction between validation-seeking and growth-seeking personal strivings is a nice way to express (1) Maslow's distinction between deficiency and growth needs and (2) Rogers' distinction between conditional positive regard and unconditional positive regard.

Causality orientations concern differences in people's understanding of what causes their behavior. For the person with an autonomy-causality orientation, behavior arises in response to needs and interests with a full sense of choice. For the person with a control-causality orientation, inner guides are relatively ignored. Instead, behavior arises in response to feelings of pressure, compliance to what is expected, and to a sense of having to. Causality orientations reflect the extent of self-determination in personality. Autonomy-oriented individuals rely on intrinsic motivation and identified regulation, whereas control-oriented individuals rely on introjected regulation and extrinsic motivators. Autonomy-oriented individuals show a strong attitude-behavior consistency, and they maintain goal-directed behavior changes over time.

Interpersonal relationships support the actualizing tendency in at least three ways: helping others (as in therapy), promoting the freedom to learn (as in education), and defining the self. Interpersonal relationships characterized by warmth, genuineness, empathy, interpersonal acceptance, and confirmation of the other person's capacity for self-determination provide the social climate that supports the actualization tendency in another person. Helping others revolves around the helper acting in a way that is honest, real, understanding, and nonauthoritarian. Freedom to learn concerns the educational relationship between "facilitator" and student and relies on autonomy support and learning rather than authoritarianism and traditional teaching. Self-definition concerns how people conceptualize who they are, and the distinction between self-definition and social definition highlights the fundamental antithesis between personal autonomy and social compliance.

The problem of evil wrestles with the questions of how much of human nature is inherently evil and why some people enjoy inflicting intentional suffering on others. While some humanistic thinkers argue that evil is not inherent in human nature, others stress that the actualizing tendency can pair itself either with a benevolent value system associated with constructive and pro-social tendencies or with a malevolent value system associated with destructive and antisocial tendencies. The chapter concludes by offering a number of criticisms of a humanistic understanding of motivation, including Pollyanna optimism, unscientific concepts, "feelingism," unknown origins of inner motivational forces, and an underappreciation of the societal contribution to personal freedom and adjustment.

RECOMMENDED READINGS

Humanistic Theorists

Hardeman, M. (1979). A dialogue with Abraham Maslow. *Journal of Humanistic Psychology, 19,* 23–28.

Maslow, A. H. (1943). A theory of motivation. *Psychological Review, 50,* 370–396.

May, R. (1982). The problem of evil: An open letter to Carl Rogers. *Journal of Humanistic Psychology, 22,* 10–21.

Rogers, C. R. (1959). A theory of therapy, personality, and interpersonal relationships, as developed in the client-centered framework. In S. Koch (Ed.), *Psychology: A study of science* (Vol. 3, pp. 184–256). New York: McGraw-Hill.

Rogers, C. R. (1969). Personal thoughts on teaching and learning. In *Freedom to learn: A view of what education might become* (Chapter 6, pp. 151–155). Columbus, OH: Merrill.

Rogers, C. R. (1995). What understanding and acceptance mean to me. *Journal of Humanistic Psychology, 35,* 7–22.

Extensions and Empirical Tests of Humanistic Hypotheses

Baumeister, R. F., & Campbell, W. K. (1999). The intrinsic appeal of evil: Sadism, sensational thrills, and threatened egotism. *Personality and Social Psychology Review, 3,* 210-221.

Deci, E. L., & Ryan, R. M. (1985). The General Causality Orientations Scale: Self-determination in personality. *Journal of Research in Personality, 19,* 109-134.

Dykman, B. M. (1998). Integrating cognitive and motivational factors in depression: Initial tests of a goal-orientation approach. *Journal of Personality and Social Psychology, 74,* 139–158.

Ford, J. G. (1991). Inherent potentialities of actualization: An initial exploration. *Journal of Humanistic Psychology, 31,* 65–88.

Jenkins, S. R. (1996). Self-definition in thought, action, and life path choices. *Personality and Social Psychology Bulletin, 22,* 99–111.

Koestner, R., Bernieri, F., & Zuckerman, M. (1992). Self-regulation and consistency between attitudes, traits, and behaviors. *Personality and Social Psychology Bulletin, 18,* 52–59.

Criticisms

Geller, L. (1982). The failure of self-actualization theory: A critique of Carl Rogers and Abraham Maslow. *Journal of Humanistic Psychology, 22,* 56–73.

Rowan, J. (1987). Nine humanistic heresies. *Journal of Humanistic Psychology, 27,* 141–157.

13

Unconscious Motivation

Imagine accompanying your friend on his visit to a psychiatrist. To begin the session, your friend undergoes hypnosis. Once hypnotized, the psychiatrist suggests that your friend brought a newspaper with him to the session and that once he awakes, he will want to read it. In actuality, your friend brought no newspaper. Further, the therapist suggests that upon his awakening, he will look for the newspaper but will be unable to find it. The therapist tells your friend that, after a couple of minutes of searching, an idea will occur to him that another person has taken his newspaper—that the other person has, in fact, stolen it. The therapist also suggests that your friend's discovery will provoke him to the point of being angry. Further, the therapist tells your friend to direct that anger toward the thief. Unfortunately for you, the psychiatrist next tells your friend that you are that thief. The therapist tells your friend that, in his fit of anger, he will first insist and then will demand that you return his newspaper. To conclude the hypnosis session, the psychiatrist tells your friend that he will forget that the source of all this (mis)information was actually a series of suggestions given to him during hypnosis by the therapist.

Your friend awakens. He begins to talk about the day's events, and then remarks, "Incidentally, that reminds me of something I read in today's newspaper. I'll show you." Your friend looks around, does not see his newspaper, and begins to search for it through his backpack. You begin to feel a hint of anxiety because you have been with your friend all day and know that he has neither read nor purchased a paper that day. Then all of a sudden, he turns toward you with piercing eyes. Accusingly, your friend pronounces that you took his newspaper, and he now wants it back. You are starting to think coming along was not such a good idea and rather sheepishly say that you know nothing of his newspaper. But your friend persists. He truly seems upset. With his anger piqued, your friend forcefully accuses you of stealing his newspaper. He goes further by saying that you took it because you are too cheap to buy one of your own. To substantiate his accusation, he says someone saw you steal his newspaper and told him about it. This is no longer funny. Your friend *really* believes you stole his newspaper, and he *really* wants it back.

What does this hypnosis session, based on Erich Fromm (1941), illustrate? The scenario illustrates that human beings can have thoughts, feelings, and emotions that subjectively feel to be their own but, in fact, have been introjected from another source. Your friend wanted something—to show you an item in the newspaper. He thought something—you stole his newspaper. And he felt something—anger against an alleged thief. But your friend's wants, thoughts, and feelings were not his own in the sense that they did not originate within him. Yet, your friend surely acted as if they were his own. Such a demonstration of the posthypnotic suggestion testifies to the paradox that while we can be sure of what we want, think, and feel, we can also have little idea as to the source of what we want, think, and feel. The whole scenario bears witness to the idea that motivation can arise from a source that lies outside of conscious awareness and volitional intent.

PSYCHOANALYTICAL PERSPECTIVE

In contrast to humanism (chapter 12), the psychoanalytic approach presents a deterministic, pessimistic image of human nature. Psychoanalysis is deterministic in that it holds that the ultimate cause of motivation and behavior derives from biologically endowed and socially acquired impulses that determine our desires, thoughts, feelings, and behaviors, whether we like it or not. Psychoanalysis is further deterministic in that personality changes little after puberty. Thus, many of the motivational impulses of an adult can be traced to events that took place in childhood. Psychoanalysis is also relatively pessimistic in its tone, including sexual and aggressive urges, conflict, repression, defense mechanisms, unconscious desires, anxiety, and other such burdens, vulnerabilities, and shortcomings of human nature. It sees anxiety as inevitable and the collapse of personality as a matter of degree rather than as an exceptional event that happens to only some of us. We are all dogged by guilt, anxiety is our constant companion, narcissism and homophobia are all too common, and distortions of reality are modus operandi. It is not a pretty picture, Freud said, but it is reality nonetheless. In his mind, Freud was not a pessimist; he was a realist.

Psychoanalysis is strangely appealing and wonderfully popular. Part of its appeal is that, in reading psychoanalytic theory, the reader comes face to face with some difficult aspects of human nature. According to psychoanalysis, people "are more interested in getting sexual pleasure than they will admit" and people have "blind rages, wild lusts, and parasitic infantile longings, any of which may or may not be present as conscious desires" (Holt, 1989). These difficult, mysterious aspects of human nature present us with a psychological riddle that pulls in our curiosity. Who can resist wanting to learn more about a theory that reveals the secrets of the mind—secret crushes and jealousies, fantasies and desires, memories of things done and not done, and all sorts of hidden intrigue and despair?

Part of the appeal of psychoanalysis is that it makes the unconscious its subject matter. Thus, psychoanalysis willingly goes "where no theory has gone before" (to paraphrase a phrase from *Star Trek)*—into dreams, hypnosis, inaccessible memories, fantasy, and all the hidden forces that shape our motives and behaviors without our awareness or consent. In doing so, psychoanalysis offers a chance to talk about what might arguably be the most interesting subject matter of all—the content of our own private subjective experience and why unwanted desires and fears make their home there.

PSYCHOANALYTIC BECOMES PSYCHODYNAMIC

A few decades ago, the terms psychoanalytic and psychodynamic could be used as synonyms. A growing number of scholars, however, found themselves in the somewhat uncomfortable (i.e., dissonance-arousing) position of accepting Freud's ideas about unconscious mental processes but rejecting some of his other ideas, such as his dual-instinct theory of motivation. Today, the term *psychoanalytic* refers to practitioners who remain committed to most traditional Freudian principles, whereas the term *psychodynamic* refers to the study of dynamic unconscious mental processes. In other words, one can study unconscious mental processes (e.g., prejudice, depression, thought suppression, defense mechanisms) inside or outside the Freudian tradition. That is, many researchers study psychodynamic processes without embracing the psychoanalytic approach. To understand the history of how psychoanalysis became psychodynamic within the study of motivation, one should be familiar with Freud's controversial dual-instinct theory. A brief review of this theory follows.

FREUD'S DUAL-INSTINCT THEORY

A physician by training, Sigmund Freud viewed motivation as regulated by impulse-driven biological forces. For Freud, the human body was a complex energy system organized for the purpose of increasing and decreasing its energies through behavior. For example, by eating and breathing, the body increases its physical energy; by working and playing, the body uses up its energy. In addition, the body regulates its mental (psychical) energy. The mind needs mental energy to perform its functions (e.g., thinking, remembering), and it draws this energy—its psychic force—from the body's physical energy. The driving force for both physical and mental energy was biological drive (or instinct), which was a biologically rooted force "emanating within the organism and penetrating to the mind" (Freud, 1915). Hence, motivation emerged from instinctual bodily demands.

For Freud, there were as many biological drives as there were different bodily demands (e.g., food, water, sleep). But Freud recognized that there were too many different bodily needs to list. Instead of compiling a taxonomy of bodily drives, Freud (1920, 1923) emphasized two general categories: the instincts for life and the instincts for death.

The first class of instincts—Eros, the life instincts—are the more easily defined of the two. Eros maintain life and ensure individual and collective (species) survival. Thus, instincts for food, water, air, sleep, and the like all contribute to the life and survival of the individual. These are instincts for self-preservation. Instincts for sex, nurturance, and affiliation contribute to the life and survival of the species, a reproductive emphasis Freud borrowed from Darwin (Ritvo, 1990). These are instincts for species-preservation. In his discussions of the life instincts, Freud gave primary emphasis to sex, though he conceptualized sex quite broadly as "pleasure seeking." Thumb-sucking; being tickled, rocked, rubbed, caressed, and tossed in the air; rhythmic stimulation; masturbation; and sexual contact were all included as gratifications of the sex (or pleasure) instinct (Freud, 1905).

The second class of instincts—Thanatos, the death instincts—push the individual toward rest, inactivity, and energy conservation. An absence of bodily disturbance and an unwavering homeostatic stability could be fully achieved only through total rest, which was death. In discussing the death instincts, Freud gave primary emphasis to aggression. When focused on the self, aggression manifests itself in self-criticism, sadism, depression, suicide, masochism, alcoholism, drug addiction, and unnecessary risk taking like gambling. When focused on others, aggression manifests itself in anger, hate, prejudice, verbal insult, cruelty, rivalry, revenge, murder, and war. For example, a hostile joke about a disliked ethnic group represents a nonphysical expression of the Thanatos (Freud, 1905).

These bodily based instinctual drives toward life and death—sex and aggression—provide the energy that motivates behavior. But people did not just impulsively act on their inborn sexual and aggressive energies. These instincts may energize behavior, but it is what the individual learned from experience that directs behavior toward need-satisfying aims. Through experience, which is essentially a synonym for "psychosexual development," the individual learns defensive reactions for managing her sexual and aggressive energies. One's habitual, learned manner of defense is much of what Freud meant by the ego. Thus, instinctual drives provide the energy for behavior, while the ego provides its direction—attain need satisfaction in the most socially adaptive, socially appropriate, and least anxiety-provoking way.

Drive or Wish?

The dual-instinct theory of motivation represents psychoanalysis, circa 1930. Few contemporary psychoanalysts understand motivation as a function of biological instincts (Kolb, Cooper, & Fishman, 1995; Westen, 1991), and this revised understanding has been true for several decades (Berkowitz, 1962). Contemporary psychoanalysts review Freud's dual-instinct theory and generally find it wanting (Holt, 1989). Unlike hunger and thirst, neither sex nor aggression conform nicely to a physiological model of drive. For instance, notice how poorly an analysis of aggression would fit into the cyclical pattern of homeostasis depicted earlier in Figure 3.2:

homeostasis → need → drive → goal-directed behavior → consummation → return to homeostasis

Physiological deprivation rarely produces aggressive urges, and the urge to aggress does not intensify with the passage of time. Further, consummatory behavior typically fuels and intensifies, rather than satiates and calms, aggressive desires. Because sex and aggression are so central to Freud's view of motivation and because sex and aggression fit the drive conceptualization so poorly, contemporary psychoanalysts drop the idea of the instinctual drive as their central motivational construct.

As a substitute motivational principle, sex and aggression are conceptualized as psychological wishes, rather than as physiological drives (Holt, 1989; Klein, 1967). The reformulated "wish model" is essentially a discrepancy theory of motivation (see chapter 7) and proposes the following: At any time, individuals are aware, consciously or unconsciously, of their present state and, on encountering almost any situation, perceive some more potentially desirable state. For example, a man goes about his daily affairs without any aggressive urge but, upon being insulted or otherwise ridiculed, perceives a potentially more favorable state of social status than his present one. Consequently, a "present state" versus "ideal state" mismatch occurs, and the aggressive wish to advance the present state closer to the ideal state arises. Contemporary psychoanalysts now propose that psychological wishes, not instinctual drives, regulate and direct human behavior (Holt, 1989). The wish retains all the spirit of Freudian motivation as people wish all too frequently for desired states in the sexual and aggressive realms, but it overcomes the contradictory evidence that sex and aggression do not function as physiological drives.

Notice the change in thinking. With wishes, motivation arises from thoughts that arise out of problems in adapting successfully to one's surroundings and interpersonal relationships. With instinctual drives, motivation arises from bodily demands. The body's energy keeps rising until one gets to the point of needing a behavioral outlet to quiet the rising demand. This change of emphasis about the origins of motivational states now leads contemporary psychoanalysts to spend time wrestling with the cognitive, social, and personal sources of wishes (Wegner, 1989; Westen, 1998), which can explain phenomena such as suicide, alcoholism, masochism, binge eating, religious fanaticism, and other such ways of coping with and adjusting to life (Baumeister, 1991).

Intrapersonal or Interpersonal?

In shifting its attention away from instinctual drives toward psychological wishes, contemporary psychoanalytic thought shifted away from that which was mostly biological to that which was mostly cognitive. A second change was a lessened reliance on an exclusive study of intrapersonal processes and a greater emphasis on interpersonal processes. Contemporary psychoanalytic therapists and researchers do not write much about ids and egos, and they do not spend most of their time undertaking archaeological-like expeditions in search of lost memories that will lead to a discovery of the developmental origins of the patient's present-day psychopathology (Kolb et al., 1995; Mitchell, 1988; Wachtel, 1993; Westen, 1998). Instead, the contemporary focus has gone decidedly interpersonal as it centers on helping people recognize, improve upon, or outright run away from problematic interpersonal styles and relationships (Hazan & Shaver, 1987; Loevinger, 1976; Scharff & Scharff, 1995; Westen et al. 1991). For example, a common problem in psychoanalytic therapy is recognizing and developing the skills necessary to overcome the chronic tendency of involving oneself in intimate relationships with the wrong kind of person (Greenberg & Mitchell, 1983; Westen et al., 1991).

The goal of psychoanalytic therapy has always been to understand the confusing activities of the unconscious so as to free the ego to deal with reality. Contemporary psychoanalytic therapists find it more profitable to understand the unconscious confusion emanating from relationships (interpersonal) rather than from instincts (intrapersonal).

CONTEMPORARY PSYCHODYNAMIC THEORY

Basically, a lot has changed since Freud. Today, there are basically four postulates that define psychodynamic theory (Westen, 1998). That these principles are contemporary, as opposed to classically Freudian, is important for two reasons. First, psychodynamic thought has had time to put Freud's insightful propositions to empirical tests to see which postulates do, and which postulates do not, stand the objective tests of time and of empirical evaluation. Second, most readers will be more familiar with Freud's classical psychoanalysis than they will be with what contemporary psychodynamic theory embraces, a fact that makes it necessary to review the following core postulates (Westen, 1998):

1. Much of mental life is unconscious.
2. Mental processes operate in parallel with one another.
3. Healthy development involves moving from an immature, socially dependent personality to one that is more mature and interdependent.
4. Mental representations of self, others, and relationships form in childhood that guide people's later social motivations.

The first postulate pertains to an emphasis on the *unconscious*. It argues emphatically that thoughts, feelings, and desires exist at the unconscious level. Thus, because unconscious mental life affects behavior, people can behave in ways that are inexplicable, even to themselves. The second postulate communicates an emphasis on the mental conflict of *psychodynamics*. It argues that motivational and emotional processes frequently operate in parallel with one another—people commonly want and fear the same thing. It is the rule, not the exception, that people have conflicting feelings that motivate them in opposing ways. Hence, people commonly harbor divergent conscious and unconscious racial (Fazio et al., 1995) and gender (Banaji & Hardin, 1996) attitudes that produce simultaneous approach and avoidance interpersonal behavior. The third postulate is an emphasis on *ego development*. While recognizing the motivational significance of sexual and aggressive energies, ego psychologists focus on how we grow, develop, and leave behind our relatively immature, fragile, egocentric, and narcissistic beginnings in life to become relatively mature, resilient, empathic, and socially responsible beings. The fourth postulate recognizes the emerging importance of *objects relations theory.* It argues that stable personality patterns begin to form in childhood as people construct mental representations of the self, others, and their relationships. Once formed, these beliefs about self and others shape motivational states and guide the course of one's interpersonal relationships.

THE UNCONSCIOUS

Scientific psychology has had a difficult time with the empirical exploration of the unconscious. After all, if the unconscious is hidden from both private consciousness and public observation, then how can a researcher ever gain access to it? This problem is not an insurmountable one, however, any more than concepts such as (inaccessible) electrons are insurmountable to those who study physics. Freud believed that the individual must express strong unconscious urges and impulses, though often in a disguised form. The unconscious is therefore a "shadow phenomenon" that cannot be known directly but can be inferred from a variety of its indirect manifestations (Erdelyi, 1985). Believing the unconscious constituted the "primary process" while consciousness was but a "secondary process," Freud and his colleagues explored the contents and processes of the unconscious in a number of ways, including hypnosis, free association, dream analysis, humor, projective tests, errors and slips of the tongue, and so-called "accidents" (Exner, 1986; Freud, 1900, 1901, 1905, 1920, 1927; Murray, 1943).

It has been a rocky and emotionally charged 100-year debate, but the conclusion that much of mental life is unconscious is now largely accepted (Westen, 1998). Instead of debating whether some of mental life is unconscious, the debate now centers on two different portrayals of the unconscious. The two views can be called the Freudian unconscious and the non-Freudian unconscious. Just as Freud used methods like hypnosis and slips of the tongue, modern-day psychologists use methods like subliminal activation, selective attention, unconscious learning, and implicit memory (Greenwald, 1992; Kihlstrom, 1987).

One question that separates the two views of the unconscious is whether the unconscious is smart or dumb (Loftus & Klinger, 1992). In the Freudian conceptualization, the unconscious is every bit as smart as is its conscious counterpart because it uses sophisticated defenses, is complex and dynamic, is flexible, manages complex bodies of knowledge, and knows how to best protect the conscious mind from injury. In other words, the Freudian unconscious is smart because of its remarkable ability to help the individual adapt successfully to the demands of the world. The more contemporary view, however, is that the unconscious is dumb. To call the unconscious dumb is to say that it is (compared to the conscious mind) simple, automatic, and performs only routine information processing. It carries out habitual or automatic processing, such as that which occurs when driving a car or playing the piano (i.e., unconscious procedural knowledge). Whenever a person engages in highly practiced actions, these performances occur without apparent mental effort and often without the ability of verbalizing or remembering what one has done. In modern-day parlance, when talking about unconscious information processing, computer terminology is favored over psychoanalytic ids and egos (Erdelyi, 1985;

Loftus & Klinger, 1992): The ego becomes the *executive process;* unconscious censoring becomes *filtering;* conflict becomes *decision modes;* conscious becomes *working memory;* and so on.

A second question that arises concerns whether the unconscious is motivationally hot and passionate or is only cognitively cold and automated. The Freudian unconscious was hot. It reeked with lust and anger; it was irrational, impulsive, primitive, demanding, and hallucinatory. The unconscious studied by present-day psychologists, however, is cold. It is mechanical and automated (Greenwald, 1992).

FREUDIAN UNCONSCIOUS

The division of mental life into what is conscious and what is unconscious is the fundamental premise of psychoanalysis (Freud, 1923). Freud rejected the idea that consciousness was the essence of mental life and therefore divided the mind into three components: conscious, preconscious, and unconscious. The conscious (i.e., "short-term memory" or "consciousness") includes all the thoughts, feelings, sensations, memories, and experiences that a person is aware of at any given time. The preconscious stores all the thoughts, feelings, and so on that are absent from immediate consciousness but can be retrieved into consciousness with a little prompting (e.g., you are aware of but are not currently thinking about your name, today's date, or what color ink these words are printed in). The most important, and by far the largest, component is the unconscious. The unconscious is the mental storehouse of inaccessible instinctual impulses, repressed experiences, childhood (before language) memories, and strong but unfulfilled wishes and desires (Freud, 1915, 1923).

To illustrate the view of the unconscious as flexible and strategic (i.e., smart), consider unconscious activity during dreaming. For Freud, daily tensions continually mounted in the unconscious and were vented during dreaming. Because dreams vent unconscious tensions, dreams provided an opportunity for accessing the wishful core of the unconscious. Assuming that the person could recall his dreams, dream analysis began by asking the individual to report a dream's story line and ended with the therapist's interpretation of the underlying meaning of the dream. A dream's story line represents its manifest content (its face value and defensive facade), while the symbolic meanings of the events in the story line represent its latent content (its underlying meaning and wishful core). Because the explicit expression of unconscious wishes would be anxiety-provoking (and would therefore awaken the dreamer), the unconscious, both strategically and defensively, expresses its impulses through the latent and symbolic, rather than the obvious and manifest.

As one illustration, consider the following dream reported by one of Freud's patients and that was analyzed with free association (Freud, 1900):

> A whole crowd of children—all of her brothers, sisters and cousins of both sexes—were romping in a field. Suddenly they all grew wings, flew away and disappeared.

The patient first had this dream as a young child and continued to have this same dream repeatedly into adulthood. In the dream, all of the patient's brothers, sisters, and cousins flew away and she alone remained in the field. According to Freud, the dream does not make much sense at the manifest level, and to gain an understanding of its meaning and significance, the analysis must take place within the latent content. At the latent level, the dream is (for this particular person) a death wish from the Thanatos that her brothers, sisters, and cousins would all sprout wings and fly away like a butterfly (a child's view of the soul leaving the body upon death), leaving her to the full attention and affection of her parents.

Before we can conclude that dreams function to vent unconscious wishes, however, we must acknowledge what 20th-century research has discovered since Freud. In addition to serving a venting function, dreams serve (1) a *neurophysiological venting function* in that the brain stem (not unconscious wishes) produces random (though rhythmic) neural excitatory inputs for the neocortex to process and make sense of (Crick & Mitchison, 1986); (2) a *memory consolidating function* as memories of the day are moved from short-term into long-term memory (Greenberg & Perlman, 1993); (3) a *stress-buffering (coping) function* by providing an opportunity to pair defense mechanisms against threatening events such as social isolation and job stress (Koulack, 1993); and (4) a *problem-solving function* in that, during dreaming, people process information, organize ideas, and arrive at creative constructions for solving their problems (Winson, 1992). While some evidence supports the idea that dreams provide an outlet for venting wishes and tensions (Fisher & Greenberg, 1996), it is also true that Freud's concept of the dream was too limited. Dreams are not only motivated events, they are also neurophysiological, cognitive, coping, and problem-solving events that have little to do with motivation. Even among psychoanalytic thinkers, the trend in thinking about dreams has been to move away from focusing on dreams as only venting, drive-reducing events in favor of highlighting the general defensive or self-protective role of the dream process (Levin, 1990; Fisher & Greenberg, 1996; Moffitt, Kramer, & Hoffman, 1993).

NON-FREUDIAN UNCONSCIOUS

The view of the unconscious that has emerged within modern-day scientific psychology offers an understanding that is quite different from what Freud and his contemporaries talked and wrote about (Greenwald, 1992; Kihlstrom, 1987; Schacter, 1992). This modern research recognizes the existence of unconscious information processing but argues that its analytic (i.e., problem-solving) capabilities are severely limited (Greenwald, 1992). The analogy to a motiveless computer is simplistic, yet vaguely fitting nonetheless. Much of the non-Freudian unconscious has little to do with motivational processes. Instead, it enacts procedural knowledge (the "how-to knowledge" underlying motor skills), recognizes events despite any conscious awareness of being previously exposed to them (Roediger, 1990), and acquires the sort of implicit, nonverbal knowledge we gain, as from listening to and becoming familiar with music (Robin, Wallace, & Houston, 1993). The argument is that Freudian views have overestimated the influence of unconscious motives on action (Jacoby & Kelly, 1992).

Subliminal information processing provides a good example in which to discuss these two contrasting views of the unconscious. To subliminally activate unconscious information, a stimulus is presented at a very weak energy level (or for only a very brief duration of time) to an unsuspecting research participant. For instance, while the person looks through a tachistoscope, the phrase "Mommy and I are one" appears for four milliseconds, which is a span of time much too brief for anyone to report actually seeing anything, much less read, recognize, and comprehend the message. Both the Freudian and the non-Freudian views of the unconscious agree that the information does get processed at an unconscious level. Just what the mind does with that unconscious information is where the two views differ dramatically.

According to the Freudian view, the phrase functions every bit as does a hypnotic suggestion in that it activates deep wishes embedded in the viewer's infant experience with a comforting, protecting, and nurturing mother. Such activation then produces positive effects, such as increased self-esteem, increased assertiveness, and decreased anxiety and depression (Hardaway, 1990; Silverman & Weinberger, 1985). A smart, adaptive unconscious indeed. According to the non-Freudian view, however, the idea that the brain can process a complex phrase like the one above with such a brief exposure is considered to be overly generous. At best, people can process a single word or perhaps an outline of a figure. Unconscious information processing is simply too basic and automatic. In this view, it is asking too much to think that just because people can respond to a subliminal message in some way (i.e., with a gut feeling of recognition) they will automatically follow its directives.

Consider the sort of subliminal information processing made popular in the 1960s when a marketing executive superimposed the very briefly flashed messages, "Eat popcorn" and "Drink Coke," over a film shown at a local theater. According to the executive, popcorn sales exploded (Morse & Stoller, 1982). Marketers have been trying to send subliminal messages into the minds of the unsuspecting masses ever since this experiment, as with department stores' antishoplifting subliminal messages broadcast over the public address system ("If you steal, you will get caught"; Loftus & Klinger, 1992). But researchers have tested whether people ever act on subliminal messages and found that people do not behave in ways consistent with the subliminal directive. The unconscious might recognize and understand the message in some way, but acting on the directive is a whole different matter. And therein lies the controversy—while subliminal marketing messages routinely fail to influence people, subliminal messages, like "Mommy and I are one," can increase self-esteem and decrease anxiety and depression.

One group of researchers tested the validity of widely available subliminal audiotapes designed to enhance memory or boost self-esteem (Greenwald, et al., 1991). The audiotapes play subliminal messages (e.g., "You're the best"; "I love you") over relaxing material (e.g., popular music, nature sounds of the forest) to improve the daily listener's self-esteem (or memory, or some other targeted purpose, such as weight loss or smoking cessation). The researchers recruited college-aged volunteers who wanted to increase their self-esteem or improve their memory. Each volunteer completed initial measures of their self-esteem and memory, listened daily to the audiotape for 5 weeks, and completed follow-up measures of their self-esteem and memory. In a nutshell, results showed that the audiotapes did not work. Like the "Eat popcorn" and "If you steal, you will get caught" messages, the "I love you" subliminal messages were not processed in a way that affected thoughts or behaviors (Greenwald et al., 1991). The fundamental question with which scientists who study unconscious processes are therefore wrestling with is whether people change either their ways of thinking, their ways of feeling, or their ways of behaving following subliminal (unconscious) activation of information or desires.

PSYCHODYNAMICS

Based on Freud's observations of people who engaged in behavior that they clearly wished not to engage in (e.g., ritualized hand washing), he reasoned that motivation must be more complex than that which follows intentional volition. Conscious volition must have to wrestle with an unconscious counterwill of some sort. Following this line of reasoning, Freud conceptualized people as being of two minds, as it were: "The mind is an arena, a sort of tumbling-ground, for the struggle of antagonistic impulses" (Freud, 1917). People have ideas and wills, but people also have counterideas and counterwills. When the conscious (ego's) will and the unconscious (id's) counterwill are of roughly equal strength, a sort of internal civil war ensues in which neither is completely satisfied. The combatants can be diagramed as follows:

will → ← counterwill

Freud's depiction of the human mind was one of conflict—idea versus counteridea, will versus counterwill, desire versus repression, excitation versus inhibition, and cathexis (sexual attraction) versus anticathexis (guilt). This clashing of forces is what is meant by the term *psychodynamics*.

For Freud, psychodynamics concerned the conflict between the personality structures of the id and ego (and superego, which is not discussed here). The motivations of the id were unconscious, involuntary, impulse-driven, and hedonistic, as the id obeyed the pleasure principle: Obtain pleasure and avoid pain and do so at all costs and without delay. The motivations of the ego were partly conscious and partly unconscious, steeped in defenses, and sought to delay gratification, as the ego obeyed the reality principle: Hold pleasure seeking at bay until an appropriate, timely, and socially acceptable need-satisfying object can be found. Today, psychoanalysts point out that wishes, fears, values, goals, emotions, thoughts, and motives are never in harmony, and mental conflict is an inevitable constant (e.g., one wants and fears the same thing, as during a job interview, a marriage proposal, or in contemplating attending classes or not). As a case in point, Drew Westen (1998) points out that children's feelings toward their parents almost have to be riddled in conflict since parents provide not only security, comfort, and love but also frustration, distress, and disappointment.

REPRESSION

When most readers think of psychodynamics, what comes to mind are concepts like the id, ego, libido, and the Oedipal complex (Boneau, 1990). But, when Freud himself defined psychodynamics, the central concept was repression (Freud, 1917). Freud envisioned the unconscious as a vastly overcrowded apartment, the conscious as a reception room to the public world, and repression as a metaphorical doorkeeper to check each unconscious thought's identification card to judge whether it was fit to invite into consciousness. Because motivations reside in the unconscious, people remain unaware of their own motivations. In addition, however, people go out of their way to remain unaware of the motivations because they cannot bear to know things about themselves that contradict public opinion or their own consciences. Awareness of one's true motives would generate conflict with either the ideal self or what society regards to be a respectable person. Thus, repression and resistance constitute the foundation of psychodynamics (Fromm, 1986).

Repression refers to the process of forgetting information or an experience by ways that are unconscious, unintentional, and automatic. (Suppression [discussed next], in contrast, refers to the process of removing a thought from attention by ways that are conscious, intentional, and deliberate; [Wegner, 1992].) Repression is the ego's psychodynamic counterforce to the id's demanding desires. It is a defensive process for keeping out of consciousness some otherwise distressing wish, desire, idea, or memory. Without repression, the ego's charge to coordinate the demands of the id, superego, and physical/ social reality would be an impossible undertaking. When unconscious thoughts and impulses begin to surface, anxiety emerges as a danger signal, and it is this anxiety that moves the unconscious mind to action—to repression and perhaps to other ways of coping as well (Freud, 1926; Holmes, 1974, 1990). But repression is tremendously difficult to study empirically because you have to ask people about things they do not remember. Studying repression is similar to figuring out whether the refrigerator light stays on when you close the door (to borrow an example from Wegner, 1989). Research on repression has not yet produced impressive understandings (Erdelyi & Goldberg, 1979; Erdelyi, 1985, 1990), but research on the related mental control process of suppression has been enlightening.

THOUGHT SUPPRESSION

The ability to stop a thought is beyond the human mind. When an unwanted thought or worry comes to mind, people generally try to control the intruder via suppression (remove or avoid it). Generally speaking, suppression fails.[1] When we try to suppress a thought, all we get for our efforts is a lesson that we have less control over our thoughts than we care to admit (Wegner, 1989).

Consider the psychodynamics of the following: (1) Do not *think* about something (try not to think about today's dental appointment, for example); (2) do not *do* something (try to go all day without smoking a cigarette, for example); (3) do not *want*

---

[1] Suppressing a thought given by an external source (i.e., another person) is that which lies beyond the human mind (e.g., try not to think about eating a candy bar). People's own intrusive thoughts are different (Kelly & Kahn, 1994). The number one strategy that works with intrusive thoughts is distraction (Wegner, 1989). With familiar intrusive thoughts, people generally have a rich network of thoughts they have used previously to distract themselves from their unwanted thoughts (Kelly & Kahn, 1994). Over time, people learn the skill and technique of thought suppression. But a psychodynamic rebound effect always occurs when thoughts are generated by an outside agent, like an experimenter saying not to think of a white bear (Wegner et al., 1987) or a friend asking you to keep a secret (Lane & Wegner, 1995). With externally induced intrusive thoughts, people lack experience in trying to suppress them, and hence, the psychodynamic mental conflict is on.

something (try not to want to eat food while on a diet, for example); and (4) do not *remember* something (try to forget about a deeply humiliating experience, for example). When such thoughts enter our consciousness, our thinking halts itself because the thought precedes something that we wish not to happen. That is, the self-instruction of "don't think about that candy bar" precedes the undesired act of eating the candy bar. With the stream of thought interrupted—in fact, halted—the unwanted thought lingers out there in consciousness all by itself with a spotlight on it. We can suppress the thought for a few seconds or perhaps for a few minutes, but there is a curious tendency for that thought to pop up again (Wegner, 1989; Wegner et al., 1987).

Consider a laboratory experiment in which college students were asked not to think of a white bear (Wegner et al., 1987). Each participant sat alone at a table with a bell on it (like those bells used in hotels for service). For the first 5 minutes, the participant said whatever popped into mind. "Free association" was easy. For the next 5 minutes, however, the participant was asked explicitly not to think of a white bear, but if she did think of the bear, she was to ring the bell as a signal that the unwanted thought had accidentally popped into her mind. The attempt at thought suppression was very difficult, and a lot of bell ringing occurred. During a final 5-minute period, each participant was asked to think about a white bear. In this last period, participants experienced a "rebound effect" in which the thought of the white bear preoccupied their attention. Bell ringing sounded like a hotel desk at check-out time.

These results contradict common sense. Thought suppression not only failed, but it produced an obsessive preoccupation about those white bears (the rebound effect).

People rely on thought suppression to control their thoughts and actions in practically all areas of life. People rely on thought suppression for behavioral self-control, as in the effort to abstain from eating certain foods (Polivy & Herman, 1985) or consuming addictive substances (Marlatt & Parks, 1982). People rely on thought suppression to keep a secret (Pennebaker, 1990) or to deceive another person (DePaulo, 1992). People rely on thought suppression for self-control over pain (Cioffi, 1991) and fear (Rachman, 1978). And people use thought suppression to avoid making public the inner workings of their mind and its socially offensive wants, desires, and intentions (Wegner & Erber, 1993). People basically rely on thought suppression for seemingly good reasons. Many of our private thoughts would produce public confusion (to put it nicely) if they were allowed to be freely expressed, such as greeting a stranger and suppressing the first impression that he is extremely attractive or unattractive. Thought suppression turns potential social conflict into a private mental struggle of wanted versus unwanted thoughts (Wegner, 1992). We learn quickly that thought suppression can be a social ally in preventing us from just blurting out our thoughts, as sometimes happens when we are stressed (Jacobs & Nadel, 1985) or impaired by drugs or alcohol (Steele & Josephs, 1990).

All this makes for interesting psychodynamics. An unwanted thought comes to mind, so we suppress it. But conscious thought suppression activates an unconscious counterprocess to keep searching and to detect any presence of the thought to be suppressed. The unconscious monitoring process ironically keeps the to-be-suppressed thought activated, which is the very thing that the conscious intention was trying to avoid. With this psychodynamic process in mind, it makes sense why research shows that the act of suppressing produces an uninvited rebound effect of the unwanted thought. Continued suppression actually, in time, builds a rather potent counterforce that drives the unwanted thought toward an obsession (e.g., the dieter who tries not to think of food is vulnerable to thinking only about food; Polivy & Herman, 1985). According to Dan Wegner (1989, 1992), the way out of the quagmire of the suppression cycle (unwanted thought → thought suppression → obsession → unwanted thought returns, and so on) is to stop suppressing and, instead, focus on and think about the unwanted thought. Paradoxically, only those thoughts that we welcome are we able to forget (Frankl, 1960).

Thought suppression does more than just illustrate interesting psychodynamics, and it does more than just explain why "you can't always think about what you want" (Wegner, 1992). Thought suppression also illustrates the basic Freudian principle that emotionally charged thoughts that are suppressed exert a continuous affective press on the mind, even outside of our conscious awareness. People who are told to suppress an exciting thought about sex, for instance, remain physiologically aroused even when they are not consciously thinking about sex, and they show heightened sexual arousal when the thought returns to consciousness (Wegner et al., 1990). Basically, thought suppression recruits unconscious counterthoughts (the rebound effect) that can lead people to thoughts, feelings, and actions that they are not aware they possess. People can feel things without knowing why they feel them, and they can act on feelings in which they are unaware they possess.

DO THE ID AND EGO ACTUALLY EXIST?

Given the preceding discussion on psychodynamics, an interesting question arises that asks: What does contemporary empirical research have to say about the scientific status of the id and ego? Is the human brain organized such that part exists as a cauldron of innate and impulsive biological desires, while another part exists as an executive control center that perceives the world and learns and adapts to it? The conscious awareness responsible for executive control is a relatively new evolutionary development that has been superimposed over a primitive, goal-directed, motivationally rich information processing system (Reber, 1992). The limbic structures of the brain—the hypothalamus, thalamus, amygdala, medial forebrain bundle, and so on—are commonly referred to as pleasure-unpleasure brain centers. Electrical stimulation of the brain reveals that some limbic areas are pleasure centers (i.e., septum, lateral hypothalamus, medial forebrain bundle), whereas other limbic areas are unpleasure centers (i.e., thalamus, amygdala, medial hypothalamus; Olds & Fobes, 1981; Stellar & Stellar, 1985; Wise & Bozarth, 1984).[2] The limbic system makes for a pretty fair id. The neocortex qualifies as the brain structure that might correspond to the ego, as it performs all those functions that reflect learning, memory, decision making, and intellectual problem solving. Further, the neural pathways and structures of the neocortex and the limbic systems are intricately interrelated. Even within the neocortex itself, and even within the limbic system itself, the interrelationships of how one structure affects the other (e.g., how the amygdala excites and inhibits the hypothalamus) are so complex as to

---

[2] As a sidenote, however, electrical brain stimulation in humans does not produce intense pleasure or rage-filled attacks but rather only mild feelings of pleasure and unpleasure (Gloor, Oliver, & Quesney, 1981; Heath, 1964; Valenstein, 1973).

defy description here. The picture that emerges corresponds to a pattern of psychodynamics, of forces and counterforces, of excitations and inhibitions.

EGO PSYCHOLOGY

Freud postulated that all psychical energy originated in the id. At birth, the infant was all id; the ego was only in the beginning processes of formation (Freud, 1923). Throughout infancy, the ego developed from perceiving instincts to controlling them, from obeying instincts to curbing them. As an infant matured, id energies were distributed, in part, to the developing ego. How much energy was distributed to the id and ego during childhood determined the relative strengths of that personality. If the id had the greater energy, adult behavior was relatively impulsive and pleasure oriented. On the other hand, if the ego had the greater energy, adult behavior was relatively realistic and characterized by the timely gratification of needs and strategic avoidance of dangers. To describe the relationship between the id and ego, Freud (1923) wrote the following:

> One might compare the relation of the ego to the id with that between a rider and his horse. The horse provides the locomotive energy, and the rider has the prerogative of determining the goal and of guiding the movements of his powerful mount towards it. . . . The ego feels itself hemmed in on three sides and threatened by three kinds of danger. . . . Goaded on by the id, hemmed in by the superego, and rebuffed by reality, the ego struggles to cope with its economic task of reducing the forces and influences which work in it and upon it to some kind of harmony (Freud, 1923).

Thus, Freud saw the ego as a personality structure that arose from id energies to mediate between id impulses, superego demands, and the dangers of the environment. The id is force; the ego becomes counterforce.

The neo-Freudians saw ego functioning as much more. Heinz Hartmann (1958, 1964), the "father of ego psychology," saw the ego involved in a process of maturation that made it increasingly independent from its id origins. For Hartmann, the ego, unlike the id, developed through learning and experience. Learning occurred because the child engaged in a tremendous amount of manipulative, exploratory, and experimental activity (such as grasping, walking, crawling, and thinking), all of which provided the ego with information about itself and its surroundings. With feedback from its manipulative, exploratory, and experimental activity, the ego began to acquire ego properties—language, memory, intentions, complex ideas, and so on—that facilitated its ability to adapt successfully to the realities, demands, and constraints of the world. Hartmann conceptualized that because of its ability to learn, adapt, and grow, the mature ego was mostly autonomous from the id. Neo-Freudians studied the motivational dynamics of the "autonomous ego."

EGO DEVELOPMENT

Defining ego is difficult because it is not so much a thing as it is a developmental process. The essence of ego development is a developmental progression toward what is possible in terms of psychological growth, maturity, adjustment, pro-social interdependence, competence, and autonomous functioning (Hartmann, 1958; Loevinger, 1976). From its infantile origins through its progression toward what is possible, the ego unfolds along the following developmental trajectory (Loevinger, 1976):

- Symbiotic
- Impulsive
- Self-Protective
- Conformist
- Conscientious
- Autonomous

During the (infantile) symbiotic stage, the ego is extremely immature, constantly overwhelmed by impulses, and exists as wholly dependent on its caretaker. With language, the symbiotic ego begins to differentiate itself from the caretaker but remains extremely immature. In the impulsive stage, external forces (parental constraints, rules) and not the ego per se, curb the child's impulses and desires. Self-control emerges when the child first anticipates consequences and understands that rules exist. The ego then internalizes these consequences and rules in guiding its self-protective defensive capabilities. During the conformist stage, the ego internalizes group-accepted rules, and the anxiety of group disapproval becomes a potent counterforce against one's impulses. The conscientious ego has a conscience, an internalized set of rules and a pro-social sense of responsibility to others that functions as internal standards for curbing and countering impulses. The conscientious ego is the modal ego stage among adults (Loevinger, 1976). The autonomous ego is one in which thoughts, plans, goals, and behaviors originate from within the ego and its resources, rather than from id impulses or from other people's (including society's) demands and pressures (Ryan, 1993).

Each ego stage is more complex than the one that precedes it. And ego development revolves around increasing the effectiveness of acquired capacities, such as impulse control, delay of gratification, finding appropriate outlets for gratification, emotional stability, active coping, emotional intelligence, environmental mastery motivation, hardiness, and autonomous self-regulation (Block & Kreman, 1996).

The developmental progression from immature ego stages to relatively more mature stages has been shown to occur in both cross-sectional studies that compare ego development in children, adolescents, and adults (Loevinger & Wessler, 1970) as well as longitudinal studies that compare the same individuals over their life courses (Redmore, 1983; Redmore & Loevinger, 1979). It is not known precisely when or why people achieve their maximum ego developmental stage, though social experiences such as going to college (Loevinger et al., 1985) and coping with divorce (Bursik, 1991) are important. What is clear is that (1) most people stabilize (halt) their ego development before the autonomous stage (Holt, 1980; Loevinger, 1976), and (2) ego strengths during preschool foreshadows ego strength during adolescence (and vice versa for ego deficits; Shoda, Mischel, & Peake, 1999).

EGO STRENGTHS

Ego development does not happen automatically, and the day-to-day existence of the ego is one of vulnerability. To overcome immaturity and a susceptibility to being overwhelmed by unacceptable desires and environmental demands, the ego must gain resources, or strengths. A mature, strong ego manifests itself in three ways: (1) Resilient defense mechanisms allow it to cope successfully with the inevitable anxieties of life; (2) a sense of effectance or competence provides it with a generative capacity for seeking out and mastering optimal challenges and for developing new skills; and (3) a sense of identity provides it with a productive and fulfilling place within the society. These three attributes correspond to ego defense, ego effectance, and ego identity.

Ego Defense

Through defense mechanisms, the ego buffers consciousness against potentially overwhelming levels of anxiety originating from conflict with id impulses (neurotic anxiety), superego demands (moral anxiety), and environmental dangers (realistic anxiety). Three signs provide evidence that an anxiety-reducing course of action is indeed a defense mechanism: (1) A defense mechanism is unconscious rather than reflective and intellectual; (2) its use is immediate rather than deliberative; and (3) it functions to deny, distort, or otherwise rearrange the person's understanding of reality so that it is less threatening. Fourteen such defense mechanisms appear in Table 13.1, along with a definition and example for each (borrowing mostly from Anna Freud, 1946).

TABLE 13.1 **Defense Mechanisms of the Ego**

DEFENSE MECHANISM	DEFINITION (WITH *EXAMPLE)*
Denial	Unpleasant external realities are ignored or their acknowledgment is refused. *Preoccupation with work so there is no attention paid to the messages of rejection coming from a problematic personal relationship.*
Fantasy	Gratifying frustrated desires by imaginary achievement. *Imagining oneself to be a courageous national hero who performs incredible feats and wins the admiration of all.*
Isolation	A form of self-censorship that prevents or keeps affect (emotion) out of consciousness while allowing the cold facts to register in consciousness. *Hearing the news of the death of a loved one and responding only cognitively (matter-of-factly) to the events that one is hearing.*
Repression	Prevents and keeps anxiety-provoking thoughts out of consciousness. *Rejecting the desire to injure another person.*
Identification	Taking on the characteristics of someone viewed as successful. *Seeing the nation adore a celebrity and then adjusting one's appearance (hair style, mode of dress, walk) to be loved and treated like the celebrity.*

TABLE 13.1 **Defense Mechanisms of the Ego** (CONTINUED)

DEFENSE MECHANISM	DEFINITION (WITH *EXAMPLE*)
Projection	Attributing one's own unacceptable desire or impulse onto someone else, often producing a mild paranoia. *The anxiety of "I am failing this course because I am unintelligent" is expressed as "This textbook is stupid" or "The teacher is an idiot."*
Reaction formation	Adopting or expressing the strong opposite of one's true feelings or motives. *Expressing and endorsing strong optimism ("Everything will work out just fine") in the face of the grim realities of world hunger, nuclear war, or interpersonal rejection.*
Regression	Returning to an earlier stage of development when experiencing stress or anxiety. *Using baby talk to gain another's nurturance and sympathy to win an anxiety-provoking argument.*
Displacement	Releasing one's anxiety against a substitute object when doing so against the source of the anxiety could be harmful. *Discharging pent-up aggressive impulses against a father figure (the boss) onto a more anxiety-manageable object, such as the household dog. The worker kicks the dog as a substitute for the father figure.*
Rationalization	Justifying a disturbing or unacceptable thought or feeling by selecting a logical reason to think or feel that way. *Producing an acceptable reason to justify one's hatred for a particular group of people, such as "because they lie and cheat all the time."*
Atonement	Undoing an anxiety-provoking thought or behavior by apologizing or repenting. *The child-neglecting, world-traveling parent brings gifts home for children to make up for the neglect.*
Compensation	Covering up a weakness or inferiority by overemphasizing the importance of a desirable trait. *The physically unattractive person develops an exceptional athletic or musical skill, or a person with feelings of inferiority may brag frequently about the status of his ancestors.*
Humor	Expression of unconscious wishes in a socially approved manner such that the person releases sexual and aggressive impulses and insults authority figures in a disguised form. *A newspaper editorial cartoon exaggerates an unflattering anatomical feature of a high-ranking politician that allows readers to laugh at the authority figure.*
Sublimation	A displacement that results in something advantageous to society. *Libidinal energy, such as a sexual impulse, is released through creative, scientific, or manual work.*

Defense mechanisms exist in a hierarchical ordering from least to most mature, from least to most adaptive (Vaillant, 1977, 1992, 1993). The essential criterion for determining how mature or adaptive a defense mechanism is depends on how much distortion or blocking of reality the defense mechanism achieves. Denial and fantasy, for instance, are the defenses of psychosis, while sublimation and humor are relatively mature ego defenses. The maturity hierarchy reflects ego strength, as a strong ego habitually relies on relatively mature defense mechanisms that allow the ego to react to the realities of life with appropriate problem-solving coping responses. In contrast, a weak ego relies on relatively immature defenses to sidestep the realities of life in ways that prevent anticipation of problems and appropriate problem solving once distress occurs.

George Vaillant (1977, 1992) classified defense mechanisms into four categories of maturity. At the most immature level, defense mechanisms deny reality or invent an imaginary one. Defense mechanisms such as denial and fantasy are the most immature because the individual fails even to recognize and attempt to cope with external reality. At the second level of maturity are defenses such as projection and identification. These defenses recognize reality, but attempts to cope with reality are accomplished by casting its disturbing aspects away from the self (as in projection) or reframing the stressor as a harmless, nonthreatening life event (as in isolation). At the third level of maturity are the most common defenses, including rationalization, regression, and reaction formation. These defenses deal effectively with short-term anxiety but fail to accomplish any longer-term gain in adjustment (because reality is repressed rather than accommodated). Rationalization, for example, temporarily excuses unacceptable desires or characteristics, but it fails to provide the means for coping with the problem that produced the anxiety in the first place. Level four defenses are the most adaptive and mature and include mechanisms such as sublimation and humor. Sublimation accepts unconscious impulses but effectively channels these impulses into socially beneficial outlets, such as the creative energy that produces a painting or a poem (making unconscious impulses both socially acceptable and personally productive). As for humor, all of us experience life stresses and psychological distresses, but people with a well-developed sense of humor suffer comparatively little maladjustment from these stresses and distresses (e.g., depression; Lefcourt & Martin, 1986; Nezu, Nezu, & Blissett, 1988).

To test his ideas that the maturity level of one's defenses reflect ego strength and thus life adjustment, Vaillant (1977) followed the lives of 56 men over a 30-year period. He interviewed each man in his college-age years, and objective testers classified each man as using predominantly mature (levels 3 and 4) or predominantly immature (levels 1 and 2) defense mechanisms as a personal style against distress and anxiety. The study sought to determine how these two groups of men would fare in life, and the research assessed each man's life adjustment 30 years later in four categories: career, social, psychological, and medical. Ego strength, as indexed by maturity level of defense mechanisms, successfully discriminated men who had career, social, psychological, and medical problems from those who did not (see Table 13.2). Mature defense mechanisms allowed the men to live a well-adjusted life, find and keep a fulfilling job, develop a rich friendship pattern, avoid divorce, avoid the need for psychiatric visits and mental illnesses, and so on. Other researchers have found that the more people rely on active, reality-confronting defenses

TABLE 13.2 **Relationship Between Maturity of Defense Mechanisms and Life Adjustment**

	Predominant Adaptive Style (%)		
	MATURE (N = 25)	IMMATURE (N =31)	SIGNIFICANCE (P)
Overall adjustment			
1) Top third in adult adjustment	60%	0%	< .01**
2) Bottom third in adult adjustment	4%	61%	< .001*
3) "Happiness" (top third)	68%	16%	< .001*
Career adjustment			
1) Income over $20,000/year	88%	48%	< .01**
2) Job meets ambition for self	92%	58%	< .001*
3) Active public service outside job	56%	29%	< .05**
Social adjustment			
1) Rich friendship pattern	64%	6%	< .001*
2) Marriage in least harmonious quartile or divorced	28%	61%	< .01**
3) Barren friendship pattern	4%	52%	< .001*
4) No competitive sports (age 40–50)	24%	77%	< .001*
Psychological adjustment			
1) 10+ psychiatric visits	0%	45%	< .01**
2) Ever diagnosed mentally ill	0%	55%	< .001*
3) Emotional problems in childhood	20%	45%	< .05**
4) Worst childhood environment (bottom fourth)	12%	39%	< .05**
5) Fails to take full vacation	28%	61%	< .05**
6) Able to be aggressive with others (top fourth)	36%	6%	< .05**
Medical adjustment			
1) 4+ adult hospitalizations	8%	26%	
2) 5+ days sick leave/year	0%	23%	< .05**
3) Recent health poor by objective exam	0%	36%	< .05**
4) Subjective health consistently judged excellent since college	68%	48%	< .05**

*Very significant difference; would occur by chance only one time in a thousand.

**Significant difference.

N=sample size; P=probability, a statistic to denote significant findings

SOURCE: From *Adaptation to Life* (p. 87), by G. E. Vaillant, 1977, Boston: Little, Brown & Company. Copyright 1977 by George E. Vaillant.

(e.g., anticipating problems, seeking out information, accepting personal responsibility), the better they are at handling life's challenges (e.g., maintain employment, resist suicide; Westen, 1998).

Ego Effectance

Ego effectance concerns the individual's competence in dealing effectively with environmental challenges, demands, and opportunities (White, 1959; Harter, 1981). Effectance motivation begins as an undifferentiated source of ego energy. With its diffuse energy, its properties (e.g., grasping, crawling, walking), and its acquired skills (e.g., language, penmanship, social skills), the ego attempts to deal satisfactorily with the circumstances and stressors that come its way. In the process of adapting and developing, the undifferentiated ego energy begins to differentiate into specific motives, such as the needs for achievement, affiliation, intimacy, and power (see chapter 6). Thus begins the development of a variety of separate ego motivations, but the core ego motivation is effectance motivation, or the desire to interact effectively with the environment (see chapter 4, especially Figure 4.1).

Ego effectance develops into more than just a defensive, reactive coping response to life's demands. As the child exercises skills, she begins to learn how to produce successful change in the environment. The child learns how to use crayons, climb trees, cross streets, hold the attention of adults, feed herself, write letters, make new friends, ride a bicycle, hit baseballs, and a hundred other tasks. When successful, such interactions produce a sense of efficacy, a perception of competence, and feelings of satisfaction and enjoyment. The ego aggregates these perceptions and feelings into a general sense of competence. Eventually, the child's cumulative history of efficacious versus inefficacious feedback yields a personal sense of competence, which is a synonym for ego strength. The greater the ego's effectance motivation, the greater the person's willingness to use ego properties proactively (not just reactively) by intentionally changing the environment for the better. With each successful transaction with the environment (a friend is made, a tree house is constructed), the ego's pooled reservoir of effectance motivation increases. The greater the effectance motivation, the stronger the desire to develop personal skills (ego properties) further and to seek out interactions with the environment in general.

With ever-strengthening ego development, the individual gains a repository of two sources of motives: id-based instinctual drives (unconscious wishes) and ego-based effectance motives. Id-based motivations are inherited and change little in the course of development. Ego-based effectance motives are acquired through environmental interactions and change markedly in the course of development (Harter, 1981). Together, these two sources of motivation explain most of human beings' energetic and directed behaviors in the psychoanalytic tradition. (A third major source of motives that will be used to complete the psychoanalytical trilogy of motivation will be identified in the section on "Object Relations Theory.")

Ego Identity

Another aspect of ego development is an emerging sense of identity, the sense of being a distinct and productive individual within a social framework (Erikson, 1959, 1963, 1964, 1968). A coherent sense of identity integrates the ego's physical, psychological, and social attributes and provides a life course characterized by both direction and commitment.

Erik Erikson describes the lifelong quest to formulate an identity by postulating an epigenetic sequence of eight developmental turning points, a theory of psychosocial lifespan development that has received a good deal of empirical support and confirmation (Whitbourne et al., 1992). With each developmental turning point comes the twofold possibility for ego growth toward greater adjustment versus ego decline toward greater maladjustment. A positive resolution (at each turning point) empowers the ego's development toward growth, strength, and adaptation; a negative resolution fosters a trajectory toward regression, fragility, and maladjustment.

During infancy, the ego is helpless and immature; it possesses literally no ego strength. Being helpless, the ego is fully dependent on its primary caregiver for need satisfaction and faces its first developmental turning point (trust versus mistrust of others). When caretakers prove themselves trustworthy, the ego gains the strength of hope and begins to exercise emerging skills, such as locomotion and language. In early childhood, the infant exercises his emerging competencies, initiates experiments on the world, and faces his second developmental turning point (autonomy versus doubt). Caretakers either support the child's emerging autonomy and endow the ego with the strength of will or greet it with punishing shame. In the preschool years, the third developmental turning point arises in which the ego develops toward either initiative or guilt. With initiative support, the ego gains the strength of purpose. During the elementary grades, the fourth developmental turning point arises in which the ego moves toward industry (i.e., effectance) or inferiority. The ego strength to be gained through industry is competence, or effectance. Industry involves competence-based development that is cognitive (development of skills and knowledge), behavioral (application of those skills and knowledge), and emotional (rewarding experiences during the acquisition and application of skills and knowledge; Kowaz & Marcia, 1991). The developmental aggregate of an ego endowed with hope, will, purpose, and competence provides an ideal platform for the ego to face its fifth developmental turning point during adolescence: identity versus role confusion.

By adolescence, the emerging ego must prove itself relevant to an adult social system, to specific adult endeavors, and to available societal roles (Baumeister, 1986, 1987; Marcia, 1994). Hence, occupational apprenticeship begins and with it a sense of individuality and identity. When adolescents search for, find, and eventually commit to a particular strategy for life, they develop an identity; when they fail to search for, find, or commit to adult roles, adolescents develop role confusion and a sense of ego uncertainty (Marcia, 1966; Meilman, 1979). Whether the adolescent ego achieves a sense of identity therefore depends in part on her own developing ego strength and resources, including hope, will, purpose, and effectance. It also, however, depends on how relevant the ego's skills and talents are in the context of social opportunities, endeavors, and roles.

Four distinct identity statuses exist: achieved, in moratorium, foreclosed, and diffuse (Marcia, 1966, 1994). Classification of identity status follows the individual's pattern of exploration and commitment in socially relevant areas of life, such as occupation and values (but other domains as well, including interests, aspirations, and sexual orientation). The adolescent with an *achieved identity* has explored actively and made personal commitments to a way of life. The adolescent with an *identity in moratorium* has explored actively but not made personal commitments (the "identity crisis"). The adolescent with a *foreclosed identity* has not explored but has committed to an identity (e.g., assimilated a parent's occupational role or values). The adolescent with a *diffuse identity* has not searched, explored, or committed to occupational choices or values. Among adults, achieved identity reflects both an integration of personal attributes and an acceptance of the social environment (i.e., the ego is characterized by independence, effectance, coherent values, and warm relationships with others). Moratorium identity reflects a lack of integration of personal attributes and a questioning of the social environment (i.e., the ego values independence and is rebellious, anxious, introspective, and open to new ideas and change). Foreclosed identity reflects an acceptance of the social environment (i.e., the ego is controlled too much and relates to people in conventional ways). And a diffuse identity reflects poor integration in the personality (i.e., the ego is conflicted, and its needs are difficult to reconcile into commitments; Helson, Stewart, & Ostrove, 1995; Kroger, 1993; Marcia, 1966, 1980; Marcia et al., 1993; Waterman, 1982).

OBJECT RELATIONS THEORY

The study of unconscious motivation began with a rather single-minded focus on sexual and aggressive drives. Over time, thinking about unconscious motivation became less biological and more interpersonal. Emphasis on the biological need for sexual gratification gave way to the psychological need for relatedness (Horney, 1939). The infant's need for attachment to the caregiver is central in the object relations theory, as is the individual's interpersonal connectedness to all the important people in his life.

"Object relations" is an awkward term used in the psychoanalytic profession. But the term is less awkward than it might at first appear to be when its etiology is told. Freud used the word "object" to refer to the target at which the individual's drives were directed for gratification (see chapter 2). Therefore, object relations theory studies how people satisfy their need for relatedness through their mental representations of and actual attachments to social and sexual objects (i.e., other people). The subject matter of object relations is (1) the need to be in relationship with others, (2) how objects are mentally represented, and (3) the quality of one's interpersonal relationships.

Objects relations theory focuses on the nature and the development of mental representations of the self and others and on the affective processes (wishes, fears) associated with these representations (Bowlby, 1969; Eagle, 1984; Greenberg & Mitchell, 1983; Scharff & Scharff, 1995; Westen, 1990). In particular, object relations theories focus on how childhood mental representations of one's caretakers are captured within the personality and persist into adulthood. What persists into adulthood are those mental representations of self and of other significant people (Main, Kaplan, & Cassidy, 1985; van IJzendoorn, 1995). What emerges as problematic are the core conflictual relationship themes that emanate out of negative mental representations of object relations (Blatt, 1994; Luborsky & Crits-Christoph, 1990; Strauman, 1992; Urist, 1980).

Object relations theories often stress the impact that parental abuse or neglect has on the infant's emerging representations of self and others. When one's primary caretaker is warm, nurturing, responsive, available, and trustworthy, the parental object satisfies the infant's need for relatedness, communicates a message of approval, and communicates a message about relationships that encourages a secure and affectionate attachment; when one's primary caretaker is cold, abusive, unresponsive, neglectful, and unpredictable, the parental object frustrates the infant's need for relatedness, communicates a message of disapproval, and communicates a message about relationships that encourages an insecure and anxiety-ridden attachment (Ainsworth et al., 1978; Sullivan, 1953). For instance, a childhood characterized by interpersonal traumas (e.g., assault, physical abuse,

Love as an Attachment Process

Question: Why would a person want to learn about the motivational states discussed in this chapter?

Answer: To understand romantic love as an attachment process.

Consider the following three-item, multiple-choice question. Read each statement carefully, and check the one that best describes you:

_____ I find it easy to get close to others. I am comfortable depending on others. And I am comfortable having other people depend on me. I don't worry about being abandoned, and I don't worry about someone getting too close to me.

_____ I am somewhat uncomfortable being close to others. I find it difficult to trust others completely, and I find it difficult to allow myself to depend on others. I become nervous when anyone gets too close. And I get nervous when others want me to be more intimate with them than I feel comfortable being.

_____ I find that others are reluctant to get as close as I would like. I worry that others don't really love me or that others don't really want to stay with me. I want to merge completely with others, especially love partners, and this desire sometimes scares people away.

Attachment theory argues that affectionate bonds develop between infants and their caretakers and that these affectionate bonds, whether positive or negative, carry forward into adulthood, affecting the adult's relationships with lovers (Bowlby, 1969, 1973, 1980). Ethologically based attachment theory is very similar to psychoanalytically based objects relations theory. In both theories, infants have a psychological need for relatedness that strongly motivates them to desire close, affectionate bonds with their caregivers. Based on the quality of that care, infants form mental models of how interaction partners relate to them that can be characterized as secure, anxious, or full of avoidance (Ainsworth et al., 1978).

Which of the three statements above best resonated with your own experience? The three statements characterize, in order, a secure, an avoidance, and an anxious attachment style. About 50% of adults classify themselves as secure, while about 25% classify themselves as anxious and as avoidance individuals, respectively (Hazan & Shaver, 1987; Shaver & Hazan, 1987).

Cindy Hazan and Phillip Shaver (1987) gave the above multiple-choice question to about 600 adults in the Denver, Colorado, area and asked them also to

serious neglect, rape, sexual molestation, and threatened with a weapon) and parental psychopathology (e.g., depression, anxiety, substance abuse, antisocial behavior, and poor and violent martial interaction) predict adulthood dysfunctional interpersonal relationships (Mickelson, Kessler, & Shaver, 1997). Further, when adults have secure mental models of self, others, and relationships, they experience greater self-esteem, more openness to experience, less neuroticism, and lessened senses that other people have control over complete questionnaires about their attachment history, beliefs about love, and experiences with a current partner. The three attachment groups experienced romantic love very differently. Securely attached lovers experienced love as a trilogy of friendship, trust, and happiness. They accepted and supported their partner, and their relationships endured over the years. Avoidance-attached lovers experienced love as an ongoing fear of intimacy and commitment, they often felt jealous, and they reported a marked absence of a positive emotion from the relationship. Their love was embedded in a defensiveness, and it was more likely to end in separation or divorce. Anxiously attached lovers experienced love as an obsession, a desire for constant reunion and reciprocation, as an extreme attraction and an extreme jealousy, and it produced emotional highs and emotional lows. Obsessive preoccupations might play out well in soap operas, but in real life, they generally lead to "needy, clingy" partners who are troubled by frequent episodes of loneliness and whose relationships are less likely to last than those of securely attached lovers.

Is there a personal continuity linking childhood attachment to adult romantic love? Infant attachment experiences do not just fast-forward into adulthood, and romantic relationships have additional features that infant-caretaker relationships do not (e.g, a two-way relationship, element of sexual attraction). But the experiences, emotions, and mental models of childhood do spill over and color adult constructions of beliefs about love (as evidenced by Hazan & Shaver's data). To articulate how infantile experiences color the adult mind, Freud used the example of comparing Ancient Rome with modern-day Rome (see *Civilization and Its Discontents,* 1930, pp. 15–20). Under the great 21st-century metropolis, now lie mostly nonexistent ruins. Early stages of the city's development are hard to find—victims of physical traumas such as fire, earthquake, and invasion. Instead, ancient features have been absorbed into later features for which they supplied the materials. Like the metaphor of Ancient Rome, infantile mental models mix with the psychological traumas of childhood to leave behind diffuse anger, frustration, sadness, craving, painful longing, and a fear of mistrust and commitment that carry forward into and color adult constructions of mental models of romantic love.

their fates (Mickelson et al., 1997). Positive mental models of one's self predict adult levels of self-reliance, social confidence, and self-esteem (Klohnen & Bera, 1998; Feeney & Noller, 1990). Similarly, secure mental models of significant others predict the quality of one's adult romantic relationships (Feeney & Noller, 1990; Hazan & Shaver, 1987), including whether that person ever marries and, if so, how long that person stays committed to that marriage (Klohnen & Bera, 1998; see "Love as an Attachment Process" box).

For a concrete example, consider a schematic of one female patient's mental representation of men, which is depicted in Figure 13.1 (Westen, 1991). The young woman suffered from rather severe depression and social isolation, and she reported a childhood history in which she characterized her parents as openly contemptuous of one another. Her mother constantly spoke of the ways in which she was victimized verbally and sexually by her husband and three sons. In the course of psychotherapy, the woman's mental representation of her expected and actual relationships with men became apparent (Figure 13.1). Her representation contains aspects of a psychological need for relatedness (closeness, sexuality), but it also contains an ample supply of conflicting fears and inhibiting affects (enslavement, rejection). The experiences and feelings associated with "relationships with men" are difficult to represent in a figure, but they too are part of the women's object ("men") relations. As you might suspect, the woman's conflicting needs, feelings, and thoughts led her to adopt an interpersonal style with men that was extremely anxious and full of avoidance.

According to objects relations theory, the quality of one's mental representations of relationships (e.g., Figure 13.1) can be characterized by three chief dimensions:

FIGURE 13.1 **One Woman's Representation of Relationships With Men**

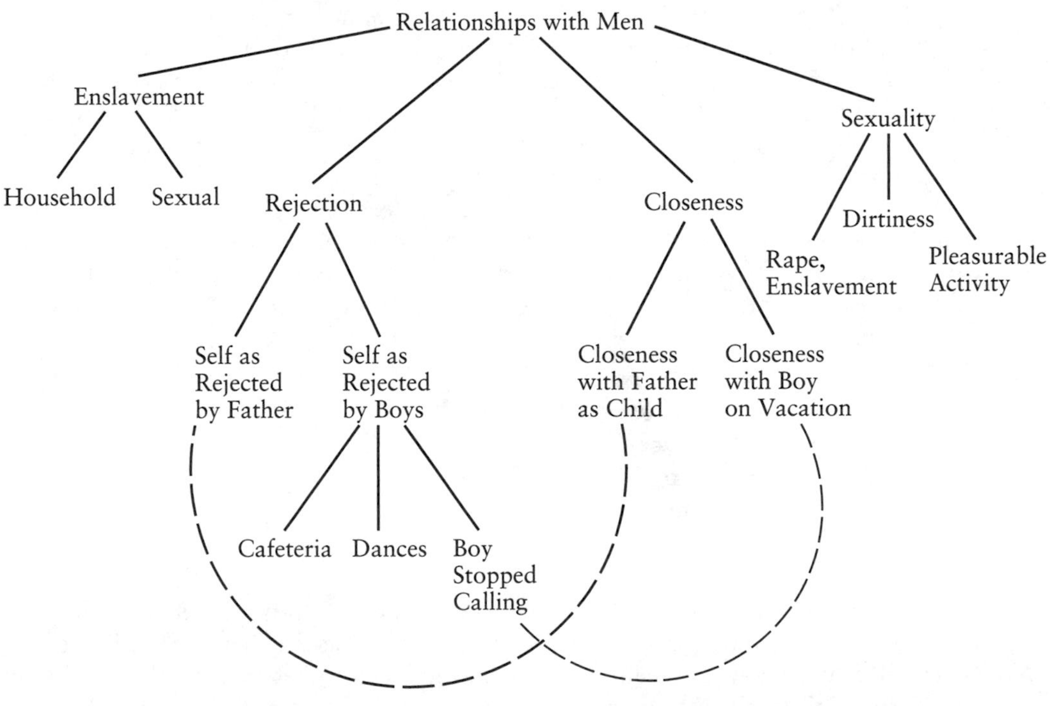

SOURCE: From "Social Cognition and Object Relations," by D. Westen, 1991, *Psychological Bulletin, 109,* pp. 429–455. Copyright 1991 by American Psychological Corporation. Reprinted with permission.

- unconscious tone (benevolent vs. malevolent)
- capacity for emotional involvement (narcissism vs. mutual concern)
- mutuality of autonomy with others

First, mental representations possess an unconscious affective tone (Westen, 1991). This affective coloring of the object world ranges from understanding relationships as malevolent versus benevolent. Second, mental representations possess an unconscious capacity for emotional involvement (Westen, 1991). This capacity ranges from a narcissistic, exploitive, need-gratifying orientation toward relationships to a more mature object relatedness based on mutual love, concern, respect, and an eagerness to invest in relationships. Third, mental representations possess an unconscious capacity for experiencing a mutuality of autonomy with others (Urist, 1980). At its higher level (mutuality of autonomy), objects are viewed as having an autonomous existence vis-à-vis one another, and relationships present no risk to the integrity of the participants; at its lower level, objects are viewed in an absence of any sense of people as autonomous agents, and relationships are seen as malevolent and overpowering (Ryan, Avery, & Grolnick, 1985; Urist, 1977).

Research on object relations theory underscores the fundamental motivational significance of people's psychological need for relatedness. When this need is nurtured through warm, responsive, and contingent care, a person develops positive mental models of himself, of significant others, and of relationships in general. Positive object relations, in turn, enable the person to develop, and to relate to others, in ways that are healthy, growth oriented, and resistant to psychopathology. When this need for relatedness is frustrated or ignored through cold, rejecting, and unpredictable care, however, a person develops maladaptive mental models that leave him vulnerable to developing motivational orientations that are unhealthy, defense oriented, and vulnerable to psychopathology.

Interestingly, in conversation, only people with a history of secure attachments recognize the debt they owe to their positive interpersonal relationships for the motivational resources they possess as adults. People with a history of insecure attachments fall back on delusional defense mechanisms and dismiss the importance of early attachment relationships (or offer unsubstantiated idealized generalizations about their parents; Main, Kaplan, & Cassidy, 1985). Discovering the origins of people's maladaptive motivational orientations is one explicit purpose of object relations therapy.

CRITICISMS

Despite its intrigue, Freud's psychoanalytic contribution to the study of human motivation is plagued by (at least) five criticisms. Contemporary research on psychodynamics has addressed and smoothed over some of these criticisms, but it helps to identify them nonetheless.

The most devastating criticism against Freud is that many of his concepts are not scientifically testable (Crews, 1996; Eysenck, 1986). Without scientific tests, such concepts are best taken with skepticism and understood metaphorically rather than as credible scientific constructs. Theoretical constructs that have not yet stood the test of objective experimentation must remain guilty until proven innocent, invalid until proven valid. For this reason, psychoanalytic thinkers have spent the last 50 years finding ways for testing his ideas and, once done, glean his many ideas into a core set of postulates like the four mentioned earlier in the chapter. Some (but certainly not all) of Freud's ideas have indeed stood the test of empirical validation (Fisher & Greenberg, 1977; Masling, 1983; Silverman, 1976). Other ideas and phenomena have been reinterpreted in ways that do not rely on psychoanalytic concepts (e.g., consider Brown's analysis of the tip-of-the-tongue phenomenon [1991] and Wegner's analysis of mental control [1994]).

Many of Freud's motivational concepts arose from case studies of disturbed individuals, and this constitutes a second criticism. It is a difficult theoretical step to suppose that the motivational dynamics of a few, single-gender adults from European background undergoing psychotherapy in the early 1900s represent the motivational dynamics of the human species in general. The criticism is one of external validity. It asks how appropriate it is to generalize the findings of a specific group to the general population (Silverman & Weinberger, 1985). For example, how comfortable would you feel with a theory of motivation derived solely from the observation of men or of adults? One probably wonders whether the motives of men apply equally to women or to children.

A third criticism is that on many points about human motivation and emotion, Freud was simply wrong (e.g., his theory of superego formation; Fisher & Greenberg, 1977). Freud placed too heavy an emphasis on biological endowment, childhood experience, and the pessimistic aspects of personality. Contemporary research now recognizes that social and cultural influences shape our motives as much as does biology, that adult experiences are as equally important as are childhood experiences, and that the optimistic view of personality has as much to offer as does the pessimistic view. In other words, even if one sees value in Freud's views of motivation, one must further recognize that there are many additional pieces of the theoretical puzzle of motivation left to be fitted into place.

A fourth criticism—a red flag of caution—arises with respect to Freud's methods of data collection. For empirical data, he used his own observations, his own dream diary, and his own memories of therapy sessions (rather than actual transcripts) and saw evidence for the death instinct from the devastation of the world wars. Such methods of data collection inherently invite personal biases, skewed interpretations, omissions and distortions (even unconscious ones), and a lack of consideration of alternative explanations. While Freud's insight was amazing, research shows that he was wrong about as often as he was right.[3]

A final criticism is that although psychoanalytic theory is a wonderful interpretive device for events that occurred in the past, it is woeful as a predictive device. For instance, suppose a person has a dream about siblings dying (as discussed earlier in the chapter). For one person, the dream might be best interpreted as a wish for her siblings to die. For a second person, however, the dream might be best interpreted (via reaction formation) as a wish for her siblings to survive. For yet another person, the siblings' deaths or survivals

[3] Perhaps the most satisfying conclusion to a critical evaluation of Freud's ideas is echoed by the words of Henry Murray, a neo-Freudian: "There is no reason for going blind and swallowing the whole indigestible bolus. . . . I, for one, prefer to take what I please, suspend judgement, reject what I please."

might represent sentiments associated with a third party, for instance, one's own children. All these post hoc (after the fact) interpretations make sense in psychoanalysis. The theory, however, is very poor at predicting a priori (before the fact) that a person will commit suicide or will have a dream about siblings sprouting wings and flying off into the sky. For the theory to be predictive, the theory must allow us to anticipate when a person will or will not have a particular type of dream (or use a particular defense mechanism or achieve a particular level of ego development or whatever). A scientific theory must be able to predict what will happen in the future. It is hard to trust a theory that explains only the past.

SUMMARY

Psychoanalysis makes for a strangely appealing study. By studying the unconscious and by embracing a rather pessimistic view of human nature, psychoanalysis opens the door to study topics such as traumatic memories, unwanted thoughts, unpleasant emotions, inexplicable addictions, anxieties about the future, dreams, hypnosis, inaccessible and repressed memories, fantasies, masochism, repression, self-defeating behaviors, suicidal thoughts, overwhelming impulses for revenge, and all the hidden forces that shape our needs, feelings, and ways of thinking and behaving that we would probably not want our neighbors to know. The subject matter of psychoanalysis strangely reflects what seems to be so popular in contemporary movies (hence, in contemporary society): sex, aggression, psychopathology, revenge, and the like.

The father of the psychoanalytic perspective was Sigmund Freud. His view of motivation presented a biologically based physiological model in which the two instinctual drives of sex and aggression supplied the body with its physical and mental energies. Contemporary psychoanalysts, however, emphasize the motivational importance of psychological wishes (rather than biological drives) and of cognitive information processing. The concept of psychological wishes retains the full spirit of Freudian motivation, but it overcomes the contradictory evidence that sex and aggression do not function like physiological drives. The study of conscious suppression (rather than unconscious repression) also exemplifies how contemporary researchers study psychoanalytic processes. Because suppression, unlike repression, involves cognitive processes that are conscious, intentional, and deliberate, it can more readily be studied empirically and objectively in the scientific laboratory.

Four postulates define contemporary psychodynamic theory. The first is that much of mental life is unconscious. This is the postulate of the primacy of the unconscious. It argues emphatically that thoughts, feelings, and desires exist at the unconscious level. Thus, because unconscious mental life affects behavior, people can behave in ways that are inexplicable, even to themselves.

The second postulate of a contemporary psychodynamic understanding of motivation and emotion is that mental processes operate in parallel with one another, such that people commonly want and fear the same thing. This is the postulate of psychodynamics. It is the rule, not the exception, that people have conflicting feelings that motivate them in opposing ways. Hence, people commonly harbor divergent conscious and unconscious racial attitudes, gender biases, and love/hate (approach/avoidance) relationships with their parents.

The third postulate of a contemporary psychodynamic understanding of motivation is that healthy development involves moving from an immature, socially dependent personality to one that is more mature and socially responsible. This is the postulate of ego development. According to neo-Freudians, the ego develops motives of its own by moving through the following developmental progression: symbiotic, impulsive, self-protective, conformist, conscientious, and autonomous. But ego development does not happen automatically. To overcome immaturity and vulnerability, the ego must gain resources and strengths, including resilient defense mechanisms for coping successfully with the inevitable anxieties of life (e.g., ego defense), a sense of competence that provides a generative capacity for changing the environment for the better (e.g., ego effectance), and a sense of distinct individuality within the larger social context (e.g., ego identity). Collectively, the ego's defenses, effectance, and identity provide the individual with a second source of motivation, as motivation derives not only from id-based wishes but also from ego-based strivings.

The fourth postulate of a contemporary psychodynamic understanding is that mental representations of self, others, and relationships form in childhood to guide adult social motivations. This is the postulate of object relations. It argues that stable personality patterns begin to form in childhood as people construct mental representations of the self, others, and relationships. Once formed, these beliefs form the basis of motivational states (e.g., relatedness, anxiety) and guide the course of the adult's interpersonal relationships. Positive mental models of oneself, for instance, predict adult levels of self-reliance, social confidence, self-esteem, and loving and committed partnerships. Negative mental models of self, others, and relationships, on the other hand, predict dysfunctional interpersonal relationships in adulthood.

RECOMMENDED READINGS

Psychodynamics and the Unconscious

Greenwald, A. (1992). New look 3: Unconscious cognition reclaimed. *American Psychologist, 47,* 766–779.

Kolb, J., Cooper, S., & Fishman, G. (1995). Recent developments in psychoanalytic technique: A review. *Harvard Review of Psychiatry, 3,* 65–74.

Silverman, L. H., & Weinberger, J. (1985). Mommy and I are one: Implications for psychotherapy. *American Psychologist, 40,* 1296–1308.

Wegner, D. M. (1992). You can't always think what you want: Problems in the suppression of unwanted thoughts. In M. P. Zanna (Ed.), *Advances in experimental social psychology* (Vol. 25, pp. 193–225). San Diego: Academic Press.

Wegner, D. M., Schneider, D. J., Carter, S., III, & White, L. (1987). Paradoxical effects of thought suppression. *Journal of Personality and Social Psychology, 53,* 5–13.

Westen, D. (1998). The scientific legacy of Sigmund Freud: Toward a psychodynamically informed psychological science. *Psychological Bulletin, 124,* 333–371.

Ego Development

Loevinger, J. (1976). Stages of ego development. In *Ego development* (Chpt. 2, pp. 13–28). San Francisco: Jossey-Bass.

Schiedel, D., & Marcia, J. (1985). Ego integrity, intimacy, sex role orientation, and gender. *Developmental Psychology, 21,* 149–160.

White, R. W. (1959). Motivation reconsidered: The concept of competence. *Psychological Review, 66,* 297–333.

Object Relations Theory

Hazan, C., & Shaver, P. (1987). Romantic love conceptualized as an attachment process. *Journal of Personality and Social Psychology, 52,* 511–524.

Mickelson, K. D., Kessler, R. C., & Shaver, P. (1997). Adult attachment in a nationally representative sample. *Journal of Personality and Social Psychology, 73,* 1092–1106.

Westen, D., Klepser, J., Ruffins, S. A., Silverman, M., Lifton, N., & Boekamp, J. (1991). Object relations in childhood and adolescence: The development of working representations. *Journal of Consulting and Clinical Psychology, 59,* 400–409.

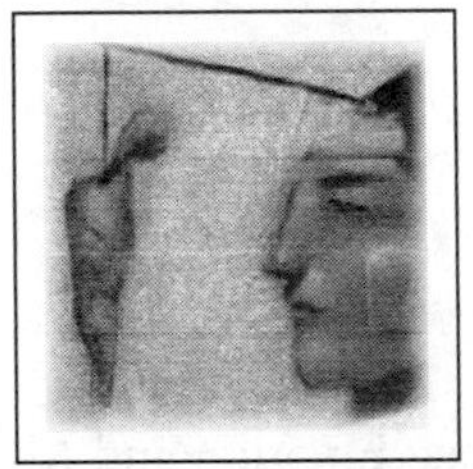

IV

Emotions

14

Nature of Emotion

As you sit reading, your friends approach, inviting you to spend the weekend skiing. The invitation—just being included in the group's plans—brings a feeling of being accepted that makes you feel happy. Your happiness ebbs into excitement as your thoughts turn to adventurous travel, snowcapped mountains, and racing freely and swiftly down the slopes. The weekend arrives. You still feel happy and excited, but your emotions change in a hurry once you hit the slopes. Worry comes first, and then it gives way to full-blown fear. The mountain slopes are a lot steeper than you expected, and moguls dot the landscape for as far as the eye can see. Your fear brings a pressing urge to flee, and this fear involuntarily expresses itself on your face, in your dry mouth and tightened voice, and in your hesitancy to begin. Then you fall, and you fall hard enough so that your face plows through the snow. Your emotion changes again—this time into distress and frustration. Embarrassment creeps in as an 8-year-old zooms by. To alleviate the distress and to cope with the frustration, you call your hotshot buddy over for a quick lesson. Luckily, the tips are excellent, and you start to improve. These glimmering signs of improvement bring a renewed sense of mastery, and your distress and frustration are replaced by hope and optimism. Suddenly, you notice the clear blue sky for the first time, and you pause to notice how pretty, fresh, and calm everything on the mountain really is.

Whether skiing or doing any number of activities, emotion is always with us, forever changing, and constantly motivating us to adapt to the situations and challenges we face. We seem to have an emotion for every situation.

Chapters 14 and 15 discuss the nature and aspects of human emotion. Emotions typically arise from situational or environmental events, express themselves uniquely, serve important purposes, and motivate a predictable way of behaving. In the preceding example, the skier's sight of the steep slopes produced fear, changes in facial expressions, a motivational urge to flee, and avoidance behaviors such as hesitancy. To understand the nature of emotion, we begin with the most fundamental of all questions: What is an emotion?

WHAT IS AN EMOTION?

Emotions are multidimensional. They exist as subjective, biological, purposive, and social phenomena. In part, emotions are subjective feelings, as they make us feel a particular way such as angry or joyful. Emotions are also biological reactions, energy-mobilizing responses that prepare the body for adapting to whatever situation one faces. Emotions are also agents of purpose, much like hunger has purpose. Anger, for instance, creates a motivational desire to do what we might not normally do, such as fight an enemy or protest an injustice. And emotions are social phenomena. When emotional, we send recognizable facial, postural, and vocal signals that communicate the quality of our emotionality to others (e.g., the movements of our eyebrows, the tones of our voices).

Given the four-part character of emotion, it is apparent that the concept of emotion is going to elude a straightforward definition. The difficulty in defining emotion might puzzle you at first because emotions seem so straightforward in everyday experiences. Everyone knows what it is like to experience joy and anger, so the reader might ask, "What's the problem with actually defining emotion?" The problem is the following: "Everyone knows what emotion is, until asked to give a definition" (Fehr & Russell, 1984). None of these separate dimensions—subjective, biological, purposive, or social—adequately defines emotion. As you shall see, one cannot equate a feeling with an emotion any more than one can equate a posed facial expression with an emotion (Russell, 1995). Each of these four dimensions simply emphasizes a different character of emotion. To understand (or define) emotion, it is necessary to study each of emotion's four dimensions and how they interact with one another.

Emotion's four dimensions (or components) appear in Table 14.1. The subjective component gives emotion its feeling, a subjective experience that has both meaning and personal significance. In both intensity and quality, emotion is felt at a subjective level.

Table 14.1 **Multidimensional Aspects of Emotion**

Dimension	Contribution to emotion	Manifestation
Subjective (Cognitive)	Feelings Phenomenological awareness	Self-report
Biological (Physiological)	Arousal Physical preparation Motor responses	Brain circuits Autonomic nervous system Endocrine (hormonal) system
Functional (Purposive)	Goal-directed motivation	Desire to engage in situationally appropriate coping responses
Expressive (Social)	Communication	Facial expressions Bodily postures Vocalizations

The biological component includes the activity of the autonomic and hormonal systems as they participate in emotion to prepare and regulate adaptive coping behavior. Neurophysiological activity is so intertwined with emotion that any attempt to imagine an angry person who is not aroused is nearly impossible.

The functional component pertains to the question of how an emotion, once experienced, benefits the individual. The person without emotions would be at a substantial evolutionary disadvantage to the rest of us. Imagine, for instance, the physical and social survival handicap of the person without the capacity for fear, interest, or love.

The expressive component is emotion's social, communicative aspect. Through postures, gestures, vocalizations, and facial expressions in particular, our private experiences are expressed and communicated to others. Emotions therefore engage our whole person—our feelings and phenomenology, our biochemistry and musculature, our desires and purposes, and our communication and interaction with others.

Notice that emotion to this point in the text has yet to be defined. One definition might be that emotions are short-lived, subjective-physiological-motivational-communicative phenomena that help us adapt to the opportunities and challenges we face during important life events. That definition is a good start, but defining emotion is a bit deceptive because *emotion* per se does not actually exist. Instead, emotion is the psychological construct that unites and coordinates the four aspects of experience outlined in Table 14.1 into a synchronized pattern. Emotion is that which choreographs the subjective, biological, functional, and expressive components into a coherent reaction to an eliciting event. For instance, in the case of fear, the eliciting event might be the steep ski slopes, while the reaction includes feelings, neurological reactions, goal-directed desires, and all-too-public nonverbal communications. Thus, the skier feels scared (subjective aspect), is "pumped up" (biological aspect), strongly desires self-protection (functional aspect), and shows tensed eyes and pulled-back corners of the mouth (expressive aspect). These synchronized, mutually supportive elements form a pattern of reactivity to an environmental danger that is the emotion of fear.

This definition of emotion highlights how different aspects of experience coordinate with one another (Averill, 1990; LeDoux, 1989). For instance, what people feel correlates with how they move the muscles of their face. As you view and smell rotten food, for instance, the way you feel and the way you wrinkle your nose and scrunch your upper lip are coordinated as a coherent feeling-expressive system (Rosenberg & Ekman, 1994). Similarly, the way you move your face is coordinated with your physiological reactivity, such that lowering your brow and pressing your lips firmly together coincides with increased heart rate and a raised skin temperature (Davidson et al., 1990). Without going into all the details, these synchronized systems coordinate subjective, biological, functional, and expressive ways of reacting to allow us to adapt successfully to life circumstances. Emotion is just the word psychologists use to name this coordinated, synchronized process.

Relationship Between Emotion and Motivation

Emotions relate to motivation in two ways. First, emotions serve as an ongoing "readout" system for indicating how well or how poorly things are going. Joy, for instance, signals progress toward goals and social inclusion, whereas distress signals failure and loss. Second, emotions are a type of motive. Like all motives (e.g., needs, cognitions), emotions energize and direct behavior. Anger, for instance, mobilizes physiological, hormonal, and muscular resources (i.e., energizes behavior) to achieve a particular goal or purpose, such as overcoming an obstacle (i.e., directs behavior).

Emotion as a Readout System

Emotions provide a readout of the status of the person's ever-changing motivational states. This is another way of saying that motivation and emotion exist as two sides of the same coin (Buck, 1988). Motives such as hunger and thirst energize the person to action, while emotions such as frustration and relief provide an ongoing progress report as to how well or how poorly these motives are being gratified. From this point of view, emotions are not motives but instead reflect the satisfied versus frustrated status of motives.

Consider sexual motivation and how emotion readout provides a progress report that facilitates some behaviors and inhibits others. During attempts at sexual gratification, positive emotions such as interest and joy signal that all is well and therefore facilitate sexual conduct. Negative emotion such as disgust, anger, and guilt signal that all is not well and therefore inhibit sexual conduct. The positive emotions experienced during attempts at involving and satisfying one's motives (i.e., interest, joy) provide a metaphorical green light for continuing to pursue one's present course of action. Negative emotions experienced during attempts at involving and satisfying one's motives (i.e., disgust, guilt), on the other hand, provide a metaphorical red light for stopping the pursuit of one's present course of action.

Emotion as a Motivational System

Most emotion researchers agree that emotions function as one type of motive. Some researchers, however, go further and argue that emotions constitute the *primary* motivational system (Tomkins, 1962, 1963, 1984; Izard, 1991).

Throughout the history of psychology, the physiological drives (hunger, thirst, sleep, sex, and pain) were considered the primary motivators (Hull, 1943, 1952). Air deprivation provides one example of a physiological motivation that can capture the person's full attention, energize the most vigorous of action, and direct behavior decidedly toward a single purpose. Air deprivation threatens the body's homeostasis, so it seems logical to conclude that air deprivation produces a potent and primary homeostatic motive for taking whatever action is necessary in gaining the air needed to reestablish homeostasis (see chapter 3). Emotion researcher Silvan Tomkins, however, called this reasoning, this apparent truism, a "radical error" (1970). The loss of air produces a strong emotional reaction of fear or terror. This terror provides the motivation to act. Thus, the terror, not the air deprivation or the homeostasis threat, is the causal and immediate source of the panicked, grasping display of motivated behavior. Using this logic, one can see emotion as the primary motivation system. Take away the emotion, and you take away the motivation.[1]

WHAT CAUSES AN EMOTION?

One central struggle emotion researchers face is understanding the cause, or causes, of an emotion. Many viewpoints come into play in this causal analysis, including those that are biological, psychoevolutionary, cognitive, developmental, psychoanalytical, social, sociological, cultural, and anthropological. Despite this diversity, understanding what causes an emotion rallies around one central debate: biology versus cognition. In essence, this debate asks whether emotions are primarily biological or primarily cognitive phenomena. If emotions are largely biological, they should emanate from a causal biological core, such as neuroanatomical brain circuits. If emotions are largely cognitive, however, they should emanate from causal mental events, such as a subjective appraisal of a particular event's meaning.

BIOLOGY VERSUS COGNITION

Together, the cognitive and biological perspectives provide a relatively comprehensive picture of the emotion process. Nonetheless, acknowledging that both cognitive and biological aspects underlie emotion begs the question as to which is primary: biological or cognitive factors (Lazarus, 1982, 1984, 1991a, 1991b; Scherer & Ekman, 1984; Zajonc, 1980, 1981, 1984). Those who argue for the primacy of cognition contend that individuals cannot respond emotionally unless they first cognitively appraise the meaning and personal significance of an event: Is an event relevant to a person's well-being? Is it relevant to that person's loved one's well-being? Is it important? beneficial? harmful? First, meaning is established, and then emotion follows accordingly. Those who argue for the

---

[1]The position taken throughout this book is that there are four primary motivational agents: needs, external events, cognitions, and emotions. Emotions are important motivators, but their status is comparable to that of needs, cognitions, and external events.

primacy of biology contend that emotional reactions do not necessarily require such cognitive evaluations. Events of a different sort, such as subcortical neural activity or spontaneous facial expressions, activate emotion. For the biological theorist, emotions can and do occur without a prior cognitive event, but they cannot occur without a prior biological event. Biology, not cognition, is therefore primary.

Biological Perspective

Four outspoken representatives for the biological perspective include Carroll Izard (1989, 1991), Paul Ekman (1992), Jaak Panksepp (1982, 1994), and Robert Zajonc (1980, 1984). Izard (1984) finds that infants respond emotionally to certain events despite their cognitive shortcomings (e.g., limited vocabulary, limited memory capacity). A 3-week-old infant, for instance, smiles in response to a high-pitched human voice (Wolff, 1969), and the 2-month-old expresses anger in response to pain (Izard et al., 1983). By the time the child acquires language and begins to use sophisticated long-term memory capacities, most emotional events then involve a great deal of cognitive processing. Nonetheless, despite the richness of cognitive activity in the emotion process, Izard (1989) insists that much of the emotional processing of external events remains noncognitive—automatic, unconscious, and mediated by subcortical structures. Infants, because they are biologically sophisticated yet cognitively limited, best demonstrate the primacy of biology in the emotion process.

Ekman (1992) points out that emotions have very rapid onsets, brief duration, and can occur automatically/involuntarily. Thus, because we act emotionally even before we are consciously aware of that emotionality, Ekman argues that it is necessary to understand that emotions evolved through their adaptive value in dealing with fundamental life tasks. Ekman, like Izard, recognizes the cognitive, social, and cultural contributions to emotional experience, but he concludes that biology—rather than learning, social interaction, or socialization processes—lies at the causal core of emotion.

For Panksepp (1982, 1994), emotions arise from genetically endowed neural circuits that regulate brain activity (e.g., biochemical and neurohormonal events). Panksepp acknowledges that it is more difficult to study the hidden recesses of brain circuits than it is to study verbally labeled feelings. He does insist, however, that brain circuits provide the essential biological underpinning for emotional experience. For instance, we (and other animals) inherit a brain-anger circuit, a brain-fear circuit, a brain-sadness circuit, and a few others. The rationale in supporting Panksepp's biological perspective comes from three important findings:

1. Because emotional states are often difficult to verbalize, they must therefore have origins that are noncognitive (not language based).
2. Emotional experience can be induced by noncognitive procedures, such as electrical stimulation of the brain or activity of the facial musculature.
3. Emotions occur in both infants and nonhuman animals.

For these reasons, Zajonc (1980) concludes that, "people do not get married or divorced, commit murder or suicide, or lay down their lives for freedom upon a detailed cognitive analysis of the pros and cons of their actions."

Cognitive Perspective

Four outspoken representatives of the cognitive perspective include Richard Lazarus (1984, 1991a, 1991b), Klaus Scherer (1994a, 1994b), Bernard Weiner (1986), and James Averill (1982, 1991). For each of these theorists, cognitive activity is a necessary prerequisite to emotion. Take away the cognitive processing, and the emotion disappears. Lazarus argues that without an understanding of the personal relevance of an event's potential impact on personal well-being, there is no reason to respond emotionally. Stimuli appraised as irrelevant do not elicit emotional reactions. For Lazarus (1991a, 1991b), the individual's cognitive appraisal of the meaning of an event (rather than the event itself) sets the stage for emotional experience. That is, a car passing you in traffic is not likely to call up your fear unless its way of passing leads you to think that your well-being has in some way been put at risk. The emotion-generating process begins not with the event itself and not with one's biological reaction to it, but instead, with the cognitive appraisal of its meaning.

Scherer (1994a) points out that people process information without necessarily experiencing an accompanying emotion. Some encounters produce emotions, whereas others do not. Those encounters that do are appraised in terms of their novelty, pleasantness, goal/need significance, coping potential, or norm compatibility. These five types of appraisal, Scherer contends, constitute the sort of cognitive processing that gives rise to emotions (as discussed later). Weiner (1986) emphasizes a different type of emotion-causing appraisal. In his attribution analysis of emotion, Weiner concentrates on the information processing that takes place after outcomes occur, such as success versus failure or inclusion versus rejection.

For Averill (1982, 1985), emotions are understood best in a social or cultural context. People show emotion to produce social effects. When angered, one can violate a social norm, deny responsibility for action (e.g., "I couldn't help it; I was overcome by anger"), and effectively communicate their intentions toward others. Consider falling in love, for example. According to Averill and Boothroyd (1977), the romantic ideal is a cultural standard by which people interpret their experiences of love. The romantic ideal holds that one is emotionally and unexpectedly overwhelmed by the (usually chance) appearance of another. Once the ideal is internalized into a belief system, people try to emulate that ideal in relationships, and they interpret their relationship behavior as either conforming or not conforming to that ideal. Once cultural standards of what love should be have been internalized, people can then figure out just what emotions they are currently feeling—is this love? lust? infatuation? The whole emotion process has little to do with biology and much to do with social and cultural expectations and understandings.

The most direct benefit to extract from the cognition versus biology debate is that both sides clearly state their respective positions. Once introduced to the thinking from both sides, the following can now be asked: What side is correct? Emotion psychologists have struggled for answers to this question to settle the debate, and three answers have emerged.

Two-Systems View

One answer to the preceding question is that both cognition and biology emotion processes are correct. According to Buck (1984), human beings have two synchronous systems that activate and regulate emotion.

One system is an innate, spontaneous, physiological system that reacts involuntarily to emotional stimuli. A second system is an experience-based cognitive system that reacts interpretatively and socially. The physiological emotion system came first in humankind's evolution (i.e., the limbic system), whereas the cognitive emotion system came later as human beings became increasingly cerebral and increasingly social (i.e., the neocortex). Together, the primitive biological system and the contemporary cognitive system combine to provide a highly adaptive, two-system emotion mechanism.

The two-systems view appears in Figure 14.1 (Buck, 1984). The lower system is biological and traces its origins to the ancient evolutionary history of the species. Sensory information is processed rapidly, automatically, and unconsciously by subcortical (i.e., limbic) structures and pathways. The second system is cognitive and depends on the unique social and cultural learning history of the individual. Sensory information is processed evaluatively, interpretatively, and consciously by cortical pathways. The two emotion systems are complementary (rather than competitive) and work together to activate and regulate emotional experience.

The case of pain provides a nice analogy for underscoring the need for a two-systems, biology-cognition model of emotion (Clark & Watson, 1994). People have both innate ways of knowing and learned ways of knowing that environmental events do and do not produce pain. The innate ways of knowing provide millisecond judgments in motivating avoidance behavior, while the acquired ways of knowing provide deliberate, reflective judgments in motivating avoidance. Possessing only innate ways of knowing or only acquired ways of knowing about pain would leave human beings ill equipped for adapting to a dangerous, complex, and ever-changing environment. A dual system, however, takes advantage of both the immediacy and reliability of biology as well as the flexibility of cognitive processing. Humans also have innate/immediate and acquired/flexible ways of knowing about fear, about anger, about joy, and so on. Like pain, emotions too operate with the immediacy of biology and the flexibility of cognition.

Robert Levenson (1994a) takes the two-systems view of emotion a bit farther by hypothesizing how the biological and cognitive emotion systems interact. Instead of existing as parallel systems, the two systems interact and influence one another. In this model, significant life events are appraised, these appraisals activate biological systems, and how these biological systems are expressed in emotion displays are filtered by cultural knowledge.

Panksepp (1994) also posits that two categories of emotion exist, such that some emotions arise primarily from the biological system whereas other emotions arise primarily from the cognitive system. Emotions such as fear and anger arise primarily from subcortical neural command circuits (from subcortical structures and pathways in Buck's terminology). Other emotions, however, cannot be well explained by subcortical neural circuits. Instead, they arise chiefly from personal experience, social modeling, and cultural contexts. This category of emotions arises primarily from appraisals, expectancies, and attributions (from cortical structures and pathways in Buck's terminology).

Chicken-and-Egg Problem

Robert Plutchik (1985) sees the cognition versus biology debate as a chicken-and-egg quandary. Emotion should not be conceptualized as cognitively caused or as biologically

FIGURE 14.1 Two-Systems View of Emotion

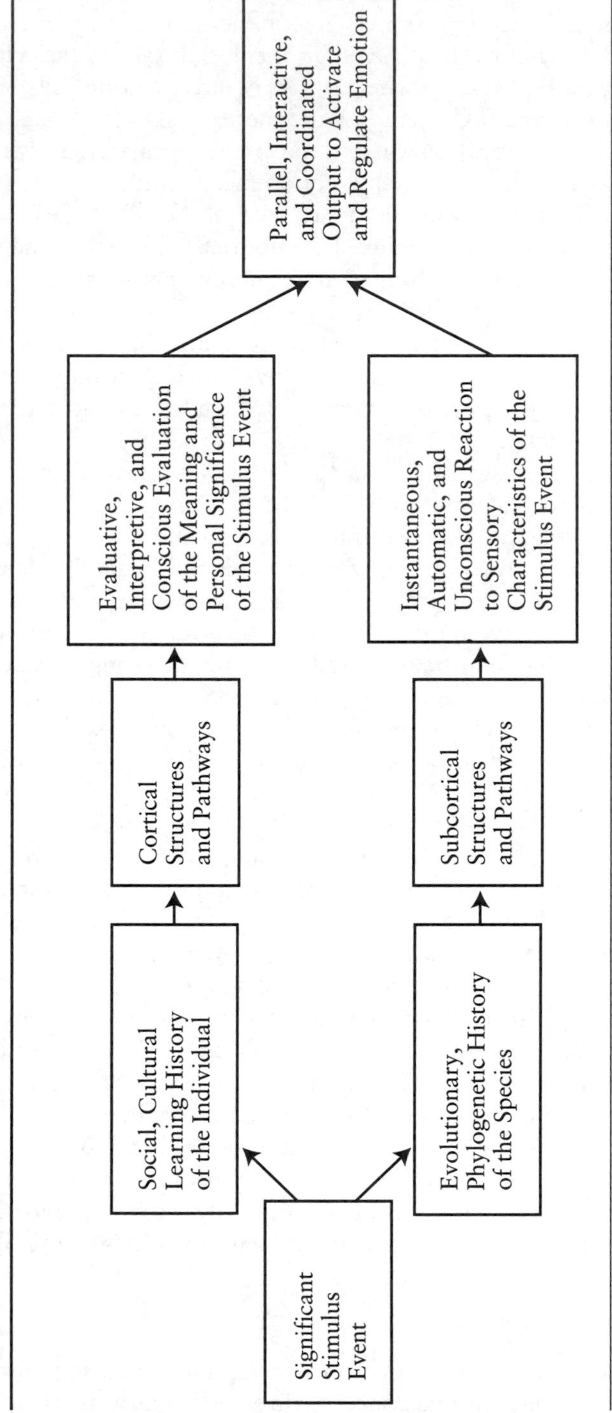

caused. Rather, emotion is a process, a chain of events that aggregate into a complex feedback system. The elements in Plutchik's feedback loop are cognition, arousal, feelings, preparations for action, expressive displays, and overt behavioral activity (i.e., recall the multidimensional aspects of emotion from Table 14.1). One possible representation of Plutchik's emotion feedback loop appears in Figure 14.2. The feedback system begins with a significant life event and concludes with emotion. Mediating between event and emotion is a complex interactive chain of events. To influence emotion, one can intervene at any point in the feedback loop. Change the cognitive appraisal from "this is beneficial" to "this is harmful," and the emotion will change. Change the quality of the arousal (as through exercise, a drug, or an electrode in the brain), and the emotion will change. Or change bodily expression (e.g., the facial musculature, bodily posture), and the emotion will change, and so on.

Plutchik's solution to the cognition-biology debate enters into the complex world of dialectics, in which each aspect of emotion is both cause and effect and the final outcome is due to the dynamic interplay among the six forces in the figure. The most important theme to extract from a chicken-and-egg analysis is that cognitions do not directly cause emotions any more than biological events do. Together, cognition, arousal, preparation for action, feelings, expressive displays, and overt behavioral activity constitute the cauldron of experience that regulates emotion. Other emotion researchers (Scherer, 1994b) echo this emotion-as-a-process view by emphasizing that all emotional experiences exist as episodes that occur over time. Over time, the different components of emotion rise and fall and exert continuous influences on one another.

FIGURE 14.2 **Feedback Loop in Emotion**

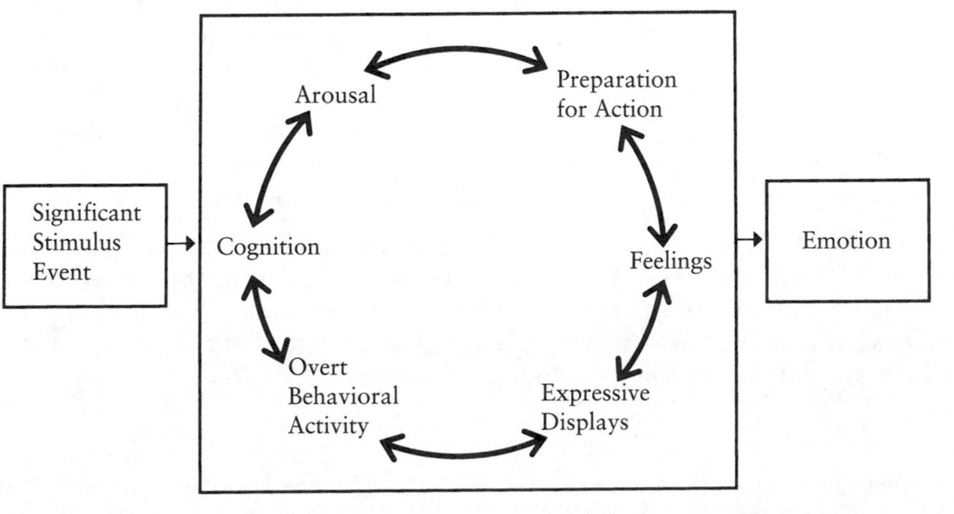

COMPREHENSIVE BIOLOGY-COGNITION MODEL

Emotions are complex (and interactive) phenomena. As with most complexities, it makes sense to work on one piece of the puzzle at a time. Generally speaking, biologists, ethologists, and neurophysiologists focus mostly on the biological aspects of emotion, whereas cognitive psychologists, social psychologists, and sociologists focus mostly on its cognitive, sociocultural aspects. For an overview of the many aspects of emotion, consider Izard's (1993) multisystem model of emotion activation that argues for the validity of each of the following causes of emotion:

Neural Systems

- Changes in neurotransmitters (e.g., decreased serotonin → depression)
- Electrical stimulation of the brain (e.g., artificial stimulation of hypothalamus → rage)

Sensorimotor Systems

- Feedback from facial expression (e.g., nose contraction → disgust)
- Feedback from body posture (e.g., slumping posture → sadness)

Motivational Systems

- Taste, odor (e.g., sweet taste → interest)
- Pain (e.g., aversive stimulation → anger)

Cognitive Systems

- Appraisal, evaluation, attribution (e.g., judging a harm as unjustified → anger)
- Memory (e.g., recall of childhood experience → sentimentality)

Social Systems

- Social contagion (e.g., another person's anxiety rubs off on you)
- Identity confirmation (e.g., a cheerleader role → excitement)

Izard (1993) actually lists only the first four systems. The fifth category—social systems—was added to this text's discussion for clarity. Izard acknowledges the contribution of social interaction and cultural influence on emotion, but he argues that social/interpersonal/cultural forces activate emotions through one of the other four systems.[2] However, the fifth category helps introduce the contents of chapter 15.

---

[2] For example, social contagion is a process by which one person mimics the facial, vocal, and postural expressions of the other and therefore "catches" that emotional experience, Hence, social systems affect the individual's sensorimotor systems (Izard's second category).

HOW MANY EMOTIONS ARE THERE?

The cognition-biology debate indirectly raises another interesting and important question: How many emotions are there? A biological orientation emphasizes primary emotions (e.g., anger, fear) and downplays the importance of secondary or acquired emotions. A cognitive orientation acknowledges the importance of the primary emotions, but it stresses that much of what is interesting about emotional experiences arises from individual, social, and cultural experiences. Ultimately, any answer to the preceding question depends on whether one favors a biological or a cognitive orientation.

Biological Perspective

The biological perspective typically emphasizes several primary emotions, with a lower limit of two (Solomon, 1980) or three (Gray, 1994) to an upper limit of ten (Izard, 1991). Each biological theorist has a very good reason for proposing a specific number of emotions, though each proposal is based on a different emphasis. Eight major research traditions in the biological study of the emotions appear in Figure 14.3. The figure identifies the number of emotions suggested by the empirical findings within that tradition, and it also adds a supportive reference citation.

Richard Solomon (1980) identifies 2 hedonic, unconscious brain systems that exist such that any pleasurable experience is automatically and reflexively opposed by a counter-aversion experience, just as any aversive experience is automatically and reflexively opposed by a counter-pleasurable process (e.g., fear is countered by, and quickly replaced by, the "opponent process" of euphoria during sky diving). Jeffrey Gray (1994) proposes 3 basic emotion systems rooted in separate brain circuits: the behavioral approach system (joy), the fight-or-flight system (anger/fear), and the behavioral inhibition system (anxiety). Jaak Panksepp (1982) proposes 4 emotions—fear, rage, panic, and expectancy—based on his finding of 4 separate neuroanatomical, emotion-generating pathways within the limbic system. Nancy Stein and Tom Trabasso (1992) stress the 4 emotions of happiness, sadness, anger, and fear because these emotions reflect reactions to the 4 possible statuses of valued goals: attainment (happiness), loss (sadness), obstruction (anger), and goal uncertainty (fear). Silvan Tomkins (1970) distinguishes 6 emotions—interest, fear, surprise, anger, distress, and joy—because he finds 6 distinct patterns of neural firing produce these different emotions (e.g., rapid increase in rate of neural firing instigates surprise). Paul Ekman (1992, 1994a) proposes 6 distinct emotions—fear, anger, sadness, disgust, enjoyment, and contempt—because he finds that each of these emotions is associated with a corresponding universal (cross-cultural) facial expression. Robert Plutchik (1980) lists 8 emotions—anger, disgust, sadness, surprise, fear, acceptance, joy, and anticipation—because each one corresponds to 1 of 8 emotion-behavior syndromes common to all living organisms (e.g., fear corresponds to protection). Finally, Carroll Izard (1991) lists 10 emotions on the basis of his differential emotions theory: anger, fear, distress, joy, disgust, surprise, shame, guilt, interest, and contempt.[3]

---

[3] Several of these theories of emotion will be discussed in chapter 15.

FIGURE 14.3 **Eight Research Traditions in the Biological Study of Emotion**

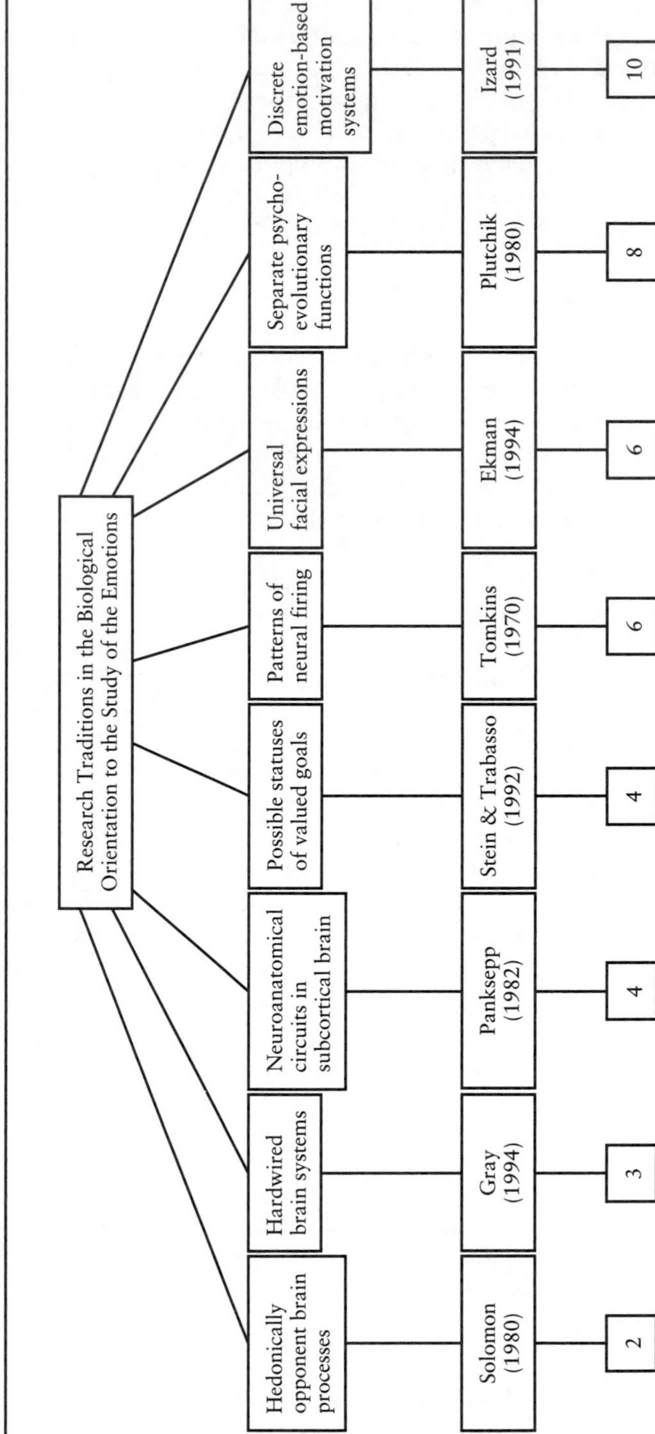

Each of these eight research traditions agree that (1) a small number of basic emotions exists, (2) basic emotions are universal to all human beings (and animals), and (3) basic emotions are products of evolution. Where the eight traditions diverge from one another is in their specifications of what constitutes the biological core that orchestrates emotional experience.

Cognitive Perspective

The cognitive perspective asserts firmly that human beings experience a greater number of emotions than the 2 to 10 highlighted by the biological tradition. Cognitive theorists grant that there are a limited number of neural circuits and bodily reactions (e.g., the fight-or-flight reaction), but they point out that several different emotions can arise from the same biological reaction. For instance, a single physiological response, such as a rapid rise in blood pressure, can serve as the biological basis for anger, jealousy, or envy. High blood pressure and a sense of injustice produce anger; high blood pressure and a belief that an object should be the self's rather than another person's produce jealousy; and high blood pressure and a belief that another is in a more favorable position than the self produce envy. For cognitive theorists, human beings experience a rich diversity of emotion because situations can be interpreted so differently (Shaver et al., 1987) and because emotion arises from a blend of cognitive interpretation (Lazarus, 1991a), language (Storm & Storm, 1987), personal knowledge (Linville, 1982), socialization (Kemper, 1987), and culture (Leavitt & Power, 1989).

Nine research traditions within the cognitive study of the emotions appear in Figure 14.4. The figure includes a supportive reference citation for each program of research. Because both people and cultures vary so much, each of these research traditions argues that the number of possible emotions is almost infinite.

As was the case with the biologically oriented emotion theorists, each cognitive theorist has good reasons for proposing an almost limitless number of human emotions. What they all have in common is the shared assumption that "emotions arise in response to the meaning structures of given situations; different emotions arise in response to different meaning structures" (Frijda, 1988). How the cognitive theories of emotion differ from one another is in how they portray the way people generate and interpret the meaning structure of a situation. The situation can provide the context to interpret one's aroused state (Schachter, 1964), the individual can interpret his or her own aroused state (Mandler, 1984), and people can be socialized to interpret his or her aroused state (Kemper, 1987). In addition, people make appraisals of whether their relationship to the environment affects their personal well-being (Lazarus, 1991a), the meaning and memories of the situations and circumstances they face (Fridja, 1993), and their attributions of why good and bad outcomes occurred (Weiner, 1986). And emotional experiences are embedded within language (Shaver et al., 1987), within socially constructed ways of acting (Averill, 1982), and within social roles like "cheerleader" and "bully" (Heise, 1989).

Reconciliation of Numbers Issue

Everyone—biologically and cognitively minded researchers—agrees that there are dozens of emotions. The debate therefore centers on whether some emotions are more fundamental

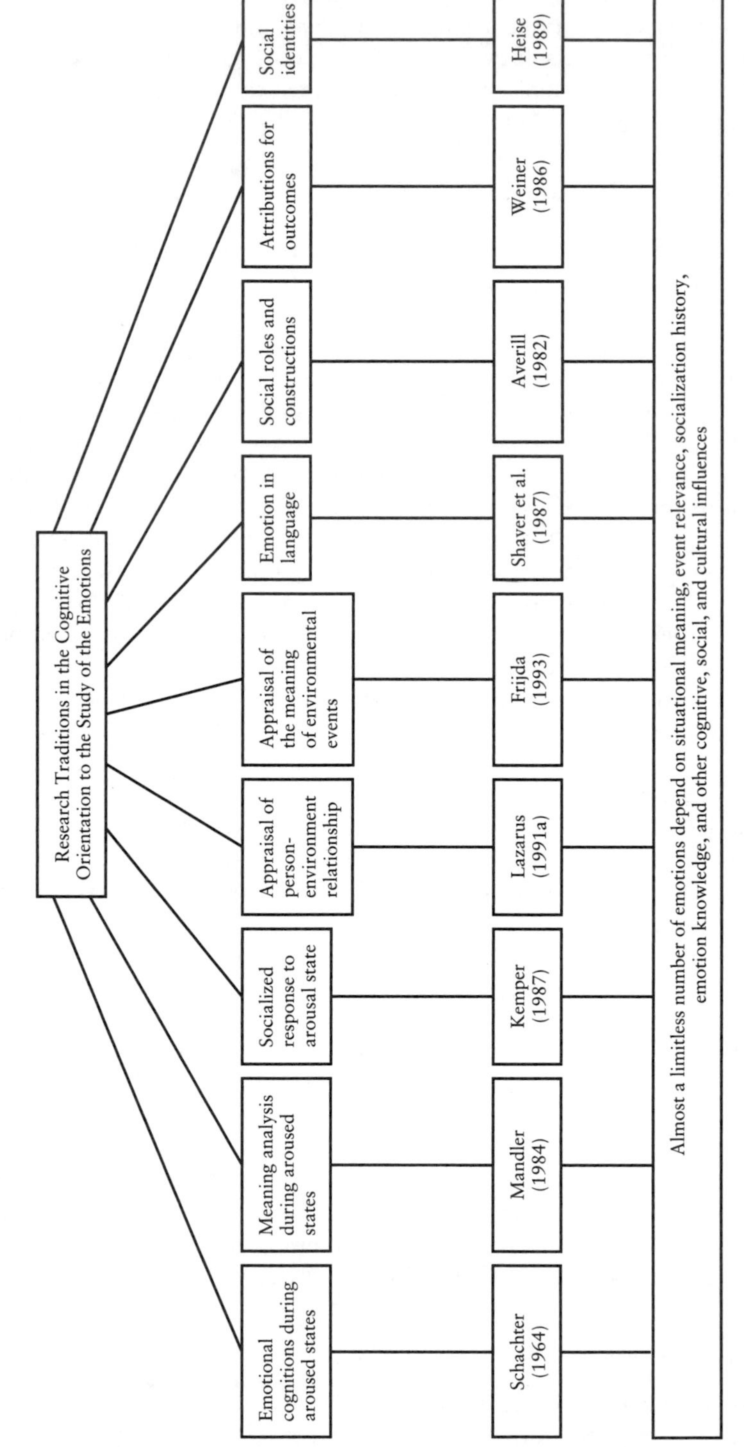

FIGURE 14.4 Nine Research Traditions in the Cognitive Study of Emotion

than others (Ekman & Davidson, 1994). A middle-ground perspective is to argue that each basic emotion is not a single emotion but rather a *family* of related emotions (Ekman, 1994a). For instance, anger is a basic emotion, but anger is also a family of emotions that includes hostility, rage, fury, outrage, annoyance, resentment, envy, and frustration. Similarly, joy is a basic emotion, but the joy emotion family further includes amusement, relief, satisfaction, contentment, and pride in achievement. Each member of a family shares many of the characteristics of the basic emotion—its physiology, its subjective feeling state, its expressive characteristics, and so on (recall Table 14.1). There are a limited number of these basic emotion families, and each emotion family features both a prototypical theme via evolution and biology and a number of variations via learning, socialization, and culture (Ekman, 1994a). There are at least five such emotion families: anger, fear, disgust, sadness, and enjoyment (Ekman, 1992, 1994a).

Emotion families can be understood from a cognitive perspective as well. An analysis of the English language led one group of researchers to conclude that emotion knowledge involves five basic emotion prototypes: anger, fear, sadness, joy, and love (Shaver et al., 1987). According to this group of researchers, people learn increasingly finer distinctions within the causes and consequences of these five basic emotions. Through experience and through socialization, people learn that different situations give rise to different variations of fear—alarm, shock, fright, horror, terror, panic, hysteria, mortification, anxiety, nervousness, tension, uneasiness, apprehension, worry, dread, and perhaps others. Thus, fear is the basic emotion, while the other variations, which include alarm, shock, fright, horror, and terror, are acquired as secondary emotions.

Basic Emotions

Any answer to the question of how many emotions there are forces one to commit to a level of specificity (Averill, 1994), which means that emotions can be conceptualized generally (at the family or prototype level; e.g., anger) or more specifically (at the situation level; e.g., hostility, envy, frustration). Here, emotions are considered at their most general level. The so-called basic emotions are those that do the following (Ekman & Davidson, 1994):

1. Are innate rather than acquired.
2. Arise from the same circumstances for all people (personal loss makes everyone sad, irrespective of their age, culture, and so on).
3. Are expressed uniquely and distinctively (as through a facial expression).
4. Evoke a distinctive physiological patterned response.

Certainly, emotions develop and change throughout life (see Szagun & Schauble's, 1997, analysis of courage). Yet, despite differences in personal experience and cultural demands, we all share an emotion commonality of these basic emotions. Some researchers argue against the idea of basic emotions (Ortony & Turner, 1990). Others offer a different list of basic emotions. Despite this diversity of opinion, no list would vary far from including the six presented here: fear, anger, disgust, sadness, joy, and interest. The following descriptive information comes from both cognitive and biological theorists (Ekman, 1992; Ellsworth & Smith, 1988a; Izard, 1991; Shaver et al., 1987; Weiner, 1986).

Fear

Fear begins with an individual's interpretation of a situation as potentially dangerous and threatening. Perceived dangers and threats can be psychological or physical. The most common fear-activating situations are those that lead the individual to anticipate physical or psychological harm, a vulnerability to danger, or an expectation that one's coping abilities will not be able to match up to forthcoming circumstances. The perception that one can do little to cope with an environmental threat or danger is at least as important a source of fear as is any actual characteristic of the threat/danger itself (Bandura, 1983).

Fear motivates defense. It functions as a warning signal for forthcoming physical or psychological harm that manifests itself in autonomic nervous system arousal (as in the flight part of the fight-or-flight response). The individual trembles, perspires, looks around, and feels nervous tension to protect the self. The protection motivation is typically manifested either through escape and withdrawal from the object(s) or by coping responses in meeting the object of fear face to face. Fleeing puts physical (or psychological) distance between the self and that which is feared. If fleeing is not possible, fear motivates coping, as by being quiet and still or perhaps by acting courageously.

On a more positive note, fear can provide the motivational support for learning new coping responses that remove the person from encountering danger in the first place. Few highway drivers in a torrential rainfall, for instance, need to be reminded to pay attention to the slippery road (fear activates coping efforts), and experienced drivers are better at coping with such a danger than are novice drivers (fear facilitates the learning of adaptive responses). Fear therefore activates coping and facilitates learning.

Anger

Anger is a ubiquitous emotion (Averill, 1982). When people are asked to describe their most recent emotional experience, anger is the one that most often comes to mind (Scherer & Tannenbaum, 1986). One reason anger is ubiquitous is that it has a number of varieties that allow it to be expressed not only as a prototype (the offended person glares, clenches, and then lashes out violently) but also as appropriate to specific situations (anger as fury, as hostility, as vengefulness, as rage, as aggravation, as wrath, and so on; Russell & Fehr, 1994).

Anger arises from the experience of restraint, as in the interpretation that one's plans and goals have been interfered with by some outside force (e.g., barriers, obstacles, interruptions). Anger also arises from a betrayal of trust, being rebuffed, receiving unwarranted criticism, a lack of consideration from others, and cumulative annoyances (Fehr et al., 1999). The essence of anger is the belief that the situation is not what it should be; that is, the restraint, interference, or criticism is illegitimate (deRivera, 1981). How the cognitive, social, developmental, and cultural aspects of anger play themselves out in everyday life appears in Table 14.2

Anger is the most passionate emotion. The angry person becomes stronger and more energized (as in the fight part of the fight-or-flight response). Anger makes people more sensitive and attuned to the injustices of what other people do (Keltner, Ellsworth, & Edwards, 1993), and the fight is directed at overcoming or righting the illegitimate restraint, interference, or criticism. This attack can be verbal or nonverbal (yelling or slamming the door) and direct or indirect (destroying the obstacle or just throwing objects about). In addition to direct and indirect aggression, some other common anger-motivated

Table 14.2 **Cognitive, Social, Developmental, and Cultural Aspects of Anger**

Anger in Infants	A babysitter grasps the arm of a one-year-old who displays anger and struggles for freedom.
Anger in Adults	A motorist yells a crude insult about a pedestrian's appearance who experiences anger as the self is demeaned.

The essence of anger is being taken for something less than one wants to be by someone who acts inconsiderately or malevolently. *Cognitively,* anger involves making appraisals of having something important at stake and then losing it in an undeserved way at the hands of an external agent. For the infant, physical restraint thwarted free movement; and for the pedestrian, the insult attacked self-esteem. *Socially,* anger involves an external agent who acts in a way that is inconsiderate or mean, especially when the offender just as easily could have been considerate or polite. *Developmentally,* anger in infants is not the same as anger in adults. Infants do not make external attributions, do not blame others as accountable, and do not experience blows to their self-esteem in the same way adults sometimes do. For these reasons, adult anger is more likely to endure and to differentiate into a more specific emotion (e.g., irritation, resentment). Coping potential constitutes an additional developmental difference in anger. When people are unable to cope with the social slights that come their way, they experience an anger that blends toward pouting. But, when coping potential is high, anger blends toward gloating. *Culturally,* the thoughts, physiology, and behavioral intentions that spring from anger are often something to be controlled. Some cultures discourage anger-generated physical attack while they accept verbal attack (e.g., middle-class Americans). Among working-class individuals (especially males) and among some ethnic groups, not responding to a social slight is unacceptable as being demeaned carries the cultural burden of physical retaliation. And what makes a person angry varies with culture, as Japanese experience more stranger-induced anger than do Americans who experience more injustice-induced anger.

responses are to express hurt feelings, talk things over, conciliate, or avoid the other person altogether (Fehr et al., 1999). Anger is potentially the most dangerous emotion, as its purpose is to destroy barriers in the environment. Sometimes, anger produces needless destruction and injury, as when we push a child, curse at a teammate, or kick a locked door. Other times, however, anger is productive, as when it energizes vigor, strength, and endurance in our efforts to cope productively as we change the world around us into what it should be. When circumstances change from what they should not be (injustice) to what they should be (justice), experienced anger fades (Lerner & Tetlock, 1998).

Disgust

Disgust involves getting rid of or getting away from a contaminated, deteriorated, or spoiled object. Just what that object is depends on development and culture (Rozin, Haidt, & McCauley, 1993; Rozin, Lowery, & Ebert, 1994). In infancy, the cause of disgust is limited to bitter or sour tastes. In childhood (age 4 through 8), disgust reactions expand to include both innate distaste and acquired revulsion. Older children show disgust in engaging any offensive stimulus (Rozin & Fallon, 1987). By adulthood, objects that elicit disgust include bodily contamination (poor hygiene, gore, death), interpersonal contamination (physical contact with undesirable people), and moral contamination (child abuse, incest, infidelity). Cultural learning determines much of what the adult considers a bodily, interpersonal, or moral contamination. Still, disgust maintains a biological core as people from most cultures rate disgusting things as those that are of animal origin and spread to contaminate other objects (e.g., a dead roach touching your food triggers core disgust and pretty much contaminates the whole plate).

The function of disgust is rejection. Through disgust, the individual actively rejects and casts off some physical or psychological aspect of the environment. Consider these environmental invasions that the person, through the disgust emotion, seeks to reject (Rozin, Lowery, & Ebert, 1994): eating something bitter (bad taste), smelling ammonia or rotten meat (bad smell), eating an apple with a worm in it (contaminated food), watching a medical dissection (body violation), thinking about a friend engaged in incest (moral violation), and sleeping in a hotel bed on which the linens have not been changed (interpersonal contamination). Because disgust is phenomenologically aversive, people learn the coping behaviors needed to prevent encountering (or creating) conditions that produce disgust. Therefore, people change personal habits and attributes, discard waste and sanitize their surroundings, and reappraise their thoughts and values; they wash the dishes, brush their teeth, take showers, and exercise to avoid an out-of-shape or "disgusting" body.

Sadness

Sadness (or distress) is the most negative, aversive emotion. Sadness arises principally from experiences of separation and failure. Separation, or the loss of a loved one through death, divorce, circumstances (e.g., travel), or argument, is distressing. One can also be separated from a valued job, position, or status. Failure too leads to sadness, as in failing an examination, losing a contest, or being rejected for a group's membership. Even failure outside of one's volitional control can cause distress, as in war, illness, accidents, and economic depression (Izard, 1991).

Sadness, because it feels so aversive, motivates the individual to initiate whatever behavior is necessary to alleviate the distress-provoking circumstances before they occur again. Sadness motivates the person to restore the environment to its state before the distressing situation. Following separation, the rejected lover apologizes, sends flowers, or telephones in an effort to repair the broken relationship. Following failure, a performer practices to restore confidence. Unfortunately, many separations and failures cannot be restored to their states before the separation or failure. Under these hopeless conditions, the person behaves not in an active, vigorous way but in an inactive, lethargic way that essentially leads to withdrawing from the distressing situation.

One beneficial aspect of sadness is that it indirectly facilitates the cohesiveness of social groups (Averill, 1968). Because separation from significant people causes sadness and because sadness is such an uncomfortable emotion, its anticipation motivates people to stay cohesive with their loved ones (Averill, 1979). If people did not miss others so much, then they would not be so motivated to go out of their way to maintain social cohesion. Similarly, if the student or athlete did not anticipate the possibility of suffering failure-induced distress, she would be less motivated to prepare and practice.

Threat and Harm

Threat and harm are the themes that unite the emotions of fear, sadness, anger, and disgust. When bad events are forecast or anticipated, we feel fear. During the struggle to reject or fight off the threat or harm, we feel disgust and anger. Once the threat or harm has occurred, we feel sadness. In response to threat and harm, fear motivates avoidance behavior—fleeing the threat. Disgust motivates rejection of the bad event or object. Anger motivates fighting and vigorous counterdefense. Sadness leads to inactivity and withdrawal and is effective when it leads one to give up coping efforts in situations that he cannot flee from, reject, or fight against. Such an analysis confirms the functional aspect of emotion in that fear, sadness, anger, and disgust work as a collective emotion system in equipping the individual to deal effectively with all aspects of threat and harm.

Joy

The events that bring joy include desirable outcomes, such as success at a task, personal achievement, progress toward a goal, getting what we want, gaining esteem, gaining respect, receiving love or affection, receiving a wonderful surprise, or experiencing pleasurable sensations (Ekman & Friesen, 1975; Izard, 1991; Shaver et al., 1987). The causes of joy—desirable outcomes related to success and belongingness—are essentially the opposite of the causes of sadness (undesirable outcomes related to failure and separation/loss). How joy affects us also seems to be the opposite of how sadness affects us. When sad, we feel lethargic and withdrawn; when joyous, we feel enthusiastic and outgoing. When sad, we are often pessimistic; when joyous, we turn optimistic.

The function of joy is twofold. On the one hand, joy facilitates our willingness to engage in social activities. Smiles of joy facilitate social interaction (Haviland & Lelivica, 1987), and if the smiles keep coming, then they help relationships form and strengthen (Langsdorf et al., 1983). Few social stimuli are as potent and as rewarding as are the smile and interpersonal inclusion. Expressed joy is therefore the social glue that bonds relationships, such as infant and mother, lovers, coworkers, and teammates. A second benefit of joy is its "soothing function" (Levenson, 1991). Joy is a positive feeling that makes life pleasant. The pleasantness of joy therefore counteracts the inevitable life experiences of frustration, disappointment, and general negative affect and allows us to preserve psychological well-being. Joy has a way of undoing the distressing effects of emotions, as when parents sing and make funny faces to soothe distressed infants and when lovers show affection to soothe away otherwise escalating negative emotional exchanges (Carstensen, Gottman, & Levenson, 1995).

Interest

Interest is the most prevalent emotion in the day-to-day functioning of human beings (Izard, 1991). Interest arises mostly from those situations that involve the person's needs or well-being (Deci, 1992b), though some level of interest is ever-present. At the neurological level, interest involves a moderate increase in the rate of neural firing. So those environmental conditions that produce a moderate increase in the rate of neural firing are the ones that arouse our interest—stimulus change, novelty, uncertainty, complexity, puzzles and curiosities, challenge, thoughts of learning, thoughts of achieving, and acts of discovery (Berlyne, 1966; Izard, 1991). Because interest is ever-present, increases and decreases in interest usually involve a shifting of interest from one event, thought, or action to another. In other words, we typically do not lose interest, but rather, we redirect it from one object or event to another.

Interest creates the desire to explore, investigate, seek out, manipulate, and extract information from the objects that surround us. Interest motivates acts of exploration, and it is in these acts of turning things around, upside down, over, and about that we gain the information we seek. Interest also underlies our desire to be creative, to learn, and to develop our competencies and skills (Renninger, Hidi, & Krapp, 1992). A person's interest in an activity determines how much attention is directed to that activity and how well that person processes, comprehends, and remembers relevant information (Hidi, 1990; Renninger, Hidi, & Krapp, 1992; Renninger & Wozniak, 1985; Schiefele, 1991; Shirey & Reynolds, 1988). Interest therefore enhances learning (Alexander, Kulikowich, & Jetton, 1994). It is difficult to learn a foreign language, allocate time to read a book, or engage in most any learning activity without emotional support from interest.

Motive Involvement and Satisfaction

Motive involvement and motive satisfaction are the themes that unite the positive emotions of interest and joy. When a beneficial event is forecast or anticipated, we feel interest as a motive becomes aroused. Once the event materializes and the motive is satisfied, we feel joy (or enjoyment). When a task or event involves a motive, interest motivates the approach and exploratory behavior necessary for promoting contact with the potentially motive-satisfying event. It is interest that prolongs our task engagement enough so we can put ourselves in a position to experience motive satisfaction. Joy adds to and somewhat replaces interest when motive satisfaction occurs (Izard, 1991). Joy then promotes ongoing task persistence and subsequent reengagement behaviors with the motive-satisfying event. Together, interest and joy are the emotions that regulate a person being fully and voluntarily involved in an activity (Reeve, 1989).

WHAT GOOD ARE THE EMOTIONS?

While feeling the subjective angst inherent in sadness, anger, or jealousy, people understandably ask themselves the following question: "What purpose do emotions serve—what good are they?" Work on the function of emotion began with Charles Darwin's *The Expression of Emotions in Man and Animals* (1872), a less famous effort than his 1859 work. In this work, Darwin argued that emotions help animals adapt to their surroundings. Displays of emotion help adaptation much in the same way that physical characteristics (e.g., height) do. For example, the dog baring its teeth in defense of its territory helps it to cope with hostile situations (by warding off opponents). Such expressiveness is functional, and emotions are therefore candidates for natural selection.

COPING FUNCTIONS

Emotions do not just occur out of the blue; they occur for a reason. From a functional point of view, emotions evolved because they helped animals deal with fundamental life tasks (Ekman, 1994a). To survive, animals must explore their surroundings, vomit harmful substances, develop and maintain relationships, attend immediately to emergencies, avoid injury, reproduce, fight, and both receive and provide care giving. Each of these behaviors is emotion produced, and each facilitates the individual's adaptation to changing physical and social environments.

Fundamental life tasks are universal human predicaments, such as loss, frustration, and achievement (Johnson-Laird & Oatley, 1992). The emotion during life tasks energizes and directs behavior in evolution-benefiting ways (e.g., after separation, crying for help proved more effective than did other courses of action). That is, emotion and emotional behavior provide animals with coherent and ingrained ways for coping with the major challenges and threats to their welfare (Tooby & Cosmides, 1990).

According to Plutchik (1970, 1980), emotions serve eight distinct purposes: protection, destruction, reproduction, reunion, affiliation, rejection, exploration, and orientation. Thus, for the purpose of protection, fear prepares the body for withdrawal and escape. To destroy some aspect of the environment (e.g., enemy, obstacle to food), anger prepares the body for attack. To explore the environment, anticipation sparks curiosity and readies the body for investigation. For every major life task, human beings evolved a corresponding, adaptive emotional reaction. The function of emotion is therefore to prepare us to respond to life's fundamental tasks in successful ways.

Some fundamental situations are paired with their adaptive emotional responses in Table 14.3, which also lists the functional aspect of the emotion. Thus, the table shows that when facing threat animals run or fly away to serve the purpose of protection. The emotion that coordinates all this running, flying, and protection is fear.

From a functional point of view, there is no such thing as a "bad" emotion. Joy is not necessarily a good emotion, and anger and fear are not necessarily bad emotions (Izard, 1982). *All* emotions are beneficial because they direct attention and channel behavior to where it is needed, given the circumstances one faces. In doing so, each emotion provides a unique readiness for responding to a particular situation. From this point of view, fear, anger, disgust, sadness, and all specific emotions are good emotions

Table 14.3 **Functional View of Emotional Behavior**

Stimulus	Responses	Function	Emotion
Threat	Running, flying away	Protection	Fear
Obstacle	Biting, hitting	Destruction	Anger
Potential mate	Courting, mating	Reproduction	Joy
Loss of valued person	Crying for help	Reunion	Sadness
Group member	Grooming, sharing	Affiliation	Acceptance
Gruesome object	Vomiting, pushing away	Rejection	Disgust
New territory	Examining, mapping	Exploration	Anticipation
Sudden novel object	Stopping, alerting	Orientation	Surprise

Source: From "Functional View of Emotional Behavior," *Emotion: A Psychoevolutionary Synthesis* (p. 289), by R. Plutchik, 1980, New York: Harper & Row. Adapted with permission.

Emotion's Role in Development

Question: Why would a person want to learn about the motivational states discussed in this chapter?

Answer: To appreciate why Vulcans could never really be smarter than humans.

In science fiction (i.e., *Star Trek*), Vulcans are a race who struggle to deny and overcome their emotions. Vulcans are also a very smart race, full of logic, intelligence, and amazing cognitive development. They accomplish these lofty attainments because they reject their emotions. But this is more fiction than it is science. The emotion system is a valued ally for the development of the cognitive system.

What if the Vulcan infant refused to smile or show spontaneous interest? One thing that would happen is that the poor little guy's quantity and quality of social interaction with caretakers would nose dive. The social smile (smile in response to another person) communicates well-being and recruits approach by others. Such displays of positive emotion bring others to us, and it is in the context of social interaction that infants gain the steady stream of stimulation and challenge that is necessary for optimal cognitive development. Interacting with others also provides the setting for developing the cognitive skills of perspective taking, role playing, and rule internalization.

What if the Vulcan could not experience interest in response to novelty and environmental change? Without interest, the Vulcan would lack an inner motivational guide to explore her physical surroundings—to pick things up, shake them, toss them, and conduct all sorts of little experiments on the world. And if the joyless infant failed to gain a secure emotional attachment to a caregiver, he would lack a secure base from which to go out into the world and explore the exciting and information-rich physical surroundings (Caruso, 1989; Carr, Dabbs, & Carr, 1975; Rheingold & Eckerman, 1970). Infants who express positive emotions bring caretakers close to them, and the relationship with an attachment figure is the infant's springboard for increasing exploration, increasing play, reducing wariness of strangers, and gaining an increased sociability with others outside the infant-caregiver relationship (Caruso, 1989).

Anger expressions during the "terrible twos" helps foster the preschool child's sense toward self-reliance (Dunn & Mum, 1987). Imagine life without the capacity for anger when goals were obstructed or blocked. Anger motivates protest against restraints and discomforts, and it provides the motivation for supporting the thinking and problem-solving necessary for figuring out how to cope best with what is happening so that one can reverse or overcome obstacles. Anger also

because fear optimally facilitates protection, disgust optimally facilitates repulsion of contaminated objects, and so forth. Plutchik's psychoevolutionary perspective on emotion encourages an understanding of the emotions as positive, functional, purposive, and adaptive organizers of behavior.

motivates discussions and negotiations in considering the perspective of others and in gaining an understanding of social rules and obligations.

Experiences and expressions of sadness, shame, guilt, sympathy, and empathy are vital ingredients in the development of prosocial behavior. Without the information provided by these emotions, a child would be slow to learn what would be wrong with taking a prized toy from another child, as she needs the capacity for both empathy and sadness in understanding the deleterious consequences to the other child (Davidson, Turiel, & Black, 1983). Shame and guilt make it painful to violate social rules (shame) and moral standards (guilt). In doing so, these emotions spotlight social rules and moral standards. When social norms or expectations are violated, shame communicates the message that one is acting in a way that is inadequate or unacceptable to others. Hence, shame motivates the person to change and improve, to be less vulnerable to such feelings in the future (Barrett, 1985). In the same spirit, guilt motivates reparative behaviors and therefore helps maintain our relationships with others (Baumeister, Stillwell, & Heatherton, 1995). Even fear can contribute productively to healthy development, at least to the extent that it helps children build a sense of conscience as parents provide gentle and informative discipline (Kochanska, 1997).

Vulcans are known for their abstract thinking, logical reasoning, and a capacity to consider multiple possible future events. Emotion researchers, however, study the positive role that emotional changes during adolescence play in facilitating cognitive development (Abe & Izard, 1999; Larson & Asmussen, 1991). One interesting analysis of this process appears in *The Diary of Anne Frank*. Her writings consistently showed that experiences of intense emotion were quickly followed by higher levels of thinking (Haviland & Kramer, 1991). Emotional experiences of anxiety, fear, anger, disgust, and sadness therefore contribute motivationally to the adolescent's active mental construction of the self-concept, the discovery of meaning, consideration of ideal and possible selves, and abstract thinking in general.

The Vulcan solution for coping with emotions like joy, interest, anger, shame, and guilt is to suppress them. The human solution is to use emotions as information regarding the progress of development and to adjust behavior to facilitate coping and developing. Hence, humans have a resource—a basis of information and a motivational guide to adaptive behavior—that Vulcans lack. Therefore, just as emotions have coping and social functions, emotions also have developmental functions.

Other biologically oriented emotion researchers stress greater flexibility in emotional readiness and in ways of coping than is otherwise apparent from Table 14.3 (Frijda, 1994). That is, while fear essentially motivates protective behavior, it also readies us for additional and more flexible actions, including preventing the dangerous event from occurring in the first place and suppressing activity until the threat passes. Likewise, anger essentially motivates destructive action, but it also prepares us to enforce social norms and to discourage anger-causing events (e.g., discourage someone from insulting us). Individual experience and cultural learning, therefore, further contribute to how we express our emotional readiness in coping with fundamental life tasks. Individual experience and cultural learning over time greatly expand the entries in the "Response" column in Table 14.3. This increased flexibility of responding is important because it makes it clear that emotional responses are more flexible than are reflexes (Scherer, 1984b).

SOCIAL FUNCTIONS

In addition to serving coping functions, emotions serve social functions (Izard, 1989; Keltner & Haidt, 1999; Manstead, 1991). Emotions:

- Communicate our feelings to others.
- Regulate how others interact with us.
- Invite and facilitate social interaction.
- Play a pivotal role in creating, maintaining, and dissolving relationships.

Emotional expressions are potent, nonverbal messages that communicate our feelings to others. Through emotional expressions, infants nonverbally communicate what they cannot communicate verbally, as through the face (Fridland, 1992), through the voice (Scherer, 1986), and through emotional behavior in general (Huebner & Izard, 1988). At birth, infants are capable of expressing pain, joy, interest, and disgust; by two months, infants can also express sadness and anger; and by six months, infants can further express fear (Izard, 1989). Throughout infancy, interest, joy, sadness, disgust, and anger represent almost 100% of emotion-based facial expressions (Izard et al., 1995). Equally important, each of these infantile expressions can be reliably recognized and interpreted by caregivers (Izard et al., 1980). Robin Huebner and Carroll Izard (1988), for instance, showed that infant facial expressions functioned as specific communication signals to guide mothers' emotion-appropriate care for their infants.

Emotional displays regulate how people interact, as the emotional expression of one person can prompt selective behavioral reactions from a second person (Camras, 1977; Coyne, 1976a, 1976b; Frijda, 1986; Klinnert et al., 1983). In a conflict situation over a toy, for instance, the child who expresses anger or sadness is much more likely to keep the toy than the child who expresses no such emotion (Camras, 1977; Reynolds, 1982). The emotional expression communicates to others what one's probable forthcoming behavior is likely to be. If the toy is taken away, the anger-expressing child communicates a probable forthcoming attack, whereas the sadness-expressing child communicates a probable barrage of tears. The signal that one is likely to attack or cry often succeeds in regaining the lost toy (or in preventing the toy from being taken in the first place). Hence, emotions expressed in a social context serve informative ("This is how I feel"), forewarning ("This is what I am about to do"), and directive ("This is what I want you to do") functions (Ekman, 1993; Schwartz & Clore, 1983). In this way, emotional expressions help people learn the beliefs and behavioral intentions of others and thus help smooth and coordinate social interactions.[4]

Emotional displays invite and facilitate social interaction. Toward this end, many emotional expressions are socially, rather than biologically, motivated. This assertion sounds strange because it is generally assumed that people smile when they feel joy and frown when they feel sad. Nonetheless, people frequently smile when they do not feel joy. People sometimes smile when they wish to facilitate social interaction.

Ethologists studying smiling in primates found that chimpanzees use the voluntary smile to deflect potentially hostile behavior from dominant animals and to maintain or increase friendly interactions (van Hooff, 1962, 1972). Just as primates smile (bare their teeth) to appease dominants, young children frequently smile when approaching a stranger, and children are more likely to approach a stranger who smiles than a stranger who does not smile (Connolly & Smith, 1972). Adults who make mistakes or who are embarrassed socially are also likely to smile, apparently in an effort to rectify the just-committed faux pas (Kraut & Johnston, 1979). In addition, the smile is a universal greeting display (Eibl-Eibesfeldt, 1972; van Hooff, 1972) that seems to say, nonverbally, "I am friendly" and "I would like us to be friendly, at least for a while." In each of these instances, smiling is socially, rather than emotionally, motivated.

The idea that a smile can be socially motivated leads to the question of whether smiling evolved as an emotional expression of joy or as a social expression of appeasement and friendliness (Fernandez-Dols & Ruiz-Belba, 1995; Kraut & Johnston, 1979). To test this hypothesis, Robert Kraut and Robert Johnston observed people smiling while bowling, while watching a hockey match, and while walking down the street. The researchers wondered whether people smiled more often when engaged in social interaction or when experiencing a joy reaction to a positive event (a good bowling score, a goal for their hockey team, sunny weather). Generally speaking, bowlers, spectators, and pedestrians were more likely to smile when engaging in social interactions than when experiencing joy.

Most emotions arise not during impersonal encounters with the environment, but instead during social interaction. If you kept track of which events and experiences caused your emotional reactions—another person's action, an action of your own, something you read or saw—you would more than likely find that interpersonal encounters triggered most of your emotional reactions (Oatley & Duncan, 1994). Emotions are intrinsic to interpersonal relationships. They also play a central role in creating, maintaining, and dissolving interpersonal relationships by regulating the distance between people, as emotions draw us together and emotions push us apart (Levenson, Carstensen, & Gottman, 1994;

---

[4]Emotional expressions usually produce desired effects as incentives and deterrents to other people's ways of interacting (Tronick, 1989), as when infantile distress vocalizations bring parental care (Fernald, 1992) and adult embarrassment brings forgiveness (Keltner & Buswell, 1997). Sometimes, however, strategic emotional expressions backfire (Coyne, 1976a). Depressed persons, for instance, sometimes present their emotional state to others to gain support and reassurance. Unfortunately, such emotional communications frequently arouse negative affect in others that leads to rejection rather than to the hoped-for reassurance. Because sad moods are intrinsically unpleasant and hence avoided, people tend to reject expressions of sad moods, especially given repeated encounters in which the sadness is expressed (Winer et al., 1981).

Levenson & Gottman, 1983). For instance, joy, sadness, and anger all work to affect the social fabric of relationships. Joy promotes the establishment of relationships. Sadness maintains relationships in times of separation (by motivating reunion). And anger motivates the action necessary to break off injurious relationships.

WHY WE HAVE EMOTIONS

Some argue that emotions serve no useful purpose, as emotions disrupt ongoing activity, disorganize behavior, and rob us of our rationality and logic (Hebb, 1949; Mandler, 1984). The argument is that while emotions once served important evolutionary functions, in the modern world, they no longer do. Others, however, argue that emotions prioritize behavior in ways that optimize our adjustment to the demands we face in the physical and social environment (Lazarus, 1991a; Levenson, 1994a, 1999; Oatley & Jenkins, 1992; Plutchik, 1980). Thus, everyone agrees that emotions affect the way we think, feel, and behave. And researchers have done a good job in detailing what happens to us during an emotional experience (e.g, blood pressure increases, we signal to others our position in the social hierarchy). Instead, the question hinges on whether emotions are adaptive and functional or are maladaptive and dysfunctional.

Life is full of challenges, stresses, and problems to be solved (e.g., avoid threats, form and maintain attachments). The reason people possess emotions is because emotions exist as solutions to these challenges, stresses, and problems (Ekman, 1992; Frijda, 1980, 1988; Lazarus, 1991a; Scherer, 1994b). By coordinating and orchestrating subjective, biological, motivational, and expressive processes, emotions "establish our position vis-à-vis our environment" (Levenson, 1999) and "equip us with specific, efficient responses that are tailored to problems of physical and social survival" (Keltner & Gross, 1999).

The reason that both sides of the "functional versus dysfunctional" question makes sense is because both are correct. Emotions exist as both a masterpiece of evolutionary design (as pointed out by emotion theorists) and also as excess baggage in the age of reason (as pointed out by Stoics, Buddhists, and others).

Human emotion operates within a two-system design (Levenson, 1999). The biological core of the emotion system is one that humans share with other animals, and this is the part of the emotion system that evolved to solve fundamental life tasks. Because only a few life tasks are truly fundamental, the emotion system responds in a prototypical/stereotypical way that recruits and orchestrates a limited but highly appropriate set of responses. This way of responding can be characterized rather like a "time-tested recipe" (to borrow an example from Levenson, 1999). These prototypical ways of responding to fundamental life tasks are the same as those listed in Table 14.3. They are automatic and highly biological. These automated ways of responding to problems, therefore, can be highly adaptive when situationally appropriate. But they can also be situationally inappropriate when activated under other circumstances (e.g., attacking one's opponents is not always the best way to handle a situation). For emotions to be adaptive across many different situations, emotions need to be regulated and controlled.

As Robert Levenson (1999) points out, in the modern world, tigers rarely jump out at us, people rarely steal our food, and beasts rarely threaten to kill our young. Today's threats are on a smaller scale and therefore do not require the same sort of massive mobilization of our emotion systems. More often than not, we need to control or reserve our full-blown emotional responses. The two primary ways we regulate our emotion systems are through cognitive appraisals and through culturally appropriate displays. For instance, instead of thinking a person cutting us off in traffic is trying to injure or kill us, we can use appraisals to interpret the behavior in a way that is less likely to cue up a threat-activated emotion system (e.g., we can reappraise what we see as a rushed attempt to make an important appointment; Lazarus, 1991b). Also, people can suppress the intensity with which they experience and express the emotions they feel (e.g., we can suppress crying during a heart-tugging movie; Gross & Levenson, 1993).

Becoming competent at emotion regulation generally improves with experience, and it constitutes a lifelong undertaking (Carstensen, 1995; Gross et al., 1997). In the end, whether emotions serve us well and facilitate adaptive coping depends on how able we are to self-regulate our emotion systems such that we experience regulation *of* emotion rather than regulation *by* emotion (Gross, 1999).

WHAT IS THE DIFFERENCE BETWEEN EMOTION AND MOOD?

A fifth fundamental question on the nature of emotion concerns the difference between emotion and mood (Ekman & Davidson, 1994; Russell & Barrett, 1999). Several distinguishing criteria can be listed (Goldsmith, 1994), but three seem especially telling: antecedents, action-specificity, and time course. First, emotions and moods arise from different causes, or antecedents. Emotions emerge from significant life situations and from appraisals of their significance to our well-being. Moods, on the other hand, emerge from processes that are ill-defined and are oftentimes unknown (Goldsmith, 1994). Second, emotions function mostly to bias behavior and to select specific courses of action, whereas moods function mostly to bias cognition and what the person thinks (Davidson, 1994). Also, emotions emanate from short-lived events that last for seconds or perhaps minutes, whereas moods emanate from mental events that last for hours or longer. Hence, the third distinguishing characteristic is time course such that moods are more enduring than are emotions (Ekman, 1994a).

Everyday, Ongoing Affective Experience

Most people have about 1,000 waking minutes in their day, but only a few of these actually include a prototypical emotion such as anger, fear, or joy (Clark, Watson & Leeka, 1989; Watson & Clark, 1994). In contrast, the average person generally experiences an ever-present stream of moods. Though emotions are relatively rare in daily experience, people are always feeling something. What they typically feel is some level of positive affect and some level of negative affect (Watson & Tellegen, 1985; Watson, Clark, & Tellegen, 1988). These moods often exist as aftereffects of episodes involving emotions (Davidson, 1994).

These two moods (positive affect and negative affect) are more independent of one another than they are opposite ways of feeling[5] (Diener & Emmons, 1984; Diener & Iran-Nejad, 1986). For example, during a job interview, people often report feeling both positive and negative affects simultaneously. Positive affect also varies systematically as a function of the individual's location in the sleep-wake cycle while negative affect does not (Watson et al., 1999). Positive affect level is quite low upon waking. It increases rapidly throughout the morning, and positive affect continues to rise gradually throughout the afternoon until it hits its peak from 6 p.m. to 9 p.m. Positive affect then declines rapidly throughout the late evening as it returns to its early-morning low level (Clark, Watson, & Leeka, 1989).

Positive affect is a dimension of pleasurable engagement. It exists as a person's current level of pleasure, enthusiasm, and progress toward goals. People who feel high positive affect typically feel enthusiastic and experience energy, alertness, and optimism, whereas those who feel low positive affect typically feel lethargic and experience apathy and boredom.

Negative affect is a dimension of an unpleasant engagement. People who feel high negative affect typically experience dissatisfaction, nervousness, and irritability, whereas those who feel low negative affect typically experience calmness and relaxation. These feelings of alertness versus boredom (extent of positive affect) and irritability versus relaxation (extent of negative affect), rather than prototypical emotional states like joy and fear, constitute the essential nature of everyday, ongoing affective experience.

The two dimensions of positive and negative affect pertain not only to moods but also to broad cognitive, motivational, biological, and behavioral systems (Clark et al., 1994). Positive affect reflects a reward-driven, appetitive motivational system (Fowles, 1988), whereas negative affect reflects a punishment-driven, aversive motivational system (Gray, 1987). Basically, positive affect supports approach behavior, while negative affect supports withdrawal (Watson et al., 1999). The positive affect system has its own neural substrate—dopaminergic pathways, and these pathways are activated by the expectancy of desirable events and produce emotions like hope and moods like positive affect (Wise, 1996; Ashby, Isen, & Turken, 1999). The negative affect system has its own neural substrate—serotonergic and noradrenergic pathways, and these pathways are activated by the expectancy of negative outcomes and produce emotions like worry and moods like negative affect (MacLeod, Byrne, & Valentine, 1996). Again, these findings point to the conclusion that positive and negative affect are more independent ways of feeling than they are opposites.

NATURE OF POSITIVE AFFECT

Positive affect refers to the everyday, low-level, general state of feeling good (Isen, 1987). It is the warm glow that so often accompanies everyday pleasant experiences such as walking in the park on a sunny day, receiving an unexpected gift or good news, listening

[5]Stated differently, positive affect and negative affect are not one-dimensional opposites (despite what their terminology implies) but are, rather, two orthogonal (independent) dimensions of experience.

to music, or making progress on a task. Although we focus on the park scenery, good news, pleasant music, or positive feedback, the mild good feeling of positive affect often arises subconsciously. We may smile more, whistle while we walk, daydream about happy memories, or talk more excitedly, but the positive feelings typically remain outside our conscious attention. In fact, if someone brings the pleasant mood to our attention, such attention paradoxically is the beginning of the end of the positive affect.

Notice that this lack of awareness of the positive affect stands in contrast to the more intense, attention-grabbing positive emotions, such as joy. The purpose of an emotion is to capture attention and direct coping behavior (so the person can adapt to situational demands effectively). Positive affect is more subtle. It generally does not affect attention and behavior. Instead, positive affect influences the information processing flow—what we think about, the decisions we make, creativity, judgments, and so on (Isen, 1987, 1996).

SOURCES OF POSITIVE AFFECT

People have difficult times explaining why they feel good. If pressed, they typically say that life is generally going well. Mood researchers, on the other hand, have learned which conditions lead people to feel good, and most of these conditions create positive affect in ways such that people remain unaware of the causal source of their good moods (Isen, 1987). Consider these positive affect-inducing experimental manipulations of a small gain, amusement, or pleasure: Find money in the coin-return slot of a public telephone (Isen & Levin, 1972), receive a gift of a bag of candy (Isen & Geva, 1987; Isen, Niedenthal & Cantor, 1992), receive a free product sample (worth a quarter; Isen, Clark, & Schwartz, 1976), receive a candy bar (Isen et al., 1985; Isen, Daubman, & Nowicki, 1987), learn that a performance was successful (Isen, 1970), receive a cookie (Isen & Levin, 1972), receive refreshments such as orange juice (Isen et al., 1985), receive positive feedback (Isen, Rosenzweig, & Young, 1991), think about positive events (Isen et al., 1985), experience sunny weather (Kraut & Johnston, 1979), watch an amusing film (Isen & Nowicki, 1981), or rate funny cartoons (Carnevale & Isen, 1986).

Once instigated by an eliciting event (e.g., receiving a small gift), the warm glow of a positive mood continues for up to 20 minutes (Isen, Clark, & Schwartz, 1976). Because we enjoy feeling good, happy people make decisions and act in ways that maintain their good moods for longer than 20 minutes (Forest et al., 1979; Isen et al., 1978). More often than not, however, some rival event or interrupting life task distracts our attention away from the positive affect-inducing event. That is, we lose our positive mood by engaging in neutral and aversive events (e.g., boring work, dense or congested traffic, bad news, a risk turned sour).

BENEFITS OF POSITIVE AFFECT

Compared to people in a neutral mood, people exposed to conditions that allow them to feel good are more likely to help others (Isen & Levin, 1972), act sociably (i.e., initiate conversations, Batson et al., 1979), express greater liking for others (Veitch & Griffitt, 1976), be more generous to others (Isen, 1970) and to themselves (Mischel, Coates, & Raskoff, 1968), take greater risks (Isen & Patrick, 1983), act more cooperatively and less aggressively (Carnevale & Isen, 1986), solve problems more creatively (Isen, Daubman, & Nowicki, 1987), persist in the face of failure feedback (Chen & Isen, 1992), make decisions more efficiently (Isen & Means, 1983), and show greater intrinsic motivation on interesting activities (Isen & Reeve, 2000). Consider the following two examples of enhanced creativity and efficient decision making.

Positive affect facilitates cognitive flexibility (Isen, Niedenthal, & Cantor, 1992) and creative problem solving (Estrada, Isen, & Young, 1997; Isen, Daubman, & Nowicki, 1987). Alice M. Isen and colleagues (1987) induced positive or neutral affect in groups of college students and then asked them to solve one of two problem-solving tasks requiring creativity—the candle task (Dunker, 1945) or the Remote Associates Test (RAT; Mednick, Mednick, & Mednick, 1964). In the candle task, the participant receives a pile of tacks, a candle, and a box of matches and the instructions to attach the candle to the wall (a cork board) so that the candle can burn without dripping wax on the floor. In the RAT, the participant sees three words (soul, busy, guard) and is asked to generate a fourth word that relates to the other three (in this case, "body"). Positive affect participants solved the creativity-demanding candle task and gave creative (unusual or "remote") associates to the RAT (Isen et al., 1987). In contrast, the candle task stumped the neutral affect participants, and they gave routine, stereotypical responses to the RAT. Thus, there are inherent processing advantages conferred by feeling good, as positive affect acts as a resource in solving problems and attaining goals (Aspenwall, 1998).

Positive affect enhances cognitive efficiency during decision making (Carnevale & Isen, 1986; Isen & Means, 1983; Isen, Rosenzweig, & Young, 1991). Feeling good biases people toward faster, more efficient, and less effortful decision-making performances. On tasks that are more structured and need to be double-checked for accuracy (e.g., geometry proofs, second drafts of a manuscript), however, positive affect individuals do not outperform their neutral affect counterparts (because their fast, efficient, effortless decision-making style makes them increasingly susceptible to error making).

The explanation as to *how* and *why* positive affect facilitates creativity, decision-making efficiency, sociability, prosocial behavior, persistence, and so on is not as straightforward as it might first appear to be. Being a mood rather than an emotion, positive affect influences cognitive processes, such as memories, judgments, and problem-solving strategies. It therefore influences the contents of working (short-term) memory by biasing what the individual thinks about and what memories and expectations come to mind (Isen, 1984, 1987). It essentially serves as a retrieval cue for positive material stored in memory (Isen et al., 1978; Laird et al., 1982; Nasby & Yando, 1982; Teasdale & Fogarty, 1979). As a result, people who feel good have ready access to happy thoughts and positive memories (compared to people who feel neutral). With happy thoughts and pleasant memories salient in one's mind, people show increased creativity, show persistence in the face of failure, make decisions efficiently, show high intrinsic motivation, and so on.

SUMMARY

This chapter addresses five questions central to understanding the nature of emotion. The first question asks, "What is an emotion?" Emotions have a four-part character in that they feature distinct subjective, biological, functional, and expressive dimensions. The subjective dimension gives an emotion its feeling state. The biological dimension gives an emotion its physiological reaction and bodily preparedness for coping with a specific situation. The functional dimension provides a motivational aspect as the emotion creates desires and purposes that channel behavior in adaptive ways. The expressive component gives emotion a social, communicative aspect. Emotion is the psychological construct that coordinates and unifies these four aspects of experience into a synchronized, adaptive pattern.

The second question asks, "What causes an emotion?" Rephrased, this question debates whether emotion is primarily a biological or a cognitive phenomenon. According to the biological perspective, emotions arise from bodily influences such as limbic neural pathways, patterns of neural firing, and facial feedback. According to the cognitive perspective, emotions arise from mental events such as appraisals, knowledge, and memory as the individual interprets the personal meanings of stimulus events. Both sides of the biology-cognition debate marshal together an impressive array of evidence in supporting their positions. Because such things as drugs, electrical brain stimulation, and facial feedback activate emotion, it is clear that biological forces cause emotional experience, with or without cognitive participation. Because people can almost always interpret the self-relevance and personal significance of an event, it is clear that cognitive forces also cause emotional experience. To resolve the biology-cognition debate, three solutions emerged. The first argues that human beings possess two parallel emotion systems—an innate, spontaneous, and primitive biological emotion system and an acquired, interpretive, and social cognitive emotion system. The second solution argues that the biology-cognition debate is fruitless, as emotion should be considered a dynamic, dialectic process rather than the output of either the biological or cognitive systems. The third solution proposes that emotions include both cognitive and biological components, and it is simply a matter of perspective as to which set of variables one wishes to emphasize and investigate.

The third question asks, "How many emotions are there?" The answer depends on one's perspective. According to the biological perspective, human beings possess several basic emotions—somewhere between 2 and 10. These researchers illustrate how primary emotions emerge from hedonically opponent processes, hardwired limbic neural pathways, patterns of neural firing, universal facial expressions, evolutionary functions, and discrete patterns of facial feedback. According to the cognitive perspective, human beings possess a much richer, more diverse emotional repertoire than just the basic emotions. These researchers illustrate how secondary emotions are acquired as the individual learns to interpret situations differently, gains experience in emotional situations, learns new emotion words, learns to manage emotion expressions, and learns cultural display rules.

The fourth question asks, "What good are the emotions?" It highlights that emotions serve a purpose. From a functional point of view, emotions evolved as biological reactions that helped us adapt successfully to fundamental life tasks, such as facing a threat. The emotion that arises during a life task energizes and directs behavior in a way that proves to be most effective. Hence, emotions possess an inherent coping function. In addition, emotions serve social purposes. Emotions communicate our feelings to others, affect how others interact with us, invite and facilitate social interaction, and play a pivotal role in creating, maintaining, and dissolving interpersonal relationships.

The final question asks, "What is the difference between emotion and mood?" Emotions arise from specific events, motivate specific adaptive behaviors, and are short-lived. Moods arise from ill-defined and often unknown sources, affect behavior only indirectly through their effects on cognitive processes, and are pervasive. To illustrate the motivational significance of moods, this chapter focuses on positive affect, which refers to the everyday, low-level, general state of feeling good. When people feel good, they are more sociable, cooperative, creative, persistent during failure, efficient in their decision making, and intrinsically motivated on interesting tasks. Positive affect exerts these effects by affecting cognitive processes such as memories and judgments. As a result, people who feel good have greater access to happy thoughts and positive memories and therefore behave in ways that reflect easy access to happy thoughts (e.g., are more sociable, more creative).

RECOMMENDED READINGS

What Are Emotions?

Izard, C. E. (1993). Four systems for emotion activation: Cognitive and noncognitive processes. *Psychological Review, 100,* 68–90.

Lazarus, R. S. (1991). Cognition and motivation in emotion. *American Psychologist, 46,* 352–367.

Oatley, K., & Duncan, E. (1994). The experience of emotions in everyday life. *Cognition and Emotion, 8,* 369–381.

Plutchik, R. (1985). On emotion: The chicken-and-egg problem revisited. *Motivation and Emotion, 9,* 197–200.

How Many Emotions Are There?

Ekman, P. (1992). An argument for basic emotions. *Cognition and Emotion, 6,* 169–200.

Kemper, T. D. (1987). How many emotions are there? Wedding the social and autonomic components. *American Sociological Review, 93,* 263–289.

Functions of Emotion

Carstensen, L. L., Gottman, J. M., & Levenson, R. W. (1995). Emotional behavior in long-term marriage. *Psychology and Aging, 10,* 140–149.

Kraut, R. E., & Johnston, R. E. (1979). Social and emotional messages of smiling: An ethological approach. *Journal of Personality and Social Psychology, 37,* 1539–1553.

Levenson, R. W. (1994). Human emotion: A functional view. In P. Ekman & R. J. Davidson (Eds.), *The nature of emotion* (pp. 123–126). New York: Oxford University Press.

Plutchik, R. (1970). Emotions, evolution, and adaptive processes. In M. B. Arnold (Ed.), *Feelings and emotions* (pp. 3–24). New York: Academic Press.

Tooby, J., & Cosmides, L. (1990). The past explains the present: Emotional adaptations and the structure of ancestral environment. *Ethology and Sociobiology, 11,* 375–424.

Mood and Positive Affect

Isen, A. M., Daubman, K. A., & Nowicki, G. P. (1987). Positive affect facilitates creative problem-solving. *Journal of Personality and Social Psychology, 51,* 1122–1131.

Watson, D., Clark, L. A., & Tellegen, A. (1988). Development and validation of brief measures of positive and negative affect: The PANAS scales. *Journal of Personality and Social Psychology, 54,* 1063–1070.

15

Aspects of Emotion

Pause for a moment and try to look sad—try to produce a sad facial expression. As you try this, attend to the changing sensations you feel from the movements of your facial musculature. If you just moved your mouth by pouting the lower lip and pulling down the corners of your mouth, then you probably did not feel too sad. So, try this again. Produce a second sad facial expression. But this time move not only your lower lip and corners of your mouth but also move your eyebrows inward at the same time. This will take some skill, so pretend that you have a couple of golf tees attached to the inner corners of the eyebrows. Pretend these golf tees are about an inch apart and pointing outward from your face (base of each tee rests on the inner eyebrow with its tip extending outward). Now move your eyebrows inward until the tips of the golf tees touch. Now try to move all three of these muscles together—touch the golf tees together, pout your lower lip, and turn the corners of your mouth down (Larsen, Kasimatis, & Frey, 1992).

Did you feel anything as you were attempting this facial expression? Does your heart rate drop? Do you sense a hint of a sad feeling coming on? Any vague urge to cry? If so, the feeling will be mild because a posed facial expression is not as authentic and emotion-producing as a spontaneous facial expression. But the mild sad feeling via a patterned facial expression is a good way to introduce one of the many aspects of emotion discussed in this chapter—in this case, the "facial feedback hypothesis."

BIOLOGICAL ASPECTS OF EMOTION

Emotions are, in part, biological reactions to important life events. Biology contributes at least five aspects of emotion, as follows:

1. Autonomic nervous system
2. Endocrine system
3. Neural brain circuits
4. Rate of neural firing
5. Facial feedback

This list is important because it identifies the body's emotion-related biological reactions to important life events. Facing a situation of personal significance (e.g., a threat), the body prepares itself to cope effectively (e.g., gets ready to run) by activating the following: (1) heart, lungs, and muscles (autonomic nervous system); (2) glands and hormones (endocrine system); (3) limbic brain structures such as the hypothalamus (neural brain circuits); (4) neural activity and the pace of information processing (rate of neural firing); and (5) discrete patterns of the facial musculature (facial feedback). With these biological systems engaged, the person is significantly more readied to cope with a threat than had these biological systems not been engaged.

Emotion study began about 100 years ago by asking what role the autonomic nervous system played in the subjective experience of emotion. The first theory of emotion, the James-Lange theory, asked whether individual emotions had particular patterned bodily reactions associated with them. When facing a threat, people feel fear and predictable bodily changes occur—the heart races, palms sweat, and breathing quickens. People in love also experience similar bodily changes. There is little doubt that fear and love feel different, but it is an interesting question whether fear and love have unique bodily reactions. Do our heart, spleen, eyes, and stomach behave one way when we are afraid yet another way when we are in love? And if so, do these biological differences explain why the emotions we experience are different?

James-Lange Theory

Personal experience suggests that we experience an emotion and that emotion is quickly followed by bodily changes. As soon as we see the flashing red lights and hear the siren of a police car, fear arises and makes our heart race and our palms sweat. The order of events seems to be stimulus → emotion → bodily reaction. William James (1884, 1890, 1894) argued against this common view. He suggested that our bodily changes do not follow the emotional experience; rather, emotional experience follows and depends on bodily and behavioral responses to the flashing lights and siren. Hence, bodily changes cause emotional experience: stimulus → bodily reaction → emotion.

James' theory rested on two assumptions: (1) The body reacts discriminatorily to different emotion-eliciting stimuli, and (2) nonemotional stimuli elicit no bodily changes. To appreciate James' hypothesis, think of the physiological responses of your body to an unexpectedly cold shower. The physiological reaction—the increased heart rate, quickened breath, and widened eyes—begins before you have time to think about why your heart is racing and your eyes are widening. James argued that such instantaneous bodily reactions occur in discernible patterns, and emotional experience is a person's way of making sense of such bodily reactions. When such physiological changes do not occur, people feel no emotion.

The James-Lange theory of emotions quickly became popular, but it also met with criticism (Cannon, 1927).[1] Critics argued that the sort of bodily reactions James referred to were actually part of the body's general mobilizing fight-or-flight response that did not vary from one emotion to the next (Cannon, 1929; Mandler, 1975; Schachter, 1964).[2] These critics also argued that emotional experience was quicker than physiological reactions. That is, while a person feels anger in a tenth of a second, it takes this person's nervous system a full second or two to activate important glands and send excitatory hormones through the bloodstream. These critics contended that the role of physiological arousal was to augment, rather than cause, emotion (Newman, Perkins, & Wheeler, 1930). Critics concluded that the contribution of physiological changes to emotional experience was small, supplemental, and relatively unimportant. The first major theory of emotion was in doubt.

CONTEMPORARY PERSPECTIVE

In the face of criticism, James' ideas faded out of favor, and rival theories of emotion emerged and became popular (Schachter & Singer, 1962). Nonetheless, his ideas continue to guide and inform contemporary study (Ellsworth, 1994; Lang, 1994), and contemporary research now finds support for physiological specificity in a few emotions (Buck, 1986; Levenson, 1992; Schwartz, 1986). Paul Ekman, Robert Levenson, and

---

[1]At the same time James presented his ideas, a Danish psychologist, Carl Lange (1885), proposed essentially the same (but more limited) theory of emotion. For this reason, the idea that emotions emanate from our interpretation of patterns of physiological arousal is traditionally called the James-Lange theory (Lange & James, 1922)

[2]For instance, does a person experience specific emotions after taking a stimulant drug known to induce bodily changes—increase heart rate, minimize gastrointestinal activity, and dilate the bronchioles? Drug-induced visceral stimulation leads people to feel "as if afraid" or "as if going to weep without knowing why" rather than afraid or sad per se (i.e., people feel generally aroused but not specifically afraid).

Wallace Friesen (1983), for example, studied whether each of several emotions does or does not have a unique pattern of bodily changes. These researchers recruited people who could experience emotions on command (professional actors) and asked each to relive five different emotions—anger, fear, sadness, joy, and disgust—while the researchers measured for emotion-specific patterns of physiological activity. Distinct differences in heart rate (HR) and skin temperature (ST) emerged. With anger, HR and ST both increased; with fear, HR increased while ST decreased; with sadness, HR increased while ST was stable; with joy, HR was stable while ST increased; and with disgust, both HR and ST decreased. Different emotions did indeed produce distinguishable physiological patterns.

The contemporary perspective on whether emotions have distinctive patterns of physiological activity is that a few emotions do, while most do not. Persuasive evidence exists for distinctive autonomic nervous system (ANS) activity associated with anger, fear, disgust, and sadness (Ekman & Davidson, 1993; Ekman, Levenson, & Friesen, 1983; Levenson, 1992; Levenson et al., 1991; Levenson, Ekman, & Friesen, 1990; Sinha & Parsons, 1996; Stemmler, 1988). These patterns of ANS activity supposedly emerged because they were able to recruit ways of behaving that proved to be adaptive. For instance, in a fight that arouses anger, increased heart rate and skin temperature facilitate strong, assertive behavior.

Not all emotions have distinct patterns of ANS activity, however. If no specific pattern of behavior has survival value for an emotion, there is little reason for the development of a specific pattern of ANS activity (Ekman, 1992, 1994a). For instance, what is the most adaptive behavioral pattern to jealousy? to envy? joy? hope? For these emotions, no single adaptive activity seems universally most appropriate. Hence, there is little reason to expect a single pattern of ANS activity to evolve.

In discussing the James-Lange theory of emotion, the fundamental question is whether the physiological arousal causes, or just follows, emotion activation. This question is important because if arousal causes emotion, then the study of physiological arousal becomes a cornerstone study for any understanding of emotion. But if arousal merely follows and augments emotion, physiological activity is therefore much less important. Contemporary researchers generally agree that physiological arousal accompanies, regulates, and sets the stage for emotion, but it does not cause it directly. The modern perspective is that emotions recruit physiological support to enable adaptive behaviors such as fighting, fleeing, and nurturing. Hence, the autonomic nervous system's role in emotion is to create the optimal biological milieu that will support the adaptive behavior called for by a life situation (Levenson, 1994b).

Specific Neural Circuits

Some researchers search for emotion-specific patterns in brain activity (Gray, 1994; LeDoux, 1987; Panksepp, 1982, 1986). For instance, Jeffrey Gray's (1994) neuroanatomical findings (with nonhuman mammals) document the existence of three distinct neural circuits in the brain, each of which regulates a distinctive pattern of emotional behavior: (1) a behavioral approach system that readies the animal to seek out and interact with attractive environmental opportunities, (2) a fight-or-flight system that

Affective Computing

Question: Why would a person want to learn about the motivational states discussed in this chapter?

Answer: To get ready for the coming technology that will read emotions.

The finding that emotions show ANS specificity has big implications for coming technology. If changes in blood pressure and skin temperature can reliably distinguish between the emotions of anger, fear, sadness, joy, and disgust, and if machines like a stethoscope and GSR (lie detector) can detect these bodily changes, then why can we not build machines that know how we feel—that read our emotions? Imagine sensors built into the steering wheel of a car to read the driver's heart rate and skin temperature. Imagine sensors built into the handles of bicycles, pilot simulators, joysticks, golf clubs, and utensils, and into the handles held by audience members during plays, lectures, musical performances, and political debates.

Actually, soon you will not need to imagine such technological inventions, as scientists in the new field of "affective computing" are hard at work building such devices (Azar, 2000; see also "Soon: Computers that know you hate them," *The New York Times,* January 6, 2000). One particularly interesting invention is the "emotion mouse." It functions like an ordinary computer mouse, except it has copper buttons and an infrared port for monitoring heart rate, skin temperature, hand movements, and electrical skin conductance. The computer monitors the data collected by the emotion mouse and analyzes this data to infer the user's emotional state.

If a computer can read a user's emotions, then a computer gains the potential capacity for adjusting to its user. A computer game can be made more or less challenging, a tutorial can be adjusted to decrease fear or to increase joy, or an online counseling session can provide emotional feedback regarding the feelings of a client at different points in the conversation. But the emotion mouse will still be limited to monitoring only the five emotions of anger, fear, sadness, joy, and disgust (i.e., only

readies the animal to flee from some aversive events but to defend aggressively against others, and (3) a behavioral inhibition system that readies the animal to freeze in the face of aversive events. These three neural circuits underlie the four emotions of joy, fear, rage, and anxiety.

Overall, four emotions possess ANS physiological specificity—anger, fear, disgust, and sadness—and four emotions possess neural circuit specificity—joy, fear, rage, and anxiety.

Neural Activation

Different emotions are activated by different rates of cortical neural firing (Tomkins, 1970). Neural firing refers to the pattern of electrocortical activity at any given time. According to Silvan Tomkins, there are three basic patterns of neural firing: activity the emotions that show ANS specificity). To expand the computer's ability to monitor and analyze additional emotions, another feature could be added—something akin to a video camera to monitor and analyze facial expressions. A video camera could monitor movements of the user's face—the user's frontalis, corrugators, orbicularis oculi, zygomaticus, nasalis, depressors, orbicularis oris, and quadratus labii (see Figure 15.3). With these facial movements, the computer gains the data necessary for inferring not only the presence of anger, fear, distress, disgust, joy, interest, and contempt (see Figure 15.5) but also the intensity of these emotions (based on the intensity of the muscular movements).

Computers can analyze and interpret a user's facial muscles because researchers have already developed an elaborate coding system for doing so called FACS, for facial action coding system (Ekman & Friesen, 1978). Software has already been developed so that computers are about as accurate as (and much faster than) people who score the same facial movements in users (Cohn et al., 1999). The computer (and human rater) must then make the leap between the movements of the face and infer the underlying emotion that causes the facial expression; but reliable heuristics for doing so have been established (Ekman & Friesen, 1975; Ekman & Rosenberg, 1997). The ability of computers to recognize the emotional facial expressions of a wide range of people is only a matter of time.

With the emotion mouse and video camera installed, the computer can make a reliable analysis of the biological aspects of the user's emotion. But emotion further features cognitive, social, and cultural aspects as well. To build technology to monitor and analyze these aspects of emotion will take even greater technology. But reading the first half of this chapter ought to help ready you for the coming technology that will read your emotions.

increases, activity decreases, or activity remains constant. Whether the rate of neural firing is increasing, decreasing, or constant depends mostly on environmental events. For example, if you are sleeping (a low rate of neural firing, as measured by the electroencephalogram, or EEG) and a cat jumps on your face (a stimulating event), the rate of neural firing will more than likely increase. If you are at a rock concert (another stimulating event) and exit to relative quiet, the rate of neural firing will decrease. Other times, neural activity is constant, as in persistent cognitive effort while reading the newspaper, for instance.

With these three basic patterns of neural firing, the person is equipped for virtually every contingency. If neural firing suddenly increases, the person experiences one class of emotions—surprise, fear, or interest—with the specific emotion depending on the suddenness of the increased rate of neural firing (i.e., gradual increase → interest, increase → fear, and sudden increase → surprise). If neural firing reaches and maintains a high level, then the constant (and high) neural firing activates either distress or anger, depending on the magnitude of the neural stimulation (i.e., continuously high → distress, continuously very high → anger). Finally, if neural firing decreases, joy is activated, as the individual laughs and smiles with relief. The relationship between each of these changes in the rate of neural firing and its associated emotion is illustrated in Figure 15.1.

Consider the neural activity of an audience watching a horror movie. First, the audience is slowly introduced to the characters, setting, and circumstances of the plot. All this new information gradually increases neural firing, and the audience becomes interested. Suddenly, the crazy man with an axe jumps out from behind the bushes, an event that drastically increases the audience's neural firing and activates surprise. Later, the audience watches the protagonist move through the dark forest, hearing unfamiliar noises and seeing strange sights. The audience's neural firing quickens and arouses fear. If the neural firing remains high, it could arouse distress. Of course, the hero and heroine conquer the crazy man in the end, a resolution that decreases the audience's rate of neural firing and activates joy.

DIFFERENTIAL EMOTIONS THEORY

Differential emotions theory takes its name from its emphasis on basic emotions serving unique, or different, motivational purposes (Izard, 1991, 1992, 1993; Izard & Malatesta, 1987). The theory endorses the following postulates (Izard, 1991):

FIGURE 15.1 **Emotion Activation as Function of Changes in Rate of Neural Firing in the Cortex**

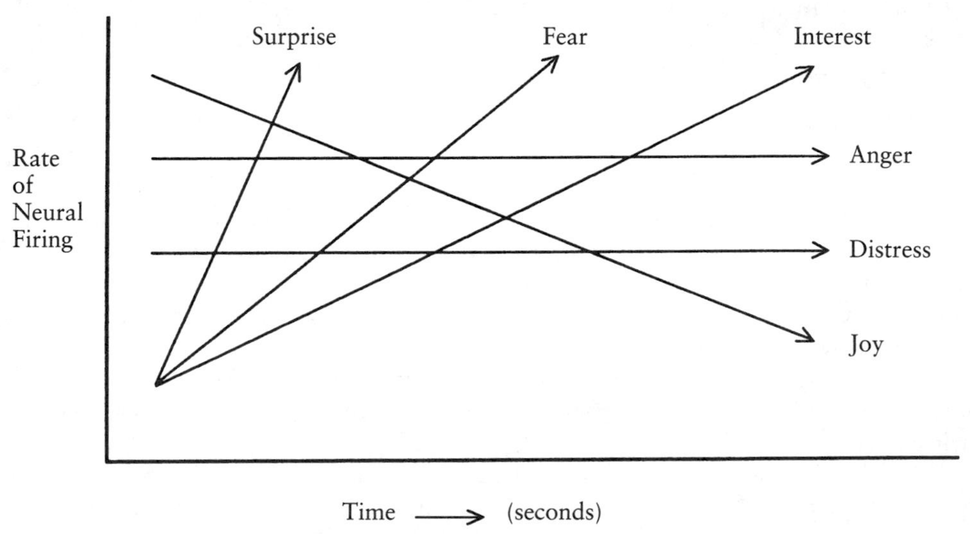

SOURCE: From "Affect as the Primary Motivational System," by S. S. Tomkins (1970) in M. B. Arnold (Ed.), *Feelings and Emotions* (pp. 101–110), New York: Academic Press.

1. Ten discrete emotions constitute the principal motivation system for human beings.
2. Each discrete emotion has a unique subjective, phenomenological quality.
3. Each discrete emotion has a unique facial-expressive pattern.
4. Each discrete emotion is sensitive to a specific rate of neural firing that automatically activates it into consciousness.
5. Each discrete emotion generates distinctive motivational properties and serves adaptive functions.

The 10 discrete emotions that fit the last four postulates above appear in Table 15.1. Each emotion, according to differential emotions theory, operates as a system of interacting experiential (postulate 2), expressive (postulate 3), neural (postulate 4), and motivational (postulate 5) components. The core understanding of the differential emotions theory is that these 10 discrete emotions are essentially motivational systems that prepare the individual for acting in adaptive ways (Izard, 1989, 1991, 1992). Each emotion has been preadapted over the course of evolution to provide an organized heuristic for dealing effectively with life tasks and problems that are both important and recurring (e.g., form social bonds, confront threats).

Seeing the list of emotions in Table 15.1 is likely to conjure up a question such as the following: Where are emotions like jealousy, hope, love, hate, smugness, and worry? Biologically minded theories generally do not count experiences such as these among the basic emotions. Paul Ekman (1992) offers seven reasons for explaining why there are only a small number of basic emotions:

1. Emotion families exist such that many nonbasic emotions are experienced-based derivatives of a single basic emotion (e.g., anxiety is a derivative of fear).
2. Many emotion terms actually better describe moods (e.g., apprehension, irritation).
3. Many emotion terms actually better describe attitudes (e.g., love, hatred).
4. Many emotion terms actually better describe personality traits (e.g., hostile).
5. Many emotion terms actually better describe disorders (e.g., depression, anxiety).
6. Some nonbasic emotions are blends of basic emotions (e.g., romantic love blends interest, joy, and the sex drive).
7. Many emotion words refer to specific aspects of a basic emotion (e.g., what elicits the emotion [homesickness] or how a person behaves [gaiety, aggression]).

TABLE 15.1 **Izard's 10 Fundamental Emotions**

POSITIVE	NEGATIVE	NEUTRAL
Interest	Fear	Surprise
Joy	Anger	
	Disgust	
	Distress	
	Contempt	
	Shame	
	Guilt	

FACIAL FEEDBACK HYPOTHESIS

According to the facial feedback hypothesis, the subjective aspect of emotion stems from feelings engendered by (1) movements of the facial musculature, (2) changes in facial temperature, and (3) changes in glandular activity in the facial skin. Therefore, emotions are "sets of muscle and glandular responses located in the face" (Tomkins, 1962). In other words, emotion is the awareness of proprioceptive feedback from facial behavior.

Upon being introduced to the hypothesis that emotion is facial feedback information, the reader might be a bit skeptical. But consider the following sequence of events to understand how sensations from the face feed back to the cortical brain to produce emotional experience. A quick increase in neural firing activates a subcortical emotion program (e.g., fear, as in Figure 15.1). The human subcortical brain possesses innate, genetically wired, emotion-specific programs. When activated, these programs generate discrete facial expressions and patterned changes in the ANS and endocrine system. Within microseconds of the displayed fear facial expression, the brain interprets the facial feedback from drawn-back corners of the mouth, decreased facial temperature, and activated glandular secretions. This particular pattern of facial feedback gives rise to the subjective feeling of fear. The whole body becomes involved in the fear emotion as the glandular-hormonal, cardiovascular, and respiratory systems become aroused and amplify and sustain the fear experience.

Facial feedback does one job: emotion activation (Izard, 1989, 1994). Facial feedback activates the subcortical emotion program. The emotion program, not the facial feedback, then arouses cognitive and bodily participation to continue the emotional experience. Thus, following emotion activation from facial feedback, a person monitors not her facial feedback but her changes in heart rate, respiratory rate, muscle tonus, and the amount of perspiration. She also monitors her posture and gestures. These bodily changes maintain the emotional experience over time. Nonetheless, it is the facial feedback that activates the chain of events that underlie the emotional experience, according to the facial feedback hypothesis. Facial action also changes brain temperature, such that facial movements associated with negative emotion (sadness) constrict breathing, raise brain temperature, and produce negative feelings, whereas facial movements associated with positive emotion (happiness) enhance breathing, cool brain temperature, and produce positive feelings (McIntosh et al., 1997; Zajonc, Murphy, & Inglehart, 1992).

The sequential process of emotional activation appears in Figure 15.2 (Izard, 1991). Internal (e.g., memory) or external (e.g., a firecracker popping) events change the gradient in neural firing (see Figure 15.1). Changes in the rate of neural firing are detected by the limbic system (where the subcortical emotion-specific programs are). Impulses go to the basal ganglia, which organize facial expressions, and excite the motor cortex and facial nerve (cranial nerve VII) to produce a specific facial expression. In the facial musculature, specific muscles are contracted and relaxed and changes in blood flow and glandular secretions occur. The trigeminal nerve (cranial nerve V) relays the changing proprioceptive stimulation to the sensory cortex. Finally, cortical integration of the proprioceptive stimulation (i.e., the "facial feedback") generates the subjective experience of emotion. It is in the frontal lobe of the neocortex that the individual eventually becomes aware of emotion at a conscious level (i.e., number 6 in Figure 15.2).

FIGURE 15.2 **Sequence of Neurological Events in the Facial Feedback Hypothesis**

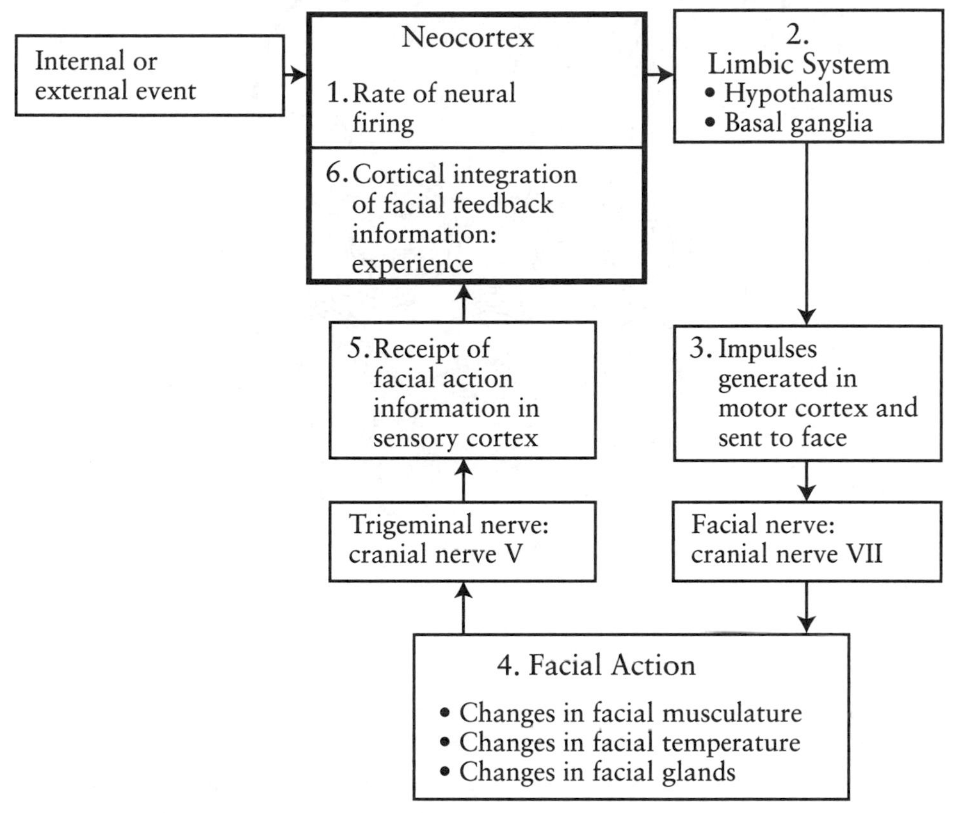

FACIAL MUSCULATURE

There are 80 facial muscles, 36 of which are involved in facial expression. For purposes of exposition, however, the 8 facial muscles shown in Figure 15.3 are sufficient for differentiating among the basic emotions (for more information, see Ekman & Friesen, 1975; Izard, 1971). The upper face (the eyes and forehead) has 3 major muscles: the frontalis (covers the forehead), corrugator (lies beneath each eyebrow), and orbicularis oculi (surrounds each eye). The middle face has 2 major muscles: the zygomaticus (extends from the corners of the mouth to the cheekbone) and the nasalis (wrinkles the nose). The lower face has 3 major muscles: the depressor (draws the corners of the mouth downward), the orbicularis oris (circular muscle surrounding the lips), and the quadratus labii (draws the corners of the mouth backward).

Patterns of facial behavior produce discrete emotions. Anger, fear, disgust, distress, and joy, for instance, are each associated with the particular patterns of facial behavior in the following list (see Figure 15.4; Ekman & Friesen, 1975).

FIGURE 15.3 **Eight Major Facial Muscles**

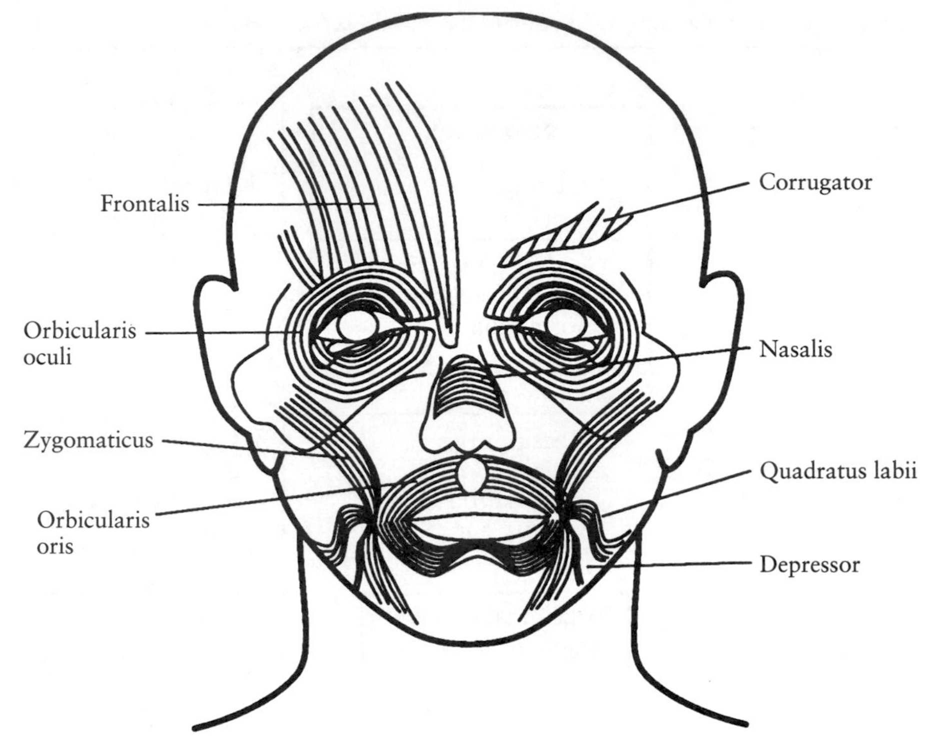

FOR ANGER:

corrugators draw eyebrows inward and downward
orbicularis oculi tense lower eyelids upward
orbicularis oris presses lips firmly together

FOR FEAR:

corrugators raise inner corners of the eyebrows
frontalis contracts to produce horizontal forehead wrinkles
orbicularis oculi raise upper eyelids and tense lower eyelids
quadratus labii pull lips tightly backwards

FOR DISGUST:

orbicularis oris raises upper lip
nasalis wrinkles nose
zygomaticus raises cheeks

FOR SADNESS:

corrugators raise and draw together inner corners of the eyelids
orbicularis oculi raise upper inner corner of eyelids
depressors pull corners of lips down

FOR JOY:

zygomaticus pulls corners of lips back and up
zygomaticus raises cheeks, producing crow's-feet wrinkles below eyes and wrinkles running down from nose to corners of lips
orbicularis oculi relax, showing wrinkles below eyelids

FIGURE 15.4 **Facial Expressions for Five Emotions**

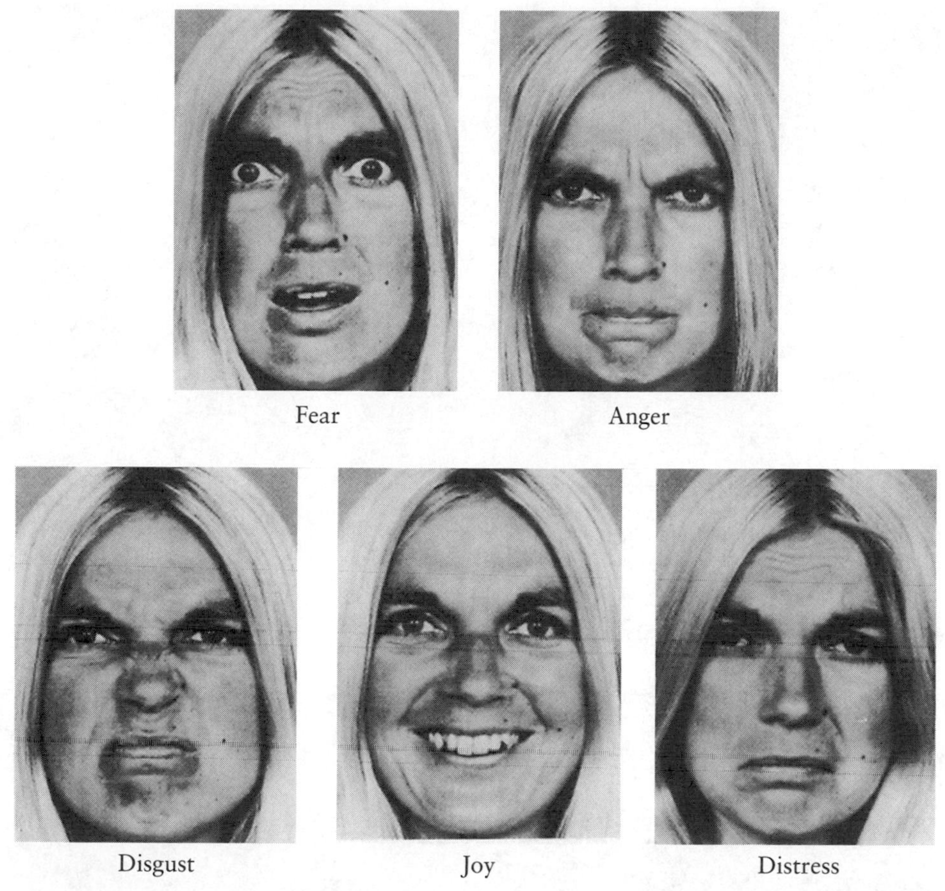

Fear Anger

Disgust Joy Distress

SOURCE: From *Unmasking the Face,* by P. Ekman and W. V. Friesen, 1975, Englewood Cliffs, NJ: Prentice Hall.

Two additional emotions are associated with a particular pattern of facial behavior: interest (Reeve, 1993) and contempt (Ekman & Friesen, 1986). The interest expression is illustrated in the majority of the faces shown in Figure 15.5 (all but the boy in the lower right corner). For interest, the orbicularis oculi open the eyelids and the orbicularis oris slightly parts the lips open. For contempt, the zygomaticus unilaterally raises the corner of one lip upwards.

TEST OF THE FACIAL FEEDBACK HYPOTHESIS

Feedback from facial behavior, when transformed into conscious awareness, constitutes the experience of emotion (Laird, 1974; Tomkins, 1962, 1963). This is the facial feedback hypothesis (FFH). The studies testing the FFH use one of two methodologies because

FIGURE 15.5 **Facial Expressions of Interest**

SOURCE: AP/Wide World Photos

there are two testable versions of the FFH—strong and weak (McIntosh, 1996; Rutledge & Hupka, 1985).

In its strong version, the FFH proposes that manipulating one's facial musculature into a pattern that corresponds to an emotion display will activate that emotional experience. In other words, frowning the lips and raising the inner eyebrows activates sadness (recall the example at the beginning of this chapter). In empirical tests, an experimenter instructs a participant to contract and relax specific muscles of the face and, with a particular facial expression displayed, complete a questionnaire to assess emotional experience. For example, in one study, participants were instructed to (1) "raise your brows and pull them together," (2) "now raise your upper eyelids," and (3) "now also stretch your lips horizontally, back towards your ears" (Ekman, Levenson, & Friesen, 1983). So posed, the participants were asked about their emotional state (fear, in this case) on a questionnaire. Research has both supported (Laird, 1974, 1984; Larsen, Kasimatis, & Frey, 1992; Rutledge & Hupka, 1985; Strack, Martin, & Stepper, 1988) and refuted (McCaul, Holmes, & Solomon, 1982; Tourangeau & Ellsworth, 1979) the strong version of the FFH. One area of consensus is that a posed facial musculature produces reliable changes in physiological reactions, such as changes in cardiovascular and respiratory rates (Tourangeau & Ellsworth, 1979; Ekman, Levenson, & Friesen, 1983). It is still debated whether the posed facial musculature produces emotional experience, but most studies suggest that it produces only a small effect (Adelmann & Zajonc, 1989; Izard, 1990; Laird, 1984; Matsumoto, 1987; Rutledge & Hupka, 1985).

In its weaker (more conservative) version, the FFH proposes that facial feedback modifies the intensity of (rather than causes) the emotion. Thus, managing one's facial musculature into a particular emotional display will augment (exaggerate) but will not necessarily activate the emotional experience. In other words, if you intentionally smile when you are already joyful, then you will feel a more intense joy. In one experiment, participants either exaggerated or suppressed their spontaneous facial expressions while watching a video, which depicted either a pleasant, neutral, or unpleasant scenario (Zuckerman et al., 1981). Exaggerating naturally occurring facial expressions did augment emotional and physiological experience, and suppressing naturally occurring facial expressions did moderate the intensity of the emotional and physiological experience (Lanzetta, Cartwright-Smith, & Kleck, 1976).

Unlike its stronger version, the weaker version of the FFH has received a consensus of support (McIntosh, 1996). Facial management does moderate emotional experience, and human beings can intensify or reduce naturally occurring emotional experience by exaggerating or suppressing facial actions. These results are important because they highlight the two-way street between the emotions we feel and the emotions we express: Emotions activate facial expressions, and facial expressions, in turn, feed back to exaggerate and suppress the emotions we feel. Critics, however, contend that the contribution of such facial feedback is small (Matsumoto, 1987), and they argue that other factors are relatively more important.

VOLUNTARY AND INVOLUNTARY FACIAL EXPRESSIONS

Infants make woeful actors. Before the age of 2, human facial expressions are largely involuntary acts. When distressed, the infant's face reflects this inner state. As infants acquire language, undergo rapid cognitive development, and become increasingly social beings, they acquire an increasing ability to control facial expressions voluntarily. By the preschool years, children can mask (inhibit) most inner states. With increased cognitive and maturational development, children become increasingly capable of voluntarily controlling their facial musculature.

Is Facial Behavior Learned or Innate?

There are two major motor systems in the nervous system. The pyramidal system controls precise and voluntary control of localized movements, such as those muscular movements involved in the intentional, socially polite smile (Rinn, 1984; Weil, 1974). The nonpyramidal system regulates nonspecific and involuntary control of general muscle movements, including those facial behaviors under involuntary control such as the spontaneous smile. The significance of the distinction between the pyramidal and nonpyramidal systems is that it directly relates to the question of whether facial expressions are innate and automated or learned and modifiable.

Much facial behavior is surely learned. It is a rare individual who has not learned to express the polite smile and to inhibit the angry face while talking with the boss. But the fact that some facial behavior is learned (and therefore under voluntary control) does not rule out the possibility that facial behavior also has a genetic, innate component (as proposed by the proponents of the FFH).

A series of cross-cultural investigations tested the proposition that human beings display similar facial expressions regardless of cultural differences (Ekman, 1972, 1994b; Izard, 1994). In each of these studies, representatives from diverse nationalities looked at three photographs, each showing a different facial expression (Ekman, 1972, 1993; Ekman & Friesen, 1971; Ekman, Sorenson, & Friesen, 1969; Izard, 1971, 1980, 1994). From these photographs, participants chose, via a multiple-choice format, the photograph they thought best expressed a particular emotion. For example, participants were shown photographs of three faces, one expressing anger, one expressing joy, and one expressing fear. The participants selected the picture they thought showed what a face would look like when the person encountered an injustice or obstacle to a goal (i.e., anger). The research question is whether persons from different cultures agree on which facial expressions correspond with which emotional experiences. The finding that people from different cultures match the same facial expressions with the same emotions is evidence that facial behavior is cross-culturally universal, which is evidence that facial behavior has an innate, unlearned component (Ekman, 1994b; Ekman & Friesen, 1971; Izard, 1971).[3]

Take a look at the photographs shown in Figure 15.6 and test yourself as the participants in the cross-cultural experiments were tested. The photographs show four different expressions of a New Guinea native. Your task is to identify the face that just encountered a contaminated object (i.e., disgust).

Typically, the involuntary (nonpyramidal) and voluntary (pyramidal) motor systems work together to produce moment-to-moment facial expressions of emotion. Almost any facial expression is the product of both systems, though their contributions are rarely equal (Rinn, 1984). In unconstrained circumstances (when we are alone), facial expressions are relatively more automated, and emotional experience corresponds highly to expression. In

---

[3]Research with infants supports the idea that facial behavior has a strong innate component (Izard et al., 1980) because pre-socialized infants show distinct, identifiable facial expressions. Blind children, who lack opportunity to learn facial expressions from others through modeling and imitation, show the same recognizable facial expressions as do children of the same age who can see (Goodenough, 1932). Severely mentally handicapped children, who have difficulty learning new motor behaviors, also show full expressions of the emotions (Eibl-Eibesfeldt, 1971).

FIGURE 15.6 **Which Facial Expression Shows Disgust?**

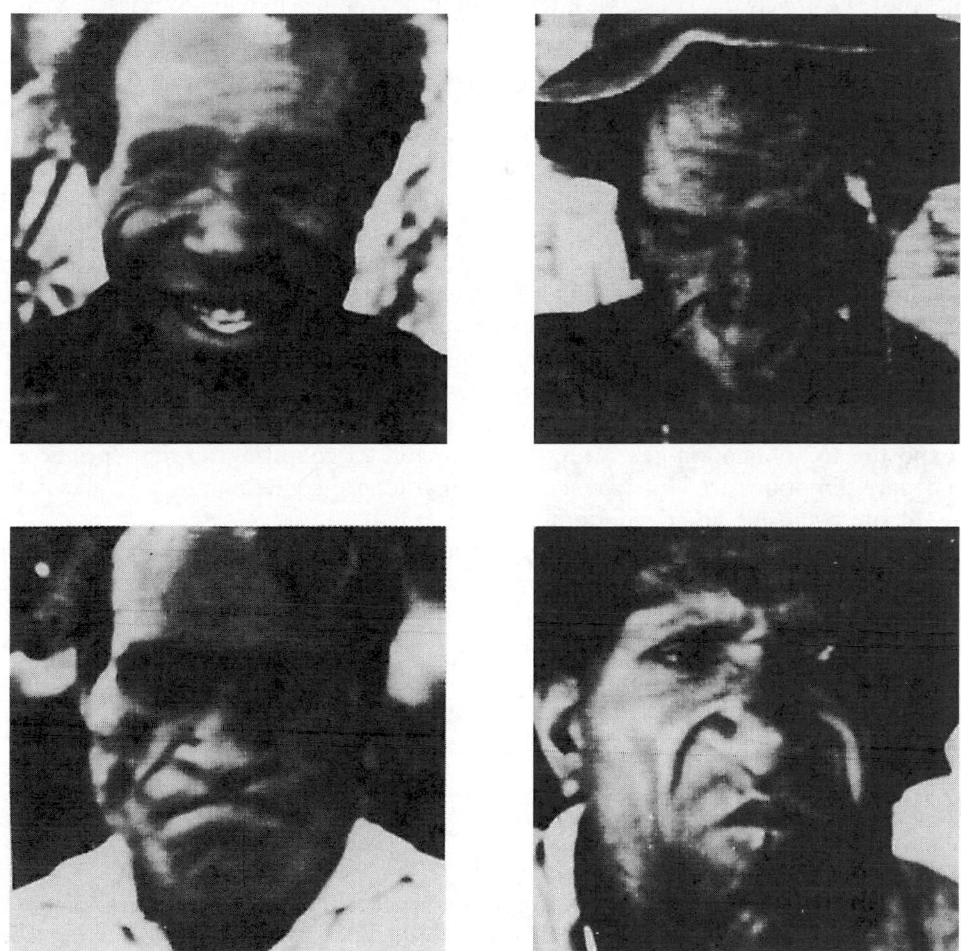

The photograph of the New Guinea native expressing disgust appears in the lower right corner. Clockwise from the bottom left are expressions of anger, joy, and distress.

SOURCE: From "Universal and Cultural Differences in Facial Expression of Emotion," by P. Ekman, 1972, in J. R. Cole (Ed.), *Nebraska Symposium on Motivation* (Vol. 19, pp. 207–283), Lincoln: University of Nebraska Press.

constrained circumstances (when we are in public), facial expressions are more managed, and emotional experience corresponds only roughly to expression. Hence, the pyramidal motor system typically dominates in social situations, whereas the nonpyramidal motor system typically dominates in nonsocial settings. But just because facial expressions can be produced by either voluntary or involuntary muscles does not mean they are interchangeable (Frank, Ekman, & Friesen, 1993). Spontaneous, joy-motivated smiles show a smoothness and more even duration than do intentional, socially motivated smiles. And observers can make distinctions between voluntary and involuntary expressions, as they rate spontaneous smiles more positively than they rate intentional smiles (Frank, Ekman, & Friesen, 1993).

CAN WE VOLUNTARILY CONTROL OUR EMOTIONS?

One intriguing question in emotion research asks, "Can we voluntarily control our emotions?" (Ekman & Davidson, 1994). The difficulty in providing a definitive answer emerges when you recall that emotions have four aspects: subjective, physiological, functional, and expressive. Emotion's multidimensional nature begs the question whether feelings, heart rate and physiological states, motivational desires, and facial expressions are controllable. In trying to answer the more general question, however, some emotions plainly just happen to us, and we therefore cannot be held responsible for the involuntary feelings, physiology, desires, and behaviors that ensue (Ekman, 1992, 1994a).[4] We all have difficulty conjuring up some emotions at will—courage, love, optimism, interest, and so on. It is very difficult to just say that you are now going to feel joy. Instead, you need an exposure to an emotion-generating event capable of conjuring up that specific emotional state. Emotions are largely reactions, and you need something to react to involuntarily before conjuring up an emotion.

If emotions are largely biological phenomena that are governed by subcortical structures and pathways, then it makes sense that much of an emotion will escape our voluntary control. If, however, emotions are largely cognitive phenomena that are governed by thoughts, beliefs, and ways of thinking, it makes sense that a good deal of emotional experience can be voluntarily controlled, at least to the point that we can voluntarily control our thoughts, beliefs, and ways of thinking.

COGNITIVE ASPECTS OF EMOTION

For those who study emotion from a cognitive, social, or cultural point of view, biological events are not necessarily the most important aspects of emotion. Emotions do emerge from biological processes, but emotions also emerge from information processing, social interaction, and cultural contexts. For instance, a purely biological analysis with a spotlight on subcortical brain circuits, autonomic and endocrine system activity, and facial expressions does not give one an understanding of emotions such as hope, pride, and alienation. "Disappointment" stems not from ANS activity or changes in facial expressions but, instead, from a cognitive understanding of not having what you hoped you would have (van Dijk, Zeelengerb, & van der Pligt, 1999). The second half of this chap-

---

[4] Daily experience confirms that we can voluntarily regulate emotions once they happen to us, at least to some extent. Intentionally, we mask and hide our fear before sky diving, and we suppress our boredom while listening to another person's conversation. Because we can regulate our emotions, through inhibition mostly (Levenson, 1994a), we are therefore somewhat responsible for our emotionality (e.g., how angry or sad we get and how long we stay that way). Therefore, the initial onset of an emotion is what is so difficult to control. But our capacity for emotional regulation allows us control over the intensity of the rise and fall of our emotions once they happen to us (Ekman, 1992; Levenson, 1994a).

ter begins with a cognitive analysis of emotion and concludes with a discussion of how social interaction and culture influence emotion.

APPRAISAL

The central construct in a cognitive understanding of emotion is appraisal (Frijda, 1993; Smith et al., 1993).[5] All cognitive emotion theorists endorse two interrelated beliefs (Frijda, 1986; Lazarus, 1991a; Ortony, Clore, & Collins, 1988; Roseman, 1984; Scherer, 1984a; Smith & Ellsworth, 1985; Weiner, 1986):

1. Emotions do not occur without an antecedent appraisal (cognition) of the life event.
2. The appraisal, not the life event itself, causes the emotion.

Consider a child who sees a man approaching. Immediately and automatically, the child appraises the meaning of the man's approach as probably good or probably bad. The appraisal is based on the salient characteristics of the man approaching (gender, facial expression, pace of approach), expectations of who might be approaching, beliefs of what approaching people typically do, and memories of people approaching in the past. It is not the approaching man per se that explains the quality of the child's emotional reaction, but rather, it is how the child thinks the approaching man will affect her well-being that gives life to her emotion. If she sees the approaching man smiling and waving and if she remembers the man as being her friend, then she will likely appraise the event as a good one. If she sees the approaching man ranting and raving and if she remembers the man as being the neighborhood bully, then she will likely appraise the event as a bad one. These appraisals cause her to experience emotion (and physiological bodily changes as well). If the child did not appraise the personal relevance of the approaching man, she would not have had an emotional reaction to the man because events that are irrelevant to well-being do not generate emotions (Lazarus, 1991a; Ortony & Clore, 1989; Ortony, Clore, & Collins, 1988).

Basically, the appraisal, and not the situation itself, determines the quality of the emotional experience. To reinforce this idea, consider the counterintuitive finding that Olympic bronze medalists experience more post-competition happiness than do Olympic silver medalists, a phenomenon that shows that the athlete's appraisal of what might have been is at least as important as what situation actually took place (e.g., "I could have won the gold" versus "I could have come up empty"; Medvec, Madey, & Gilovich, 1995). The same sort of cognitive construal also works in emotions such as shame ("If only I weren't . . .") and guilt ("If only I hadn't . . ."; Niedenthal, Tangney, & Gavanski, 1994). Emotions follow appraisals. Change the appraisal, and you change the emotion.

One of the earliest appraisal theorists was Magda Arnold (1960, 1970). She specified how cognition, neurophysiology, and arousal work together to produce the experience and expression of emotion by focusing on three questions: (1) How does the perception of an object or event produce a good or bad appraisal; (2) how does the appraisal generate emotion; and (3) how does felt emotion express itself in action?

---

[5] An appraisal is an estimate of the value or significance of something. Thus, enviromental objects are appraised as significant or not and as valuable or not, and these appraisals activate the emotion process.

From Perception to Appraisal

According to Arnold, people categorically appraise stimulus events and objects as positive or negative. To substantiate her ideas, Arnold paid particularly close detail to the neurological pathways in the brain. In all encounters with the environment, limbic system brain structures (the amygdala) automatically appraise the hedonic tone of sensory information. For instance, a harsh sound instantaneously is appraised as intrinsically unpleasant (bad), while the smell of a rose is appraised as intrinsically pleasant (good). Recent neuroanatomical research confirms Arnold's claim that the limbic system (and amygdala in particular) is the focal brain center that appraises the emotional significance of sensory stimuli (LeDoux, 1992a, 1992b). In addition, most stimuli are further appraised cortically by adding information processing and hence expectations, memories, beliefs, goals, judgments, and attributions. Full appraisal therefore draws on both subcortical (limbic system) and cortical interpretations and evaluations.

From Appraisal to Emotion

Once an object has been appraised as good or bad (as beneficial or harmful), an experience of liking or disliking follows immediately and automatically. For Arnold, the liking or disliking is the felt emotion.

From Felt Emotion to Action

Liking generates a motivational tendency to approach the emotion-generating object; disliking generates a motivational tendency to avoid it. During appraisal, the individual relies on memory and imagination to generate a number of possible courses of action in dealing with the liked or disliked object. When a particular course of action is decided upon, the hippocampal brain circuit activates the motor cortex, which leads to behavioral action. Contemporary research adds that the limbic system also has direct access to the muscles that control facial expressions (Holstedge, Kuypers, & Dekker, 1977), autonomic and endocrine system reactions (Kapp, Pascoe, & Bixler, 1984; LeDoux et al., 1988), and general arousal systems (brain stem; Krettek & Price, 1978). Through its effects on these biological systems, emotions produce action.[6]

PRIMARY AND SECONDARY APPRAISALS

Like Arnold, Richard Lazarus emphasized the cognitive processes that intervene between environmental conditions and behavioral and physiological reactivity. While following Arnold's ideas as a road map, he supplemented her general good/bad appraisal with a

---

[6] One important feature of Arnold's theory is that emotion is defined in terms of motivation. The tendency to approach or avoid gives the emotion a directional force, while the physiological changes in the muscles and viscera give emotion its energy. A second important feature of Arnold's theory treats emotion as a unitary construct, as she preferred to talk about emotion forces of approach and avoidance, of attraction and repulsion, and of liking and disliking more than she did of specific emotions such as anger, sadness, or pride.

more complex conceptualization of the appraisal process (Lazarus, 1968, 1991a; Lazarus & Folkman, 1984). In articulating a more comprehensive view of appraisal, Lazarus pointed out that people evaluate whether the situation they face has personal relevance for their well-being. When well-being is at stake, people then evaluate the potential harm, threat, or benefit they face. For Lazarus (1991a), appraisals take the form of questions such as the following: Is this situation relevant to my well-being? If relevant, is this situation congruent or incongruent with the goals I seek? How deeply does this event touch my self-esteem? Given these appraisals of relevance, goal congruence, and ego involvement, people appraise situations as particular kinds of harm, as particular kinds of threat, or as particular kinds of benefit (see Table 15.2; Lazarus, 1991a, 1994).

The appraisal process does not end with an assessment of personal relevance. Perceived coping abilities continue to alter how people interpret (appraise) the situations they face (Folkman & Lazarus, 1990; Lazarus, 1991a, 1991b). For instance, once insulted and thus potentially harmed, people cope by (1) taking action to change the harmful relationship, (2) denying its importance (psychological avoidance), or (3) changing the appraisal itself (e.g., "That comment is not really harmful; actually, it's beneficial because I can learn from it"). Thus, coping changes the way a situation is appraised, and a changed appraisal leads to a changed emotion. Overall, then, people first appraise their

Table 15.2 **Types of Primary Appraisal and Related Emotions**

Primary appraisal category	Emotion
Type of Harm:	
Being demeaned by a personal offense	Anger
Transgressing against a moral imperative	Guilt
Failing to live up to an ego ideal	Shame
Experiencing an irrevocable loss	Sadness
Taking in or being too close to an indigestible object or idea	Disgust
Type of Threat:	
Facing an uncertain, nonspecific threat	Anxiety
Facing immediate overwhelming physical danger	Fright
Wanting what someone else has	Envy
Resenting a rival	Jealousy
Type of Benefit:	
Making progress toward a goal	Happiness
Taking credit for an achievement	Pride
Improving a distressing condition	Relief
Feeling confident of a desired outcome	Hope
Sharing affection	Love
Being moved by another person's suffering and wanting to help	Compassion

Source: From *Emotion and Adaptation,* by R. S. Lazarus, 1991, New York: Oxford University Press. Adapted with permission.

relationship to the situation ("primary appraisal") and then they appraise their coping potential within that situation ("secondary appraisal").

Primary Appraisal

Primary appraisal involves an estimate of whether one has anything at stake in the encounter (Folkman et al., 1986). The following are potentially at stake in primary appraisal: (1) physical well-being, (2) self-esteem, (3) a goal, (4) financial state, (5) respect for another person, and (6) well-being of a loved one. In other words, primary appraisals ask whether one's physical or psychological well-being, goals and financial status, or interpersonal relationships are at stake during this particular encounter with the environment. For instance, when driving a car and it swerves on the ice, the cognitive system immediately generates the primary appraisal that much is now at stake—personal health, reputation as a skillful driver, getting to work on time, a valuable possession (the car), and the physical and psychological well-being of one's passenger. Not all primary appraisals involve such high stakes, but the example communicates the essence of primary appraisal. Also, in some encounters, nothing related to well-being is at stake (e.g., hearing today's weather forecast for Sydney, Australia; participating in an athletic contest after the championship has been ensured). Events appraised as irrelevant do not cause emotions.

Secondary Appraisal

Secondary appraisal, which occurs after some reflection, involves the person's assessment for coping with the emotion-generating event (Folkman & Lazarus, 1990). Coping involves the person's cognitive, emotional, and behavioral efforts to manage specific external and internal demands. Personal abilities, skills, and strategies are the resources that enable a person to affect a change in the environment or to manage their emotional, cognitive, and physiological reactions to that change. For instance, imagine the coping options for a musician scheduled to perform for an audience. The musician might solicit advice from a friend, practice throughout the night, withdraw and escape, make a plan of action and follow through, copy another musician's style, joke and make light of the event's significance, and so forth. Whichever way of coping seems most adaptive for that situation will likely be used.

Appraisal Model of Emotion

Lazarus' emotion model appears in Figure 15.7. Given an encounter with the environment, the individual first makes a primary appraisal pertaining to its personal significance and meaning in terms of physical, psychological, or social well-being. Personally significant events are evaluated either as a threat, harm, or benefit, which causes autonomic nervous system (ANS) discharge in the form of sympathetic activation, as the individual prepares to adapt to the stimulus (Tomaka et al., 1993). Sympathetic activation, in turn, activates secondary appraisal. Secondary appraisals produce voluntary coping responses. If the coping responses are successful, the emotion-generating event loses its status as a potential threat or harm. If coping responses are unsuccessful, the ANS activation continues until

FIGURE 15.7 Lazarus' Conceptualization of Emotion as a Process

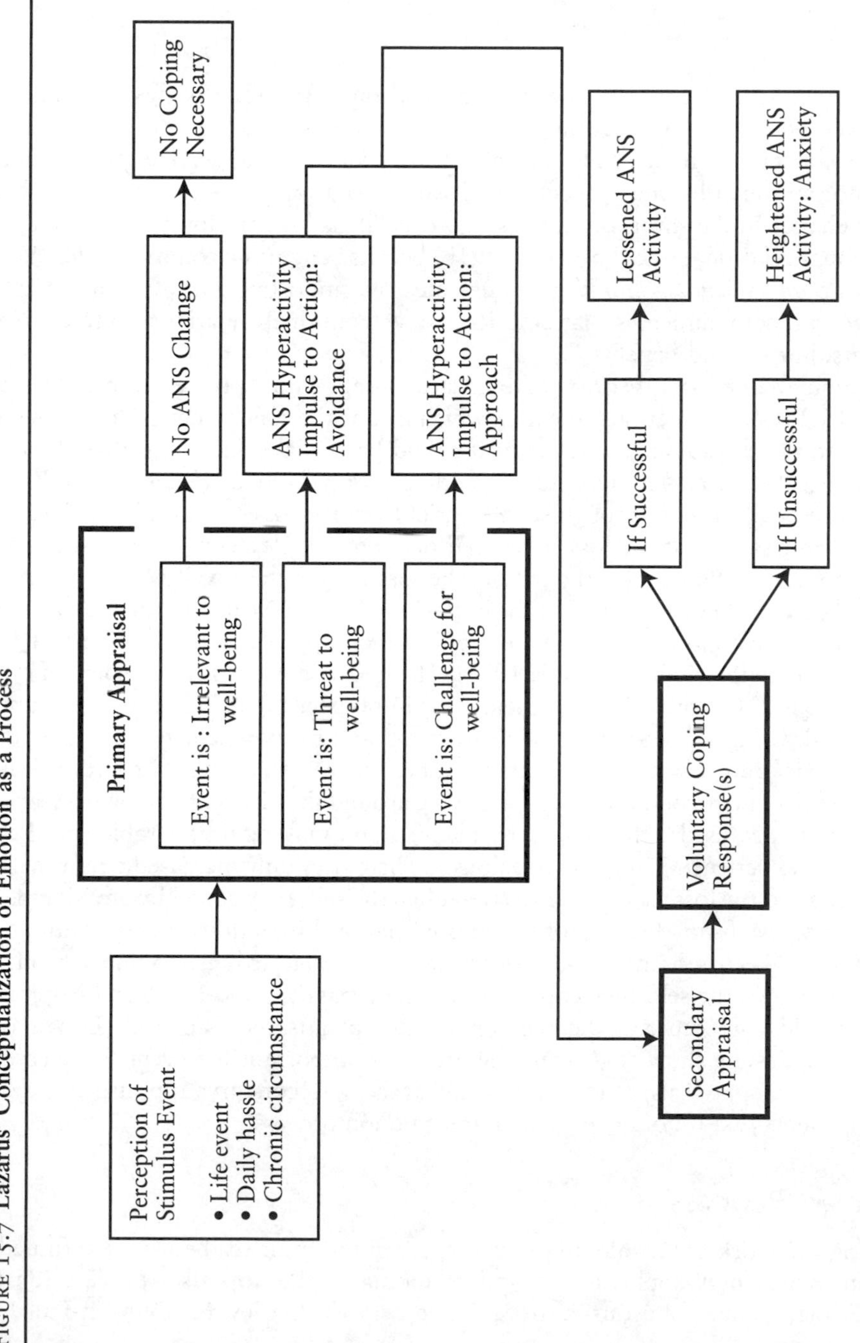

either the emotion-generating event goes away, coping is successful, or the ANS fails from exhaustion.

Motivation

Lazarus' portrayal of emotion is a motivational one. A person brings personal motives (goals, well-being) into a situation. When motives are at stake, emotions follow. Further, emotions constantly change as appraisals of the situation change. The process is characterized not so much by the sequence of situation → appraisal → emotion as it is by the ongoing change in the status of motives. Lazarus labels his emotion theory as a cognitive-motivational-relational one (Lazarus, 1991b) because *cognitive* communicates the importance of appraisal, *motivational* communicates the importance of goals and well-being, and *relational* communicates that emotions arise from one's relationship to environmental threats, harms, and benefits.

A synonym appraisal theorists (like Lazarus) use for the "primary appraisal category" in Table 15.2 is "core relational theme," which means the fundamental ("core") ways people relate to the threatening, harm-inducing, and beneficial elements of their environment (Lazarus, 1991a, 1991b). The virtue of adding core relational themes to understanding emotion can be illustrated through sadness-grief from the loss of a loved one. Everyone experiences sadness-grief at the loss of a loved one, but people's core relational themes—the primary appraisals they make about how the loss affects their well-being—determine the emotional course of events following the initial loss. For two years, one group of researchers followed adults who lost a loved one to monitor their appraisals and well-being from their loss (Bonanno, Mihalecz, & LeJeune, 1999). The meaning of the loss for some of the adults revolved around the core relational theme (CRT) of "sharing affection." They coped with the loss by drawing strength from the relationship and by experiencing love. Months later, both their grief and somatic complaints (e.g., headaches, sleeplessness) decreased. Another group of adults understood the loss as revolving around the CRTs of "being demeaned" and "resenting the deceased"; they coped by blaming and making unfavorable social comparisons and by experiencing anger and jealously. Their grief only increased over time. A third group appraised the loss as a trigger to strengthen the self; they coped by envisioning a safer and more positive future because of their prior relationship with the deceased and by experiencing relief. Their grief decreased over time. Finally, a fourth group understood the loss as a weakening of the self; they coped by becoming passive, uncertain, and helpless. Their grief increased over time, as did the somatic complaints they suffered (Bonanno et al., 1999). These results show that while the loss is an important life event for everyone, the CRT (primary appraisals) and coping effectiveness (secondary appraisals) explain the course of events that unfold over time in the emotion process.

APPRAISAL PROCESS

Following the work of Arnold and Lazarus, cognition-minded theorists continued to develop an increasingly sophisticated understanding of the appraisal process (de Rivera, 1977; Frijda, 1986; Johnson-Laird & Oatley, 1989; Oatley & Johnson-Laird, 1987;

Ortony, Clore, & Collins, 1988; Roseman, 1984, 1991; Scherer, 1984, 1997; Smith & Ellsworth, 1985; Weiner, 1986). Each theorist embraces the stimulus event → appraisal → emotion sequence, but they differ on how many dimensions of appraisal are necessary for explaining emotional experience. Arnold used appraisal to explain two emotions (like and dislike), Lazarus' primary and secondary appraisals explain approximately 15 emotions (see Table 15.2), yet cognitive emotion theorists ultimately seek to explain all emotions. These theorists believe each emotion can be described by a unique pattern of appraisal. That is, if one knew the full pattern of the person's appraisals, then it would be a rather straightforward task in predicting one's ensuing, specific emotion.

To explain the full complexity of emotions, theorists have argued for the importance of additional dimensions of appraisal. One such list begins with goal significance and coping potential (Lazarus' primary and secondary appraisals) but also adds appraisals of the stimulus event's unexpectedness, intrinsic pleasantness, and compatibility with internalized standards (Scherer, 1997). Another such list features certainty, anticipated effort to goal, attention, pleasantness, and legitimacy (Smith & Ellsworth, 1985). It is difficult to say how many dimensions of appraisal exist or which appraisals are most fundamental and which are of only a peripheral importance. The following list of appraisals, however, represents the thinking of most cognition-minded emotion theorists (these dimensions are a combination of those proposed by Roseman, 1984, 1991; Smith & Ellsworth, 1985; Scherer, 1984a, 1997):

Pleasantness	Is the event good or bad?
Relevance	Is well-being of self or others at stake?
Coping ability	Can I cope successfully with the situation?
Anticipated effort	How much coping effort will be needed?
Responsibility	Who caused the event—self, others, or circumstances?
Compatibility with self/society's standards	Is this event okay on a moral level?
Expectancy	Did I expect this event to happen?
Legitimacy	Is what happened fair or deserved?

Consider how a combination of several different appraisals can produce one specific emotion. Anger, for instance, is a combination of the following four appraisals: (1) A valued goal is at stake (relevance); (2) the goal was lost (pleasantness); (3) someone blocked my goal attainment (responsibility); and (4) the loss was undeserved (legitimacy). Any event that leads to the appraisals of high relevance, coping potential, expectancy, pleasantness, and compatibility with standards produces "sentimentality." Change one appraisal, and the experienced emotion will also change. That is, change coping ability from high to low (while keeping the other four appraisals constant) and "sentimentality" changes to "longing."

Perhaps the ultimate goal of the appraisal emotion theorists is now apparent. They are hard at work to construct a decision tree in which all possible patterns of appraisal lead to a single emotion (Scherer, 1993, 1997). That is, if the person makes appraisals X, Y, and Z, then emotion A must surely and inevitably follow.

Emotion Differentiation

The strong suit of an appraisal theory of emotion is its ability to explain emotion differentiation processes (e.g., how people experience different emotions to the same event). For instance, Figure 15.8 depicts how any pattern among 6 appraisal dimensions can differentiate among 17 different emotions (Roseman, Antoniou, & Jose, 1996). The appraisal dimensions are shown on the border of the figure, while the differentiated emotions appear in the boxes inside the figure. The appraisal dimensions on the left side of the figure are responsibility (circumstance-caused, other-caused, self-caused), expectancy (unexpected), and certainty (uncertain, certain). The appraisal dimensions on the top of the figure are goal/need at stake (motive-consistent, motive-inconsistent) and pleasantness (appetitive, aversive). The appraisal dimension on the right side of the figure is coping ability (low versus high control potential). And the appraisal dimension on the bottom of the figure is source of problem (noncharacterological, characterological).

FIGURE 15.8 **Appraisal Theory of Emotion to Differentiate Among 17 Different Emotions**

	Positive Emotions Motive-Consistent		Negative Emotions Motive-Inconsistent		
	Appetitive	Aversive	Appetitive	Aversive	
Circumstance-Caused Unexpected	Surprise				
Uncertain	Hope		Fear		Low Control Potential
Certain	Joy	Relief	Sadness	Distress	
Uncertain	Hope		Frustration	Disgust	High Control Potential
Certain	Joy	Relief			
Other-Caused Uncertain	Liking		Dislike		Low Control Potential
Certain					
Uncertain			Anger	Contempt	High Control Potential
Certain					
Self-Caused Uncertain	Pride		Regret		Low Control Potential
Certain					
Uncertain			Guilt	Shame	High Control Potential
Certain					
			Noncharacterological	Characterological	

SOURCE: From "Appraisal Determinants of Emotions: Constructing a More Accurate and Comprehensive Theory," by I. J. Roseman, A. A. Antoniou, and P. E. Jose, 1996, *Cognition and Emotion, 10,* pp. 241–277.

Some emotions require knowing only two appraisals to predict their activation. Surprise, for instance, arises from appraisals of expectancy and responsibility (i.e., an unexpected, circumstance-caused event). Other emotions, however, involve several appraisal dimensions to differentiate them. Sadness, for instance, involves the five dimensions of goal/need at stake, pleasantness, responsibility, certainty, and coping ability (e.g., sadness arises from being denied a pleasant [appetitive] event with certainty and knowing that circumstances caused the event and that one can do little about [low control potential]).

An appraisal decision tree such as the one depicted in Figure 15.8 will never predict ensuing emotions correctly 100% of the time (Oatley & Duncan, 1994). Appraisal theorists generally agree that knowing a person's particular configuration of appraisal allows them about a 65 to 70% accuracy level in predicting people's emotions (Reisenzein & Hofmann, 1993). Four reasons explain why appraisal theory cannot explain emotional reactions with 100% accuracy (Fischer et al., 1990; Reisenzein & Hofmann, 1993; Scherer, 1997):

1. Processes other than appraisal contribute to emotion (as discussed in the first half of this chapter).
2. While each specific emotion has a unique pattern of appraisals associated with it, the patterns of appraisals for many emotions overlap and create some confusion (e.g., guilt and shame, like anger and disgust, have very similar patterns of appraisal).
3. Developmental differences exist among people such that children generally experience basic, general emotions (e.g., joy), whereas socialized adults generally experience a richer variety of appraisal-specific emotions (e.g., pride, relief, gratitude).
4. Emotion knowledge and attributions (the next two topics in this chapter) represent additional cognitive factors beyond appraisal that affect emotion.

This fourth point recognizes that cognition (appraisal) precedes emotion, but it adds that cognition also follows emotion. Emotions cause changes in cognition, such as attributions, coping, self-monitoring, and the retrieval of memories. As these new cognitive elements are added to the experience, emotion results from an accumulation of not only appraisal but these additional cognitive elements as well (Frijda, 1993).

Emotion Knowledge

Infants and young children understand and distinguish between only a few basic emotions. They learn to name the few basic emotions of anger, fear, sadness, joy, and love (Kemper, 1987; Shaver et al., 1987). As people gain experience with different situations, they learn to discriminate shades within the same emotion. The shades of joy, for instance, include happiness, relief, optimism, pride, contentment, and gratitude (Ellsworth & Smith, 1988b). The shades of anger include fury, hostility, vengefulness, rage, aggravation, and wrath (Russell & Fehr, 1994). These distinctions are stored cognitively in hierarchies of basic emotions and their derivatives. Thus, the number of different emotions any one person can distinguish constitutes her *emotion knowledge* (Shaver et al., 1987). Through experience, we construct a mental representation of the different emotions and how each relates to other emotions and to the situations that produce them.

One person's hypothetical (computer-generated) emotion knowledge appears in Figure 15.9. One level includes basic emotion categories of love, joy, surprise, anger, sadness, and fear. With experience, the individual learns shades of these basic emotions (listed on the lower part of the figure). For instance, the individual depicted in the figure understands three shades of love—affection, lust, and longing—and six shades of sadness—suffering, depression, disappointment, shame, neglect, and sympathy. The asterisk in each column of emotion words denotes the prototype within the shades of that emotion.

Much of the diversity of emotion experience comes from learning fine distinctions among emotions and the specific situations that cause them. Appraisal theorists believe that there are as many emotions as there are cognitive appraisal possibilities of a situation (Ellsworth & Smith, 1988a; Smith & Ellsworth, 1985, 1987). For example, an individual who has just lost out to a rival might potentially experience distress, anger, fear, disgust, and jealousy (Hupka, 1984). One learns that these emotions can coincide and are therefore related to one another (as in the jealousy complex; Hupka, 1984; White, 1981). One also learns that other emotions (e.g., love, joy) are far removed from this cluster of emotional experience. Finally, one learns the differences between shades of anger—the differences among jealousy, hate, irritation, and so on. Eventually, such learning produces a highly personal emotion knowledge, which enables the individual to appraise situations with high discrimination and therefore to respond with situationally appropriate emotions (rather than with general ones).

Knowledge in the more general sense is also important to emotional experience (Clore, 1994). We use our knowledge of the world to endow events with positive or negative values (primary appraisal). We also use our knowledge of the world to predict the probable effects of our coping efforts (secondary appraisal). While driving in traffic and the snow starts falling, for instance, our knowledge of having new tires and four-wheel drive allows us to ward off the thought of potential harm so that we can consider the snow's potential benefits (scenery, skiing). Without new tires or four-wheel drive, our knowledge of the difficulty of driving on the curvy road, how poorly we have driven in snow in the past, and how serious an accident can be can further affect our emotions. Knowledge, in fact, plays such an intricate role in practically all our environmental interactions that some researchers conceptualize emotions themselves as mental states (Clore, 1994; Clore, Ortony, & Foss, 1987; Sabini & Silver, 1987).

ATTRIBUTIONS

Appraisal theorists begin their analysis with relatively simple appraisals, such as whether an event signifies harm, threat, or danger (Lazarus, 1991a). They continue with progressively more complex appraisals (Ellsworth & Smith, 1988a) and then add emotion knowledge to explain how people make fine-tuned appraisals. In his attributional analysis, Bernard Weiner (1982, 1986) adds yet one more type of appraisal to help explain emotional processes. People make appraisals not only before (primary) and during (secondary) their interactions with the event, but people also make appraisals following an event's outcome. In other words, people evaluate why they experienced harm, a threat, or a benefit. This post-outcome appraisal is termed an attribution (see chapter 9).

FIGURE 15.9 Hypothetical Representation of One Person's Emotion Knowledge

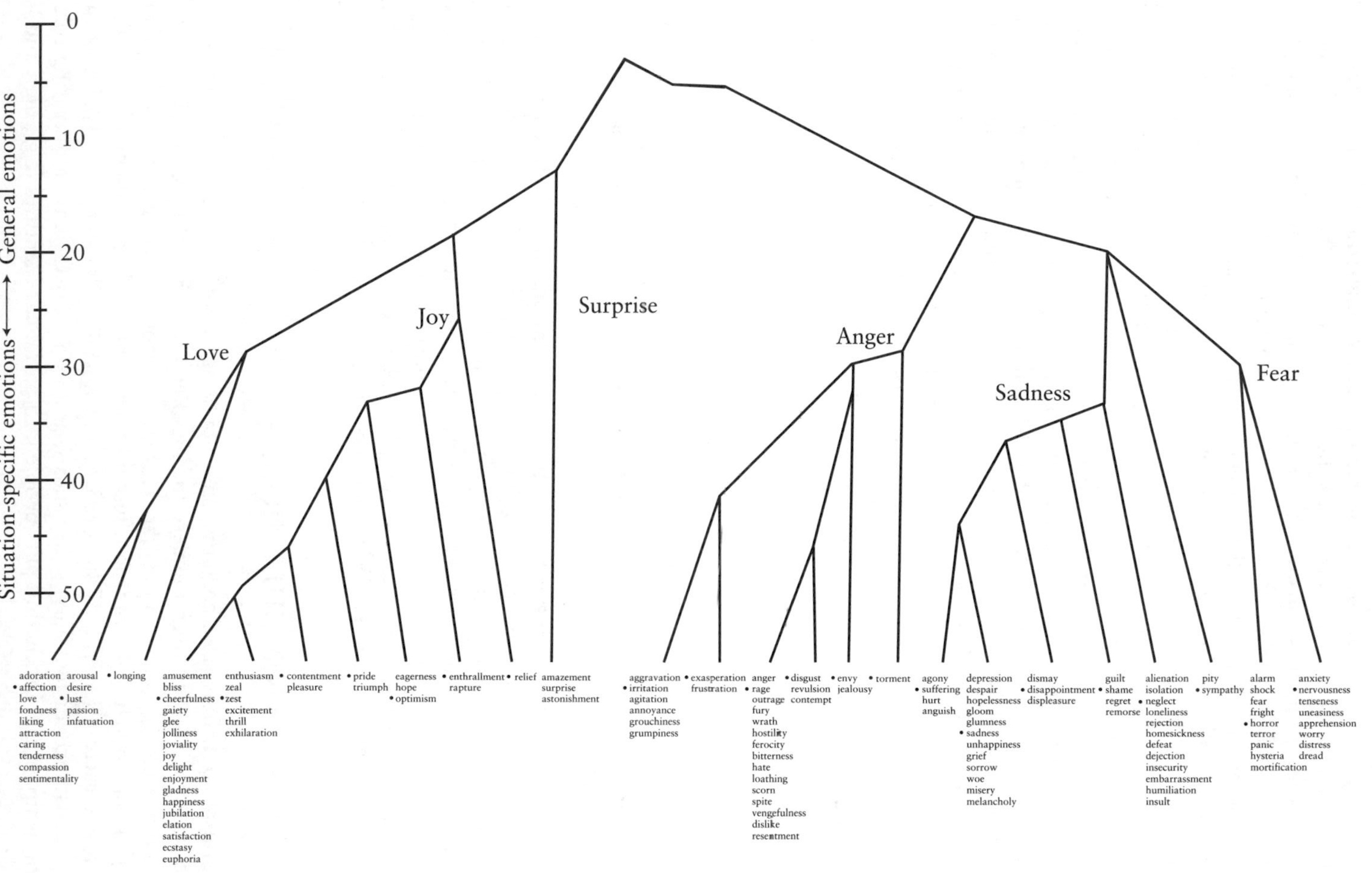

SOURCE: From "Emotion knowledge: Further exploration of a prototype approach," by P. Shaver, J. Schwartz, D. Kirson, and C. O'Connor, 1987, *Journal of Personality and Social Psychology, 52*, pp. 1061-1086. Copyright © 1987 by American Psychological Association. Adapted with permission.

According to attribution theory, the emotion-generating sequence within appraisal is the following: situation → outcome → attribution → emotion (Weiner, 1985, 1986). The attribution to explain why an outcome occurred is the cognitive mechanism (the appraisal) that produces emotion. Hence, after winning a contest and attributing the victory to talent and ability, the individual experiences pride. If the attribution for winning was different, the emotion following the victory would also be different. If the victory was attributed to help from a teammate, for instance, the emotion would be gratitude, not pride. The strength of adding attribution theory to a cognitive understanding of emotion is that it points out that people can experience different emotions in response to the same situation, even to the same outcome in that situation. It is the attribution (the cognitive event), rather than the situation or its outcome, that causes the specific emotion. As discussed in chapter 9, the attributional dimensions of locus, stability, and controllability explain the emotional experiences of pride, gratitude, hope, anger, pity, shame, and guilt (see Figure 9.1; Weiner, 1985, 1986; Weiner & Graham, 1989). The limitation of attribution theory is that while it explains some post-outcome emotions well (e.g., anger, guilt), it remains necessary to add pre-outcome appraisals (e.g., those in Table 15.2) to fully explain and predict the emotions people experience (Leon & Hernandez, 1998).

Disappointment and regret illustrate attribution-generated emotional processes (van Dijk, van der Pligt, & Zeelenberg, 1999). Disappointment and regret arise when we invest effort in vain. Suppose you experienced something similar to the following (from van Dijk, van der Pligt, and Zeelenberg, 1999):

> Friday Susan has a date with a man she really likes. They would meet in a good restaurant, where they would have dinner. After dinner they planned to go somewhere else for a drink. (Susan bought something new to wear and she even went to the hairdresser.) On Friday evening Susan gets a phone call from her date that he has to cancel the date because he has fallen ill. How would Susan feel?

The researchers included the parenthetical phrase (about the new purchase and hairdresser visit) in the experimental condition, and they excluded it in the control group. Hence, Susan either did or did not invest effort in vain. Investing effort in vain intensified the severity of both disappointment and regret. Investing effort does typically make desired outcomes more likely (and, hence, keep emotions like disappointment, regret, shame, and guilt at bay). But this effort also has the disadvantage of intensifying disappointment and regret when the desired outcome does not materialize.

SOCIAL AND CULTURAL ASPECTS OF EMOTION

As appraisal contributes to a cognitive understanding of emotion, social interaction contributes to a social and cultural understanding of emotion. Social psychologists, sociologists, anthropologists, and others argue that emotion is not necessarily a private, biological, intrapsychic phenomenon. Instead, they contend that most emotions originate in social interaction (Averill, 1980, 1983; Kemper, 1987; Manstead, 1991). Embarrassment, for instance, displays low social status, and sympathy displays a nurturing role in a relationship. Social interaction puts people into particular identities (e.g., high and low status), and it is within the context of social interaction that events such as exchange, reciprocity, and equity stir people to emotion.

Those who study the social construction of emotion point out that if you changed the situation you were in, then your emotions would also change. Think about the typical emotions experienced at a playground, at work, at a weekend party, at the theater, at a sporting event, cleaning the bathroom, attending a church or synagogue, during a fist-fight, and so on. Situations define what emotions are most appropriate and expected, and because people know which emotions are likely to occur in which settings, they can select a setting and therefore "construct" a particular emotional experience. If you want to construct joy, for example, you go to a weekend party; if you want to construct disgust, you clean the bathroom. Also, think about the typical emotions experienced while interacting with someone with superior status (boss, parent), with someone of equal status (friend, spouse), or with someone of inferior status (child, new employee). Status differences between interactants define what emotions are appropriate and expected, and because people know which emotions go with which interactants, they can select interaction partners and therefore "construct" a particular emotional experience.

SOCIAL INTERACTION

Other people are typically our most frequent source of day-to-day emotion (Oatley & Duncan, 1994). We experience more frequent emotions when interacting with others than when we are alone.

Other people not only cause emotions to stir in us, but they also affect us indirectly, as through *emotional contagion*, which is "the tendency to automatically mimic and synchronize expressions, vocalizations, postures, and movements with those of another person and, consequently, to converge emotionally" (Hatfield, Cacioppo, & Rapson, 1993a). The three propositions of mimicry, feedback, and contagion explain how the emotions of others create emotions in us through social interaction (Hatfield, Cacioppo, & Rapson, 1993b):

MIMICRY: "In conversation, people automatically and continuously mimic and synchronize their movements with the facial expressions, voices, postures, movements, and instrumental behaviors of other people."

FEEDBACK: "Subjective emotional experience is affected, moment to moment, by the activation of and feedback from facial, vocal, postural, and movement mimicry."

CONTAGION: "Consequently, people tend, from moment to moment, to 'catch' other people's emotions."

As we are exposed to the emotional expressions of others, we tend to mimic their facial expressions (Dimberg, 1982; Strayer, 1993), speech style (Hatfield et al., 1995), and posture (Bernieri & Rosenthal, 1991). Once mimicry occurs, the facial feedback hypothesis illustrates how mimicry (of not only the face, but also voice and posture) can affect the observer's emotional experience, and hence lead to a contagion effect.

During social interaction, we not only expose ourselves to emotional contagion effects, but we also put ourselves into a conversational context that provides an opportunity to re-experience and relive past emotional experiences, a process referred to as "the social sharing of emotion" (Rimé et al., 1991). Social sharing of emotional conversations usually take place later in the day and when in the company of intimates (close friend, love partner, teammates). When people share their emotions, they typically do so by sharing the full account of what happened, what it meant, and how the person felt throughout (Rimé et al., 1991). It is in these times of sharing our emotions that we build and maintain the relationships that are central to our lives (Edwards, Manstead & McDonald, 1984), such as marital relationships (Noller, 1984). And social sharing of emotion pays off. An empathic other person can offer support or assistance, divert attention, provide tips about impression management, strengthen coping responses, help make sense of the emotional experience, and reconfirm the self-concept (Lehman, Ellard, & Wortman, 1986; Thoits, 1984).

EMOTIONAL SOCIALIZATION

Emotional socialization occurs as adults tell children what they ought to know about emotion. Emotional socialization occurs among adults as well, but the process is best illustrated when adults interact with children for the explicit purpose of teaching socialization to the children (Pollak & Thoits, 1989). Adults show disgust facial expressions to sanction children's misbehavior (Rozin, Haidt, & McCauley, 1999), and adults tell children about the situations that cause emotions, about how emotion expresses itself, and about emotion words or labels. In turn, children learn that a basic emotion can be differentiated into specific emotions (emotion knowledge; Shaver et al., 1987), that certain expressive displays can and should be controlled (expression management; Saarni, 1979), and that negative emotions can be manipulated deliberately into neutral or positive emotions (emotion control; McCoy & Masters, 1985).

Consider the socialization that occurs in settings such as daycare centers, preschools, and elementary schools (Denham et al., 1997; Pollak & Thoits, 1989). During an emotional episode of a child, a caretaker or teacher might explain the child's feelings, point out the causes of an emotion, and instruct the child about which expressive displays are most and least appropriate. Consider an example of emotion knowledge—how adults tell children about the causes of emotion (Pollak & Thoits, 1989):

GIRL (SEVERAL TIMES): *My mom is late.*
STAFF MEMBER: Does that make you *mad*?
GIRL: Yes.
STAFF MEMBER: Sometimes kids get *mad* when their *moms are late to pick them up.*

Consider an example of expression management—how adults tell children to express their emotions (Pollak & Thoits, 1989):

STAFF MEMBER, WHILE HOLDING A KICKING, SCREAMING BOY IN TIME-OUT: Robert, I see you're *very angry.*

Consider an example of emotion control—how adults teach children to control their emotional displays (Pollak & Thoits, 1989):

During circle, Alec tried to climb all over John, a volunteer.

JOHN: If you want *to be close,* there are some things you could do. . . . You could *sit next to me and we could hold hands,* or I could put my arm around you, or *you could sit on my lap.*

Societies clearly socialize their members' emotional experiences and expressions. Still, limits exist as to how much a culture can socialize particular emotions into its constituents. Consider the claim that in some cultures people exchange romantic partners without jealousy. Evolution- and biology-minded theorists argue that sharing a sexual partner would surely produce jealously, and appraisal theorists might make a similar argument (see Table 15.2). But can people be socialized not to feel jealous? The short answer is, basically, no (Reis, 1986). Cultures *do* vary as to which behaviors signal jealousy, which signs of affection justify jealousy, and how people express jealousy, but sexual jealousy occurs in all cultures (Reis, 1986). A middle-ground conclusion is that while jealousy is universal, many of its nuances (causes, expressions) vary from one culture to the next.

MANAGING EMOTIONS

Emotional socialization pressures surround professionals such as airline flight attendants (Hochschild, 1983), hair stylists (Parkinson, 1991), and physicians (Smith & Kleinman, 1989). These pressures mostly revolve around a theme of coping with aversive feelings in ways that are both socially desirable and personally adaptive (Saarni, 1997). Physicians, for instance, are not supposed to feel either attraction or disgust for their patients. Therefore, during their medical school training, physicians must learn affective neutrality, a detached concern for their patients. In medical school, they learn how to manage their emotions in ways that are appropriate with their social position.

Imagine being a medical student asked to conduct pelvic, rectal, and breast examinations and perform surgery, dissections, and autopsies. For two years, researchers interviewed medical students to identify the emotion-management strategies they learned to achieve affective neutrality (Smith & Kleinman, 1989). Medical students learned to manage their emotions by (1) transforming the contact (e.g., mentally transform intimate bodily contact into something qualitatively different, such as a step-by-step procedure), (2) accentuating the positive (e.g., identify the satisfaction in learning or the opportunity to practice medicine), (3) using the patient (e.g., shift awareness of uncomfortable feelings onto the patient, as in projection or in blame), (4) laughing about it (e.g., joking exempts the doctor from admitting weakness), and (5) avoiding the contact (e.g., keep the patient covered, look elsewhere, or hurry through the procedure). These five emotion-management strategies illustrate the culture that is Western medicine. When students rely on that culture for guidance to manage their emotions, they in effect reproduce the culture for the next generation of students (Smith & Kleinman, 1989).

Consider hair stylists (Parkinson, 1991). To be professionally successful, hair stylists need to develop an open communication style characterized by expressiveness, affect intensity, empathy, poise, frequent positive facial expressions, and a concealment of negative emotions. Further, the more natural and spontaneous the hair stylist appears to clients, the better the job goes. How do hair stylists learn to manage their emotions? The problem is, essentially, how to acquire an open interaction style with clients who are often uptight and socially remote (Straub & Roberts, 1983). Hair stylists who develop these social skills report high job satisfaction, whereas those hair stylists who fail to do so report feeling deceptive and experience low job satisfaction.

A flight attendant needs to adopt an open interaction style similar to that of the hair stylist. To do so, the flight attendant frequently uses "deep-acting" methods in which she replaces her natural and spontaneous emotional reactions with constant courtesy to clients (Hochschild, 1983). In all these cases—medical students, hair stylists, and flight attendants—people learn to manage their private, spontaneous feelings and express them as public, scripted ways of acting. Doing so facilitates smooth social interaction, at least with clients and strangers (Manstead, 1991).

INFERRING IDENTITIES FROM EMOTIONAL DISPLAYS

People react emotionally to the events in their lives, and how people react emotionally tells us something about what kind of people they are. For instance, weeping has traditionally communicated weakness, whereas laughter communicates health (Labott et al., 1991). According to affect control theory (chapter 10), emotional displays confirm or disconfirm our identities (Heise, 1989). Emotional displays function as public expressions (as "readouts") of a person's underlying identity. A man who disparages a woman and then expresses joy disconfirms his identity as a "man." His emotional display leads the culture to believe that his underlying identity must be something closer to "assassin." A neutral expression would lead members of the culture to think that his underlying identity must be something like an "ogre" or a "monster." Displaying disgust suggests that his underlying identity must be that of "boss" or "supervisor" (Heise, 1989).

Recall that affect control theory expresses identities, behaviors, and emotions in terms of EPA (evaluation, potency, activity) profiles. For instance, the identity of a *man* is slightly good, slightly powerful, and slightly active (EPA = 1.1, 1.1, 0.6), and the behavior of a *kiss* is quite good, slightly powerful, and slightly active (EPA = 2.3, 1.0, 0.8). Given these cultural perceptions of "who a man is" and "what a kiss is," consider the consequences of a man kissing a woman and then expressing either joy, calm, or disgust (Heise, 1989):

AFTER KISSING, HE EXPRESSES:	HIS NEW EPA PROFILE BECOMES:	THEREFORE, HIS NEW IDENTITY IS:
Joy	3.4, 0.3, –0.1	gentleman
Calm	1.0, 1.5, –1.1	advisor
Disgust	–2.4, 0.8, –0.5	snob

The brief preceding list implies that a joy expression (after a man kisses a woman) raises the man's goodness (from 1.1 to 3.4) and lowers his power (from 1.1 to 0.3) and liveliness (from 0.6 to –0.1) so that the culture reevaluates his identity from *man* to *gen-*

tleman or *mate*. The calm expression slightly increases his power and rather dramatically decreases his liveliness so that the culture reevaluates his identity to be an *advisor* or *grown-up* (from 1.1, 1.1, 0.6 to 1.0, 1.5, –1.1). The disgust expression drastically decreases the man's goodness and somewhat decreases his liveliness so that the culture reevaluates his identity to be a *snob* or *killjoy* (from 1.1, 1.1, 0.6 to –2.4, 0.8, –0.5).

During social interaction, each person uses emotional expression information to infer the other person's underlying identity and probable future behaviors. Legal trials provide an excellent illustration of this process, as judges and jurors must (1) observe a person they know little about (the defendant), (2) infer his character (identity), and (3) predict what the defendant's likely future behavior will be so that they can make sentencing recommendations if necessary (Robinson, Smith-Lovin, & Tsoudis, 1994). When people speak of their deviant acts (as does a defendant in a court case), their behaviors endow them with a corresponding identity such as thief, murderer, or freeloader. The speaker's emotional expressions signal a confirmation or disconfirmation of that inferred identity. The sobbing, remorseful, grief-stricken thief somehow is a regular sort of guy who got involved in an accident, while the relaxed, cold-hearted thief somehow is a devilish rogue who performed a crime. When a person engages in a bad act and shows no sign of remorse, the observer infers that this is surely a bad person; but when a person engages in a bad act and does show remorse, the observer infers that this person must not be so bad after all (Robinson et al., 1994).

SUMMARY

Emotions are, in part, biological reactions to important life events. They serve coping functions that allow the individual to prepare herself in adapting effectively to important life circumstances. Emotions energize and direct bodily actions (e.g., running, fighting) by affecting (1) the autonomic nervous system and its regulation of the heart, lungs, and muscles; (2) the endocrine system and its regulation of glands, hormones, and organs; (3) neural brain circuits such as those in the limbic system; (4) the rate of neural firing and therefore the pace of information processing; and (5) facial feedback and discrete patterns of the facial musculature.

Research on the James-Lange theory of emotion confirms that four emotions show a unique pattern of ANS physiology specificity: anger, fear, disgust, and sadness. Research on neural circuits in the brain confirms that four emotions possess neural circuit specificity: joy, fear, rage, and anxiety. According to differential emotions theory, there are 10 fundamental emotions. An emotion is "fundamental" to the extent that it (1) has a unique experiential quality, (2) has a unique facial expression, (3) is highly sensitive to a specific pattern of neural firing, and (4) has distinctive motivational properties that serve adaptive functions. The central assertion of the differential emotions theory is that each fundamental emotion is inherently adaptive and provides the individual with an organized heuristic in dealing effectively with recurring and important life tasks and problems. The 10 fundamental emotions that meet these criteria include interest, joy, fear, anger, disgust, distress, contempt, shame, guilt, and surprise.

The facial feedback hypothesis asserts that the subjective aspect of emotion is actually the awareness of proprioceptive feedback from facial action. The facial feedback hypothesis appears in two forms: weak and strong. According to its strong version, posed facial expressions activate specific emotions, such that a full smile activates joy. According to its weak version, exaggerated and suppressed facial expressions augment and attenuate naturally occurring emotion. Although research is mixed on the strong version, considerable evidence confirms the validity of the weaker version of the facial feedback hypothesis. Facial management does moderate emotional experience, and human beings can intensify or reduce naturally ongoing emotional experience by exaggerating or suppressing their facial actions.

The central construct in a cognitive understanding of emotion is appraisal. Two types of appraisal—primary and secondary—regulate the emotion process. Primary appraisal evaluates whether or not anything important is at stake in a situation—physical well-being, self-esteem, a goal, financial state, respect from another person, or the well-being of a loved one. Secondary appraisal occurs after some reflection and revolves around an assessment of how to cope with the harmful, threatening, or beneficial situation. The ultimate goal appraisal theorists pursue is the construction of a decision-tree in which knowing all appraisals the person makes will yield a prediction of which emotion must inevitably be experienced (e.g., something is at stake, it was lost, and it was lost because of an outside and illegitimate force → anger).

In addition to the appraisal of a life event, emotion is also embedded in cognition via emotion knowledge and attributions. Emotion knowledge involves learning fine distinctions among basic emotions and learning which situations cause which emotions. Sophisticated emotion knowledge enables the individual to appraise a situation with high discrimination and therefore respond with highly appropriate emotions. An attributional analysis focuses on post-outcome emotions for explaining when and why people experience pride, gratitude, or hope following positive outcomes and when and why people experience guilt, shame, anger, and pity following negative outcomes.

In a social and cultural analysis of emotion, other people are our richest sources of emotional experiences, as most emotions arise during social interaction. During social interaction, we often "catch" other people's emotions through a process of emotion contagion that involves mimicry, feedback, and, eventually, contagion. We also share and relive our recent emotional experiences during conversations with others, a process referred to as the social sharing of emotion. And the culture socializes its members to experience and express emotions in particular ways. Other people instruct us about the causes of our emotions (emotion knowledge), how we should express our emotions (expression management), and how and when we should control our emotions (emotion management). And how people react emotionally to the events in their lives tells us something about the kind of people they are, which illustrates a process in which private identities are inferred from public emotional displays.

Recommended Readings

Biological Aspects of Emotion

Ekman, P. (1993). Facial expression and emotion. *American Psychologist, 48,* 384–392.

Izard, C. E. (1989). The structure and functions of emotions: Implications for cognition, motivation, and personality. In I. S. Cohen (Ed.), *The G. Stanley Hall lecture series* (Vol. 9, pp. 39–73). Washington, DC: American Psychological Association.

Laird, J. D. (1974). Self-attribution of emotion: The effects of expressive behavior on the quality of emotional experience. *Journal of Personality and Social Psychology, 29,* 475–486.

Larsen, R. J., Kasimatis, M., & Frey, K. (1992). Facilitating the furrowed brow: An unobtrusive test of the facial feedback hypothesis applied to unpleasant affect. *Cognition and Emotion, 6,* 321–338.

Levenson, R. W. (1992). Autonomic nervous system differences among emotions. *Psychological Science, 3,* 23–27.

McIntosh, D. N. (1996). Facial feedback hypotheses: Evidence, implications, and directions. *Motivation and Emotion, 20,* 121-147

Zajonc, R. B. (1980). Feeling and thinking: Preferences need no inferences. *American Psychologist, 35,* 151–175.

Cognitive Aspects of Emotion

Lazarus, R. S. (1991). Progress on a cognitive-motivational-relational theory of emotion. *American Psychologist, 46,* 819–834.

Lazarus, R. S., & Smith, C. A. (1988). Knowledge and appraisal in the cognition-emotion relationship. *Cognition and Emotion, 2,* 281–300.

Scherer, K. R. (1993). Studying the emotion-antecedent appraisal process: An expert system approach. *Cognition and Emotion, 7,* 325–355.

Shaver, P., Schwartz, J., Kirson, D., & O'Connor, C. (1987). Emotion knowledge: Further exploration of a prototype approach. *Journal of Personality and Social Psychology, 52,* 1061–1086.

Smith, C. A., & Ellsworth, P. C. (1985). Patterns of cognitive appraisal in emotion. *Journal of Personality and Social Psychology, 48,* 813–838.

Weiner, B., & Graham, S. (1989). Understanding the motivational role of affect: Life-span research from an attributional perspective. *Cognition and Emotion, 3,* 401–419.

Cultural Aspects of Emotion

Averill, J. A. (1983). Studies on anger and aggression. *American Psychologist, 38,* 1145–1160.

Hatfield, E., Cacioppo, J. T., & Rapson, R. L. (1993). Emotional contagion. *Current Directions in Psychological Science, 2,* 96–99.

Pollak, L. H., & Thoits, P. A. (1989). Processes in emotional socialization. *Social Psychology Quarterly, 52,* 22–34.

Smith, A. C., III, & Kleinman, S. (1989). Managing emotions in medical school: Students' contacts with the living and the dead. *Social Psychology Quarterly, 52,* 56–69.

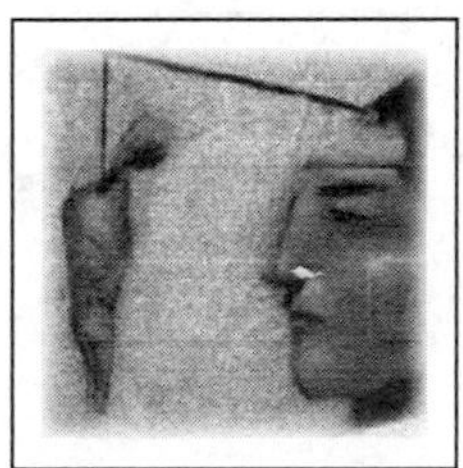

Conclusion

16

Conclusion

Imagine your next-door neighbor drops by for a visit. She tells you that her daughter, who attends the local public school, has been doing marginal while making acceptable grades. But your friend would very much like to see her daughter improve. You soon find out that this visit has a purpose. Your neighbor seeks advice, "How can I motivate my daughter?" What would you recommend?

After 15 years in school and 15 chapters in a book entitled, *Understanding Motivation and Emotion,* it has come to the following: What can you recommend to motivate your neighbor's daughter?

Fittingly, this preceding scenario has no ending. Rather, it asks whether or not you can generate answers, solutions, and ways of understanding that are both empirically grounded and psychologically satisfying to motivational problems in people's lives. Would you suggest offering the young scholar monetary incentives, say $10 for every *A* on future report cards? The mother and daughter could then talk about things like the grades she will need to get into college. Would offering incentives and emphasizing collegiate standards constitute a good strategy? What might be wrong with this approach? Alternatively, would you recommend that the mother have a heart-to-heart talk with her daughter about what school means to her? They could talk about things like interest, competence, the value of school, possible selves the daughter might embrace, and the quality of her relationship with her teacher. Would this be a good strategy? What might be wrong with this approach? Can you suggest something better? What if the person being motivated was a factory worker, a collegiate athlete, or your own daughter—would your advice be any different?

UNDERSTANDING AND APPLICATION

At this point in the text, you should feel confident of your understanding of motivation and emotion. Just how much confidence you currently possess will depend on the extent to which you can do the following:

1. Explain why people do what they do.
2. Predict how various conditions will affect motivation and emotion.
3. Apply motivational principles to everyday situations.

In the spirit of asking about such things, this chapter has three goals. First, this opening section checks on your understanding of motivation, asking questions such as the following: Why do we do what we do? What are the antecedents to motivational and emotional states? Can you solve practical motivational problems? The second section looks back on the first 15 chapters to identify those motivational constructs that emerge to attain a status of "core unifying constructs." This section also emphasizes the "big picture" in understanding motivation and emotion. The third and last section adopts a practical tone and asks you to take your knowledge about motivation into everyday life to create productive ways of motivating both self and others.

WHY WE DO WHAT WE DO

Explaining the reasons for behavior—explaining why we do what we do—requires the ability to generate psychologically satisfying answers to questions such as, Why did he do that? and Why does she want to do that? Answers to these questions lie in understanding the source of motivation and how motives, once aroused, intensify, change, and fade.

To explain why we do what we do, chapter 1 listed two dozen theories of motivation (see Table 1.2, page 22). Each of these theories provides a piece of the puzzle in the grand effort to explain human wants, desires, fears, and strivings. Working down the list of theories in Table 1.1, for instance, achievement motivation theory explains why people when challenged by a standard of excellence sometimes show positive emotion and approach the challenge before them but other times show negative emotion and seek to avoid it. The other theories apply to a different set of motivation-generating conditions. Collectively, the theories address most of the circumstances in which the reader might be interested. For instance, why do people do what they do when their identities are threatened (see self-schema consistency, affect control theory), when working in unresponsive, unpredictable environments (see learned helplessness theory, reactance theory), and so on? Taken together, theories in motivation provide a means of explaining and understanding why we do what we do.

IDENTIFYING ANTECEDENTS

Motivation study pays close attention to the conditions that give rise to motivational and emotional states, asking, Which antecedent conditions energize and direct behavior? An understanding of motivation and emotion includes the ability to use motivation theories to predict what effect environmental, interpersonal, intrapsychic, and physiological conditions will have on motivation and emotion.

Consider, for instance, that a teacher wants to know *in advance* what effect report cards will have on students' motivation in the classroom. Cognitive evaluation theory (chapter 5) explains how any external event effects students' psychological needs, intrinsic motivation, and extrinsic motivation. In this example, the external event is a course grade, and cognitive evaluation theory explains that if the grades are administered to students in an informational way ("We'll have a test, so you can get some feedback about the progress you are making"), then competence-affirming grades will increase intrinsic motivation, whereas competence-frustrating grades will decrease intrinsic motivation. If the grades are administered in a controlling way ("We'll have a test so that I can tell whether or not you have been reading the book"), then grades will decrease self-determination, decrease intrinsic motivation, and increase extrinsic motivation.

The important point here is that while motivation theories are based on past research findings, once validated they can be used to predict how conditions/variables will affect motivation and emotion. Test yourself on a few antecedents. For each of the following, ask if any theory comes to mind to help predict what effect the condition will have on a person's motivation:

- hours of deprivation
- lack of insulin
- taking a stimulant or depressant
- presence of a warm, genuine, and empathic friend
- exposure to an inspirational role model
- smiling face
- violent television show
- cultural pressures toward thinness or toward one sexual orientation
- evolutionary pressures toward obesity or toward one sexual orientation
- social expectations entrenched in conditions of worth
- choice
- optimal challenge
- standard of excellence
- short-term goal
- potential mate
- social interaction

- negative reinforcer
- uncontrollable, traumatic environmental conditions
- autonomy-supportive environment
- attractive incentive
- high task difficulty
- particular social role
- obstacle
- failure
- finding money in the coin return of a public phone
- positive feedback
- sudden increase in the rate of neural firing
- movement in the facial musculature
- all those ways of thinking that we harbor within ourselves, such as a pessimistic explanatory style, illusions of control, ideal states of body and performance, self-schemas, situational appraisals of benefit and harm, self-efficacy beliefs, unconscious defense mechanisms, and self-actualizing growth strivings

SOLVING PROBLEMS

An understanding of motivation and emotion also includes the ability to put theories into practice to promote optimal experience and functioning. The effort to apply motivational principles asks, "How do I motivate myself, and how do I motivate others?"

Improving human welfare involves the two complementary quests to (1) improve functioning and (2) overcome pathologies. Consider first the effort to improve human functioning—to increase effort in school, performance in athletics, productivity at work, wellness in therapy, personal growth in old age, environmental mastery, and so on. Each chapter of this book provides some insight into the practical task of promoting human welfare. The following are a few reminders:

- promote resilient self-efficacy beliefs (chapter 8)
- generate attractive possible selves (chapter 10)
- gain ego strength and effectance motivation (chapters 4, 13)
- cultivate rich personal autonomy and self-determination (chapter 4)
- nurture self-actualization and the actualizing tendency's development toward becoming a fully functioning individual (chapter 12)
- set up conditions that promote the flow experience (chapter 4)
- develop and maintain warm interpersonal relationships (chapters 4, 12)
- cultivate talent and creativity (chapters 4, 12)
- nurture growth needs (chapters 5, 12)
- develop a mastery motivational orientation (chapters 4, 9)
- promote intrinsic interest (chapter 4)
- adopt positive social identities (chapter 10)
- set difficult, specific goals (chapter 8)
- encourage learning goals over performance goals (chapter 6)
- encourage incremental theories over entity theories (chapter 10)

- encourage differentiation and integration of the self (chapter 10)
- nurture mature ego development (chapter 13)
- improve decision-making efficiency (chapters 8, 15)
- create conditions that allow the freedom to learn (chapters 4, 12)
- promote consistency between attitudes and behaviors (chapter 7)
- promote self-definition over social definition (chapter 12)
- establish, maintain, and restore personal control beliefs (chapters 8, 9)

Consider also how motivational principles can be applied to overcome motivational pathologies—student apathy, achievement anxiety, helplessness, depression, immature coping strategies, challenge avoidance, worker absenteeism, breakdowns in relationships, and breakdowns in regulation such as ignoring physiological cues for regulating eating or ignoring personal preferences in favor of conditions of worth. Once again, the following are a few reminders:

- promote a constructive rather than destructive reaction to failure (chapters 8, 9)
- avoid the hidden costs of reward (chapter 5)
- reverse the restraint release that leads to binge eating (chapter 3)
- channel acts of aggression into appropriate outlets (chapter 13)
- reverse decision making that is doubt-plagued and fear-dominated (chapter 8)
- prevent learned helplessness and its deficits (chapter 8)
- challenge entity theorists to find value in effort (chapter 10)
- redefine the meaning of failure (chapters 8, 10)
- reverse pessimistic expectancies and explanatory styles (chapter 9)
- overcome addictions (chapters 3, 13)
- manage emotions and identities (chapters 10, 15)
- deal with the problem of evil (chapter 12)
- solve the paradox of thought suppression (chapter 13)
- identify immature defense mechanisms and find the courage to give them up (chapters 12, 13)

Motivational principles offer the potential for improving the human condition. These principles are remarkable in their breadth, as they relate to all aspects of life, including education, work, sports, therapy, and relationships.

SUBJECT MATTER

Motivation study is more than just the development and application of its theories.

In some sense, theories come and go. For a science to make progress, its theories actually *must* come and go. Over the years, theories rise in popularity and then fade away, and they do so because new questions get asked and new data surface to challenge the theories to improve and refine to better explain the data. So in some sense, theories are just ways of understanding motivational phenomenon. As new data and new questions emerge to improve the theories, therefore, the understanding of motivation increases in kind.

The heart and soul of the subject matter of motivation study are the agents of motivation themselves: needs, cognitions, emotions, and external events. Specific phenomena—motivational agents—energize and direct behavior. So motivation study centers on these motivational agents, while the theories tell us how these motivational agents produce energy and direction. The full range of motivational agents appears in Table 16.1 on page 480. Figure 16.1, which follows the organization of chapters 3 through 15, organizes the sources of human motivation into four categories.

Motivation study is about appreciating the contribution to our lives of wants, desires, wishes, strivings, hopes, goals, aspirations, longings, feelings, and emotions. The roots of such phenomena are needs, cognitions, emotions, and external events. As represented in Figure 16.1, needs arise from physiological and psychological sources, and psychological needs can be innate and organismic, situational and quasi, or acquired and social. Cognitions exist as several different types of mental states, including discrepancies (plans, goals), expectations, attributions, and the self. Emotions and moods constitute a third class of motivational agents, and emotions can be understood as those that are mostly basic and biological (e.g., fear, disgust) and those that are complex and sociocognitive (e.g., pride, regret). External events exist as either situationally specific, single events (e.g., incentives, consequences) or more generally as social contexts (e.g., climates, relationships, cultures).

CORE THEMES

Theories (Table 1.2) and motivational agents (Figure 16.1) provide the nuts and bolts of motivation study. Assembling these nuts and bolts together allows the big picture of motivation study to emerge. It is difficult to say precisely what the big picture of motivation is because different readers and different researchers bring in a diversity of priorities, methodologies, and philosophical orientations. What appears in the following sections is a list of themes with which most participants in the study of motivation and emotion would agree. Maybe all readers and researchers would not include all five themes—adaptation, hedonism, optimal experience, human nature, and mastery—and most readers and researchers surely would want an additional theme or two added to the list. That not withstanding, these five themes help articulate what the study of motivation is about. And with these unifying themes, readers can take motivation themes into other courses of study, into their vocational aspirations and settings, and into their lives.

ADAPTATION

Motives exist for a reason. They have utility. Motives are useful and beneficial because opportunities to involve, nurture, and satisfy one's motives lead to high productivity, positive well-being, and successful adaptation. In a very real sense, that is why we have motives, namely to enhance our capacity to adapt successfully to the changing and often stressful circumstances we face. When people suffer motivational pathologies (e.g., helplessness, doubt, apathy) and when people intentionally ignore their motivations and emotions (as during dieting, conditions of worth, introjected regulation), adaptation suffers, as do productivity and well-being. At a basic, biological, and evolutionary level, motives such as

FIGURE 16.1 **Sources of Motivation**

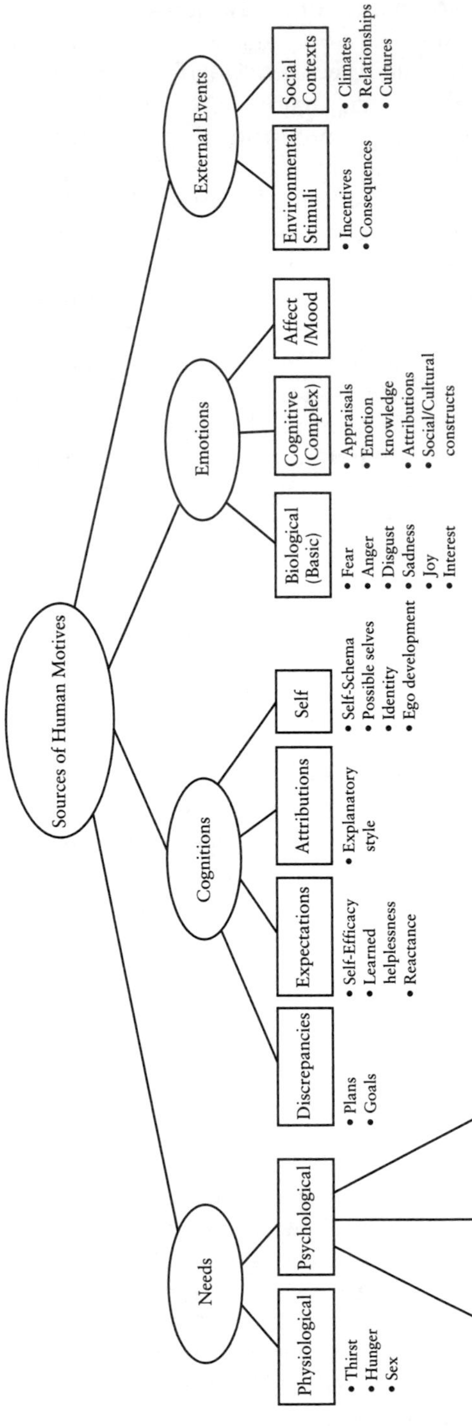

hunger, competence, and disgust are valuable allies we depend on to adapt successfully to important life events. At a cognitive and sociocultural level, motives such as relatedness, learning goals, self-efficacy beliefs, attractive possible selves, and emotions like shame and guilt are valuable allies we depend on to adapt to relationships and cultural demands.

The surest way to appreciate the important role motives play in our ongoing effort to adapt is to imagine not having these inner motivational allies. Imagine having a nervous system incapable of generating hunger, an emotional system incapable of generating fear, a family incapable of nurturing children's psychological needs, or a culture that offered its members no attractive possible selves to pursue. Imagine how adaptation would go awry, how productivity would suffer, and how well-being would sour if we lived a life in which our motives were continuously neglected, suppressed, or thwarted. Therefore, one core theme that runs throughout any motivational analysis is that motives serve us well.

Hedonism

People are always approaching or avoiding something, and this core principle of motivation can be expressed as hedonism—as pleasure versus pain, reward versus aversion, hope versus fear, and approach versus avoidance. Hedonism (approach pleasure, avoid pain) is central to understanding want, desire, and motivation in general. Constructs like reward, pleasure, and hope constitute the essence of why people are approaching something, whereas constructs like aversion, pain, and fear constitute the essence of why people are avoiding something.

Reward and aversion are experiences that can be investigated and understood at several levels of analysis. Reward and aversion have their physiological underpinnings in electrical stimulation of specific brain sites, in neural circuits within the limbic system, in neurochemical pathways, and in hedonically opponent processes in the brain. In a need analysis, reward experiences arise from need involvement and the perception of making progress toward fulfilling one's needs, whereas aversion experiences arise from need frustration, neglect, and from the perception of a lack of progress toward need fulfillment. In a cognitive analysis, reward and aversion arise from mental events such as appraisals of benefit versus harm and attributions of why a certain outcome might have occurred. Emotion researchers highlight interest and joy as approach-based emotions and fear and disgust as avoidance-based emotions. Mood researchers highlight the role of positive affect and negative affect on approach and avoidance. Pleasure and aversion also explain personality processes such as the reactions of the sensation seeker and sensation avoider toward the prospect of jumping out of an airplane. And pleasure and aversion are basic to psychoanalytic thinking via the instincts toward pleasure (Eros) and displeasure (Thanatos). Thus, irrespective of which motive one seeks to understand or which level of analysis one favors (physiology, need, cognition, emotion, culture), hedonic forces help explain why people are always approaching or avoiding something.

Enjoyment, Happiness, and Optimal Experience

Hedonism concerns pleasure, but contemporary motivation study is actually more about the pursuit of enjoyment than the pursuit of pleasure per se. Contemporary researchers study the role that motivation and emotion play in enabling people to regulate their behavior in ways that produce enjoyment—good feelings, optimal experience, happiness, and the liberation of states like creativity, effectance, and talent development (Seligman & Csikszentmihalyi, 2000). Enjoyment in one sense is, in fact, the transcendence of pleasure, as people strive to break through the limits of their hedonically based homeostatic motivations to produce experiences in their lives that make personal growth and positive well-being possible.

The study of motivation helps us to understand what makes people happy and which experiences make optimal functioning more likely. One ingredient to happiness and well-being is the establishment, maintenance, and growth of close relationships. Those who need to belong, those who establish mutual friendships, and those who marry are generally happier than those who do not (Myers, 2000). Those who construct a lifestyle rich in challenge and stimulation show more optimal experience (characterized by concentration, absorption, and intrinsic motivation) than those who fall into a lifestyle low in challenge and intellectual stimulation (Csikszentmihalyi, 1990; Larson, 2000). Those who are surrounded by social contexts that support and nurture their psychological needs and intrinsic motivation show greater vitality, experience personal growth, and thrive more than those who are surrounded by social contexts offering neglect and frustration of these needs (Ryan & Deci, 2000). Those who cultivate a sociocognitive world of optimism (Peterson, 2000), mature defense mechanisms (Vaillant, 2000), and positive illusions about the future (Taylor, 1989) show not only more positive daily moods but also enduring persistence, high achievement, and greater physical well-being than their pessimistic, immature, and more realistic counterparts. Those who experience positive mood states show better health than those that experience negative mood states, even in the face of life-threatening illnesses (Salovey et al., 2000). And those who actively construct meaning in their lives and those who gain a sense of control over their fates are more likely to be happy and live optimally (Frankl, 1963; Fromm, 1986; Taylor et al., 2000).

HUMAN NATURE

A fourth theme speaks to the question of human nature: Are people essentially good or evil? Are people by nature active or passive? Is psychological growth inherent in development? What do human beings really want, desire, and fear? Theories of motivation do a good job in revealing what is common within the strivings of all human beings. Differences in personality and culture are certainly important, but much can be gained by focusing on our shared strivings, wants, and fears. All of us harbor physiological needs such as hunger, biological dispositions such as temperament, prewired neural circuits in the brain for pleasure and aversion, basic emotions such as anger and joy, psychological needs such as belongingness and competence, intrinsic motivation to explore and pursue what is interesting, unconscious desires and fears, and developmental tendencies to actualize our inherent potentialities.

Because people differ in their genetic endowments, life experiences, and cultural demands, people show wide individual differences in the beliefs they hold, the expectations they bring to a task, the explanatory styles they rely on to interpret the world, the goals they value and seek, and the social needs that guide their desires and make them happy. Other motivational forces have origins that are clearly outside the realm of human nature, as their origins can be traced reliably to environmental, social, and cultural forces (e.g., incentives, reinforcers, socially inspired possible selves, cultural roles). Motivation study informs us of what part of want and desire stem from human nature and what part of want and desire arise from personal, social, and cultural experiences.

MASTERY

Mastery serves as a fifth theme that runs throughout most approaches to motivation. Mastery typically manifests itself in discussions of gaining competence and exercising control, especially on those occasions in which we try to adapt to life's challenges and demands. Thus, it is fitting to feature adaptation as the first core theme and mastery as the final core theme.

As a need, competence generates the desire to seek out and master optimal challenges. As cognition, competence generates perceptions of high self-efficacy that encourages effort, persistence, and task reengagement. Competence is also central to constructs such as effectance motivation/ego strength, intrinsic motivation, mastery motivation, flow, need for achievement, self-actualization, and the fully functioning individual. Each of these constructs has in common the idea that pleasure and reward that is earned (through intentional effort and effective performance) is qualitatively richer and more meaningful than is pleasure and reward that is not earned (a gift, a sunny day). The reason that earned competence generates greater vitality is that it involves and nurtures some inner motivational resource of the person, such as her self-concept, an organismic need for competence, personal control beliefs, positively evaluated identity, or ego strength.

Many theories of motivation include a construct to represent perceptions of control (Bandura, 1997; Peterson et al., 1993; Skinner et al., 1998). Control beliefs enable people to shape their surrounding environment in ways that fit their particular needs and development potentials. Control beliefs therefore include motivational constructs such as self-efficacy, locus of causality, desire for control, agency, mastery motivational orientation, and the social need for power—all aspects of motivation that people rely on to generate energy and direction in their behavior to effect intentional changes in their physical and interpersonal environments. Constructs such as attribution, explanatory style, illusion of control, and locus of control contribute to a mastery theme because people continually appraise how much or how little control they have over what happens to them. Even an emotion like hope is not the loosey-goosey emotion that people sometimes make it out to be because hope is about having goals and finding ways in achieving these goals (Snyder et al., 1991). Rises and falls in personal control beliefs lead to motivational phenomena such as mastery motivation versus learned helplessness, illusion of control versus depression, coping efficaciously versus being overwhelmed, optimism versus pessimism, achievement motivation versus fear of failure, performance-approach goals versus performance-avoidance goals, and vitality versus eating disorders such as anorexia and bulimia.

MOTIVATING SELF AND OTHERS

Much of the appeal in studying motivation lies in its potential to speak to motivating ourselves and others. We want to promote effort, achievement, challenge seeking, and excellence in self, and we want to promote these aims for those who are important to us. And we want to help self and others reverse and overcome pessimism, anxiety and doubt, apathy and helplessness.

MOTIVATING SELF

Motivation study is complex. Its complexity stems, in part, from the fact that motivation has many sources—needs, cognitions, emotions, and external events. Within each source, different facets can be identified (see Figure 16.1). For instance, within needs, the motivational dynamics vary for physiological, organismic, quasi, and social needs. Similarly, the motivational problems to be solved can be, and usually are, complex. Student listlessness and worker apathy, for instance, might have their roots in needs, in cognitions, in emotions, or in the supportiveness versus neglect of the school or workplace environment. The effort to motivate self might therefore strike the reader as overwhelming, complex, and something best left to the experts. But this need not be the case.

A straightforward framework for organizing one's thoughts about motivational problems appears in Table 16.1. The framework's purpose is to help you think about, diagnose, and eventually solve problems such as absenteeism, fear of public speaking, and lackluster effort as a student, worker, or athlete.

For instance, imagine that you cannot generate within yourself the motivation to study, exercise, or practice. How do you motivate yourself? To start, diagnose the problem. Ask about the status of your needs, cognitions, emotions, and external environment. Consider whether your needs, cognitions, emotions, and external environment are contributing positively (+) or negatively (−) to your motivation. That is, in Table 16.1 simply circle, after some reflection, a + or − sign for each question posed under the four columns of needs, cognitions, emotions, and supporting environment.

As one illustration, consider a motivational problem of hesitancy, procrastination, and outright avoidance in not really wanting to practice a skill, such as improving your face-to-face communication/conversational skills. Need-supported motivation might arise from a perception of competence, a need for relatedness with your interaction partner, or a need for achievement in the challenge to improve. Cognition-supported motivation might arise from self-efficacy beliefs, mastery or performance-approach goals, or an optimistic explanatory style. Emotion-supported motivation might arise from interest, hope, and joy. Environment-supported motivation might arise from an autonomy-supportive interaction partner, informational and timely feedback, and an empathic ear. On the other hand, need-depleting motivation might stem from incompetence, fear of failure, and an avoidance attachment style. Cognition-depleting motivation might stem from doubt, a performance-avoidance goal, and pessimistic explanatory style. Emotion-depleting motivation might stem from fear, anger, and embarrassment. Environment-depleting motivation might stem from a controlling interaction partner, ego-involving feedback, or a closed ear.

TABLE 16.1 **A Framework for Motivating the Self**

	NEED (N)	COGNITION (C)	EMOTION (E)	SUPPORTING ENVIRONMENT (SE)
	Does this activity involve and satisfy a need that is important to me (e.g., competence, intimacy)?	Does this activity conjure up positive expectations and beliefs (e.g., self-efficacy, personal control, energy-mobilizing values)?	Does this activity conjure up positive emotions and moods (e.g., interest, joy, positive affect)?	Is the social context supportive of my agenda (e.g., responsive, stimulating, autonomy supportive)?
ACTIVITY				
Studying	+ or −	+ or −	+ or −	+ or −
Exercising	+ or −	+ or −	+ or −	+ or −
Practicing	+ or −	+ or −	+ or −	+ or −
etc.				

For example, a N+ C+ E+ SE+ status is not the answer to every motivational problem, but seeking to turn the minuses into pluses does help make some sense in the struggle to diagnose and potentially solve motivational problems. While N+ C+ E+ SE+ might constitute an ideal profile, the presence of a minus sign is not all that problematic, as it likely just reflects the complexity of motivational problems. In fact, numerous scenarios fit a C+ E− pattern ("My control beliefs are high, but I'm just not interested in the subject matter") or C− E+ pattern ("The task is fun, but I don't want to do it because I lack sufficient self-efficacy"). Such a profile yields a motivational ambiguity that is only sometimes a problem. A problem exists, however, when the majority of elements are negative. Not living up to potential, a poor performance, apathy, and disengagement follow from a majority of minus signs for any activity included in Table 16.1.

Sometimes progress can be made on a motivational problem by breaking the problem down into smaller parts. Consider a fear of public speaking that motivates avoidance behavior, which is one motivational problem that typically involves needs, cognitions, emotions, and environments. Is part of the problem a need-based lack of relatedness or affiliation with the audience (N−)? Is part of the problem a cognition-based lack of self-efficacy in coping with the demands and uncertainties of public speaking (C−)? Is part of the problem an emotion-based fear or anxiety in facing an evaluative situation (E−)? Or is part of the problem an environment-based perception of speaking to a hostile, critical, controlling, or competitive audience (JE−)? Once the problem has been diagnosed, a plan of action—an intervention—can be created. Hopefully, chapters 3 through 15 provide some helpful leads to pursue.

MOTIVATING OTHERS

Motivating others is even more difficult and complex than is motivating self. In practice, most attempts to motivate others take place in relationships that involve interpersonal power differentials between the motivator and the person being motivated (Deci & Ryan, 1987). For example, consider the following interpersonal relationships in which the first person has some responsibility for motivating the other: teachers motivating students, parents motivating children, employers motivating employees, doctors motivating patients, therapists motivating clients, coaches motivating athletes, clergy motivating parishioners, experts motivating novices, and therapists motivating clients. In each case, the first person has some influence over the second, whether the basis of that influence manifests itself in expertise, rewards, force, status, or position. Consequently, the person who is one down in the relationship is vulnerable to being controlled by the person who is one up in power. Powerful people sometimes motivate others in ways that simply produce compliance (i.e., the desired, or compliant, behavior). To achieve compliance, an authority figure or an expert (teacher, coach, therapist) often uses extrinsic incentives to direct the other person's way of thinking, feeling, or behaving.

The directive, take-charge approach to motivating others manifests itself in a great variety of different relationships, but it is especially evident in military leaders, hard-line employers, extremely competitive athletic coaches, controlling teachers, take-charge politicians, authoritarian parents, patronizing doctors, and in all those relationships steeped in a doctrine of "my way or the highway." This traditional approach has some appeal mostly because experience teaches us that others can indeed be externally regulated. People will work hard when they desire approval, seek rewards, or fear punishment. In the words of the old Irish poet, "Nothing focuses the mind like the threat of hanging."

When directive supervisors try to motivate others, a paradoxical course of events typically unfolds. Directive supervisors typically begin their motivational attempt by inadvertently undermining the inner motivational states of those they are trying to motivate. That is, by using strong, attention-getting incentives and consequences (e.g., the sergeant yelling in the private's ear, the boss threatening to fire the tardy employee, the teacher telling students to read because of a test), the motivator ignores and even bulldozes over the very needs, cognitions, and emotions capable of motivating action. When the dust settles, directive supervisors focus on promoting desirable *behavior,* not desirable *motivation.*

An alternative approach is to support people's motivation from within. This approach focuses on latent inner motivational states, and it seeks to support and nurture these resources. Instead of seeking compliance, the supervisor supports the other person's motivation to enable an increased capacity for self-regulation. With self-regulation, the individual accepts personal responsibility for generating his or her own motivation from within. Hence, motivating others does not mean outwardly controlling them by providing substitutes (e.g., money, rewards) for absent inner motivation. Instead, the fundamental rationale for motivating others in this approach is to cultivate strong and resilient inner motivational resources to energize, direct, and regulate behavior.

Inner resources—growth-promoting needs, resilient and optimistic cognitions, and approach-oriented emotions—provide motivational support for people facing challenges, problems, or opportunities. When people set goals, encounter failure feedback, or need to marshal great efforts to face the challenges in their lives, it helps if they have inner motivational resources to buffer the stress, silence the doubt, maintain positive emotionality, initiate energetic action, and maintain a sense of purpose. For instance, imagine the positive role the following needs, cognitions, and emotions can play in a person's life when owned and cultivated by the individual: self-determination, competence, relatedness, self-efficacy, personal control beliefs, achievement strivings, optimistic explanatory style, mastery motivational orientation, an attractive possible self, curiosity, interest, and positive affect. Thus, the effort to motivate others becomes the effort to figure out how to support and nurture these potential inner motivational resources.

Most of us find the task of motivating others to be challenging, however, and we seem to prefer strategies that work in a hurry. We sometimes treat others the way Colonel Tom Parker (the man who supposedly discovered Elvis Presley) treated his "Incredible Dancing Chickens" at the State Fair—hook up the metaphorical electrified floor so they will dance on command. In other words, we reach for external resources to turn on motivation (e.g., directives, incentives, rewards) the way we might reach for a switch to turn on a light. At first glance, these incentives seem to work just fine—workers arrive on time, complete their projects, and act as employers request. But neglecting inner motivational resources and pursuing the motivational agenda of another is not all it is cracked up to be, even if we get paid a lot of money or attention for doing so. Compared with those who pursue intrinsic goals (e.g., personal growth), people who pursue extrinsic goals (e.g., money, fame, image) have significantly less vitality and significantly more narcissism, negative emotionality, and physical distress (Kasser & Ryan, 1993, 1996). When others control us, or when we allow others to control us, we pay a hidden toll (Kohn, 1993).

When trying to motivate others, first ask three questions:

1. Who is motivating the person?
2. Is the social context supporting the person's inner motivational resources, or is it robbing this person of these assets?
3. Is the focus on supporting motivation, or is it only on gaining compliant behavior?

As to the first question, the motivator will be either the person himself, or it will be some outside force, such as a supervisor or coach. The second question presents the social context as a two-edged sword that can either support *or* undermine the person's motivation. The third question seeks to take some of the attention off the intensity of the behavior and put it on the quality of the motivation that regulates that behavior.

If you find merit in asking these three questions, then the following conclusion about motivating self and others will emerge. Motivating self and others is not so much a situational event as it is a developmental undertaking. That is, the goal of motivating self and others is less about generating energy and direction in a particular situation than it is about developing rich inner resources for both the present and future.

Fostering healthy development in self and others is as much an art as it is a science. But, even artists need feedback to refine their skills. Emotion, behavior, and well-being are excellent sources of feedback information to help the person develop the art of motivating self and others. Recall from chapter 14 that emotions function as a readout of the status of a person's motivational status. Chapter 2 presented the idea that behavior varies in its effortfulness, latency, persistence, choice of direction, probability of occurrence, expressiveness in the face and body, and engagement. Changes in vitality and well-being signal progress and growth versus stagnation and regression. When the reader relies on her knowledge of theories to generate motivational strategies, she can then attend closely to emotional, behavioral, and well-being feedback to signal how things are going (and whether changes need to be made) in the art of motivating others. Once done, the reader will begin to realize the amazing capacity that an understanding of motivation and emotion has to improve people's lives.

References

Abe, J. A. A., & Izard, C. E. (1999). The developmental functions of emotions: An analysis in terms of differential emotions theory. *Cognition and Emotion, 13,* 523–549.

Abele, A. (1985). Thinking about thinking: Causal, evaluative and finalistic cognitions about social situations. *European Journal of Social Psychology, 15,* 315–332.

Abramson, L. Y., & Alloy, L. B. (1980). Judgment of contingency: Errors and their implications. In A. Baum & J. Singer (Eds.), *Advances in environmental psychology: Applications of personal control* (Vol. 2, pp. 111-130). Hillsdale, NJ: Lawrence Erlbaum.

Abramson, L. Y., Matalsky, G. I., & Alloy, L. B. (1989). Hopelessness depression: A theory-based subtype of depression. *Psychological Review, 96,* 358–372.

Abramson, L. Y., Seligman, M. E. P., & Teasdale, J. (1978). Learned helplessness in humans: Critique and reformulation. *Journal of Abnormal Psychology, 87,* 49–74.

Adelmann, P. K., & Zajonc, R. B. (1989). Facial efference and the experience of emotion. *Annual Review of Psychology, 40,* 249–280.

Adkins, K. K., & Parker, W. (1996). Perfectionism and suicidal preoccupation. *Journal of Personality, 64,* 529–543.

Adolph, E. F. (1980). Intakes are limited: Satieties. *Appetite, 1,* 337–342.

Ainsworth, M. D. S. (1989). Attachments beyond infancy. *American Psychologist, 44,* 709–716.

Ainsworth, M. D. S., Blehar, M. C., Waters, E., & Wall, S. (1978). *Patterns of attachment: A psychological study of the strange situation.* Hillsdale, NJ: Lawrence Erlbaum.

Alexander, P. A., Kulikowich, J. M., & Jetton, T. L. (1994). The role of subject-matter knowledge and interest in the processing of linear and nonlinear text. *Review of Educational Research, 64,* 201–252.

Allender, J. S., & Silberman, M. L. (1979). Three variations of student-directed learning: A research report. *Journal of Humanistic Psychology, 19,* 79–83.

Alloy, L. B., & Abramson, L. T. (1979). Judgment of contingency in depressed and nondepressed students: Sadder but wiser? *Journal of Experimental Psychology: General, 108,* 441–485.

Alloy, L. B., & Abramson, L. T. (1982). Learned helplessness, depression, and the illusion of control. *Journal of Personality and Social Psychology, 42,* 1114–1126.

Alloy, L. B., & Seligman, M. E. P. (1979). On the cognitive component of learned helplessness and depression. *The Psychology of Learning and Motivation, 13,* 219–276.

Altmaier, E. M., & Happ, D. A. (1985). Coping skills training's immunization effects against learned helplessness. *Journal of Social and Clinical Psychology, 3,* 181–189.

Amabile, T. M. (1985). Motivation and creativity: Effect of motivational orientation on creative writers. *Journal of Personality and Social Psychology, 48,* 393–399.

Amabile, T. M., DeJong, W., & Lepper, M. R. (1976). Effects of externally-imposed deadlines on subsequent intrinsic motivation. *Journal of Personality and Social Psychology, 34,* 92–98.

Amabile, T. M., Hennessey, B. A., & Grossman, B. S. (1986). Social influences on creativity: The effects of contracted-for reward. *Journal of Personality and Social Psychology, 50,* 14–23.

Amari, A., Grace, N. C., & Fisher, W. W. (1995). Achieving and maintaining compliance with the ketogenic diet. *Journal of Applied Behavior Analysis, 28,* 341–342.

Ames, C. A. (1987). Enhancing student motivation. In M. Maehr & D. Kleiber (Eds.), *Recent advances in motivation and achievement: Enhancing motivation* (Vol. 5, pp. 123–148). Greenwich, CT: JAI Press.

Ames, C. A., & Archer, J. (1988). Achievement goals in the classroom: Student learning strategies and motivational processes. *Journal of Educational Psychology, 80,* 260–267.

Ames, R., & Ames, C. A. (1984). Introduction. In R. Ames & C. A. Ames (Eds.), *Research on motivation in education: Student motivation* (Vol. 1, pp. 1–11). Orlando, FL: Academic Press.

Anand, B. K., Chhina, G. S., & Singh, B. (1962). Effect of glucose on the activity of hypothalamic feeding centers. *Science, 138, 597–598.*

Anastasi, A. (1982). *Psychological testing* (5th ed.). New York: Macmillan.

Andersen, B. L., & Cyranowski, J. M. (1994). Women's sexual self-schema. *Journal of Personality and Social Psychology, 67,* 1079–1100.

Anderson, C. A. (1989). Temperature and aggression: Ubiquitous effects of heat on occurrence of human violence. *Psychological Bulletin, 106,* 74–106.

Anderson, D. C., & Jennings, D. L. (1980). When experiences of failure promote expectations of success: The impact of attributing failure to ineffective strategies. *Journal of Personality, 48,* 393–407.

Anderson, G., & Brown, R. I. (1984). Real and laboratory gambling sensation seeking and arousal. *British Journal of Psychology, 5,* 401–411.

Anderson, J. R. (1995a). *Cognitive psychology and its implications* (4th ed.). New York: Freeman.

Anderson, J. R. (1995b). *Learning and memory.* New York: John Wiley & Sons.

Anderson, K. J. (1990). Arousal and the inverted-U hypothesis: A critique of Neiss's Reconceptualizing arousal. *Psychological Bulletin, 107,* 96–100.

Anderson, R., Manoogian, S. T., & Reznick, J. S. (1976). The undermining and enhancing of intrinsic motivation in preschool children. *Journal of Personality and Social Psychology, 34,* 915–922.

Andreassi, J. L. (1986). *Psychophysiology: Human behavior and physiological response* (2nd ed.). Hillsdale, NJ: Lawrence Erlbaum.

Andrews, G. R., & Debus, R. L. (1978). Persistence and the causal perception of failure: Modifying cognitive attributions. *Journal of Educational Psychology, 70,* 154–166.

Appley, M. H. (1991). Motivation, equilibration, and stress. In R. A. Dienstbier (Ed.), *Nebraska symposium on motivation* (Vol. 38, pp. 1–67). Lincoln: University of Nebraska Press.

Arkin, R. M., Cooper, H., & Kolditz, T. (1980). A statistical review of the literature concerning the self-serving bias in interpersonal influence situations. *Journal of Personality, 48,* 435–448.

Arnett, J. (1991). Still crazy after all these years: Reckless behavior among young adults aged 23–27. *Personality and Individual Differences, 12,* 1305–1313.

Arnold, M. B. (1960). *Emotion and personality* (Vols. 1 & 2). New York: Columbia University Press.

Arnold, M. B. (1970). Perennial problems in the field of emotion. In M. B. Arnold (Ed.), *Feelings and emotions* (pp. 169–185). New York: Academic Press.

Aronson, E. (1969). The theory of cognitive dissonance: A current perspective. In L. Berkowitz (Ed.), *Advances in experimental social psychology* (Vol. 4, pp. 1–34). New York: Academic Press.

Aronson, E. (1988). *The social animal* (5th ed.). San Francisco: W. H. Freeman.

Aronson, E. (1992). The return of the repressed: Dissonance theory makes a comeback. *Psychological Inquiry, 3,* 303–311.

Aronson, E. (1999). Dissonance, hypocrisy, and the self-concept. In E. Harmon-Jones & J. Mills (Eds.), *Cognitive dissonance: Progress on a pivotal theory in social psychology* (pp. 103–126). Washington, DC: American Psychological Association.

Aronson, E., Fried, C. B., & Stone, J. (1991). Overcoming denial and increasing the intention to use condoms through the induction of hypocrisy. *American Journal of Public Health, 81,* 1636–1637.

Aronson, E., & Mills, J. (1959). The effect of severity of initiation on liking for a group. *Journal of Abnormal and Social Psychology, 59,* 177–181.

Ashby, F. G., Isen, A. M., & Turken, A. U. (1999). A neuropsychological theory of positive affect and its influence on cognition. *Psychological Review, 106,* 529–550.

Aspinwall, L. G. (1998). Rethinking the role of positive affect in self-regulation. *Motivation and Emotion, 22,* 1–32.

Atkinson, J. W. (1957). Motivational determinants of risk-taking behavior. *Psychological Review, 64,* 359–372.

Atkinson, J. W. (1964). A theory of achievement motivation. In *An introduction to motivation* (pp. 240–268). New York: Van Nostrand.

Atkinson, J. W. (1981). Studying personality in the context of an advanced motivational psychology. *American Psychologist, 36,* 117–128.

Atkinson, J. W. (1982). Motivational determinants of thematic apperception. In A. J. Stewart (Ed.), *Motivation and society* (pp. 3–40). San Francisco: Jossey-Bass.

Atkinson, J. W., & Birch, D. (Eds.). (1970). *The dynamics of action.* New York: Wiley.

Atkinson, J. W., & Birch, D. (1974). The dynamics of achievement-oriented activity. In J. W. Atkinson & J. O. Raynor (Eds.), *Motivation and achievement* (pp. 271–325). Washington, DC: Van Nostrand Reinhold.

Atkinson, J. W., & Birch, D. (1978). *Introduction to motivation* (2nd ed.). New York: Van Nostrand.

Atkinson, J. W., Bongort, K., & Price, L. H. (1977). Explorations using computer simulation to comprehend TAT measurement of motivation. *Motivation and Emotion, 1,* 1–27.

Atkinson, J. W., Heyns, R. W., & Veroff, J. (1954). The effect of experimental arousal of the affiliation motive on thematic apperception. *Journal of Abnormal and Social Psychology, 49,* 405–410.

Austira, J., Hatfield, D. B., Grindle, A. C., & Bailey, J. S. (1993). Increasing recycling in office environments: The effects of specific, informative cues. *Journal of Applied Behavior Analysis, 26,* 247–253.

Averill, J. R. (1968). Grief: Its nature and significance. *Psychological Bulletin, 70,* 721–748.

Averill, J. R. (1979). The functions of grief. In C. Izard (Ed.), *Emotions in personality and psychopathology* (pp. 339–368). New York: Plenum.

Averill, J. R. (1980). A constructivist view of emotion. In R. Plutchik & H. Kellerman (Eds.), *Theories of emotion* (pp. 305–340). New York: Academic Press.

Averill, J. R. (1982). *Anger and aggression: An essay on emotion.* New York: Springer-Verlag.

Averill, J. R. (1983). Studies on anger and aggression. *American Psychologist, 38,* 1145–1160.

Averill, J. R. (1985). The social construction of emotion: With special reference to love. In K. Gergen & K. Davis (Eds.), *The social construction of the person* (pp. 89–109). New York: Springer-Verlag.

Averill, J. R. (1990). Emotions as related to systems of behavior. In N. L. Stein, B. Leventhal, & T. Trabasso (Eds.), *Psychological and biological approaches to emotion* (pp. 385–404). Hillsdale, NJ: Lawrence Erlbaum.

Averill, J. R. (1991). Emotions as episodic dispositions, cognitive schemas, and transitory social roles: Steps toward an integrated theory of emotion. In D. Ozer, J. M. Healy Jr., & A. J. Stewart (Eds.), *Perspectives in personality* (Vol. 32, pp. 139–167). London: Jessica Kingsley.

Averill, J. R. (1994). In the eyes of the beholder. In P. Ekman & R. J. Davidson (Eds.), *The nature of emotion: Fundamental questions* (pp. 7–14). New York: Oxford University Press.

Averill, J. R., & Boothroyd, P. (1977). On falling in love in conformance with the romantic ideal. *Motivation and Emotion, 1,* 235–247.

Azar, B. (1994, October). Seligman recommends a depression vaccine. *APA Monitor, 27,* 4.

Azar, B. (2000, January). Two computer programs 'face' off. *Monitor on Psychology,* 48–49.

Azrin, N. H., Rubin, H., O'Brien, F., Ayllon, T., & Roll, D. (1968). Behavioral engineering: Postural control by a portable operant apparatus. *Journal of Applied Behavior Analysis, 2,* 39–42.

Bailey, J. M., Gavlin, S., Agyei, Y., & Gladue, B. A. (1994). Effects of gender and sexual orientation on evolutionary relevant aspects of human mating psychology. *Journal of Personality and Social Psychology, 66,* 1081–1093.

Bailey, J. M., & Pillard, R. C. (1991). A genetic study of the male sexual orientation. *Archives of General Psychiatry, 48,* 1089–1096.

Bailey, J. M., Pillard, R. C., Neale, M. C., & Agyei, Y. (1993). Heritable factors influence sexual orientation in women. *Archives of General Psychiatry, 50,* 217–223.

Baldwin, J. D., & Baldwin, J. I. (1986). *Behavior principles in everyday life* (2nd ed.). Englewood Cliffs, NJ: Prentice-Hall.

Banaji, M., & Hardin, C. (1996). Automatic stereotyping. *Psychological Science, 7,* 136–141.

Bandura, A. (1977). Self-efficacy: Toward a unifying theory of behavioral change. *Psychological Review, 84,* 191–215.

Bandura, A. (1982). Self-efficacy mechanism in human agency. *American Psychologist, 37,* 122–147.

Bandura, A. (1983). Self-efficacy mechanisms of anticipated fears and calamities. *Journal of Personality and Social Psychology, 45,* 464–469.

Bandura, A. (1986). Self-efficacy. In *Social foundations of thought and action: A social cognitive theory* (pp. 390–453). Englewood Cliffs, NJ: Prentice-Hall.

Bandura, A. (1988). Self-efficacy conception of anxiety. *Anxiety Research, 1,* 77–98.

Bandura, A. (1989). Human agency in social cognitive theory. *American Psychologist, 44,* 1175–1184.

Bandura, A. (1990). Conclusion: Reflections on nonability determinants of competence. In R. J. Sternberg & J. Kolligian Jr. (Eds.), *Competence considered* (pp. 315–362). New Haven, CT: Yale University Press.

Bandura, A. (1991). Self-regulation of motivation through anticipatory and self-regulatory mechanisms. In R. A. Dienstbier (Ed.), *Nebraska symposium on motivation: Perspectives on motivation* (Vol. 38, pp. 69–164). Lincoln: University of Nebraska Press.

Bandura, A. (1993). Perceived self-efficacy in cognitive development and functioning. *Educational Psychologist, 28,* 117–148.

Bandura, A. (1997). *Self-efficacy: The exercise of control.* New York: W. H. Freeman.

Bandura, A. (1998). Health promotion from the perspective of social cognitive theory. *Psychological Health, 13,* 623–649.

Bandura, A. (1999). Moral disengagement in the perpetration of inhumanities. *Personality and Social Psychology Review, 3,* 193–209.

Bandura, A., & Adams, N. E. (1977). Analysis of self-efficacy theory of behavioral change. *Cognitive Therapy and Research, 1,* 287–308.

Bandura, A., Adams, N. E., Hardy, A. B., & Howells, G. N. (1980). Tests of the generality of self-efficacy theory. *Cognitive Therapy and Research, 4,* 39–66.

Bandura, A., & Cervone, D. (1983). Self-evaluative and self-efficacy mechanisms governing the motivational effects of goal systems. *Journal of Personality and Social Psychology, 45,* 1017–1028.

Bandura, A., & Cervone, D. (1986). Differential engagement of self-reactive influences in cognitive motivation. *Organizational Behavior and Human Decision Processes, 38,* 92–113.

Bandura, A., Cioffi, D., Taylor, C. B., & Brouillard, M. E. (1988). Perceived self-efficacy in coping with cognitive stressors and opioid activation. *Journal of Personality and Social Psychology, 55,* 479–488.

Bandura, A., Reese, L., & Adams, N. E. (1982). Microanalysis of action and fear arousal as a function of differential levels of perceived self-efficacy. *Journal of Personality and Social Psychology, 43,* 5–21.

Bandura, A., & Schunk, D. H. (1981). Cultivating competence, self-efficacy, and intrinsic interest through proximal self-motivation. *Journal of Personality and Social Psychology, 41,* 586–598.

Bandura, A., Taylor, C. B., Williams, S. L., Mefford, I. N., & Barchas, J. D. (1985). Catecholamine secretion as a function of perceived coping self-efficacy. *Journal of Consulting and Clinical Psychology, 53,* 406–414.

Bandura, A., & Wood, R. E. (1989). Effect of perceived controllability and performance standards on self-regulation of complex decision making. *Journal of Personality and Social Psychology, 56,* 805–814.

Bandura, M., & Dweck, C. S. (1985). *The relationship of conceptions of intelligence and achievement goals to achievement-related cognition, affect, and behavior.* Unpublished manuscript, Harvard University.

Barrett, K. C. (1995). A functionalist approach to shame and guilt. In J. P. Tangney & K. W. Fischer (Eds.), *Self-conscious emotions: The psychology of shame, guilt, embarrassment, and pride* (pp. 25–63). New York: Guilford Press.

Bassett, G. A. (1979). A study of the effects of task goal and schedule choice on work performance. *Organizational Behavior and Human Performance, 24,* 202–227.

Basso, M. R., Schefft, B. K., & Hoffman, R. G. (1994). Mood-moderating effects of affect intensity of cognition: Sometimes euphoria is not beneficial and dysphoria is not detrimental. *Journal of Personality and Social Psychology, 66,* 363–368.

Batson, C. D., Coke, J. S., Chard, F., Smith, D., & Taliaferro, A. (1979). Generality of the "glow of goodwill": Effects of mood on helping and information acquisition. *Social Psychology Quarterly, 42,* 176–179.

Baucom, D. H., & Aiken, P. A. (1981). Effect of depressed mood on eating among obese and nonobese dieting and nondieting persons. *Journal of Personality and Social Psychology, 41,* 577–585.

Baumeister, R. F. (1986). *Identity: Cultural change and the struggle for self.* New York: Oxford University Press.

Baumeister, R. F. (1987). How the self became a problem: A psychological review of historical research. *Journal of Personality and Social Psychology, 52,* 163–176.

Baumeister, R. F. (1991). *Escaping the self: Alcoholism, spirituality, masochism, and other flights from the burden of selfhood.* New York: Basic Books.

Baumeister, R. F., & Campbell, W. K. (1999). The intrinsic appeal of evil: Sadism, sensational thrills, and threatened egotism. *Personality and Social Psychology Review, 3,* 210–221.

Baumeister, R. F., Heatherton, T. F., & Tice, D. M. (1994). *Losing control: How and why people fail at self-regulation.* San Diego: Academic Press.

Baumeister, R. F., & Leary, M. R. (1995). The need to belong: Desire for interpersonal attachments as a fundamental human motivation. *Psychological Bulletin, 117,* 497–529.

Baumeister, R. F., Smart, L., & Boden, J. M. (1996). Relation of threatened egotism to violence and aggression: The dark side of self-esteem. *Psychological Review, 103,* 5–33.

Baumeister, R. F., Stillwell, A. M., & Heatherton, T. F. (1995). Interpersonal aspects of guilt: Evidence from narrative studies. In J. P. Tangney & K. W. Fischer (Eds.), *Self-conscious emotions: The psychology of shame, guilt, embarrassment, and pride* (pp. 255–273). New York: Guilford Press.

Beach, F. A. (1955). The descent of instinct. *Psychological Review, 62,* 401–410.

Beatty, J. (1982). Task-evoked pupillary response, processing load, and the structure of processing resources. *Psychological Bulletin, 91,* 276–292.

Beatty, J. (1986). The pupillary system. In M. G. H. Coles, E. Ponchin, & S. W. Proges (Eds.), *Psychophysiology: Systems, processes, and applications* (pp. 43–50). New York: Guilford Press.

Beatty, W. W. (1982). Dietary variety stimulates appetite in females but not in males. *Bulletin of the Psychonomic Society, 19,* 212–214.

Beauvois, J. L., & Joule, R. V. (1996). *A radical dissonance theory.* London: Taylor & Francis.

Beck, A. T. (1967). *Depression: Clinical, experimental, and theoretical aspects.* New York: Hoeber.

Beck, A. T. (1976). *Cognitive therapy and the emotional disorders.* New York: International Universities Press.

Beck, A. T. (1984). Cognition and therapy. *Archives of General Psychiatry, 41,* 1112–1114.

Beck, A. T., Rush, A. J., Shaw, B. F., & Emery, G. (1979). *Cognitive therapy of depression.* New York: Guilford Press.

Beck, R. C. (1979). Roles of taste and learning in water regulation. *Behavioral and Brain Sciences, 1,* 102–103.

Beck, S. P., Ward-Hull, C. I., & McLear, P. M. (1976). Variable related to women's somatic preferences of the male and female body. *Journal of Personality and Social Psychology, 34,* 1200–1210.

Becker, L. J. (1978). Joint effect of feedback and goal setting on performance: A field study of residential energy conservation. *Journal of Applied Psychology, 63,* 428–433.

Beecher, H. K. (1956). Relationship of significance of wound to pain experienced. *Journal of the American Medical Association, 161,* 1609–1613.

Bell, A. P., Weinberg, M. S., & Hammersmith, S. K. (1981). *Sexual preference: Its development in men and women.* Bloomington: Indiana University Press.

Bellak, L. (1993). *The T.A.T., C.A.T., and S.A.T. in clinical use.* Needham Heights, MA: Allyn and Bacon.

Bem, D. J. (1967). Self-perception: An alternative interpretation of cognitive dissonance phenomena. *Psychological Review, 74,* 183–200.

Bem, D. J. (1972). Self-perception theory. In L. Berkowitz (Ed.), *Advances in experimental social psychology* (Vol. 6, pp. 1–62). New York: Academic Press.

Bem, D. J., & McConnell, H. K. (1970). Testing the self-perception explanation of dissonance phenomena: On the salience of premanipulation attitudes. *Journal of Personality and Social Psychology, 14,* 23–31.

Benjamin, L. T., Jr., & Jones, M. R. (1978). From motivational theory to social cognitive development:

Twenty-five years of the Nebraska Symposium. *Nebraska symposium on motivation* (Vol. 26, pp. ix–xix). Lincoln: University of Nebraska Press.

Benware, C., & Deci, E. L. (1984). The quality of learning with an active versus passive motivational set. *American Educational Research Journal, 21,* 755–765.

Berenbaum, S. A., & Snyder, E. (1995). Early hormonal influences on childhood sex-typed activity and playmate preferences: Implications for the development of sexual orientation. *Developmental Psychology, 31,* 31–42.

Bergmann, G., & Spence, K. W. (1941). Operationalism and theory construction. *Psychological Review, 48,* 1–14.

Berkowitz, L. (1962). *Aggression: A social psychological analysis.* New York: McGraw-Hill.

Berlyne, D. E. (1966). Curiosity and exploration. *Science, 153,* 25–33.

Berlyne, D. E. (1967). Arousal and reinforcement. In D. Levine (Ed.), *Nebraska symposium on motivation* (Vol. 15, pp. 1–110). Lincoln: University of Nebraska Press.

Berlyne, D. E. (1975). Behaviourism? Cognitive theory? Humanistic psychology? To Hull with them all. *Canadian Psychological Review, 16,* 69–80.

Bernard, L. L. (1924). *Instinct: A study of social psychology.* New York: Holt.

Bernieri, F. J., & Rosenthal, R. (1991). Interpersonal coordination: Behavior matching and interactional synchrony. In R. S. Feldman & B. Rimeí (Eds.), *Fundamentals of nonverbal behavior* (pp. 401–432). New York: Cambridge University Press.

Berry, D. S., & McArthur, L. Z. (1985). Some components and consequences of a babyface. *Journal of Personality and Social Psychology, 48,* 312–323.

Berry, D. S., & McArthur, L. Z. (1986). Perceiving character in faces: The impact of age-related craniofacial changes on social perception. *Psychological Bulletin, 100,* 3–18.

Berry, J. M., & West, R. L. (1993). Cognitive self-efficacy in relation to personal mastery and goal setting across the life span. *International Journal of Behavioral Development, 16,* 351–379.

Berry, S. L., Beatty, W. W., & Klesges, R. C. (1985). Sensory and social influences on ice cream consumption by males and females in a laboratory setting. *Appetite, 6,* 41–45.

Berscheid, E., Graziano, W., Monson, T., & Dermer, M. (1976). Outcome dependency: Attention, attribution, and attraction. *Journal of Personality and Social Psychology, 34,* 978–989.

Betz, N. E., & Hackett, G. (1986). Applications of self-efficacy theory to understanding career choice behavior. *Journal of Social and Clinical Psychology, 4,* 279–289.

Bexton, W. H., Heron, W., & Scott, T. H. (1954). Effects of decreased variation in the sensory environment. *Canadian Journal of Psychology, 8,* 70–66.

Beyer, S. (1995). Maternal employment and children's academic achievement: Parenting styles as mediating variables. *Development Review, 15,* 212–253.

Bindra, D. (1959). *Motivation: A systematic reinterpretation.* New York: Ronald Press.

Biner, P. M., Angle, S. T., Park, J. H., Mellinger, A. E., & Barber, B. C. (1995). Need state and the illusion of control. *Personality and Social Psychology Bulletin, 21,* 899–907.

Biner, P. M., & Hua, D. M. (1995). Determinants of the magnitude of goal valence: The interactive effects of need, instrumentality, and the difficulty of goal attainment. *Basic and Applied Social Psychology, 16,* 53–74.

Biner, P. M., Huffman, M. L., Curran, M. A., & Long, K. R. (1998). Illusory control as a function of motivation for a specific outcome in a chance-based situation. *Motivation and Emotion, 22,* 277–292.

Birch, H. G. (1956). Sources of odor in maternal behavior in animals. *American Journal of Orthopsychiatry, 26,* 279–284.

Birch, L. L., & Fisher, J. A. (1996). The role of experience in the development of children's eating behavior. In E. D. Capaldi (Ed.), *Why we eat what we eat: The psychology of eating.* Washington, DC: American Psychological Association.

Birch, L. L., Johnson, S. L., Anderson, G., Peters, J. C., & Schulte, M. C. (1991). The variability of young children's energy-intake. *New England Journal of Medicine, 324,* 232–235.

Birch, L. L., Zimmerman, S. I., & Hind, H. (1980). The influence of social affective context on the formation of children's food preferences. *Child Development, 51,* 856–861.

Birney, R. C., Burdick, H., & Teevan, R. C. (1969). *Fear of failure.* New York: Van Nostrand.

Blai, B., Jr. (1964). An occupational study of job satisfaction and need satisfaction. *Journal of Experimental Education, 32,* 383–388.

Blais, M. R., Sabourin, S., Boucher, C., & Vallerand, R. J. (1990). Toward a motivational model of couple happiness. *Journal of Personality and Social Psychology, 59,* 1021–1031.

Blank, P. D., Reis, H. T., & Jackson, L. (1984). The effects of verbal reinforcements on intrinsic motivation for sex-linked tasks. *Sex Roles, 10,* 369–387.

Blankenship, V. (1987). A computer-based measure of resultant achievement motivation. *Journal of Personality and Social Psychology, 53,* 361–372.

Blascovich, J., Brennan, K., Tomaka, J., Kelsey, R. M., Hughes, P., Coad, M. L., & Adlin, R. (1992). Affect intensity and cardiac arousal. *Journal of Personality and Social Psychology, 63,* 164–174.

Blasi, A. (1976). Concept of development in personality theory. In J. Loevinger (Ed.), *Ego development* (pp. 29–53). San Francisco: Jossey-Bass.

Blass, E. M., & Hall, W. G. (1976). Drinking termination: Interactions among hydrational, orogastric, and behavioral controls in rats. *Psychological Review, 83,* 356–374.

Blatt, S. J. (1994). *Therapeutic change: An objects relations approach.* New York: Plenum.

Blatt, S. J. (1995). The destructiveness of perfectionism: Implications for the treatment of depression. *American Psychologist, 50,* 1003–1020.

Block, J., & Kremen, A. M. (1996). IQ and ego-resiliency: Conceptual and empirical connections and separateness. *Journal of Personality and Social Psychology, 70,* 349–361.

Boggiano, A. K., & Barrett, M. (1985). Performance and motivational deficits of helplessness: The role of motivational orientations. *Journal of Personality and Social Psychology, 49,* 1753–1761.

Boggiano, A. K., Barrett, M., Weiher, A. W., McClelland, G. H., & Lusk, C. M. (1987). Use of the maximal-operant principle to motivate children's intrinsic interest. *Journal of Personality and Social Psychology, 53,* 866–879.

Boggiano, A. K., Flink, C., Shields, A., Seelbach, A., & Barrett, M. (1993). Use of techniques promoting students' self-determination: Effects on students' analytic problem-solving skills. *Motivation and Emotion, 17,* 319–336.

Boggiano, A. K., Main, D. S., & Katz, P. A. (1988). Children's preference for challenge: The role of perceived competence and control. *Journal of Personality and Social Psychology, 54,* 134–141.

Boggiano, A. K., & Ruble, D. N. (1979). Competence and the overjustification effect: A developmental study. *Journal of Personality and Social Psychology, 37,* 1462–1468.

Bohner, G., Bless, H., Schwarz, N., & Strack, F. (1988). What triggers causal attributions? The impact of valence and subjective probability. *European Journal of Social Psychology, 18,* 335–345.

Bolles, R. C. (1975). *A theory of motivation* (2nd ed.). New York: Harper & Row.

Bolles, R. C., & Fanselow, M. S. (1980). A perceptual-defensive-recuperative model of fear and pain. *Behavioral and Brain Sciences, 3,* 291–323.

Bolm-Avdorff, J., Schwammle, J., Ehlenz, K., & Kaffarnik, H. (1989). Plasma level of catecholamines and lipids when speaking before an audience. *Work and Stress, 3,* 249–253.

Bonanno, G. A., Mihalecz, M. C., & LeJeune, J. T. (1999). The core emotion themes of conjugal loss. *Motivation and Emotion, 23,* 175–202.

Boneau, C. A. (1990). Psychological literacy: A first approximation. *American Psychologist, 45,* 891–900.

Booth, A., Shelley, G., Mazur, A., Tharp, G., & Kittok, R. (1989). Testosterone and winning and losing in human competition. *Hormones and Behavior, 23,* 556–571.

Borecki, I. B., Rice, T., Peírusse, L., Bouchard, C., & Rao, D. C. (1995). Major gene influence on the proximity to store fat in trunk versus extremity depots: Evidence from the Quebec family study. *Obesity Research, 3,* 1–8.

Bowlby, J. (1969). *Attachment and loss: Vol. 1. Attachment.* New York: Basic Books.

Bowlby, J. (1973). *Attachment and loss: Vol. 2. Separation: Anxiety and anger.* New York: Basic Books.

Boyatzis, R. E. (1972). *A two factor theory of affiliation motivation.* Unpublished doctoral dissertation, Harvard University.

Boyatzis, R. E. (1973). Affiliation motivation. In D. C. McClelland & R. S. Steele (Eds.), *Human motivation: A book of readings.* Morristown, NJ: General Learning Press.

Bradley, R. H., & Caldwell, B. M. (1979). Home environment and locus of control. *Journal of Clinical Child Psychology, 8,* 107–111.

Brehm, J. W. (1956). Postdecision changes in the desirability of alternatives. *Journal of Abnormal and Social Psychology, 52,* 384–389.

Brehm, J. W. (1966). *A theory of psychological reactance.* New York: Academic Press.

Brehm, S. S., & Brehm, J. W. (1981). *Psychological reactance: A theory of freedom and control.* New York: Academic Press.

Brewer, M. B. (1979). Ingroup bias in the minimal intergroup situation: A cognitive-motivational analysis. *Psychological Bulletin, 86,* 307–324.

Brewin, C. R. (1985). Depression and causal attribution: What is their relation? *Psychological Bulletin, 98,* 297–309.

Brigham, T. A., Maier, S. M., & Goodner, V. (1995). Increased designated driving with a program of prompts and incentives. *Journal of Applied Behavior Analysis, 28,* 8384.

Broadbent, D. E., Cooper, P. F., FitzGerald, P., & Parkes, K. R. (1982). The cognitive failures questionnaire (CFQ). *British Journal of Clinical Psychology, 21,* 1–16.

Brobeck, J. R. (1960). Food and temperature. *Recent Progress in Hormone Research, 16,* 439.

Brophy, J. (1981). Teacher praise: A functional analysis. *Review of Educational Research, 51,* 5–32.

Brophy, J. (1999). Toward a model of the value aspects of motivation in education: Developing appreciation for particular learning domains and activities. *Educational Psychologist, 34,* 75–85.

Brothers, K. J. (1994). Office paper recycling: A function of container proximity. *Journal of Applied Behavior Analysis, 27,* 153–160.

Brouwers, M., & Wiggum, C. D. (1993). Bulimia and perfectionism: Developing the courage to be imperfect. *Journal of Mental Health Counseling, 15,* 141–149.

Brown, A. S. (1991). A review of the tip-of-the-tongue experience. *Psychological Bulletin, 109,* 204–223.

Brown, I., Jr., & Inouye, D. K. (1978). Learned helplessness through modeling: The role of perceived similarity in competence. *Journal of Personality and Social Psychology, 36,* 900–908.

Brown, J. S. (1961). *The motivation of behavior.* New York: McGraw-Hill.

Brown, L. T., Ruder, V. G., Ruder, J. H., & Young, S. D. (1974). Stimulation seeking and the change seeker index. *Journal of Consulting and Clinical Psychology, 42,* 311.

Brownell, K. D. (1982). The addictive disorders. In C. M. Franks, B. T. Wilson, P. C. Kendall, & K. D. Brownell (Eds.), *Annual review of behavior therapy: Theory and practice* (Vol. 8, pp. 208-272). New York: Guilford Press.

Brownell, K. D. (1991). Dieting and the search for the perfect body: Where physiology and culture collide. *Behavior Therapy, 22,* 1–12.

Bryne, D. (1961). Anxiety and the experimental arousal of affiliation need. *Journal of Abnormal and Social Psychology, 63,* 660–662.

Buck, R. (1984). *The communication of emotion.* New York: Guilford Press.

Buck, R. (1986). The psychology of emotion. In J. LeDoux & W. Hirst (Eds.), *Mind and brain: Dialogues in cognitive neuroscience* (pp. 275–300). New York: Cambridge University Press.

Buck, R. (1988). *Human motivation and emotion.* New York: John Wiley & Sons.

Buckner, C. E., & Swann, Jr., W. B. (1995, August). *Physical abuse in close relationships: The dynamic interplay of couple characteristics.* Paper presented at the annual meeting of the American Psychological Association, Washington, DC.

Bugental, J. F. T. (1967). *Challenges and humanistic psychology.* New York: McGraw-Hill.

Bugental, J. F. T. (1970). The humanistic ethic: The individual in psychotherapy as a societal change agent. *Journal of Humanistic Psychology, 10,* 11–25.

Burger, J. M. (1984). Desire for control, locus of control, and proneness to depression. *Journal of Personality, 52,* 71–89.

Burger, J. M. (1985). Desire for control and achievement-related behaviors. *Journal of Personality and Social Psychology, 48,* 1520–1533.

Burger, J. M. (1986). Desire for control and illusion of control: The effects of familiarity and sequence of outcomes. *Journal of Research in Personality, 20,* 66–76.

Burger, J. M. (1990). Desire for control and interpersonal interaction style. *Journal of Research in Personality, 24,* 32–44.

Burger, J. M. (1992). *Desire for control: Personality, social, and clinical perspectives*. New York: Plenum.

Burger, J. M., & Arkin, R. M. (1980). Prediction, control, and learned helplessness. *Journal of Personality and Social Psychology, 38,* 482–491.

Burger, J. M., & Cooper, H. M. (1979). The desirability of control. *Motivation and Emotion, 3,* 381–393.

Burger, J. M., Oakman, J. A., & Bullard, N. G. (1983). Desire for control and the perception of crowding. *Personality and Social Psychology Bulletin, 9,* 475–479.

Burger, J. M., & Schnerring, D. A. (1982). The effects of desire for control and extrinsic rewards on the illusion of control and gambling. *Motivation and Emotion, 6,* 329–335.

Burris, C. T., Harmon-Jones, E., & Tarpley, W. R. (1997). "By faith alone": Religious agitation and cognitive dissonance. *Basic and Applied Social Psychology, 19,* 17–31.

Bursik, K. (1991). Adaptation to divorce and ego development in adult women. *Journal of Personality and Social Psychology, 60,* 300–306.

Buss, D. M., & Schmitt, D. P. (1993). Sexual strategies theory: An evolutionary perspective on human mating. *Psychological Review, 100,* 204–232.

Bussey, K., & Bandura, A. (1999). Social cognitive theory of gender development and differentiation. *Psychological Review, 106,* 676–713.

Byrne, B. M. (1984). The general/academic self-concept nomological network: A review of construct validation research. *Review of Educational Research, 54,* 427–456.

Byrne, B. M. (1986). Self-concept/academic achievement relations: An investigation of dimensionality, stability, and causality. *Canadian Journal of Behavioral Science, 18,* 173–186.

Byrne, B. M. (1996). Academic self-concept: Its structure, measurement, and relation with academic achievement. In B. A. Bracken (Ed.), *Handbook of self-concept*. New York: Wiley.

Cabanac, M., & Duclaux, P. (1970). Obesity: Absence of satiety aversion to sucrose? *Science, 168,* 496–497.

Cacioppo, J. T., Petty, R. E., Losch, M. E., & Kim, H. S. (1986). Electromyographic activity over facial muscle regions can differentiate the valence and intensity of affective reactions. *Journal of Personality and Social Psychology, 50,* 260–268.

Calhoon, L. L. (1988). Explorations in the biochemistry of sensation seeking. *Personality and Individual Differences, 9,* 941–949.

Cameron, J., & Pierce, W. D. (1994). Reinforcement, reward, and intrinsic motivation: A meta-analysis. *Review of Educational Research, 64,* 363–423.

Campfield, L. A., Smith, F. J., & Burn, P. (1997a). The OB protein (leptin) pathway: A link between adipose tissue mass and central neural networks. *Hormone and Metabolic Research, 28,* 619–632.

Campfield, L. A., Smith, F. J., & Burn, P. (1997b). OB protein: A hormonal controller of central neural networks mediating behavioral, metabolic and neuroendocrine responses. *Endocrinology and Metabolism, 4,* 81–102.

Campfield, L. A., Smith, F. J., & Burn, P. (1998). Strategies and potential molecular targets for obesity treatment. *Science, 280,* 1383–1387.

Campfield, L. A., Smith, F. J., Rosenbaum, M., & Hirsch, J. (1996). Human eating: Evidence for a physiological basis using a modified paradigm. *Neuroscience and Biobehavioral Reviews, 20,* 133–137.

Campion, M. A., & Lord, R. G. (1982). A control systems conceptualization of the goal-setting and changing process. *Organizational Behavior and Human Performance, 30,* 265–287.

Camras, L. (1977). Facial expressions used by children in a conflict situation. *Child Development, 48,* 1431–1435.

Cannon, W. B. (1927). The James-Lange theory of emotion: A critical examination and an alternative theory. *American Journal of Psychology, 39,* 106–124.

Cannon, W. B. (1929). *Bodily changes in pain, hunger, fear, and rage*. New York: Appleton.

Cannon, W. B. (1932). *The wisdom of the body*. New York: W. W. Norton.

Cantor, N., Markus, H., Niedenthal, P., & Nurius, P. (1986). On motivation and the self-concept. In R. M. Sorrentino & E. T. Higgins (Eds.), *Handbook of motivation and cognition* (Vol. 1, pp. 96–121). New York: Guilford Press.

Carlsmith, J. M., Ellsworth, P. C., & Aronson, E. (1976). *Methods of research in social psychology*. New York: Random House.

Carlson, N. C. (1988). *Discovering psychology.* Boston: Allyn & Bacon.

Carnelley, K. B., Pietromonaco, P. R., & Jaffe, K. (1994). Depression, working models of others, and relationship functioning. *Journal of Personality and Social Psychology, 66,* 127–140.

Carnevale, P. J. D., & Isen, A. M. (1986). The influence of positive affect and visual access on the discovery of integrative solutions in bilateral negotiation. *Organizational Behavior and Human Decision Processes, 37,* 1–13.

Carpenter, S., & Halberstadt, A. G. (1996). What makes people angry? Layperson's and psychologists' categorizations of anger in the family. *Cognition and Emotion, 10,* 627–656.

Carstensen, L. L. (1993). Motivation for social contact across the life span. In J. Jacobs (Ed.), *Nebraska Symposium on Motivation: Developmental perspectives on motivation* (Vol. 40, pp. 209–254). Lincoln: University of Nebraska Press.

Carstensen, L. L. (1995). Evidence for a life-span theory of socioemotional selectivity. *Current Directions in Psychological Science, 4,* 151–156.

Carstensen, L. L., Gottman, J. M., & Levenson, R. W. (1995). Emotional behavior in long-term marriage. *Psychology and Aging, 10,* 140–149.

Carver, C. S., & Blaney, P. H. (1977). Avoidance behavior and perceived control. *Motivation and Emotion, 1,* 61–63.

Carver, C. S., & Scheier, M. F. (1981). *Attention and self-regulation: A control theory approach to human behavior.* New York: Springer-Verlag.

Carver, C. S., & Scheier, M. F. (1982). Control theory: A useful conceptual framework for personality: Social, clinical, and health psychology. *Psychological Bulletin, 92,* 111–135.

Carver, C. S., & Scheier, M. F. (1990). Origins and functions of positive and negative affect: A control-process view. *Psychological Review, 97,* 19–35.

Chen, M., & Isen, A. M. (1992). *The influence of positive affect and success on persistence on a failed task.* Unpublished manuscript, Cornell University.

Cialdini, R. B., Petty, R. E., & Cacioppo, J. T. (1981). Attitudes and attitude change. *Annual Review of Psychology, 32,* 357–404.

Cioffi, D. (1991). Beyond attentional strategies: A cognitive-perceptual model of somatic interpretation. *Psychological Bulletin, 109,* 25–41.

Clark, L. A., & Watson, D. (1994). Distinguishing functional from dysfunctional affective responses. In P. Ekman & R. J. Davidson (Eds.), *The nature of emotion: Fundamental questions* (pp. 131–136). New York: Oxford University Press.

Clark, L. A., Watson, D., & Leeka, J. (1989). Diurnal variation in the positive affects. *Motivation and Emotion, 13,* 205–234.

Clark, L. A., Watson, D., & Mineka, S. (1994). Temperament, personality, and the mood and anxiety disorders. *Journal of Abnormal Psychology, 103,* 103–116.

Clark, M. S. (1984). Record keeping in two types of relationships. *Journal of Personality and Social Psychology, 47,* 549–557.

Clark, M. S., & Mills, J. (1979). Interpersonal attraction in exchange and communal relationships. *Journal of Personality and Social Psychology, 37,* 12–24.

Clark, M. S., Mills, J., & Powell, M. C. (1986). Keeping track of needs in communal and exchange relationships. *Journal of Personality and Social Psychology, 51,* 333–338.

Clark, M. S., Ouellette, R., Powell, M. C., & Milberg, S. (1987). Recipient's mood, relationship type, and helping. *Journal of Personality and Social Psychology, 53,* 94–103.

Clarke, R. A. (1973). Measures of achievement and affiliation motivation. *Review of Educational Research, 43,* 41–51.

Clement, R., & Jonah, B. A. (1984). Field dependence, sensation seeking and driving behavior. *Personality and Individual Differences, 5,* 87–93.

Clifford, M. M. (1984). Thoughts on a theory of constructive failure. *Educational Psychologist, 19,* 108–120.

Clifford, M. M. (1988). Failure tolerance and academic risk-taking in ten- to twelve-year-old students. *British Journal of Educational Psychology, 58,* 15–27.

Clifford, M. M. (1990). Students need challenge, not easy success. *Educational Leadership, 48,* 22–26.

Clore, G. L. (1994). Why emotions require cognition. In P. Ekman & R. J. Davidson (Eds.), *The nature of emotion: Fundamental questions* (pp. 181–191). New York: Oxford University Press.

Clore, G. L., Ortony, A., & Foss, M. (1987). The psychological foundations of the affective lexicon. *Journal of Personality and Social Psychology, 53,* 751–766.

Cofer, C. N., & Appley, M. H. (1964). *Motivation: Theory and research.* New York: John Wiley.

Cohen, S., Sherrod, D. R., & Clark, M. S. (1986). Social skills and the stress-protective role of social support. *Journal of Personality and Social Psychology, 50,* 963–973.

Cohn, J. F., Zlochower, A. J., Lien, J., & Kanade, T. (1999). Automated face analysis by feature point tracking has high concurrent validity with manual FACS coding. *Psychophysiology, 36,* 35–43.

Coles, M. G. H., Ponchin, E., & Porges, S. W., (Eds.) (1986). *Psychophysiology: Systems, processes, and applications.* New York: Guilford Press.

Condry, J. (1977). Enemies of exploration: Self-initiated versus other-initiated learning. *Journal of Personality and Social Psychology, 35,* 459–477.

Condry, J. (1987). Enhancing motivation: A social development perspective. *Advances in motivation and achievement: Enhancing motivation, 5,* 23–49.

Condry, J., & Chambers, J. (1978). Intrinsic motivation and the process of learning. In M. R. Lepper & D. Greene (Eds.). *The hidden costs of reward: New perspectives on the psychology of human motivation.* Hillsdale, NJ: Lawrence Erlbaum.

Condry, J., & Stokker, L. G. (1992). Overview of special issue on intrinsic motivation. *Motivation and Emotion, 16,* 157–164.

Connell, J. P. (1990). Context, self, and action: A motivational analysis of self-system processes across the life-span. In D. Cicchetti (Ed.), *The self in transition: From infancy to childhood* (pp. 61–97). Chicago: University of Chicago Press.

Connell, J. P., & Wellborn, J. G. (1991). Competence, autonomy, and relatedness: A motivational analysis of self-system processes. In M. R. Gunnar & L. A. Sroufe (Eds.), *Self processes in development: Minnesota symposium on child psychology* (Vol. 23, pp. 167–216). Chicago: University of Chicago Press.

Connolly, K., & Smith, P. K. (1972). Reactions of pre-school children to a strange observer. In N. G. Blurton-Jones (Ed.), *Ethological studies of child behavior.* Cambridge: Cambridge University Press.

Conti, R., Amabile, T. M., & Pollak, S. (1995). The positive impact of creative activity: Effects of creative task engagement and motivational focus on college students learning. *Personality and Social Psychology Bulletin, 21,* 664–675.

Cooper, K. H. (1968). *Aerobics.* New York: Bantam Books.

Cooper, M. L., Frone, M. R., Russell, M., & Mudar, P. (1995). Drinking to regulate positive and negative emotions: A motivational model of alcohol use. *Journal of Personality and Social Psychology, 69,* 990–1005.

Cooper, W. H. (1983). An achievement motivation nomological network. *Journal of Personality and Social Psychology, 44,* 841–861.

Cordova, D. I., & Lepper, M. R. (1996). Intrinsic motivation and the process of learning: Beneficial effects of contextualization, personalization, and choice. *Journal of Educational Psychology, 88,* 715–730.

Costa, P. T., Jr., & McCrae, R. R. (1980). Influence of extraversion and neuroticism on subjective well-being: Happy and unhappy people. *Journal of Personality and Social Psychology, 38,* 668–678.

Costa, P. T., Jr., & McCrae, R. R. (1988). From catalogue to classification: Murray's needs and the five-factor model. *Journal of Personality and Social Psychology, 55,* 258–265.

Costello, C. G. (1978). A critical review of Seligman's laboratory experiments on learned helplessness and depression in humans. *Journal of Abnormal Psychology, 87,* 21–31.

Cotton, J. L. (1981). A review of research on Schachter's theory of emotion and the misattribution of arousal. *European Journal of Social Psychology, 11,* 365–397.

Covington, M. (1984a). The self-worth theory of achievement motivation: Findings and implications. *The Elementary School Journal, 85,* 5–20.

Covington, M. (1984b). Motivation for self-worth. In R. Ames & C. A. Ames (Eds.), *Research on motivation in education* (Vol. 1, pp. 77–113). New York: Academic Press.

Covington, M. W., & Omelich, C. L. (1984). Task-oriented versus competitive learning structures: Motivational and performance consequences. *Journal of Educational Psychology, 76,* 1038–1050.

Cox, R. (1987). The rich harvest of Abraham Maslow. In A. Maslow *Motivation and personality* (3rd ed., pp. 245–271). New York: Harper & Row.

Coyne, J. C. (1976a). Towards an interactional description of depression. *Psychiatry, 39,* 28–40.

Coyne, J. C. (1976b). Depression and the response of others. *Journal of Abnormal Psychology, 85,* 186–193.

Coyne, J. C., & DeLongis, A. (1986). Going beyond social support: The role of social relationships in adaptation. *Journal of Consulting and Clinical Psychology, 54,* 454–460.

Crago, M., Yates, A., Beutler, L. E., & Arizmendi, T. G. (1985). Height-weight ratios among female athletes: Are collegiate athletics the precursors to an anorexic syndrome? *International Journal of Eating Disorders, 4,* 79–87.

Crandall, C. S. (1988). Social cognition of binge eating. *Journal of Personality and Social Psychology, 55,* 588–598.

Crary, W. G. (1966). Reactions to incongruent self-experiences. *Journal of Consulting Psychology, 30,* 246–252.

Crews, F. (1996). The verdict on Freud. *Psychological Science, 7,* 63–67.

Crick, F., & Mitchison, G. (1986). REM sleep and neural networks. *Journal of Mind and Behavior, 7,* 229–250.

Cross, P. (1977). Not can but will college teaching be improved? *New Directions for Higher Education, 17,* 1–15.

Cross, S. E., & Markus, H. R. (1991). Possible selves across the life span. *Human Development, 34,* 230–255.

Cross, S. E., & Markus, H. R. (1994). Self-schemas, possible selves, and competent performance. *Journal of Educational Psychology, 86,* 423–438.

Crowne, D. P., & Marlowe, D. (1964). *The approval motive.* New York: Wiley.

Croyle, R. T., & Cooper, J. (1983). Dissonance arousal: Physiological evidence. *Journal of Personality and Social Psychology, 45,* 782–791.

Csikszentmihalyi, M. (1975). *Beyond boredom and anxiety: The experience of flow in work and play.* San Francisco: Jossey-Bass.

Csikszentmihalyi, M. (1982). Toward a psychology of optimal experience. *Review of Personality and Social Psychology, 3,* 13–36.

Csikszentmihalyi, M. (1990). *Flow: The psychology of optimal experience.* New York: Harper & Row.

Csikszentmihalyi, M. (1997). *Finding flow: The psychology of engagement with everyday life.* New York: Basic Books.

Csikszentmihalyi, M., & Csikszentmihalyi, I. (Eds.) (1988). *Optimal experiences: Psychological studies of flow in consciousness.* New York: Cambridge University Press.

Csikszentmihalyi, M., & LeFevre, J. (1989). Optimal experience in work and leisure. *Journal of Personality and Social Psychology, 56,* 815–822.

Csikszentmihalyi, M., & Nakamura, J. (1989). The dynamics of intrinsic motivation: A study of adolescents. In C. A. Ames & R. Ames (Eds.), *Research on motivation in education* (Vol. 3, pp. 45–61). San Diego: Academic Press.

Csikszentmihalyi, M., & Rathunde, K. (1993). The measurement of flow in everyday life: Toward a theory of emergent motivation. In J. E. Jacobs (Ed.), *Nebraska symposium on motivation: Developmental perspectives on motivation* (Vol. 40, pp. 57–97). Lincoln: University of Nebraska Press.

Csikszentmihalyi, M., Rathunde, K., & Whalen, S. (1993). *Talented teenagers: The roots of success and failure.* New York: Cambridge University Press.

Cunningham, M. R. (1986). Measuring the physical in physical attractiveness: Quasi-experiments on the sociobiology of female facial beauty. *Journal of Personality and Social Psychology, 50,* 925–935.

Cunningham, M. R., Barbee, A. P., & Pike, C. L. (1990). What do women want? Facialmetric assessment of multiple motives in the perception of male facial physical attractiveness. *Journal of Personality and Social Psychology, 59,* 61–62.

Cunningham, M. R., Roberts, A. R., Barbee, A. P., Druen, P. B., & Wu, C. (1995). Their ideas of beauty are, on the whole, the same as ours: Consistency and variability in the cross-cultural perception of female physical attractiveness. *Journal of Personality and Social Psychology, 68,* 261–279.

D'Amato, M. R. (1974). Derived motives. *Annual Review of Psychology, 25,* 83–106.

Daniels, M. (1988). The myth of self-actualization. *Journal of Humanistic Psychology, 28,* 7–38.

Darwin, C. A. (1859). *On the origin of species by means of natural selection.* London: John Murray; New York: Modern Library, 1936.

Darwin, C. A. (1872). *The expression of the emotions in man and animals.* London: John Murray.

Davidson, P., Turiel, E., & Black, A. (1983). The effects of stimulus familiarity in the use of criteria and justification in children's social reasoning. *British Journal of Developmental Psychology, 1,* 49–65.

Davidson, R. J. (1994). On emotion, mood, and related affective constructs. In P. Ekman & R. J. Davidson (Eds.), *The nature of emotion: Fundamental questions* (pp. 51–55). New York: Oxford University Press.

Davidson, R. J., Ekman, P., Saron, C., Senulis, J., & Friesen, W. V. (1990). Approach/withdrawal and cerebral asymmetry. *Journal of Personality and Social Psychology, 58,* 330–341.

Day, J. D., Borkowski, J. G., Punzo, D., & Howsepian, B. (1994). Enhancing possible selves in Mexican American students. *Motivation and Emotion, 18,* 79–103.

Deaux, K., Reid, A., Mizrahi, K., & Ethier, K. A. (1995). Parameters of social identity. *Journal of Personality and Social Psychology, 53,* 281–295.

DeCastro, J. M., & Brewer, E. M. (1991). The amount eaten in meals by humans is a power function of the number of people present. *Physiology and Behavior, 51,* 121–125.

deCharms, R. (1976). *Enhancing motivation: Change in the classroom.* New York: Irvington.

deCharms, R. (1984). Motivation enhancement in educational settings. In R. E. Ames & C. A. Ames (Eds.), *Research on motivation in education: Student motivation* (Vol. 1, pp. 275–310). New York: Academic Press.

deCharms, R., & Moeller, G. H. (1962). Values expressed in American children's readers: 1800–1950. *Journal of Abnormal and Social Psychology, 64,* 136–142.

Deci, E. L. (1971). Effects of externally mediated rewards on intrinsic motivation. *Journal of Personality and Social Psychology, 18,* 105–115.

Deci, E. L. (1972). Intrinsic motivation, extrinsic reinforcement, and inequity. *Journal of Personality and Social Psychology, 22,* 113–120.

Deci, E. L. (1975). *Intrinsic motivation.* New York: Plenum.

Deci, E. L. (1980). *The psychology of self-determination.* Lexington, MA: Lexington Books.

Deci, E. L. (1992a). On the nature and function of motivation theories. *Psychological Science, 3,* 167–171.

Deci, E. L. (1992b). The relation of interest to the motivation of behavior: A self-determination theory perspective. In K. A. Renninger, S. Hidi, & A. Krapp (Eds.), *The role of interest in learning and development* (pp. 43–60). Hillsdale, NJ: Erlbaum.

Deci, E. L. (1995). *Why we do what we do: Understanding self-motivation.* New York: Penguin Books.

Deci, E. L., Betley, G., Kahle, J., Abrams, L., & Porac, J. (1981). When trying to win: Competition and intrinsic motivation. *Personality and Social Psychology Bulletin, 7,* 79–83.

Deci, E. L., & Casio, W. F. (1972, April). *Changes in intrinsic motivation as a function of negative feedback and threats.* Paper presented at the meeting of the Eastern Psychological Association, Boston, MA.

Deci, E. L., Connell, J. P., & Ryan, R. M. (1989). Self-determination in a work organization. *Journal of Applied Psychology, 74,* 580–590.

Deci, E. L., Driver, R. E., Hotchkiss, L., Robbins, R. J., & Wilson, I. M. (1993). The relation of mother's controlling vocalizations to children's intrinsic motivation. *Journal of Experimental Child Psychology, 55,* 151–162.

Deci, E. L., Eghrari, H., Patrick, B. C., & Leone, D. R. (1994). Facilitating internalization: The self-determination theory perspective. *Journal of Personality, 62,* 119–142.

Deci, E. L., Koestner, R., & Ryan, R. M. (1999a). A meta-analytic review of experiments examining the effects of extrinsic rewards on intrinsic motivation. *Psychological Bulletin, 125,* 627–668.

Deci, E. L., Koestner, R., & Ryan, R. M. (1999b). The undermining effect is a reality after all: Extrinsic rewards, task interest, and self-determination: Reply to Eisenberger, Pierce, and Cameron (1999) and Lepper, Henderlong, and Gingras (1999). *Psychological Bulletin, 125,* 692–700.

Deci, E. L., & Olson, B. C. (1989). Motivation and competition: Their role in sports. In J. H. Goldstein (Ed.), *Sports, games, and play: Social and psychological viewpoints* (2nd ed., pp. 83-110). Hillsdale, NJ: Erlbaum.

Deci, E. L., & Ryan, R. M. (1980). The empirical exploration of intrinsic motivational processes. In

L. Berkowitz (Ed.), *Advances in experimental social psychology* (Vol. 13, pp. 39–80). New York: Academic Press.

Deci, E. L., & Ryan, R. M. (1985a). *Intrinsic motivation and self-determination in human behavior.* New York: Plenum.

Deci, E. L., & Ryan, R. M. (1985b). The General Causality Orientations Scale: Self-determination in personality. *Journal of Research in Personality, 19,* 109–134.

Deci, E. L., & Ryan, R. M. (1987). The support of autonomy and the control of behavior. *Journal of Personality and Social Psychology, 53,* 1024–1037.

Deci, E. L., & Ryan, R. M. (1991). A motivational approach to self: Integration in personality. In R. Dienstbier (Ed.), *Nebraska symposium on motivation: Perspectives on motivation* (Vol. 38, pp. 237–288). Lincoln: University of Nebraska Press.

Deci, E. L., & Ryan, R. M. (1995). Human autonomy: The basis for true self-esteem. In M. Kernis (Ed.), *Efficacy, agency, and self-esteem* (pp. 31–49). New York: Plenum.

Deci, E. L., Ryan, R. M., & Williams, G. C. (1995). Need satisfaction and the self-regulation of learning. *Learning and Individual Differences, 8,* 165–183.

Deci, E. L., Schwartz, A., Scheinman, L., & Ryan, R. M. (1981). An instrument to assess adult's orientations toward control versus autonomy in children: Reflections on intrinsic motivation and perceived competence. *Journal of Educational Psychology, 73,* 642–650.

Deci, E. L., Spiegel, N. H., Ryan, R. M., Koestner, R., & Kauffman, M. (1982). Effects of performance standards on teaching styles: Behavior of controlling teachers. *Journal of Educational Psychology, 74,* 852–859.

Delgado, J. M. R., & Anand, B. K. (1953). Increased food intake induced by electrical stimulation of the lateral hypothalamus. *American Journal of Physiology, 172,* 162–168.

Delisle, J. (1986). Death with honors: Suicide among gifted adolescents. *Journal of Counseling and Development, 64,* 558–560.

DeLongis, A., Coyne, J. C., Dakof, G., Folkman, S., & Lazarus, R. S. (1982). Relations of daily hassles, uplifts, and major life events to health status. *Health Psychology, 1,* 119–136.

DeLongis, A., Folkman, S., & Lazarus, R. S. (1988). The impact of daily stress and mood: Psychological and social resources as mediators. *Journal of Personality and Social Psychology, 54,* 486–495.

Dember, W. N. (1965). The new look in motivation. *American Scientist, 53,* 409–427.

Dember, W. N. (1974). Motivation and the cognitive revolution. *American Psychologist, 29,* 161–168.

Dembroski, T. M., MacDougall, J. M., & Musante, L. (1984). Desirability of control versus locus of control: Relationship to paralinguistics in the Type A interview. *Health Psychology, 3,* 15–26.

Dempsey, E. W. (1951). Homeostasis. In S. S. Stevens (Ed.), *Handbook of experimental psychology* (pp. 209–235). New York: John Wiley.

Denham, S. A., Mitchell-Copeland, J., Strandberg, K., Auerbach, S., & Blair, K. (1997). Parental contributions to preschooler's emotional competence: Direct and indirect effects. *Motivation and Emotion, 21,* 65–86.

DePaulo, B. (1992). Nonverbal behavior and self-presentation. *Psychological Bulletin, 111,* 203–243.

Depue, R. A., & Monroe, S. M. (1978). Learned helplessness in the perspective of the depressive disorders: Conceptual and definitional issues. *Journal of Abnormal Psychology, 87,* 3–20.

de Rivera, J. (1977). *A structural theory of the emotions.* New York: International Universities Press.

de Rivera, J. (1981). The structure of anger. In J. de Rivera (Ed.), *Conceptual encounter: A method for the exploration of human experience.* Washington, DC: University Press of America.

Derryberry, D., & Rothbart, M. K. (1988). Arousal, affect, and attention as components of temperament. *Journal of Personality and Social Psychology, 55,* 958–966.

Deutsch, J. A., & Gonzalez, M. F. (1980). Gastric nutrient content signals satiety. *Behavior Neural Biology, 30,* 113–116.

Deutsch, J. A., Young, W. G., & Kalogeris, T. J. (1978). The stomach signals satiety. *Science, 201,* 165–167.

DeVillis, R. F., DeVillis, B. M., & McCauley, C. (1978). Vicarious acquisition of learned helplessness. *Journal of Personality and Social Psychology, 36,* 894–899.

Dickerson, C., Thibodeau, R., Aronson, E., & Miller, D. (1992). Using cognitive dissonance theory to encourage water conservation. *Journal of Applied Social Psychology, 22,* 841–854.

Diener, C. I., & Dweck, C. S. (1978). An analysis of learned helplessness: Continuous changes in performance, strategy, and achievement cognitions following failure. *Journal of Personality and Social Psychology, 36,* 451–462.

Diener, C. I., & Dweck, C. S. (1980). An analysis of learned helplessness: II. The processing of success. *Journal of Personality and Social Psychology, 39,* 940–952.

Diener, E., & Emmons, R. A. (1984). The independence of positive and negative affect. *Journal of Personality and Social Psychology, 47,* 105–1117.

Diener, E., & Iran-Nejad, A. (1986). The relationship in experience between various types of affect. *Journal of Personality and Social Psychology, 50,* 1031–1038.

Diener, E., Larsen, R. J., Levine, S., & Emmons, R. A. (1985). Frequency and intensity: The underlying dimensions of affect. *Journal of Personality and Social Psychology, 48,* 1253–1265.

Dienstbier, R. A. (1991). Introduction. In R. A. Dienstbier (Ed.), *Nebraska symposium on motivation* (Vol. 38, pp. ix–xiv). Lincoln: University of Nebraska Press.

Dimberg, U. (1982). Facial reactions to facial expressions. *Psychophysiology, 19,* 643–647.

Dimsdale, J. E., & Moss, J. (1980). Plasma catecholamines in stress and exercise. *The Journal of the American Medical Association, 243,* 340–342.

Diserens, C. M. (1925). Psychological objectivism. *Psychological Review, 32,* 121–125.

Dollinger, S. J., & Thelen, M. H. (1978). Overjustification and children's intrinsic motivation: Comparative effects of four rewards. *Journal of Personality and Social Psychology, 36,* 1259–1269.

Donahue, M. J. (1985). Intrinsic and extrinsic religiousness: Review and meta-analysis. *Journal of Personality and Social Psychology, 48,* 400–419.

Donovan, J. M., Hill, E., & Jankowiak, W. R. (1989). Gender, sexual orientation, and truth-or-consequences in studies of physical attractiveness. *Journal of Sex Research, 26,* 264–271.

Druss, R. G., & Silverman, J. A. (1979). Body image and perfectionism of ballerinas. *General Hospital Psychiatry, 2,* 115–121.

Duffy, E. (1957). Psychological significance of the concept of arousal or activation. *Psychological Review, 64, 265–275.*

Dunker, K. (1945). On problem-solving. *Psychological Monographs, 58,* Whole No. 5.

Dunlap, K. (1919). Are there any instincts? *Journal of Abnormal Psychology, 14,* 35–50.

Dunn, J., & Munn, P. (1987). Development of justification in disputes with mother and sibling. *Developmental Psychology, 23,* 791–798.

Dunning, D. (1993). Words to live by: The self and definitions of social concepts and categories. In J. Suls (Ed.), *Psychological perspectives on the self* (Vol. 4, pp. 99–126). Hillsdale, NJ: Lawrence Erlbaum.

Dunning, D., Leuenberger, A., & Sherman, D. A. (1995). A new look at motivated inference: Are self-serving theories of success a product of motivational forces? *Journal of Personality and Social Psychology, 69,* 58–68.

Dunning, D., Meyerowitz, J. A., & Holzberg, A. D. (1989). Ambiguity and self-evaluation: The role of idiosyncratic trait definitions in self-serving assessments of ability. *Journal of Personality and Social Psychology, 57,* 1082–1090.

Dunning, D., Perie, M., & Story, A. L. (1991). Self-serving prototypes of social categories. *Journal of Personality and Social Psychology, 61,* 957–968.

Durkheim, E. (1951). *Suicide.* New York: Free Press.

Dweck, C. S. (1975). The role of expectancies and attributions in the alleviation of learned helplessness. *Journal of Personality and Social Psychology, 31,* 674–685.

Dweck, C. S. (1986). Motivational processes affecting learning. *American Psychologist, 41,* 1040–1048.

Dweck, C. S. (1990). Motivation. In R. Glaser & A. Lesgold (Eds.), *Foundations for a cognitive psychology of education.* Hillsdale, NJ: Lawrence Erlbaum.

Dweck, C. S. (1999). *Self-theories: Their role in motivation, personality, and development.* Philadelphia: Psychology Press.

Dweck, C. S., & Elliot, E. S. (1983). Achievement motivation. In P. Mussen & E. M.Hetherington (Eds.), *Handbook of child psychology* (pp. 643–692). New York: Wiley.

Dweck, C. S., & Leggett, E. L. (1988). A social-cognitive approach to motivation and personality. *Psychological Review, 95,* 256–273.

Dweck, C. S., & Repucci, N. D. (1973). Learned helplessness and reinforcement responsibility in children. *Journal of Personality and Social Psychology, 25,* 109–116.

Dworetzkey, J. P. (1988). *Psychology* (3rd ed.). St. Paul, MN: West.

Dykman, B. M. (1998). Integrating cognitive and motivational factors in depression: Initial tests of a goal-orientation approach. *Journal of Personality and Social Psychology, 74,* 139–158.

Earley, P. C., & Perry, B. C. (1987). Work plan availability and performance: An assessment of task strategy priming on subsequent task completion. *Organizational Behavior and Human Decision Processes, 39,* 279–302.

Earley, P. C., Connolly, T., & Ekegren, G. (1989). Goals, strategy development and task performance: Some limits on the efficacy of goal setting. *Journal of Applied Psychology, 74,* 24–33.

Earley, P. C., Wojnaroski, P., & Prest, W. (1987). Task planning and energy expended: Exploration of how goals influence performance. *Journal of Applied Psychology, 72,* 107–113.

Eaves, L. J., Eysenck, H. J., & Martin, N. G. (1989). *Genes, culture, and personality: An empirical approach.* San Diego: Academic Press.

Eccles, J. S. (1984a). Sex differences in achievement patterns. In T. Sonderegger (Ed.), *Nebraska symposium on motivation: Psychology and gender* (Vol. 32, pp. 97–132). Lincoln: University of Nebraska Press.

Eccles, J. S. (1984b). Sex differences in mathematics participation. In M. Steinkamp & M. L. Maehr (Eds.), *Advances in motivation and achievement* (Vol. 2, pp. 93–137). Lincoln: University of Nebraska Press.

Eccles, J. S., Adler, T. F., Futterman, R., Goff, S. B., Kaczala, C. M., Meece, J. L., & Midgley, C. (1983). Expectancies, values, and academic behaviors. In J. T. Spence (Ed.), *Achievement and achievement motivation* (pp. 75–146). San Francisco: W. H. Freeman.

Eccles, J. S., & Wigfield, A. (1995). In the mind of the achiever: The structure of adolescents' academic achievement related-beliefs and self-perceptions. *Personality and Social Psychology Bulletin, 21,* 215–225.

Eccles-Parsons, J. E., Adler, T. F., & Kaczala, C. M. (1982). Socialization of achievement attitudes and beliefs: Parental influences. *Child Development, 53,* 310–321.

Eccleston, C., & Crombez, G. (1999). Pain demands attention: A cognitive-affective model of the interruptive function of pain. *Psychological Bulletin, 125,* 356–366.

Eckelman, J. D., & Dyck, D. G. (1979). Task- and setting-related cues in immunization against learned helplessness. *American Journal of Psychology, 92,* 653–667.

Eckenrode, J. (1984). Impact of chronic and acute stressors on daily reports of mood. *Journal of Personality and Social Psychology, 46,* 907–918.

Edwards, A. L. (1959). *Manual for the Edwards Personal Preference Schedule.* New York: The Psychology Corporation.

Edwards, R., Manstead, A. S. R., & MacDonald, C. J. (1984). The relationship between children's sociometric status and ability to recognize facial expressions of emotion. *European Journal of Social Psychology, 14,* 235–238.

Eibl-Eibesfeldt, I. (1971). *Love and hate.* London: Methuen.

Eibl-Eibesfeldt, I. (1972). Similarities and differences between cultures in expressive movements. In R. A. Hinde (Ed.), *Nonverbal communication.* Cambridge: Cambridge University Press.

Eibl-Eibesfeldt, I. (1989). *Human ethology.* New York: Aldine De Gruyter.

Eidelson, R. J. (1980). Interpersonal satisfaction and level of involvement: A curvilinear relationship. *Journal of Personality and Social Psychology, 39,* 460–470.

Eisen, S. V. (1979). Actor-observer differences in information inferences and causal attribution. *Journal of Personality and Social Psychology, 37,* 261–272.

Eisenberger, R., Pierce, W. D., & Cameron, J. (1999). Effects of reward on intrinsic motivation: Negative, neutral, and positive: Comment on Deci, Koestner, and Ryan (1999). *Psychological Bulletin, 125,* 677–691.

Eisenstadt, D., & Leippe, M. R. (1994). The self-comparison process of self-discrepant feedback: Consequences of learning you are what you thought you were not. *Journal of Personality and Social Psychology, 67,* 611–626.

Ekman, P. (1972). Universal and cultural differences in facial expression of emotion. In J. R. Cole

(Ed.), *Nebraska symposium on motivation* (Vol. 19, pp. 207–284). Lincoln: University of Nebraska Press.

Ekman, P. (1992). An argument for basic emotions. *Cognition and Emotion, 6,* 169–200.

Ekman, P. (1993). Facial expression and emotion. *American Psychologist, 48,* 384–392.

Ekman, P. (1994a). All emotions are basic. In P. Ekman & R. J. Davidson (Eds.), *The nature of emotion: Fundamental questions* (pp. 15–19). New York: Oxford University Press.

Ekman, P. (1994b). Strong evidence for universals in facial expressions: A reply to Russell's mistaken critique. *Psychological Bulletin, 115,* 268–287.

Ekman, P., & Davidson, R. J. (1993). Voluntary smiling changes regional brain activity. *Psychological Science, 4,* 342–345.

Ekman, P., & Davidson, R. J. (Eds.). (1994). *The nature of emotion: Fundamental questions* (pp. 20–24). New York: Oxford University Press.

Ekman, P., & Friesen, W. V. (1971). Constants across cultures in facial expressions of emotion. In J. K. Cole (Ed.), *Nebraska symposium on motivation* (pp. 207–283). Lincoln: University of Nebraska Press.

Ekman, P., & Friesen, W. V. (1975). *Unmasking the face.* Englewood Cliffs, NJ: Prentice-Hall.

Ekman, P., & Friesen, W. V. (1978). *Facial action coding system.* Palo Alto, CA: Consulting Psychologists Press.

Ekman, P., & Friesen, W. V. (1986). A new pan-cultural facial expression of emotion. *Motivation and Emotion, 10,* 159–168.

Ekman, P., Levenson, R. W., & Friesen, W. V. (1983). Autonomic nervous system activity distinguishes between emotions. *Science, 221,* 1208–1210.

Ekman, P., & Rosenberg, E. (1997). *What the face reveals.* New York: Oxford University Press.

Ekman, P., Sorenson, E. R., & Friesen, W. V. (1969). Pan-cultural elements in facial displays of emotion. *Science, 164,* 86–88.

Elkin, R., & Leippe, M. (1986). Physiological arousal, dissonance, and attitude change: Evidence for a dissonance-arousal link and a "don't remind me" effect. *Journal of Personality and Social Psychology, 51,* 55–65.

Elliot, A. J. (1997). Integrating the "classic" and "contemporary" approaches to achievement motivation: A hierarchical model of approach and avoidance achievement motivation. In M. L. Maehr & P. R. Pintrich (Eds.), *Advances in motivation and achievement* (Vol. 10, pp. 143–179). Greenwich, CT: JAI Press.

Elliot, A. J. (1999). Approach and avoidance motivation and achievement goals. *Educational Psychologist, 34,* 169–189.

Elliot, A. J., & Church, M. (1997). A hierarchical model of approach and avoidance achievement motivation. *Journal of Personality and Social Psychology, 72,* 218–232.

Elliot, A. J., & Devine, P. G. (1994). On the motivational nature of cognitive dissonance: Dissonance as psychological discomfort. *Journal of Personality and Social Psychology, 66,* 382–394.

Elliot, A. J., & Harackiewicz, J. (1996). Approach and avoidance goals and intrinsic motivation: A mediational analysis. *Journal of Personality and Social Psychology, 70,* 461–475.

Elliot, A. J., & McGregor, H. (1999). Test anxiety and the hierarchical model of approach and avoidance achievement motivation. *Journal of Personality and Social Psychology, 76,* 628–644.

Elliot, A. J., & Sheldon, K. (1997). Avoidance achievement motivation: A personal goals analysis. *Journal of Personality and Social Psychology, 73,* 171–185.

Elliot, A. J., Sheldon, K., & Church, M. (1997). Avoidance personal goals and subjective well-being. *Personality and Social Psychology Bulletin, 23,* 915–927.

Elliot, E., & Dweck, C. (1988). Goals: An approach to motivation and achievement. *Journal of Personality and Social Psychology, 54,* 5–12.

Ellsworth, P. C. (1994). William James and emotion: Is a century of fame worth a century of misunderstanding? *Psychological Review, 101,* 222–229.

Ellsworth, P. C., & Smith, C. A. (1988a). From appraisal to emotion: Differences among unpleasant feelings. *Motivation and Emotion, 12,* 271–302.

Ellsworth, P. C., & Smith, C. A. (1988b). Shades of joy: Patterns of appraisal differentiating pleasant emotions. *Cognition and Emotion, 2,* 301–331.

Elman, D., & Killebrew, T. J. (1978). Incentives and seat belts: Changing a resistant behavior through extrinsic motivation. *Journal of Applied Social Psychology, 8,* 73–83.

Emmons, R. A. (1986). Personal strivings: An approach to personality and subjective well-being. *Journal of Personality and Social Psychology, 51,* 1058–1068.

Emmons, R. A. (1989). The personal striving approach to personality. In L. A. Pervin (Ed.), *Goal concepts in personality and social psychology* (pp. 87–126). Hillsdale, NJ: Lawrence Erlbaum.

Emmons, R. A. (1991). Personal strivings, daily life events, and psychological and physical well-being. *Journal of Personality, 59,* 453–472.

Emmons, R. A. (1996). Striving and feeling: Personal goals and subjective well-being. In P. M. Gollwitzer & J. A. Bargh (Eds.), *The psychology of action: Linking cognition and motivation to behavior* (pp. 313–337). New York: Guilford Press.

Emmons, R. A., & Diener, E. (1986). Influence of impulsivity and sociability on subjective well-being. *Journal of Personality and Social Psychology, 50,* 1211–1215.

Emmons, R. A., & McAdams, D. P. (1991). Personal strivings and motive dispositions: Exploring the links. *Personality and Social Psychology Bulletin, 17,* 648–654.

Engberg, L. A., Hansen, G., Welker, R. L., & Thomas, D. R. (1972). Acquisition of key-pecking via autoshaping as a function of prior experience: Learned laziness? *Science, 178,* 1002–1004.

Entwistle, D. R. (1972). To dispel fantasies about fantasy-based measures of achievement motivation. *Psychological Bulletin, 77,* 377–391.

Epstein, A. N. (1973). Epilogue: Retrospect and prognosis. In A. N. Epstein, H. R. Kissileff, & E. Stellar (Eds.), *The neuropsychology of thirst: New findings and advances in concepts* (pp. 315–332). New York: Wiley.

Epstein, J. A., & Harackiewicz, J. H. (1992). Winning is not enough: The effects of competition and achievement orientation on intrinsic interest. *Personality and Social Psychology Bulletin, 18,* 128–138.

Erdelyi, M. H. (1990). Repression, reconstruction, and defense: History and integration of the psychoanalytic and experimental frameworks. In J. L. Singer (Ed.), *Repression and dissociation* (pp. 1–31). Chicago: University of Chicago Press.

Erdelyi, M. H. (1985). *Psychoanalysis: Freud's cognitive psychology.* New York: W. H. Freeman.

Erez, M. (1977). Feedback: A necessary condition for the goal setting performance relationship. *Journal of Applied Psychology, 62,* 624–627.

Erez, M., Earley, P. C., & Hulin, C. L. (1985). The impact of participation on goal acceptance and performance: A two-step model. *Academy of Management Journal, 28,* 50–66.

Erez, M., & Kanfer, F. H. (1983). The role of goal acceptance in goal setting and task performance. *Academy of Management Review, 8,* 454–463.

Erez, M., & Zidon, I. (1984). Effects of goal acceptance on the relationship to goal difficulty and performance. *Journal of Applied Psychology, 60,* 69–78.

Erikson, E. H. (1959). Identity and the life cycle. *Psychological Issues, 1,* 1–171.

Erikson, E. H. (1963). *Childhood and society* (2nd ed.). New York: Norton.

Erikson, E. H. (1964). *Insight and responsibility.* New York: Norton.

Erikson, E. H. (1968). *Identity, youth, and crisis.* New York: Norton.

Estrada, P., Arsenio, W. F., Hess, R. D., & Holloway, S. D. (1987). Affective quality of the mother-child relationship: Longitudinal consequences for children's school-relevant cognitive functioning. *Developmental Psychology, 23,* 210–215.

Ethington, C. A. (1991). A test of a model of achievement behaviors. *American Educational Research Journal, 28,* 155–172.

Evans, G. E., Shapiro, D. H., & Lewis, M. (1993). Specifying dysfunctional mismatches between different control dimensions. *British Journal of Psychology, 84,* 255–273.

Exline, R. V. (1962). Need affiliation and initial communication behavior in problem solving groups characterized by low interpersonal visibility. *Psychological Reports, 10,* 79–89.

Exner, J. E., Jr. (1986). *The Rorschach: A comprehensive system* (Vol. 1, 2nd ed.). New York: Wiley-Interscience.

Eysenck, H. J. (1967). *The biological basis of personality.* Springfield, IL: Charles C. Thomas.

Eysenck, H. J. (1971). *Readings in extraversion-introversion: II. Fields of application.* London: Staples.

Eysenck, H. J. (1986). Can personality study ever be scientific? *Journal of Social Behavior and Personality, 1,* 3–19.

Eysenck, H. J. & Eysenck, S. B. G. (1968). *Manual of the Eysenck Personality Inventory.* London: University of London Press.

Eysenck, H. J., & Eysenck, S. B. G. (1969). *Personality structure and measurement.* New York: Routledge, Chapman, & Hall.

Eysenck, H. J., & Eysenck, S. B. G. (1985). *Personality and individual differences.* New York: Plenum.

Fanselow, M. S. (1985). Odors released by stressed rats produce opioid analgesia in unstressed rats. *Behavioral Neuroscience, 99,* 589–592.

Faust, I. M., Johnson, P. R., & Hirsch, J. (1977a). Adipose tissue regeneration following lipectomy. *Science, 197,* 391–393.

Faust, I. M., Johnson, P. R., & Hirsch, J. (1977b). Surgical removal of adipose tissue alters feeding behavior and the development of obesity in rats. *Science, 197,* 393–396.

Fazio, R. H., & Cooper, J. (1983). Arousal in the dissonance process. In J. T. Cacioppo & R. E. Petty (Eds.), *Social psychophysiology: A sourcebook* (pp. 122-152). New York: Guilford.

Fazio, R. H., Jackson, J. R., Dunton, B., & Williams, C. J. (1995). Variability in automatic activation as an unobtrusive measure of racial attitudes: A bona fide pipeline? *Journal of Personality and Social Psychology, 69,* 1013–1027.

Fazio, R. H., Zanna, M., & Cooper, J. (1977). Dissonance and self-perception: An integrative view of each theory's proper domain of application. *Journal of Experimental Social Psychology, 13,* 464–479.

Fazio, R. H., Zanna, M., & Cooper, J. (1979). On the relationship of data to theory: A reply to Ronis and Greenwald. *Journal of Experimental Social Psychology, 15,* 70–66.

Feather, N. T. (1961). The relationship of persistence at a task to expectation of success and achievement related motives. *Journal of Abnormal and Social Psychology, 63,* 552–561.

Feather, N. T. (1963). Persistence at a difficult task with alternative tasks of intermediate difficulty. *Journal of Abnormal and Social Psychology, 66,* 604–609.

Feather, N. T. (1966). Effects of prior success and failure on expectations of success and subsequent performance. *Journal of Personality and Social Psychology, 3,* 287–298.

Feather, N. T. (1992). Values, valences, expectations, and actions. *Journal of Social Issues, 48,* 109–124.

Feather, N. T. (1995). Values, valences, and choices: The influence of values on the perceived attractiveness of choice of alternatives. *Journal of Personality and Social Psychology, 68,* 1135–1151.

Feather, N. T., & Newton, J. W. (1982). Values, expectations, and the prediction of social action: An expectancy-value analysis. *Motivation and Emotion, 6,* 217–244.

Feather, N. T., & Saville, M. R. (1967). Effects of amount of prior success and failure on expectations of success and subsequent task performance. *Journal of Personality and Social Psychology, 5,* 226–232.

Feeney, J. A., & Noller, P. (1990). Attachment style as a predictor of adult romantic relationships. *Journal of Personality and Social Psychology, 58,* 281–291.

Fehr, B., Baldwin, M., Collins, L., Patterson, S., & Benditt, R. (1999). Anger in close relationships: An interpersonal script analysis. *Personality and Social Psychology Bulletin, 25,* 299–312.

Fehr, B., & Russell, J. A. (1984). Concept of emotion viewed from a prototype perspective. *Journal of Experimental Psychology: General, 113,* 464–486.

Felson, R. B. (1984). The effect of self-appraisals of ability on academic performance. *Journal of Personality and Social Psychology, 47,* 944–952.

Feltz, D. L. (1992). Understanding motivation in sport: A self-efficacy perspective. In G. C. Roberts (Ed.), *Motivation in sport and exercise* (pp. 93–105). Champaign, IL: Human Kinetics.

Fenigstein, A., Scheier, M. F., & Buss, A. H. (1975). Public and private self-consciousness: Assessment and theory. *Journal of Consulting and Clinical Psychology, 43,* 522–527.

Fernald, A. (1992). Human maternal vocalizations to infants as biologically relevant signals: An evolutionary perspective. In J. H. Barkow, L. Cosmides, & J. Tooby (Eds.), *The adapted mind* (pp. 391–428). New York: Oxford University Press.

Fernandez-Dols, J. M., & Ruiz-Belba, M. A. (1995). Are smiles a sign of happiness? Gold medal winners at the Olympic games. *Journal of Personality and Social Psychology, 69,* 1113–1119.

Feshbach, S. (1984). The personality of personality theory and research. *Personality and Social Psychology Bulletin, 10,* 446–456.

Festinger, L. (1957). *A theory of cognitive dissonance.* Stanford: Stanford University Press.

Festinger, L., & Carlsmith, J. M. (1959). Cognitive consequences of forced compliance. *Journal of Abnormal and Social Psychology, 58,* 203–210.

Festinger, L., Riecken, H. W., & Schachter, S. (1956). *When prophecy fails.* Minneapolis: Minnesota University Press.

Festinger, L., Riecken, H. W., & Schachter, S. (1958). When prophecy fails. In E. E. Maccoby, T. M. Newcomb, & E. L. Hartley (Eds.), *Readings in social psychology* (pp. 156–163). New York: Holt, Rinehart & Winston.

Findley, M. J., & Cooper, H. M. (1983). Locus of control and academic achievement: literature review. *Journal of Personality and Social Psychology, 44,* 419–427.

Fineman, S. (1977). The achievement motive construct and its measurement: Where are we now? *British Journal of Psychology, 68,* 1–22.

Fischer, K. W., Shaver, P. R., & Carnochan, P. (1990). How emotions develop and how they organise development. *Cognition and Emotion, 4,* 81–127.

Fisher, C. D. (1978). The effects of personal control, competence, and extrinsic reward systems on intrinsic motivation. *Organizational Behavior and Human Performance, 21,* 273–288.

Fisher, S., & Greenberg, R. P. (1977). *The scientific credibility of Freud's theories and therapy.* New York: Basic Books.

Fisher, S., & Greenberg, R. P. (1996). *Freud scientifically reappraised: Testing the theories and therapy.* New York: John Wiley & Sons.

Fisher, W., Piazza, C., Cataldo, M., Harrell, R., Jefferson, G., & Comer, R. (1993). Functional communication training with and without extinction and punishment. *Journal of Applied Behavior Analysis, 26,* 23–36.

Fiske, S. T., & Taylor, S. E. (1984). *Social cognition.* Reading, MA: Addison-Wesley.

Fletcher, G. J. O. (1983). The analysis of verbal explanations for marital separation: Implications for attribution theory. *Journal of Applied Social Psychology, 13,* 245–258.

Fletcher, G. J. O., Fernandez, G., Peterson, D., & Reeder, G. D. (1986). Attributional complexity: An individual difference measure. *Journal of Personality and Social Psychology, 51,* 875–884.

Flink, C., Boggiano, A. K., & Barrett, M. (1990). Controlling teaching strategies: Undermining children's self-determination and performance. *Journal of Personality and Social Psychology, 59,* 916–924.

Flink, C., Boggiano, A. K., Main, D. S., Barrett, M., & Katz, P. A. (1992). Children's achievement-related behaviors: The role of extrinsic and intrinsic motivational orientations. In A. K. Boggiano & T. S. Pittman (Eds.), *Achievement and motivation: A social-developmental perspective* (pp. 189–214). New York: Cambridge University Press.

Foch, T. T., & McClearn, G. E. (1980). Genetics, body weight, and obesity. In A. E. Stunkard (Ed.), *Obesity* (pp. 48–61). Philadelphia: W. B. Saunders.

Foder, E. M., & Farrow, D. L. (1979). The power motive as an influence on the use of power. *Journal of Personality and Social Psychology, 37,* 2091–2097.

Foder, E. M., & Smith, T. (1982). The power motive as an influence on group decision making. *Journal of Personality and Social Psychology, 42,* 178–185.

Folkman, S., & Lazarus, R. S. (1985). If it changes it must be a process: Study of emotion and coping during three stages of a college examination. *Journal of Personality and Social Psychology, 48,* 150–170.

Folkman, S., & Lazarus, R. S. (1990). Coping and emotion. In N. Stein, B. Leventhal, & T. Trabasso (Eds.), *Psychological and biological approaches to emotion* (pp. 313–332). Hillsdale, NJ: Lawrence Erlbaum.

Folkman, S., Lazarus, R. S., Dunkel-Schetter, C., DeLongin, A., & Gruen, R. J. (1986). Dynamics of a stressful encounter: Cognitive appraisal, coping, and encounter outcomes. *Journal of Personality and Social Psychology, 50,* 992–1003.

Foote, N. N. (1951). Identification as the basis for a theory of motivation. *American Sociological Review, 16,* 14–21.

Ford, J. G. (1991a). Inherent potentialities of actualization: An initial exploration. *Journal of Humanistic Psychology, 31,* 65–88.

Ford, J. G. (1991b). Rogerian self-actualization: A clarification of meaning. *Journal of Humanistic Psychology, 31,* 101–111.

Ford, J. G. (1995). The temperament/actualization concept: A perspective on constitutional integrity and psychological health. *Journal of Humanistic Psychology, 35,* 57–67.

Forest, D., Clark, M. S., Mills, J., & Isen, A. M. (1979). Helping as a function of feeling state and nature of the helping behavior. *Motivation and Emotion, 3,* 161–169.

Forsterling, F. (1985). Attribution retraining: A review. *Psychological Bulletin, 98,* 495–512.

Fowles, D. C. (1983). Motivational effects of heart rate and electrodermal activity: Implications for research on personality and psychopathology. *Journal of Research in Personality, 17,* 48–61.

Fowles, D. C. (1988). Psychophysiology and psychopathology: A motivational approach. *Psychophysiology, 25,* 373–391.

Fowles, D. C., Fisher, A. E., & Tranel, D. T. (1982). The heart beats to reward: The effect of monetary incentive on heart rate. *Psychophysiology, 19,* 506–513.

Frank, M. G., Ekman, P., & Friesen, W. V. (1993). Behavioral markers and recognizability of the smile of enjoyment. *Journal of Personality and Social Psychology, 64,* 83–93.

Frankl, V. E. (1960). Paradoxical intention: A logotherapeutic technique. *American Journal of Psychotherapy, 14,* 520–525.

Frankl, V. E. (1963). *Man's search for meaning.* New York: Washington Square Press.

Freud, A. (1946). *The ego and mechanisms of defense.* New York: International Universities Press.

Freud, S. (1914). *Psychopathology of everyday life* (A. A. Brill, Trans.). New York: Macmillan. (Original work published 1901)

Freud, S. (1917). *Wit and its relation to the unconscious* (A. A. Brill, Trans.). New York: Moffat, Yard. (Original work published 1905)

Freud, S. (1920). *A general introduction to psychoanalysis* (J. Rivieíre, Trans.). New York: Liverright. (Original work published 1917)

Freud, S. (1922). *Beyond the pleasure principle* (J. Strachey, Trans.). London: Hogarth. (Original work published 1920)

Freud, S. (1927). *The ego and the id* (J. Rivieíre, Trans.). London: Hogarth. (Original work published 1923)

Freud, S. (1930). *Civilization and its discontents* (J. Rivieíre, Trans.). London: Hogarth Press. (Original work published 1930)

Freud, S. (1932). *The interpretation of dreams* (A. A. Brill, Trans.). London: Allen & Irwin. (Original work published 1900)

Freud, S. (1949). Instincts and their vicissitudes. In J. Rivieíre (Trans.), *Collected papers of Sigmund Freud* (Vol. 4, pp. 60–83). London: Hogarth. (Original work published 1915)

Freud, S. (1959). Inhibitions, symptoms, and anxiety (A. Strachey & J. Strachey, Trans.). In J. Strachey (Ed.) *The standard edition of the complete psychological works of Sigmund Freud* (Vol. 20). London: Hogarth Press. (Original work published 1926)

Freud, S. (1961). Humour (J. Rivieíre & J. Strachey, Trans.). In J. Strachey (Ed.) *The standard edition of the complete psychological works of Sigmund Freud* (Vol. 21). London: Hogarth press. (Original work published 1927)

Fridlund, A. J. (1992). The behavioral ecology and sociality of human faces. In M. S. Clark (Ed.), *Emotion.* Newbury Park, CA: Sage.

Fridlund, A. J. & Izard, C. E. (1983). Electromyographic studies of facial expressions of emotions. In J. T. Cacioppo & R. E. Petty (Eds.), *Social psychophysiology.* New York: Guilford Press.

Fried, C. B., & Aronson, E. (1995). Hypocrisy, misattribution, and dissonance reduction. *Personality and Social Psychology Bulletin, 21,* 925–933.

Frijda, N. H. (1986). *The emotions.* New York: Cambridge University Press.

Frijda, N. H. (1988). The laws of emotion. *American Psychologist, 43,* 349–358.

Frijda, N. H. (1993). The place of appraisal in emotion. *Cognition and Emotion, 7,* 357–388.

Frijda, N. H. (1994). Universal antecedents exist, and are interesting. In P. Ekman & R. J. Davidson (Eds.), *The nature of emotion: Fundamental questions* (pp. 155–162). New York: Oxford University Press.

Fromm, E. (1941). *Escape from freedom.* New York: Rinehart.

Fromm, E. (1956). *The art of loving.* New York: Harper & Brothers.

Fromm, E. (1964). *The heart of man.* New York: Harper & Row.

Fromm, E. (1986). *For the love of life.* New York: The Free Press.

Frost, R. O., Marten, P., Lahart, C., & Rosenblate, R. (1990). The dimensions of perfectionism. *Cognitive Therapy and Research, 14,* 449–468.

Funder, D. C. (1987). Errors and mistakes: Evaluating the accuracy of social judgment. *Psychological Bulletin, 101,* 75–90.

Gagnon, J. H. (1974). Scripts and the coordination of sexual conduct. In J. K. Cole & R. Diensteiber (Eds.), *Nebraska symposium on motivation* (Vol. 21, pp. 27–59). Lincoln: University of Nebraska Press.

Gagnon, J. H. (1977). *Human sexualities.* Glenview, IL: Scott Foresman.

Gale, A. (1973). The psychophysiology of individual differences: Studies of extraversion and the EEG. In P. Kline (Ed.), *New approaches in psychological measurement.* London: Wiley.

Gale, A. (1983). Electroencephalogram studies of extraversion-introversion: A case study in the psychophysiology of individual differences. *Personality and Individual Differences, 4,* 371–380.

Gale, A., Coles, M. G. H., & Blaydon, J. (1969). Extraversion-introversion and the EEG. *British Journal of Psychology, 60,* 209–223.

Gale, A., & Edwards, J. A. (1986). Individual differences. In M. G. H. Coles, E. Donchin, & S. W. Proges (Eds.), *Psychophysiology: Systems, processes, and applications* (pp. 431–507). New York: Guilford Press.

Garbarino, J. (1975). The impact of anticipated reward upon cross-aged tutoring. *Journal of Personality and Social Psychology, 32,* 421–428.

Gardner, H. (1985). *The mind's new science: A history of the cognitive revolution.* New York: Basic Books.

Gecas, V., & Burke, P. J. (1995). Self and identity. In K. S. Cook, G. A. Fine, & J. S. House (Eds.), *Sociological perspectives on social psychology* (pp. 41–67). Boston: Allyn & Bacon.

Geller, E. S., Altomari, M. G., & Russ, N. W. (1984). *Innovative approaches to drunk driving prevention.* Warren, MI: Societal Analysis Department, General Motors Research Laboratories.

Geller, E. S., Casali, J. G., & Johnson, R. P. (1980). Seat belt usage: A potential target for applied behavior analysis. *Journal of Applied Behavior Analysis, 13,* 669–675.

Geller, E. S., Rudd, J. R., Kalsher, M. J., Streff, F. M., & Lehman, G. R. (1987). Employer-based programs to motivate safety-belt use: A review of short-term and long-term effects. *Journal of Safety Research, 18,* 1–17.

Geller, L. (1982). The failure of self-actualization theory: A critique of Carl Rogers and Abraham Maslow. *Journal of Humanistic Psychology, 22,* 56–63.

Gendolla, G. H. E. (1997). Surprise in the context of achievement: The role of outcome valence and importance. *Motivation and Emotion, 21,* 165–193.

Gerard, H. (1992). Dissonance theory: A cognitive psychology with an engine. *Psychological Inquiry, 3,* 323–327.

Gergen, K. J. (1971). *The concept of self.* New York: Holt.

Gibson, E. J. (1988). Exploratory behavior in the development of perceiving, acting and the acquiring of knowledge. *Annual Review of Psychology, 39,* 1–41.

Gill, D. L., Ruder, K., & Gross, J. B. (1982). Open-ended attributions in team competition. *Journal of Sport Psychology, 4,* 159–169.

Gilovich, T., Medvec, V. H., & Chen, S. (1995). Commission, omission, and dissonance reduction: Coping with regret in the Monty Hall problem. *Personality and Social Psychology Bulletin, 21,* 182–190.

Gjesme, T. (1981). Is there any future in achievement motivation? *Motivation and Emotion, 5,* 115–138.

Gloor, P., Oliver, A., & Quesney, L. F. (1981). The role of the amygdala in the expression of psychic phenomena in temporal lobe seizures. In Y. Ben-Ari (Ed.), *The amygdaloid complex* (pp. 489-498). New York: Elsevier.

Goebel, B. L., & Brown, D. R. (1981). Age differences in motivation related to Maslow's need hierarchy. *Developmental Psychology, 17,* 809–815.

Goethals, G. R., Cooper, J., & Naficy, A. (1979). Role of foreseen, foreseeable, and unforeseeable consequences in the arousal of cognitive dissonance. *Journal of Personality and Social Psychology, 37,* 1179–1185.

Goffman, E. (1959). *The presentation of self in everyday life.* Garden City, NY: Doubleday.

Goldberg, C. (1995). The daimenic development of the malevolent personality. *Journal of Humanistic Psychology, 35,* 7–36.

Goldsmith, H. H. (1994). Parsing the emotional domain from a developmental perspective. In P. Ekman & R. J. Davidson (Eds.), *The nature of emotion: Fundamental questions* (pp. 68–73). New York: Oxford University Press.

Goldstein, K. (1939). *The organism.* New York: American Book Company.

Gollwitzer, P. M. (1993). Goal achievement: The role of intentions. In W. Stroebe & M. Hewstone (Eds.), *European review of social psychology* (Vol. 4, pp. 141-185). Chichester, England: Wiley.

Gollwitzer, P. M. (1996). The volitional benefits of planning. In P. M. Gollwitzer & J. A. Bargh (Eds.), *The psychology of action: Linking cognition and emotion to behavior* (pp. 287–312). New York: Guilford Press.

Gollwitzer, P. M. (1999). Implementation intentions: Strong effects of simple plans. *American Psychologist, 54,* 493–503.

Gollwitzer, P. M., & Bargh, J. A. (Eds.). (1996). *The psychology of action: Linking cognition and motivation to behavior.* New York: Guilford Press.

Gollwitzer, P. M., & Brandstatter, V. (1997). Implementation intentions and effective goal pursuit. *Journal of Personality and Social Psychology, 73,* 186–199.

Gollwitzer, P. M., & Moskowitz, G. B. (1996). Goal effects on action and cognition. In E. T. Higgins & A. W. Kruglanski (Eds.), *Social psychology: Handbook of basic principles* (pp. 361–399). New York: Guilford Press.

Gonas, G. (1977). Situation versus frame: The interactionist and the structuralist analysis of everyday life. *American Sociological Review, 42,* 854–867.

Goodenough, F. L. (1932). Expressions of emotions in a blind-deaf child. *Journal of Abnormal and Social Psychology, 27,* 328–333.

Goodenow, C. (1993). The psychological sense of school membership among adolescents: Scale development and educational correlates. *Psychology in the Schools, 30,* 79–90.

Goodman, R. A. (1968). On the operationality of Maslow's need hierarchy. *British Journal of Industrial Relations, 6,* 51–57.

Gottfried, A. (1985). Academic intrinsic motivation in elementary and junior high school students. *Journal of Educational Psychology, 77,* 631–645.

Gough, H. G. (1964). A cross-sectional study of achievement motivation. *Journal of Applied Psychology, 48,* 191–196.

Gould, D., Hodge, K., Peterson, K., & Giannini, J. (1989). An exploratory examination of strategies used by elite coaches to enhance self-efficacy in athletes. *Journal of Sport and Exercise Psychology, 11,* 128–140.

Gould, R., & Sigall, H. (1977). The effects of empathy and outcome on attribution: An examination of the divergent-perspectives hypothesis. *Journal of Experimental Social Psychology, 13,* 480–491.

Gray, J. A. (1987). *The psychology of fear and stress* (2nd ed.). New York: Cambridge University Press.

Gray, J. A. (1994). Three fundamental emotion systems. In P. Ekman & R. J. Davidson (Eds.), *The nature of emotion: Fundamental questions* (pp. 243–247). New York: Oxford University Press.

Green, C. W., Reid, D. H., White, L. K., Halford, R. C., Brittain, D. P., & Gardner, S. M. (1988). Identifying reinforcers for persons with profound handicaps: Staff opinion versus systematic assessment of preferences. *Journal of Applied Behavior Analysis, 21,* 31–43.

Greenberg, J. R., & Mitchell, S. (1983). *Object relations in psychoanalytic theory.* Cambridge, MA: Harvard University Press.

Greenberg, J. R., & Pyszczynski, T. (1985). Compensatory self-inflation: A response to the threat to self-regard of public failure. *Journal of Personality and Social Psychology, 49,* 273–280.

Greenberg, J. R., Pyszcynski, T., & Solomon, S. (1982). The self-serving attributional bias: Beyond self-presentation. *Journal of Experimental Social Psychology, 18,* 56–67.

Greenberg, J. R., Solomon, S., Pyszczynski, T., Rosenblatt, A., Burling, J., Lyon, D., Simon, L., & Pinel, E. (1992). Why do people need self-esteem? Converging evidence that self-esteem serves an anxiety-buffering function. *Journal of Personality and Social Psychology, 63,* 913–922.

Greenberg, R., & Pearlman, C. (1993). An integrated approach to dream theory: Contributions from sleep research and clinical practice. In A. Moffitt, M. Kramer, & R. Hoffman (Eds.), *The functions of dreaming* (pp. 363–380). Albany: State University of New York.

Greene, D., & Lepper, M. R. (1974). Effects of extrinsic rewards on children's subsequent intrinsic interest. *Child Development, 45,* 1141–1145.

Greening, T. (1995). Commentary. *Journal of Humanistic Psychology, 35,* 1–6.

Greeno, C. G., & Wing, R. R. (1994). Stress-induced eating. *Psychological Bulletin, 115,* 444–464.

Greenwald, A. G., (1992). New look 3: Unconscious cognition reclaimed. *American Psychologist, 47,* 766–779.

Greenwald, A. G., Spangenberg, E. R., Pratkanis, A. R., & Eskenazi, J. (1991). Double-blind tests of subliminal self-help audiotapes. *Psychological Science, 2,* 119–122.

Gregory, L. W., Cialdini, R. B., & Carpenter, K. M. (1982). Self-relevant scenarios as mediators of likelihood estimates and compliance: Does imagining make it so? *Journal of Personality and Social Psychology, 43,* 89–99.

Grilo, C. M., & Pogue-Geile, M. F. (1991). The nature of environmental influences on weight and obesity: A behavior genetics analysis. *Psychological Bulletin, 110,* 520–537.

Grilo, C. M., Shiffman, S., & Wing, R. R. (1989). Relapse crises and coping among dieters. *Journal of Consulting and Clinical Psychology, 57,* 488–495.

Grolnick, W. S., Deci, E. L., & Ryan, R. M. (1997). Internalization within the family: The self-determination perspective. In J. E. Grusec & L. Kuczynski (Eds.), *Parenting and children's internalization of values: A handbook of contemporary theory* (pp. 135–161). New York: Wiley.

Grolnick, W. S., Frodi, A., & Bridges, L. (1984). Maternal control styles and the mastery motivation of one-year-olds. *Infant Mental Health Journal, 5,* 72–82.

Grolnick, W. S., & Ryan, R. M. (1987). Autonomy in children's learning: An experimental and individual difference investigation. *Journal of Personality and Social Psychology, 52,* 890–898.

Grolnick, W. S., & Ryan, R. M. (1989). Parent style associated with children's self-regulation and competence: A social contextual perspective. *Journal of Educational Psychology, 81,* 143–154.

Grolnick, W. S., Ryan, R. M., & Deci, E. L. (1989). Inner resources for school achievement: Motivational mediators of children's perception of their parents. *Journal of Educational Psychology, 83,* 508–517.

Grolnick, W. S., Ryan, R. M., & Deci, E. L. (1991). Inner resources for school achievement: Motivational mediators of children's perceptions of their parents. *Journal of Educational Psychology, 83,* 508–517.

Gross, J. J. (1999). Emotion regulation: Past, present, future. *Cognitive and Emotion, 13,* 551–573.

Gross, J. J., Carstensen, L. L., Pasupathi, M., & Tsai, J. (1997). Emotion and aging: Experience, expression, and control. *Psychology and Aging, 12,* 590–599.

Gross, J. J., & Levenson, R. W. (1993). Emotional suppression: Physiology, self-report, and expressive behavior. *Journal of Personality and Social Psychology, 64,* 970–986.

Gross, N., Mason, W. S., & McEachern, A. W. (1958). *Explorations in role analysis: Studies of the school superintendency role.* New York: Wiley.

Gruen, A. (1976). Autonomy and compliance: The fundamental antithesis. *Journal of Humanistic Psychology, 16,* 61–69.

Guisinger, S., & Blatt, S. J. (1994). Individuality and relatedness: Evolution of a fundamental dialectic. *American Psychologist, 49,* 104–111.

Guthrie, E. R. (1959). Association by contiguity. In S. Koch (Ed.), *Psychology: A study of a science* (Vol. 2, pp. 158–195). New York: McGraw-Hill.

Hackett, G. (1985). The role of mathematics self-efficacy in the choice of math-related majors of college women and men: A path analysis. *Journal of Counseling Psychology, 32,* 47–56.

Hall, H. K., & Byrne, A. T. J. (1988). Goal setting in sport: Clarifying recent anomalies. *Journal of Sport and Exercise Psychology, 10,* 184–198.

Hall, J. F. (1961). *Psychology of motivation.* Philadelphia: J. B. Lippincott.

Hall, R. V., Axelrod, S., Tyler, L., Grief, E., Jones, F. C., & Robertson, R. (1972). Modification of behavior problems in the home with a parent as observer and experimenter. *Journal of Applied Behavior Analysis, 5,* 53–64.

Hall, W. G. (1973). A remote stomach clamp to evaluate oral and gastric controls of drinking in the rat. *Physiology and Behavior, 173,* 897–901.

Hamachek, D. E. (1978). Psychodynamics of normal and neurotic perfectionism. *Psychology, 15,* 27–33.

Hamer, D. H., Hu, S., Magnuson, V. L., Hu, N., & Pattatucci, A. M. L. (1993). A linkage between DNA markers on the X chromosome and male sexual orientation. *Science, 261,* 321–327.

Hansford, B. C., & Hattie, J. A. (1982). The relationship between self and achievement/performance measures. *Review of Educational Research, 52,* 123–142.

Hapidou, E. G., & deCatanzaro, D. (1992). Responsiveness to laboratory pain in women as a function of age and childbirth pain experience. *Pain, 48,* 177–181.

Harackiewicz, J. (1979). The effects of reward contingency and performance feedback on intrinsic motivation. *Journal of Personality and Social Psychology, 37,* 1352–1363.

Harackiewicz, J. M., Barron, K. E., Carter, S. M., Lehto, A. T., & Elliot, A. J. (1997). Predictors and consequences of achievement goals in the college classroom: Maintaining interest and making the grade. *Journal of Personality and Social Psychology, 73,* 1284–1295.

Harackiewicz, J. M., & Elliot, A. J. (1993). Achievement goals and intrinsic motivation. *Journal of Personality and Social Psychology, 65,* 904–915.

Harackiewicz, J. M., & Manderlink, G. (1984). A process analysis of the effects of performance-contingent rewards on intrinsic motivation. *Journal of Experimental Social Psychology, 20,* 531–551.

Harackiewicz, J. M., Sansone, C., & Manderlink, G. (1985). Competence, achievement orientation, and intrinsic motivation: A process analysis. *Journal of Personality and Social Psychology, 48,* 493–508.

Hardaway, R. A. (1990). Subliminally activated symbiotic fantasies: Facts and artifacts. *Psychological Bulletin, 107,* 177–195.

Hardeman, M. (1979). A dialogue with Abraham Maslow. *Journal of Humanistic Psychology, 19,* 23–28.

Harlow, H. F. (1953). Motivation as a factor in the acquisition of new responses. In M. R. Jones (Ed.), *Nebraska symposium on motivation* (Vol. 1, pp. 24–49). Lincoln: University of Nebraska Press.

Harmon-Jones, E., & Mills, J. (1999). An introduction to cognitive dissonance theory and an overview of current perspectives on the theory. In E. Harmon-Jones & J. Mills (Eds.), *Cognitive dissonance: Progress on a pivotal theory in social psychology* (pp. 3–21). Washington, DC: American Psychological Association.

Harper, F. B. W. (1975). The validity of some alternative measurements of achievement motivation. *Educational and Psychological Measurement, 35,* 905–909.

Harris, R. N., & Snyder, C. R. (1986). The role of uncertain self-esteem in self-handicapping. *Journal of Personality and Social Psychology, 51,* 451–458.

Harter, S. (1974). Pleasure derived by children from cognitive challenge and mastery. *Child Development, 45,* 661–669.

Harter, S. (1978a). Effectance motivation reconsidered: Toward a developmental model. *Human Development, 21,* 34–64.

Harter, S. (1978b). Pleasure derived from optimal challenge and the effects of extrinsic rewards on children's difficulty level choices. *Child Development, 49,* 788–799.

Harter, S. (1981). A model of mastery motivation in children: Individual differences and developmental changes. In W. A. Collin (Ed.), *Aspects of the development of competence* (Vol. 14, pp. 215–255). Hillsdale, NJ: Erlbaum.

Harter, S. (1988). The construction and conservation of the self: James and Cooley revisited. In D. K. Lapsle & F. C. Power (Eds.), *Self, ego, and identity: Integrative approaches* (pp. 43–60). New York: Springer-Verlag.

Harter, S. (1990). Causes, correlates and the functional role of global self-worth: A life-span perspective. In R. J. Sternberg & J. Kolligian, Jr. (Eds.), *Competence considered* (pp. 67–97). New Haven, CT: Yale University Press.

Harter, S. (1993). Visions of self: Beyond the me in the mirror. In J. E. Jacobs (Ed.), *Nebraska symposium on motivation: Developmental perspectives on motivation* (Vol. 40, pp. 99–144). Lincoln: University of Nebraska Press.

Harter, S., & Park, R. (1984). The pictorial perceived competence scale for young children. *Child Development, 55,* 1969–1982.

Hartmann, H. (1958). *Ego psychology and the problem of adaptation* (D. Rapaport, Trans.). New York: International Universities Press.

Hartmann, H. (1964). *Essays on ego psychology: Selected problems in psychoanalytic theory.* New York: International Universities Press.

Harvey, J. H., & Weary, G. (1981). *Perspectives on attributional processes.* Dubuque, IA: Wm. C. Brown.

Hatfield, E., Cacioppo, J. T., & Rapson, R. L. (1993a). *Emotional contagion.* Cambridge: Cambridge University Press.

Hatfield, E., Cacioppo, J. T., & Rapson, R. L. (1993b). Emotional contagion. *Current Directions in Psychological Science, 2,* 96–99.

Hatfield, E., Hsee, C. K., Costello, J., Weisman, M. S., & Denney, C. (1995). The impact of vocal feedback on emotional experience and expression. *Journal of Social Behavior and Personality, 10,* 293–312.

Haviland, J. J., & Lelwica, M. (1987). The induced affect response: Ten-week old infants' responses to three emotion expressions. *Developmental Psychology, 23,* 997–1004.

Haviland, J. M., & Kramer, D. A. (1991). Affect-cognition relationships in adolescent diaries: The case of Anne Frank. *Human Development, 34,* 143–159.

Hazan, C., & Shaver, P. (1987). Romantic love conceptualized as an attachment process. *Journal of Personality and Social Psychology, 52,* 511–524.

Heath, R. G. (1964). Pleasure response of human subjects to direct stimulation of the brain. In R. G. Heath (Ed.), *The role of pleasure in behavior* (pp. 219–243). New York: Harper & Row.

Heatherton, T. F., Herman, C. P., & Polivy, J. (1991). Effects of physical threat and ego threat on eating behavior. *Journal of Personality and Social Psychology, 60,* 138–143.

Heatherton, T. F., & Nichols, P. A. (1994). Personal accounts of successful versus failed attempts at life change. *Personality and Social Psychology Bulletin, 20,* 664–675.

Heatherton, T. F., Polivy, J., & Herman, C. P. (1989). Restraint and internal responsiveness: Effects of placebo manipulations of hunger state on eating. *Journal of Abnormal Psychology, 98,* 89–92.

Hebb, D. O. (1949). *The organization of behavior.* New York: Wiley.

Hebb, D. O. (1955). Drives and the C.N.S.: Conceptual nervous system. *Psychological Review, 62,* 245–254.

Heckhausen, H. (1967). *The anatomy of achievement motivation.* New York: Academic Press.

Heckhausen, H. (1977). Achievement motivation and its constructs: A cognitive model. *Motivation and Emotion, 1,* 283–329.

Heckhausen, H. (1980). *Motivation and Handeln.* New York: Springer-Verlag.

Heckhausen, H. (1982). The development of achievement motivation. In W. W. Harup (Ed.), *Review of child development research* (Vol. 6, pp. 600–668). Chicago: University of Chicago Press.

Heider, F. (1958). *The psychology of interpersonal relations.* New York: John Wiley.

Heise, D. R. (1979). *Understanding events: Affect and the construction of social action.* New York: Cambridge University Press.

Heise, D. R. (1985). Affect control theory: Respecification, estimation, and tests of the formal model. *Journal of Mathematical Sociology, 1,* 191–222.

Heise, D. R. (1989). Effects of emotion displays on social identification. *Social Psychology Quarterly, 52,* 10–21.

Heise, D. R. (1991). *INTERACT 2: A computer program for studying cultural meanings and social interaction.* Department of Sociology, University of Indiana: Bloomington, IN.

Helmke, A., & van Aken, M. A. G. (1995). The causal ordering of academic achievement and self-concept of ability during elementary school: A longitudinal study. *Journal of Educational Psychology, 87,* 624–637.

Helson, R., Stewart, A. J., & Ostrove, J. (1995). Identity in three cohorts of midlife women. *Journal of Personality and Social Psychology, 69,* 544–557.

Hendrick, S. S., & Hendrick, C. (1987). Love and sexual attitudes, self-disclosure, and sensation seeking. *Journal of Social and Personal Relationships, 4,* 281–297.

Herman, C. P., & Mack, D. (1975). Restrained and unrestrained eating. *Journal of Personality, 43,* 647–660.

Herman, C. P., Polivy, J., & Esses, J. M. (1987). The illusion of counter-regulation. *Appetite, 9,* 161–169.

Hermans, H. J. M. (1970). A questionnaire measure of achievement motivation. *Journal of Applied Psychology, 54,* 353–363.

Heron, W. (1957). The pathology of boredom. *Scientific American, 196,* 52–56.

Hess, E. H. (1975). *The tell-tale eye.* New York: Van Nostrand Reinhold.

Hewitt, P. L., & Dyck, D. G. (1986). Perfectionism, stress, and vulnerability to depression. *Cognitive Therapy and Research, 10,* 137–142.

Hewitt, P. L., & Flett, G. L. (1991a). Dimensions of perfectionism in unipolar depression. *Journal of Abnormal Psychology, 100,* 98–101.

Hewitt, P. L., & Flett, G. L. (1991b). Perfectionism in the self and social contexts: Conceptualization, assessment, and association with psychopathology. *Journal of Personality and Social Psychology, 60,* 456–470.

Heyman, G. D., & Dweck, C. S. (1992). Achievement goals and intrinsic motivation: Their relation and their role in adaptive motivation. *Motivation and Emotion, 16,* 231–247.

Heyns, R. W., Veroff, J., & Atkinson, J. W. (1958). A scoring manual for the affiliation motive. In J. W. Atkinson (Ed.), *Motives in fantasy, action, and society.* Princeton, NJ: Van Nostrand.

Hidi, S. (1990). Interest and its contribution as a mental resource for learning. *Review of Educational Research, 60,* 549–571.

Hilgard, E. R., & Hilgard, J. R. (1975). *Hypnosis in the relief of pain.* Los Altos, CA: William Kaufmann.

Hilgard, E. R., & Hilgard, J. R. (1983). *Hypnosis in the relief of pain* (Rev. ed.). Los Altos, CA: William Kaufmann.

Hill, J. O., Pagliassotti, M. J., & Peters, J. C. (1994). In C. Bouchard (Ed.), *Genetic determinants of obesity* (pp. 35–48). Boca Raton, FL: CRC Press.

Hill, J. O., & Peters, J. C. (1998). Environmental contributions to the obesity epidemic. *Science, 280,* 1371–1374.

Hiroto, D. S. (1974). Locus of control and learned helplessness. *Journal of Experimental Psychology, 102,* 187–193.

Hiroto, D. S., & Seligman, M. E. P. (1975). Generality of learned helplessness in man. *Journal of Personality and Social Psychology, 31,* 311–327.

Hirt, M., & Genshaft, J. L. (1981). Immunization and reversibility of cognitive deficits due to learned helplessness. *Personality and Individual Differences, 2,* 191–196.

Hochschild, A. R. (1983). *The managed heart.* Berkeley: University of California Press.

Hodgins, H. S., Koestner, R., & Duncan, N. (1996). On the compatibility of autonomy and relatedness. *Personality and Social Psychology Bulletin, 22,* 227–237.

Hodgson, R., & Rachman, S. (1974). Desynchrony in measures of fear. *Behaviour Research and Therapy, 12,* 319–326.

Hokoda, A., & Fincham, F. D. (1995). Origins of children's helpless and mastery achievement patterns in the family. *Journal of Educational Psychology, 87,* 375–385.

Holahan, C. K., & Holahan, C. J. (1987). Self-efficacy, social support, and depression in aging: A longitudinal analysis. *Journal of Gerontology, 42,* 65–68.

Hollender, M. H. (1965). Perfectionism. *Comprehensive Psychiatry, 6,* 94–103.

Holmes, D. S. (1974). Investigation of repression: Differential recall of material experimentally or naturally associated with ego threat. *Psychological Bulletin, 81,* 632–653.

Holmes, D. S. (1990). The evidence for repression: An examination of sixty years of research. In J. L. Singer (Ed.), *Repression and dissociation* (pp. 85–102). Chicago: University of Chicago Press.

Holmes, T. H., & Rahe, R. H. (1967). The social readjustment rating scale. *Journal of Psychosomatic Research, 11,* 213–218.

Holstedge, G., Kuypers, H. G. J. M., & Dekker, J. J. (1977). The organization of the bulbar fibre connections to the trigeminal, facial, and hypoglossal motor nuclei: II. An autoradiographic tracing study in cat. *Brain, 100,* 265–286.

Holt, E. B. (1931). *Animal drive and the learning process.* New York: Holt.

Holt, R. R. (1980). Loevinger's measure of ego development: Reliability and national norms for male and female short forms. *Journal of Personality and Social Psychology, 39,* 909–920.

Holt, R. R. (1989). *Freud reappraised: A fresh look at psychoanalytic theory.* New York: Guilford Press.

Hom, H. L., Jr. (1994). Can you predict the overjustification effect? *Teaching of Psychology, 21,* 36–37.

Horney, K. (1939). *New ways in psychoanalysis.* New York: Norton.

Horowitz, M. J., Wilner, N., Kaltreidr, N., & Alvarez, W. (1980). Signs and symptoms of post-traumatic stress disorder. *Archives of General Psychology, 37,* 85–92.

Horvath, P., & Zuckerman, M. (1993). Sensation seeking, risk appraisal, and risky behavior. *Personality and Individual Differences, 14,* 41–52.

Horvath, T. (1979). Correlates of physical beauty in men and women. *Social Behavior and Personality, 7,* 145–151.

Horvath, T. (1981). Physical attractiveness: The influence of selected torso parameters. *Archives of Sexual Behavior, 10,* 21–24.

Huber, V. L. (1985). Effects of task difficulty, goal setting, and strategy on performance of a heuristic task. *Journal of Applied Psychology, 70,* 492–504.

Hudley, C., & Graham, S. (1993). An attributional intervention to reduce peer-directed aggression among African-American boys. *Child Development, 64,* 124–138.

Huebner, R. R., & Izard, C. E. (1988). Mothers responses to infants facial expressions of sadness, anger, and physical distress. *Motivation and Emotion, 12,* 185–196.

Hull, C. L. (1943). *Principles of behavior.* New York: Appleton-Century-Crofts.

Hull, C. L. (1952). *A behavior system: An introduction to behavior theory concerning the individual organism.* New Haven, CT: Yale University Press.

Hull, J. G. (1981). A self-awareness model of the causes and effects of alcohol consumption. *Journal of Abnormal Psychology, 90,* 586–600.

Hunt, J. M. (1965). Intrinsic motivation and its role in psychological development. In D. Levine (Ed.), *Nebraska symposium on motivation* (Vol. 13, pp. 189–282). Lincoln: University of Nebraska Press.

Hupka, R. B. (1984). Jealousy: Compound emotion or label for a particular situation. *Motivation and Emotion, 8,* 141–155.

Hymbaugh, K., & Garrett, J. (1974). Sensation seeking among skydivers. *Perceptual and Motor Skills, 38,* 1–18.

Isen, A. M. (1970). Success, failure, attention, and reactions to others: The warm glow of success. *Journal of Personality and Social Psychology, 15,* 294–301.

Isen, A. M. (1984). Toward understanding the role of affect in cognition. In R. Wyer & T. Srull (Eds.), *Handbook of social cognition* (pp. 179–236). Hillsdale, NJ: Erlbaum.

Isen, A. M. (1987). Positive affect, cognitive processes, and social behavior. In L. Berkowitz (Ed.), *Advances in experimental social psychology* (Vol. 20, pp. 203–253). New York: Academic Press.

Isen, A. M. (1999). Positive affect. In T. Dalgleish & M. Power (Eds.), *The handbook of cognition and emotion* (pp. 521–539). New York: Wiley.

Isen, A. M., Clark, M. S., & Schwartz, M. F. (1976). Duration of the effects of good mood on helping: Footprints in the sands of time. *Journal of Personality and Social Psychology, 34,* 385–393.

Isen, A. M., Daubman, K. A., & Nowicki, G. P. (1987). Positive affect facilitates creative problem-solving. *Journal of Personality and Social Psychology, 51,* 1122–1131.

Isen, A. M., & Geva, N. (1987). The influence of positive affect on acceptable level of risk: The person with a large canoe has a large worry. *Organizational Behavior and Human Decision Processes, 39,* 145–154.

Isen, A. M., Johnson, M. M. S., Mertz, E., & Robinson, G. F. (1985). The influence of positive affect on the unusualness of word associations. *Journal of Personality and Social Psychology, 48,* 1413–1426.

Isen, A. M., & Levin, P. F. (1972). The effect of feeling good on helping: Cookies and kindness. *Journal of Personality and Social Psychology, 21,* 384–388.

Isen, A. M., & Means, B. (1983). The influence of positive affect on decision-making strategy. *Social Cognition, 2,* 18–31.

Isen, A. M., Niedenthal, P., & Cantor, N. (1992). An influence of positive affect on social categorization. *Motivation and Emotion, 16,* 65–68.

Isen, A. M., & Nowicki, G. P. (1981). *Positive affect and creative problem solving.* Paper presented at the annual meeting of the Cognitive Science Society, Berkeley, CA.

Isen, A. M., & Patrick, R. (1983). The effect of positive feelings on risk-taking: When the chips are down. *Organizational Behavior and Human Performance, 31,* 194–202.

Isen, A. M., & Reeve, J. (2000). *The influence of positive affect on intrinsic motivation.* Unpublished manuscript, Cornell University.

Isen, A. M., Rosenzweig, A. S., & Young, M. J. (1991). The influence of positive affect on clinical problem solving. *Medical Decision Making, 11,* 221–227.

Isen, A. M., Shalker, T., Clark, M., & Karp, L. (1978). Affect, accessibility of material in memory, and behavior: A cognitive loop? *Journal of Personality and Social Psychology, 36,* 1–12.

Iso-Ahola, S. E. (1977). Immediate attributional effects of success and failure in the field: Testing some laboratory hypotheses. *European Journal of Social Psychology, 7,* 275–296.

Iversen, L., & Sabroe, S. (1989). Psychological well-being among unemployed and employed people after a company closes down: A longitudinal study. *Journal of Social Issues, 44,* 141–152.

Iwata, B. A. (1987). Negative reinforcement in applied behavior analysis: An emerging technology. *Journal of Applied Behavior Analysis, 20,* 361–378.

Izard, C. E. (1971). *The face of emotion.* New York: Appleton-Century-Crofts.

Izard, C. E. (1980). Cross-cultural perspectives on emotion and emotion communication. In H. Triandis & W. J. Lonner (Eds.), *Handbook of cross-cultural psychology* (Vol. 3). Boston: Allyn & Bacon.

Izard, C. E. (1982). Comments on emotion and cognition: Can there be a working relationship? In M. S. Clark & S. T. Fiske (Eds.), *Affect and cognition.* Hillsdale, NJ: Lawrence Erlbaum.

Izard, C. E. (1989). The structure and functions of emotions: Implications for cognition, motivation, and personality. In I. S. Cohen (Ed.), *The G. Stanley Hall lecture series* (Vol. 9, pp. 39–63). Washington, DC: American Psychological Association.

Izard, C. E. (1990). Facial expressions and the regulation of emotions. *Journal of Personality and Social Psychology, 58,* 487–498.

Izard, C. E. (1991). *The psychology of emotions.* New York: Plenum.

Izard, C. E. (1992). Basic emotions, relations among the emotions, and emotion-cognition relations. *Psychological Review, 99,* 561–565.

Izard, C. E. (1993). Four systems for emotion activation: Cognitive and noncognitive development. *Psychological Review, 100,* 68–90.

Izard, C. E. (1994). Innate and universal facial expressions: Evidence from developmental and cross-cultural research. *Psychological Bulletin, 115,* 288–299.

Izard, C. E., Fantauzzo, C. A., Castle, J. M., Haynes, O. M., Rayias, M. F., & Putnam, P. H. (1995). The ontogeny and significance of infants' facial expressions in the first nine months of life. *Developmental Psychology, 31,* 997–1013.

Izard, C. E., Hembree, E. A., Dougherty, L. M., & Spizzirri, C. C. (1983). Changes in facial expressions of 2- to 19-month-old infants following acute pain. *Developmental Psychology, 19,* 418–426.

Izard, C. E., Huebner, R. R., Risser, D., McGinnes, G., & Dougherty, L. (1980). The young infant's ability to reproduce discrete emotion expressions. *Developmental Psychology, 16,* 132–140.

Izard, C. E., & Malatesta, C. Z. (1987). Perspectives on emotional development: I. Differential emotions theory of early emotional development. In J. D. Osotsky (Ed.), *Handbook of infant development* (2nd ed., pp. 494–554). New York: Wiley-Interscience.

Jackson, D. N. (1974). *Manual for the Personality Research Form.* Goshen, NY: Research Psychologists Press.

Jacobs, K. W., & Koeppel, J. C. (1974). Psychological correlates of the mobility decision. *Bulletin of the Psychodynamic Society, 3,* 330–332.

Jacobs, W. J., & Nadel, L. (1985). Stress-induced recovery of fears and phobias. *Psychological Review, 92,* 512–531.

Jacoby, L., & Kelly, C. M. (1992). A process-dissociation framework for investigating unconscious influences: Freudian slips, projective tests, subliminal perception, and signal detection theory. *Current Directions in Psychological Science, 1,* 174–179.

James, W. (1884). What is an emotion? *Mind, 9,* 188–205.

James, W. (1890). *The principles of psychology* (2 Vols.). New York: Henry Holt.

James, W. (1894). The physical basis of emotion. *Psychological Review, 1,* 516–529.

Janis, I. L., & Field, P. B. (1959). The Janis and Field Personality Questionnaire. In C. I. Hovland & I. L. Janis (Eds.), *Personality and persuasibility* (pp. 300–305). New Haven: Yale University Press.

Jeffrey, D. B., & Knauss, M. R. (1981). The etiologies, treatments, and assessments of obesity. In S. N. Haynes & L. Gannon (Eds.), *Psychosomatic disorders: A psychophysiological approach to etiology and treatment* (pp. 269–319). New York: Praeger.

Jenkins, S. R. (1987). Need for achievement and women's careers over 14 years: Evidence for occupational structural effects. *Journal of Personality and Social Psychology, 53,* 922–932.

Jenkins, S. R. (1996). Self-definition in thought, action, and life path choices. *Personality and Social Psychology Bulletin, 22,* 99–111.

Jessell, T. M., & Kelly, D. D. (1991). Pain and analgesia. In E. R. Kandel, J. H. Schwartz, & T. M.

Jessell (Eds.), *Principles of neural science* (3rd ed., pp. 385–399). Norwalk, CT: Appleton & Lange.

Jobe, J. B., Holgate, S. H., & Sorapansky, T. A. (1983). Risk-taking as motivation for volunteering for a hazardous experiment. *Journal of Personality, 51,* 95–107.

John, O. P., & Robins, R. W. (1994). Accuracy and bias in self-perception: Individual differences in self-enhancement and the role of narcissism. *Journal of Personality and Social Psychology, 66,* 206–219.

Johnson, D. W., & Johnson, R. T. (1985). Motivational processes in cooperative, competitive, and individualistic learning situations. In C. A. Ames & R. Ames (Eds.), *Research on motivation in education: The classroom milieu* (Vol. 2, pp. 249–286). Orlando, FL: Academic Press.

Johnson, R. W., Kelly, R. J., & LeBlanc, B. A. (1995). Motivational basis of dissonance: Aversive consequences or inconsistency. *Personality and Social Psychology Bulletin, 21,* 850–855.

Johnson-Laird, P. N., & Oatley, K. (1989). The language of emotions: An analysis of a semantic field. *Cognition and Emotion, 3,* 81–123.

Johnson-Laird, P. N., & Oatley, K. (1992). Basic emotions, rationality and folk theory. *Cognition and Emotion, 6,* 201–223.

Jones, E. E. (1985). Major developments in social psychology during the past five decades. In G. Lindzey & E. Aronson (Ed.), *Handbook of social psychology: Theory and method* (Vol. 1, pp. 47–107). New York: Random House.

Jones, E. E., & Davis, K. E. (1965). From acts to dispositions: The attribution process in person perception. In L. Berkowitz (Ed.), *Advances in experimental social psychology* (Vol. 2, pp. 214–266). New York: Academic Press.

Jones, E. E., & Gerard, H. B. (1967). *Foundations of social psychology*. New York: Wiley.

Jones, E. E., & Nisbett, R. E. (1971). *The actor and the observer: Divergent perceptions of the causes of behavior.* Morristown, NJ: General Learning Press.

Jones, E. E., & Nisbett, R. E. (1972). The actor and the observer: Divergent perceptions of the causes of behavior. In E. E. Jones, D. E. Kanouse, H. H. Kelley, R. E. Nisbett, S. Valins, & B. Weiner (Eds.), *Attribution: Perceiving the causes of behavior.* Morristown, NJ: General Learning Press.

Jones, S. L., Nation, J. R., & Massad, P. (1977). Immunization against learned helplessness in man. *Journal of Abnormal Psychology, 86,* 75–83.

Josephs, R. A., Markus, H. R., & Tafarodi, R. W. (1992). Gender and self-esteem. *Journal of Personality and Social Psychology, 63,* 391–402.

Kagan, J. (1972). Motives and development. *Journal of Personality and Social Psychology, 22,* 51–66.

Kahneman, D. (1973). *Attention and effort.* Englewood Cliffs, NJ: Prentice-Hall.

Kapp, B. S., Pascoe, J. P., & Bixler, M. A. (1984). The amygdala: A neuroanatomical systems approach to its contributions to aversive conditioning. In N. Buttlers & L. R. Squire (Eds.), *Neuropsychology of memory* (pp. 473–488). New York: Guilford Press.

Karabenick, S. A., & Yousseff, Z. I. (1968). Performance as a function of achievement level and perceived difficulty. *Journal of Personality and Social Psychology, 10,* 414–419.

Karniol, R., & Ross, M. (1977). The effect of performance-relevant and performance-irrelevant rewards on children's intrinsic motivation. *Child Development, 48,* 482–487.

Karoly, P. (1993). Mechanisms of self-regulation: An overview. *Annual Review of Psychology, 44,* 23–52.

Kasser, T., & Ryan, R. M. (1993). A dark side of the American dream: Correlates of financial success as a central life aspiration. *Journal of Personality and Social Psychology, 65,* 410–422.

Kasser, T., & Ryan, R. M. (1996). Further examining the American dream: Differential correlates of intrinsic and extrinsic goals. *Personality and Social Psychology Bulletin, 22,* 280–287.

Kasser, V. G., & Ryan, R. M. (1999). The relation of psychological needs for autonomy and relatedness to vitality, well-being, and mortality in a nursing home. *Journal of Applied Social Psychology, 29,* 935–954.

Kassirer, J. P., & Angell, M. (1998). Losing weight: An ill-fated new year's resolution. *New England Journal of Medicine, 338,* 52–54.

Kast, A., & Connor, K. (1988). Sex and age differences in response to informational and controlling feedback. *Personality and Social Psychology Bulletin, 14,* 514–523.

Katzell, R. A., & Thompson, D. E. (1990). Work motivation: Theory and practice. *American Psychologist, 45,* 144–153.

Katzman, M., & Wolchik, S. (1984). Bulimia and binge eating in college women: A comparison of personality and behavioral characteristics. *Journal of Consulting and Clinical Psychology, 52,* 423–428.

Kazdin, A. E. (1979). Imagery elaboration and self-efficacy in the covert modeling treatment of unassertive behavior. *Journal of Consulting and Clinical Psychology, 47,* 725–733.

Kazdin, A. E. (1980). *Behavior modification in applied settings* (rev. ed.). Homewood, IL: Dorsey Press.

Keating, C. F., Mazur, A., & Segall, M. H. (1981). A cross-cultural exploration of physiognomic traits of dominance and happiness. *Ethology and Sociobiology, 2,* 41–48.

Keesey, R. E. (1980). A set-point analysis of the regulation of body weight. In A. J. Stunkard (Ed.), *Obesity* (pp. 144–165). Philadelphia: Saunders.

Keesey, R. E., Boyle, P. C., Kemnitz, J. W., & Mitchell, J. S. (1976). The role of the lateral hypothalamus in determining the body weight set point. In D. Novin, W. Wyrwicka, & G. A. Bray (Eds.), *Hunger: Basic mechanisms and clinical implications.* New York: Raven Press.

Keesey, R. E., & Powley, T. L. (1975). Hypothalamic regulation of body weight. *American Scientist, 63,* 558–565.

Kelley, H. H. (1967). Attribution theory in social psychology. In D. Levine (Ed.), *Nebraska symposium on motivation* (Vol. 15, pp. 192–238). Lincoln: University of Nebraska Press.

Kelley, H. H. (1973). The process of causal attribution. *American Psychologist, 28,* 107–128.

Kelly, A. E., & Kahn, J. H. (1994). Effects of suppression of personal intrusive thought. *Journal of Personality and Social Psychology, 66,* 998–1006.

Kelly, D. D. (1991). Sexual differentiation of the nervous system. In E. R. Kandel, J. H. Schwartz, & T. M. Jessell (Eds.), *Principles of neural science* (3rd ed., pp. 959–973). Norwalk, CT: Appleton & Lange.

Keltner, D., & Buswell, B. N. (1997). Embarrassment: Its distinct form and appeasement functions. *Psychological Bulletin, 122,* 250–270.

Keltner, D., Ellsworth, P. C., & Edwards, K. (1993). Beyond simple pessimism: Effects of sadness and anger on social perception. *Journal of Personality and Social Psychology, 64,* 740–752.

Keltner, D., & Gross, J. J. (1999). Functional accounts of emotions. *Cognitive and Emotion, 13,* 467–480.

Keltner, D., & Haidt, J. (1999). Social functions of emotions at four levels of analysis. *Cognitive and Emotion, 13,* 505–521.

Kemper, T. D. (1987). How many emotions are there? Wedding the social and the autonomic components. *American Sociological Review, 93,* 263–289.

Kihlstrom, J. F. (1987). The cognitive unconscious. *Science, 237,* 1445–1452.

Kihlstrom, J. F., & Cantor, N. (1984). Mental representations of the self. In L. Berkowitz (Ed.), *Advances in experimental and social psychology* (Vol. 17, pp. 2–47). New York: Academic Press.

Kimble, G. A. (1990). Mother nature's bag of tricks is small. *Psychological Science, 1,* 36–41.

Kirkpatrick, L. A., & Shaver, P. (1988). Fear and affiliation reconsidered from a stress and coping perspective: The importance of cognitive clarity and fear reduction. *Journal of Social and Clinical Psychology, 7,* 214–233.

Kirschbaum, C., Wolf, O. T., May, M., Wippich, W., & Hellhammer, D. H. (1996). Stress and treatment-induced elevations of control levels associated with impaired declarative memory in healthy adults. *Life Sciences, 58,* 1475–1483.

Kirschenbaum, D. S. (1987). Self-regulatory failure: A review with clinical implications. *Clinical Psychology Review, 7,* 77–104.

Klein, C. S. (1967). Peremptory ideation: Structure and force in motivated ideas. In R. R. Holt (Ed.), Motives and thought: Psychoanalytic essays in honor of David Rapaport. *Psychological Issues, 5* (Monograph No. 18/19), 80–128.

Klein, D. C., & Seligman, M. E. P. (1976). Reversal of performance deficits in learned helplessness and depression. *Journal of Abnormal Psychology, 85,* 11–26.

Klein, H. J. (1991). Control theory and understanding motivated behavior: A different conclusion. *Motivation and Emotion, 15,* 29–44.

Klesges, R. C., Coates, T. J., Brown, G., Sturgeon-Tillisch, J., Moldenhauer-Klesges, L. M., Holzer, B., Woolfrey, J., & Vollmer, J. (1983). Parental influences on children's eating behavior and relative weight. *Journal of Applied Behavioral Analysis, 16,* 371–378.

Klien, G. (1954). Need and regulation. In M. R. Jones (Ed.), *Nebraska symposium on motivation* (Vol. 2, pp. 224–274). Lincoln: University of Nebraska Press.

Klinnert, M. D., Campos, J. J., Sorce, J. F., Emde, R. N., & Suejda, M. (1983). Emotions as behavior regulators: Social referencing in infancy. In R. Plutchik & H. Kellerman (Eds.), *Emotion: Theory, research, and experience, emotions in early development* (Vol. 2, pp. 57–86). New York: Academic Press.

Klohnen, E. C., & Bera, S. (1998). Behavioral and experiential patterns of avoidantly and securely attached women across adulthood: A 31-year longitudinal perspective. *Journal of Personality and Social Psychology, 74,* 211–223.

Klose, D. A. (1995). M. Scott Peck's analysis of human evil: A critical review. *Journal of Personality and Social Psychology, 35,* 37–66.

Knox, R. E., & Inkster, J. A. (1968). Postdecision dissonance at post time. *Journal of Personality and Social Psychology, 8,* 319–323.

Kochanska, G. (1993). Toward a synthesis of parental socialization and child temperament in early development of conscience. *Child Development, 64,* 325–347.

Kochanska, G. (1997). Multiple pathways to conscience for children with different temperaments: From toddlerhood to age 5. *Developmental Psychology, 33,* 228–240.

Koestner, R., Bernieri, F., & Zuckerman, M. (1992). Self-regulation and consistency between attitudes, traits, and behaviors. *Personality and Social Psychology Bulletin, 18, 52–59.*

Koestner, R., Losier, G. F., Vallerand, R. J., & Carducci, D. (1996). Identified and introjected forms of political internalization: Extending self-determination theory. *Journal of Personality and Social Psychology, 70,* 1025–1036.

Koestner, R., Ryan, R. M., Bernieri, F., & Holt, K. (1984). Setting limits on children's behavior: The differential effects of controlling versus informational styles on intrinsic motivation and creativity. *Journal of Personality, 52,* 233–248.

Koestner, R., Zuckerman, M., & Koestner, J. (1987). Praise, involvement, and intrinsic motivation. *Journal of Personality and Social Psychology, 53,* 383–390.

Kohn, A. (1993). *Punished by rewards: The trouble with gold stars, incentive plans, A's, praise, and other bribes.* Boston: Houghton Mifflin.

Kohut, H. (1971). *The analysis of self.* New York: International Universities Press.

Kolb, J., Cooper, S, & Fishman, G. (1995). Recent developments in psychoanalytic technique: A review. *Harvard Review of Psychiatry, 3,* 65–74.

Koulack, D. (1993). Dreams and adaptation to contemporary stress. In A. Moffitt, M. Kramer, & R. Hoffman (Eds.), *The functions of dreaming* (pp. 321–340). Albany: State University of New York Press.

Kowaz, A. M., & Marcia, J. E. (1991). Development and validation of a measure of Eriksonian industry. *Journal of Personality and Social Psychology, 60,* 390–397.

Kramer, R. (1995). The birth of client-centered therapy: Carl Rogers, Otto Rank, and "The Beyond." *Journal of Humanistic Psychology, 35,* 54–110.

Krantz, P. J., & McClannahan, L. E. (1993). Teaching children with autism to initiate to peers: Effects of a script-fading procedure. *Journal of Applied Behavior Analysis, 26,* 121–132.

Kraut, R. E., & Johnston, R. E. (1979). Social and emotional messages of smiling: An ethological approach. *Journal of Personality and Social Psychology, 37,* 1539–1553.

Krettek, J. E., & Price, J. L. (1978). Amygdaloid projections to subcortical structures within the basal forebrain and brainstem in the rat and cat. *Journal of Comparative Neurology, 178,* 225–254.

Kroger, J. (1993). The role of historical context in the identity formation process of late adolescence. *Youth and Society, 24,* 363–376.

Kuhl, J. (1978). Standard setting and risk preference: An elaboration of the theory of achievement motivation and an empirical test. *Psychological Review, 85,* 239–248.

Kuhl, J., & Blankenship, V. (1979). The dynamic theory of achievement motivation. *Psychological Review, 86,* 141–151.

Kuhlman, D. M. (1975). Individual differences in casino gambling? In N. R. Eadington (Ed.), *Gambling and society.* Springfield, IL: Thomas.

Kuhn, T. S. (1962). *The structure of scientific revolutions.* Chicago: University of Chicago Press.

Kulik, J. A., Mahler, H. I. M., & Earnest, A. (1994). Social comparison and affiliation under threat: Going beyond the affiliative-choice paradigm. *Journal of Personality and Social Psychology, 66,* 301–309.

Kunda, Z. (1990). The case for motivated reasoning. *Psychological Bulletin, 108,* 480–498.

Kuo, Z. Y. (1921). Giving up instincts in psychology. *Journal of Philosophy, 17,* 645–664.

Labott, S. M., Martin, R. B., Eason, P. S., & Berkey, E. Y. (1991). Social reactions to the expression of emotion. *Cognition and Emotion, 5,* 397–417.

Lacey, J. I., Kagan, J., Lacey, B. C., & Moss, H. A. (1963). The visceral level: Situational determinants and behavioral correlates of autonomic responses. In P. Knapp (Ed.), *Expression of the emotions in man.* New York: International Universities Press.

Laird, J. D. (1974). Self-attribution of emotion: The effects of expressive behavior on the quality of emotional experience. *Journal of Personality and Social Psychology, 29,* 475–486.

Laird, J. D. (1984). Facial response and emotion. *Journal of Personality and Social Psychology, 47,* 909–917.

Laird, J. D., Wagener, J. J., Halal, M., & Szegda, M. (1982). Remembering what you feel: The effects of emotion on memory. *Journal of Personality and Social Psychology, 42,* 646–657.

Lane, J. D., & Wegner, D. M. (1995). The cognitive consequences of secrecy. *Journal of Personality and Social Psychology, 69,* 237–253.

Lang, P. J. (1994). The varieties of emotional experience: A mediation of James-Lange theory. *Psychological Review, 101,* 211–221.

Lange, C. (1922). The emotions. In K. Dunlap (Ed.), *The emotions* (Istar A. Haupt, Trans.; pp. 33–90). Baltimore: Williams & Wilkins. (Original work published 1885).

Lange, R. D., & James, W. (1922). *The emotions.* Baltimore: Williams & Wilkins.

Langer, E. (1975). The illusion of control. *Journal of Personality and Social Psychology, 32,* 311–328.

Langer, E., & Rodin, J. (1976). The effects of choice and enhanced personal responsibility for the aged: A field experiment in an institutionalized setting. *Journal of Personality and Social Psychology, 34,* 191–198.

Langsdorff, P., Izard, C. E., Rayias, M., & Hembree, E. (1983). Interest expression, visual fixation, and heart rate changes in 2- to 8-month old infants. *Developmental Psychology, 19,* 375–386.

Lansing, J. B., & Heyns, R. W. (1959). Need affiliation and frequency of four types of communication. *Journal of Abnormal and Social Psychology, 58,* 365–372.

Lanzetta, J. T., Cartwright-Smith, J. E., & Kleck, R. E. (1976). Effects of nonverbal dissimulation of emotional experience and autonomic arousal. *Journal of Personality and Social Psychology, 33,* 354–370.

LaPointe, K. A., & Crandell, C. J. (1980). Relationship of irrational beliefs to self-reported depression. *Cognitive Therapy and Research, 4,* 247–250.

Lapore, S. J. (1992). Social conflict, social support, and psychological distress: Evidence of cross-domain buffering effects. *Journal of Personality and Social Psychology, 63,* 857–867.

LaPorte, R. E., & Nath, R. (1976). Role of performance goals in prose learning. *Journal of Educational Psychology, 68,* 260–264.

Larson, R., & Asmussen, L. (1991). Anger, worry, and hurt in early adolescence: An enlarging world of negative emotion. In M. Colton & S. Gore (Eds.), *Adolescent stress: Causes and consequences* (pp. 21–42). New York: Aldine de Gruyter.

Larsen, R. J. (1988, June). *Individual differences in affect intensity.* Paper presented at the *Motivation and Emotion* conference at Nags Head, NC.

Larsen, R. J., & Diener, E. (1987). Affect intensity as an individual difference characteristic: A review. *Journal of Research in Personality, 21,* 1–39.

Larsen, R. J., Diener, E., & Cropanzano, R. S. (1987). Cognitive operations associated with individual differences in affect intensity. *Journal of Personality and Social Psychology, 53,* 767–774.

Larsen, R. J., Diener, E., & Emmons, R. A. (1986). Affect intensity and reactions to daily life events. *Journal of Personality and Social Psychology, 51,* 803–814.

Larsen, R. J., Kasimatis, M., & Frey, K. (1992). Facilitating the furrowed brow: An unobtrusive test of the facial feedback hypothesis applied to unpleasant affect. *Cognition and Emotion, 6,* 321–338.

Larsen, R. J., & Ketelaar, T. (1991). Personality and susceptibility to positive and negative emotional states. *Journal of Personality and Social Psychology, 61,* 132–140.

Larsen, R. W. (2000). Toward a psychology of positive youth development. *American Psychologist, 55,* 170–183.

Latham, G. P., & Baldes, J. J. (1975). The practical significance of Locke's theory of goal setting. *Journal of Applied Psychology, 60,* 122–124.

Latham, G. P., Erez, M., & Locke, E. A. (1988). Resolving scientific disputes by the joint design of crucial experiments by the antagonists: Application to the Erez-Latham dispute regarding participation in goal setting. *Journal of Applied Psychology, 73,* 753–772.

Latham, G. P., & Locke, E. A. (1975). Increasing productivity with decreasing time limits: A field replication of Parkinson's law. *Journal of Applied Psychology, 60,* 524–526.

Latham, G. P., Mitchell, T. R., & Dossett, D. L. (1978). Importance of participative goal setting and anticipated rewards on goal difficulty and job performance. *Journal of Applied Psychology, 63,* 163–171.

Latham, G. P., & Saari, L. M. (1979). Importance of supportive relationships in goal setting. *Journal of Applied Psychology, 64,* 151–156.

Latham, G. P., & Yukl, G. A. (1975). Assigned versus participative goal setting with educated and uneducated woods workers. *Journal of Applied Psychology, 60,* 299–302.

Latham, G. P., & Yukl, G. A. (1976). Effects of assigned and participative goal setting on performance and job satisfaction. *Journal of Applied Psychology, 61,* 166–171.

Lau, R. R., & Russell, D. (1980). Attributions in the sports pages. *Journal of Personality and Social Psychology, 39,* 29–38.

Lavrakas, P. J. (1975). Female preferences for male physiques. *Journal of Research in Personality, 9,* 324–334.

Law, A., Logan, H., & Baron, R. S. (1994). Desire for control, felt control, and stress inoculation training during dental treatment. *Journal of Personality and Social Psychology, 67,* 926–936.

Lazarus, R. S. (1966). *Psychological stress and the coping process.* New York: McGraw-Hill.

Lazarus, R. S. (1968). Emotions and adaptation: Conceptual and empirical relations. In W. J. Arnold (Ed.), *Nebraska symposium on motivation* (Vol. 16, pp. 175–266). Lincoln: University of Nebraska Press.

Lazarus, R. S. (1982). Thoughts on the relations between emotion and cognition. *American Psychologist, 37,* 1019–1024.

Lazarus, R. S. (1983). The costs and benefits of denial. In S. Bresnitz (Ed.), *The denial of stress* (pp. 1–32). New York: International Universities Press.

Lazarus, R. S. (1984). On the primacy of cognition. *American Psychologist, 39,* 124–129.

Lazarus, R. S. (1991a). *Emotion and adaptation.* New York: Oxford University Press.

Lazarus, R. S. (1991b). Progress on a cognitive-motivational-relational theory of emotion. *American Psychologist, 46,* 819–834.

Lazarus, R. S. (1994). Universal antecedents of the emotions. In P. Ekman & R. J. Davidson (Eds.), *The nature of emotion: Fundamental questions* (pp. 163–171). New York: Oxford University Press.

Lazarus, R. S., & DeLongis, A. (1983). Psychological stress and coping in aging. *American Psychologist, 38,* 245–254.

Lazarus, R. S., & Folkman, S. (1984). *Stress, appraisal, and coping.* New York: Springer-Verlag.

Lazarus, R. S., & Smith, C. A. (1988). Knowledge and appraisal in the cognition-emotion relationship. *Cognition and Emotion, 2,* 281–300.

Leary, M. R. (1983). Social anxiousness: The construct and its measurement. *Journal of Personality Assessment, 47,* 66–75.

Leavitt, R. L., & Power, M. B. (1989). Emotional socialization in the postmodern era: Children and day care. *Social Psychology Quarterly, 52,* 35–43.

LeDoux, J. E. (1987). Emotion. In F. Plum (Ed.), *Handbook of psychology: I. The nervous system* (pp. 419–460). Bethesda, MD: American Physiological Society.

LeDoux, J. E. (1989). Cognitive-emotional interactions in the brain. *Cognition and Emotion, 3,* 267–289.

LeDoux, J. E. (1992a). Brain mechanisms of emotion and emotional learning. *Current Opinion in Neurobiology, 2,* 191–198.

LeDoux, J. E. (1992b). Emotion and the amygdala. In J. P. Aggleton (Ed.), *The amygdala: Neurobiological aspects of emotion, memory, and mental dysfunction* (pp. 339–351). New York: Wiley-Liss.

LeDoux, J. E., Iwata, J., Cicchetti, P., & Reis, D. J. (1988). Different projections of the central amygdaloid nucleus mediate autonomic and behavioral correlates of conditioned fear. *Journal of Neuroscience, 8,* 2517–2529.

Lefcourt, H. M., & Martin, R. A. (1986). *Humor and life stress: An antidote to adversity.* New York: Springer-Verlag.

Lehman, D. R., Ellard, D. R., & Wortman, C. B. (1986). Social support for the bereaved: Recipients and providers perspectives on what is helpful. *Journal of Consulting and Clinical Psychology, 54,* 438–446.

Leippe, M. R., & Eisenstadt, D. (1994). Generalization of dissonance reduction: Decreasing prejudice through induced compliance. *Journal of Personality and Social Psychology, 67,* 395–413.

Leon, I., & Hernandez, J. A. (1998). Testing the role of attribution and appraisal in predicting own and other's emotions. *Cognition and Emotion, 12,* 27–43.

Lepper, M. R. (1983). Social-control processes and the internalization of social values: An attributional perspective. In E. T. Higgins, D. N. Ruble, & W. W. Hartup (Eds.), *Social cognition and social development* (pp. 294–330). New York: Cambridge University Press.

Lepper, M. R., & Cordova, D. I. (1992). A desire to be taught: Instructional consequences of intrinsic motivation. *Motivation and Emotion, 16,* 187–208.

Lepper, M. R., & Greene, D. (1975). Turning play into work: Effects of adult surveillance and extrinsic rewards on children's intrinsic motivation. *Journal of Personality and Social Psychology, 31,* 479–486.

Lepper, M. R., & Greene, D. (Eds.). (1978). *The hidden costs of reward.* Hillsdale, NJ: Erlbaum.

Lepper, M. R., Greene, D., & Nisbett, R. E. (1973). Undermining children's intrinsic interest with extrinsic rewards: A test of the overjustification hypothesis. *Journal of Personality and Social Psychology, 28,* 129–137.

Lerner, J. S., Goldberg, J. H., & Tetlock, P. E. (1999). Sober second thought: The effects of accountability, anger, and authoritarianism on attributions of responsibility. *Personality and Social Psychology Bulletin, 24,* 563–574.

Lester, L. S., & Fanselow, M. S. (1985). Exposure to a cat produces opioid analgesia in rats. *Behavioral Neuroscience, 99,* 756–759.

Levenson, H. M. (1981). Differentiating among internality, powerful others, and chance. In H. M. Lefcourt (Ed.), *Research with the locus of control construct: Vol. 1. Assessment methods* (pp. 15–63). New York: Academic Press.

Levenson, R. W. (1992). Autonomic nervous system differences among emotions. *Psychological Science, 3,* 23–27.

Levenson, R. W. (1994a). Human emotion: A functional view. In P. Ekman & R. J. Davidson (Eds.), *The nature of emotion: Fundamental questions* (pp. 123–126). New York: Oxford University Press.

Levenson, R. W. (1994b). The search for autonomic specificity. In P. Ekman & R. J. Davidson (Eds.), *The nature of emotion: Fundamental questions* (pp. 252–257). New York: Oxford University Press.

Levenson, R. W. (1999). The intrapersonal functions of emotion. *Cognitive and Emotion, 13,* 481–504.

Levenson, R. W., Carstensen, L. L., & Gottman, J. M. (1994). Influence of age and gender on affect, physiology, and their interrelations: A study of long-term marriages. *Journal of Personality and Social Psychology, 67,* 56–68.

Levenson, R. W., Carstensen, L. L., Friesen, W. V., & Ekman, P. (1991). Emotion, physiology, and expression in old age. *Psychology and Aging, 6,* 28–35.

Levenson, R. W., Ekman, P., & Friesen, W. V. (1990). Voluntary facial action generates emotion-specific autonomic nervous system activity. *Psychophysiology, 27,* 363–384.

Levenson, R. W., & Gottman, J. M. (1983). Marital interaction: Physiological linkage and affective exchange. *Journal of Personality and Social Psychology, 45,* 587–597.

Leventhal, H., & Everhart, D. (1979). Emotion, pain, and physical illness. In C. E. Izard (Ed.), *Emotions in personality and psychopathology* (pp. 263–299). New York: Plenum.

Levin, R. (1990). Psychoanalytic theories of the function of dreaming: A review of the empirical literature. In J. Masling (Ed.), *Empirical studies of psychoanalytic theories* (Vol. 3, pp. 1–53). Hillsdale, NJ: Analytic Press.

Lewin, K. (1935). *A dynamic theory of personality.* New York: McGraw-Hill.

Lewinsohn, P. M., Mischel, W., Chaplin, W., & Barton, R. (1980). Social competence and depression:

The role of illusory self-perceptions. *Journal of Abnormal Psychology, 89,* 203–212.

Lindgren, H. C. (1976). Measuring need to achieve by NachNaff scale: A forced choice questionnaire. *Psychological Reports, 39,* 907–910.

Lindsley, D. B. (1957). Psychophysiology and motivation. In M. R. Jones (Ed.), *Nebraska symposium on motivation* (Vol. 5, pp. 44–105). Lincoln: University of Nebraska Press.

Lindzey, G. (Ed.). (1958). *Assessment of human motives.* New York: Rinehart.

Linehan, M. M. (1997). Self-verification and drug abusers: Implications for treatment. *Psychological Science, 8,* 181–183.

Linville, P. W. (1982). Affective consequences of complexity regarding the self and others. In M. S. Clark & S. T. Fiske (Eds.), *Affect and cognition* (pp. 79–109). Hillsdale, NJ: Erlbaum.

Litle, P., & Zuckerman, M. (1986). Sensation seeking and music preferences. *Personality and Individual Differences, 4,* 575–578.

Lockard, J. S., Allen, D. J., Schielle, B. J., & Wiemer, M. J. (1978). Human postural signals: Stance, weight-shifts and social distance as intention movements to depart. *Animal Behavior, 26,* 219–224.

Locke, E. A. (1968). Toward a theory of task motivation and incentives. *Organizational Behavior and Human Performance, 3,* 157–189.

Locke, E. A., & Bryan, J. F. (1969). The directing function of goals in task performance. *Organizational Behavior and Human Performance, 4,* 35–42.

Locke, E. A., Chah, D. O., Harrison, S., & Lustgarten, N. (1989). Separating the effects of goal specificity from goal level. *Organizational Behavior and Human Decision Processes, 43,* 270–287.

Locke, E. A., & Kristof, A. L. (1996). Volitional choices in the goal achievement process. In P. M. Gollwitzer & J. A. Bargh (Eds.), *The psychology of action: Linking cognition and motivation to behavior.* New York: Guilford Press.

Locke, E. A., & Latham, G. P. (1984). *Goal-setting: A motivational technique that works!* Englewood Cliffs, NJ: Prentice Hall.

Locke, E. A., & Latham, G. P. (1990). *A theory of goal setting and task performance.* Englewood Cliffs, NJ: Prentice Hall.

Locke, E. A., Shaw, K. N., Saari, L. M., & Latham, G. P. (1981). Goal setting and task performance: 1969–1980. *Psychological Bulletin, 90,* 125–152.

Loevinger, J. (1976). Stages of ego development. In J. Loevinger (Ed.), *Ego development* (pp. 13–28). San Francisco: Jossey-Bass.

Loevinger, J., Cohn, L., Bonneville, L., Redmore, C., Streich, D., & Sargent, M. (1985). Ego development in college. *Journal of Personality and Social Psychology, 48,* 947–962.

Loevinger, J., & Wessler, R. (1970). *Measuring ego development: Vol. 1. Construction and use of a sentence completion test.* San Francisco: Jossey-Bass.

Loftus, E. F., & Klinger, M. R. (1992). Is the unconscious smart or dumb? *American Psychologist, 47,* 761–765.

Londerville, S., & Martin, M. (1981). Security of attachment, compliance, and maternal training methods in the second year of life. *Developmental Psychology, 17,* 289–299.

Lorenz, K. (1965). *Evolution and modification of behavior: A critical examination of the concepts of the "learned" and the "innate" elements of behavior.* Chicago: The University of Chicago Press.

Losch, M., & Cacioppo, J. (1990). Cognitive dissonance may enhance sympathetic tonus, but attitudes are changed to reduce negative affect rather than arousal. *Journal of Personality and Social Psychology, 51,* 55–65.

Lowe, M. R. (1993). The effects of dieting on eating behavior: A three-factor model. *Psychological Bulletin, 114,* 100–121.

Luborsky, L., & Crits-Christoph, P. (1990). *Understanding transference: The core conflictual relationship theme method.* New York: Basic Books.

MacKinnon, N. J. (1994). *Symbolic interactionism as affect control.* Albany, NY: SUNY Press.

MacLeod, A. K, Byrne, A., & Valentine, J. D. (1996). Affect, emotional disorder, and future-directed thinking. *Cognition and Emotion, 10,* 69–86.

Madsen, K. B. (1959). *Theories of motivation.* Copenhagen: Munksgaard.

Maehr, M. L., & Kleiber, D. A. (1980). The graying of achievement motivation. *American Psychologist, 36,* 787–793.

Mahoney, E. R. (1983). *Human sexuality.* New York: McGraw-Hill.

Main, M., Kaplan, N., & Cassidy, J. (1985). Security in infancy, childhood, and adulthood: A move to the level of representation. In I. Bretherton & E. Waters (Eds.), Growing points of attachment theory and research. *Monographs of the Society for Research in Child Development, 50,* 67–104.

Malmo, R. B. (1959). Activation: A neurological dimension. *Psychological Review, 66,* 367–386.

Manderlink, G., & Harackiewicz, J. M. (1984). Proximal versus distal goal setting and intrinsic motivation. *Journal of Personality and Social Psychology, 47,* 918–928.

Mandler, G. (1975). *Mind and emotion.* New York: John Wiley & Sons.

Mandler, G. (1984). *Mind and body: Psychology of emotion and stress.* New York: Norton.

Manstead, A. S. R. (1991). Emotion in social life. *Cognition and Emotion, 5,* 353–362.

Marcia, J. E. (1966). Development and validation of ego identity status. *Journal of Personality and Social Psychology, 3,* 551–558.

Marcia, J. E. (1980). Identity in adolescence. In J. Adelson (Ed.), *Handbook of adolescent psychology.* New York: Wiley.

Marcia, J. E. (1994). The empirical study of ego identity. In H. A. Bosma, T. L. G. Graffsma, H. D. Grotevant, & D. J. de Levita (Eds.), *Identity and development: An interdisciplinary approach* (pp. 67–80). Thousand Oaks, CA: Sage.

Marcia, J. E., Waterman, A. S., Matteson, D. R., Archer, S. L., & Orlofsky, J. L. (1993). *Ego identity: A handbook for psychosocial research.* New York: Springer-Verlag.

Markus, H. (1977). Self-schemata and processing information about the self. *Journal of Personality and Social Psychology, 35,* 63–68.

Markus H. (1983). Self-knowledge: An expected view. *Journal of Personality, 51,* 543–565.

Markus, H., Cross, S., & Wurf, E. (1990). The role of self-esteem in competence. In R. J. Sternberg & J. Kolligian (Eds.), *Competence considered* (pp. 205–225). New Haven: Yale University Press.

Markus, H., & Nurius, P. (1986). Possible selves. *American Psychologist, 41,* 954–969.

Markus, H., & Sentisk, K. (1982). The self in social information processing. In J. Suls (Ed.), *Psychological perspectives on the self* (Vol. 1, pp. 41–60). Hillsdale, NJ: Erlbaum.

Markus, H., & Wurf, E. (1987). The dynamic self-concept: A social psychological perspective. *Annual Review of Psychology, 38,* 299–337.

Marlatt, G. P., & Parks, G. A. (1982). Self-management of addictive behaviors. In P. Karoly & F. H. Kanfer (Eds.), *Self-management and behavior change* (pp. 443–488). New York: Pergamon.

Marsh, H. W. (1990). Causal ordering of academic self-concept and academic achievement: A multivariate, longitudinal panel analysis. *Journal of Educational Psychology, 82,* 646–656.

Masling, J. (Ed.). (1983). *Empirical studies of psychoanalytic theories.* Hillsdale, NJ: Analytic Press.

Maslow, A. H. (1943). A theory of human motivation. *Psychological Review, 50,* 370–396.

Maslow, A. H. (1954). *Motivation and personality.* New York: Harper.

Maslow, A. H. (1968). *Toward a psychology of being.* New York: Van Nostrand.

Maslow, A. H. (1971). *The farther reaches of human nature.* New York: Viking Press.

Maslow, A. H. (1987). *Motivation and personality* (3rd ed.). New York: Harper & Row.

Mason, A., & Blankenship, V. (1987). Power and affiliation motivation, stress, and abuse in intimate relationships. *Journal of Personality and Social Psychology, 52,* 203–210.

Masters, W. H., & Johnson, V. E. (1966). *Human sexual response.* Boston: Little, Brown.

Mathes, E. W. (1981). Maslow's hierarchy of needs as a guide for living. *Journal of Humanistic Psychology, 21,* 69–72.

Mathews, J. R., Hodson, G. D., Crist, W. B., & LaRoche, G. R. (1992). Teaching young children to use contact lenses. *Journal of Applied Behavior Analysis, 25,* 229–235.

Matsumoto, D. (1987). The role of facial response in the experience of emotion: More methodological problems and a meta-analysis. *Journal of Personality and Social Psychology, 52,* 769–774.

May, R. (Ed.). (1961). *Existential psychology.* New York: Random House.

May, R. (1982). The problem of evil: An open letter to Carl Rogers. *Journal of Humanistic Psychology, 22,* 10–21.

Mayer, D. J. (1952). The glucostatic theory of regulation of food intake and the problem of obesity. *Bulletin of the New England Medical Center, 14,* 43.

Mayer, D. J. (1953). Glucostatic mechanism of regulation of food intake. *New England Journal of Medicine, 249,* 13–16.

Mayer, D. J., Wolfe, T. L., Akil, H., Carder, B., & Liebeskind, J. C. (1971). Analgesia from electrical stimulation in the brainstem of the rat. *Science, 174,* 1351–1354.

McAdams, D. P. (1980). A thematic coding system for the intimacy motive. *Journal of Research in Personality, 14,* 413–432.

McAdams, D. P. (1982a). Intimacy motivation. In A. J. Stewart (Ed.), *Motivation and society.* San Francisco: Jossey-Bass.

McAdams, D. P. (1982b). Experiences of intimacy and power: Relationships between social motives and autobiographical memory. *Journal of Personality and Social Psychology, 42,* 292–302.

McAdams, D. P., & Constantian, C. A. (1983). Intimacy and affiliation motives in daily living: An experience sampling analysis. *Journal of Personality and Social Psychology, 45,* 851–861.

McAdams, D. P., Healy, S., & Krause, S. (1984). Social motives and patterns of friendship. *Journal of Personality and Social Psychology, 47,* 828–838.

McAdams, D. P., Jackson, R. J., & Kirshnit, C. (1984). Looking, laughing, and smiling in dyads as a function of intimacy motivation and reciprocity. *Journal of Personality, 52,* 261–273.

McAdams, D. P., & Losoff, M. (1984). Friendship motivation in fourth and sixth graders: A thematic analysis. *Journal of Social and Personal Relationships, 1,* 11–27.

McAdams, D. P., & Powers, J. (1981). Themes of intimacy in behavior and thought. *Journal of Personality and Social Psychology, 40,* 573–587.

McAdams, D. P., & Vaillant, G. E. (1982). Intimacy motivation and psychosocial adaptation: A longitudinal study. *Journal of Personality Assessment, 46,* 586–593.

McAuley, E., & Tammen, V. V. (1989). The effect of subjective and objective competitive outcomes on intrinsic motivation. *Journal of Sport and Exercise Psychology, 11,* 84–93.

McCaul, K. D., Holmes, D. S., & Solomon, S. (1982). Facial expression and emotion. *Journal of Personality and Social Psychology, 42,* 145–152.

McCaul, K. D., & Malott, J. M. (1984). Distraction and coping with pain. *Psychological Bulletin, 95,* 516–533.

McClelland, D. C. (Ed.). (1955). *Studies in motivation.* New York: Appleton-Century-Crofts.

McClelland, D. C. (1961). *The achieving society.* Princeton, NJ: Van Nostrand.

McClelland, D. C. (1965). Achievement and entrepreneurship: A longitudinal study. *Journal of Personality and Social Psychology, 1,* 389–392.

McClelland, D. C. (1975). *Power: The inner experience.* New York: Irvington.

McClelland, D. C. (1978). Managing motivation to expand human freedom. *American Psychologist, 33,* 201–210.

McClelland, D. C. (1980). Motive dispositions: The merits of operant and respondent measures. In L. Wheeler (Ed.), *Review of Personality and Social Psychology* (Vol. 1). Beverly Hills, CA: Sage.

McClelland, D. C. (1982). The need for power, sympathetic activation, and illness. *Motivation and Emotion, 6,* 31–41.

McClelland, D. C. (1985). *Human motivation.* San Francisco: Scott, Foresman.

McClelland, D. C. (1987). Characteristics of successful entrepreneurs. *The Journal of Creative Behavior, 21,* 219–233.

McClelland, D. C., Atkinson, J. W., Clark, R. A., & Lowell, E. L. (1953). *The achievement motive.* New York: Appleton-Century-Crofts.

McClelland, D. C., Atkinson, J. W., Clark, R. A., & Lowell, E. L. (1958). A scoring manual for the achievement motive. In J. W. Atkinson (Ed.), *Motives in fantasy, action, and society* (pp. 179–204). Princeton, NJ: D. Van Nostrand.

McClelland, D. C., & Burnham, D. H. (1976, March–April). Power is the great motivator. *Harvard Business Review, 100–110,* 159–166.

McClelland, D. C., Constantian, C., Pilon, D., & Stone, C. (1982). Effects of child-rearing practices on adult maturity. In D. C. McClelland (Ed.), *The development of social maturity.* New York: Irvington.

McClelland, D. C., Davis, W. B., Kalin, R., & Wanner, E. (1972). *The drinking man: Alcohol and human motivation.* New York: Free Press.

McClelland, D. C., & Pilon, D. A. (1983). Sources of adult motives in patterns of parent behavior in early childhood. *Journal of Personality and Social Psychology, 44,* 564–574.

McClelland, D. C., & Teague, G. (1975). Predicting risk preferences among power-related tasks. *Journal of Personality, 43,* 266–285.

McClelland, D. C., & Watson, R. I., Jr. (1973). Power motivation and risk-taking behavior. *Journal of Personality, 41,* 121–139.

McCombs, B. L., & Pope, J. E. (1994). *Motivating hard to reach students.* Washington, DC: American Psychological Association.

McCoy, C. L., & Masters, J. C. (1985). The development of children's strategies for the social control of emotion. *Child Development, 56,* 1214–1222.

McDougall, W. (1908). *Introduction to social psychology.* London: Methuen.

McDougall, W. (1926). *Introduction to social psychology.* Boston: Luce and Co.

McDougall, W. (1933). *The energies of men.* New York: Scribner.

McFarlin, D. B., & Blascovich, J. (1981). Effects of self-esteem and performance feedback on future affective preferences and cognitive expectations. *Journal of Personality and Social Psychology, 40,* 521–531.

McGinley, H., McGinley, P., & Nicholas, K. (1978). Smiling, body position and interpersonal attraction. *Bulletin of the Psychonomics Society, 12,* 21–24.

McGraw, K. O. (1978). The detrimental effects of reward on performance: A literature review and a prediction model. In M. R. Lepper & D. Greene (Eds.), *The hidden costs of reward* (pp. 33–60). New York: John Wiley.

McGraw, K. O., & McCullers, J. C. (1979). Evidence of detrimental effects of extrinsic incentives on breaking a mental set. *Journal of Experimental Social Psychology, 15,* 285–294.

McHugh, P. R., & Moran, T. H. (1985). The stomach: A conception of its dynamic role in satiety. In J. M. Sprague & A. N. Epstein (Eds.), *Progress in psychobiology and physiological psychology* (Vol. 11, pp. 197–232). Orlando, FL: Academic Press.

McIntosh, D. N. (1996). Facial feedback hypotheses: Evidence, implications, and directions. *Motivation and Emotion, 20,* 121–147.

McIntosh, D. N., Zajonc, R. B., Vig, P. S., & Emerick, S. W., (1997). Facial movement, breathing, temperature, and affect: Implications of the vascular theory of emotional efference. *Cognition and Emotion, 11,* 171–195.

McKeachie, W. J. (1976). Psychology in America's bicentennial year. *American Psychologist, 31,* 819–833.

McKeachie, W. J., Lin, Y., Milholland, J., & Issacson, R. (1966). Student affiliation motives, teacher warmth, and academic achievement. *Journal of Personality and Social Psychology, 4,* 457–461.

McNulty, S. E., & Swann, W. B., Jr. (1994). Identity negotiation in roommate relationships: The self as architect and consequence of social reality. *Journal of Personality and Social Psychology, 67,* 1012–1023.

Mednick, M. T., Mednick, S. A., & Mednick, E. V. (1964). Incubation of creative performance and specific associative priming. *Journal of Abnormal and Social Psychology, 69,* 84–88.

Medvec, V. H., Madey, S. F., & Gilovich, T. (1995). When less is more: Counterfactual thinking and satisfaction among Olympic medalists. *Journal of Personality and Social Psychology, 69,* 603–610.

Meece, J., Blumenfeld, P., & Hoyle, R. (1988). Students' goal orientations and cognitive engagement in classroom activities. *Journal of Educational Psychology, 80,* 514–523.

Mehrabian, A. (1968). Male and female scales of the tendency to achieve. *Educational and Psychological Measurement, 28,* 493–502.

Mehrabian, A., & Bank, L. (1975). *Manual for the Mehrabian measure of achieving tendency.* Unpublished manuscript, University of California at Los Angeles.

Meilman, P. W. (1979). Cross-sectional age changes in ego identity status during adolescence. *Developmental Psychology, 15,* 230–231.

Mellstrom, M., Jr., Cicala, G. A., & Zuckerman, M. (1976). General versus specific trait anxiety measures in the prediction of fear of snakes, heights, and darkness. *Journal of Consulting and Clinical Psychology, 44,* 83–91.

Mento, A. J., Steel, R. P., & Karren, R. J. (1987). A meta-analytic study of the effects of goal setting on task performance: 1966–1984. *Organizational Behavior and Human Decision Processes, 39,* 52–83.

Meskin, B. B., & Singer, J. L. (1974). Daydreaming, reflective thought, and laterality of eye movements. *Journal of Personality and Social Psychology, 30,* 64–71.

Meuhlenhard, C. L., & Kimes, L. A. (1999). The social construction of violence: The case of sexual and domestic violence. *Personality and Social Psychology Review, 3,* 234–245.

Mickelson, K. D., Kessler, R. C., & Shaver, P. R. (1997). Adult attachment in a nationally representative sample. *Journal of Personality and Social Psychology, 73,* 1092–1106.

Mikulincer, M. (1986). Motivational involvement and learned helplessness: The behavioral effects of the importance of uncontrollable events. *Journal of Social and Clinical Psychology, 4,* 402–422.

Mikulincer, M. (1988). The relationship of probability of success and performance following failure: Reactance and helplessness effects. *Motivation and Emotion, 12,* 139–152.

Mikulincer, M. (1994). *Human learned helplessness: A coping perspective.* New York: Plenum Press.

Miller, D. L., & Kelley, M. L. (1994). The use of goal setting and contingency contracting for improving children's homework performance. *Journal of Applied Behavior Analysis, 27,* 73–84.

Miller, D. T., & Ross, M. (1975). Self-serving bias in the attribution of causality: Fact or fiction? *Psychological Bulletin, 82,* 213–215.

Miller, G. A., Galanter, E. H., & Pribrum, K. H. (1960). *Plans and the structure of behavior.* New York: Holt, Rinehart & Winston.

Miller, I. W., & Norman, W. H. (1981). Effects of attributions for success on the alleviation of learned helplessness and depression. *Journal of Abnormal Psychology, 90,* 113–124.

Miller, N. E. (1948). Studies of fear as an acquirable drive: 1. Fear as motivation and fear-reduction as reinforcement in the learning on new responses. *Journal of Experimental Psychology, 38,* 89–101.

Miller, N. E. (1959). Liberalization of basic S-R concepts: Extensions to conflict behavior, motivation, and social learning. In S. Koch (Ed.), *Psychology: A study of a science* (Vol. 2, pp. 196–292). New York: McGraw-Hill.

Miller, N. E. (1960). Motivational effects of brain stimulation and drugs. *Federation Proceedings, Federation of American Societies for Experimental Biology, 19,* 846–853.

Millon, T. (1990). The disorders of personality. In L. A. Pervin (Ed.), *Handbook of personality: Theory and research* (pp. 339–370). New York: Guilford Press.

Mills, J., & Clark, M. S. (1982). Communal and exchange relationships. In L. Wheeler (Ed.), *Review of personality and social psychology* (Vol. 3, pp. 121–144). Beverly Hills, CA: Sage.

Mischel, H. N., & Mischel, W. (1983). The development of children's knowledge of self-control strategies. *Child Development, 54,* 603–619.

Mischel, W. (1996). From good intentions to willpower. In P. M. Gollwitzer & J. A. Bargh (Eds.), *The psychology of action: Linking cognition and motivation to behavior.* New York: Guilford Press.

Mischel, W., Coates, B., & Raskoff, A. (1968). Effects of success and failure on self-gratification. *Journal of Personality and Social Psychology, 10,* 381–390.

Mischel, W., Shoda, Y., & Rodriguez, M. L. (1989). Delay of gratification in children. *Science, 244,* 933–938.

Miserandino, M. (1996). Children who do well in school: Individual differences in perceived competence and autonomy in above-average children. *Journal of Educational Psychology, 88,* 203–214.

Mitchell, M., & Jolley, J. (1988). *Research design explained.* New York: Holt, Rinehart & Winston.

Mitchell, S. (1988). *Relational concepts in psychoanalysis.* Cambridge, MA: Harvard University Press.

Mitchell, T. R. (1974). Expectancy models of job satisfaction, occupational preference and effort: A theoretical, methodological, and empirical appraisal. *Psychological Bulletin, 81,* 1053–1077.

Mittelman, W. (1991). Maslow's study of self-actualization: A reinterpretation. *Journal of Humanistic Psychology, 31,* 114–135.

Moffitt, A., Kramer, M., & Hoffman, R. (1993). *The functions of dreaming.* Albany: State University of New York.

Moltz, H. (1965). Contemporary instinct theory and the fixed action pattern. *Psychological Review, 72,* 27–47.

Money, J. (1988). *Gay, straight, and in-between: The sexology of erotic orientation.* New York: Oxford University Press.

Money, J., & Ehrhardt, A. A. (1972). *Man and woman, boy and girl.* Baltimore: Johns Hopkins University Press.

Money, J., Wiedeking, C., Walker, P. A., & Gain, D. (1976). Combined antiandrogenic and counseling program for treatment of 46 XY and 47 XYY sex offenders. In E. J. Sachar (Ed.), *Hormones, behavior, and psychopathology, 66,* 105–109.

Monson, T. C., & Snyder, M. (1977). Actors, observers, and the attribution process: Toward a reconceptualization. *Journal of Experimental Social Psychology, 13,* 89–111.

Mook, D. G. (1988). On the organization of satiety. *Appetite, 11,* 27–39.

Mook, D. G. (1996). *Motivation: The organization of action* (2nd ed.). New York: W. W. Norton.

Mook, D. G., & Kozub, F. J. (1968). Control of sodium chloride intake in the nondeprived rat. *Journal of Comparative and Physiological Psychology, 66,* 105–109.

Mook, D. G., & Wagner, S. (1989). Orosensory suppression of saccharin drinking in rat: The response, not the taste. *Appetite, 13,* 1–13.

Morgan, C. T., & Murray, H. A. (1935). A method for investigating fantasies. *Archives of Neurology and Psychiatry, 34,* 289–306.

Morse, R. C., & Stoller, D. (1982, September). The hidden message that breaks habits. *Science Digest,* 28.

Moruzzi, G., & Magoun, H. W. (1949). Brain stem reticular formation and activation of the EEG. *EEG and Clinical Neurophysiology, 1,* 455–473.

Mossholder, K. W. (1980). Effects of externally mediated goal setting on intrinsic motivation: A laboratory experiment. *Journal of Applied Psychology, 65,* 202–210.

Mueller, C. M., & Dweck, C. S. (1997). *Implicit theories of intelligence: Malleability beliefs, definitions, and judgments of intelligence.* Unpublished data.

Murray, H. A. (1937). Facts which support the concept of need or drive. *Journal of Personality, 3,* 115–143.

Murray, H. A. (1938). *Explorations in personality.* New York: Oxford University Press.

Murray, H. A. (1943). *Thematic apperception test.* Cambridge: Harvard University Press.

Myers, D. G. (2000). The funds, friends, and faith of happy people. *American Psychologist, 55,* 56–67.

Nasby, W., & Yando, R. (1982). Selective encoding and retrieval of affectively information. *Journal of Personality and Social Psychology, 43,* 1244–1255.

Neary, R. S., & Zuckerman, M. (1976). Sensation-seeking, trait and state anxiety, and the electrodermal orienting reflex. *Psychophysiology, 13,* 205–211.

Neemann, J., & Harter, S. (1986). *The self-perception profile for college students.* [Manual]. Denver: University of Denver.

Neher, A. (1991). Maslow's theory of motivation: A critique. *Journal of Humanistic Psychology, 31,* 89–112.

Neiss, R. (1988). Reconceptualizing arousal: Psychobiological states in motor performance. *Psychological Bulletin, 103,* 345–366.

Neisser, U. (1967). *Cognitive psychology.* Englewood Cliffs, NJ: Prentice-Hall.

Newcomb, M. D., & McGee, L. (1991). Influence of sensation seeking on general deviance and specific problem behaviors from adolescence to young adulthood. *Journal of Personality and Social Psychology, 61,* 614–628.

Newell, A., Shaw, J. C., & Simon, H. A. (1958). Elements of a theory of human problem solving. *Psychological Review, 65,* 151–166.

Newman, E. B., Perkins, F. T., & Wheeler, R. H. (1930). Cannon's theory of emotion: A critique. *Psychological Review, 37,* 305–326.

Newman, R. S. (1991). Goals and self-regulated learning: What motivates children to seek academic help? In M. L. Maehr & P. R. Pintrich (Eds.), *Advances in motivation and achievement* (Vol. 7, pp. 151–183). Greenwich, CT: JAI Press.

Nezu, A. M., Nezu, C. M., & Blissett, S. E. (1988). Sense of humor as a moderator of the relation between stressful events and psychological distress: A prospective analysis. *Journal of Personality and Social Psychology, 54,* 520–525.

Nicholls, J. G. (1978). The development of the concepts of effort and ability, perceptions of academic achievement, and the understanding that difficult tasks require more ability. *Child Development, 49,* 800–814.

Nicholls, J. G. (1979). Development of perception of own attainment and causal attributions for success and failure in reading. *Journal of Educational Psychology, 71,* 94–99.

Nicholls, J. G. (1984). Achievement motivation: Conceptions of ability, subjective experience, task choice, and performance. *Psychological Review, 91,* 328–346.

Niedenthal, P. M., Tangney, J. P., & Gavanski, I. (1994). "If only I weren't" versus "If only I hadn't": Distinguishing shame and guilt in counterfactual thinking. *Journal of Personality and Social Psychology, 67,* 585–595.

Nisbett, R. E., & Ross, L. (1980). *Human inference: Strategies and shortcomings of social judgment.* Englewood Cliffs, NJ: Prentice-Hall.

Nisbett, R. E., & Wilson, T. D. (1977). Telling more than we can know: Verbal reports on mental processes. *Psychological Review, 84,* 231–259.

Nolen-Hoeksema, S., Wolfson, A., Mumme, D., & Guskin, K. (1995). Helplessness in children of depressed and nondepressed mothers. *Developmental Psychology, 31,* 377–387.

Noller, P. (1984). *Nonverbal communication and marital interaction.* Oxford: Pergamon.

Notermans, S. L. H., & Tophoff, M. M. W. A. (1975). Sex differences in pain tolerance and pain apperception. In M. Weisenberg (Ed.), *Pain: Clinical and experimental perspectives.* St. Louis, MO: Mosby.

Nowicki, S., & Schneewind, K. A. (1982). Relation of family climate variables to locus of control in German and American students. *Journal of Genetic Psychology, 141,* 277–286.

Nurius, P. (1991). Possible selves and social support: Social cognitive resources for coping and striving. In J. A. Howard & P. L. Callero (Eds.), *The self-society interface: Cognition, emotion, and action* (pp. 239–258). New York: Cambridge University Press.

Nystul, M. S. (1984). Positive parenting leads to self-actualized children. *Individual Psychology, 40,* 177–183.

Oatley, K., & Duncan, E. (1994). The experience of emotions in everyday life. *Cognition and Emotion, 8,* 369–381.

Oatley, K., & Jenkins, J. M. (1992). Human emotions: Function and dysfunction. *Annual Review of Psychology, 43,* 55–85.

Oatley, K., & Johnson-Laird, P. N. (1987). Toward a cognitive theory of emotions. *Cognition and Emotion, 1,* 29–50.

Oettingen, G. (1995). Positive fantasy and motivation. In P. M. Gollwitzer & J. A. Bargh (Eds.), *The psychology of action: Linking cognition and motivation to behavior* (pp. 236–259). New York: Guilford Press.

O'Hara, M. (1989). When I use the term humanistic psychology . . . *Journal of Humanistic Psychology, 29,* 263–273.

Okano, K. (1981). The effects of extrinsic reward on intrinsic motivation. *Journal of Child Development, 17,* 11–23.

Oldham, G. R. (1975). The impact of supervisory characteristics on goal acceptance. *Academy of Management Journal, 18,* 461–475.

Olds, J. (1956a). *The growth and structure of motives.* Glencoe, IL: Free Press.

Olds, J. (1956b). A preliminary mapping of electrical reinforcing effects in the rat brain. *Journal of Comparative and Physiological Psychology, 49,* 281–285.

Olds, J. (1969). The central nervous system and the reinforcement of behavior. *American Psychologist, 24,* 114–132.

Olds, J., & Milner, P. (1954). Positive reinforcement produced by electrical stimulation of septal area and other regions in the rat brain. *Journal of Comparative and Physiological Psychology, 47,* 419–427.

Olds, M. E., & Fobes, J. L. (1981). The central basis of motivation: Intracranial self-stimulation studies. *Annual Review of Psychology, 32,* 523–574.

Oliveras, J. L., Kedjemi, F., Guilbaud, G., & Besson, J. M. (1975). Analgesia induced by electrical stimulation of the inferior centralis nucleus of the raphe in the cat. *Pain, 1,* 139–145.

Olson, B. C. (1985). *The effects of informational and controlling feedback on intrinsic motivation in competition.* Unpublished doctoral dissertation, Texas Christian University, Fort Worth, TX.

O'Malley, M. N., & Becker, L. A. (1984). Removing the egocentric bias: The relevance of distress cues to evaluation of fairness. *Personality and Social Psychology Bulletin, 10,* 235–242.

Orbach, I., & Hadas, Z. (1982). The elimination of learned helplessness deficits as a function of induced self-esteem. *Journal of Research in Personality, 16,* 511–523.

Orbell, S., Hodgkins, S., & Sheeran, P. (1997). Implementation intentions and the theory of planned behavior. *Personality and Social Psychology Bulletin, 23,* 945–954.

Orbell, S., & Sheeran, P. (1998). "Inclined abstainers": A problem for predicting health-related behavior. *British Journal of Social Psychology, 37,* 151–165.

Orbell, S., & Sheeran, P. (In press). Motivation and volitional processes in action initiation: A field study of the role of implementation intentions. *Journal of Applied Social Psychology.*

Orlick, T. D., & Mosher, R. (1978). Extrinsic rewards and participant motivation in a sport related task. *International Journal of Sport Psychology, 9,* 27–39.

Ortony, A., & Clore, G. L. (1989). Emotion, mood, and conscious awareness. *Cognition and Emotion, 3,* 125–137.

Ortony, A., Clore, G. L., & Collins, A. (1988). *The cognitive structure of emotions.* Cambridge: Cambridge University Press.

Ortony, A., & Turner, T. J. (1990). What's basic about basic emotions? *Psychological Review, 97,* 315–331.

Osgood, C. E., May, W. H., & Miron, M. S. (1975). *Cross-cultural universals of affective meaning.* Urbana: University of Illinois Press.

Osgood, C. E., Suci, G. C., & Tannenbaum, P. H. (1957). *The measurement of meaning.* Urbana: University of Illinois Press.

Oyserman, D., & Markus, H. (1990). Possible selves and delinquency. *Journal of Personality and Social Psychology, 59,* 112–125.

Ozer, E. M., & Bandura, A. (1990). Mechanisms governing empowerment effects: A self-efficacy analysis. *Journal of Personality and Social Psychology, 58,* 472–486.

Pace, G. M., Ivancis, M. T., Edwards, G. L., Iwata, B. A., & Page, T. J. (1985). Assessment of stimulus preference and reinforcer value with profoundly retarded individuals. *Journal of Applied Behavior Analysis, 18,* 249–255.

Pallak, S. R., Costomiris, S., Sroka, S., & Pittman, T. S. (1982). School experience, reward characteristics, and intrinsic motivation. *Child Development, 53,* 1382–1391.

Panksepp, J. (1982). Toward a general psychobiological theory of emotions. *Behavioral and Brain Science, 5,* 407–467.

Panksepp, J. (1986). The anatomy of emotions. In R. Plutchik & H. Kellerman (Eds.), *Emotion: Theory, research, and experience: Biological foundations of emotions* (Vol. 5, pp. 91–124). New York: Academic Press.

Panksepp, J. (1994). The basics of basic emotion. In P. Ekman & R. J. Davidson (Eds.), *The nature of emotion: Fundamental questions* (pp. 20–24). New York: Oxford University Press.

Parkes, A. S., & Bruce, H. M. (1961). Olfactory stimuli in mammalian reproduction. *Science, 134,* 1049–1054.

Parkes, M. C., Benjamin, B., & Fitzgerald, R. G. (1969). Broken heart: A statistical study of increased mortality among widowers. *British Journal of Medicine, 1,* 740–743.

Parkinson, B. (1991). Emotional stylists: Strategies of expressive management among trainee hairdressers. *Social Psychology Quarterly, 5,* 419–434.

Parsons, J. E., & Ruble, D. N. (1977). The development of achievement-related expectancies. *Child Development, 48,* 1975–1979.

Patrick, B. C., Skinner, E. A., & Connell, J. P. (1993). What motivates children's behavior and emotion? Joint effects of perceived control and autonomy in the academic domain. *Journal of Personality and Social Psychology, 65,* 781–791.

Patterson, C. J., & Mischel, W. (1976). Effects of temptation-inhibiting and task-facilitating plans on self-control. *Journal of Personality and Social Psychology, 33,* 209–217.

Paul, J. P. (1993). Childhood cross-gender behavior and adult homosexuality: The resurgence of biological models of sexuality. *Journal of Homosexuality, 24,* 41–54.

Pederson, N. C., Plomin, R., McClearn, G. E., & Friberg, L. (1988). Neuroticism, extraversion, and related traits in adult twins reared apart and reared together. *Journal of Personality and Social Psychology, 55,* 950–957.

Pennebaker, J. W. (1990). *Opening up.* New York: Morrow.

Perls, F. S. (1969). *Gestalt therapy verbatim.* Lafayette, CA: Real People Press.

Person, J. B., & Rao, P. A. (1985). Longitudinal study of cognitions, life events, and depression in psychiatric in-patients. *Journal of Abnormal Psychology, 94,* 51–63.

Peters, R. S. (1958). *The concept of motivation.* London: Routledge and Kegan Paul.

Peterson, C. (2000). The future of optimism. *American Psychologist, 55,* 44–55.

Peterson, C., & Barrett, L. C. (1987). Explanatory style and academic performance among university freshmen. *Journal of Personality and Social Psychology, 53,* 603–607.

Peterson, C., Maier, S. F., & Seligman, M. E. P. (1993). *Learned helplessness: A theory for the age of personal control.* New York: Oxford University Press.

Peterson, C., & Seligman, M. E. P. (1984). Causal explanations as a risk factor for depression: Theory and evidence. *Psychological Review, 91,* 347–374.

Peterson, C., Seligman, M. E. P., & Vaillant, G. E. (1988). Pessimistic explanatory style is a risk factor for physical illness: A thirty-five year longitudinal study. *Journal of Personality and Social Psychology, 55,* 23–27.

Peterson, C., Semmel, A., von Baeyer, C., Abramson, L. Y., Metalsky, G. I., & Seligman, M. E. P. (1982). The Attributional Style Questionnaire. *Cognitive Therapy and Research, 6,* 287–299.

Peterson, C., & Villanova, P. (1988). An expanded Attributional Style Questionnaire. *Journal of Abnormal Psychology, 97,* 87–89.

Pfaffman, C. (1960). The pleasures of sensation. *Psychological Review, 67,* 253–268.

Pfaffmann, C. (1961). The sensory and motivating properties of the sense of taste. In M. R. Jones (Ed.), *Nebraska symposium on motivation* (Vol. 9, pp. 71–108). Lincoln: University of Nebraska Press.

Pfaffmann, C. (1982). Taste: A model of incentive motivation. In D. W. Pfaff (Ed.), *The physiological mechanisms of motivation* (pp. 61–97). New York: Springer-Verlag.

Pham, L. B., & Taylor, S. E. (1999). From thought to action: Effects of process- versus outcome-based mental simulations on performance. *Personality and Social Psychology Bulletin, 25,* 250–260.

Philips, D. A., & Zimmerman, M. (1990). The developmental course of perceived competence and incompetence among competent children. In R. J. Sternberg & J. Kolligian (Eds.), *Competence considered.* New Haven, CT: Yale University Press.

Phillips, D. (1984). The illusion of incompetence among academically competent children. *Child Development, 55,* 2000–2016.

Pierce, G. R., Sarason, B. R., & Sarason, I. G. (1991). General and specific support expectations and stress as predictors of perceived supportiveness: An experimental study. *Journal of Personality and Social Psychology, 63,* 297–307.

Pierce, K. L., & Schreibman, L. (1994). Teaching daily living skills to children with autism in unsupervised settings through pictorial self-management. *Journal of Applied Behavior Analysis, 27,* 471–481.

Pittman, T. S., Boggiano, A. K., & Ruble, D. N. (1983). Intrinsic and extrinsic motivational orientations: Limiting conditions on the undermining and enhancing effects of reward on intrinsic motivation. In J. Levine & M. Wang (Eds.), *Teacher and student perceptions: Implications for learning* (pp. 319–340). Hillsdale, NJ: Erlbaum.

Pittman, T. S., Davey, M. E., Alafat, K. A., Wetherill, K. V., & Kramer, N. A. (1980). Informational versus controlling verbal rewards. *Personality and Social Psychology Bulletin, 6,* 228–233.

Pittman, T. S., Emery, J., & Boggiano, A. K. (1982). Intrinsic and extrinsic motivational orientations: Reward induced changes in preference for complexity. *Journal of Personality and Social Psychology, 42,* 789–797.

Pittman, T. S., & Heller, J. F. (1988). Social motivation. *Annual Review of Psychology, 38,* 461–489.

Plutchik, R. (1970). Emotions, evolution, and adaptive processes. In M. B. Arnold (Ed.), *Feelings and emotions* (pp. 3–24). New York: Academic Press.

Plutchik, R. (1980). *Emotion: A psychoevolutionary analysis.* New York: Harper & Row.

Plutchik, R. (1985). On emotion: The chicken-and-egg problem revisited. *Motivation and Emotion, 9,* 197–200.

Polivy, J. (1976). Perception of calories and regulation of intake in restrained and unrestrained subjects. *Addictive Behaviors, 1,* 237–243.

Polivy, J., & Herman, C. P. (1976a). Clinical depression and weight change: A complex relation. *Journal of Abnormal Psychology, 85,* 338–340.

Polivy, J., & Herman, C. P. (1976b). Effect of alcohol on eating behavior: Influences of mood and perceived intoxication. *Journal of Abnormal Psychology, 85,* 601–606.

Polivy, J., & Herman, C. P. (1983). *Breaking the diet habit.* New York: Basic Books.

Polivy, J., & Herman, C. P. (1985). Dieting and binging. *American Psychologist, 40,* 193–201.

Pollak, L. H., & Thoits, P. A. (1989). Processes in emotional socialization. *Social Psychology Quarterly, 52,* 22–34.

Pope, L. T., & Smith, C. A. (1994). On the distinct meanings of smiles and frowns. *Cognition and Emotion, 8,* 65–72.

Powley, T. L., & Keesey, R. E. (1970). Relationship of body weight to the lateral hypothalamus feeding syndrome. *Journal of Comparative and Clinical Psychology, 70,* 25–36.

Premack, D. (1959). Toward empirical behavior laws: I. Positive reinforcement. *Psychological Review, 66,* 219–233.

Price, D. D. (1988). Classical and current theories of pain mechanisms. In D. D. Price (Ed.), *Psychological and neural mechanisms of pain* (pp. 212–231). New York: Raven Press.

Price, R. A. (1987). Genetics of human obesity. *Annals of Behavioral Medicine, 9,* 9–14.

Pritchard, R. D., Campbell, K. M., & Campbell, D. J. (1977). Effects of extrinsic financial rewards on intrinsic motivation. *Journal of Applied Psychology, 62,* 9–15.

Pyszczynski, T., & Greenberg, J. (1981). Role of disconfirmed expectations in the instigation of attributional processing. *Journal of Personality and Social Psychology, 40,* 31–38.

Quattrone, C. A. (1982). Overattribution and unit information: When behavior engulfs the person. *Journal of Personality and Social Psychology, 42,* 593–607.

Quattrone, C. A. (1985). On the congruity between internal states and action. *Psychological Bulletin, 98,* 3–40.

Rachman, S. (1978). *Fear and courage.* San Francisco: Freeman.

Rachman, S., & Hodgson, R. I. (1974). Synchrony and desynchrony in fear and avoidance. *Behaviour Research and Therapy, 12,* 311–318.

Ramirez, E., Maldonado, A., & Markus, R. (1992). Attributions modulate immunization against learned helplessness in humans. *Journal of Personality and Social Psychology, 62,* 139–146.

Rand, A. (1964). The objectivist ethics. In *The virtue of selfishness.* New York: Signet.

Rapaport, D. (1960). On the psychoanalytic theory of motivation. *Nebraska symposium on motivation* (Vol. 8, pp. 173–247). Lincoln: University of Nebraska Press.

Raskin, D. C. (1973). Attention and arousal. In W. F. Prokasy & D. C. Raskin (Eds.), *Electrodermal activity in psychological research.* New York: Academic Press.

Ravlin, S. B. (1987). A computer model of affective reactions to goal-relevant events. Unpublished master's thesis, University of Illinois, Urbana-Champaign. As cited in A. Ortony, G. L. Clore, & A. Collins (Eds.), *The cognitive structure of emotions.* Cambridge: Cambridge University Press.

Raynor, J. O. (1969). Future orientation and motivation of immediate activity: An elaboration of the theory of achievement motivation. *Psychological Review, 76,* 606–610.

Raynor, J. O. (1970). Relationship between achievement-related motives, future orientation, and academic performance. *Journal of Personality and Social Psychology, 15,* 28–33.

Raynor, J. O. (1974). Future orientation in the study of achievement motivation. In J. W. Atkinson & J. O. Raynor (Eds.), *Motivation and achievement.* Washington, DC: V. H. Winston.

Raynor, J. O., & Entin, E. E. (1982). *Motivation, career striving, and aging.* New York: Hemisphere.

Reber, A. (1992). The cognitive unconscious: An evolutionary perspective. *Consciousness and Cognition, 1,* 93–133.

Redmore, C. (1983). Ego development in the college years: Two longitudinal studies. *Journal of Youth and Adolescence, 12,* 301–306.

Redmore, C., & Loevinger, J. (1979). Ego development in adolescence: Longitudinal studies. *Journal of Youth and Adolescence, 8,* 1–20.

Reeve, J. (1989). The interest-enjoyment distinction in intrinsic motivation. *Motivation and Emotion, 13,* 83–103.

Reeve, J. (1993). The face of interest. *Motivation and Emotion, 17,* 353–375.

Reeve, J. (1996). *Motivating others: Nurturing inner motivational resources.* Needham Heights, MA: Allyn and Bacon.

Reeve, J., & Deci, E. L. (1996). Elements of the competitive situation that affect intrinsic motivation. *Personality and Social Psychology Bulletin, 22,* 24–33.

Reeve, J., Olson, B. C., & Cole, S. G. (1985). Motivation and performance: Two consequences of winning and losing in competition. *Motivation and Emotion, 9,* 291–298.

Reifman, A. S., Larrick, R. P., & Fein, S. (1991). Temper and temperature on the diamond: The heat-aggression relationship in major league baseball. *Personality and Social Psychology Bulletin, 17,* 580–585.

Reis, I. L. (1986). A sociological journey into sexuality. *Journal of Marriage and the Family, 48,* 233–242.

Reisenzein, R., & Hofman, T. (1993). Discriminating emotions from appraisal-relevant situational information: Baseline data for structural models of cognitive appraisals. *Cognition and Emotion, 7,* 271–293.

Renninger, K. A., Hidi, S., & Krapp, A. (Eds.). (1992). *The role of interest in learning and development.* Hillsdale, NJ: Lawrence Erlbaum.

Renninger, K. A., & Wozniak, R. H. (1985). Effect of interest on attentional shift, recognition, and recall in young children. *Developmental Psychology, 21,* 624–632.

Revelle, W., Amaral, P., & Turriff, S. (1976). Introversion/extraversion, time stress, and caffeine: Effect on verbal performance. *Science, 192,* 149–150.

Reynolds, P. C. (1982). Affect and instrumentality: An alternative view on Eibl-Eibesfeldt's human ethology. *Behavioral and Brain Science, 5,* 267–268.

Rheingold, H., & Eckerman, C. (1970). The infant separates himself from his mother. *Science, 168,* 78–83.

Riess, M., & Taylor, J. (1984). Ego-involvement and attributions for success and failure in a field setting. *Personality and Social Psychology Bulletin, 10,* 536–543.

Rigby, C. S., Deci, E. L., Patrick, B. P., & Ryan, R. M. (1992). Beyond the intrinsic-extrinsic dichotomy: Self-determination in motivation and learning. *Motivation and Emotion, 16,* 165–185.

Rimé, B., Mesquita, B., Philippot, P., & Boca, S. (1991). Beyond the emotional event: Six studies on the social sharing of emotion. *Cognition and Emotion, 5,* 435–465.

Rinn, W. E. (1984). The neuropsychology of facial expression: A review of the neurological and psychological mechanisms for producing facial expressions. *Psychological Bulletin, 95,* 52–67.

Riordan, C. A., Thomas, J. S., & James, M. K. (1985). Attributions in a one-on-one sports competition: Evidence for self-serving biases and gender differences. *Journal of Sport Behavior, 8,* 42–53.

Riskind, J. H., & Gotay, C. C. (1982). Physical posture: Could it have regulatory or feedback effects on motivation? *Motivation and Emotion, 6,* 273–298.

Ritcher, C. P. (1957). On the phenomenon of sudden death in animals and man. *Psychosomatic Medicine, 19,* 191–198.

Ritvo, L. B. (1990). *Darwin's influence on Freud: A tale of two sciences.* New Haven, CT: Yale University Press.

Rizley, R. (1978). Depression and distortion in the attribution of causality. *Journal of Abnormal Psychology, 87,* 32–48.

Roberts, G. C. (Ed.). (1992). *Motivation in sport and exercise.* Champaign, IL: Human Kinetics Books.

Robertson, L. S., Kelley, A. B., O'Neil, B., Wixom, C. W., Eiswirth, R. S., & Haddon, W. (1974). A controlled study of the effect of television messages on safety belt use. *American Journal of Public Health, 64,* 1071–1080.

Robins, C. J. (1988). Attribution and depression: Why is the literature so inconsistent? *Journal of Personality and Social Psychology, 54,* 880–889.

Robinson, D. T., & Smith-Lovin, L. (1992). Selective interaction as a strategy for identity maintenance: An affect control model. *Social Psychology Quarterly, 55,* 12–28.

Robinson, D. T., Smith-Lovin, L., & Tsoudis, O. (1994). Heinous crime or unfortunate accident? The effects of remorse on responses to mock criminal confessions. *Social Forces, 73,* 175–190.

Rodin, J. (1981). Current status of the external-internal hypothesis for obesity. *American Psychologist, 36,* 361–372.

Rodin, J. (1982). Obesity: Why the losing battle? In B. B. Wolman (Ed.), *Psychological aspects of obesity: A handbook* (pp. 30–87). New York: Van Nostrand Reinhold.

Rodin, J., & Langer, E. J. (1977). Long-term effects of a control-relevant intervention with the institutionalized aged. *Journal of Personality and Social Psychology, 35,* 897–902.

Roediger, H. L. (1990). Implicit memory: Retention without remembering. *American Psychologist, 45,* 1043–1056.

Rofeí, Y. (1984). Stress and affiliation: A utility theory. *Psychological Review, 91,* 251–268.

Rogers, C. R. (1951). *Client-centered therapy: Its current practice, implications, and theory.* Boston: Houghton Mifflin.

Rogers, C. R. (1959). A theory of therapy, personality, and interpersonal relationships, as developed in the client-centered framework. In S. Koch (Ed.), *Psychology: A study of a science* (Vol. 3, pp. 184–256). New York: McGraw-Hill.

Rogers, C. R. (1961). *On becoming a person.* Boston: Houghton Mifflin.

Rogers, C. R. (1963). Actualizing tendency in relation to motives and to consciousness. *Nebraska symposium on motivation* (Vol. 11, pp. 1–24). Lincoln: University of Nebraska Press.

Rogers, C. R. (1966). *A therapist's view of personal goals* [A Pendle Hill pamphlet, #108]. Wallingford, PA: Pendle Hill.

Rogers, C. R. (1969). *Freedom to learn: A view of what education might become.* Columbus, OH: Merrill.

Rogers, C. R. (1973). My philosophy of interpersonal relationships and how it grew. *Journal of Humanistic Psychology, 13,* 3–15.

Rogers, C. R. (1980). *A way of being.* Boston: Houghton Mifflin.

Rogers, C. R. (1982). Notes on Rollo May. *Journal of Humanistic Psychology, 22,* 8–9.

Rogers, C. R. (1995). What understanding and acceptance mean to me. *Journal of Humanistic Psychology, 35,* 7–22.

Rolls, B. J. (1979). How variety and palatability can stimulate appetite. *Nutrition Bulletin, 5,* 78–86.

Rolls, B. J., Rowe, E. T., & Rolls, E. T. (1982). How sensory properties of food affect human feeding behavior. *Physiology and Behavior, 29,* 409–417.

Rolls, B. J., Wood, R. J., & Rolls, E. T. (1980). Thirst: The initiation, maintenance, and termination of drinking. In J. M. Sprague & A. N. Epstein (Eds.), *Progresses in psychobiology and physiological psychology* (Vol. 9, pp. 263–321). New York: Academic Press.

Roney, C., Higgins, E. T., & Shah, J. (1995). Goals and framing: How outcome focus influences motivation and emotion. *Personality and Social Psychology Bulletin, 21,* 1151–1160.

Ronis, D., & Greenwald, A. (1979). Dissonance theory revised again: Comment on the paper by Fazio, Zanna, and Cooper. *Journal of Experimental Social Psychology, 15,* 62–69.

Rose, S., Frieze, I. H. (1989). Young singles scripts for a first date. *Gender and Society, 3,* 258–268.

Roseman, I. J. (1984). Cognitive determinants of emotion: A structural theory. In P. Shaver (Ed.), *Review of personality and social psychology: Emotions, relationships, and health* (Vol. 5, pp. 11–36). Beverly Hills, CA: Sage.

Roseman, I. J. (1991). Appraisal determinants of discrete emotions. *Cognition and Emotion, 5,* 161–200.

Roseman, I. J., Antoniou, A. A., & Jose, P. E. (1996). Appraisal determinants of emotions: Constructing a more accurate and comprehensive theory. *Cognition and Emotion, 10,* 241–277.

Rosen, B., & D'Andrade, R. C. (1959). The psychological origins of achievement motivation. *Sociometry, 22,* 185–218.

Rosenberg, E. L., & Ekman, P. (1994). Coherence between expressive and experiential systems in emotion. *Cognition and Emotion, 8,* 201–229.

Rosenberg, M. (1965). *Society and the adolescent self-image.* Princeton, NJ: Princeton University Press.

Rosenfeld, P., Giacalone, R. A., & Tedeschi, J. T. (1984). Cognitive dissonance and impression management explanations for effort justification. *Personality and Social Psychology Bulletin, 10,* 394–401.

Rosenhan, D. L., & Seligman, M. E. P. (1984). *Abnormal psychology.* New York: W. W. Norton.

Rosenholtz, S. J., & Rosenholtz, S. H. (1981). Classroom organization and the perception of ability. *Sociology of Education, 54,* 132–140.

Ross, L. (1977). The intuitive psychologist and his shortcomings: Distortions in the attribution process. In L. Berkowitz (Ed.), *Advances in experimental and social psychology* (Vol. 10, pp. 173–220). New York: Academic Press.

Ross, M., & Shulman, R. (1973). Increasing the salience of initial attitudes: Dissonance versus self-perception theory. *Journal of Personality and Social Psychology, 28,* 138–144.

Rothkopf, E. Z., & Billington, M. J. (1979). Goal-guided learning from text: Inferring a descriptive processing model from inspection times and eye movements. *Journal of Educational Psychology, 71,* 310–327.

Rotter, J. B. (1966). Generalized expectancies for internal and external control of reinforcement. *Psychological Monographs,* Whole No. 80.

Rowan, J. (1987). Nine humanistic heresies. *Journal of Humanistic Psychology, 27,* 141–157.

Rozin, P. (1999). The process of moralization. *Psychological Science, 10,* 218–221.

Rozin, P., & Fallon, A. E. (1987). A perspective on disgust. *Psychological Review, 94,* 23–41.

Rozin, P., Haidt, J., & McCauley, C. R. (1993). Disgust. In M. Lewis & J. Haviland (Eds.), *Handbook of emotions* (pp. 575–594). New York: Guilford Press.

Rozin, P., Haidt, J., McCauley, C. R., Dunlop, L., & Ashmore, M. (1999). Individual differences in disgust sensitivity: Comparisons and evaluations of paper-and-pencil versus behavioral measures. *Journal of Research in Personality, 33,* 330–351.

Rozin, P., Lowery, L., & Ebert, R. (1994). Varieties of disgust faces and the structure of disgust. *Journal of Personality and Social Psychology, 66,* 870–881.

Rozin, P., Markwith, M., & Stoess, C. (1997). Moralization and becoming a vegetarian: The transformation of preferences into values and the recruitment of disgust. *Psychological Science, 8,* 67–73.

Rozin, P., & Singh, L. (in press). The moralization of cigarette smoking in America. *Journal of Consumer Behavior.*

Ruble, D. N., Crosovsky, E. H., Frey, K. S., & Cohen, R. (1992). Developmental changes in competence assessment. In A. Boggiano & T. S. Pittman (Eds.), *Motivation and achievement: A social-developmental perspective* (pp. 138–166). New York: Cambridge University Press.

Ruble, D. N., Parsons, J., & Ross, J. (1976). Self-evaluative responses of children in an achievement setting. *Child Development, 47,* 990–997.

Ruckmick, C. A. (1936). *The psychology of feeling and emotion.* New York: McGraw-Hill.

Rudd, J. R., & Geller, E. S. (1985). A university-based incentive program to increase safety belt use: Towards cost-effective institutionalization. *Journal of Applied Behavior Analysis, 18,* 215–226.

Ruderman, A. J., & Wilson, G. T. (1979). Weight, restraint, cognitions, and counter-regulation. *Behaviour Therapy and Research, 17,* 581–590.

Rummel, A., & Feinberg, R. (1988). Cognitive evaluation theory: A meta-analytic review of the literature. *Social Behavior and Personality, 16,* 147–164.

Russek, M. (1971). Hepatic receptors and the neurophysiological mechanisms controlling feeding behavior. In S. Ehrenpreis (Ed.), *Neuroscience research.* New York: Academic Press.

Russell, J. A. (1995). Facial expressions of emotion: What lies beyond minimal universality? *Psychological Bulletin, 118,* 379–391.

Russell, J. A., & Barrett, L. F. (1999). Core affect, prototypical emotional episodes, and other things call emotion: Dissecting the elephant. *Journal of Personality and Social Psychology, 76,* 805–819.

Russell, J. A., & Fehr, B. (1994). Fuzzy concepts in a fuzzy hierarchy: Varieties of anger. *Journal of Personality and Social Psychology, 67,* 186–205.

Russell, J. A., & Fernandez-Dols, J. M. (1997). *The psychology of facial expression.* New York: Cambridge University Press.

Rutledge, L. L., & Hupka, R. B. (1985). The facial feedback hypothesis: Methodological concerns and new supporting evidence. *Motivation and Emotion, 9,* 219–240.

Ryan, E. D., & Kovacic, C. R. (1975). Pain tolerance and athletic participation. In M. Weisenberg (Ed.), *Pain: Clinical and experimental perspectives.* St. Louis: Mosby.

Ryan, E. D., & Lakie, W. L. (1965). Competitive and noncompetitive performance in relation to achievement motive and manifest anxiety. *Journal of Personality and Social Psychology, 1,* 342–345.

Ryan, R. M. (1982). Control and information in the intrapersonal sphere: An extension of cognitive evaluation theory. *Journal of Personality and Social Psychology, 43,* 450–461.

Ryan, R. M. (1991). The nature of the self in autonomy and relatedness. In J. Strauss & G. R. Goethals (Eds.), *The self: Interdisciplinary approaches* (pp. 208–238). New York: Springer-Verlag.

Ryan, R. M. (1993). Agency and organization: Intrinsic motivation, autonomy, and the self in psychological development. In J. E. Jacobs (Ed.), *Nebraska symposium on motivation: Developmental perspectives on motivation* (Vol. 40, pp. 1–56). Lincoln: University of Nebraska Press.

Ryan, R. M. (1995). Psychological needs and the facilitation of integrative processes. *Journal of Personality, 63,* 397–427.

Ryan, R. M., Avery, R. R., & Grolnick, W. S. (1985). A Rorschach assessment of children's mutuality of autonomy. *Journal of Personality Assessment, 49,* 6–12.

Ryan, R. M., & Connell, J. P. (1989). Perceived locus of causality and internalization: Examining reasons for acting in two domains. *Journal of Personality and Social Psychology, 57,* 749–761.

Ryan, R. M., Connell, J. P., & Grolnick, W. S. (1992). When achievement is not intrinsically motivated: A theory of internalization and self-regulation in school. In A. K. Boggiano & T. S. Pittman (Eds.), *Achievement and motivation: A social-development perspective* (pp. 167–188). New York: Cambridge University Press.

Ryan, R. M., & Deci, E. L. (2000). Self-determination theory and the facilitation of intrinsic motivation, social development, and well-being. *American Psychologist, 55,* 68–78.

Ryan, R. M., & Frederick, C. M. (1997). On energy, personality, and health: Subjective vitality as a dynamic reflection of well-being. *Journal of Personality, 65,* 529–565.

Ryan, R. M., Frederick, C. M., Lepes, D., Rubio, N., & Sheldon, K. M. (1997). Intrinsic motivation and exercise adherence. *International Journal of Sport Psychology, 28,* 335–354.

Ryan, R. M., & Grolnick, W. S. (1986). Origins and pawns in the classroom: Self-report and projective assessments of individual differences in children's perceptions. *Journal of Personality and Social Psychology, 50,* 550–558.

Ryan, R. M., Koestner, R., & Deci, E. L. (1991). Ego-involved persistence: When free-choice behavior is not intrinsically motivated. *Motivation and Emotion, 15,* 185–205.

Ryan, R. M., & Lynch, J. (1989). Emotional autonomy versus detachment: Revisiting the vicissitudes of adolescent and young adulthood. *Child Development, 60,* 340–356.

Ryan, R. M., Mims, V., & Koestner, R. (1983). Relation of reward contingency and interpersonal context to intrinsic motivation: A review and test using cognitive evaluation theory. *Journal of Personality and Social Psychology, 45,* 736–750.

Ryan, R. M., Plant, R. W., & O'Malley, S. (1995). Initial motivations for alcohol treatment: Relations with patient characteristics, treatment involvement and dropout. *Addictive Behaviors, 20,* 586–596.

Ryan, R. M., & Powelson, C. L. (1991). Autonomy and relatedness as fundamental to motivation and education. *Journal of Experimental Education, 60,* 49–66.

Ryan, R. M., Rigby, S., & King, K. (1993). Two types of religious internalization and their relations to religious orientations and mental health. *Journal of Personality and Social Psychology, 65,* 586–596.

Ryan, R. M., Stiller, J., & Lynch, J. H. (1994). Representations of relationships to teachers, parents, and friends as predictors of academic motivation and self-esteem. *Journal of Early Adolescence, 14,* 226–249.

Ryff, C. D. (1989). Happiness is everything, or is it? Explorations on the meaning of psychological well-being. *Journal of Personality and Social Psychology, 57,* 1069–1081.

Ryff, C. D. (1995). Psychological well-being in adult life. *Current Directions in Psychological Science, 4,* 99–104.

Ryff, C. D., & Keyes, C. L. M. (1995). The structure of psychological well-being revisited. *Journal of Personality and Social Psychology, 69,* 719–727.

Saarni, C. (1979). Children's understanding of display rules for expressive behavior. *Developmental Psychology, 15,* 424–429.

Saarni, C. (1997). Coping with aversive feelings. *Motivation and Emotion, 21,* 45–63.

Sabini, J., & Silver, M. (1987). Emotions, responsibility, and character. In F. Schoeman (Ed.), *Responsibility, character, and the emotions: New essays in moral psychology* (pp. 165–175). Cambridge: Cambridge University Press.

Sackeim, H. A. (1983). Self-deception, self-esteem, and depression: The adaptive value of lying to oneself. In J. Masling (Ed.), *Empirical studies of psychoanalytic theories* (Vol. 1, pp. 101–157). Hillsdale, NJ: Analytic Press.

Sackeim, H. A., Gur, R. C., & Saucy, M. C. (1978). Emotions are expressed more intensely on the left side of the face. *Science, 202,* 434–435.

Sacks, C. H., & Bugental, D. B. (1987). Attributions as moderators of affective and behavioral responses to social failure. *Journal of Personality and Social Psychology, 53,* 939–947.

Sakurai, T., Amemiya, A., Ishii, M., Matsuzaki, I., Chemelli, R. M., Tanaka, H., Williams, S. C., Richardson, J. A., Kozlowski, G. P., Wilson, S., Arch, J. R. S., Buckingham, R. E., Haynes, A. C., Carr, S. A., Annan, R. S., McNulty, D. E., Liu, W. S., Terrett, J. A., Elshourbagy, N. A., Bergsma, D. J., & Yanagisawa, M. (1998). Orexins and orexin receptors: A family of hypothalamic neuropeptides and G protein-coupled receptors that regulate feeding behavior. *Cell, 92,* 573–585.

Salomon, G. (1984). Television is easy and print is tough: The differential investment of mental effort in learning as a function of perceptions and attributions. *Journal of Educational Psychology, 76,* 647–658.

Salovey, P., Rothman, A. J., Detweiler, J. B., & Steward, W. T. (2000). Emotional states and physical health. *American Psychologist, 55,* 110–121.

Sansone, C. (1989). Competence feedback, task feedback, and intrinsic interest: The importance of context. *Journal of Experimental Social Psychology, 25,* 343–361.

Sanz, J. (1996). Memory biases in social anxiety and depression. *Cognition and Emotion, 10,* 87–105.

Sarason, B. R., Pierce, G. R., Shearin, E. N., Sarason, I. G., Waltz, J. A., & Poppe, L. (1991). Perceived social support and working models of self and actual others. *Journal of Personality and Social Psychology, 60,* 273–287.

Sarason, I. G. (1977). The test anxiety scale: Concept and research. In C. D. Spielberger & I. G. Sarason (Eds.), *Stress and anxiety* (Vol. 5, pp. 193–216). Washington, DC: Hemisphere.

Schaal, B., & Gollwitzer, P. M. (1999). *Implementation intentions and resistance to temptation.* Unpublished manuscript, New York University.

Schacter, D. L. (1992). Understanding implicit memory: A cognitive neuroscience approach. *American Psychologist, 47,* 559–569.

Schachter, S. (1959). *The psychology of affiliation.* Stanford, CA: Stanford University Press.

Schachter, S. (1964). The interaction of cognitive and physiological determinants of emotion. In L. Berkowitz (Ed.), *Advances in experimental social psychology* (Vol. 1, pp. 49–80). New York: Academic Press.

Schachter, S., & Singer, J. E. (1962). Cognitive, social, and physiological determinants of emotional states. *Psychological Review, 69,* 379–399.

Scharff, J. S., & Scharff, D. E. (1995). *The primer of object relations therapy.* Northvale, NJ: Jason Aronson.

Scheier, M. A., & Kraut, R. E. (1979). Increasing educational achievement via self-concept change. *Review of Educational Research, 49,* 131–150.

Scheier, M. F., & Carver, C. S. (1985). Optimism, coping, and health: Assessment and implications of generalized outcome expectations. *Health Psychology, 4,* 219–247.

Scheier, M. F., & Carver, C. S. (1988). A model of behavioral self-regulation: Translating intention into action. In L. Berkowitz (Ed.), *Advances in experimental social psychology* (Vol. 21, pp. 303–346). New York: Academic Press.

Scherer, K. R. (1984a). Emotion as a multicomponent process: A model and some cross-cultural data. In P. Shaver (Ed.), *Review of personality and social psychology* (Vol. 5, pp. 37–63). Beverly Hills, CA: Sage.

Scherer, K. R. (1984b). On the nature and function of emotion: A component process approach. In K. Scherer & P. Ekman (Eds.), *Approaches to emotion* (pp. 293–318). Hillsdale, NJ: Erlbaum.

Scherer, K. R. (1986). Vocal affect expression: A review and a model for future research. *Psychological Bulletin, 99,* 143–165.

Scherer, K. R. (1993). Studying the emotion-antecedent appraisal process: An expert systems approach. *Cognition and Emotion, 7,* 325–355.

Scherer, K. R. (1994a). An emotion's occurrence depends on the relevance of an event to the organism's goal/need hierarchy. In P. Ekman & R. J. Davidson (Eds.), *The nature of emotion: Fundamental questions* (pp. 227–231). New York: Oxford University Press.

Scherer, K. R. (1994b). Toward a concept of modal emotions. In P. Ekman & R. J. Davidson (Eds.), *The nature of emotion: Fundamental questions* (pp. 25–31). New York: Oxford University Press.

Scherer, K. R. (1997). Profiles of emotion-antecedent appraisal: Testing theoretical predictions across cultures. *Cognition and Emotion, 11,* 113–150.

Scherer, K. R., & Ekman, P. (1984). *Approaches to emotion.* Hillsdale, NJ: Lawrence Erlbaum.

Scherer, K. R., & Tannenbaum, P. H. (1986). Emotional experience in everyday life. *Motivation and Emotion, 10,* 295–314.

Scherhorn, G., & Grunert, S. C. (1988). Using the causality orientations concept in consumer behavior research. *Journal of Consumer Psychology, 13,* 33–39.

Schiefele, U. (1991). Interest, learning, and motivation. *Educational Psychologist, 26,* 299–323.

Schierman, M. J., & Rowland, G. L. (1985). Sensation seeking and selection of entertainment. *Personality and Individual Differences, 6,* 599–603.

Schmale, A., & Iker, H. (1966). The psychological setting of uterine cervical cancer. *Annals of the New York Academy of Sciences, 125,* 807–813.

Schmalt, H. D. (1982). Two concepts of fear of failure motivation. *Advances in Test Anxiety Research, 1,* 45–52.

Schmalt, H. D. (1999). Assessing the achievement motive using the grid technique. *Journal of Research in Personality, 33,* 109–130.

Schmitt, M. (1973). Influences of hepatic portal receptors on hypothalamic feeding and satiety centers. *American Journal of Physiology, 225,* 1089–1095.

Schmitz, B., & Skinner, E. A. (1993). Perceived control, effort, and academic performance: Interindividual, intraindividual, and multivariate time-series analyses. *Journal of Personality and Social Psychology, 64,* 1010–1028.

Schooler, C., Zahn, T. P., Murphy, D. L., & Buchsbaum, M. S. (1978). Psychological correlates of monoamine oxidase in normals. *Journal of Nervous and Mental Disease, 166,* 177–186.

Schultz, D. P. (1987). *A history of modern psychology* (4th ed.). San Diego, CA: Harcourt Brace Jovanovich.

Schunk, D. H. (1989a). Self-efficacy and achievement behaviors. *Educational Psychology Review, 1,* 173–208.

Schunk, D. H. (1989b). Self-efficacy and cognitive skill learning. In C. A. Ames & R. Ames (Eds.), *Research on motivation in education: Goals and cognition* (Vol. 3, pp. 13–44). San Diego: Academic Press.

Schunk, D. H. (1991). Self-efficacy and academic motivation. *Educational Psychologist, 26,* 207–231.

Schunk, D. H., & Cox, P. D. (1986). Strategy training and attributional feedback with learning disabled students. *Journal of Educational Psychology, 78,* 201–209.

Schunk, D. H., & Hanson, A. R. (1989). Self-modeling and children's cognitive skill learning. *Journal of Educational Psychology, 83,* 155–163.

Schwab, D. P., Olian-Gottlieb, J. D., & Heneman, H. G., III (1979). Between-subjects expectancy theory research: A statistical review of studies predicting effort and performance. *Psychological Bulletin, 86,* 139–147.

Schwartz, G. E. (1986). Emotion and psychophysiological organization: A systems approach. In M. G. H. Coles, E. Ponchin, & S. W. Proges (Eds.), *Psychophysiology: Systems, processes, and applications* (pp. 354–377). New York: Guilford Press.

Schwartz, G. E., Brown, S. L., & Ahern, G. L. (1980). Facial muscle patterning and subjective experience during affective imagery: Sex differences. *Psychophysiology, 17,* 75–82.

Schwartz, M. W., & Seeley, R. J. (1997). Neuroendocrine responses to starvation and weight loss. *New England Journal of Medicine, 336,* 1802–1811.

Schwartz, N., & Clore, G. L. (1983). Mood, misattribution, and judgments of well-being: Informative and directive functions of affective states. *Journal of Personality and Social Psychology, 45,* 513–523.

Sclafani, A. (1980). Dietary obesity. In A. J. Stunkard (Ed.), *Obesity* (pp. 166–181). Philadelphia: W. B. Saunders.

Sclafini, A., & Springer, D. (1976). Dietary obesity in adult rats: Similarities to hypothalamic and human obesity syndromes. *Physiology and Behavior, 17,* 461–471.

Seligman, M. E. P. (1975). *Helplessness: On depression, development, and death.* San Francisco: W. H. Freeman.

Seligman, M. E. P. (1991). *Learned optimism.* New York: Alfred A. Knopf.

Seligman, M. E. P., Abramson, L. Y., Semmel, A., & von Baeyer, C. (1979). Depressive attributional style. *Journal of Abnormal Psychology, 88,* 242–247.

Seligman, M. E. P., Castellon, C., Cacciola, J., Schulman, P., Luborsky, L., Ollove, M., & Downing, R. (1988). Explanatory style change during cognitive therapy for unipolar depression. *Journal of Abnormal Psychology, 97,* 13–18.

Seligman, M. E. P., & Csikszentmihalyi, M. (2000). Positive psychology: An introduction. *American Psychologist, 55,* 5–14.

Seligman, M. E. P., & Maier, S. F. (1967). Failure to escape traumatic shock. *Journal of Experimental Psychology, 94,* 1–9.

Seligman, M. E. P., & Schulman, P. (1986). Explanatory style as a predictor of productivity and quitting among life insurance agents. *Journal of Personality and Social Psychology, 50,* 832–838.

Sepple, C. P., & Read, N. W. (1989). Gastrointestinal correlates of the development of hunger in man. *Appetite, 13,* 183–191.

Seyle, H. (1956). *The stress of life.* New York: McGraw-Hill.

Seyle, H. (1976). *Stress in health and disease.* Reading, MA: Butterworth.

Shaalvik, E. M., & Hagtvet, K. A. (1990). Academic achievement and self-concept. *Journal of Personality and Social Psychology, 58,* 292–307.

Shaffer, D. (1977). Suicide in childhood and early adolescence. *Journal of Child Psychology and Psychiatry, 45,* 406–451.

Shapira, Z. (1976). Expectancy determinants of intrinsically motivated behavior. *Journal of Personality and Social Psychology, 34,* 1235–1244.

Shapiro, D. H., Potkin, S., Jin, Y., Brown, B., & Carreon, D. (1993). Measuring the psychological construct of control: Discriminant, divergent, and incremental validity of the Shapiro Control Inventory and Rotter's and Wallston's locus of control scales. *International Journal of Psychosomatics, 40,* 35–46.

Shapiro, D. H., Schwartz, C. E., & Astin, J. A. (1996). Controlling ourselves, controlling our world: Psychology's role in understanding positive and negative consequences of seeking and gaining control. *American Psychologist, 51,* 1213–1230.

Shaver, P., & Hazan, C. (1987). Being lonely, falling in love: Perspectives from attachment theory. *Journal of Social Behavior and Personality, 2,* 105–124.

Shaver, P., Schwartz, J., Kirson, D., & O'Connor, C. (1987). Emotion knowledge: Further exploration of a prototype approach. *Journal of Personality and Social Psychology, 52,* 1061–1086.

Sheeran, P., & Orbell, S. (1999). Implementation intentions and repeated behaviors: Augmenting the predictive validity of the theory of planned behavior. *European Journal of Social Psychology, 29,* 349–370.

Sheffield, F. D., & Roby, T. B. (1950). Reward value of a non-nutritive sweet taste. *Journal of Comparative and Physiological Psychology, 43,* 471–481.

Sheldon, K. M., & Kasser, T. (1994). Coherence and congruence: Two aspects of personality integration. *Journal of Personality and Social Psychology, 68,* 531–543.

Sheldon, K. M., Ryan, R. M., & Reis, H. T. (1996). What makes for a good day? Competence and autonomy in the day and in the person. *Personality and Social Psychology Bulletin, 22,* 1270–1279.

Shields, J. (1976). Heredity and environment. In H. J. Eysenck & G. D. Wilson (Eds.), *A textbook of human psychology.* Baltimore: University Park Press.

Shipley, T. E., Jr., & Veroff, J. (1952). A projective measure of need for affiliation. *Journal of Experimental Psychology, 43,* 349–356.

Shirey, L. L., & Reynolds, R. E. (1988). Effect of interest on attention and learning. *Journal of Educational Psychology, 80,* 159–166.

Shoda, Y., Mischel, W., & Peake, P. (1990). Predicting adolescent cognitive and self-regulatory competencies from preschool delay of gratification: Identifying diagnostic conditions. *Developmental Psychology, 26,* 978–986.

Shostrom, E. L. (1964). An inventory for the measurement of self-actualization. *Educational and Psychological Measurement, 24,* 207–218.

Shostrom, E. L. (1974). *Manual for the Personal Orientation Inventory.* San Diego, CA: EDITS.

Sid, A. K. W., & Lindgren, H. C. (1981). Sex differences in achievement and affiliation motivation among undergraduates majoring in different academic fields. *Psychological Reports, 48,* 539–542.

Silverman, L. H. (1976). Psychoanalytic theory: The reports of my death are greatly exaggerated. *American Psychologist, 31,* 621–637.

Silverman, L. H., & Weinberger, J. (1985). Mommy and I are one: Implications for psychotherapy. *American Psychologist, 40,* 1296–1308.

Simon, L., Greenberg, J., & Brehm, J. (1995). Trivialization: The forgotten mode of dissonance reduction. *Journal of Personality and Social Psychology, 68,* 247–260.

Simon, W., & Gagnon, J. H. (1986). Sexual scripts: Permanence and change. *Archives of Sexual Behavior, 15,* 97–120.

Singh, D. (1993a). Adaptive significance of female physical attractiveness: Role of waist-to-hip ratio. *Journal of Personality and Social Psychology, 65,* 293–307.

Singh, D. (1993b). Body shape and women's attractiveness: The critical role of waist-to-hip ratio. *Human Nature, 4,* 297–321.

Singh D. (1995). Female judgment of male attractiveness and desirability for relationships: Role of waist-to-hip ratio and financial status. *Journal of Personality and Social Psychology, 69,* 1089–1101.

Sinha, R., & Parsons, O. A. (1996). Multivariate response patterning of fear and anger. *Cognition and Emotion, 10,* 173–198.

Skinner, B. F. (1938). *The behavior of organisms.* New York: Appleton-Century-Crofts.

Skinner, B. F. (1953). *Science and human behavior.* New York: Macmillan.

Skinner, B. F. (1986). What is wrong with daily life in the Western world? *American Psychologist, 41,* 568–574.

Skinner, E. A. (1985). Action, control judgments, and the structure of control experience. *Psychological Review, 92,* 39–58.

Skinner, E. A. (1986). The origins of young children's perceived control: Caregivers contingent and sensitive behavior. *International Journal of Behavioral Development, 9,* 359–382.

Skinner, E. A. (1991). Development and perceived control: A dynamic model of action in context. In M. Gunnar & L. A. Sroufe (Eds.), *Minnesota Symposium on Child Psychology* (Vol. 23). Hillsdale, NJ: Erlbaum.

Skinner, E. A. (1995). *Perceived control, motivation, and coping.* Newbury Park, CA: Sage.

Skinner, E. A., & Belmont, M. J. (1993). Motivation in the classroom: Reciprocal effects of teacher behavior and student engagement across the school year. *Journal of Educational Psychology, 85,* 571–581.

Skinner, E. A., Chapman, M., & Baltes, P. B. (1988). Control, means-ends, and agency beliefs: A new conceptualization and its measurement during childhood. *Journal of Personality and Social Psychology, 54,* 117–133.

Skinner, E. A., Zimmer-Gembeck, M. J., & Connell, J. P. (1998). Individual differences and the development of perceived control. *Monographs of the Society for Research in Child Development, 63,* Serial number 254.

Sklar, L. S., & Anisman, H. (1979). Stress and coping factors influence tumor growth. *Science, 205,* 513–515.

Slade, L. A., & Rush, M. C. (1991). Achievement motivation and the dynamics of task difficulty choices. *Journal of Personality and Social Psychology, 60,* 165–172.

Smith, A. C., III, & Kleinman, S. (1989). Managing emotions in medical school: Students' contacts with the living and the dead. *Social Psychology Quarterly, 52,* 56–69.

Smith, C. A., & Ellsworth, P. C. (1985). Patterns of cognitive appraisal in emotion. *Journal of Personality and Social Psychology, 48,* 813–838.

Smith, C. A., & Ellsworth, P. C. (1987). Patterns of appraisal and emotion related to taking an exam. *Journal of Personality and Social Psychology, 52,* 475–488.

Smith, C. A., Haynes, K. N., Lazarus, R. S., & Pope, L. K. (1993). In search of the "hot" cognitions: Attributions, appraisals, and their relation to emotion. *Journal of Personality and Social Psychology, 65,* 916–929.

Smith, C. P. (Ed.). (1992). *Motivation and personality: Handbook of thematic content analysis.* New York: Cambridge University Press.

Smith, E. R., & Miller, F. D. (1978). Limits on perception of cognitive processes: A reply to Nisbett and Wilson. *Psychological Review, 85,* 355–362.

Smith, R. A., Wallston, B. S., Wallston, K. A., Forsberg, P. R., & King, J. E. (1984). Measuring desire for control of health care processes. *Journal of Personality and Social Psychology, 47,* 415–426.

Smith, R. G., Iwata, B. A., & Shore, B. A. (1995). Effects of subject- versus experimenter-selected reinforcers on the behavior of individuals with profound developmental disabilities. *Journal of Applied Behavior Analysis, 28,* 61–71.

Smith-Lovin, L. (1990). Emotion as confirmation and disconfirmation of identity: An affect control model. In T. D. Kemper (Ed.), *Research agendas in the sociology of emotions.* New York: SUNY Press.

Smith-Lovin, L. (1991). An affect control view of cognition and emotion. In J. A. Howard & P. L. Callero (Eds.), *The self-society dynamic: Cognition, emotion, and action* (pp. 143–169). New York: Cambridge University Press.

Smith-Lovin, L., & Heise, D. R. (Eds.). (1988). *Analyzing social interaction: Advances in affect control theory.* New York: Gordon & Breach.

Snyder, C. R., Harris, C., Anderson, J. R., Holleran, S. A., Irving, L. M., Sigmon, S. T., Yoshinobu, L.,

Gibb, J., Langelle, C., & Harney, P. (1991). The will and the ways: Development and validation of an individual-differences measure of hope. *Journal of Personality and Social Psychology, 60,* 570–585.

Snyder, M., & Ebbesen, E. B. (1972). Dissonance awareness: A test of dissonance theory versus self-perception theory. *Journal of Experimental Social Psychology, 8,* 502–517.

Sobal, J., & Stunkard, A. J. (1989). Socioeconomic status and obesity: A review of the literature. *Psychological Bulletin, 105,* 260–275.

Solomon, R. L. (1980). The opponent-process theory of motivation: The costs of pleasure and the benefits of pain. *American Psychologist, 35,* 691–712.

Solomon, S., Greenberg, J., & Pyszczynski, T. (1991). A terror management theory of social behavior: The psychological functions of self-esteem and cultural worldviews. In M. P. Zanna (Ed.), *Advances in experimental social psychology* (Vol. 24, pp. 93–159). San Diego: Academic Press.

Sorrentino, R. M., & Higgins, E. T. (1986). Motivation and cognition. In R. M. Sorrentino & E. T. Higgins (Eds.), *Handbook of motivation and cognition: Foundations of social behavior* (pp. 3–19). New York: Guilford Press.

Spangler, W. D., & House, R. J. (1991). Presidential effectiveness and the leadership motive profile. *Journal of Personality and Social Psychology, 60,* 439–455.

Spence, J. T., & Helmreich, R. L. (1983). Achievement-related motives and behavior. In J. T. Spence (Ed.), *Achievement and achievement motives: Psychological and sociological approaches* (pp. 10–74). San Francisco: W. H. Freeman.

Spencer, J. A., & Fremouw, W. J. (1979). Binge eating as a function of restrained and weight classification. *Journal of Abnormal Psychology, 88,* 262–267.

Spielberger, C. D., & Starr, L. M. (1994). Curiosity and exploratory behavior. In H. F. O'Neil Jr., & M. Drillings (Eds.), *Motivation: Theory and research* (pp. 221–243). Hillsdale, NJ: Lawrence Erlbaum.

Spink, K. S. (1978). Win-lose causal attributions of high school basketball players. *Canadian Journal of Applied Sports Sciences, 3,* 195–201.

Spitzer, L., & Rodin, J. (1981). Human eating behavior: A critical review of studies in normal weight and overweight individuals. *Appetite, 2,* 293–329.

Sprecher, S., Sullivan, Q., & Hatfield, E. (1994). Mate selection preferences: Gender differences examined in a national sample. *Journal of Personality and Social Psychology, 66,* 1074–1080.

Squire, S. (1983). *The slender balance.* New York: Pinnacle.

Stacey, C. L., & DeMartino, M. F. (Eds.). (1958). *Understanding human motivation.* Cleveland, OH: Howard Allen.

Stagner, R. (1977). Homeostasis, discrepancy, dissonance: A theory of motives and motivation. *Motivation and Emotion, 1,* 103–138.

Staub, E. (1999). The roots of evil: Social conditions, culture, personality, and basic human needs. *Personality and Social Psychology Review, 3,* 179–192.

Steele, C. M. (1988). The psychology of self-affirmation: Sustaining the integrity of the self. In L. Berkowitz (Ed.), *Advances in experimental social psychology* (Vol. 20, pp. 261–302). New York: Academic Press.

Steele, C. M., & Josephs, R. A. (1990). Alcohol myopia: Its prized and dangerous effects. *American Psychologist, 45,* 921–933.

Steele, R. S. (1977). Power motivation, activation, and inspirational speeches. *Journal of Personality, 45,* 53–64.

Stein, G. L., Kimiecik, J. C., Daniels, J., & Jackson, S. A. (1995). Psychological antecedents of flow in recreational sport. *Personality and Social Psychology Bulletin, 21,* 125–135.

Stein, N. L., & Trabasso, T. (1992). The organisation of emotional experience: Creating links among emotion, thinking, language and intentional action. *Cognition and Emotion, 6,* 225–244.

Stellar, J. R., & Stellar, E. (1985). *The neurobiology of motivation and reward.* New York: Springer-Verlag.

Stemmler, G. (1989). The autonomic differentiation of emotions revisited: Convergent and discriminant validity. *Psychophysiology, 26,* 617–632.

Stepper, S., & Strack, F. (1993). Proprioceptive determinants of emotional and nonemotional feelings. *Journal of Personality and Social Psychology, 64,* 211–220.

Stern, J. A., Walrath, L. C., & Goldstein, R. (1984). The endogenous eyeblink. *Psychophysiology, 21,* 22–33.

Stern, J. S., & Lowney, P. (1986). Obesity: The role of physical activity. In K. D. Brownell & J. P. Foreyt (Eds.), *Handbook of eating disorders: Physiology, psychology, and treatment of obesity, anorexia, and bulimia* (pp. 145–158). New York: Basic Books.

Stevens, J., Cai, J. W., Pamuk, E. R., Williamson, D. F., Thun, M. J., & Wood, J. L. (1998). The effect of age on the association between body-mass index and mortality. *New England Journal of Medicine, 338,* 1–7.

Stevenson, J. A. F. (1969). Neural control of food and water intake. In W. Haymaker, E. Anderson, & W. J. H. Nauta (Eds.), *The hypothalamus.* Springfield, IL: Thomas.

Stewart, A. J. (1992). Self-definition and social definition: Personal styles reflected in narrative style. In C. P. Smith (Ed.), *Motivation and personality: Handbook of thematic content analysis.* New York: Cambridge University Press.

Stewart, A. J., & Rubin, Z. (1976). Power motivation in the dating couple. *Journal of Personality and Social Psychology, 34,* 305–309.

Stewart, A. J., & Winter, D. G. (1974). Self-definition and social definition in women. *Journal of Personality, 42,* 238–259.

Stipek, D. J. (1980). A causal analysis of the relationship between locus of control and academic achievement in the first grade. *Contemporary Educational Psychology, 5,* 90–99.

Stipek, D. J. (1983). A developmental analysis of pride and shame. *Human Development, 26,* 42–56.

Stipek, D. J. (1984). Young children's performance expectations: Logical analysis or wishful thinking? In J. G. Nicholls (Ed.), *The development of achievement motivation* (pp. 33–56). Greenwich, CT: JAI.

Stipek, D. J., & Gralinski, H. (1996). Children's beliefs about intelligence and school performance. *Journal of Educational Psychology, 88,* 397–407.

Stipek, D. J., & Kowalski, P. S. (1989). Learned helplessness in task-orienting versus performance-orienting testing conditions. *Journal of Educational Psychology, 81,* 384–391.

Stokols, D. (1972). On the distinction between density and crowding: Some implications for future research. *Psychological Review, 79,* 275–277.

Storm, C., & Storm, T. (1987). A taxonomic study of the vocabulary of emotions. *Journal of Personality and Social Psychology, 53,* 805–816.

Storms, M. D. (1973). Videotape and the attribution process: Reversing actors' and observers' points of view. *Journal of Personality and Social Psychology, 27,* 165–175.

Strack, F., Martin, L. L., & Stepper, S. (1988). Inhibiting and facilitating conditions of the human smile: Unobtrusive test of the facial feedback hypothesis. *Journal of Personality and Social Psychology, 54,* 768–777.

Strang, H. R., Lawrence, E. C., & Fowler, P. C. (1978). Effects of assigned goal level and knowledge of results on arithmetic computation: A laboratory study. *Journal of Applied Psychology, 63,* 446–450.

Straub, R. R., & Roberts, D. M. (1983). Effects of nonverbal oriented social awareness training program on social interaction ability of learning disabled children. *Journal of Nonverbal Behavior, 7,* 195–201.

Straub, W. F., & Williams, J. M. (Eds.). (1984). *Cognitive sport psychology.* Lansing, NY: Sport Science Associates.

Strauman, T. (1992). Self-guides, autobiographical memory, and anxiety and dysphoria: Toward a cognitive model of vulnerability to emotional distress. *Journal of Abnormal Psychology, 101,* 87–95.

Strayer, J. (1993). Children's concordant emotions and cognitions in response to observed emotions. *Child Development, 64,* 188–201.

Strube, M. J., Boland, S. M., Manfredo, P. A., & Al-Falaij, A. (1987). Type A behavior pattern and the self-evaluation of abilities: Empirical tests of the self-appraisal model. *Journal of Personality and Social Psychology, 52,* 956–974.

Stunkard, A. J. (1988). Some perspectives on human obesity: Its causes. *Bulletin of New York Academy of Medicine, 64,* 902–923.

Sullivan, H. S. (1953). *The interpersonal theory of psychiatry.* New York: Norton.

Sutherland, S. (1993). Impoverished minds. *Nature, 364,* 767.

Swann, W. B., Jr. (1983). Self-verification: Bringing social reality into harmony with self. In J. Suls & A. Greenwald (Eds.), *Psychological perspectives on the self* (Vol. 2, pp. 33–66). Hillsdale, NJ: Lawrence Erlbaum.

Swann, W. B., Jr. (1985). The self as architect of social reality. In B. Schlenker (Ed.), *The self and social life* (pp. 100–125). New York: McGraw-Hill.

Swann, W. B., Jr. (1987). Identity negotiation: Where two roads meet. *Journal of Personality and Social Psychology, 53,* 1038–1051.

Swann, W. B., Jr. (1990). To be adored or to be known: The interplay of self-enhancement and self-verification. In R. M. Sorrentino & E. T. Higgins (Eds.), *Handbook of motivation and cognition: Foundations of social behavior* (Vol. 2, pp. 408–448). New York: Guilford Press.

Swann, W. B., Jr. (1992a). Why people self-verify. *Journal of Personality and Social Psychology, 62,* 392–401.

Swann, W. B., Jr. (1992b). Seeking truth, finding despair: Some unhappy consequences of a negative self-concept. *Current Directions in Psychological Science, 1,* 15–18.

Swann, W. B., Jr. (1997). The trouble with change: Self-verification and allegiance to the self. *Psychological Science, 8,* 177–180.

Swann, W. B., Jr., & Hill, C. A. (1982). When our identities are mistaken: Reaffirming self-conceptions through social interactions. *Journal of Personality and Social Psychology, 43, 59–66.*

Swann, W. B., Jr., Hixon, J. G., & De La Ronde, C. (1992). Embracing the bitter "truth": Negative self-concepts and marital commitment. *Psychological Science, 3,* 118–121.

Swann, W. B., Jr., Hixon, J. G., Stein-Seroussi, A., & Gilbert, D. T. (1990). The fleeting gleam of praise: Behavioral reactions to self-relevant feedback. *Journal of Personality and Social Psychology, 59,* 17–26.

Swann, W. B., Jr., Pelham, B. W., & Krull, D. S. (1989). Agreeable fancy or disagreeable truth: Reconciling self-enhancement and self-verification. *Journal of Personality and Social Psychology, 57,* 782–791.

Swann, W. B., Jr., & Pittman, T. S. (1977). Initiating play activity in children: The moderating influence of verbal cues on intrinsic motivation. *Child Development, 48,* 1125–1132.

Swann, W. B., Jr., & Predmore, S. C. (1985). Intimates as agents of social support: Sources of consolation or despair? *Journal of Personality and Social Psychology, 49,* 1609–1617.

Swann, W. B., Jr., & Schroeder, D. G. (1995). The search for beauty and truth: A framework for understanding reactions to evaluations. *Personality and Social Psychology Bulletin, 21,* 1307–1318.

Swann, W. B., Jr., Stein-Seroussi, A., & Giesler, B. (1992). Why people self-verify. *Journal of Personality and Social Psychology, 62,* 392–401.

Swann, W. B., Jr., Wenzlaff, R. M., & Tafarodi, R. W. (1992). Depression and the search for negative evaluations: More evidence of the role of self-verification strivings. *Journal of Abnormal Psychology, 101,* 314–317.

Sweeney, P. D., Anderson, K., & Bailey, S. (1986). Attributional style in depression: A meta-analytic review. *Journal of Personality and Social Psychology, 50,* 974–991.

Symons, D. (1992). What do men want? *Behavioral and Brain Sciences, 15,* 113.

Szagun, G., & Schauble, M. (1997). Children's and adults' understanding of the feeling experience of courage. *Cognition and Emotion, 11,* 291–306.

Taubes, G. (1998). Obesity rates rise, experts struggle to explain why. *Science, 280,* 1367–1368.

Tauer, J. M., & Harackiewicz, J. M. (1999). Winning isn't everything: Competition, achievement orientation, and intrinsic motivation. *Journal of Experimental Social Psychology, 35,* 209–238.

Taylor, C. B., Bandura, A., Ewart, C. K., Miller, N. H., & DeBusk, B. F. (1985). Exercise testing to enhance wives' confidence in their husbands' cardiac capabilities soon after clinically uncomplicated acute myocardial infarction. *American Journal of Cardiology, 55,* 635-638.

Taylor, S. E. (1989). *Positive illusions: Creative self-deception and the healthy mind.* New York: Basic Books.

Taylor, S. E., & Brown, J. D. (1988). Illusion and well-being: A social psychological perspective on mental health. *Psychological Bulletin, 103,* 193–210.

Taylor, S. E., & Brown, J. D. (1994). Positive illusions and well-being revisited: Separating fact from fiction. *Psychological Bulletin, 116,* 21–27.

Taylor, S. E., & Fiske, S. T. (1978). Salience, attention, and attribution: Top of the head phenomena.

In L. Berkowitz (Ed.), *Advances in experimental social psychology* (Vol. 11, pp. 249–288). New York: Academic Press.

Taylor, S. E, & Gollwitzer, P. M. (1995). The effects of mind-sets on positive illusions. *Journal of Personality and Social Psychology, 69,* 213–226.

Taylor, S. E., Kemeny, M. E., Reed, G. M., Bower, J. E., & Gruenewald, T. L. (2000). Psychological resources, positive illusions, and health. *American Psychologist, 55,* 99–109.

Taylor, S. E., Pham, L. B., Rivkin, I. D., & Armor, D. A. (1998). Harnessing the imagination: Mental simulation, self-regulation, and coping. *American Psychologist, 53,* 429–439.

Teasdale, J. D., & Fogarty, S. J. (1979). Differential effects of induced mood on retrieval of pleasant and unpleasant events from episodic memory. *Journal of Abnormal Psychology, 88,* 248–257.

Teichman, Y. (1973). Emotional arousal and affiliation. *Journal of Experimental Social Psychology, 9,* 591–605.

Tennen, H., & Affleck, G. (1987). The costs and benefits of optimistic explanations and dispositional optimism. *Journal of Personality, 55,* 377–393.

Tennen, H., & Eller, S. J. (1977). Attributional components of learned helplessness and facilitation. *Journal of Personality and Social Psychology, 35,* 265–271.

Terasaki, M., & Imada, S. (1988). Sensation seeking and food preferences. *Personality and Individual Differences, 9,* 87–93.

Terborg, J. R. (1976). The motivational components of goal setting. *Journal of Applied Psychology, 61,* 613–621.

Terhune, K. W. (1968). Studies of motives, cooperation, and conflict within laboratory microcosms. In G. H. Snyder (Ed.), *Studies in international conflict* (Vol. 4, pp. 29–58). Buffalo, NY: University of Buffalo.

Tesser, A. (1988). Toward a self-evaluation maintenance model of social behavior. In L. Berkowitz (Ed.), *Advances in experimental social psychology* (Vol. 21, pp. 181–227). New York: Academic Press.

Thibodeau, R., & Aronson, E. (1992). Taking a closer look: Reasserting the role of the self-concept in dissonance theory. *Personality and Social Psychology Bulletin, 18,* 591–602.

Thoits, P. A. (1984). Coping, social support, and psychological outcomes. In P. Shaver (Ed.), *Review of personality and social psychology* (Vol. 5, pp. 219–238). Beverly Hills, CA: Sage.

Thompson, S. (1981). Will it hurt less if I can control it? A complex answer to a simple question. *Psychological Bulletin, 90,* 89–101.

Thorton, J. W., & Jacobs, P. D. (1971). Learned helplessness in human subjects. *Journal of Experimental Psychology, 87,* 369–372.

Thorton, J. W., & Powell, G. D. (1974). Immunization to and alleviation of learned helplessness in man. *American Journal of Psychology, 87,* 351–367.

Tiggenmann, M., & Winefield, A. H. (1987). Predictability and timing of self-report in learned helplessness experiments. *Personality and Social Psychology Bulletin, 13,* 253–264.

Timberlake, W. (1980). A molar equilibrium theory of learned performance. In G. H. Bower (Ed.), *The psychology of learning and motivation* (Vol. 14, pp. 1–58). San Diego: Academic Press.

Timberlake, W., & Allison, J. (1974). Response deprivation: An empirical approach to instrumental performance. *Psychological Review, 81,* 146–164.

Timberlake, W., & Farmer-Dougan, V. A. (1991). Reinforcement in applied settings: Figuring out ahead of time what will work. *Psychological Bulletin, 110,* 379–391.

Timpe, R. L. (1989). Perfectionism: Positive possibility or personal pathology. *Journal of Psychology and Christianity, 8,* 23–24.

Toates, F. M. (1979). Homeostasis and drinking. *Behavior and Brain Science, 2,* 95–139.

Tolman, E. C. (1923). The nature of instinct. *Psychological Bulletin, 20,* 200–218.

Tolman, E. C. (1925). Purpose and cognition: The determinants of animal learning. *Psychological Review, 32,* 285–297.

Tolman, E. C. (1932). *Purposive behavior in animals and man.* New York: Century.

Tolman, E. C. (1938). The determinants of behavior at a choice point. *Psychological Review, 45,* 1–44.

Tolman, E. C. (1959). Principles of purposive behavior. In S. Koch (Ed.), *Psychology: A study of a science* (Vol. 2, pp. 92–157). New York: McGraw-Hill.

Tolman, E. C., Ritchie, B. F., & Kalish, D. (1946a). Studies in spatial learning: 1. Orientation and the short cut. *Journal of Experimental Psychology, 36,* 13–24.

Tolman, E. C., Ritchie, B. F., & Kalish, D. (1946b). Studies in spatial learning: 2. Place learning versus response learning. *Journal of Experimental Psychology, 36,* 221–229.

Tomaka, J., Blascovich, J., Kelsey, R. M., & Leitten, C. L. (1993). Subjective, physiological, and behavioral effects of threat and challenge appraisals. *Journal of Personality and Social Psychology, 65,* 248–260.

Toman, W. (1960). *An introduction to the psychoanalytic theory of motivation.* New York: Pergamon Press.

Tomkins, S. S. (1962). *Affect, imagery, and consciousness: The positive affects* (Vol. 1). New York: Springer.

Tomkins, S. S. (1963). *Affect, imagery, and consciousness: The negative affects* (Vol. 2). New York: Springer.

Tomkins, S. S. (1970). Affect as the primary motivational system. In M. B. Arnold (Ed.), *Feelings and emotions* (pp. 101–110). New York: Academic Press.

Tomkins, S. S. (1984). Affect theory. In K. R. Scherer & P. Ekman (Eds.), *Approaches to emotion* (pp. 163–196). Hillsdale, NJ: Lawrence Erlbaum.

Tooby, J., & Cosmides, L. (1990). The past explains the present: Emotional adaptations and the structure of ancestral environment. *Ethology and Sociobiology, 11,* 375–424.

Tourangeau, R., & Ellsworth, P. C. (1979). The role of facial response in the experience of emotion. *Journal of Personality and Social Psychology, 37,* 1519–1531.

Tranel, D. T., Fisher, A. E., & Fowles, D. C. (1982). Magnitude of incentive on heart rates. *Psychophysiology, 19,* 514–519.

Trice, A. D., & Ogdon, E. P. (1986). Informed consent: I. The institutional nonliability clause as a liability in recruiting research subjects. *Journal of Social Behavior and Personality, 1,* 391–396.

Tronick, E. Z. (1989). Emotions and emotional communication in infants. *American Psychologist, 44,* 112–119.

Trope, Y. (1975). Seeking information about one's own ability as a determinant of choice among tasks. *Journal of Personality and Social Psychology, 32,* 1004–1013.

Trope, Y. (1983). Self-assessment in achievement behavior. In J. Suls & A. G. Greenwald (Eds.), *Psychological perspectives on the self* (Vol. 2, pp. 93–121). Hillsdale, NJ: Lawrence Erlbaum.

Trope, Y., & Brickman, P. (1975). Difficulty and diagnosticity as determinants of choice among tasks. *Journal of Personality and Social Psychology, 31,* 918–925.

Trudewind, C. (1982). The development of achievement motivation and individual differences: Ecological determinants. In W. Hartrup (Ed.), *Review of Child Development Research* (Vol. 6, pp. 669–703). Chicago: University of Chicago Press.

Tubbs, M. E. (1986). Goal-setting: A meta-analytic examination of the empirical evidence. *Journal of Applied Psychology, 71,* 474–483.

Turner, J. H. (1987). Toward a sociological theory of motivation. *American Sociological Review, 52,* 15–27.

Urist, J. (1977). The Rorschach test and the assessment of object relations. *Journal of Personality Assessment, 41,* 3–9.

Urist, J. (1980). Object relations. In R. W. Woody (Ed.), *Encyclopedia of clinical assessment* (Vol. 2, pp. 821–833). San Francisco: Jossey-Bass.

Vaillant, G. E. (1977). *Adaptation to life.* Boston: Little, Brown, & Company.

Vaillant, G. E. (1992). *Ego mechanisms of defense: A guide for clinicians and researchers.* Washington, DC: American Psychiatric Association.

Vaillant, G. E. (1993). *The wisdom of the ego.* Cambridge, MA: Harvard University Press.

Vaillant, G. E. (2000). Adaptive mental mechanisms: Their role in a positive psychology. *American Psychologist, 55,* 89–98.

Valenstein, E. S. (1973). *Brain control.* New York: Wiley.

Vallerand, R. J., Deci, E. L., & Ryan, R. M. (1985). Intrinsic motivation in sport. In K. B. Pandolf (Ed.), *Exercise and sport sciences reviews* (Vol. 15, pp. 389–425). New York: Macmillan.

Vallerand, R. J., Gauvin, L. I., & Halliwell, W. R. (1986). Negative effects of competition on children's intrinsic motivation. *Journal of Social Psychology, 126,* 649–656.

Vallerand, R. J., Fortier, M. S., & Guay, F. (1997). Self-determination and persistence in a real-life setting: Toward a motivational model of high school dropout. *Journal of Personality and Social Psychology, 72,* 1161–1176.

Vallerand, R. J., Pelletier, L. G., Blais, M. R., Briere, N. M., Senecal, C., & Vallieres, E. F. (1992). The Academic Motivation Scale: A measure of intrinsic, extrinsic, and amotivation in education. *Educational and Psychological Measurement, 52,* 1003–1017.

Vallerand, R. J., & Reid, G. (1984). On the causal effects of perceived competence on intrinsic motivation: A test of cognitive evaluation theory. *Journal of Sport Psychology, 6,* 94–102.

Van Der Plight, J., & Eiser, J. R. (1983). Actors and observers attributions, self-serving bias, and positivity bias. *European Journal of Social Psychology, 13,* 95–104.

van Dijk, W. W., Zeelenberg, M., & van Der Plight, J. (1999). Not having what you want versus having what you do not want: The impact of type of negative outcome on the experience of disappointment and related emotions. *Cognition and Emotion, 13,* 129–148.

van Dijk, W. W., van Der Plight, J., & Zeelenberg, M. (1999). Effort invested in vain: The impact of effort on the intensity of disappointment and regret. *Motivation and Emotion, 23,* 203–220.

van Hooff, J. A. R. A. M. (1962). Facial expressions in higher primates. *Symposium of the Zoological Society of London, 8,* 97–125.

van Hooff, J. A. R. A. M. (1972). A comparative approach to the phylogeny of laughter and smiling. In R. A. Hinde (Ed.), *Non-verbal communication.* Cambridge: Cambridge University Press.

van IJzendoorn, M. H. (1995). Adult attachment representations, parental responsiveness, and infant attachment: A meta-analysis on the predictive validity of the adult attachment interview. *Psychological Bulletin, 117,* 387–403.

Veitch, R., & Griffitt, W. (1976). Good news bad news: Affective and interpersonal effects. *Journal of Applied Social Psychology, 6,* 69–75.

Veroff, J. (1957). Development and validation of a projective measure of power motivation. *Journal of Abnormal and Social Psychology, 54,* 1–8.

Veroff, J., Depner, C., Kulka, R., & Douvan, E. (1980). Comparison of American motives: 1957 versus 1976. *Journal of Personality and Social Psychology, 39,* 1249–1262.

Verplanken, B., & Faes, S. (1999). Good intentions, bad habits, and effects of forming implementation intentions on healthy eating. *European Journal of Social Psychology, 29,* 591–604

Viken, R. J., Rose, R. J., Kaprio, J., & Kosken, V. U. O. (1994). A developmental genetic analysis of adult personality: Extraversion and neuroticism from 18 to 59 years of age. *Journal of Personality and Social Psychology, 66,* 722–730.

Visintainer, M., Volpicelli, J. R., & Seligman, M. E. P. (1982). Tumor rejection in rats after inescapable or escapable shock. *Science, 216,* 437–439.

Volmer, F. (1986). Why do men have higher expectancy than women? *Sex Roles, 14,* 351–362.

Vroom, V. H. (1964). *Work and motivation.* New York: Wiley.

Wachtel, P. (1993). *Therapeutic communication.* New York: Guilford Press.

Wahba, M. A., & Bridwell, L. G. (1976). Maslow reconsidered: A review of research on the need hierarchy theory. *Organizational Behavior and Human Performance, 15,* 212–240.

Waterman, A. S. (1982). Identity development from adolescence to adulthood: An extension of theory and a review of research. *Developmental Psychology, 18,* 341–358.

Waterman, A. S. (1988). Identity status theory and Erikson's theory: Commonalities and differences. *Developmental Review, 8,* 185–208.

Watson, D., & Clark, L. A. (1994). The vicissitudes of mood: A schematic model. In P. Ekman & R. J. Davidson (Eds.), *The nature of emotion: Fundamental questions* (pp. 400–405). New York: Oxford University Press.

Watson, D., Clark, L. A., McIntyre, C. W., & Hamaker, S. (1992). Affect, personality, and social activity. *Journal of Personality and Social Psychology, 63,* 1011–1025.

Watson, D., Clark, L. A., & Tellegen, A. (1988). Development and validation of brief measures of positive and negative affect: The PANAS scales. *Journal of Personality and Social Psychology, 54,* 1063–1070.

Watson, D., & Tellegen, A. (1985). Toward a consensual structure of mood. *Psychological Bulletin, 98,* 219–235.

Watson, D., Wiese, D., Vaidya, J., & Tellegen, A. (1999). The two general activation systems of affect: Structural findings, evolutionary considerations, and psychobiological evidence. *Journal of Personality and Social Psychology, 76,* 820–838.

Watson, J. B. (1919). *Psychology from the standpoint of a behaviorist.* Philadelphia: Lippincott.

Watson, J. B. (1924). *Behaviorism.* New York: W. W. Norton.

Wegner, D. M. (1989). *White bears and other unwanted thoughts.* New York: Guilford Press.

Wegner, D. M. (1992). You can't always think what you want: Problems in the suppression of unwanted thoughts. In M. P. Zanna (Ed.), *Advances in experimental social psychology* (Vol. 25, pp. 193–225). San Diego: Academic Press.

Wegner, D. M. (1994). Ironic processes of mental control. *Psychological Review, 101,* 34–52.

Wegner, D. M., & Erber, R. (1993). Hyperaccessibility of suppressed thoughts. *Journal of Personality and Social Psychology, 63,* 903–912.

Wegner, D. M., Schneider, D. J., Carter, S., III, & White, T. (1987). Paradoxical effects of thought suppression. *Journal of Personality and Social Psychology, 53,* 5–13.

Wegner, D. M., Shortt, J., Blake, A. W., & Page, M. S. (1990). The suppression of exciting thoughts. *Journal of Personality and Social Psychology, 58,* 409–418.

Weil, J. L. (1974). *A neurophysiological model of emotional and intentional behavior.* Springfield, IL: Charles C. Thomas.

Weinberg, R. S., Bruya, L., & Jackson, A. (1985). The effects of goal proximity and goal specificity on endurance performance. *Journal of Sport Psychology, 7,* 296–305.

Weinberg, R. S., Bruya, L., Longino, J., & Jackson, A. (1988). Effect of goal proximity and specificity on endurance performance of primary-grade children. *Journal of Sport and Exercise Psychology, 10,* 81–91.

Weinberg, R. S., Gould, D., & Jackson, A. (1979). Expectations and performance: An empirical test of Bandura's self-efficacy theory. *Journal of Sport Psychology, 1,* 320–331.

Weiner, B. (1972). *Theories of motivation: From mechanism to cognition.* Chicago: Rand McNally.

Weiner, B. (1974). An attributional interpretation of expectancy-value theory. In B. Weiner (Ed.), *Cognitive views of human motivation* (pp. 51–69). New York: Academic Press.

Weiner, B. (1979). A theory of motivation for some classroom experiences. *Journal of Educational Psychology, 71,* 3–25.

Weiner, B. (1980). *Human motivation.* New York: Holt, Rinehart & Winston.

Weiner, B. (1982). The emotional consequences of causal attributions. In M. S. Clark & S. T. Fiske (Eds.), *Affect and cognition* (pp. 185-209). Hillsdale, NJ: Lawrence Erlbaum.

Weiner, B. (1985). An attributional theory of achievement motivation and emotion. *Psychological Review, 92,* 548–573.

Weiner, B. (1986). *An attributional theory of motivation and emotion.* New York: Springer-Verlag.

Weiner, B. (1990). History of motivational research in education. *Journal of Educational Psychology, 82,* 616–622.

Weiner, B., Frieze, I., Kukla, A., Reed, L., Rest, S., & Rosenbaum, R. M. (1971). *Perceiving the causes of success and failure.* In E. E. Jones, D. E. Kanouse, H. H. Kelley, R. E. Nisbett, S. Valins, & B. Weiner (Eds.), *Attribution: Perceiving the causes of behavior.* Morristown, NJ: General Learning Press.

Weiner, B., & Graham, S. (1989). Understanding the motivational role of affect: Life-span research from an attributional perspective. *Cognition and Emotion, 3,* 401–409.

Weiner, B., Russell, D., & Learman, D. (1978). Affective consequences of causal ascriptions. In J. Harvey, W. J. Ickes, & R. F. Kidd (Eds.), *New directions in attribution research* (Vol. 2, pp. 59–88). Hillsdale, NJ: Erlbaum.

Weiner, B., Russell, D., & Learman, D. (1979). The cognition-emotion process in achievement-related context. *Journal of Personality and Social Psychology, 37,* 1211–1220.

Weingarten, H. P. (1985). Stimulus control of eating: Implications for a two-factor theory of hunger. *Appetite, 6,* 387–401.

Weinstein, N. D. (1984). Why it won't happen to me: Perceptions of risk factors and susceptibility. *Health Psychology, 3,* 431–457.

Weinstein, N. D. (1993). Optimistic biases about personal risks. *Science, 155,* 1232–1233.

Weiss, J. M. (1972). Psychological factors in stress and disease. *Scientific American, 226,* 104–113.

Weiss, J. M., Glazer, H. I., & Pohorecky, L. A. (1976). Coping behavior and neurochemical changes in rats: An alternative explanation for the original learned helplessness experiments. In G. Serban & A. King (Eds.), *Animal models in human psychobiology.* New York: Plenum.

Weiss, J. M., Stone, E. A., & Harrell, N. (1970). Coping behavior and brain norepinephrine level in rats. *Journal of Comparative and Physiological Psychology, 72,* 153–160.

Wellborn, J. G. (1991). *Engaged and disaffected action: The conceptualization and measurement of motivation in the academic domain.* Unpublished doctoral dissertation, University of Rochester.

Wertheimer, M. (1978). Humanistic psychology and the humane but tough-minded psychologist. *American Psychologist, 33,* 739–745.

Westen, D. (1990). Psychoanalytic approaches to personality. In L. Pervin (Ed.), *Handbook of personality: Theory and research* (pp. 21–65). New York: Guilford Press.

Westen, D. (1991). Social cognition and object relations. *Psychological Bulletin, 109,* 429–455.

Westen, D. (1998). The scientific legacy of Sigmund Freud: Toward a psychodynamically informed psychological science. *Psychological Bulletin, 124,* 333–371.

Westen, D., Klepser, J., Ruffins, S. A., Silverman, M., Lifton, N., & Boekamp, J. (1991). Object relations in childhood and adolescence: The development of working representations. *Journal of Consulting and Clinical Psychology, 59,* 400–409.

Wheeler, L., Reis, H. T., & Nezlek, J. (1983). Loneliness, social interaction, and sex roles. *Journal of Personality and Social Psychology, 45,* 943–953.

Whitbourne, S. K., Zuschlag, M. K., Elliot, L. B., & Waterman, A. S. (1992). Psychosocial development in adulthood: A 22-year sequential study. *Journal of Personality and Social Psychology, 63,* 260–271.

White, G., & Gerard, H. (1983). Post-decision reevaluation of choice alternatives. *Personality and Social Psychology Bulletin, 9,* 365–369.

White, G. L. (1981). A model of romantic jealousy. *Motivation and Emotion, 5,* 295–310.

White, H. R., Labourvie, E. N., & Bates, M. E. (1985). The relationship between sensation seeking and delinquency: A longitudinal analysis. *Journal of Research in Crime and Delinquency, 22,* 197–211.

White, R. W. (1959). Motivation reconsidered: The concept of competence. *Psychological Review, 66,* 297–333.

White, R. W. (1960). Competence and the psychosexual stages of development. In M. R. Jones (Ed.), *Nebraska symposium on motivation* (Vol. 8, pp. 97–141) Lincoln: University of Nebraska Press.

Wicker, A. W. (1969). Attitudes versus action: The relationship of verbal and overt behavioral responses to attitude objects. *Journal of Social Issues, 25,* 41–68.

Wiersma, U. J. (1992). The effects of extrinsic rewards in intrinsic motivation: A meta-analysis. *Journal of Occupational and Organizational Psychology, 65,* 101–114.

Wigfield, A. (1994). Expectancy-value theory of achievement motivation: A developmental perspective. *Educational Psychology Review, 6,* 49–78.

Wigfield, A., & Eccles, J. S. (1992). The development of achievement task values: A theoretical analysis. *Developmental Review, 12,* 265–310.

Wigfield, A., & Eccles, J. S. (2000). Expectancy-value theory of achievement motivation. *Contemporary Educational Psychology, 25,* 68–81.

Wilder, D. A., & Thompson, J. E. (1980). Intergroup contact with independent manipulations of in-group and out-group interaction. *Journal of Personality and Social Psychology, 38,* 589–603.

Williams, D. G. (1990). Effects of psychoticism, extraversion, and neuroticism in current mood: A statistical review of six studies. *Personality and Individual Differences, 11,* 615–630.

Williams, D. R., & Teitelbaum, P. (1956). Control of drinking by means of an operant conditioning technique. *Science, 124,* 1294–1296.

Williams, G. C., & Deci, E. L. (1996). Internalization of biopsychological values by medical students: A test of self-determination theory. *Journal of Personality and Social Psychology, 70,* 767–779.

Williams, G. C., Grow, V. M., Freedman, Z. R., Ryan, R. M., & Deci, E. L. (1996). Motivational predictors of weight loss and weight-loss maintenance. *Journal of Personality and Social Psychology, 70,* 115–126.

Williams, J. G., & Solano, C. H. (1983). The social reality of feeling lonely: Friendship and reciprocation. *Personality and Social Psychology Bulletin, 9,* 237–242.

Wilson, T. D., & Linville, P. W. (1982). Improving the academic performance of college freshman:

Attribution therapy revisited. *Journal of Personality and Social Psychology, 42,* 367–376.

Wilson, T. D., & Linville, P. W. (1985). Improving the performance of college freshman with attributional techniques. *Journal of Personality and Social Psychology, 49,* 287–293.

Winchie, D. B., & Carment, D. W. (1988). Intention to migrate: A psychological analysis. *Journal of Applied Psychology, 18,* 727–736.

Windle, M. (1992). Temperament and social support in adolescence: Interrelations with depression and delinquent behavior. *Journal of Youth and Adolescence, 21,* 1–21.

Winefield, A. H. (1982). Methodological differences in demonstrating learned helplessness in humans. *Journal of General Psychology, 107,* 255–266.

Winefield, A. H., Barnett, A., & Tiggemann, M. (1985). Learned helplessness deficits: Uncontrollable outcomes or perceived failure? *Motivation and Emotion, 9,* 185–195.

Winer, D. L., Bonner, T. O., Jr., Blaney, P. H., & Murray, E. L. (1981). Depression and social attraction. *Motivation and Emotion, 5,* 153–166.

Winson, J. (1992). The function of REM sleep and the meaning of dreams. In J. W. Barron, M. N. Eagle, & D. L. Wolitzky (Eds.), *Interface of psychoanalysis and psychology* (pp. 347–356). Washington, DC: American Psychological Association.

Winter, D. G. (1973). *The power motive.* New York: Free Press.

Winter, D. G. (1987). Leader appeal, leader performance, and the motive profiles of leaders and followers: A study of American presidents and elections. *Journal of Personality and Social Psychology, 52,* 196–202.

Winter, D. G. (1988). The power motive in women and men. *Journal of Personality and Social Psychology, 54,* 510–519.

Winter, D. G. (1993). Power, affiliation, and war: Three tests of a motivational model. *Journal of Personality and Social Psychology, 65,* 532–545.

Winter, D. G., & Stewart, A. J. (1978). Power motivation. In H. London & J. Exner (Eds.), *Dimensions of personality.* New York: Wiley.

Winterbottom, M. (1958). The relation of need for achievement to learning experience in independence and mastery. In J. Atkinson (Ed.), *Motives in fantasy, action, and society* (pp. 453–478). Princeton, NJ: Van Nostrand.

Wise, R. A. (1996). Addictive drugs and brain stimulation reward. *Annual Review of Neuroscience, 19,* 319–340.

Wise, R. A., & Bozarth, M. A. (1984). Brain reward circuitry: Four circuit elements wired in apparent series. *Brain Research Bulletin, 12,* 203–208.

Wittrock, M. C. (1992). An empowering conception of educational psychology. *Educational Psychologist, 27,* 129–142.

Wolff, P. H. (1969). The natural history of crying and other vocalizations in early infancy. In B. M. Foss (Ed.), *Determinants of infant behavior* (pp. 81–109). London: Methuen.

Wong, M. M., & Csikszentmihalyi, M. (1991). Affiliation motivation and daily experience: Some issues on gender differences. *Journal of Personality and Social Psychology, 60,* 154–164.

Wong, P. T. P., & Weiner, B. (1981). When people ask "why" questions and the heuristics of attributional search. *Journal of Personality and Social Psychology, 40,* 650–663.

Wood, R. E., & Bandura, A. (1989). Impact of conceptions of ability on self-regulatory mechanisms and complex decision making. *Journal of Personality and Social Psychology, 56,* 407–415.

Wood, R. E., Bandura, A., & Bailey, T. (1990). Mechanisms governing organizational performance in complex decision-making environments. *Organizational Behavior and Human Decision Processes, 46,* 181–201.

Wood, R. E., Mento, A. J., & Locke, E. A. (1987). Task complexity as a moderator of goal effects: A meta-analysis. *Journal of Applied Psychology, 72,* 416–425.

Woods, D. J., Beecher, G. P., & Ris, M. D. (1978). The effects of stressful arousal on conjugate lateral eye movement. *Motivation and Emotion, 2,* 345–353.

Woods, D. J., & Steigman, K. B. (1978). Conjugate lateral eye movement and interpersonal arousal: Effects of interviewer sex and topic intimacy. *Personality and Social Psychology Bulletin, 4,* 151–154.

Woods, S. C., Seeley, R. J., Porte, D., Jr., & Schwartz, M. W. (1998). Signals that regulate food intake and energy homeostasis. *Science, 280,* 1378–1383.

Woodworth, R. S. (1918). *Dynamic psychology.* New York: Columbia University Press.

Woody, E. Z., Costanzo, P. R., Leifer, H., & Conger, J. (1981). The effects of taste and caloric perceptions on the eating behavior of restrained and unrestrained subjects. *Cognitive Research and Therapy, 5,* 381–390.

Wortman, C. B., & Brehm, J. W. (1975). Responses to uncontrollable outcomes: An integration of reactance theory and the learned helplessness model. In L. Berkowitz (Ed.), *Advances in experimental social psychology* (Vol. 8, pp. 277–336). New York: Academic Press.

Wortruba, T. R., & Price, K. F. (1975). Relationships among four measures of achievement motivation. *Educational and Psychological Measurement, 35,* 911–914.

Wyrwicka, W. (1988). *Brain and feeding behavior.* Springfield, IL: Charles C. Thomas.

Yaksh, T. L., & Rudy, T. A. (1976). Analgesia mediated by a direct spinal action of narcotics. *Science, 192,* 1357–1358.

Yerkes, R. M., & Dodson, J. D. (1908). The relation of strength of stimulus to repidity of habit formation. *Journal of Comparative Neurology and Psychology, 18,* 459–482.

Young, P. T. (1961). *Motivation and emotion: A survey of the determinants of human and animal activity.* New York: Wiley.

Younger, J. C., Walker, L., & Arrowood, A. J. (1977). Postdecision dissonance at the fair. *Personality and Social Psychology Bulletin, 3,* 284–287.

Zajonc, R. B. (1980). Feeling and thinking: Preferences need no inferences. *American Psychologist, 35,* 151–175.

Zajonc, R. B. (1981). A one-factor mind about mind and emotion. *American Psychologist, 36,* 102–103.

Zajonc, R. B. (1984). On the primacy of affect. *American Psychologist, 39,* 117–123.

Zajonc, R. B., Murphy, S. T., & Inglehart, M. (1989). Feeling and facial efference: Implications of the vascular theory of emotions. *Psychological Review, 96,* 395–416.

Zanna, M. P., & Cooper, J. (1976). Dissonance and the attribution process. In J. H. Harvey, W. J. Ickes, & R. F. Kidd (Eds.), *New directions in attribution research* (Vol. 1, pp. 199–217). Hillsdale, NJ: Lawrence Erlbaum.

Zoeller, C. J., Mahoney, G., Weiner, B. (1983). Effects of attribution training on the assembly task performance of mentally retarded adults. *American Journal of Mental Deficiency, 88,* 109–112.

Zubek, J. P. (Ed.). (1969). *Sensory deprivation.* New York: Appleton-Century-Crofts.

Zuckerman, M(arvin). (1978). Sensation seeking. In H. London & J. E. Exner (Eds.), *Dimensions of personality* (pp. 487–559). New York: John Wiley.

Zuckerman, M. (1979). *Sensation-seeking: Beyond the optimal level of arousal.* Hillsdale, NJ: Erlbaum.

Zuckerman, M. (1994). *Behavioral expressions and biosocial bases of sensation seeking.* New York: Cambridge University Press.

Zuckerman, M., Ball, S., & Black, J. (1990). Influences of sensation seeking, gender, risk appraisal, and situational motivation on smoking. *Addictive Behaviors, 15,* 209–220.

Zuckerman, M., Bone, R. N., Neary, R., Mangelsdorff, D., & Brustman, B. (1972). What is the sensation seeker? Personality trait and experience correlates of the Sensation Seeking Scale. *Journal of Clinical Counseling Psychology, 39,* 308–321.

Zuckerman, M., Buchsbaum, M. S., & Murphy, D. L. (1980). Sensation seeking and its biological correlates. *Psychological Bulletin, 88,* 187–214.

Zuckerman, M., & Neeb, M. (1980). Demographic influences in sensation seeking and expressions of sensation seeking in religion, smoking, and driving habits. *Personality and Individual Differences, 1,* 197–206.

Zuckerman, M., Tushup, R., & Finner, S. (1976). Sexual attitudes and experience: Attitude and personality correlates and changes produced by a course in sexuality. *Journal of Consulting and Clinical Psychology, 44,* 7–19.

Zuckerman, M(iron). (1979). Attribution of success and failure revisited, or: The motivational bias is alive and well in attribution theory. *Journal of Personality, 47,* 245–287.

Zuckerman, M., Gioioso, C., & Tellini, S. (1988). Control orientation, self-monitoring, and preference for image versus quality approach to advertising. *Journal of Research in Personality, 22,* 89–100.

Zuckerman, M., Klorman, R., Larrance, D. T., & Spiegel, N. H. (1981). Facial, autonomic, and subjective components of emotion: The facial feedback hypothesis versus the externalizer-internalizer distinction. *Journal of Personality and Social Psychology, 41,* 929–944.

Zuckerman, M., Kieffer, S. C., & Knee, C. R. (1998). Consequences of self-handicapping effects on coping, academic performance, and adjustment. *Journal of Personality and Social Psychology, 74,* 1619–1628.

Zuckerman, M., Porac, J., Lathin, D., Smith, R., & Deci, E. L. (1978). On the importance of self-determination for intrinsically motivated behavior. *Personality and Social Psychology Bulletin, 4,* 443–446.

Zullow, H. M., Oettingen, G., Peterson, C., & Seligman, M. E. P. (1988). Pessimistic explanatory style in the historical record: CAVing LBJ, presidential candidates, and East versus West Berlin. *American Psychologist,* 43, 673–682.

CREDITS

Figure 1.2 Birch, D. et al., "Cognitive Control of Action" in B. Weiner (Ed.), *Cognitive View of Human Motivation.* Copyright © 1974 Academic Press. Reprinted by permission.

Figure 3.4 From "Emotion, Pain and Physical Illness" by H. Leventhal and D. Everhart, in *Emotions in Personality and Psychopathology,* C.E. Izard, ed. Copyright © 1979 Plenum Publishing. Reprinted by permission.

Figure 3.5 C. Pfaffmann, "The Pleasures of Sensation," *Psychological Review,* Vol. 67, 1960, pp. 253-268.

Table 3.1 From "Sensory and Social Influence on Ice Cream Consumption by Males and Females in a Laboratory Setting" by S.L. Berry et al., *Appetite,* Vol. 6, 1985, pp. 41-45. Copyright 1985 by Academic Press, Ltd. Reprinted by permission.

Figure 3.6 "Measuring the Physical in Physical Attractiveness: Quasi-Experiments on the Sociobiology of Female Facial Beauty" by M.R. Cunningham, *Journal of Personality and Social Psychology,* Vol. 50, pp. 925-935. Copyright © 1986 by the American Psychological Association. Reprinted with permission.

Figure 3.7 "Scripts and the Coordination of Sexual Conduct" by H. Gagnon, in J. K. Cole & R. Diensteiber (eds.) *Symposium on Motivation,* Vol. 21, pp. 27-59. Copyright © 1974 University of Nebraska Press. Reprinted by permission.

Table 3.2 "Mate Selection Preferences: Gender Differences Examined in a National Sample" by S. Sprecher et al., *Journal of Personality and Social Psychology,* Vol. 66, pp. 1074-1080. Copyright © 1994 by the American Psychological Association. Reprinted with permission.

Figure 4.1 "Expectancy Determinants of Intrinsically Motivated Behavior" by Z. Shapira, *Journal of Personality and Social Psychology,* Vol. 34, pp. 1235-1244. Copyright © 1976 by the American Psychological Association. Reprinted with permission.

Figure 4.2 "Self-determination and Persistence in a Real-life Setting" by R.J. Vallerand et al., *Journal of Personality and Social Psychology,* Vol. 72, pp. 1161-1172. Copyright © 1997 by the American Psychological Association. Reprinted with permission.

Figure 4.3 "Motivating Others: Nurturing Inner Motivational Resources" by J. Reeve. Copyright © 1996 by Allyn and Bacon. Reprinted by permission.

Figure 4.4 Adapted from "Beyond Boredom and Anxiety: The Experience of Flow in Work and Play" by M. Scikszentmihalyi (San Francisco: Jossey-Bass, 1975).

Figure 5.1 From "A University-Based Incentive Program to Increase Safety Belt Use" by J.R. Rudd and G.S. Geller, *Journal of Applied Behavior Analysis,* Vol. 18, 1985, pp. 215-226. Copyright © 1985 by the Journal of Applied Behavior Analysis. Reprinted by permission.

Figure 5.2 From "Behavioral Engineering: Postural Control by a Portable Operant Apparatus," N.H. Azrin et al., *Journal of Applied Behavior Analysis,* Vol. 2, 1968, pp. 39-42. Copyright ©

1968 by the Journal of Applied Behavior Analysis. Reprinted by permission.

Figure 5.3 Adapted from *Behavior Modification in Applied Settings,* Revised Edition, by A.E. Kazdin. Copyright 1975 and 1980 by Dorsey Press. Used with permission of Brooks/Cole Publishing Corp., Pacific Grove, CA 93950.

Figure 5.4 From "Modification of Behavior Problems in the Home With a Parent as Observer and Experimenter," R.V. Hall et al., *Journal of Applied Behavior Analysis,* Vol. 5, 1972, pp. 53-64. Copyright © 1972 by the *Journal of Applied Behavior Analysis.* Reprinted by permission.

Table 5.1 Adapted from *Intrinsic Motivation and Self-Determination in Human Behavior* by E.L. Deci and R.M. Ryan. Copyright © 1985 Plenum Publishing. Reprinted by permission.

Figure 5.5 "Self-Determination Theory and the Facilitation of Intrinsic Motivation, Social Development, and Well-Being" by R.M. Ryan and E.L. Deci, *American Psychologist,* Vol. 55, pp. 68-78. Copyright © 2000 by the American Psychological Association. Reprinted with permission.

Figure 6.1 "A Computer-Based Measure of Resultant Achievement Motivation" by V. Blankenship, *Journal of Personality and Social Psychology,* Vol. 53, pp. 361-372. Copyright © 1987 by the American Psychological Association. Reprinted with permission.

Figure 6.2 "A Hierarchical Model of Approach and Avoidance Achievement Motivation" A.J. Elliot and M. Church, *Journal of Personality and Social Psychology,* Vol. 72, pp. 218-232. Copyright © 1997 by the American Psychological Association. Reprinted with permission.

Table 6.2 "Achievement Goals in the Classroom: Students' Learning Strategies and Motivational Processes" by C.A. Ames and J. Archer, *Journal of Educational Psychology,* Vol. 80, pp. 260-267. Copyright © 1988 by the American Psychological Association. Reprinted with permission.

Table 6.3 "Approach and Avoidance Motivation and Achievement Goals" by A.J. Elliot, *Educational Psychologist,* Vol. 34, 1999, pp. 169-189. Reprinted by permission of Lawrence Erlbaum Associates, Inc.

Figure 7.3 Adapted from "A Computer Model of Affective Reactions to Goal-Relevant Events" by S.B. Ravlin, unpublished master's thesis. Cited in A. Ortony, G.L. Clore, and A. Collins (Eds.), *The Cognitive Structure of Emotions,* 1987, New York: Cambridge University Press.

Figure 8.2 "Effects of Prior Success and Failure on Expectancies of Success and Subsequent Failure," N.T. Feather, *Journal of Personality and Social Psychology,* Vol. 3, pp. 287-298. Copyright © 1966 American Psychological Association.

Figure 8.3 From *Discovering Psychology* by N.C. Carlson. Copyright © 1988 by Allyn and Bacon. Adapted by permission.

Figure 8.4 "An Analysis of Learned Helplessness: Continuous Changes in Performance, Strategy and Achievement Cognition Following Failure," C.I. Diener and C.S. Dweck, *Journal of Personality and Social Psychology,* Vol. 36, pp. 451-462. Copyright © 1978 by the American Psychological Association. Reprinted with permission.

Figure 8.5 Psychological Factors in Stress and Disease" J.M. Weiss, *Scientific American,* Vol. 225, 1972, pp. 104-113. Illustration adapted with permission by Eric Mose.

Figure 8.6 "Judgment on Contingency in Depressed and Nondepressed Students: Sadder but Wiser?" L.B. Alloy and L.T. Abramson, *Journal of Experimental Psychology: General,* Vol. 108, pp. 441-485. Copyright © 1979 American Psychological Association. Adapted by permission.

Figure 8.8 "Responses to Uncontrollable Outcomes; An Integration of Reactance Theory and the Learned Helplessness Model" C.B. Wortman and J.W. Brehm, in L. Berkowitz (Ed.), *Advances in Experimental Social Psychology,* Vol. 8, 1975, pp. 277-336. Copyright © 1975 Academic Press. Reprinted by permission.

Box 8 Adapted from "Controlling Ourselves, Controlling Our World: Psychology's Role in Understanding Positive and Negative Consequences of Seeking and Gaining Control" D.H. Shapiro, Jr. et al., *American Psychologist,* Vol. 51, pp. 1213-1230. Copyright © 1996 American Psychological Association. Reprinted by permission.

Table 9.1 Adapted from "Pessimistic Explanatory Style is a Risk Factor for Physical Illness" C. Peterson et al., *Journal of Personality and Social Psychology,* Vol. 55, pp. 23-27. Copyright © 1988 American Psychological Association. Reprinted by permission.

Figure 10.1 "Self-Verification: Bringing Social Reality into Harmony with Self" by W.B. Swann, Jr, in J. Sius and A. Greenwald (Eds.), *Psychological Perspectives on the Self,* Vol. 2, 1983, pp. 33-66. Reprinted by permission of Lawrence Erlbaum Associates, Inc.

Figure 11.2 "Drive and the C.N.S.—Conceptual Nervous System" D.O. Hebb, *Psychological Review,* Vol. 62, 1955, pp. 245-254.

Figure 11.3 "The Pathology of Boredom" W. Heron, *Scientific American,* Vol. 196, 1957, pp. 52-56. Illustration reprinted by permission of Eric Mose.

Figure 11.4 "Affect Intensity as an Individual Difference Characteristic: A Review," R.J. Larsen and E. Diener, *Journal of Research in Personality,* Vol. 21, 1987, pp. 1-39. Copyright © 1987 Academic Press. Reprinted by permission.

Figure 11.5 "Can Personality Study Ever Be Scientific?" H.J. Eysenck, *Journal of Social Behavior and Personality,* Vol. 1, 1986, pp. 3-19. Copyright © 1986 Select Press. Reprinted by permission.

Figure 11.6 "Individual Differences" A. Gale and J.A. Edwards in M.G. Coles et al., (Eds.), *Psychophysiology: Systems, Processes, and Applications,* pp. 431-507. Copyright © 1986 Guilford Press. Reprinted by permission.

Figure 11.7 *Experiments With Drugs: Studies in the Relation Between Personality, Learning, Theory, and Drug Action*, H.J. Eysenck, Copyright © 1963 Pergamon Press. Reprinted by permission of the author.

Table 11.1 "Sensation Seeking" M. Zuckerman in H. London & J.E. Exner, Jr. (Eds.) *Dimensions Of Personality,* pp. 487-559. Copyright © 1978 John Wiley & Sons. Reprinted by permission.

Table 11.2 "What Is the Sensation-Seeker?" M. Zuckerman et al., *Journal of Clinical and Counseling Psychology,* Vol. 39, pp. 308-321. Copyright © 1972 by the American Psychological Association. Reprinted with permission.

Figure 11.8 Adapted from "Individual Differences in Affect Intensity" by R.J. Larsen, 1988 paper presented at the annual meeting of the Motivation and Emotion Conference at Nags Head, Nags Head, NC.

Figure 11.9 "Affect Intensity and Reactions to Daily Life Events," R.J. Larsen et al., *Journal of Personality and Social Psychology,* Vol. 51, pp. 803-814. Copyright © 1987 by the American Psychological Association. Reprinted with permission.

Figure 11.10a "Perceived Control, Effort, and Academic Performance," B. Schmitz and E. Skinner, *Journal of Personality and Social Psychology,* Vol. 64, pp. 1010-1028. Copyright © 1993 by the American Psychological Association. Reprinted with permission.

Figure 11.10b "Development and Perceived Control," E. Skinner in M. Gunnar and L.A. Sroufe (Eds.), *Minnesota Symposium on Child Development,* Vol. 23, 1991. Reprinted by permission of Lawrence Erlbaum Associates, Inc.

Table 11.3 "Engaged and Disaffected Action," J.G. Wellborn, 1991, from unpublished doctoral dissertation, University of Rochester, NY. Reprinted by permission of the author.

Figure 11.11 "Desire for Control and Achievement-Related Behaviors" J.M. Burger, *Journal of Personality and Social Psychology,* Vol. 48, pp. 1520-1533. Copyright © 1985 by the American Psychological Association. Reprinted with permission.

Table 11.4 "Desire for Control and the Perception of Crowding," J.M. Burger et al., *Personality and Social Psychology Bulletin,* Vol. 9, pp. 475-479. Copyright © 1983 Sage Publications. Reprinted by permission of Sage Publications.

Table 12.1 "A Theory of Metamotivation" from *The Farther Reaches Of Human Nature* by A.H. Maslow. Copyright © 1971 by Bertha G. Maslow. Used by permission of Viking Penguin, a division of Penguin Putnam Inc.

Table 12.2 "Age Differences in Motivation Related to Maslow's Need Hierarchy," B.L. Goebel and D.R. Brown, *Developmental Psychology,* Vol. 17, pp. 809-815. Copyright © 1981 by the American Psychological Association. Reprinted with permission.

Table 12.4 "Integrating Cognitive and Motivational Factors in Depression" B.M. Dykman, *Journal of Personality and Social Psychology,* Vol. 74, pp. 139-158. Copyright © 1998 by the American Psychological Association. Reprinted with permission.

Figure 12.4 "Motivational Predictors of Weight Loss and Weight-Loss Maintenance" G.C. Williams et al., *Journal of Personality and Social Psychology,* Vol. 70, pp. 115-126. Copyright © 1996 by the American Psychological Association. Reprinted with permission.

Table 13.2 *Adaptation To Life* by G.E. Vaillant. Copyright © 1977 by George E. Vaillant. Reprinted by permission of the author.

Figure 13.1 "Social Cognition and Object Relations," D. Westen, *Psychological Bulletin,* Vol. 109, pp. 429-455. Copyright © 1991 by the American Psychological Association. Reprinted with permission.

Table 14.3 From *Emotion: A Psychoevolutionary Synthesis* by Robert Plutchik. Copyright ©1980 Individual Dynamics, Inc. Reprinted by permission of Addison-Wesley Educational Publishers, Inc.

Figure 15.1 "Affect as the Primary Motivational System" S.S. Tomkins, in M.B. Arnold (Ed.), *Feelings And Emotions,* pp. 101-110. Copyright © 1970 Academic Press, Inc. Reprinted by permission.

Table 15.2 *Emotion And Adaptation* by Richard S. Lazarus. Copyright © 1991 Oxford University Press, Inc. Reprinted by permission of Oxford University Press, Inc.

Figure 15.4 "Five Facial Expressions" from *Unmasking The Face* by P. Ekman and W.V. Friesen. Copyright © 1975 Prentice Hall, Inc. Reprinted by permission of the author.

Figure 15.6 "Universal and Cultural Difference in Facial Expression of Emotion" by P. Ekman in J.R. Cole & R. Diensteiber (Eds.), *Nebraska Symposium on Motivation,* Vol. 19, 1972, pp. 207-283. Copyright © 1972 University of Nebraska Press. Reprinted by permission of the author.

Figure 15.8 "Appraisal Determinants of Emotions," I.J. Rosenman et al., *Cognition and Emotion,* Vol. 10, 1996, pp. 241-277. Copyright 1996, reprinted by permission of Psychology Press Ltd.

Figure 15.9 "Emotion Knowledge: Further Exploration of a Prototype Approach," P. Shaver et al., *Journal of Personality and Social Psychology,* Vol. 52, pp. 1061-1086. Copyright © 1987 by the American Psychological Association. Reprinted with permission.

Name Index